TENTH EDITION

Macroeconomics

Richard G. Lipsey

Simon Fraser University

Paul N. Courant

The University of Michigan

Douglas D. Purvis

Queen's University

Peter O. Steiner

Emeritus, The University of Michigan

 HarperCollinsCollegePublishers

Executive Editor: John Greenman
Development Editor: Mimi Melek
Production Coordination and Text Design: Publication Services, Inc.
Cover Design: Edward Smith Design, Inc.
Cover Illustration/Photo: © 1992 Comstock
Text art: John Callahan
Production Administrator: Jeffrey Taub
Compositor: Publication Services, Inc.
Printer and Binder: R. R. Donnelley & Sons Company
Cover Printer: The Lehigh Press, Inc.

MACROECONOMICS, Tenth Edition

Library of Congress Cataloging-in-Publication Data
Macroeconomics / Richard G. Lipsey . . . [et al.] — 10th ed.
    p.   cm.
   Includes index.
   ISBN 0-06-501023-X
   1. Macroeconomics.   I. Lipsey, Richard G., 1928-   .
HB171.5.L733   1993
330—dc20   92-33069
                                        CIP

92 93 94 95 9 8 7 6 5 4 3 2 1

Contents

In this volume, Chapter 5 is followed by Chapter 23.

The HarperCollins Series in Economics

Preface

Economics is a living discipline, changing and evolving in response to developments in the world economy and in response to the research of many thousands of economists throughout the world. Through 10 editions, *Economics* has evolved with the discipline. Our purpose in this edition, as in the previous 9, is to provide students with an introduction to the major issues facing the world's economies, to the methods that economists use to study those issues, and to the policy problems that those issues create. Our treatment is everywhere guided by three important principles:

1. Economics is a science, in the sense that it progresses through the systematic confrontation of theory by evidence. Neither theory nor data alone can tell us much about the world, but combined they tell us a great deal.
2. Economics is, and should be seen by students to be, useful. Economic theory and knowledge about the economy have important implications for economic policy. Although we stress these implications, we are also careful to point out cases where too little is known to support strong statements about public policy. Appreciating what is not known is as important as learning what is known.
3. We strive always to be honest with our readers. Although we know that economics is not always easy, we do not approve of glossing over hard bits of analysis without letting readers see what is happening and what has been assumed. We always take whatever space is needed to explain *why* economists draw their conclusions, rather than just asserting the conclusions. We also take pains to avoid simplifying matters so much that students would have to unlearn what they have been taught if they continue their study beyond the introductory course. In short, we have tried to follow Albert Einstein's advice:

    Everything should be made as simple as possible, but not simpler.

The Economic Issues of the 1990s

In writing the tenth edition we have tried to reflect the major economic issues of the last decade of the twentieth century.

Globalization and Growth

Enormous changes have occurred throughout the world over the last 20 or so years. Flows of trade and investment between countries have risen so dramatically that it is now common to speak of the "globalization" of the world economy. Today it is no longer possible to study any economy without taking into account developments in the rest of the world.

What is true for most countries is also true for the United States. Not so long ago it was possible to learn most of the principles of economics by studying the U.S. economy in isolation—or, as economists put it, by treating the United States as a closed economy. Many economics textbooks are still written on that premise. Today, however, economic relations between the United States and the rest of the world have a significant impact on most of the major "domestic" issues in the news. Here are four examples that we discuss, along with many others, in the tenth edition of *Economics*.

1. Throughout most of this century, Americans and Europeans have each regarded the policies that they adopted to support their farmers as strictly their own concern. Now, with the globalization of agricultural markets, what one country does to support its own agricultural sector impacts greatly on farmers in other countries. No longer is any one nation an island unto itself. Each nation's agricultural policies affect agricultural producers throughout the world and therefore concern all countries.

2. The automobile industry is one of the most important industries in the United States, in terms of both employment and the income that it generates. In 1960 the U.S. auto industry sold the vast majority of all cars used in the United States. Today Japanese and European cars are sold in profusion in the United States—and would be sold in much larger numbers were it not for government-sanctioned restrictions on imports. Abroad, foreign auto companies are beginning to establish production facilities in the emerging markets of Southeast Asia. Some economists worry that the U.S. auto industry is making a serious strategic mistake by not investing in these Asian countries at the early stages of their development. Whether or not that is correct, what is going on in Southeast Asia today will affect the employment opportunities and incomes of North American workers over the next several decades.

3. Throughout most of the twentieth century, successive generations in the United States have found themselves, on average, substantially better off than their parents as a result of the nation's economic growth. Over the last two decades, however, this generation-by-generation advance has applied to only the top income levels; for the rest, average incomes are little higher, and sometimes lower, compared with the previous generation. Although some of the causes are peculiar to the U.S. economy, many have to do with worldwide changes in technology and in patterns of international trade.

4. Americans worry about large federal budget deficits. They wonder if the failure to balance the budget will lead to higher taxes in the future. Japanese, European, and U.S. firms worry about how the deficit affects the value of the U.S. dollar and about how the value of the dollar affects their competitive positions. Developing countries worry about the extent to which the U.S. deficit absorbs investment funds that might otherwise have flowed to them, contributing to their economic development.

The Triumph of Market Capitalism

Since the last edition of this book was published, the century-long ideological conflict between capitalism and communism has virtually ended. The most powerful communist economy in the world, the USSR, has disappeared, both as a nation and as a planned economy. Mixed capitalism, the system of economic organization that has long prevailed in much of the industrialized world, now prevails in virtually all of

it. Many of the less-developed economies are also moving in this direction. The reasons for the failure of the planned economies of Eastern Europe are discussed in Chapter 1 as a contrast to the reasons for the relative success of mixed capitalism.

Declining Growth in Market Economies

At the same time that the once communist world of Eastern Europe has begun to establish free markets, the economies of western Europe, the United States, and Japan have experienced a marked reduction in economic growth.

In the United States average real wages, which rose steadily from 1900 to 1970, have remained nearly constant since the mid-1970s. Over the lifetimes of you who are now using this book, in contrast to readers of our first edition, steadily rising personal incomes have been the exception rather than the rule. Issues raised by the changing U.S. growth performance are discussed frequently in this book.

A Globalized Economics Textbook

Economic growth and the implications of the globalization of the world's economy are pressing issues of the day. Much of our study of economic principles and the U.S. economy has been shaped by these issues.

In the Appendix to Chapter 4, foreign trade provides an example of supply and demand in action. Foreign direct investment and transnational corporations receive detailed attention in many chapters, including Chapter 35 on economic growth, Chapter 37 on trade policy, and Chapter 40 on economic development. The newer method of "lean production" or "flexible manufacturing," first developed in Japan and now displacing the older mass production techniques developed by Henry Ford, is discussed in connection with economic growth (Chapter 35), and with economic development (Chapter 40).

Our basic framework for macroeconomic theory and policy is also organized around globalization and growth. In Chapters 23–28 we develop the theory of national income determination in an economy that is open to foreign trade and investment almost from the outset—rather than starting, as is so often done, with a closed economy and opening it to international trade and investment many chapters later. These chapters also discuss the long-run effects of national saving and net exports on economic growth.

Our analysis of the theory and practice of monetary policy in Chapters 29–31 now highlights the role of exchange rates. Chapter 34, on federal budget policy, covers the effects of the budget balance on the balance of trade (the "twin deficits"). We treat international trade theory, trade policy, and international finance in four chapters. In Chapter 35 we study growth to an extent that is unusual in introductory texts. Chapter 37 provides a detailed discussion of commercial policies that interfere with the free flow of international trade, and of trade-liberalizing arrangements such as the GATT and the North American Free Trade Agreement (NAFTA). Chapter 39 continues with a comprehensive treatment of macroeconomic policy in an open economy. This treatment culminates in Chapter 40, which continues the growth theme with regard to less-developed economies with a major study of the newly emerging views concerning the effects of trade and foreign investment on growth of the poorer nations.

In addition to specific coverage of growth and internationally oriented topics, growth and globalization appear naturally throughout the book in the treatment of many topics once thought to be entirely "domestic."

Macroeconomics: Structure and Coverage

In Part 1 we introduce the issues of scarcity and choice and then briefly discuss comparative economic systems. The problems of converting command economies to market economies will be with us for some time, and comparisons with command economies help to establish what a market economy is *by showing what it is not*. In the last part of Chapter 1 we survey a number of national and international trends to introduce students to many of the issues studied in detail later in the book. Chapter 2 makes the important distinction between positive and normative inquiries and goes on to an elementary discussion of the construction and testing of economic theories.

Our treatment of macroeconomics proper is divided into four parts: national income and fiscal policy; money, banking, and monetary policy; macro-economic problems and policies; and international economics. The themes of internationalization and economic growth are interwoven throughout all four parts.

The first macro chapter, Chapter 23, identifies economic growth and the level of potential national income as the major determinants of a society's material standards of living. Following the change undertaken late in 1991 by the U.S. Department of Commerce, we discuss national income in terms of *gross domestic product* (GDP) rather than *gross national product* (GNP). The discussion of national income accounting in Chapter 24 provides a thorough treatment of what has been, until recently, a somewhat unfamiliar set of national income concepts built around the GDP.

In the core macro chapters (25–28) we develop what has become the standard aggregate-demand–aggregate-supply approach—an approach which this was one of the first elementary textbooks to pioneer. We start with a detailed exposition of the fixed-price (Keynesian cross) model of the determination of equilibrium income in Chapters 25 and 26. In Chapter 25 we consider a simplified economy, one with no international sector or government, in order to make equilibrium income and the multiplier as teachable as possible. In Chapter 26 we add government and the international sector, thus opening our model economy to international trade at an early point.

In Chapters 25 and 26 we develop the saving-investment approach to equilibrium. This allows us to highlight the key temporal relationship between national savings and the accumulation of capital, both at home and abroad, that is a major source of economic growth. We also use the saving-investment approach to discuss the relationship between international trade and an economy's net accumulation of capital.

From the beginning of our treatment of macroeconomics, in contrast to many other introductory texts, we are careful to distinguish short-run *fluctuations* around equilibrium national income from the long-term *growth* of potential national income. This reflects our desire to emphasize economic growth and to avoid trivializing it by confusing it with the rise in income caused by the removal of a recessionary gap.

In Chapter 27 we develop the aggregate demand (*AD*) curve and the short-run aggregate supply curve. Since we discuss the role of wealth in the consumption function in Chapter 25 and the international sector in Chapter 26, there is no mystery about why the *AD* curve slopes down—unlike other treatments where the *AD* curve is introduced prior to discussing these issues. Chapter 28 completes the core model by deriving the vertical long-run aggregate supply curve, which allows us to discuss the different effects of *AD* shifts in the short and long run. This leads directly to an introduction to fiscal policy and a discussion of business cycles in which both stabilization and growth are treated.

Part 8 focuses on the role of money and financial systems. Chapter 29 discusses the nature of money, including an overview of the evolution from metallic money to our modern system of fiat currency and deposit money. The chapter concludes with descriptions of the various components of the money supply and the commercial banking system and of the Federal Reserve System. In Chapter 30 we review the determinants of the demand for money and then turn to a detailed discussion of the link between changes in the money supply on the one hand and interest rates, the exchange rate, national income, and the price level on the other hand. This chapter builds directly on the material in Chapters 27 and 28, with an emphasis on the distinction between short-run and long-run effects. In Chapter 31 we discuss monetary policy, covering the Fed's use of open market operations and other instruments of monetary policy, and how the Fed chooses its policy stance. The chapter ends with a review of monetary policy in action over the past 40 years. This provides some important historical context for policy discussions in later parts, as well as an opportunity to draw some general conclusions about the operation of monetary policy.

Part 9, Macroeconomic Problems and Policies, deals with some of today's most pressing issues for economic policy. It contains separate chapters on inflation, unemployment, budget deficits, and economic growth, all major concerns of the 1990s. Chapter 34, on budget deficits, stresses problems in the measurement of deficits and the effect of deficits on national saving and long-term growth. It also discusses various policies that were intended to limit deficits, including Gramm-Rudman-Hollings and its replacement, the Budget Enforcement Act of 1990, as well as proposals to require budget balance in the Constitution. The chapter also contains a brief discussion of the issue of the persistence of deficits in the face of their nearly universal condemnation by the public and politicians.

Chapter 35 provides a comprehensive summary of what is and is not currently known about the causes of economic growth. Although some of the

discussion ties directly into the emphasis of previous chapters on national saving, much of it examines current research on induced technological innovation, technological diffusion, and the role of transnational corporations. The issue of globalization is returned to in a long section relating growth to international competitiveness. *Our treatment of economic growth— which we regard as one of the most important macroeconomic issues facing the United States and the world today—goes well beyond the coverage in most other introductory texts.*

Virtually every macroeconomic chapter contains at least some discussion of international issues. However, the final part of *Economics* focuses primarily on international economics. Chapter 36 gives the basic treatment of international trade, developing both the traditional theory of static comparative advantage and newer theories based on imperfect competition and dynamic comparative advantage. Chapter 37 discusses both the positive and normative aspects of commercial policy, as well as current GATT negotiations and prospects for regional free-trade areas.

Chapter 38 introduces the basic elements of the balance of payments and international finance. Chapter 39 integrates the international material with the macroeconomic model developed earlier, thus providing an up-to-date discussion of open-economy macroeconomic policy, both monetary and fiscal. The discussion in Chapter 39 reemphasizes the distinction between the short run and the long run stressed in many earlier chapters. In addition to covering new open-economy issues, this chapter also reviews and integrates the macroeconomic theory and applications presented earlier.

Finally, Chapter 40 provides a summary of current views about economic growth in less-developed countries. We place emphasis on new views concerning the policies most effective for growth, on the part of both developed and less-developed countries. The discussion of economic development is structured to provide direct links to earlier discussions of trade, economic growth, foreign investment, and transnational corporations.

Changes in Macroeconomics

• Chapter 1 gives a new introduction to the importance of growth as a major long-run determinant of living standards and the globalization of markets, thus introducing themes that are carried throughout the whole book.

- In Chapter 3 we have added a new box on comparative advantage that introduces students to the idea of gains from specialization.

- In light of the Commerce Department's change in procedures, the entire discussion now takes place in terms of GDP rather than GNP, with a thorough discussion of the difference between the two terms.

- The material from the chapters on business cycles and fiscal policy from the ninth edition have been woven throughout Chapters 23–28, and some of the fiscal policy material is covered in Chapter 34 on budget deficits.

- The entire income-expenditure model with fixed prices is covered in two chapters (25 and 26). The saving-investment approach is fully developed along with the aggregate expenditure model. This allows us to deal explicitly with the effect of saving and investment on economic growth.

- In Chapter 25 we develop a model of a closed economy without government, which enables students to more easily understand the model and see the extensive treatment of the saving-investment balance.

- In Chapter 26 we add trade and government to the model developed in Chapter 25. Government surpluses are interpreted as public saving, and the relationship between national saving and growth is introduced here.

- We have substantially rewritten all three chapters in Part 8, Money, Banking, and Monetary Policy, to make them simpler and shorter. The new, streamlined material is better integrated with earlier material on macro theory and with later material on inflation, in Chapter 34. International issues are also given greater emphasis.

- In Chapter 32 we've added a section on expectations formation dealing with rational expectations and a new flow chart to provide a guide to the discussion of demand and supply shocks.

- Chapter 33 has been extensively rewritten to give it a purely macro cast, which helps to fit it into the rest of the macro chapters.

- In Chapter 34 we stress the role of the deficit in affecting economic growth and tie the chapter to the core macro model and to the discussion on growth in Chapter 35. Two new figures support and extend the discussion of the relationships among deficits, crowding out of investment, crowding out of net exports, and economic growth.

- Chapter 35 has been completely rewritten to provide a comprehensive and current summary of the causes of growth. The discussion examines current research on induced technological innovation, diffusion, and the role of transnational corporations.

- Chapter 36 offers a new discussion of the market processes that arise when countries go from no trade to free trade. This is designed to show students how markets will operate to ensure that the potential gains from specialization will be realized.

- Chapter 39 fully integrates international material with the new core macroeconomic model, which stresses trade, thus providing an up-to-date discussion of monetary and fiscal macroeconomic policy in an open economy.

- Chapter 40 focuses on economic development, tying together earlier discussions of trade, economic growth, foreign investment, and transnational corporations (TNCs). It discusses the Washington consensus on the importance of free-market forces to economic development together with the controversies concerning the possible need for active government policies to assist growth within the framework of free markets.

Supplements

Our book is accompanied by a workbook, *Study Guide and Problems,* by Fredric C. Menz and John H. Mutti. The workbook can be used either in the classroom or by the students on their own. It offers additional study support for each text chapter, including chapter overviews, objectives, multiple-choice questions, exercises, short problems, and answers. It is available in one- or two-volume editions.

An *Instructor's Manual,* prepared by us, includes an explanation of the approach used in each text chapter, along with a chapter overview, answers to all end-of-chapter questions, and additional teaching suggestions. Also provided are answers to all problems and cases in the student *Study Guide.*

Test Bank I, by Vikram Kumar, contains 2,400 updated and revised multiple-choice questions. *Test Bank II,* by Robert Graham and Clark Ross, offers 2,400 updated and revised multiple-choice questions. Both test banks are free to adopters. The *Test Banks* are also available in a microcomputerized version for IBM PCs or Macintosh computers called *Test Master,* which provides customized testing capabilities.

The Lipsey Disk 10: Key Concepts for Review, revised by William Davis, a computerized student review tool, provides 15 crucial multiple-choice questions for each chapter in the text. If an incorrect answer is given, the student is referred to specific text pages for further study. Free to adopters, it is available for use with IBM PCs and compatibles. *Lipsey MACROVIEW Simulation* is a software package that gives students hands-on experience in dealing with macro problems and variables. *Lipsey Micro Tutorial* is an interactive software tutorial package that helps students review microeconomic concepts in 10 key areas. Both of these programs are available free to adopters for use with IBM PCs and compatibles.

For this edition, over 100 illustrations in 18 key theory chapters are reproduced as four-color transparency acetates. In addition, the remaining figures in the text are reproduced in the form of transparency masters. All of these are available free to adopters.

Those Who Helped with This Edition

We are most grateful for all the helpful suggestions provided by the following individuals, who reviewed various drafts of the tenth edition of *Economics:* Dale Bails, Memphis State University; Lauri Bassi, Georgetown University; Donald N. Baum, University of Nebraska, Omaha; Dennis Byrne, University of Akron; Than Van Cao, Eastern Montana College; John Caskey, Swarthmore College; Celia Chen, University of Pennsylvania; Shih-Fan Chu, University of Nevada, Reno; Richard Claycombe, Western Maryland College; Richard Cornwall, Middlebury College; Robert Dolan, University of Richmond; Edwin T. Fujii, University of Hawaii; K. K. Fung, Memphis State University; Gary A. Gigliotti, Rutgers University; Sarah L. Glavin, Boston College; Fred C. Graham, The American University; Edward Gramlich, University of Michigan; Ralph Gunderson, University of Wisconsin at Oshkosh; Ronald Harstedt, Virginia Commonwealth University; Fred N. Hendon, Samford University; Carol Hogan, University of Michigan, Dearborn; Jack Hou, California State University, Long Beach; Saul Hymans,

University of Michigan; Arvind Jaggi, Franklin and Marshall College; Elaine Koppana, College of William and Mary; Jim Lee, Fort Hays State University; Mei-Hsiu Lin, State University of New York, Albany; Denton Marks, University of Wisconsin, Whitewater; W. Douglas Morgan, University of California, Santa Barbara; Max Moszer, Virginia Commonwealth University; Patrick B. O'Neill, University of North Dakota; Jeff Pliskin, Hamilton College; Malcolm Robinson, University of Cincinnati; Christine D. Romer, University of California, Berkeley; Niles C. Schoening, University of Alabama, Huntsville; Sanjay Shah, State University of New York, Albany; Stephen C. Sheppard, Oberlin College; Steve Venti, Dartmouth College; and Thomas E. Weisskopf, University of Michigan. We are most grateful to all of these people for their helpful suggestions.

The new edition has benefited greatly from the research assistance of Rachel Cohen, Patricia Casey-Purvis, and David Scoones. We are especially grateful to the students and teaching assistants in Economics 202 at the University of Michigan for invaluable comments and feedback. Ellen McKay and Robyn Wills handled with skill and patience our mountains of manuscript and innumerable revisions. Weidenfeld and Nicholson generously gave permission to use material first prepared for the seventh edition of *An Introduction to Positive Economics* by R. G. Lipsey and the second edition of *First Principles of Economics* by R. G. Lipsey and C. Harbury.

Richard G. Lipsey
Paul N. Courant
Douglas D. Purvis
Peter O. Steiner

Acknowledgments

So many teachers, colleagues, students, and friends contributed to the original book and to its continuing revision that it is impossible for us to acknowledge our debt to all of them individually. Hundreds of users, both teachers and students, have written us with specific suggested improvements, and much of the credit for the fact that the book has become more teachable belongs to them. We are listing here the names of all those who reviewed the first through the ninth editions.

Robert M. Aduddell
Phillip Allman
Wells Allred
Richard Anderson
Ernest Ankrim
G. C. Archibald
Christine Augustyniak
Douglas A. L. Auld
Stephen A. Baker
Bixio Barenco
Peter S. Barth
Willie J. Belton
Maurice C. Benewitz
Robert M. Bernado
Jeff Blais
George S. Bohler
Tom Bonsor
Charles Britton
Charles Brown
Owen M. Brovles
James L. Butkiewicz
Conrad Caligaris
Trudy Cameron
James T. Campen
Kathleen A. Carroll
Ira C. Castles
Richard J. Cebula
Robert J. Cheney
Charles Chittle
Wallace Cohen
John R. Coleman
Cynthia Cross
Robert Crouch
David H. Dean
David Denslow
Robert Dernberger

Charles Donahue, Jr.
Kenneth G. Elzinga
Carl E. Enomoto
Frances Esposito
Patricia Euzent
Jerry Evensky
Francis Flanagan
Belton M. Fleischer
Dascomb R. Forbush
Dorothy F. Forbush
Virginia L. Galbraith
Louis C. Gasper
J. Fred Giertz
E. Kenneth Grant
Eric Gustafson
Malcom D. Gutter
Scott D. Hakala
Hiroaki Hayakawa
Bruce Herrick
Stephen A. Hoenack
Emily Hoffman
John Isbister
Taka Ito
Janice Jacobson
William R. Johnson
Edward J. Kane
Bruce E. Kaufman
Ziad Keilany
Allen C. Kelley
Dennis Koepke
Kenneth J. Kopecky
Arthur Kruger
Michael Kupilik
Jerome K. Laurent
Luther D. Lawson

Thea M. Lee
Rodney H. Mabry
Richard McIntyre
A. McKee
John Madden
James R. Marsden
Gerald M. Miller
Felipe Montt
Theodore J. Morgan
W. Douglas Morgan
Edward J. Mulholland
Edwin Nadel
Stephen Nord
James Nordyke
Gerald T. O'Boyle
Kenji Okuda
Kent Olsen
Michael Perelman
Charlotte Phelps
George B. Pidot
Mark W. Plant
Joseph E. Pluta
Richard C. Porter
James Price
Robert C. Puth
Joe Rabianski
Maury Rabinowitz
Stephen E. Reynolds
Randolph Rice
Richard Rosenberg
Louis Rossiter
Bernard Saffran
B. Sahni
Arnold W. Sametz
Terrance Sandalow

Joseph L. Sax
W. M. Scammell
Elliot Schlar
Harvey Schwartz
Nancy Schwartz
Stuart O. Schweitzer
Frank A. Scott, Jr.
Joseph J. Seneca
Donald Shoup
Donald H. Silva
A. P. Simson
Murray Smith
William Doyle Smith
Gordon R. Sparks
Frank Stafford
Dennis Starleaf
M. Stelcner
Courtenay Stone
Kenneth Strand
William J. Swift
Josephine K. Tan
David Terkla
John Throckmorton, Jr.
John M. Trapani, III
W. R. Trenton
Laura Tyson
Charles Vars
Gerald Visgilio
Robert F. Wallace
Stanislaw Wasowski
Pamela Weidler
Mira Wilkins
C. R. Winegarden
Jeffrey Wolcowitz
William C. Wood
Habib A. Zuberi

To the Student

A good course in economics will give you insight into how an economy functions and into some currently debated policy issues. Like all rewarding subjects, economics will not be mastered without effort. A book on economics must be worked at. It cannot be read like a novel.

Each of you must develop an individual technique for studying, but the following suggestions may prove helpful. It is usually a good idea to read a chapter quickly in order to get the general run of the argument. At this first reading, you may want to skip the boxes and any footnotes. Then, after reading the Topics for Review and the Discussion Questions, reread the chapter more slowly, making sure that you understand each step of the argument. With respect to the figures and tables, be sure you understand how the conclusions that are stated in the brief tag lines with each table or figure have been reached. You must not skip the captions. They provide the core of economic reasoning. You should be prepared to spend time on difficult sections; occasionally, you may spend an hour on only a few pages. Paper and a pencil are indispensable equipment in your reading. It is best to follow a difficult argument by building your own diagram while the argument unfolds rather than by relying on the finished diagram as it appears in the book. It is often helpful to invent numerical examples to illustrate general propositions. The end-of-chapter questions require you to apply what you have studied. We advise you to outline answers to some of the questions. In short, you should seek to understand economics, not to memorize it.

After you have read each part in detail, reread it quickly from beginning to end. It is often difficult to understand why certain things are done when they are viewed as isolated points, but when you reread a whole part, much that did not seem relevant or entirely comprehensible will fall into place in the analysis.

We call your attention to the glossary at the end of the book. Any time that you encounter a concept that seems vaguely familiar but is not clear to you, check the glossary. The chances are that it will be there and that its definition will remind you of what you once understood. If you are still in doubt, check the index entry to find where the concept is discussed more fully. Incidentally, the glossary, along with the captions that accompany figures and tables and the end-of-chapter summaries, may prove to be very helpful when you are reviewing for examinations.

The bracketed colored numbers in the text itself refer to a series of 47 mathematical notes that are found starting on page M-1 at the end of the book. For those of you who like mathematics or prefer mathematical argument to verbal or geometric exposition, these may prove useful. Others may ignore them.

We hope that you will find the book rewarding and stimulating. Students who used earlier editions made some of the most helpful suggestions for revision, and we hope that you will carry on the tradition. If you are moved to write to us, please do.

THE NATURE OF ECONOMICS

1

The Economic Problem

Turn on the TV news, read your local newspaper or the *New York Times,* glance at *Time* or *Newsweek* magazines, and you will see for yourself that many of the world's most pressing problems are economic.

Why did communism fail to deliver acceptable living standards to the citizens of the countries of Eastern Europe and the republics of the former USSR? Are the developed nations right in making the adoption of more market-oriented economic policies a precondition of increased foreign aid to the less developed countries of the world? What is the impact of the growth of vast transnational corporations that conduct business over much of the world? Will the population explosion cause the growth of mouths to feed to outrun the growth of food to feed those mouths? Are economists right in urging that environmental protection is often best accomplished using market-price incentives rather than direct government intervention?

Your media survey of press, radio, and TV will also show the importance of economic issues in the problems facing the United States today.

How is it that when the average U.S. citizen enjoys one of the highest living standards the world has ever seen, a standard vastly higher than has been achieved by most of the people who have ever lived on the earth, so many U.S. citizens should feel economically harassed and worry about how to pay the bills? Is the United States right to feel threatened by Japanese economic power? Will a North American Free Trade Agreement (NAFTA) be a good or a bad thing for the average U.S. citizen?

Does the size of the massive U.S. government budget deficit affect the average citizen's living standards? Is the Federal Reserve System right in believing that a low inflation rate is good for the economy? Why has the distribution of income in the United States become more unequal over the past two decades? Does it pay you to go on to higher education? Does it pay the nation to subsidize you to do so?

Of course, not all the world's problems are primarily economic. Political, biological, social, cultural, and philosophical issues often predominate. However, as the following examples suggest, no matter how "noneconomic" a particular problem may seem, it will almost always have a significant economic dimension.

1. The crises that lead to wars often have economic roots. Nations often fight for oil and rice and land to live on, although the rhetoric of their leaders evokes God, Glory, and the Fatherland.
2. It took 100,000 years, from the time *Homo sapiens* first appeared on earth until about 1800, for the human population to reach 1 billion. In the next hundred years a second billion was added. Three billion more came in the next 80 years. The world's population is estimated to be over 10 billion well before the middle of the next century.

The economic consequences are steady pressures on the environment and the food supply. Unless the human race can find ways to deal with these pressures, increasing millions face starvation and increasing billions face rising levels of environmental degradation.

3. The *greenhouse effect* describes the possibility of a gradual warming of the earth's climate due to a cumulative buildup of CO_2 in the atmosphere. If the possibility proves a reality, the warming will have significant economic consequences, changing both production possibilities and consumption patterns.

What Is Economics?

So far we have identified a handful of the important current issues on which economics can shed some light. One way to define *economics* is to say that it is the social science that deals with such problems. Another definition, perhaps better known, is Alfred Marshall's: "Economics is a study of mankind in the ordinary business of life." A more penetrating definition might be the following:

Economics is the study of the use of scarce resources to satisfy unlimited human wants.

Scarcity is inevitable and is central to economic problems. What are society's resources? Why is scarcity inevitable? What are the consequences of scarcity?

Resources and Commodities

A society's resources consist of natural endowments such as land, forests, and minerals; human resources, both mental and physical; and manufactured aids to production such as tools, machinery, and buildings. Economists call such resources **factors of production**[1] because they are used to produce the outputs that people desire. We call these outputs **commodities** and divide them into goods and services. **Goods** are tangible (e.g., cars and shoes), and **services** are intangible (e.g., haircuts and education).

Notice the implication of positive value contained in the terms *goods* and *services*. (Compare the terms *bads* and *disservices*.)

People use goods and services to satisfy many of their wants. The act of making them is called **production,** and the act of using them to satisfy wants is called **consumption.** Goods are valued for the services they provide. An automobile, for example, helps to satisfy its owner's desires for transportation, mobility, and possibly status.

Scarcity

For most of the world's $5\frac{1}{2}$ billion human beings, scarcity is real and ever present. In relation to desires (for more and better food, clothing, housing, schooling, entertainment, and so forth), existing resources are woefully inadequate; there are enough to produce only a small fraction of the goods and services that are wanted.

But, one might ask, are not the advanced industrialized nations rich enough that scarcity is nearly banished? After all, they have been characterized as affluent societies. Whatever affluence may mean, it does not mean the end of the problem of scarcity. Most households that earn $60,000 a year (a princely amount by world standards) have no trouble spending it on things that seem useful to them. Yet it would take twice the present output of the U.S. economy to produce enough to allow all U.S. households to earn that amount.

Choice

Because resources are scarce, all societies face the problem of deciding what to produce and how much each person will consume.[2] Societies differ in who makes the choices and how they are made, but the need to choose is common to all. Just as scarcity

---

[1] Definitions of the terms in boldface type can be found in the glossary at the back of the book.

[2] There is a partial exception, which is studied later. This occurs when there is a recession in business activity of such severity that there are unemployed amounts of *all* resources. By putting these resources back to work, it is possible for societies to have more of what they now produce without having less of any other production. Even in such a situation, however, many important choices must be made. For example, those receiving incomes must decide what to buy with these incomes, and the government must decide how much of total national production to allocate to the support of those who are unemployed.

implies the need for choice, so choice implies the existence of cost. A decision to have more of something requires a decision to have less of something else. The less of "something else" can be thought of as the cost of having the more of something.

Scarcity implies that choices must be made, and making choices implies the existence of costs.

SCARCITY → CHOICE → COSTS

Opportunity Cost

To see how choice implies cost we look first at a trivial example and then at one that vitally affects all of us; both examples involve precisely the same fundamental principles.

Consider the choice that must be made by a small boy who has 50 cents to spend and who is determined to spend it all on candy. For him there are only two kinds of candy in the world: gumdrops, which sell for 5 cents each, and chocolates, which sell for 10 cents each. The boy would like to buy 10 gumdrops and 10 chocolates, but he knows (or will soon discover) that this is not possible: It is not an *attainable combination* given his scarce resources. However, several combinations are attainable: 8 gumdrops and 1 chocolate, 4 gumdrops and 3 chocolates, 2 gumdrops and 4 chocolates, and so on. Some of these combinations leave him with money unspent, and he is not interested in them. Only six combinations, as shown in Figure 1-1, are both attainable and use all his money.

After careful thought, the boy has almost decided to buy 6 gumdrops and 2 chocolates, but at the last moment he decides that he simply must have 3 chocolates. What will it cost him to get this extra chocolate? One answer is 2 gumdrops. As seen in the figure, this is the number of gumdrops he must forgo to get the extra chocolate. Economists describe the 2 gumdrops as the *opportunity cost* of the third chocolate.

Another answer is that the cost of the third chocolate is 10 cents. However, given the boy's budget and his intentions, this answer is less revealing than the first one. Where the real choice is between more of this and more of that, the cost of "this" is usefully viewed as what you cannot have of "that."

The idea of opportunity cost is one of the central insights of economics.

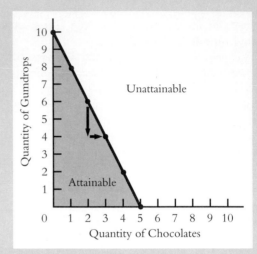

FIGURE 1-1
A Choice Between Gumdrops and Chocolates

A limited amount of money forces a choice among alternatives. Six combinations of gumdrops and chocolates are attainable and use all of the boy's money. The negatively sloped line provides a boundary between attainable and unattainable combinations. The arrows show that the opportunity cost of 1 more chocolate is 2 gumdrops. In this example the opportunity cost is constant, and therefore the boundary is a straight line.

The **opportunity cost** of using resources for a certain purpose is the benefit given up by not using them in an alternative way; that is, it is the cost measured in terms of other commodities that could have been obtained instead. If, for example, resources that could have produced 20 miles of road are used instead to produce two small hospitals, the opportunity cost of a hospital is 10 miles of road; looked at the other way round, the opportunity cost of one mile of road is one-tenth of a hospital.

Every time a choice must be made, opportunity costs are incurred.

Production Possibilities

Although the choice between gumdrops and chocolates is a minor consumption decision, the essential nature of the decision is the same whatever the choice being made. Consider, for example, the important choice between military and civilian goods.

If resources are fully employed, it is not possible to have more of both. However, if the government feels able to lower its arms production, this will free up the resources needed to produce more civilian goods. The opportunity cost of increased civilian goods is the forgone production of arms.

The choice is illustrated in Figure 1-2. Because resources are limited, some combinations—those that would require more than the total available supply of resources for their production—cannot be attained. The negatively sloped curve on the graph divides the combinations that can be attained from those that cannot. Points above and to the right of this curve cannot be attained because there are not enough resources; points below and to the left of the curve can be attained without using all of the available resources; and points on the curve can just be attained if all the available resources are used. The curve is called the **production possibility boundary** or **production possibility curve.** It has a negative slope because, when all resources are being used, having more of one kind of good requires having less of the other kind.

A production possibility boundary illustrates three concepts: scarcity, choice, and opportunity cost. *Scarcity* **is indicated by the unattainable combinations above the boundary;** *choice,* **by the need to choose among the alternative attainable points along the boundary; and** *opportunity cost,* **by the negative slope of the boundary.**

The shape of the production possibility boundary in Figure 1-2 implies that more and more civilian goods must be given up to achieve equal successive increases in military goods. This shape, referred to as *concave* to the origin, indicates that the opportunity cost of either good grows larger and larger as we increase the amount of it that is produced. A straight-line boundary, as in Figure 1-1, indicates that the opportunity cost of one good in terms of the other stays constant, no matter how much of it is produced. As we shall see later, the case of rising opportunity cost applies to many important choices.

Four Key Economic Problems

Most problems studied by economists can be grouped under four main headings.

1. What Is Produced and How?

The allocation of scarce resources among alternative uses, called **resource allocation,** determines the quantities of various goods that are produced. Choosing to produce a particular combination of goods means choosing a particular allocation of resources among the industries or regions producing the goods. This is because producing much of one good requires that many resources be allocated to its production.

Further, because resources are scarce, it is desirable that they be used efficiently. Hence it matters

---

FIGURE 1-2
A Production Possibility Boundary

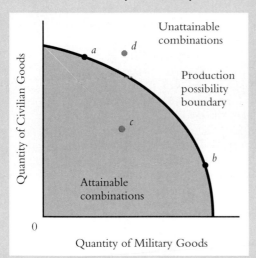

The negatively sloped boundary shows the combinations that are just attainable when all of the society's resources are effeciently employed. The quantity of military goods produced is measured along the horizontal axis, the quantity of civilian goods along the vertical axis. Thus any point on the diagram indicates some amount of each kind of good produced. The production possibility boundary separates the attainable combinations of goods, such as *a, b,* and *c,* from unattainable combinations, such as *d.* It is negatively sloped because resources are scarce: When resources are fully employed, more of one kind of good can be produced only if resources are freed by producing less of the other kind of good. Points *a* and *b* represent full and efficient use of society's resources. Point *c* represents either inefficient use of resources or failure to use all the available resources.

which of the available methods of production is used to produce each of the goods.

2. What Is Consumed and by Whom?

What is the relationship between an economy's production of commodities and the consumption enjoyed by its citizens? Economists seek to understand what determines the distribution of a nation's total output among its people. Who gets a lot, who gets a little, and why? What role does international trade play in this?

Questions 1 and 2 fall within **microeconomics**, the study of the allocation of resources and the distribution of income as they are affected by the working of the price system and government policies that seek to influence it.

3. How Much Unemployment and Inflation Exist?

When an economy is in a recession, unemployed workers would like to have jobs, the factories in which they could work are available, the managers and owners would like to be able to operate their factories, raw materials are available in abundance, and the goods that could be produced by these resources are wanted by individuals in the community, but for some reason resources remain unemployed. This means that the economy is operating within its production possibility boundary, at a point such as *c* in Figure 1-2.

The world's economies have often experienced bouts of prolonged and substantial changes in price levels. In recent decades the course of prices has almost always been upward. The 1970s and early 1980s saw accelerating inflation, not only in the United States but also in most other parts of the world. Then inflation slowed while unemployment soared. Were these two events related? Why do governments worry that reductions in either unemployment or inflation may be at the cost of a temporary increase in the other?

4. Is Productive Capacity Growing?

The capacity to produce commodities to satisfy human wants grows rapidly in some countries, slowly in others, and actually declines in still others. Growth in productive capacity can be represented by an outward shift of the production possibility boundary, as shown in Figure 1-3. If an economy's capacity to produce goods and services is growing, combinations that are

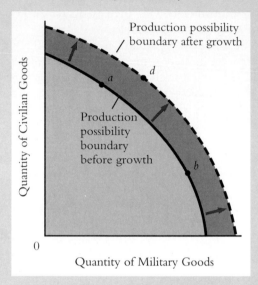

FIGURE 1-3
The Effect of Economic Growth on the Production Possibility Boundary

Economic growth shifts the boundary outward and makes it possible to produce more of all commodities. Before growth in productive capacity, points *a* and *b* were on the production possibility boundary and point *d* was an unattainable combination. After growth, as shown by the dark shaded band, point *d* and many other previously unattainable combinations are attainable.

unattainable today will become attainable tomorrow. Growth makes it possible to have more of all goods.

Questions 3 and 4 fall within **macroeconomics**, the study of the determination of economic aggregates such as total output, total employment, the price level, and the rate of economic growth.

Alternative Economic Systems

An economic system is a distinctive method of providing answers to the basic economic questions just discussed. All such systems are complex. They include producers of every sort—publicly and privately owned, as well as domestically owned and foreign-owned, producers. They include consumers of every sort: young and old, rich and poor, working and nonworking. They include laws—such as those relating to property rights—rules, regulations, taxes, subsidies, and everything else that governments use to influence what is produced, how it is produced, and who gets it. They also include customs of every conceivable kind, and the entire range of contemporary mores and values.

Types of Economic Systems

Although every economy is in some ways distinct, it is helpful to distinguish three pure types, called *traditional, command,* and *market* economies. These economies differ in the way in which economic decisions are *coordinated.* All real economies contain some elements of each method.

Traditional Systems

A traditional economic system is one in which behavior is based primarily on tradition, custom, and habit. Young men follow their fathers' occupations—hunting, fishing, and so on. Women do what their mothers did—typically cooking and field work. There is little change in the pattern of goods produced from year to year, other than those imposed by the vagaries of nature. The techniques of production also follow traditional patterns, except when the effects of an occasional new invention are felt. Finally, production is allocated among the members according to long-established traditions. In short, the answers to the economic questions of what to produce, how to produce, and how to distribute are determined by traditions.

Such a system works best in an unchanging environment. Under static conditions, a system that does not continually require people to make choices can prove effective in meeting economic and social needs.

Traditional systems were common in earlier times. The feudal system, under which most people lived in medieval Europe, was a largely traditional society. Peasants, artisans, and most others living in villages inherited their positions in that society. They also usually inherited their specific jobs, which they handled in traditional ways. For example, the blacksmith made customary charges for dealing with horses brought to him, and it would have been unthinkable for him to decline his services to any villager who requested them.

Today only a few small, isolated, self-sufficient communities still retain mainly traditional systems.

Examples can be found in the Canadian Arctic and in Patagonia. Also, in many less-developed countries significant aspects of economic behavior are still governed by traditional patterns.

Command Systems

In command systems, economic behavior is determined by some central authority, which makes most of the necessary decisions on what to produce, how to produce it, and who gets it. Such economies are characterized by the *centralization* of decision making. Because centralized decision makers usually lay down elaborate and complex plans for the behavior that they wish to impose, the terms **command economy** and **centrally planned economy** are usually used synonymously.

The sheer quantity of data required for central planning of an entire economy is enormous, and the task of analyzing it to produce a fully integrated plan can hardly be exaggerated. Moreover, the plan must be a rolling process, continually changing to take account not only of current data but also of future trends in labor supplies, technological developments, and people's tastes for various goods and services. Doing so involves the planners in *forecasting.* This is a notoriously difficult business, not least because of the unavailability of all essential, accurate, and up-to-date information.

A decade ago over one-third of the world's population lived in countries that relied heavily on central planning to deal with the basic economic questions. Today the number of such countries is small. Even in countries where planning is the proclaimed system, as in China, increasing amounts of market determination are being quietly permitted.

Market Systems

In the third type of economic system, the decisions about resource allocation are made without any central direction. Instead, they result from innumerable, independent decisions made by individual producers and consumers; such a system is known as a **free-market economy** or, more simply, a **market economy**. In such an economy, decisions relating to the basic economic issues are decentralized. They are nonetheless coordinated. The main coordinating device is the set of market-determined prices—which is why free-market systems are often called *price systems.* Because much of this book is devoted to studying how market systems work, little more needs to be said about them at this point.

Mixed Systems

Economies that are fully traditional, or fully centrally controlled, or wholly free-market are pure types that are useful for studying basic principles. When we look in detail at *any* real economy, however, we discover that its economic behavior is the result of some mixture of central control and market determination, with a certain amount of traditional behavior as well. In practice, every economy is a **mixed economy** in the sense that it combines significant elements of all three systems—traditional, command, and market—in determining economic behavior.[3]

Furthermore, within any economy, the degree of the mix will vary from sector to sector. For example, in some planned economies the command principle was used more often to determine behavior in heavy goods industries, such as steel, than in agriculture. Farmers were often given substantial freedom to produce and sell what they wished in response to varying market prices.

When we speak of a particular economy as being a centrally planned economy, we mean only that the degree of the mix is weighted heavily toward the command principle. When we speak of an economy as being a market economy, we mean only that the degree of the mix is weighted heavily toward decentralized decision making in response to market signals. It is important to realize that such distinctions are always matters of degree, and that almost every conceivable mix can be found across the spectrum of the world's economies.

Although no country offers an example of either system working alone, some economies, such as those of the United States, France, and Singapore, rely much more heavily on market decisions than others, such as the economies of China, North Korea, and Cuba. Yet even in the United States, the command principle has some sway. Minimum wages, rules and regulations for environmental protection, quotas on some agricultural outputs, and restrictions on the import of items such as textiles, cheap shoes, and sugar are the obvious examples.

Ownership of Resources

We have seen that economies differ as to the principle used for coordinating their economic decisions. They also differ as to who owns their productive resources. Who owns a nation's farms and factories, its coal mines and forests? Who owns its railways, streams, and golf courses? Who owns its houses and hotels?

In a private-ownership economy, the basic raw materials, the productive assets of the society, and the goods produced in the economy, are predominantly privately owned. By this standard the United States has primarily a private-ownership economy. However, even in the United States, public ownership extends beyond the usual basic services such as schools and local transportation systems to include such other activities as housing projects, forest and range land, and electric power utilities.

In contrast, a public-ownership economy is one in which the productive assets are predominantly publicly owned. This was true of the former USSR, and it is true to a great extent in present-day China. In China, however, private ownership exists in many sectors—including the rapidly growing part of the manufacturing sector that is foreign owned, mainly by Japanese and by Chinese from Taiwan, Hong Kong, and Singapore.

The Coordination-Ownership Mix

Leaving aside tradition because it is not the predominant coordinating method in any modern market economy, there are four possible combinations of coordination and ownership principles. Of the two most common combinations, the first is the private-ownership market economy, in which the market principle is the main coordinating mechanism and the majority of productive assets are privately owned. The second most common combination during the twentieth century has been the public-ownership planned economy, in which central planning is the primary means of coordinating economic decisions and property is primarily publicly owned.

The two other possible combinations are a market economy in which the resources are publicly owned and a command economy in which the resources are privately owned. No modern economy has acheived either of these two hybrid types. Nazi Germany from 1932 to 1945 went some way toward combining private ownership with the command principle. The United Kingdom from 1945 to 1980 went quite a way toward a public-ownership market economy, because many industries and much housing were publicly owned. On balance, however, Germany and the United Kingdom were still best described as private-ownership market economies. (The United Kingdom's privatization program in

---

[3] Although tradition influences behavior in all societies, we shall have little to say about it in the rest of this chapter because we are primarily interested in the consequences of making economic decisions through the market and the command principles.

the 1980s returned most publicly owned assets to private ownership, thus firmly placing that country back in the ranks of private-ownership market economies.)

Command Versus Market Determination

For over a century a great debate raged on the relative merits of the command principle versus the market principle for coordinating economic decisions in practice. The USSR, the countries of Eastern Europe, and China were command economies for much of this century. The United States and most of the countries of Western Europe were, and are, primarily market economies. The successes of the USSR and China in the early stages of industrialization suggested to many observers earlier in this century that the command principle was at least as good for organizing economic behavior as the market principle, if not better. In the long haul, however, planned economies proved a failure of such disastrous proportions as to seriously depress the living standards of their citizens.

Rarely in human history has such a decisive verdict been delivered on two competing systems. Box 1-1 gives some of the reasons why central planning was a failure in Eastern Europe and the USSR. The discussion is of more than purely historical interest because the reasons for the failure of planned economies give insight into the reasons for the relative success of free market economies.

The Lessons from the Failure of Command Systems

The failure of planned economies suggests the superiority of decentralized markets over centrally planned ones as coordinating and signaling devices. Put another way, it demonstrates the superiority of mixed economies with substantial elements of market determination over fully planned command economies. However, it does *not* demonstrate, as some have asserted, the superiority of completely free market economies over mixed economies.

There is no guarantee that free markets will handle, on their own, such urgent matters as controlling pollution and producing sustainable growth. (Indeed, as we shall see in later chapters, much economic theory is devoted to explaining why free markets often fail to do these things.) Mixed economies, with

significant degrees of government intervention, are needed to do these jobs.

Furthermore, acceptance of the free market over central planning does not provide an excuse to ignore a country's pressing social issues. Acceptance of the benefits of the free market still leaves plenty of scope to debate the kinds, amounts, and directions of government interventions into the workings of our market-based economy that will help to achieve social goals.

It follows that there is still room for disagreement about the *degree* of the mix of market and government determination in any modern mixed economy—room enough to accommodate such divergent views as could be expressed by the Republican and Democratic parties in the United States and conservative and social democratic parties in Europe. People can accept the free market as an efficient way of organizing economic affairs and still disagree about many things. A partial list includes the optimal amount and types of government regulation of, and assistance to, the functioning of the economy; the types of measures needed to protect the environment; whether health care should be provided by the public or the private sector; and the optimal amount, and design, of social services and other policies intended to redistribute income from more to less fortunate citizens. Some of the issues that arise when we debate the value of alternative economic systems in general, or of specific policies in particular, are discussed in Box 1-2.

Aspects of a Modern Economy

Throughout this book we study the functioning of a modern, market-based, mixed economy, security such as is found in the United States today. By way of introduction, this section introduces a few salient aspects that should be kept in mind from the outset.

Origins

The modern market economies that we know today first arose in Europe out of the ashes of the feudal system. As we have already mentioned, the feudal system was a traditional one in which people did jobs based on heredity (the miller's son became the next generation's miller) and received shares of their

Box 1-1

The Failure of Central Planning

The year 1989 signaled to the world what many economists had long argued: the superiority of a market-oriented price system over central planning as a method of organizing economic activity. The failure of central planning had many causes, but four were particularly significant.

The Failure of Coordination

In centrally planned economies a body of planners tries to coordinate all the economic decisions about production, investment, trade, and consumption that are likely to be made by the producers and consumers throughout the country. This proved impossible to do with any reasonable degree of efficiency. Bottlenecks in production, shortages of some goods, and gluts of others plagued the Soviet economy for decades. For example, in 1989 much of a bumper harvest rotted on the farm because of shortages of storage and transportation facilities, and for years there was an ample supply of black-and-white television sets and severe shortages of toilet paper and soap.

Failure of Quality Control

Central planners can monitor the number of units produced by any factory and reward those who over-fulfill their production targets and punish those who fall short. It is much harder, however, for them to monitor quality. A constant Soviet problem, there-fore, was the production of poor-quality products. Factory managers were concerned with meeting their quotas by whatever means were available, and once the goods passed out of their factory, what happened to them was someone else's headache. The quality problem was so serious that very few Eastern European-manufactured products were able to stand up to the newly permitted competition from superior goods produced in the advanced market societies.

In market economies, poor quality is punished by low sales, and retailers soon give a signal to factory managers by shifting their purchases to other suppliers. The incentives that obviously flow from such private-sector purchasing discretion are generally absent from command economies, where purchases and sales are planned centrally.

Misplaced Incentives

In market economies, relative wages and salaries provide incentives for labor to move from place to place, and the possibilty of losing one's job provides an incentive to work diligently. This is a harsh mechanism that punishes losers with loss of income (although social programs provide floors to the amount of economic punishment that can be suffered). In planned economies, workers usually have complete job security. Industrial unemployment is rare, and even when it does occur, new jobs are usually found for those who lose theirs. Although the high level of

village's total output that were based on custom. Peasants were tied to the land. Much land was owned by the crown and granted to the lord of the manor in return for military services. Some of it was made available for the common use of all villagers. Property such as the village mill and blacksmith's shop never belonged to those who worked there and could therefore never be bought and sold by them.

In contrast, modern economies are based on market transactions between people who voluntarily decide whether or not to engage in them. They have the right to buy and sell what they wish, to accept or refuse offered work, and to move to where they want when they want. Key institutions are private property and freedom of contract, both of which must be maintained by active government policies. The government creates laws of ownership security is attractive to many, it proved impossible to provide sufficient incentives for reasonably hard and efficient work under such conditions. In the words of Oxford historian Timothy Garton Ash, who wrote eyewitness chronicles of the developments in Eastern Europe from 1980 to 1990, the social contract between the workers and the government in the Eastern countries was "We pretend to work, and you pretend to pay us."

Because of the absence of a work-oriented incentive system, income inequalities do not provide the normal free-market incentives. Income inequalities were used instead to provide incentives for party members to toe the line. The major gap in income standards was between party members on the one hand and non–party members on the other. The former had access to such privileges as special stores where imported goods were available, special hospitals providing sanitary and efficient medical care, and special resorts where good vacations were available. In contrast, nonmembers had none of these things.

Environmental Degradation

Fulfilling production plans became the all-embracing incentive in planned economies, to the exclusion of most other considerations, including the environment. As a result, environmental degradation occurred in all the countries of Eastern Europe on a scale unknown in advanced Western nations. A particularly disturbing example occured in central Asia, where high quotas for cotton output led to indiscriminate use of pesticides and irrigation. Birth defects are now found in nearly one child in three, and the vast Aral Sea has been half drained, causing incalculable environmental effects.

The failure to protect the environment stems from a combination of the pressure to fulfill plans and the lack of a political marketplace where citizens can express their preferences for the environment over economic gain. Imperfect though the system may be in democratic market economies, their record of environmental protection has been vastly better than that of comand economies.

The Price System

In contrast to the failures of command economies, the performance of the free market price system is impressive. One theme of this book is *market success:* how the price system works to coordinate with relative efficiency the decentralized decisions made by private consumers and producers, providing the right quantities of relatively high-quality outputs and incentives for efficient work. It is important, however, not to conclude that doing things better means doing things perfectly. Another theme of this book is *market failure:* how and why the unaided price system sometimes fails to produce efficient results and fails to take account of social values that cannot be expressed through the marketplace.

and contract and then provides the courts to enforce these laws.

Living Standards

The material living standards of any society depend on how much it can produce. What there is to consume depends on what is produced. If the productive capacity of a society is small, then the living standards of its typical citizen will be low. Only by raising that productive capacity can average living standards be raised. No society can generate increased real consumption merely by voting its citizens higher money incomes.

How much a society can produce depends both on how many of its citizens are at work producing things and on their productivity in their work. How

Box 1-2

Ends and Means

To understand debates about relative desirability of different systems—as well as countless other debates about economic matters—we need first to distinguish between the goals of our actions and the means that we use to achieve those goals. Our goals are called **ends**; they are the things that we strive for. The things that we use to achieve our ends are our **means**; they are the methods of achieving our goals.

In the economic aspects of life, most people's ends include (1) achieving a satisfactory and, ideally, a rising living standard, (2) maintaining a reasonable quality of the environment in which they live, and (3) as far as possible, protecting themselves and others from the consequences of such serious disasters as the loss of their job, the onset of a major disability, or the bankruptcy of their employer.

All three examples represent a broad group of ends. The first relates to our material living standards. The second relates to the quality of the environment in which we live and work. The third relates to our social welfare system—the system that is intended to shield citizens from the worst consequences of disasters and to provide a "living-standard safety net" below which no one should be forced to sink for any reason. Although many others exist, these are three of our most important economic ends.

Debates over Means

Many political and economic debates relate to the alleged potency of alternative means to achieve agreed ends. Consider some examples.

The two great systems of command and free-market economies were both seen as means to higher living standards and better control over our environment. Starting in 1989, the countries of Eastern Europe made the choice to move toward a free-market system, in part because their citizens thought

that it was, among other things, a superior means to the end of higher living standards.

Many U.S. citizens support government intervention into the markets for privately rented accommodations (rent controls) and farm production (price supports and subsidies). This is not because they value intervention for its own sake. Instead, they hope that such intervention will be a means toward higher incomes for producers or lower prices to consumers, which in turn means a rise in the living standards of those concerned. Opponents agree that a rise in living standards is desirable but argue that these means are inappropriate to the ends. They say, for example, that the long-term result of government intervention into agricultural markets is that consumers will be worse off and only a few farmers better off than if the market had been left alone.

Debates over Ends

The interests of various groups who are pursuing different ends can also conflict. Everyone may agree, for example, that a particular agricultural policy makes farmers better off, but at the expense of consumers who must pay higher prices for their products. In this case, there is a real conflict between groups. The issue then becomes deciding between competing ends—improving the lot of farmers or that of consumers—rather than judging between alternative means to agreed ends.

Conflicts can also emerge over ends because different groups put different values on alternative ends. When environmental groups oppose the establishment of a local pulp mill while potential employees support it, the two groups are applying different values to two competing ends: more local job creation and more environmental protection.

well has the U.S. economy performed in each of these dimensions?

Jobs

In spite of some short-term ups and downs, the trend of total employment has been upward over most of modern U.S. history. For example, in 1951 there were 60 million U.S. citizens in civilian employment (excluding the armed forces), whereas in 1991 the figure was 117 million. This is a net creation of 57 million new jobs over that 40-year period.

These new jobs provided employment for a rising population and for the increasing proportion of that population who wished to work. The percentage of the population over 16 who were in the labor force (i.e., either working or looking for work) rose from 59 percent in 1951 to 66 percent in 1991. This modest overall increase masked large off-setting movements in male and female participation in the labor force. Over that period, the percentage of women over 16 who were in the labor force rose from 35 to 57 percent, whereas the percentage of men fell from 86 to 76 percent.

Labor Productivity

Labor productivity refers to the amount produced per hour of work. Rising living standards are closely linked to the rising productivity of the typical worker. If each worker produces more, then (other things being equal) there will be more production in total, and hence more for each person to consume on average.

In the period from 1750 to 1850 the market economies in Europe and the United States became industrial economies. With industrialization, modern market economies have raised ordinary people out of poverty by raising productivity at rates that appear slow from year to year but that have dramatic effects on living standards when sustained over long periods of time.

> Over a year, or even over a decade, the economic gains [of the late eighteenth and the nineteenth centuries], after allowing for the growth of population, were so little noticeable that it was widely believed that the gains were experienced only by the rich, and not by the poor. Only as the West's compounded growth continued through the twentieth century did its breadth become clear. It became obvious that Western working classes were increasingly well off and that the Western middle classes were prospering and growing as a proportion of the whole population. Not

that poverty disappeared. The West's achievement was not the abolition of poverty but the reduction of its incidence from 90 percent of the population to 30 percent, 20 percent, or less, depending on the country and one's definition of poverty. . . . [4]

Figure 1-4 shows the rise in the productivity of U.S. labor from 1889 to 1990. In spite of many short-term variations, the general trend is unmistakably upward. The trend in productivity of 1.9 percent from 1898 to 1938 doubles output per worker in a little less than 40 years. The trend of 3 percent from 1938 to 1974 doubles it in a little less than 25 years! (A helpful device is the *rule of 72*: Divide 72 by the annual growth rate, and the result is approximately the number of years required for income to double.) **[1]**[5]

These are potent sources of increases in living standards. Over the long period of rising productivity, U.S. citizens (as well as the citizens of most industrial countries) got used to each generation being substantially better off than each preceding generation. In the middle period from 1938 to 1974, children whose income relative to their contemporaries was the same as their parents' could expect to earn about twice the real income their parents had enjoyed.

Then in the mid-1970s, this productivity growth fell substantially to around 0.9 percent. Currently the typical child 25 years younger than his or her parents can expect to be no more than 20 percent better off than his or her parents. This is a remarkable reduction in the rate that each generation is becoming better off materially. Over long periods of time, however, even 0.9 percent productivity growth is still a potent force for change because it doubles real output per worker about every 80 years, or one human lifetime.

Distribution of Income

What we have just said is not the end of the story. Not only has the rate of increase in aggregate income slowed dramatically in recent years, but the way in which that income is distributed among the various income groups has also altered significantly.

---

[4] N. Rosenberg and L. E. Birdzell, Jr., *How the West Grew Rich* (New York: Basic Books, 1986).

[5] Notes giving mathematical demonstrations of the concepts presented in the text are designated by boldface reference numbers. These notes can be found at the end of the book beginning on page M-1.

FIGURE 1-4
Growth in Labor Productivity

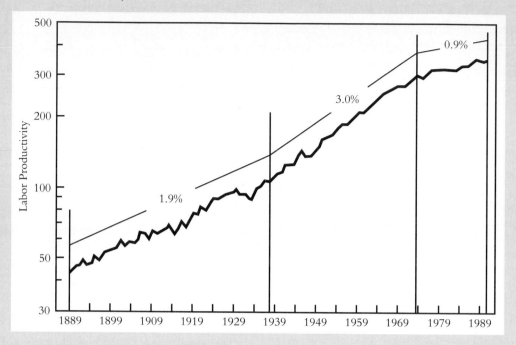

Labor productivity has grown over the time shown but at significantly different rates. From 1889 to 1937, the underlying rate of growth of output per worker, which is called labor productivity, was 1.9 percent. From then until 1974, it was 3.0 percent. After 1974, the rate slowed dramatically to 0.9 percent. It may turn out that the nontypical period is the postwar period with its rapid 3 percent growth rate that tended to double labor productivity every quarter of a century. The chart uses an index number that shows percentage changes with 1929 taken as equal to 100. The vertical axis is plotted on a logarithmic scale, which has the effect of making equal percentage changes have equal distances. (For further discussion of logarithmic scales see pages 41–42.) (*Source: Economic Report of the President, 1992, p. 91.*)

In the United States, incomes became progressively more equally distributed up through the 1960s. After that, the trend reversed. Over the 1970s, 1980s, and 1990s the distribution of income has slowly become more unequal. For example, the share of income received by the lowest 20 percent in the income distribution rose from 5.0 percent in 1947 to 5.7 percent in 1968, then fell to 4.6 percent in 1990. That is a 20 percent decrease in the share of total income going to the poorest group over a 25-year period. At the other end of the distribution, the share of income going to the highest 20 percent on the income scale fell from 43.0 percent in 1947 to 40.5 percent in 1968, then rose to 44.3 percent by 1990. That is close to a 10 percent increase in the share of total income going to the richest group in the society. (Similar changes have been observed in several advanced industrial economies, suggesting that the explanation is not solely due to special circumstances found only in the United States.)

This growing inequality in the distribution of income seems to a great extent to be due to the increasing need for, and hence higher earnings of, relatively well-educated workers. This in turn is associated with changes in many production processes that demand higher and higher levels of skill. Henry Ford boasted just before 1914 that any job on his assembly line could be taught in 15 minutes to an immigrant worker with an imperfect command of English. Today many jobs cannot be taught at all unless the workers have many years of education, followed by months of on-the-job training.

Figure 1-5 illustrates these changes by showing the incomes (adjusted for inflation) of 25- to 34-year-old males in successive 5-year intervals. Incomes of both high school dropouts and those with

FIGURE 1-5
Earnings of Young Men, 1975–1990

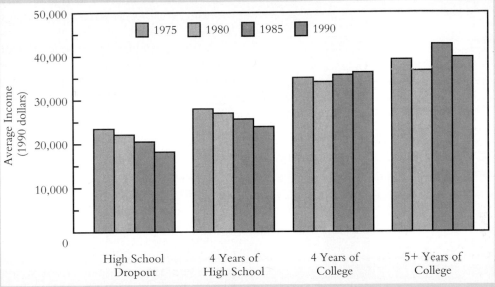

The wages of young men with lower educational attainment have declined over the period studied, while the wages of young men with higher educational attainments have tended to rise. The figure shows the average earnings for men in the age bracket 25–34 in four periods, each of which is five years apart. High school dropouts in that age bracket earned about $24,000 in 1975, but this fell steadily until 1990, when high school dropouts in the same age bracket were only earning an average of about $19,000. Although the earnings were a bit more erratic for those with four or more years of college, both groups earned more in 1990 than in 1975.

The income figures are the average for those in each group expressed in 1990 dollars. This means that the dollar values for earlier years are changed so as to give the equivalent in purchasing power in 1990. (*Source: Economic Report of the President*, 1992, p. 99.)

only a high school diploma fell steadily over the 15 years covered by the graph. Incomes of those with higher education, although showing ups and downs, generally rose over the period.

Thus the last few decades have shown two important trends. First, average incomes have risen much less rapidly than in earlier decades. Second, the shift in income distribution from poorer- to better-educated workers means that many of those at the low end of the scale have actually suffered declines in their income compared to what their parents earned.

Ongoing Change

The growth in incomes over the centuries since market economies first arose has been accompanied by continual technological change. Our technologies are our ways of doing things. New ways of doing old things, and new things to do, are continually being invented and brought into use. These technological changes make labor more productive, and they are constantly changing the nature of our economy. Old jobs are destroyed and new jobs are created as the technological structure slowly evolves.

Job Structure

The most dramatic change in the structure of jobs in the earlier part of this century was in agriculture. In 1900 over 40 percent of the U.S. population lived on farms. Today, this figure is less than 3 percent.

Figure 1-6 shows the change in occupational structure of the nonagricultural labor force over the decades since the end of the Second World War. The most dramatic changes are associated with the decline of jobs in manufacturing and the rise in service industries. The change has been so dramatic

FIGURE 1-6
The Changing Composition of the Nonagricultural Labor Force

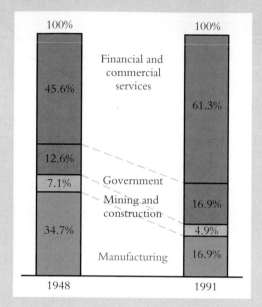

Over the decades, major shifts occur in labor utilization. In 1948 over 40 percent of the non-agricultural labor force was in the industrial sectors (largely blue collar), including manufacturing, mining, and construction. This figure had been halved, to just over 20 percent, by 1991. The shift was to the public and private service-oriented sectors (largely white collar). This process of deindustrialization has been especially dramatic over the past two decades. From 1970 to 1979, employment rose by 16 million in the service sector (public and private) but by only 800,000 in the goods sector. From 1980 to 1991, employment rose by over 21 million in services and actually fell by 1.8 million in goods.

that many observers speak of the deindustrialization of the U.S. economy. If that term applies to the U.S. economy, it also applies to the economies of most Western European countries, where similar changes have been observed.

Services in manufacturing. The enormous growth in what are recorded as service jobs overstates the decline in the importance of the manufacturing of goods in our economy. This is because many of the jobs recorded as service jobs in fact are an integral part of the production of manufactured goods.

First, some of the growth has occurred because services that used to be produced within the manufacturing firms have now been decentralized to specialist firms. These often include design, quality control, accounting, legal services, and marketing (e.g., for the first time in its 10 editions, the manuscript of this book was copyedited by an independent firm rather than in-house). Indeed, one of the most significant of the new developments in production is the breakdown of the old hierarchial organization of firms and the development of the production unit as a loosely knit grouping of organizations, each responsible for part of the total activities; some units are owned by the firms but many are on contract to it.

Second, as a result of the rapid growth of international trade, production and sales have required growing quantities of service inputs for such things as transportation, insurance, banking, and marketing.

Third, as more and more products become high-tech, increasing amounts are spent on product design at one end and customer liaison at the other end. These activities, which are all related to the production and sale of goods, are often recorded as service activities.

Services for final consumption. As households' incomes have risen over the decades, households have spent a rising proportion of their incomes on consuming services rather than goods. Today, for example, eating out is common; for our grandparents, it was a luxury. This does not mean, however, that we spend more on food. The extra expenditure goes to pay for the services of those who prepare and serve in restaurants the same ingredients that our grandparents prepared for themselves at home. Young people spend far more on attending live concerts than they used to, and all of us spend vastly more on travel. In 1890 the salesman in a small town was likely to be *the* well-traveled citizen because he had gone 250 miles by train to the state capital. Today, such a person would be regarded by many as an untraveled stay-at-home.

New Products

When we talk of each generation having more real income than previous generations, we must not think of just having more and more money to spend on the same set of products that our parents or grandparents consumed. In fact, we consume very few of the products that were the mainstays of expenditure for our great grandparents.

One of the most important aspects of the change that permeates market economies is the continual introduction of new products. It was not until well into this century that president Franklin Roosevelt earned the undying thanks of men and women on farms by bringing electricity to rural areas. Most of the myriad instruments and tools in a modern dentist's office, doctor's office, and hospital did not exist 50 years ago. Penicillin, painkillers, bypass operations, movies, stereos, videocassettes and recorders, pocket calculators, computers, ballpoint pens, compact discs, and fast, safe travel by jet aircraft, have all been introduced within living memory. So also have the products that have eliminated much of the drudgery formerly associated with housework. Dishwashers, detergents, disposable diapers, washing machines, vacuum cleaners, refrigerators, deep freezers, and their complement, the supermarket, were not there to help your great grandparents when they first set up house.

Globalization

Another aspect of the constant change that occurs in evolving market economies is the globalization that has been occurring at an accelerating rate over the last two decades. At the heart of globalization lies the rapid reduction in transportation costs and the revolution in information technology. The cost of moving products around the world has fallen greatly in recent decades. More dramatically, our ability to transmit and to analyze data have been *increasing* dramatically, while the costs of doing so have been *decreasing* equally dramatically.

Many *markets* are globalizing; for example, as some tastes become universal to young people, we can see the same designer jeans and leather jackets in virtually all big cities. Many *corporations* are globalizing, as they increasingly become what are called *transnationals.* These are massive firms with a physical presence in many countries and an increasingly decentralized management structure. Many *labor markets* are globalizing, as the revolutions in communications and transportation allow the various components of any one product to be produced all over the world. A typical compact disc player, TV set, or automobile will contain components made in literally dozens of different countries. We still know where a product is assembled, but it is becoming increasingly difficult to say where it is *made.*

One result of this globalization of production is that components that can be produced by unskilled labor can now be produced in any low-wage country around the world, where previously they were usually produced in the country that did the assembly. This has proven valuable for developing countries. They have a better chance of becoming competitive in a small range of components than in the integrated production of whole commodities. However, unskilled labor in developed countries is losing (relatively, and possibly absolutely for a while), as their labor becomes less scarce relative to the need for it. In short, the market for unskilled labor is globalizing, throwing unskilled labor in advanced countries into direct competition with unskilled labor in poorer countries.

The globalization of the world economy has had profound effects on the United States. In 1959 exports only amounted to 4.1 percent of *total U.S. production* (as measured by what is called its GDP). The rest was used domestically. In 1991 the figure was 10.4 percent. The proportion of total U.S. production of *goods* that is exported is much larger than 10 percent. Without the export market, many of the existing sources of U.S. employment and income would not exist.

On the investment side, the most important result of globalization is that large firms are seeking a physical presence in many major countries. In the 1950s and 1960s most foreign investment was made by U.S. firms investing abroad to establish a presence in foreign markets. Today most developed countries see major flows of investment in *both directions,* inward as foreign firms invest in their markets, and outward as their own firms invest abroad.

The United States has been no exception to this rule. In 1967, 50 percent of all outward-bound foreign investment came from the United States and went to many foreign countries. In 1989, according to United Nations figures, the United States accounted for less than 30 percent of all outward-bound foreign investment. At the same time the United Kingdom accounted for 16 percent, while Japan and Germany accounted for just less than 10 percent each.

On the inward-bound side, the change is more dramatic. In 1967, the United States attracted only 9 percent of all foreign investment made in that year. In 1989, however, the United States attracted 27 percent. Not only do U.S. firms hold massive foreign investments in foreign countries, but foreign firms now hold massive investments in the United States.

As a result, many U.S. citizens work for British, Japanese, German, Dutch, and French firms—just as many of the citizens of these other countries work for U.S. firms.

The world is truly globalizing in both its trade and investment flows. Today no country can take an isolationist economic stance and hope to take part in the global economy where an increasing share of jobs and incomes are created.

Conclusion

In this last part of the chapter, we have briefly discussed how people's living standards are affected by the availability of jobs, the productivity of labor in those jobs, and the distribution of the income produced by those jobs. We have seen how the economy is characterized by ongoing change in the structure of jobs, in the production techniques used by the workers, and in the kinds of goods and services produced. We have also seen that these changes exist in the context of a rapidly globalizing economy—one in which events occuring in any one country have major consequences in many other countries.

These issues will arise at many places throughout this book. We will study what is happening in more detail and will use economic theory to explain why it is happening. Because most of them are interrelated, it helps to know the basic outlines of all of them before studying any one in more depth.

SUMMARY

1. Most of the world's pressing problems have an economic aspect, and many are primarily economic. A common feature of such problems is that they concern the use of limited resources to satisfy virtually unlimited human wants.

2. Scarcity is a fundamental problem faced by all economies. Not enough resources are available to produce all the goods and services that people would like to consume. Scarcity makes it necessary to choose. All societies must have a mechanism for choosing what commodities will be produced and in what quantities.

3. The concept of opportunity cost emphasizes the problem of scarcity and choice by measuring the cost of obtaining a unit of one commodity in terms of the number of units of other commodities that could have been obtained instead.

4. Four basic questions must be answered in all economies: What commodities are to be produced and how? What commodities are to be consumed and by whom? What will the unemployment and inflation rates be? Will productive capacity change?

5. Different economies resolve these questions in different ways and with varying degrees of efficacy. Economists study how these problems are addressed in various societies and the consequences of using one method rather than another to provide solutions.

6. We can distinguish three pure types of economies: traditional, command, and free market. In practice, all economies are mixed economies in that their economic behavior responds to mixes of tradition, government command, and price incentives.

7. In the late 1980s events in Eastern Europe and the USSR led to the general acceptance that the system of fully centrally planned economies had failed to produce minimally acceptable living standards for its citizens. All of these countries are now moving toward greater market determination and less state command in their economies.

8. Market economies are based on private property and freedom of contract. They have generated sustained growth, which, over long periods, has raised material living standards massively.

9. Recently the rapid growth in labor productivity has slowed and the distribution of income has become more unequal.

10. Market economies are characterized by constant change in such things as the structure of jobs, the structure of production, the technologies in use, and the types of products produced.

11. Driven by the revolution in transportation and communications, the world economy is rapidly globalizing. National and regional boundaries are becoming less important as transnational corporations locate the production of each component part of a commodity in the country that can produce it at the best quality and the least cost.

12. As part of this globalization, the United States is much more heavily involved in foreign trade than in the past. It is also both a host country for much investment by foreign firms and a source country for much investment located in foreign countries around the world.

TOPICS FOR REVIEW

Scarcity and the need for choice

Choice and opportunity cost

Production possibility boundary

Resource allocation

Growth in productive capacity

Traditional economies

Command economies

Market economies

Globalization

DISCUSSION QUESTIONS

1. What does each of the following questions tell you about the policy conflicts perceived by the person making the statement and about how that person has resolved them?

   a. "It is an industry worth several hundred jobs to our state; we cannot afford to forgo it." A state governor explaining the decision to organize a killing of wolves in his state so that more game animals could grow up to be shot by hunters.

   b. "The annual seal hunt must be stopped, even if it destroys the livelihood of the seal hunters." An animal rights advocate opposing the seal hunt in Canada.

   c. "Considering our limited energy resources and the growing demand for electricity, the United States really has no choice but to use all of its possible domestic energy sources, including nuclear energy. Despite possible environmental and safety hazards, nuclear power is a necessity." A representative of the electricity industry replying to critics.

d. "The proposed pulp mills must be opposed because of the pollution they cause, even though they bring new, diversified jobs and even though they are based on the most advanced, pollution-minimizing technologies." An opponent of the proposal to construct new pulp and paper mills in the Peace River District of northern Canada during the 1990s.

e. "Damn the pollution—we want the jobs." A labor leader in Brazil advocating permission to build new pulp mills in his country.

2. What is the difference between scarcity and poverty? If everyone in the world had enough to eat, could we say that food was no longer scarce?

3. Consider the right to free speech in political campaigns. Suppose that the Flat Earth Society, the Communists, the Republicans, and the Democrats all demand equal time on network television in an election campaign. What economic questions are involved? Can there be freedom of speech without free access to the scarce resources needed to make one's speech heard?

4. How do you answer someone who wants to go back to the good old days in 1900 when a cup of coffee only cost a nickel and a whole meal could be bought for 30 cents?

5. Evidence accumulates that the use of chemical fertilizers, which increases agricultural production greatly, damages water quality. Show the choice between more food and cleaner water involved in using such fertilizers. Use a production possibility curve with agricultural output on the vertical axis and water quality on the horizontal axis. In what ways does this production possibility curve reflect scarcity, choice, and opportunity cost? How would an improved fertilizer that increased agricultural output without further worsening water quality affect the curve? Suppose that a pollution-free fertilizer were developed; would this mean that there would no longer be any opportunity cost in using it?

6. Identify the coordinating principle and the incentive system suggested by each of the following:

a. Some countries have very high taxes on tobacco and alcohol compared to the United States.

b. Many U.S. policymakers advocate raising taxes on gas to encourage higher-mileage cars.

c. Production targets are assigned to a Chinese factory manager by the state planning agency.

d. Legislation establishes minimum wages to be paid to everyone in a state.

e. Many state governments direct their agencies to use local suppliers of goods rather than buying from other states.

f. Legislation prohibits the sale and use of cocaine.

g. Rent controls are combined with government subsidization of the building of rental accommodations.

7. Pick one of the major socialist countries that have recently introduced market-oriented reforms and discuss the start-up problems that the reforms encounter. Explain why you think these problems will or will not persist over the next few years.

8. "The introduction of these new machines must be stopped at all costs; they will destroy our jobs"—a local labor leader. Who gains and who loses if the introduction of new machines is prevented by a strong union? Does the globalization of the world's economy affect your answer? What would have happened if such sentiments had generally prevailed in the early part of this century?

9. Discuss the following statement by Professor Paul McCracken, a former chairman of the U.S. President's Council of Economic Advisers: "One of the mysteries of semantics is why the government-managed economies ever came to be called *planned,* and the market economies *unplanned.* It is the former that are in chronic chaos, in which buyers stand in line hoping to buy some toilet paper or soap. It is the latter that are in reasonable equilibrium—where if you want a cake of soap or a steak or a shirt or a car, you can go to the store and find that the item is magically there for you to buy. It is the liberal economies that reflect a highly sophisticated planning system, and the government-managed economies that are primitive and unplanned."

2

Economics as a Social Science

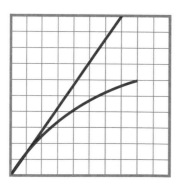

Economics is generally regarded as a social science. What does it mean to be scientific? Can economics hope to be in any way "scientific" in its study of human behavior?

The Distinction Between Positive and Normative

The success of modern science rests partly on the ability of scientists to separate their views on what *does* happen from their views on what they *would like* to happen.

Positive statements concern what is, was, or will be. Positive statements, assertions, or theories may be simple or complex, but they are basically about matters of fact. Positive statements assert things about the world. If it is possible for a positive statement to be proved wrong by empirical evidence, we call it a *testable statement*.

Many positive statements are testable, and disagreements over such statements are appropriately handled by an appeal to the facts.

Normative statements concern what one believes ought to be. They state, or are based on, judgments about what is good and what is bad (called *value judgments*). They are thus bound up with philosophical, cultural, and religious systems.

Normative statements are not testable. Disagreements over such normative statements as "It is wrong to steal" or "It is immoral to have sexual relations out of wedlock" cannot be settled by an appeal to empirical observations.

Different techniques are needed for studying normative and positive questions.

It is therefore useful to separate normative and positive inquiries. We do this not because we think one is less important than the other but merely because they must be handled in different ways.

Some related issues concerning disagreements among economists are discussed in Box 2-1.

The Distinction Illustrated

The statement "It is impossible to break up atoms" is a positive statement that can quite definitely be (and of course has been) refuted by empirical observations. In contrast, the statement "Scientists ought not to break up atoms" is a normative statement that involves ethical judgments. The questions "What government policies will reduce unemployment?" and "What policies will prevent inflation?" are positive ones, whereas the question "Should we be more concerned about unemployment than about inflation?" is a normative one.

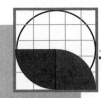

Box 2-1

Why Economists Disagree

If you listen to a discussion among economists on "Meet the Press" or "The MacNeil/Lehrer News Hour," or if you read about their debates in the daily press or weekly magazines, you will find that economists frequently disagree with each other. Why do economists disagree, and what should we make of this fact?

In a *Newsweek* column, Charles Wolf, Jr. suggested four reasons: (1) Different economists use different benchmarks (e.g., inflation is down compared with last year but up compared with the 1950s). (2) Economists fail to make it clear to their listeners whether they are talking about short-term or long-term consequences (e.g., tax cuts will stimulate consumption in the short run and investment in the long run). (3) Economists often fail to acknowledge the full extent of their ignorance. (4) Different economists have different values, and these normative views play a large part in most public discussions of policy.

There is surely some truth in each of these assessments, but there is also a fifth reason: the public's *demand for disagreement*. For example, suppose that most economists were in fact agreed on some proposition such as the following: Unions are not a major cause of inflation. This view would be unpalatable to some individuals. Those who are hostile to unions, for instance, would like to blame inflation on them and would be looking for an intellectual champion. Fame and fortune would await the economist who espoused their cause, and a champion would soon be found.

Notice also that any disagreement that does exist will be exaggerated, possibly unintentionally, by the media. When the media cover an issue, they naturally wish to give both sides of it. Normally, the public will hear one or two economists on each side of a debate, regardless of whether the profession is divided right down the middle or is nearly unanimous in its support of one side. Thus the public will not know that in one case a reporter could have chosen from dozens of economists to present each side, whereas in another case the reporter had to spend three days finding someone willing to take a particular side because nearly all the economists contacted thought it was wrong. In their desire to show both sides of all cases, however, the media present the public with the appearance of a profession equally split over all matters.

Thus anyone seeking to discredit some particular economist's advice by showing that there is disagreement among economists will have no trouble finding evidence of some disagreement. But those who wish to know if there is a majority view or even a strong consensus will find one on a surprisingly large number of issues. For example, a survey published in the *American Economic Review* showed strong agreement among economists on many propositions such as "Rent control leads to a housing shortage" (85 percent yes).

These results illustrate that economists do agree on many issues—where the balance of evidence seems to strongly support certain predictions that follow from economic theories.

The Importance of the Distinction

As an example of the importance of this distinction, consider the question "Has the payment of generous unemployment benefits increased the amount of unemployment?" This positive question can be turned into a testable hypothesis such as "The higher the benefits paid to the unemployed, the higher will be the total amount of unemployment." If we are not careful, however, attitudes and value judgments may get in the way of the study of this hypothesis. Some people are opposed to all welfare measures and believe in an individualistic self-help ethic. They may hope that the hypothesis is correct because its truth could then be used as an argument against welfare measures in general. Others feel that welfare measures are desirable, reducing misery and contributing to human dignity. They may hope that the hypothesis is wrong because they do not want any welfare measures to come under attack. In spite of different value judgments and social attitudes, however, evidence is accumulating on this particular hypothesis. As a result, we have more knowledge than we had 20 years ago of why and by how much unemployment benefits increase unemployment. This evidence could never have been accumulated or accepted if investigators had not been able to distinguish their feelings about how they wanted the answer to turn out from their assessment of evidence on how people actually behaved.[1]

The distinction between positive and normative statements allows us to keep our views on how we would like the world to work separate from our views on how the world actually does work. We may be interested in both. It can only obscure the truth, however, if we let our views on what we would like to be bias our investigations of what actually is. For this reason, the separation of positive from normative statements is one of the foundation stones of science. It is also for this reason that scientific inquiry, as it is normally understood, is usually confined to positive questions. Some important limitations on the distinction between positive and normative are discussed in Box 2-2.

Positive and Normative Statements in Economics

We have seen that normative questions cannot be settled by a mere appeal to facts. In democracies, normative questions relating to government policies are often settled by voting. So on the one hand, we look to observations to shed light on the issue of the extent to which unemployment insurance deters people from working. On the other hand, we use the political process to decide whether or not, when all the pros and cons are considered, we should have such insurance.

Economists need not confine their discussions to positive, testable statements. Economists can usefully hold and discuss value judgments. Indeed, the pur-

suit of what appears to be a normative statement, such as "unemployment insurance ought to be abolished," will often turn up positive hypotheses that underlie the normative judgment. In this case, there are probably relatively few people who believe that government provision of unemployment insurance is in itself good or bad. Their advocacy or opposition will be based on beliefs that can be stated as positive rather than normative hypotheses; for example, "Unemployment insurance causes people to remain unemployed when they would otherwise take a job" or "Unemployment insurance increases the chance that workers will locate the jobs to which they are best suited by supporting them while they search for the right job."

The Scientific Approach

An important aspect of the scientific approach consists of relating questions to evidence. When presented with a controversial issue, investigators, whether in the natural or the social sciences, will look for relevant evidence.

In some fields scientists are able to generate observations that provide evidence for use in testing their hypotheses. Experimental sciences such as chemistry and some branches of psychology have an advantage because it is possible for them to produce relevant evidence through controlled laboratory experiments.

Other sciences, such as astronomy, cannot do this. They must wait for natural events to produce observations that can be used as evidence in testing their theories. The evidence that then arises does not come from laboratory conditions under which everything is held constant except the forces being studied. Instead, it arises from situations in which many things are changing at the same time, and great care is therefore needed in drawing conclusions from what is observed.

Not long ago economics would have been put wholly in the group of nonexperimental sciences. It is still true that the majority of evidence economists use is generated by observing what happens in the economy from day to day. However, a significant and growing amount of evidence is now being generated under controlled laboratory conditions. In the introductory treatment of this book we concentrate on the nonlaboratory aspects of economic evidence, both because this is still the predominant aspect and because the sig-

---

[1] Of course, economists, like all scientists, are not immune from the possibility that what they find will be influenced by what they want to find. For a study of this problem in a different context, see Stephen Jay Gould, *The Mismeasure of Man* (New York: W. W. Norton, 1981). The more likely it is that value judgments will affect our judgments of positive issues, the more important it is that the test of consistency with facts be accepted as an important criterion for the acceptance of theories.

Box 2-2

Limits on the Positive-Normative Distinction

Although the distinction between positive and normative statements is useful, it has a number of limitations.

The classification is not exhaustive. The classifications *positive* and *normative* do not cover all statements that can be made. For example, there is an important class, called *analytic statements*, whose validity depends only on the rules of logic. Thus the sentence "If all humans are immortal and if you are a human, then you are immortal" is a valid analytic statement. It tells us that *if* two things are true, *then* a third thing must also be true. The validity of this statement is not dependent on whether or not its individual parts are in fact true. Indeed, the sentence "All humans are immortal" is a positive statement that has been decisively refuted. Yet no amount of empirical evidence on the mortality of humans can upset the truth of the *if-then* sentence quoted. Analytic statements—which proceed by logical analysis—play an important role in scientific work and form the basis of much of our ability to theorize.

Not all positive statements are testable. A positive statement asserts something about some aspect of the universe in which we live. It may be empirically true or false in the sense that what it asserts may or may not be true of the world. If it is true, it adds to our knowledge of what can and cannot happen. Many positive statements are refutable: If they are wrong, this can be ascertained (within a margin for error of observation) by checking them against data. For example, the positive statement that the earth is less than 5,000 years old was tested and refuted by a mass of evidence accumulated in the eighteenth and nineteenth centuries.

The statement "Extraterrestrials exist and frequently visit the earth in visible form" is also a positive statement. It asserts something about the universe, but we could never refute this statement with evidence because, no matter how hard we searched, believers could argue that we did not look in the right places or in the right way, that extraterrestrials do not reveal themselves to nonbelievers, or a host of other reasons. Thus some positive statements are irrefutable.

The distinction is not unerringly applied. The fact that the positive-normative distinction aids the advancement of knowledge does not necessarily mean that all scientists automatically and unerringly apply it. Scientists are human beings. Many have strongly held values, and they may let their value judgments get in the way of their assessment of evidence. Nonetheless, the desire to separate what is from what we would like to be is a guiding light, an ideal, of all science. The ability to do so, albeit imperfectly, is attested to by the acceptance, first by scientists and then by the general public, of many ideas that were initially extremely unpalatable—ideas such as the close relationship between humans and other primates.

nificance of laboratory-generated evidence remains controversial.

Later in this chapter we will consider some of the problems that arise when analyzing evidence generated by observing day-to-day behavior that does not take place under controlled laboratory conditions. For the moment, however, we shall consider some general problems that are more or less common to all sciences and are particularly important in the social sciences.

Is Human Behavior Predictable?

Social scientists seek to understand and to predict human behavior. A scientific prediction is based on discovering stable response patterns, but are such patterns possible with anything so complex as human beings?

Does human behavior show sufficiently stable responses to factors influencing it to be predictable within some stated margin of error? This positive question can be settled only by an appeal to evidence and not by armchair speculation. The question itself might concern either the behavior of groups or that of isolated individuals.

Group Behavior Versus Individual Behavior

There are many situations in which group behavior can be predicted accurately without certain knowledge of individual behavior. The warmer the weather, for example, the more people visit the beach and the higher the sales of ice cream. It may be hard to say if or when one individual will buy an ice cream cone, but a stable response pattern can be seen among a large group of individuals. Although social scientists cannot predict which particular individuals will be involved in auto accidents during the next holiday weekend, they can come very close to knowing the total number who will. The more objectively measurable data they have (e.g., the state of the weather on the days in question and the trend in gasoline prices), the more closely they will be able to predict total accidents.

Economists can also predict with fair accuracy what employees as a group will do when their take-home pay rises. Although some individuals may do surprising and unpredictable things, the overall response of workers in spending more when their take-home pay rises is predictable within quite a narrow margin of error. This relatively stable response is the basis of economists' ability to predict successfully the outcome of major changes in income-tax rates that permanently alter people's take-home pay.

Nothing we have said implies that people never change their minds or that future events can be foretold simply by projecting past trends. For example, we cannot safely predict that people will increase their spending next year just because they increased their spending this year. The stability we are discussing relates to a cause-effect response. For example, the next time take-home pay rises significantly (cause), spending by employees will rise (effect).

The "Law" of Large Numbers

Successfully predicting the behavior of large groups of people is made possible by the statistical "law" of large numbers. Broadly speaking, this law asserts that random movements of many individual items tend to offset one another.

What is implied by this law? Ask any one person to measure the length of a room, and it will be almost impossible to predict in advance what sort of error of measurement will be made. Dozens of things will affect the accuracy of the measurement; furthermore, the person may make one error today and a quite different one tomorrow. But ask 1,000 people to measure the length of the same room, and we can predict within a small margin just how this *group* will make its errors. We can assert with confidence that more people will make small errors than will make large errors; that the larger the error, the fewer will be the number making it; that roughly the same number of people will overstate as will understate the distance; and that the larger the number of people making the measurement, the smaller the average of their errors will tend to be.

If a common cause acts on each member of the group, the average behavior of the group can be predicted even though any one member may act in a surprising fashion. For example, let each of the 1,000 individuals be given a tape measure that understates "actual" distances. On the average, the group will now understate the length of the room. It is, of course, quite possible that one member who had in the past been reading her tape measure correctly will now read more than it measures as a result of developing an eye defect. However, something else may have happened to another individual that causes him to underread his tape measure where before he was reading it correctly. Individuals may alter their behavior for many different reasons, but the group's behavior, when the inaccurate tape is substituted for the accurate one, is predictable precisely because the odd things that one individual does tend to cancel out the odd things that some other individual does.

Irregularities in individual behavior tend to cancel each other out, and the regularities tend to show up in repeated observations.

The Importance of Theories

When some regularity between two or more things is observed, curious people ask why. A *theory* provides an explanation, and by doing so, it enables us to predict as yet unobserved events.

For example, the simple theory of market behavior that we will study in Part 2 shows how the output of a product affects the price at which it sells, and hence affects the incomes of those who produce it. As we will see in Chapter 6, this theory allows us to predict (among other things) that a partial failure of the potato crop will cause an increase in the income of the average potato farmer.

Theories are used in explaining existing observations. A successful theory enables us to predict things we have not yet seen.

Any explanation whatsoever of how given observations are linked together is a theoretical construction. Theories are used to impose order on our observations, to explain how what we see is linked together. Without theories, there would be only a shapeless mass of observations.

The choice is not between theory and observation but between better or worse theories to explain observations.

To illustrate this point, think about the common observation that something is "true in theory but not in practice." The next time you hear someone say this (or, indeed, the next time you say it yourself), you might reply, "All right, then, tell me what does happen in practice." Usually you will not be told mere facts, but you will be given an alternative theory—a different explanation of the facts. The speaker should have said, "The theory in question provides a poor explanation of the facts in question or is contradicted by some other facts. I have a different theory that does a much better job."

The Structure of Theories

A theory consists of (1) a set of definitions that clearly define the *variables* to be used, (2) a set of *assumptions* about the behavior of the variables, and (3) *predictions* (often called *hypotheses*) that are deduced from the assumptions of the theory and can be tested against actual empirical observations. We shall consider these constituents one by one.

Variables

A **variable** is a magnitude that can take on different possible values. Variables are the basic elements of theories, and each one needs to be carefully defined.

Price is an example of an important economic variable. The price of a commodity is the amount of money that must be given up to purchase one unit of that commodity. To define a price, we must first define the commodity to which it is attached. Such a commodity might be one dozen grade A large eggs. The price of such eggs sold in, say, supermarkets in Fargo, North Dakota defines a variable. The particular values taken on by that variable might be $1.22 on July 1, 1990, $1.29 on July 8, 1991, and $1.25 on July 15, 1992.

There are many distinctions between kinds of variables; we shall discuss only one at this time.

Endogenous and exogenous variables. An **endogenous variable** is a variable that is explained within a theory. An **exogenous variable** influences endogenous variables but is itself determined by factors outside the theory.

Consider the theory that the price of apples in Seattle, Washington on a particular day depends on several things, one of which is the weather in the Yakima Valley during the previous apple-growing season. We can safely assume that the state of the weather is not determined by economic conditions. The price of apples in this case is an endogenous variable—something determined within the framework of the theory. The state of the weather in the Yakima Valley is an exogenous variable; changes in it influence prices because the changes affect the output of apples, but the state of the weather is not influenced by apple prices.

Other words are sometimes used for the same distinction. One frequently used pair is *induced* for endogenous and *autonomous* for exogenous; another is *dependent* for endogenous and *independent* for exogenous.

Assumptions

A key element of any theory is a set of assumptions about the behavior of the variables in which we are interested. Usually these state how the behavior of two or more variables relate to each other.

In some cases, these linkages are provided by physical laws. One such case is the relation between the resources each firm uses, which economists call inputs, and that firm's output. In the case of the egg farmer, the output of eggs is related to the inputs of chicken feed, farm labor, and all the other things the farmer uses.

In other cases, these linkages are provided by human behavior. For example, economists make two basic assumptions about consumers. The first concerns how each consumer's satisfaction, or utility, is related to the quantities of all the goods and services that they consume. The second is that in making their choices on how much to consume, people seek to maximize the satisfaction they gain from that consumption.

Although assumptions are an essential part of all theories, students are often concerned about those that seem unrealistic. An example will illustrate some of the issues involved. Much of the theory that we are going to study in this book uses the assumption that the sole motive of the owners of firms is to make as much money as they possibly can, or, as economists put it, firms are assumed to *maximize their profits*. The assumption of profit maximization allows economists to make predictions about the behavior of firms. They study the effects that the choices open to firms would have on profits. They then predict that the alternative that produces the most profits will be the one selected.

Profit maximization may seem like a rather crude assumption. Surely, for example, the managers of firms sometimes choose to protect the environment rather than pursue certain highly polluting, but profitable, opportunities. Does this not discredit the assumption of profit maximization by showing it to be unrealistic?

The answer is "no"; to make successful predictions, the theory does not require that managers be solely and unwaveringly motivated by the desire to maximize profits. All that is required is that profits be a sufficiently important consideration that a theory based on the assumption of profit maximization will produce explanations and predictions that are substantially correct.

This illustration shows that it is not always appropriate to criticize a theory because its assumptions seem unrealistic. All theory is an abstraction from reality. If it were not, it would merely duplicate the world in all its complexity and would add nothing to our understanding of it. A good theory abstracts in a useful way; a poor theory does not. If a theory has ignored some genuinely important factors, its predictions will be contradicted by the evidence—at least where an ignored factor exerts an important influence on the outcome.

Predictions

A theory's predictions are the propositions that can be deduced from that theory; they are often called *hypotheses*. An example of a prediction would be a deduction that *if* firms maximize their profits and *if*

certain other assumptions of the theory hold true, *then* an increase in the going wage for labor will lower the amount of labor employed.

When the predictions of a theory have been confirmed in a large number of specific cases, they are sometimes referred to as "laws."

A scientific prediction is a conditional statement that takes the following form: *If this occurs, then* such and such will follow.

For example, *if* a city government forces down the rents on residential accommodation (through a policy called *rent control*) *then* a housing shortage will develop.

It is important to realize that this prediction is different from the statement "I prophesy that in two years' time there will be a housing shortage in my city because I believe its municipal government will decide to impose rent controls." The government's decision to introduce rent controls in two years' time will be the outcome of many influences, both economic and political. If the economist's prophecy about a housing shortage turns out to be wrong because in two years' time the government does not impose rent controls, then all that has been learned is that the economist is not a good guesser about the behavior of the government. However, *if* the government does impose rent controls (in two years' time or at any other time) and *then* a housing shortage does not develop, a conditional (if-then) prediction based on economic theory will have been contradicted.

Expressing Relations Among Variables

Economists deal with many relations among variables. A **function**, also known as a *functional relation*, is a formal expression of a relationship between two or more variables.[2]

The prediction that the quantity of eggs people want to buy is negatively related to the price of eggs is an example of a functional relation in economics. In its most general form, it merely says that quantity produced is related to price. The more specific hy-

---

[2] When two variables are related in such a way that an increase in one is associated with an increase in the other, they are said to be *positively related*. When two variables are related in such a way that an increase in one is associated with a decrease in the other, they are said to be *negatively related*.

pothesis is that as the price of eggs rises, the quantity of desired purchases falls.

In many relations of this kind, economists can be even more specific about the nature of the functional relation. On the basis of detailed factual studies, economists often have a pretty good idea of by how much the quantity demanded will change as a result of specified changes in price; that is, they can predict magnitude as well as direction.

Testing Theories

A theory is tested by confronting its predictions with evidence. It is necessary to discover if certain events are followed by the outcomes predicted by the theory. For example, is an increase in the wage rate followed by a decline in amount of labor employed? Theories are sometimes tested in conscious attempts to do just that. They are also tested every time an economist uses one to predict the outcome of some specific event. If economists continued to be mistaken every time they used some theory to make predictions, the theory would eventually be called into question.

Theories tend to be abandoned when they are no longer useful, and theories cease to be useful when they cannot predict the outcomes of actions better than the next best alternative. When a theory consistently fails to predict better than the available alternatives, it is either modified or replaced. Figure 2-1 summarizes the discussion of theories and their testing.

Refutation or Confirmation

An important part of a scientific approach to any issue consists of setting up a theory that will explain it and then seeing if that theory can be refuted by evidence.

The alternative to this approach is to set up a theory and then look for confirming evidence. Such an approach is hazardous because the world is sufficiently complex that some confirming evidence can be found for any theory, no matter how unlikely the theory may be. For example, flying saucers, the Loch Ness monster, fortune telling, and astrology all have their devotees who can quote confirming evidence in spite of the failure of attempts to discover systematic, objective evidence for these things.

An example of the unfruitful approach of seeking confirmation is frequently seen when a leader—be it a U.S. president or a foreign dictator—is surrounded by followers who provide only evidence that confirms the leader's existing views. This approach is usually a road to disaster, because the leader becomes more and more out of touch with reality.

A wise leader adopts a scientific approach instinctively, constantly checking the realism of accepted views by encouraging subordinates to criticize him or her. This tests how far the leader's existing views correspond to all available evidence and encourages amendment in the light of evidence that conflicts with the current views.

Statistical Analysis

Statistical analysis is used to test the hypothesis that two or more things are related and to estimate the numerical values of the function that describes the relation.

In practice, the same data can be used simultaneously to test whether a relationship exists and, if it does exist, to provide a measure of it.

Because economics is primarily a nonlaboratory science, it must utilize the millions of uncontrolled experiments that are going on every day. Households are deciding what to purchase given changing prices and incomes; firms are deciding what to produce and how to produce it; and governments are involved in the economy through their various taxes, subsidies, and controls. Because all these activities can be observed and recorded, a mass of data is continually being produced by the economy.

The variables that interest economists, such as the volume of unemployment, the price of wheat, and the output of automobiles, are generally influenced by many forces that vary simultaneously. If economists are to test their theories about relations among variables in the economy, they must use statistical techniques designed for situations in which other things cannot be held constant.

Fortunately, such techniques exist—although their application is often neither simple nor straightforward. The appendix to this chapter provides a discussion of some tabular and graphical techniques for describing the data and displaying some of the more obvious relationships. Further examination of the data involves techniques studied in elementary statistics courses. More advanced courses in econometrics deal with the array of techniques designed to test economic hypotheses and to measure economic

FIGURE 2-1
The Interaction of Deduction and Measurement in Theorizing

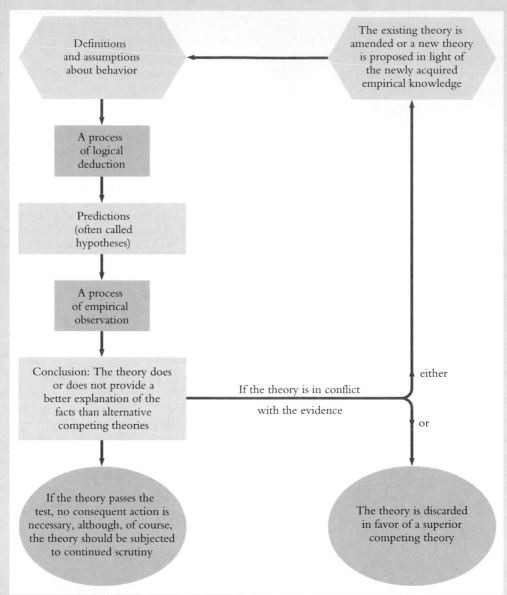

Theory and observation are in continuous interaction. Starting (at the top left) with the assumptions of a theory and the definitions of relevant terms, the theorist deduces by logical analysis everything that is implied by the assumptions. These implications are the predictions of the theory. The theory is then tested by confronting its predictions with evidence. If the theory is in conflict with facts, it will usually be amended to make it consistent with those facts (thereby making it a better theory); in extreme cases it will be discarded to be replaced by a superior alternative. The process then begins again: The new or amended theory is subjected first to logical analysis and then to empirical testing.

relations in the complex circumstances in which economic evidence is often generated.

The Decision to Reject or Accept

There is no absolute certainty in any knowledge. No doubt some of the things we now think are true will eventually turn out to be false, and some of the things we currently think are false will eventually turn out to be true. Yet even though we can never be certain, we can assess the balance of available evidence. Some hypotheses are so unlikely to be true, given current evidence, that for all practical purposes we may regard them as false. Other hypotheses are so unlikely to be false, given current evidence, that for all practical purposes we may regard them as true. This kind of practical decision must always be regarded as tentative. Every once in a while we will find that we have to change our mind. Something that looked right will begin to look doubtful, or something that looked wrong will begin to look possible.

Making the decisions just discussed requires accepting some theories (to act as if they were true) and rejecting others (to act as if they were false). Just as a jury can make two kinds of errors (finding an innocent person guilty or letting a guilty person go free), so statistical decision makers can make two kinds of errors. They can reject hypotheses that are true, and they can accept hypotheses that are false. Fortunately, like a jury, they can also make correct decisions—and indeed, they expect to do so most of the time.

Although the possibility of error cannot be eliminated when testing theories against observations, it can be controlled.

The method of control is to decide in advance how large a risk to take in accepting a hypothesis that is in fact false.[3] Conventionally in statistics, this risk is often set at 5 percent or 1 percent. When the 5 percent cutoff point is used, we will accept the hypothesis if the results that appear to establish it could have happened by chance no more than 1 time in 20. Using the 1 percent decision rule gives the hypothesis a more difficult test. A hypothesis is accepted only if the results that appear to establish it

could have happened by chance no more than 1 time in 100.

Consider the hypothesis that a certain coin is "loaded," favoring heads over tails. The test consists of flipping the coin 100 times. Say that on a single test, the coin comes up heads 53 times. This result is not strong evidence in favor of the hypothesis because such an unbalanced result could happen by chance in more than 22 percent of such tests. Thus the hypothesis of a head-biased coin would not be accepted on the basis of this evidence using either a 1 percent or a 5 percent cutoff. Had the test produced 65 heads and 35 tails, a result that would occur by chance in less than 1 percent of such tests, we would (given either a 1 percent or a 5 percent cutoff) accept the hypothesis of the coin being loaded.[4]

When action must be taken, some rule of thumb is necessary, but it is important to understand, first, that no one can ever be certain about being right in rejecting any hypothesis and, second, that there is nothing magical about arbitrary cutoff points. Some cutoff point must be used whenever decisions have to be made.

Finally, recall that the rejection of a hypothesis is seldom the end of inquiry. Decisions can be reversed if new evidence comes to light. Often the result of a statistical test of a theory suggests a new hypothesis that "fits the facts" better than the old one.

Can Economics Be Made Value-Free?

We have made two key statements about the positive-normative distinction. First, the ability to distinguish positive from normative questions is a key part of the foundation of science. Second, economists, in common with all scientists, seek to answer positive questions.

Some people who have accepted these points have gone on to argue that there can be a completely value-free inquiry into any branch of science, including economics. After long debate over this issue, the conclusion that most people seem to accept is that a *completely* value-free inquiry is impossible.

Our values become involved at all stages of any enquiry. For example, we must allocate our scarce

---

[3] Return to the jury analogy: Our notion of a person's being innocent unless the jury is persuaded of guilt "beyond a reasonable doubt" rests on our wishing to take only a small risk of accepting the hypothesis of guilt if the person tried is in fact innocent.

[4] The actual statistical testing process is more complex than this example suggests but must be left to a course in statistics.

time. This means that we choose to study some problems rather than other problems. This choice is often influenced by our value judgments about the relative importance of various problems. Also, evidence is never conclusive and so is always open to more than one interpretation. It is difficult to assess such imperfect evidence without giving some play to our values. Further, when reporting the results of our studies, we must use words that we know will arouse various emotions in those who read them. So the words we choose and the emphasis we give to the available evidence (and to the uncertainties surrounding it) will influence the impact that the study has.

For these and many other reasons, most people who have discussed this issue believe that there can be no totally value-free study of economics.

This does not mean that economists and other scientists should conclude that *everything* is a matter of subjective value judgments. The very real

advancements of knowledge in all sciences, natural and social, show that science is not just a matter of opinion or of deciding between competing value judgments.

Science has been successful in spite of the fact that individual scientists have not always been totally objective. Individual scientists have sometimes passionately resisted the apparent implications of evidence. The rules of the scientific game—that facts cannot be ignored and must somehow be fitted into the accepted theoretical structure—tend to produce scientific advance in spite of what might be thought of as unscientific, emotional attitudes on the part of many scientists.

But if those engaged in scientific debate, in economics or any other science, ever succeed in changing the rules of the game to allow inconvenient facts to be ignored or defined out of existence, a major blow would be dealt to scientific inquiry in economics.

SUMMARY

1. It is possible, and useful, to distinguish between positive and normative statements. Positive statements concern what is, was, or will be, whereas normative statements concern what ought to be. Disagreements over positive, testable statements are appropriately settled by an appeal to the facts. Disagreements over normative statements cannot be settled in this way.

2. Successful scientific inquiry requires separating positive questions about the way the world works from normative questions about how one would like the world to work, formulating positive questions precisely enough so that they can be settled by an appeal to evidence, and then finding means of gathering the necessary evidence.

3. Social scientists have observed many stable human behavior patterns. These form the basis for successful predictions of how people will behave under certain conditions.

4. The fact that people sometimes act strangely, even capriciously, does not destroy the possibility of scientific study of group behavior. The odd and inexplicable things that one person does will tend to cancel out the odd and inexplicable things that another person does.

5. Theories are designed to give meaning and coherence to observed sequences of events. A theory consists of a set of definitions of the variables to be employed and a set of assumptions about how things behave. Any theory has certain logical implications that must be true if the theory is true. These are the theory's predictions.

6. A theory is *conditional* in the sense that it provides predictions of the type "*if* one event occurs, *then* another event will also occur." An important method of testing theories is to confront their predictions with evidence.

7. The progress of any science lies in finding better explanations of events than are now available. Thus in any developing science, one must expect to discard some present theories and replace them with demonstrably superior alternatives.

8. Theories are tested by checking their predictions against evidence. In some sciences these tests can be conducted under laboratory conditions in which only one thing changes at a time. In other sciences, testing must be done using the data produced by the world of ordinary events. (The appendix to this chapter provides a brief discussion of some of the elementary statistical techniques used to test hypotheses when many variables are changing at once.)

9. Although distinguishing positive from normative questions and seeking to answer positive questions are important aspects of science, it does not follow that economic inquiry can be totally value free. Although values intrude at almost all stages of scientific inquiry, the rule that theories should be judged against evidence wherever possible tends to produce advances of positive knowledge over time.

TOPICS FOR REVIEW

Positive and normative statements

Testable statements

The law of large numbers and the predictability of human behavior

Variables, assumptions, and predictions in theorizing

Functional relations

Conditional prediction versus prophecy

DISCUSSION QUESTIONS

1. What are some of the positive and normative issues that lie behind the disagreements in the following cases?
   a. Economists disagree on whether President Bush should stimulate the economy in 1992.
   b. European and U.S. negotiators disagree over the desirability of reducing European farm subsidies.
   c. Economists argue about the merits of a voucher system that allows parents to choose the schools their children will attend.

2. What groups are likely to have a self-interest in a proposal to severely restrict the ability of Japanese-made cars to compete against U.S.-made cars in the U.S. market? What are some of the positive issues that might be relevant to deciding on this proposal?

3. A baby doesn't "know" of the theory of gravity, yet in walking and eating the child soon begins to use the principles of gravity. Distinguish between behavior and the explanation of behavior. Does a business executive or a farmer have to understand economic theory to behave in a pattern consistent with economic theory?

4. "If human behavior were completely capricious and unpredictable, life insurance could not be a profitable business." Explain. Can you think of any businesses that do *not* depend on predictable human behavior?

5. Write five statements about unemployment. Classify each statement as positive or normative. If your list contains only one type of statement, try to add a sixth statement of the other type.

6. Each of the following unrealistic assumptions is sometimes made. See if you can visualize situations in which each of them might be useful.
   a. The earth is flat.
   b. There are no differences between men and women.
   c. There is no tomorrow.
   d. People are wholly selfish.

7. What may at first appear to be untestable statements can often be reworded so that they can be tested by an appeal to evidence. How might you do that with respect to each of the following assertions?
   a. The U.S. economic system is the best in the world.
   b. Unemployment insurance is eroding the work ethic and encouraging people to become wards of the state rather than productive workers.
   c. Robotics ought to be outlawed, because it will destroy the future of working people.
   d. Laws requiring equal pay for work of equal value will spell disaster for women.

8. "The simplest way to see that capital punishment is a strong deterrent to murder is to ask yourself whether you might be more inclined to commit murder if you knew in advance that you ran no risk of ending in the electric chair, in the gas chamber, or on the gallows." Comment on the methodology of social investigation implied by this statement. What alternative approach would you suggest?

9. There are hundreds of eyewitnesses to the existence of flying saucers and other UFOs. There are films and eyewitness accounts of Nessie, the Loch Ness monster. Are you persuaded of their existence? If not, what would it take to persuade you? If so, what would it take to make you change your mind?

APPENDIX TO CHAPTER

2

Graphing Relations Among Variables

The popular saying "The facts speak for themselves" is almost always wrong when there are many facts. Theories are needed to explain how facts are linked together, and summary measures are needed to assist in sorting out what facts show in relation to theories. The simplest means of providing compact summaries of a large number of observations is the use of tables and graphs. Graphs play an important role in economics by representing geometrically both observed data and the relations among variables that are the subject of economic theory.

Because the surface of a piece of paper is two-dimensional, a graph may readily be used to represent pictorially any relation between two variables. Flip through this book and you will see dozens of examples. Figure 2A-1 shows generally how a coordinate graph can be used to represent any two measurable variables.[1]

---

[1] Economics is often concerned only with the positive values of variables, and the graph is confined to the upper right-hand (or "positive") quadrant. Whenever a variable has a negative value, one or more of the other quadrants must be included.

FIGURE 2A-1
A Coordinate Graph

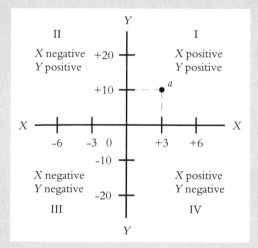

The axes divide the total space into four quadrants according to the signs of the variables. In the upper right-hand quadrant, both X and Y are greater than zero; this is usually called the *positive quadrant*. Point *a* has *coordinates* $X = 3$ and $Y = 10$ in the coordinate graph. These coordinates *define* point *a*.

FIGURE 2A-2
The Relationship Between the Price of Carrots and the Quantity of Carrots That Purchasers Wish to Buy: A Numerical Illustration

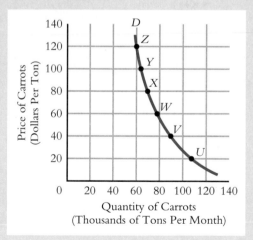

A two-dimensional graph can show how two variables are related. The two variables, the price of carrots and the quantity that people wish to purchase, are shown by the downward-sloping curve labeled D. Particular points on the curve are labeled U through Z. For example, point Z shows that at a price of $120, the demand to purchase carrots is 60,000 tons per month.

Representing Theories on Graphs

Figure 2A-2 shows a simple two-variable graph, which will be analyzed in detail in Chapter 4. For now it is sufficient to notice that the graph permits us to show the relationship between two variables, the price of carrots on the vertical axis and the *quantity* of carrots per month on the horizontal axis.[2] The downward-sloping curve, labeled *D* for a *demand curve*, shows the relationship between the price of carrots and the quantity of carrots that buyers wish to purchase.

Figure 2A-3 is very much like Figure 2A-2, with one difference. It generalizes from the specific example of carrots to an unspecified commodity and focuses on the slope of the demand curve rather than on specific numerical values. Note that the quantity labeled q_0 is associated with the price p_0, and the quantity q_1 is associated with the price p_1.

Straight Lines and Their Slopes

Figure 2A-4 illustrates a variety of straight lines. They differ according to their slopes. **Slope** is defined as the ratio of the vertical change to the corresponding horizontal change as one moves along a curve.

---

[2] The choice of which variable to put on which axis is discussed in footnote 3 on page 93 and in math note 9 (regarding math notes, see footnote 5 on page 13).

FIGURE 2A-3
The Relationship Between the Price of a Commodity and the Quantity of the Commodity That Purchasers Wish to Buy

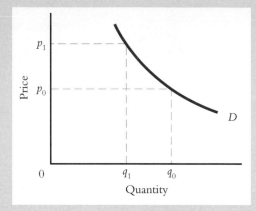

Graphs can illustrate general relationships between variables as well as between specific quantities. Here, in contrast to Figure 2A-2, price and quantity are shown as general variables. The demand curve illustrates a quantitatively unspecified *negative* relationship between price and quantity. For example, at the price p_0 the quantity that purchasers demand is q_0, whereas at the higher price of p_1 purchasers demand the lower quantity of q_1.

The symbol **Δ** (which is the Greek letter capital delta) is used to indicate a change in any vari-

FIGURE 2A-4
Four Straight Lines with Different Slopes

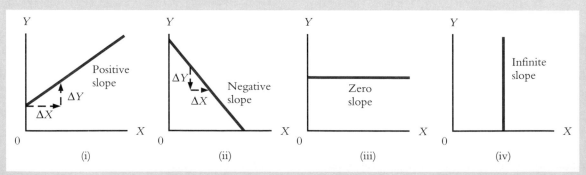

The slope of a straight line is constant but can vary from one line to another. The direction of slope of a straight line is characterized by the signs of the ratio $\Delta Y/\Delta X$. In part (i) that ratio is positive because X and Y vary in the same direction; in part (ii) the ratio is negative because X and Y vary in opposite directions; in part (iii) it is zero because Y does not change as X changes; in part (iv) it is infinite.

able. Thus ΔX means "the change in X," and ΔY means "the change in Y." The ratio $\Delta Y/\Delta X$ is the slope of a straight line. When they increase or decrease together, the ratio is positive and the line is positively sloped, as in part (i) of Figure 2A-4. When ΔY and ΔX have opposite signs, that is, when one increases while the other decreases, the ratio is negative and the line is negatively sloped, as in part (ii). When ΔY does not change, the line is horizontal, as in part (iii), and the slope is zero. When ΔX is zero, the line is vertical, as in part (iv), and the slope is often said to be infinite, although the ratio $\Delta Y/\Delta X$ is indeterminate. **[2]**

Slope is a quantitative measure, not merely a qualitative one. For example, in Figure 2A-5 two upward-sloping straight lines have different slopes. Line A has a slope of 2 ($\Delta Y/\Delta X = 2$); line B has a slope of 1/2 ($\Delta Y/\Delta X = 0.5$).

Curved Lines and Their Slopes

Figure 2A-6 shows four curved lines. The line in part (i) is plainly upward sloping; the line in part (ii) is downward sloping. The other two change from one to the other, as the labels indicate. Unlike a straight line, which has the same slope at every point on the line, the slope of a curve changes. The slope of a curve must be measured at a particular point and is defined as *the slope of a straight line that just touches (is tangent to) the straight line at that point.* This is illustrated

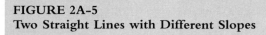

FIGURE 2A-5
Two Straight Lines with Different Slopes

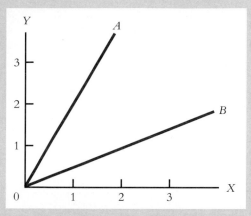

Slope is a quantitative measure. Both lines have positive slopes and thus are similar to Figure 2A-4(i). However, line A is steeper (i.e., has a greater slope) than line B. For each 1-unit increase in X, the value of Y increases by 2 units along line A but only 1/2 unit along line B. The ratio $\Delta Y/\Delta X$ is 2 for line A and 1/2 for B.

in Figure 2A-7. The slope at point A is measured by the slope of the tangent line a. The slope at point B is measured by the slope of the tangent line b.

FIGURE 2A-6
Four Curved Lines

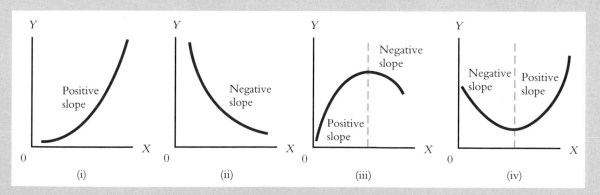

The slope of a curved line is not constant and may change direction. The slopes of the curves in parts (i) and (ii) change in size but not in direction, whereas those in parts (iii) and (iv) change in both size and direction. Unlike that of a straight line, the slope of a curved line cannot be defined by a single number because it changes as the value of X changes.

FIGURE 2A-7
Defining the Slope of a Curve

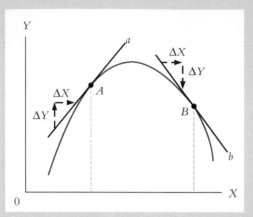

The slope of a curve at any point on the curve is defined by the slope of the straight line that is tangent to the curve at that point. The slope of the curve at point *A* is defined by the slope of the line *a*, which is tangent to the curve at point *A*. The slope of the curve at point *B* is defined by the slope of the tangent line *b*.

FIGURE 2A-8
A Scatter Diagram Relating Taxes Paid to Family Income

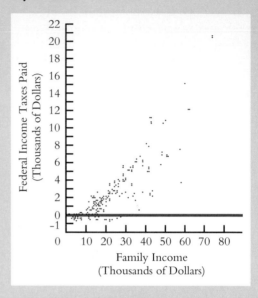

The scatter pattern shows a clear tendency for taxes paid to rise with family income. Family income is measured along the horizontal axis, and federal income taxes paid are measured along the vertical axis. Each dot represents a single family in the sample and is located on the graph according to the family's income and taxes paid. The dots fall mainly within a narrow, rising band, suggesting the existence of a systematic relationship between income and taxes paid, but they do not fall along a single line, which suggests that things other than family income affect taxes paid. The data are for 1979. (Negative amounts of tax liability arise because of such things as capital losses that may be carried forward.)

Graphing Observations

A coordinate graph such as that shown in Figure 2A-1 can be used to show the observed values of two variables as well as the theoretical relationships between them. For example, curve *D* in Figure 2A-2 might have arisen as a freehand line drawn to generalize actual observations of the points labeled *U, V, W, X, Y,* and *Z.*

Although that graph was not constructed from actual observations, many graphs are. To illustrate, we take the very simple hypothesis that the income taxes paid by families increase as their incomes increase.

To test the hypothesis about taxes, we have chosen a random sample of 212 families from data collected by the Survey Research Center of the University of Michigan. We have recorded each family's income and the federal income tax it pays.

One way in which the data may be used to evaluate the hypothesis is to draw what is called a **scatter diagram**, which plots paired values of two variables. Figure 2A-8 is a scatter diagram that relates family income to federal income tax payments. Income is measured on the horizontal axis and taxes paid on the vertical axis. Any point in the diagram represents a particular family's income combined with the tax payment of that family. Thus each family for which there are observations can be represented on the diagram by a dot, the coordinates of which indicate the family's income and the amount of taxes paid in 1979.

The scatter diagram is useful because if there is a simple relationship between the two variables, it will be apparent to the eye once the data are plotted. For example, Figure 2A-8 makes it apparent that more taxes tend to be paid as income rises. It also makes it apparent that the relationship between taxes and income is approximately linear. A rising straight line fits the data reasonably well between about $10,000 and $40,000 of income. Above $40,000 and below $10,000 the line does not fit the data as well, but because more than two-thirds of the families sampled have incomes in the $10,000-to-$40,000 range, we may conclude that the straight line provides a fairly good description of the basic relationship for middle-income families.

The graph also gives some idea of the strength of the relationship. If income were the only determinant of taxes paid, all the dots would cluster closely around a line or a smooth curve. As it is, the points are somewhat scattered, and several households with the same income show different amounts of taxes paid.

There is some scattering of the dots because the relationship is not "perfect"; in other words, there is some variation in tax payments that cannot be associated with variations in family income. These variations in tax payments occur mainly for two reasons. First, factors other than income influence tax payments, and some of these other factors will undoubtedly have varied among the families in the sample. Second, there will inevitably be some errors in measurement. For example, a family might have incorrectly reported its tax payments to the person who collected our data.

Time-Series Data

The data used in the example of Figure 2A-8 are *cross-sectional data* (several measurements or observations made at the same point in time) because the incomes of and taxes paid by different households are compared over a single period of time—the year 1979. Scatter diagrams may also be drawn for a number of observations taken on two variables at successive periods of time.

For example, if we wanted to know whether there was any simple relationship between personal income and personal consumption in the United States between 1965 and 1991, data would be collected for the levels of personal income and expenditure per capita in each year from 1965 to 1991, as is done in Table 2A-1. This information could be plotted on a scatter diagram, with consumption on the X axis and income on the Y axis. The data are plotted in Figure 2A-9, and they do indeed suggest a systematic, almost linear relationship.

Figure 2A-9 is a scatter diagram of observations taken repeatedly over successive periods of time. Such data are called **time-series data**, and plotting them

TABLE 2A-1 Personal Income and Consumption, 1965-1991 (*in 1987 dollars*)

Year	Disposable personal income per capita	Personal consumption expenditures per capita
1965	$ 8,508	$ 7,703
1966	8,822	8,005
1967	9,114	8,163
1968	9,399	8,506
1969	9,606	8,737
1970	9,875	8,842
1971	10,111	9,022
1972	10,414	9,425
1973	11,013	9,752
1974	10,832	9,602
1975	10,906	9,711
1976	11,192	10,121
1977	11,406	10,425
1978	11,851	10,744
1979	12,039	10,876
1980	12,005	10,746
1981	12,156	10,770
1982	12,146	10,782
1983	12,349	11,179
1984	13,029	11,617
1985	13,258	12,015
1986	13,552	12,336
1987	13,545	12,568
1988	13,890	12,903
1989	14,030	13,027
1990	14,154	13,051
1991	13,987	12,889

Source: Economic Report of the President, 1991.

Real disposable income per capita and real personal consumption expenditures have both grown since 1965. The former has increased by 64 percent from $8,508 to $13,987 over the period, while the latter grew by 67 percent from $7,703 to over $12,889.

on a scatter diagram involves no new techniques. When cross-sectional data are plotted, each point gives the values of two variables for a particular unit (say, a family); when time-series data are plotted, each point tells the values of two variables for a particular year.

Instead of studying the relationship between income and consumption suggested in the preceding paragraph, a study of the pattern of the changes in either one of these variables over time could be made. Figure 2A-10 shows this information for con-

FIGURE 2A-9
A Scatter Diagram Relating Consumption and Disposable Income

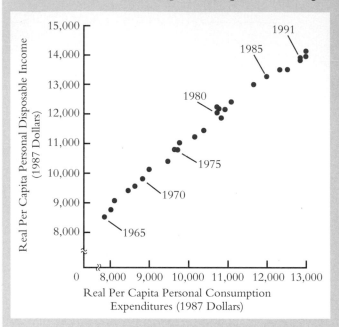

This scatter diagram shows paired values of two variables. The data of Table 2A-1 are plotted here. Each dot shows the values of per capita personal consumption expenditures and per capita disposable income for a given year. A close, positive, linear relationship between the two variables is obvious. Note that in this diagram the axes are shown with a break in them to indicate that not all the values of the variables between $8,000 and zero are given. Since no *observations* occurred in those ranges, it was unnecessary to provide space for them.

FIGURE 2A-10
A Time Series of Consumption Expenditures, 1965–1991

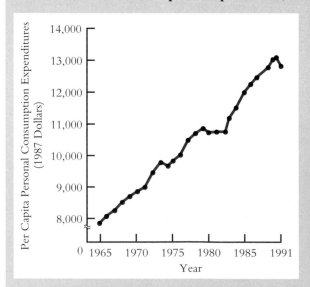

A time series plots values of a single variable in chronological order. This graph shows that with only minor interruptions, consumption measured in 1987 dollars rose from 1965 to 1991. The data are given in Table 2A-1.

sumption. Time is one variable, and consumption expenditure is the other. However, time is a special variable; the order in which successive events happen is important. The year 1991 followed 1990; they were not two independent and unrelated years. In contrast, two randomly selected households are independent and unrelated. For this reason, it is customary to draw in the line segments connecting the successive points, as has been done in Figure 2A-10.

Such a figure is called a *time-series graph* or a **time series.** This kind of graph makes it easy to see if the variable being considered has changed in a systematic way over the years or if its behavior has been more or less erratic.

Ratio (Logarithmic) Scales

All the foregoing graphs use axes that plot numbers on a natural arithmetic scale, with distances between two values shown by the size of the numerical difference. If *proportionate* rather than *absolute* changes in variables are important, it is more revealing to use a ratio scale than a natural scale. On a **natural scale** the distance between numbers is proportionate to the absolute difference between those numbers. Thus 200 is placed halfway between 100 and 300. On a **ratio scale**, the distance between numbers is proportionate to the percentage difference between the two numbers (which can also be measured as the absolute difference between their logarithms). Equal distances anywhere on a ratio scale represent equal percentage changes rather than equal absolute changes. On a ratio scale, the distance between 100 and 200 is the same as the distance between 200 and 400, between 1,000 and 2,000, and between

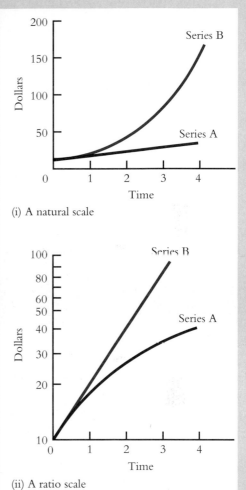

FIGURE 2A-11
The Difference Between Natural and Ratio Scales

(i) A natural scale

(ii) A ratio scale

On the natural scale, equal distances represent equal amounts; on a ratio scale, equal distances represent equal percentage changes. The two series in Table 2A-2 are plotted in each chart. Series A, which grows at a constant absolute amount, is shown by a straight line on a natural scale but by a curve of diminishing slope on a ratio scale because the same absolute growth represents a decreasing percentage growth. Series B, which grows at a rising absolute rate but a constant percentage rate, is shown by a curve of increasing slope on a natural scale but by a straight line on a ratio scale.

TABLE 2A-2   Two Series

Time period	Series A	Series B
0	$10	$ 10
1	18	20
2	26	40
3	34	80
4	42	160

Series A shows constant absolute growth ($8 per period) but declining percentage growth. Series B shows constant percentage growth (100 percent per period) but rising absolute growth.

FIGURE 2A-12
A Contour Map of a Small Mountain

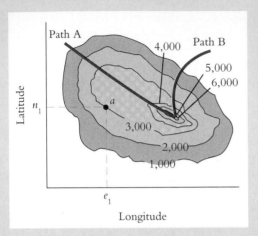

A contour map shows three variables in two-dimensional space. This familiar kind of three-variable graph shows latitude and longitude on the axes and altitude on the contour lines. The contour line labeled 1,000 connects all locations with an altitude of 1,000 feet, the contour line labeled 2,000 connects those with an altitude of 2,000 feet, and so forth. Point a, for example, has latitude n_1, longitude e_1, and an altitude of 3,000 feet. Where the lines are closely bunched, they represent a steep ascent; where they are far apart, a gradual one. Clearly, path A is a gentler climb from 3,000 to 4,000 feet on this mountain than path B.

FIGURE 2A-13
Three Variables Shown in Two Dimensions

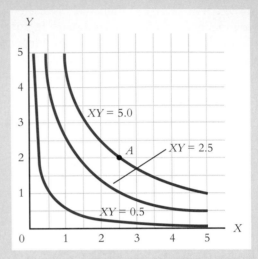

This graph illustrates examples of the three-variable function $XY = a$. The function $XY = a$ is called a *rectangular hyperbola*. The figure shows three members of the family. For example, point A represents $Y = 2.0$, $X = 2.5$, and $a = 5.0$.

any two numbers that stand in the ratio 1:2 to each other. A ratio scale is also called a **logarithmic scale**.

Table 2A-2 shows two series, one growing at a constant absolute amount of 8 units per period and the other growing at a constant rate of 100 percent per period. In Figure 2A-11 the series are plotted first on a natural scale and then on a ratio scale.

The natural scale makes it easy for the eye to judge absolute variations, and the logarithmic scale makes it easy for the eye to judge proportionate variations.[3]

Graphing Three Variables in Two Dimensions

Often we want to show graphically more than two dimensions. For example, a topographic map shows latitude, longitude, and altitude on a two-dimensional page. This is done by using contour lines, as in Figure 2A-12. Now consider the function $XY = a$, where X, Y, and a are variables. Figure 2A-13 plots this function for three different values of a. The variables X and Y are represented on the two axes. The variable a is represented by the labels on the curves. Several examples of this procedure occur throughout the book (see, for example, the discussion of indifference curves in Chapter 8 and isoquants in the Appendix to Chapter 11).

---

[3] Graphs with a ratio scale on one axis and a natural scale on the other are frequently encountered in economics. In the case just illustrated, there is a ratio scale on the vertical axis and a natural scale on the horizontal (or time) axis. Such graphs are often called *semi-log graphs*. In scientific work, graphs with ratio scales on both axes are frequently encountered. Such graphs are often referred to as *double-log graphs*.

3

An Overview of the Market Economy

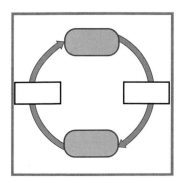

Until about 10,000 years ago, all human beings were hunter-gatherers, providing for their wants and needs with foods that were freely provided in nature. The Neolithic agricultural revolution changed all that. People gradually abandoned their nomadic life of hunting and food gathering and settled down to tend crops and domesticated animals. Since that time, all societies have faced the problem of choice under conditions of scarcity.

Specialization, Surplus, and Trade

Along with permanent settlement, the agricultural revolution brought surplus production. Farmers could produce substantially more than they needed for survival. The agricultural surplus allowed the creation of new occupations. Freed from having to grow their own food, new classes—such as artisans, soldiers, priests, and government officials—turned their talents to performing specialized services and producing goods other than food. They also produced more than they themselves needed and traded the excess to obtain other goods.

The allocation of different jobs to different people is called **specialization of labor.** Specialization has proved to be extraordinarily efficient compared with self-sufficiency, for at least two reasons.

First, individual talents and abilities differ, and specialization allows each person to do the job he or she can do best, while leaving everything else to be done by others. That production is greater with specialization than with self-sufficiency is one of the most fundamental principles in economics. It is called the *principle of comparative advantage.* An example is given in Box 3-1, and a much fuller discussion is found in Chapter 36.

Second, a person who concentrates on one activity becomes better at it than could a jack-of-all-trades. This is called "learning by doing." It was a factor much stressed by early economists. Modern research into what are called "learning curves" shows that learning by doing is important in many industries.

The exchange of goods and services in early societies commonly took place by simple mutual agreement among neighbors. In the course of time, however, trading became centered in particular gathering places called markets. Today we use the term *market economy* to refer to a society in which people specialize in productive activities and satisfy most of their material wants through exchanges.

Specialization must be accompanied by trade. People who produce only one thing must trade much of their production in order to obtain all the other things they require.

Box 3-1

Absolute and Comparative Advantage

A simple case will illustrate the important principles involved in the gains from specialization.

Absolute Advantage

Suppose that, working full time on his own, Jacob can produce 100 pounds of potatoes *or* 40 sweaters per year, whereas Maria can produce 400 pounds of potatoes *or* 10 sweaters. Maria has an absolute advantage in producing potatoes because she can make more per period than Jacob. However, Jacob has an absolute advantage over Maria in producing sweaters for the same reason. If they both spend *half* their time producing each commodity, the results will be as given in Table 1.

Now let Jacob specialize in sweaters, producing 40 of them, and Maria specialize in potatoes, producing 400 pounds. Production of both

commodities has risen because each person is better than the other person at his or her specialty.

Comparative Advantage

Now make things a little less obvious by giving Maria an absolute advantage over Jacob in both commodities. We do this by making Maria more productive in sweaters so that she can produce 48 of them per year, with all other productivities remaining the same. Table 2 gives the outputs when Jacob and Maria each divide their time equally between the two products. Now compared with Jacob, Maria is four times more efficient at producing potatoes and 20 percent more efficient at producing sweaters.

It is possible to increase their combined production of both commodities by having Maria increase

TABLE 1   Production of Potatoes and Sweaters with Each Person's Time Divided Equally Between the Two Commodities

	Potatoes	Sweaters
Jacob	50	20
Maria	200	5
Total	250	25

TABLE 2   Production of Potatoes and Sweaters with Each Person's Time Divided Equally Between the Two Commodities

	Potatoes	Sweaters
Jacob	50	20
Maria	200	24
Total	250	44

The earliest market economies depended to some considerable extent on **barter,** the trading of goods directly for other goods.[1] However, barter can

be a costly process in terms of the time spent searching out satisfactory exchanges. the evolution of money has made trading easier. Money eliminates the inconvenience of barter by allowing the two sides of the barter transaction to be separated. Farmers who have wheat and want hammers do not have to search for individuals who have hammers and want wheat. They take money in exchange, then find people who wish to trade hammers, and offer money for the hammers.

---

[1] Not only was barter common in the earliest societies that flourished before the invention of money and in medieval villages, it survived in isolated cases into more recent times. For example, much of the early North American fur trade was barter—trinkets, gems, cloths, and firearms being traded directly for furs.

her production of potatoes and Jacob increase his production of sweaters. Table 3 gives an example in which Jacob specializes fully in sweater production and Maria spends 25 percent of her time on sweaters and 75 percent on potatoes. (Her outputs of sweaters and potatoes are thus 25 percent and 75 percent of what she could produce of these commodities if she worked full time on one or the other.) Table 3 shows the results.

In this latter example, Maria is absolutely more efficient than Jacob in both lines of production, but her margin of advantage is greater in potatoes than in sweaters. Economists say that Maria has a **comparative advantage** over Jacob in the line of production in which her margin of advantage is greatest (potatoes, in this case) and that Ja-

cob has a comparative advantage over Maria in the line of production in which his margin of disadvantage is least (sweaters, in this case). This is only an illustration: the principles can be generalized as follows.

Absolute efficiencies are not necessary for there to be gains from specialization.

Gains from specialization occur whenever there are *differences* in the margin of advantage one person enjoys over another in various lines of production.

Total production can always be increased when each person specializes in the production of the commodity in which he or she has a comparative advantage.

A more detailed study of the important concept of comparative advantage and its many applications to international trade and specialization must await the chapter on international trade (which is sometimes studied in courses on microeconomics and sometimes in courses on macroeconomics). In the meantime it is worth noting that the comparative advantage of individuals and of whole nations may change. Maria may learn new skills and develop a comparative advantage in sweaters that she does not currently have. Similarly, whole nations may develop new abilities and know-how that will change their pattern of comparative advantage.

TABLE 3   Production of Potatoes and Sweaters with Jacob Fully Specialized and Maria Spending 25 Percent of Her Time on Sweaters and 75 Percent on Potatoes

	Potatoes	Sweaters
Jacob	—	40
Maria	300	12
Total	300	52
Increase over Table 2	50	8

By eliminating the need for barter, money greatly facilitates trade and specialization.

The Division of Labor

Market transactions in early economies mainly involved consumption goods. Producers specialized in making a commodity and then traded it for the other products they needed. Over the past several hundred years, many technical advances in methods of pro-

duction have made it efficient to organize agriculture and industry on a large scale. These technical developments have made use of what is called the **division of labor,** which is a further step in the specialization of labor involving specialization within the production process of a particular commodity. The labor involved is divided into a series of repetitive tasks, and each individual performs a single task that may be just one of hundreds of tasks necessary to produce the commodity.

Box 3-2

The Division of Labor

Adam Smith begins his classic *The Wealth of Nations* (1776) with a long study on the division of labor.

> The greatest improvements in the productive powers of labour...have been the effects of the division of labour.
>
> To take an example...the trade of the pinmaker; a workman not educated to this business (which the division of labour has rendered a distinct trade), nor acquainted with the use of the machinery employed in it could scarce, perhaps, with his utmost industry, make one pin in a day, and certainly could not make twenty. But in the way in which this business is now carried on...it is divided into a number of branches....One man draws out the wire, another straightens it, a third cuts it, a fourth points it, a fifth grinds it at the top for receiving the head; to make the head requires two or three distinct operations; to put it on is a peculiar business, to whiten the pins is another; it is even a trade by itself to put them into the paper; and the important business of making a pin is, in this manner, divided into about eighteen distinct operations, which, in some manufactories, are all performed by distinct hands, though in others the same man will sometimes perform two or three of them.

Smith observes that even in smallish factories, where the division of labor is exploited only in part, output is as high as 4,800 pins per person per day!

Later, Smith discusses the general importance of the division of labor and the forces that limit its application:

> Each animal is still obliged to support and defend itself, separately and independently, and derives no sort of advantage from that variety of talents with which nature has distinguished its fellows. Among men, on the contrary, the most dissimilar geniuses are of use to one another; the different produces of their respective talents, by the general disposition of truck, barter, and exchange, being brought, as it were, into a common stock, where every man may purchase whatever part of the produce of other men's talents he has occasion for.
>
> As it is the power of exchanging that gives occasion to the division of labour, so the extent of this division must always be limited by the extent of that power, or, in other words, by the extent of the market. When the market is very small, no person can have any encouragement to dedicate himself entirely to one employment for want [i.e., lack] of the power to exchange all that surplus part of the produce of his own labour, which is over and above his own consumption, for such parts of the produce of other men's labour as he has occasion for.

Smith notes that there is no point in specializing to produce a large quantity of pins, or anything else, unless there are enough persons making other commodities to provide a market for all the pins that are produced. Thus the larger the market, the greater is the scope for the division of labor and the higher are the resulting opportunities for efficient production.

To gain the advantages of the division of labor, it became necessary to organize production in large factories. The typical workers no longer earned their incomes by selling commodities they personally had produced; rather, they sold their labor services to firms and received money wages in return. With this development, most urban workers lost their status as artisans and became dependent on their ability to sell their labor. Adam Smith, the great eighteenth century Scottish political economist, was the first to study the division of labor in detail, as discussed in Box 3-2.

Interestingly, recent changes have led to an increased number of self-employed workers who are more like the artisans of old than like factory workers. These important developments are further discussed in Chapter 9. Even within the factory a new organizational principle called "lean production" or "flexible manufacturing," which was pioneered by Japanese auto manufacturers, has led back to a more craft-based form of organization within the factory. In this technique, also discussed in Chapter 9, employees work as a team; each employee is able to do every team member's job rather than one very specialized task at one point on the assembly line.

Markets and Resource Allocation

As explained in Chapter 1, *resource allocation* refers to the distribution of the available factors of production among the various uses to which they might be put. There are not enough resources to produce all the goods and services that could be consumed. It is therefore necessary to allocate the available resources among their various possible uses and in so doing to choose what to produce and what not to produce. In a market economy, millions of consumers decide what commodities to buy and in what quantities; a vast number of firms produce these commodities and buy the factor services that are needed to make them; and millions of factor owners decide to whom they will sell these services. These individual decisions collectively determine the economy's allocation of resources.

In a market economy, the allocation of resources is the outcome of countless independent decisions made by consumers and producers, all acting through the medium of markets.

This chapter provides an overview of the market mechanism.

The Decision Makers

Economics is about the behavior of people. Much that we observe in the world and that economists assume in their theories can be traced back to decisions made by individuals. There are millions of individuals in most economies. To make a systematic study of their behavior more manageable, economists categorize them into three important groups: households, firms, and the government, collectively known as **agents.**[2] Members of these groups are economic theory's cast of characters.

Households

A **household** is defined as all the people who live under one roof and who make joint financial decisions or are subject to others who make such decisions for them. The members of households are often referred to as *consumers* because they buy and consume most of the consumption goods and services. Economic theory gives households a number of attributes.

First, economists assume that each household makes consistent decisions, as though it were composed of a single individual. Thus, in analyzing markets, economists ignore many interesting problems of how each household reaches its decisions, including family conflicts and the moral and legal problems concerning parental control over minors.[3]

Second, economists assume that when buying commodities and selling factor services, households are the principal owners of factors of production. They sell the services of these factors to firms and receive their incomes in return.

Motivation.   Economists assume that each household seeks maximum *satisfaction* or *well-being* or *utility,* as the concept is variously called. The household tries to do this within the limits set by its available resources.

Firms

A **firm** is defined as the unit that employs factors of production to produce commodities that it sells to other firms, to households, or to government. For obvious reasons a firm is often called a producer. Elementary economic theory gives firms several attributes.

---

[2] Although we can get away with just three sets of decision makers, it is worth noting that there are others. Probably the most important of those omitted are nonprofit organizations such as private universities and hospitals, charities such as the American Cancer Society, and funding organizations such as the Ford Foundation. These bodies have a significant influence on the allocation of the economy's resources.

[3] Some economists have studied resource allocation within households. This field of study, pioneered by University of Chicago economist Gary Becker, is often treated in advanced courses in labor economics.

First, in elementary economic theory each firm is assumed to make consistent decisions, as though it were composed of a single individual. This strand of theory ignores the internal problems of how particular decisions are reached by assuming that the firm's internal organization is irrelevant to its decisions. This allows the firm to be treated, at least in elementary theory, as the unit of behavior on the production or supply side of commodity markets, just as the household is treated as the unit of behavior on the consumption or demand side.[4]

Second, economists assume that in their role as producers, firms are the principal users of the services of factors of production. In "factor markets" where factor services are bought and sold, the roles of firms and households are thus reversed from what they are in commodity markets: In factor markets, firms do the buying and households do the selling.

Motivation.   Economists assume that most firms make their decisions with a single goal in mind: to make as much profit as possible. This goal of *profit maximization* is analogous to the household's goal of utility maximization.

Government

The term **government** is used in economics in a broad sense to include all public officials, agencies, government bodies, and other organizations belonging to or under the direct control of federal, state, and local governments. For example, in the United States, the term *government* includes, among others, the president, the Federal Reserve System, city councils, commissions and regulatory bodies, legislative bodies, and police forces. It is not important to draw up a comprehensive list, but one should have in mind a general idea of the organizations that have legal and political power to exert control over individual decision makers and over markets.

It is *not* a basic assumption of economics that the government always acts in a consistent fashion. Three important reasons for this may be mentioned here.

First, what we call "the government" has many levels and many branches. For example, the mayor of Los Angeles, a Utah state legislator, and a United States senator from Maine represent different constituencies, whereas the Federal Departments of State, Commerce, and Housing and Urban Development represent different interests, each with its own goals. Therefore, different and conflicting views and objectives are typically found within "the government."

Second, decisions on interrelated issues of policy are made by many different bodies. Federal and state legislatures pass laws, the courts interpret laws, governments decide which laws to enforce with vigor and which not to enforce, the Treasury and the Federal Reserve Board influence monetary conditions, and a host of other agencies and semiautonomous bodies determine actions in respect to different aspects of policy goals. Because of the multiplicity of decision makers, it would be amazing if fully consistent behavior resulted.

Third, the U.S. system of checks and balances is designed to set one part of the government against another, thereby producing the characteristic U.S. division of authority and responsibility among branches of government.

Motivation.   Individual public servants, whether elected or appointed, have personal objectives (such as staying in office, promotion, power, prestige, and personal aggrandizement) as well as public service objectives. Although the balance of importance given to the two kinds of objectives will vary among persons and among types of office, both will almost always have some influence. For example, most senators would not vote against a measure that slightly reduced the "public good" if this vote almost guaranteed defeat during the next election. ("After all," the senator reasons, "if I am defeated, I won't be around to vote against *really* bad measures.")

As this discussion reveals, an important goal of legislators and political officials is the electoral success of themselves and their political party. As a result, measures that impose large costs and few obvious benefits over the short run are unlikely to find favor, even when the long-term benefits may be large. In other words, there tends to be a bias toward short-sightedness in an elective system. Although much of this bias reflects a selfish unwillingness to look beyond the present, some of it reflects genuine uncertainty about the future. These issues of government motivation are further discussed in Chapter 20.

---

[4] At the more advanced level, many studies look within the firm to ask questions such as: Does the firm's internal organization affect its behavior? We briefly consider such questions in Chapter 16.

Markets and Economies

If households, firms, and the government are the main actors, then markets are the stage on which their drama takes place.

Markets

Originally *markets* were places where goods were bought and sold. The Fulton fishmarket in New York City is a modern example of a market in the everyday sense, and many cities have their own fruit and vegetable markets. Much early economic theory explained price behavior in just such markets. Why, for example, can you get great bargains at the end of some days, but at the end of other days you buy at prices that appear exorbitant compared to the prices quoted only a few hours earlier?

As theories of market behavior were developed, they were extended to cover commodities such as wheat. Wheat produced anywhere in the world can be purchased almost anywhere else in the world, and the price of a given grade of wheat tends to be nearly uniform. When we talk about the wheat market, the concept of a market has been extended well beyond the idea of a single place to which the producer, the storekeeper, and the householder go to sell and buy.

Similarly, the "foreign exchange market" has no specific location. Instead it operates through international telephone and computer networks whereby dealers buy and sell dollars, sterling, francs, yen, and other national currencies. Markets may indeed use all conceivable means of communication, including the press, as in the case of the markets for many secondhand goods such as automobiles. If you have a car to sell or want to buy one, you will discover that "the market" comprises the local press, specialized magazines, and used-car dealers.

In the modern sense, a **market** refers to any situation in which buyers and sellers can negotiate the exchange of some commodity. In the past, high transportation costs and perishability made many markets quite local. Fresh fruits and vegetables, for example, would only be sold close to their points of production. Today, advances in preservation, the falling cost of transportation, and the development of worldwide communications networks have led to the globalization of many markets. A visit to the supermarket will confirm, for example, that food products such as Bulgarian jam, Chilean apples, and Indian rice are no longer confined to markets within their country of origin.

Economies

An **economy** is rather loosely defined as a set of interrelated production and consumption activities. It may refer to this activity in a region of one country (e.g., the economy of New England), in a country (the U.S. economy), or in a group of countries (the economy of Western Europe). In any economy the allocation of resources is determined by the production, sales, and purchase decisions made by firms, households, and governments.

In Chapter 1 we learned three important things about economies. First, a *free-market economy* is one in which the decisions of individual households and firms (as distinct from the government) exert the major influence over the allocation of resources. Second, the opposite of a free-market economy is a *command economy,* in which the major decisions about the allocation of resources are made by the government and in which firms produce and households consume only as directed. Third, in practice, all economies are *mixed economies* in that some decisions are made by firms, households, and the government acting through markets, whereas other decisions are made by the government using the command principle.

Sectors of an Economy

Parts of an economy are usually referred to as **sectors** of that economy. For example, the agricultural sector is the part of the economy that produces agricultural commodities.

Market and Nonmarket Sectors

Producers make commodities. Consumers use them. Commodities may pass from one group to the other in two ways. They may be sold by producers and bought by consumers through markets, or they may be given away.

When commodities are bought and sold, producers expect to cover their costs with the revenue they obtain from selling the product. We call this *marketed production,* and we refer to this part of the economy's activity as belonging to the **market**

sector. When the product is given away, the costs of production must be covered from some source other than sales revenue. We call this *nonmarketed production,* and we refer to this part of the economy's activity as belonging to the **nonmarket sector.**

In the case of private charities, the money required to pay for factor services may be raised from the public by voluntary contributions. In the case of production by the government—which accounts for the bulk of nonmarketed production—the money is provided from government revenue, which in turn comes mainly from taxes.

Whenever a government enterprise *sells* its output, its production is in the market sector. Most of the government's output, however, is in the nonmarket sector, often by the very nature of the product provided. For example, one could hardly expect the criminal to pay the judge for providing the service of criminal justice. Other products are in the nonmarket sector because governments have decided that there are advantages to removing them from the market sector. This is the case, for example, with public school education. Public policy places it in the nonmarket sector even though much of it could be provided by the market sector.

The economic significance of this distinction lies in the "bottom line." (In accounting, the bottom line refers to profits.) In the market sector firms face the "bottom line" test of profitability. If a product cannot be sold for a price that will cover its costs and provide sufficient profit for those who make it, the product will not be made. Production in the nonmarket sector faces no such profitability test. Since the product is provided free and its costs are met by contribution, the decision to produce it depends on the willingness of the government and private bodies to pay its costs and not on its ability to be sold at a cost-covering price.

Private and Public Sectors

An alternative division of an economy's productive activity is between private and public sectors. The **private sector** refers to all production that is in private hands, and the **public sector** refers to all production that is in public hands, that is, owned by the government. The distinction between the two sectors depends on the legal distinction of ownership. In the private sector, the organization that does the producing is owned by households or other firms; in the public sector, it is owned and controlled by the government. The public sector includes all production of goods and services by the government plus all production of all publicly owned companies and other government-operated industries that is sold to consumers through markets.

The distinction between market and nonmarket sectors is economic; it depends on whether or not producers cover their costs from revenue earned by selling output to users. The distinction between the private and the public sectors is legal; it depends on whether the producing organizations are privately or publicly owned.

Some examples will illustrate these important decisions. General Motors is in the private and market sectors; a Salvation Army soup kitchen is in the private and nonmarket sectors. A municipally owned bus company is in the public and market sectors. Finally, the Navy is in the public and nonmarket sectors.

Microeconomics and Macroeconomics

As we saw in Chapter 1, there are two different but complementary ways of viewing the economy. The first, *microeconomics,* studies the detailed workings of individual markets and interrelationships among markets. The second, *macroeconomics,* suppresses much of the detail and concentrates on the behavior of broad aggregates.[5]

Microeconomics and macroeconomics differ in the questions each asks and in the level of aggregation each uses. Microeconomics deals with the determination of prices and quantities in individual markets and with the relationships among these markets. Thus it looks at the details of the market economy. It asks, for example, how much labor is employed in the fast-food industry and why the amount is increasing. It asks about the determinants of the output of broccoli, pocket calculators, automobiles, and hamburgers. It asks, too, about the prices of these goods—why some prices go up and others down. For

---

[5] The prefixes *micro-* and *macro-* derive from the Greek words *mikros* for small and *makros* for large.

example, economists interested in microeconomics analyze how a new invention, a government subsidy, or a drought will affect the price and output of wheat and the employment of farm workers.

In contrast, macroeconomics focuses on much broader aggregates. It looks at such things as the total number of people employed and unemployed, the average level of all prices, national output, and aggregate consumption. Macroeconomics asks what determines these aggregates and how they respond to changing conditions. Whereas microeconomics looks at demand and supply with regard to particular commodities, macroeconomics looks at aggregate demand and aggregate supply.

An Overview of Microeconomics

Early economists observed the market economy with wonder. They saw that even though commodities were made by many independent producers, the amounts of commodities produced approximately equaled the amounts people wanted to purchase. Natural disasters aside, there were neither vast surpluses nor severe shortages of products. They also saw that in spite of the ever-changing geographical, industrial, and occupational patterns of demand for labor services, most laborers were able to sell their services to employers most of the time. Visitors from highly regulated economies often have a similar reaction. How, they ask, can there be such an abundance of the right things, produced at the right time, and delivered to the right place—something that planned economies have conspicuously failed to do?

How does the market produce this order in the absence of conscious coordination? It is one thing to have the same good produced year in and year out when people's wants and incomes do not change; it is quite another thing to have production adjusting continually to changing wants, incomes, and techniques of production. Yet this adjustment is accomplished relatively smoothly by markets—albeit with occasional, and sometimes serious, interruptions.

Markets work without conscious central control because individual agents make their private decisions in response to publicly known signals such as prices, wages, and profits, and these signals, in turn, respond to the collective actions entailed by the sum of all individual decisions. In short:

The great discovery of eighteenth century economists was that the price system is a social control mechanism that coordinates decentralized decision making.

In *The Wealth of Nations,* Adam Smith spoke of the price system as "the invisible hand." The system allows decision making to be decentralized under the control of millions of individual producers and consumers but nonetheless to be coordinated. An example may help to illustrate how this coordination occurs.[6]

An Example

Suppose that under prevailing conditions, farmers find it equally profitable to produce either of two crops, carrots or broccoli. As a result they are willing to produce some of both commodities, thereby satisfying the demands of households to consume both. Now suppose that consumers develop a greatly increased desire for broccoli and a diminished desire for carrots. This change might have occurred because of the discovery of hitherto unsuspected nutritive or curative powers of broccoli.

When consumers buy more broccoli and fewer carrots, a shortage of broccoli and a surplus of carrots develop. To unload their surplus stocks of carrots, merchants reduce the price of carrots because it is better to sell them at a reduced price than not to sell them at all. Merchants find, however, that they are unable to satisfy all their customers' demands for broccoli. Broccoli has become more scarce, so merchants charge more for it. As the price rises, fewer people are willing and able to purchase broccoli. Thus the rise in its price limits the quantity demanded to the available supply.

Farmers see that broccoli production has become more profitable than in the past because the costs of producing broccoli remain unchanged while its market price has risen. Similarly, they see that carrot production has become less profitable than in the past because costs are unchanged while the price has fallen. Attracted by high profits in broccoli and deterred by low profits or potential losses in carrots, farmers expand the production of broccoli and curtail the production of carrots. Thus the change in consumers' tastes, working through the price system, causes a reallocation of resources—land and

---

[6] The example is meant to give some feeling for how the price system works. This intuition is given a more formal expression in the theory laid out in Part 2 of this book.

labor—out of carrot production and into broccoli production.

The reaction of the market to a change in demand leads to a reallocation of resources. Carrot producers reduce their production; they will therefore be laying off workers and generally demanding fewer factors of production. Broccoli producers expand production; they will therefore be hiring workers and generally increasing their demand for factors of production.

Labor can probably switch from carrot to broccoli production without much difficulty. Certain types of land, however, may be better suited for growing one crop than the other. When farmers increase their broccoli production, their demands for the factors especially suited to growing broccoli also increase—and this creates a shortage of these resources and a consequent rise in their prices. Meanwhile, with carrot production falling, the demand for land and other factors of production especially suited to carrot growing is reduced. A surplus results, and the prices of these factors are forced down.

Thus factors particularly suited to broccoli production will earn more and will obtain a higher share of total national income than before. Factors particularly suited to carrot production, however, will earn less and will obtain a smaller share of the total national income than before.

All of the changes illustrated in this example will be studied more fully in subsequent parts of this book; the important thing to notice now is how changes in demand cause reallocations of resources in the directions required to cater to the new levels of demand.

This example illustrates the point made earlier: *The price system is a mechanism that coordinates individual, decentralized decisions.*

An Overview of Macroeconomics

We can group together all the buyers of the nation's output and call their total desired purchases *aggregate demand.* We can also group together all the producers of the nation's output and call their total desired sales *aggregate supply.*

Major changes in aggregate demand are called *demand shocks,* and major changes in aggregate supply are called *supply shocks.* Shocks cause important changes in the broad averages and aggregates that are the concern of macroeconomics, including total out-

put, total employment, and average levels of prices and wages. Government actions sometimes *cause* demand or supply shocks; at other times, governments are *reacting to* the shocks. In the latter case, the government may attempt to cushion, or to change, the effects of a demand or a supply shock.

The Circular Flow of Income

One way to gain insight into aggregate demand and aggregate supply is to view the economy as a giant set of flows. We build up a picture of such flows in stages.

In Figure 3-1, all *producers* of goods and services are grouped together in the lower colored area, labeled producers. All *consumers* of goods and services are grouped together in the upper colored area, labeled consumers.[7]

The interactions between producers and consumers take place through two kinds of markets. Goods and services that are produced by firms are sold in markets that are usually referred to as *goods markets.* The services of factors of production (land, labor, and capital) are sold in markets called *factor markets.* The interactions involve flows going in two directions. Flows of goods and services, called real flows, are shown flowing counterclockwise in part (i) of the figure. Flows of payments for these goods and services, called money flows, are shown flowing clockwise in part (ii) of the figure.

We may now look in a little more detail at the relations just outlined.

Goods markets.   The outputs of commodities flow from producers to consumers through what are usually known as **goods markets** (or product markets), although that term covers both goods and services. Note that the term is used in the plural form, *goods markets.* Just as firms produce many products, so are there many markets in which products are sold. Households constitute one major group of consumers—indeed the largest, by amount consumed. They buy, for their own use, goods and services such as food, clothing, train journeys, compact discs, and cars. Other "consumers" include firms that purchase capital goods produced by yet other firms and include foreigners who purchase exports.

---

[7] Most individuals and firms have a double role. As buyers of goods and services, they play a part in consuming that output; as sellers of factor services and other inputs, they play a part in producing that output.

FIGURE 3-1
Real and Money Flows

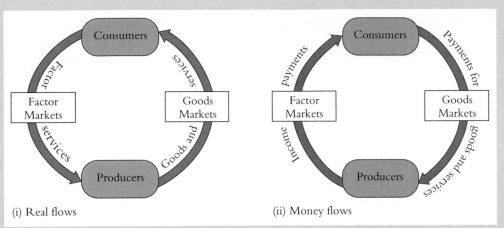

(i) Real flows

(ii) Money flows

Real flows of goods and services go in one direction between producers and consumers, whereas money flows of payments go in the opposite direction. The blue arrows in part (i) show real flows. Goods and services made by producers are sold to those who consume them, and factor services owned by consumers are sold to producers. The red arrows in part (ii) show money flows. Income payments go to consumers in return for the factor services that they sell. Expenditures flow from consumers to producers in return for the goods and services they buy.

Factor markets. Most people earn their incomes by selling factor services to producers. (Exceptions are people receiving payments from such schemes as pension plans and unemployment insurance; they receive an income but not in return for providing their factor services to help in current production.) Most of those who do sell factor services are employees. They sell their labor services to firms in return for wages. Some others own capital and receive interest or profits for providing it. Others own land and derive rents from it. The buying and selling of these factor services takes place in factor markets. The buyers are producers. They use the services that they purchase as inputs for the production of goods and services that are sold to consumers.

The circular flow. What we have just described involves two circular *flows.* This concept of a circularity in economic relations is a critical one. It helps us to understand how the separate parts of the economy are related to each other in a system of mutual interaction. For example, the activities of producers affect households, since the wages they pay affect people's incomes. The activities of households affect firms, since the goods they buy affect the sales revenues of firms.

The two parts of Figure 3-1 provide alternative ways of looking at the same transactions. Every market transaction is a two-sided exchange in the sense that for every sale, there is a purchase and, for every seller, there is a buyer. The buyer receives goods or services and parts with money; the seller receives money and parts with goods or services.

The blue arrows in part (i) of the figure show the flows of goods and services through markets. They are shown flowing counterclockwise, from consumers to producers and from producers to consumers. The red arrows in part (ii) of the figure show the corresponding flows of money payments. Flows of payments are going in the opposite direction, that is, clockwise. Payments flow from producers to consumers in order to pay for factor services, and they flow from consumers to producers to pay for goods and services.[8]

To distinguish these two sets of flows, each of which is the counterpart of the other, the blue flows

---

[8] The direction—clockwise or counterclockwise—is of no significance. What is significant is that the real and the money flows are in *opposite directions.* Any real flow is matched by a corresponding money flow going in the other direction.

in part (i) are called *real flows* and the red flows in part (ii) are called money, or *nominal,* flows.

Both of these ways of looking at the flows of economic transactions carry an important message. When firms produce goods and services, they create through factor payments the incomes needed to purchase their outputs; when users buy the outputs of firms, their payments create the incomes that firms need to pay for the factors of production that they employ. The main circular flow is shown passing from domestic producers to domestic households and back again. On the way, however, there are several leakages from, and additions to, this flow around the main circuit.

Other Flows

Figure 3-2 elaborates on the money flows shown in part (ii) of Figure 3-1 (still omitting much of the detail). It does so by allowing for private-sector saving and investment, for government taxing and spending, and for foreign trade. Since we are going to allow for foreign trade, the bottom box is labeled "Domestic Producers" to distinguish them from foreign producers. In addition, since we are going to allow for several classes of consumers of output, the top box is now labeled "Domestic Households" to distinguish that important group from the other purchasers of domestic output: foreigners, the government, and firms that purchase capital goods.

FIGURE 3-2
The Circular Flow Elaborated

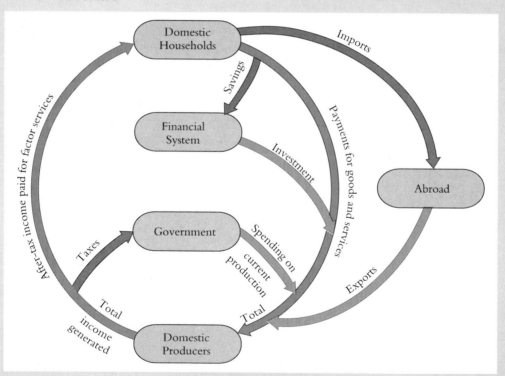

Taxes, savings, and imports withdraw expenditures from the circular flow; government purchases, investment, and exports inject expenditures into the circular flow. From the total income created by domestic producers, some leaks out of the circular flow because of government taxes on incomes. In this simplified version, the rest reaches domestic households as their disposable incomes. Some household income leaks out of the circular flow because of savings and imports; the rest is spent on purchasing the output of domestic firms. To these purchases are also added three injections: investment, government expenditure, and exports. Together these injections, plus household expenditure on domestic output, account for the total purchases of domestic output.

Leakages. As shown in Figure 3-2, payments flow from domestic producers to domestic households by way of payments for factor services. On the way, however, some leaks out of the circular flow because of government taxes, which reduce the flow of income payments that would otherwise go to households.

Payments pass from domestic households to domestic producers when households spend their incomes to buy goods and services made by producers. Some household income leaks out of the circular flow when households save part of their incomes. The part that is saved is not spent on goods and services. Instead it is shown flowing into the financial system, which happens, for example, when households deposit their savings in banks, at savings and loan associations, or with investment trust companies. Money payments also leak out of the flow because of imports, which are purchases by domestic consumers that create incomes for *foreign* producers.

Injections. The spending of domestic households on domestically produced output creates income for domestic producers. Income is also created by three additional expenditures, often called *injections,* that cause additions to the circular flow. The first is investment expenditure, which goes to purchase the output of other firms. It is expenditure that firms make on capital goods such as machinery or factories that are produced by other firms. This expenditure is shown as a flow coming from the financial system. Such investment expenditures include a firm financing its own investment with funds raised by selling stocks or bonds to households, which is done through intermediary agents, or directly borrowing money from a bank or other financial institution. The second injection is the funds that the government spends on a whole range of goods and services, from national defense through the provision of justice to the building of schools and roads. The third injection comes from the selling of exports in response to the demand from foreign consumers for the output of domestic producers.

Together, the expenditure of domestic households, the investment expenditure of domestic firms, government purchases of goods and services, and exports constitute the aggregate demand for domestic output.[9] When any one of these elements of aggregate demand changes, aggregate output and total income earned by households are likely to change as a result. Thus, studying the determinants of total consumption, investment, government spending, and imports and exports is crucial to understanding the causes of changes both in the nation's total output and in the employment generated by the production of that output.

The Next Step

Soon you will be going on to study microeconomics or macroeconomics. Whichever branch of the subject you study next, it is important to remember that microeconomics and macroeconomics are complementary, not competing, views of the economy. Both are needed for a full understanding of the functioning of a modern economy.

---

[9] Figure 3-2 highlights some of the main flows by omitting others. Two of the most important omissions, both of which are added during the study of elementary macroeconomics, are the following: (i) Governments add directly to the incomes of domestic households through what are called transfer payments, which include unemployment insurance and social security payments, and (ii) some of the money that firms spend on investment comes, not from the financial system, but from their own profits that they reinvest rather than paying out as dividends.

SUMMARY

1. Modern market economies are based on the specialization and division of labor, which necessitate the exchange of goods and services. Exchange takes place in markets and is facilitated by the use of money. Much of economics is devoted to the study of how markets work to coordinate millions of individual, decentralized decisions.

2. In economic theory, three groups of agents make the relevant decisions. Households, firms, and government all interact with each other in markets. Households are assumed to maximize their satisfaction and firms to maximize their profits. Government may have multiple objectives.

3. A free-market economy is one in which the allocation of resources is determined by production, sales, and purchase decisions made by firms and households acting in response to such market signals as prices and profits.

4. Economies are commonly divided into market and nonmarket sectors and into public and private sectors. These divisions cut across each other; the first is based on the economic distinction of how costs are covered, and the second is based on a legal distinction of ownership.

5. A key difference between microeconomics and macroeconomics is in the level of aggregation. Microeconomics looks at prices and quantities in individual markets and how they respond to various shocks that impinge on those markets. Macroeconomics looks at broader aggregates such as aggregate consumption, employment and unemployment, and the price level.

6. The questions asked in microeconomics and macroeconomics differ, but they are complementary parts of economic theory. They study different aspects of a single economic system, and both are needed for an understanding of the whole.

7. Microeconomics deals with the determination of prices and quantities in individual markets and the relationships among those markets. It shows how the price system provides signals that reflect changes in demand and supply and to which producers and consumers react in an individual but nonetheless coordinated manner.

8. The macroeconomic interactions between households and firms through markets may be illustrated in a circular flow diagram that traces money flows between producers and consumers. These flows are the starting point for studying the circular flow of aggregate income that is the key element of macroeconomics.

9. The circular flow of payments from domestic households to domestic firms and back again is not a closed system for two reasons. First, there are leakages from it in the form of taxes, savings, and imports, all of which cause the spending of domestic households on domestic output to be less than the income that they earn. Second, there are injections in the form of government spending on goods, services, investment, and exports, all of which cause the receipts of domestic firms to be greater than the spending of domestic households on domestic output.

TOPICS FOR REVIEW

Specialization and division of labor
Economic decision makers
Markets and market economies
Market and nonmarket sectors
Private and public sectors
The price system as a social control mechanism
Microeconomics and macroeconomics
Circular flow of income

DISCUSSION QUESTIONS

1. In recent years many productive activities have been moved out of the public and nonmarket sector. Can you give examples of some that have gone to the public and market sector and the private and market sector? What activities currently in the public and nonmarket sector could be moved into the private and market sector? Do you think such a move would be desirable?

2. Suggest some examples of specialization and division of labor among people you know.

3. There is a greater variety of specialists and specialty stores in large cities than in small towns having populations with the same average income. Explain this in economic terms.

4. Define the household of which you are a member. Consider your household's income last year. What proportion of it came from the sale of factor services? Identify other sources of income. Approximately what proportion of the expenditures by your household became income for firms?

5. "It is not from the benevolence of the butcher, the brewer, or the baker that we expect our dinner, but from their regard to their self-interest. We address ourselves, not to their humanity, but to their self-love, and never talk to them of our necessities, but of their advantages." Do you agree with this quotation from *The Wealth of Nations*? How are "our dinner" and their "self-interest" related to the price system? What are assumed to be the motives of firms and of households?

6. Trace the effect of a sharp change in consumer demand away from fatty red meat and toward skinless poultry as a result of continuing reports that too much fatty red meat in a diet is unhealthy.

7. Trace out some significant microeconomic and macroeconomic effects of an aging population, such as is predicted for many industrialized countries in the twenty-first century.

8. Which, if any, of the arrows in Figure 3-2 does each of the following affect initially?
   a. Households increase their consumption expenditures by reducing saving.
   b. The government lowers income-tax rates.
   c. Because of a recession, firms decide to postpone production of some new products.
   d. Consumers like the new model cars and borrow money from the banking system to buy them in record numbers. (Hint: Borrowing may be thought of as negative saving.)

PART TWO

A GENERAL VIEW OF THE PRICE SYSTEM

4

Demand, Supply, and Price

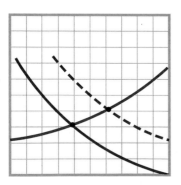

S ome people believe that economics begins and ends with the "laws" of supply and demand. However, "economics in one lesson" is, of course, too much to hope for. (An unkind critic of a book with that title remarked that the author needed a second lesson.) Still, the so-called laws of supply and demand are an important part of our understanding of the market system.

As a first step, we need to understand what determines the demand for and the supply of particular goods or services. Then we can see how demand and supply together determine the prices of goods and services and the quantities that are bought and sold. Finally, we examine how the price system allows the economy to respond to the many changes that impinge on it. Demand and supply help us understand the price system's successes and its failures. They also help us understand the consequences of such government intervention as price controls, minimum wage laws, and sales taxes.

Demand

What determines the composition of consumer expenditure in the United States? Why does it change? Why did the fraction of total consumer expenditure for food decline from more than one-quarter in 1955 to less than one-fifth by 1991? Why has the proportion of income spent on services increased from under one-third to over one-half? How have Americans reacted to the large changes in fuel prices that occurred in the last quarter century?

To see what determines the demand for various goods and services, we consider some typical *commodity*.

Quantity Demanded

The total amount of any particular commodity that all households wish to purchase in some time period is called the **quantity demanded** of that commodity.[1] It is important to notice three things about this concept.

First, quantity demanded is a *desired* quantity. It is the amount households wish to purchase, given the price of the commodity, other prices, their incomes, their tastes, and so on.[2] It may be different from the amount

---

[1] In this chapter we concentrate on the demand of *all* households for commodities. Of course, what all households do is only the sum of what each individual household does. In Chapters 7 and 8 we study the behavior of individual households in more detail.

[2] When economists say that something is "given," they do not mean that it is provided free! Instead they mean that the quantity is held constant. The expression "given the price of the commodity" therefore means that the price of the commodity is assumed not to change during the period under discussion.

that households actually succeed in purchasing. If sufficient quantities are not available, the amount that households wish to purchase may exceed the amount they actually purchase. To distinguish these two concepts, the term *quantity demanded* is used to refer to desired purchases, and a phrase such as *quantity actually bought* or *quantity exchanged* is used to refer to actual purchases.

Second, *desired* does not refer to idle dreams but to *effective demands*—that is, to the amounts people are willing to buy, given the price they must pay for the commodity.

Third, quantity demanded refers to a continuous *flow* of purchases. It must, therefore, be expressed as so much per period of time: 1 million units per day, 7 million per week, or 365 million per year. For example, being told that the quantity of new television sets demanded (at current prices) in the United States is 500,000 means nothing unless you are also told the period of time involved. Five hundred thousand television sets demanded per day would be an enormous rate of demand; 500,000 per year would be a very small rate. (The important distinction between stocks and flows is discussed in Box 4-1.)

Box 4-1

Stock and Flow Variables

One important conceptual issue that arises frequently in economics is the distinction between stock and flow variables. Economic theories use both, and it takes a little practice to keep them straight.

As noted in the text, *a flow variable has a time dimension*; it is so much per unit of time. For example, the quantity of grade A large eggs purchased in Fargo is a flow variable. No useful information is conveyed if we are told that the number purchased was 2,000 dozen eggs unless we are also told the period of time over which these purchases occured. Two thousand dozen per hour would indicate an active market in eggs, whereas 2,000 dozen per month would indicate a sluggish market.

A stock variable has no time dimension; it is just so much. Thus, the number of eggs in the egg producer's coop warehouse—for example, 20,000 dozen eggs—is a stock variable. All those eggs are there at one time, and they remain there until something happens to change the stock held by the coop. The stock variable is just a number, not a rate of flow of so much per day or per month.

The terminology of stocks and flows can be understood in terms of an analogy to a bathtub. At any moment, the tub holds so much water. This is the *stock*, and it can be measured in terms of the volume of water, say 25 gallons. There might also be water flowing into the tub from the tap, or flowing out of the tub through the drain; this *flow* is measured as so much water per unit time, say 200 gallons per hour.

The distinction between stocks and flows is important. Failure to keep them straight is a common source of confusion and even error. Note, for example, that because they have different dimensions, a stock variable and a flow variable cannot be added together without specifying some time period for which the flow persists. One cannot add 25 gallons of water in the tub plus a flow of 200 gallons per hour to get 225 gallons. The new stock of water will depend upon how long the flow goes on; if it lasts for half an hour, the new stock will be 125 gallons; if the flow persists for two hours, the new stock will be 425 gallons.*

In economics, the amount of income earned is a flow; there is so much per year or per month or per hour. The amount of a household's expenditure is also a flow—so much spent per week or per month or per hour. The amount of money in a bank account or a miser's hoard (earned, perhaps, in the past but unspent) is a stock—just so many thousands of dollars. The key test is always whether a time dimension is required to give the variable meaning.

---

* Unless, of course, the tub overflows before that volume is reached!

What Determines Quantity Demanded?

The amount of some commodity that all households wish to buy in a given time period is influenced by the following important variables: [3]

> Commodity's own price
>
> Average household income
>
> Prices of related commodities
>
> Tastes
>
> Distribution of income among households
>
> Population size

It is difficult to determine the separate influence of each of these variables if we consider what happens when everything changes at once. Instead, we consider the influence of the variables one at a time. To do this, we hold all but one of them constant. Then we let the selected variable vary and study how it affects quantity demanded. We can do the same for each of the other variables in turn, and in this way we can come to understand the importance of each.[3] Once this is done, we can combine the separate influences of the variables to discover what happens when several things change at the same time—as they often do.

Holding all other influencing variables constant is often described by the words "other things being equal," "other things given," or by the equivalent Latin phrase **ceteris paribus.** When economists speak of the influence of the price of wheat on the quantity of wheat demanded, *ceteris paribus,* they refer to what a change in the price of wheat would do to the quantity of wheat demanded if all other forces that influence the demand for wheat did not change.

Demand and Price

We are interested in developing a theory of how prices are determined. To do this we need to study the relationship between the quantity demanded of each commodity and that commodity's own price. This requires that we hold all other influences constant and ask: How will the quantity of a commodity demanded vary as its own price varies?

A basic economic hypothesis is that the price of a commodity and the quantity that will be demanded are related *negatively,* other things being equal.[4] That is, the lower the price, the higher is the quantity demanded, and the higher the price, the lower the quantity demanded.

Why might this be so? Commodities are used to satisfy desires and needs, and there is almost always more than one commodity that will satisfy any desire or need. Hunger may be alleviated by meat or vegetables; a desire for green vegetables can be satisfied by broccoli or spinach. The need to keep warm at night may be satisfied by several woolen blankets, by one electric blanket, or by a sheet and an overworked furnace. The desire for a vacation may be satisfied by a trip to the seashore or to the mountains; the need to get there may be satisfied by different airlines, a bus, a car, or a train. For any general desire or need, there are many different commodities that will satisfy it.

Now consider what happens if income, tastes, population, and the prices of all other commodities remain constant and the price of only one commodity changes. As the price goes up, that commodity becomes an increasingly expensive way to satisfy a want. Some households will stop buying it altogether; others will buy smaller amounts; still others may continue to buy the same quantity. Because many households will switch wholly or partly to other commodities to satisfy the same want, less will be bought of the commodity whose price has risen. As meat becomes more expensive, for example, households may to some extent switch to meat substitutes; they may also forgo meat at some meals and eat less meat at others.

Conversely, as the price goes down, the commodity becomes a cheaper method of satisfying a want. Households will buy more of it. Consequently,

---

[3] A relationship in which many variables (in this case, average income, population, tastes, and many prices) influence a single variable (in this case, quantity demanded) is called a *multivariate* relationship. The technique of studying the effect of each of the influencing variables one at a time, while holding the others constant, is common in mathematics, and there is a specific concept, the *partial derivative,* designed to measure such effects.

[4] The famous British economist Alfred Marshall called this fundamental relation the "law of demand." In Box 4-2 we discuss the relationship between laws, predictions, and hypotheses. In Chapters 7 and 8 we derive the "law of demand" as a prediction that follows from more basic assumptions about consumers' tastes.

they will buy less of similar commodities whose prices have not fallen and which as a result have become expensive *relative to* the commodity in question. When a bumper tomato harvest drives prices down, shoppers switch to tomatoes and cut their purchases of many other vegetables that now look relatively more expensive.

The Demand Schedule and the Demand Curve

A **demand schedule** is one way of showing the relationship between quantity demanded and the price of that commodity, other things being equal. It is a numerical tabulation showing the quantity that is demanded at selected prices.

Table 4-1 is a hypothetical demand schedule for carrots. It lists the quantity of carrots that would be demanded at various prices on the assumption that all other influences on quantity demanded are held constant. We note in particular that average household income is fixed at $30,000 because later we will want to see what happens when income changes. The table gives the quantities demanded for six selected prices, but in fact a separate quantity would be demanded at each possible price from one cent to several hundreds of dollars.

A second method of showing the relationship between quantity demanded and price is to draw a graph. The six price-quantity combinations shown

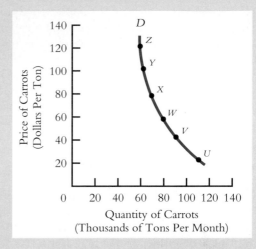

FIGURE 4-1
A Demand Curve for Carrots

This demand curve relates quantity of carrots demanded to the price of carrots; its downward slope indicates that quantity demanded increases as price falls. The six points correspond to the price-quantity combinations shown in Table 4-1. Each row in the table defines a point on the demand curve. The smooth curve drawn through all of the points and labeled D is the demand curve.

in Table 4-1 are plotted on the graph shown in Figure 4-1. Price is plotted on the vertical axis, and quantity is plotted on the horizontal axis. The smooth curve drawn through these points is called a **demand curve.** It shows the quantity that purchasers would like to buy at each price. The negative slope of the curve indicates that the quantity demanded increases as the price falls.

Each point on the demand curve indicates a single price-quantity combination. The demand curve as a whole shows something more.

The demand curve represents the relationship between quantity demanded and price, other things being equal.

When economists speak of the demand in a particular market as being given or known, they are referring not just to the particular quantity being demanded at the moment (i.e., not just to one point on the demand curve) but, instead, to the entire demand curve—to the relationship between desired purchases and all the possible alternative prices of the commodity.

TABLE 4-1 A Demand Schedule for Carrots

	Price per ton	Quantity demanded when average household income is $30,000 per year (thousands of tons per month)
U	$ 20	110.0
V	40	90.0
W	60	77.5
X	80	67.5
Y	100	62.5
Z	120	60.0

The table shows the quantity of carrots that would be demanded at various prices, *ceteris paribus.* For example, row *W* indicates that if the price of carrots were $60 per ton, consumers would desire to purchase 77,500 tons of carrots per month, given the values of the other varibles that affect quantity demanded, including average household income.

Thus the term **demand** refers to the entire relationship between the quantity demanded of a commodity and the price of that commodity (as shown, for example, by the demand schedule in Table 4-1 or the demand curve in Figure 4-1). In contrast, a single point on a demand schedule or curve is the *quantity demanded* at that point. (For example, point W in Figure 4-1 corresponds to row W in Table 4-1. At W, 77,500 tons of carrots a month are demanded at a price of $60 per ton.)

Shifts in the Demand Curve

The demand schedule is constructed and the demand curve is plotted on the assumption of *ceteris paribus*. But what if other things change, as surely they must? For example, what if a household finds itself with more income? If it spends its extra income, it will buy additional quantities of many commodities *even though the prices of those commodities are unchanged.*

If households increase their purchases of any one commodity whose price has not changed, the purchases cannot be represented by points on the original demand curve. They must be represented on a new demand curve, which is to the right of the old curve. Thus the rise in household income shifts the demand curve to the right, as shown in Figure 4-2. This illustrates the operation of an important general rule.

A demand curve is drawn on the assumption that everything except the commodity's own price is held constant. A change in any of the variables previously held constant will shift the demand curve to a new position.

A demand curve can shift in many ways; two of them are particularly important. In the first case, more is bought at *each* price, and the demand curve shifts rightward so that each price corresponds to a higher quantity than it did before. In the second case, less is bought at *each* price, and the demand curve shifts leftward so that each price corresponds to a lower quantity than it did before.

The influence of changes in variables other than price may be studied by determining how changes in each variable shift the demand curve. Any change will shift the demand curve to the right if it increases the amount that households wish to buy, other things remaining equal. It will shift the demand curve to the left if it decreases the amount that households wish to buy, other things remaining equal. Note that

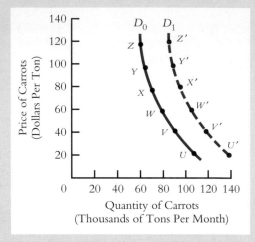

FIGURE 4-2
Two Demand Curves for Carrots

The rightward shift in the demand curve from D_0 to D_1 indicates an increase in the quantity demanded at each price. The lettered points correspond to those in Table 4-2. A rightward shift in the demand curve indicates an increase in demand in the sense that more is demanded at each price and that a higher price would be paid for each quantity.

changes in people's *expectations* about *future* values of variables such as income and prices can influence demand; however, for simplicity we consider only the influence of changes in the current values of these variables.

Average household income. If households receive more income on average, they can be expected to purchase more of most commodities even though commodity prices remain the same.[5] For such commodities we would thus expect that, at any given price, a larger quantity will be demanded than was demanded previously. This change in demand is illustrated in Table 4-2 and Figure 4-2.

A rise in average household income shifts the demand curve for most commodities to the right. This indicates that more will be demanded at each price.

[5] Such commodities are called *normal goods.* Commodities for which the amount purchased falls as income rises are called *inferior goods.* These concepts are defined and discussed in Chapter 5.

TABLE 4-2   Two Alternative Demand Schedules for Carrots

Price per ton p	Quantity demanded when average household income is $30,000 per year (thousands of tons per month) D_0		Quantity demanded when average household income is $36,000 per year (thousands of tons per month) D_1	
$ 20	110.0	U	140.0	U'
40	90.0	V	116.0	V'
60	77.5	W	100.8	W'
80	67.5	X	87.5	X'
100	62.5	Y	81.3	Y'
120	60.0	Z	78.0	Z'

An increase in average household income increases the quantity demanded at each price. When average income rises from $30,000 to $36,000 per year, quantity demanded at a price of $60 per ton rises from 77,500 tons per month to 100,800 tons per month. A similar rise occurs at every other price. Thus the demand schedule relating columns p and D_0 is replaced by one relating columns p and D_1. The graphical representations of these two functions are labeled D_0 and D_1 in Figure 4-2.

Other prices.   We saw that the negative slope of a commodity's demand curve occurs because the lower its price, the cheaper the commodity becomes relative to other commodities that can satisfy the same needs or desires. These other commodities are called **substitutes.** Another way for the same change to come about is for the price of the substitute commodity to rise. For example, carrots can become cheap relative to cabbage either because the price of carrots falls or because the price of cabbage rises. Either change will increase the amount of carrots that households wish to buy.

A rise in the price of a substitute for a commodity shifts the demand curve for the commodity to the right. More will be purchased at each price.

For example, a rise in the price of cabbage could cause the demand curve for carrots to shift to the right, as in Figure 4-2.

Complements are commodities that tend to be used jointly. Cars and gasoline are complements;

so are golf clubs and golf balls, electric stoves and electricity, and airplane flights to Denver and lift tickets at Vail. Because complements tend to be consumed together, a fall in the price of either one will increase the demand for both.

A fall in the price of a complementary commodity will shift a commodity's demand curve to the right. More will be purchased at each price.

For example, a fall in the price of airplane trips to Denver will lead to a rise in the demand for lift tickets at Vail, even though the price of those lift tickets is unchanged.

Tastes.   Tastes have an effect on people's desired purchases. A change in tastes may be long-lasting, such as the shift from fountain pens to ballpoint pens or from typewriters to word processors; or it may be a fad such as hula hoops or CB radios. In either case, a change in tastes in favor of a commodity shifts the demand curve to the right. More will be bought at each price.

Distribution of income.   If a constant total of income is redistributed among the population, demands may change. If, for example, the government increases the deductions that may be taken for children on income tax returns and compensates by raising basic tax rates, income will be transferred from childless persons to households with large families. Demands for commodities more heavily bought by childless persons will decline, while demands for commodities more heavily bought by households with large families will increase.

A change in the distribution of income will cause a rightward shift in the demand curves for commodities bought most by households whose incomes increase and a leftward shift in the demand curves for commodities bought most by households whose incomes decrease.

Population.   Population growth does not by itself create new demand. The additional people must have purchasing power before demand is changed. Extra people of working age who are employed, however, will earn new income. When this happens, the demands for all the commodities purchased by the new income earners will rise. Thus the following statement is usually true:

An increase in population will shift the demand curves for most commodities to the right, indicating that more will be bought at each price.

The reasons that demand curves shift are summarized in Figure 4-3.

Movements Along the Demand Curve Versus Shifts of the Whole Curve

Suppose you read in today's newspaper that the soaring price of carrots has been caused by a greatly increased demand for carrots. Then tomorrow you read that the rising price of carrots is greatly reducing the typical household's purchases of carrots, as shoppers switch to potatoes, yams, and peas. The two stories appear to contradict each other. The first associates a rising price with a rising demand; the second associates a rising price with a declining demand. Can both statements be true? The answer is yes, because they refer to different things. The first describes a shift in the demand curve; the second describes a movement along a demand curve in response to a change in price.

Consider first the statement that the increase in the price of carrots has been caused by an increased demand for carrots. This statement refers to a shift in the demand curve for carrots. In this case the demand curve must have shifted to the right, indicating more carrots demanded *at each price*. This shift, as we will see later in this chapter, will increase the price of carrots.

Now consider the statement that fewer carrots are being bought because carrots have become more expensive. This refers to a movement along a given demand curve and reflects a change between two specific quantities being bought—one before the price rose and one afterward.

Possible explanations for the two stories are given in the following:

1. A rise in the population is shifting the demand curve for carrots to the right as more carrots are demanded at each price. This in turn is raising the price of carrots (for reasons we will soon study in detail). This was the first newspaper story.
2. The rising price of carrots is causing each individual household to cut back on its purchase of carrots. This causes an upward movement to the left along any particular demand curve for carrots. This was the second newspaper story.

To prevent the type of confusion caused by our two newspaper stories, economists use a specialized vocabulary to distinguish between shifts of curves and movements along curves.

We have seen that *demand* refers to the *whole* demand curve, whereas *quantity demanded* refers to a specific quantity that is demanded at a specified price, as indicated by a particular point on the demand curve. In Figure 4-1, for example, demand is given by the curve *D*; at a price of $40, the quantity demanded is 90 tons, as indicated by the point *V*.

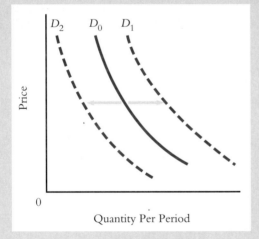

FIGURE 4-3
Shifts in the Demand Curve

The rightward shift in the demand curve from D_0 to D_1 indicates an increase in demand; a leftward shift from D_0 to D_2 indicates a decrease in demand. An increase in demand means that more is demanded at each price. Such a rightward shift can be caused by a rise in income, a rise in the price of a substitute, a fall in the price of a complement, a change in tastes that favors that commodity, an increase in population, or a redistribution of income toward groups that favor the commodity.

A decrease in demand means that less is demanded at each price. Such a leftward shift can be caused by a fall in income, a fall in the price of a substitute, a rise in the price of a complement, a change in tastes that disfavors the commodity, a decrease in population, or a redistribution of income away from groups that favor the commodity.

Economists reserve the term **change in demand** to describe a shift in the whole demand curve, that is, a change in the amount that will be bought at *every* price. The term **change in quantity demanded** refers to a change from one point on a demand curve to another point, either on the original demand curve or on a new one.

A change in quantity demanded can result from a change in demand, with the price constant; from a movement along a given demand curve due to a change in the price; or from a combination of the two. [4]

We consider each of these possibilities in turn.

An increase in demand means that the whole demand curve shifts to the right; a decrease in demand means that the whole demand curve shifts to the left. At a given price, an increase in demand causes an increase in quantity demanded, whereas a decrease in demand causes a decrease in quantity demanded.

For example, in Figure 4-2, the shift in the demand curve from D_0 to D_1 represents an increase in demand, and at a price of $40, quantity demanded increases from 90,000 tons to 116,000 tons, as indicated by the move from V to V'.

A movement down and to the right along a demand curve causes an increase in quantity demanded; a movement up and to the left along a demand curve causes a decrease in quantity demanded.

For example, in Figure 4-2, with demand given by the curve D_1, an increase in price from $40 to $60 causes a movement along D_1 from V' to W', and quantity demanded decreases from 116,000 tons to 100,800 tons.

When there is a change in demand *and* a change in the price, the change in quantity demanded is the net effect of the shift in the demand curve and the movement along the new demand curve.

Figure 4-4 shows the combined effect of a rise in demand, shown by a rightward shift in the whole

FIGURE 4-4
Shifts of and Movements Along the Demand Curve

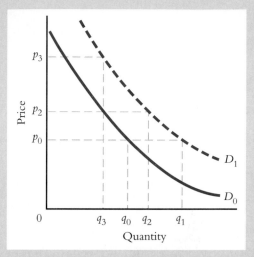

An increase in demand means that the demand curve shifts to the right, and hence quantity demanded will be higher at each price. A rise in price causes an upward movement to the left along the demand curve, and hence quantity demanded will fall.

The demand curve is originally D_0 and price is p_0, which means that quantity demanded is q_0. Suppose that demand increases to D_1, which means that at any particular price, there is a larger quantity demanded; for example, at p_0, quantity demanded is now q_1. Now suppose that the price rises above p_0. This causes a movement up and to the left along D_1, and quantity demanded falls below q_1.

The net effect of these two changes can be either an increase or a decrease in the quantity demanded. In this figure, a rise in price to p_2 means that the quantity demanded, q_2, is still in excess of the original quantity demanded, q_0; a rise in price to p_3 means that the final quantity demanded, q_3, is below the original quantity demanded, q_0.

demand curve, and an upward movement to the left along the new demand curve due to an increase in price. The rise in demand causes an increase in quantity demanded at the initial price, whereas the movement along the demand curve causes a decrease in the quantity demanded. Whether quantity demanded rises or falls overall depends on the relative magnitudes of these two changes.

Supply

The U.S. private sector produced goods and services worth nearly $5 trillion in 1991. Economists have as many questions to ask about production and its changing composition as they do about consumption. What determines the amount produced? What determines its composition? Why does the supply of goods and services produced change? Why has manufacturing output fallen from almost 30 percent of total private-sector production in 1955 to less than 20 percent in 1991? Why have agriculture, forestry, and fisheries, as a group, fallen from almost 5 percent in 1955 to just about 2 percent in 1991? Why have services grown from under 50 percent to over 60 percent in the same period?

Dramatic changes have occurred within each of these market categories. Why, for example, did the aluminum industry grow much faster than the steel industry? Even within any single industry, some firms prosper and grow while others decline. A large fraction of the firms in a typical industry at the beginning of any decade are no longer present at the end of that decade. Why and how do new jobs, new firms, and new industries come into being while other jobs, firms, and industries shrink or disappear altogether?

All of these questions and many others are aspects of a single question: *What determines the quantities of commodities that will be produced and offered for sale?*

A full discussion of these questions of supply will come later (in Part 4). For now it suffices to examine the basic relationship between the price of a commodity and the quantity produced and offered for sale and to understand what forces lead to shifts in this relationship.

Quantity Supplied

The amount of a commodity that firms wish to sell in some time period is called the **quantity supplied** of that commodity. Quantity supplied is a flow; it is so much per unit of time. Note also that quantity supplied is the amount that firms are willing to offer for sale; it is not necessarily the amount they succeed in selling, which is expressed by the term *quantity actually sold* or the term *quantity exchanged*. Although households may desire to purchase an amount that differs from what firms desire to sell, they obviously cannot succeed in buying what someone else does not sell. A purchase and a sale are merely two sides of the same transaction. Viewed from the buyer's side, there is a purchase; viewed from the seller's side, there is a sale.

Because desired purchases do not have to equal desired sales, quantity demanded does not have to equal quantity supplied. However, the quantity actually purchased must equal the quantity actually sold because whatever someone buys, someone else must sell.

What Determines Quantity Supplied?

The amount of a commodity that firms will be willing to produce and offer for sale is influenced by the following important variables:[5]

    Commodity's own price

    Prices of inputs

    Goals of firms

    State of technology

The situation with supply is the same as with demand: There are several influencing variables, and we will not get far if we try to discover what happens when they all change at the same time. So, again, we use the convenient *ceteris paribus* technique to study the influence of the variables one at a time.

Supply and Price

In order to develop a theory of how commodities get priced, we study the relationship between the quantity supplied of each commodity and that commodity's own price. We start by holding all other influences constant and asking: How do we expect the quantity of a commodity supplied to vary with its own price?

A basic hypothesis of economics is that, for many commodities, the price of the commodity and the quantity that will be supplied are related *positively*, other things being equal.[6]

---

[6] In Box 4-2, we contrast laws, predictions, and hypotheses. In this chapter, we introduce this key relation as a hypothesis. In later chapters, we will derive it as a prediction from more basic assumptions about the behavior of firms.

That is to say, **the higher the commodity's own price, the more its producers will supply, and the lower the price, the less its producers will supply.**

Why might this be so? It is true because the profits that can be earned from producing a commodity will almost certainly increase if the price of that commodity rises while the costs of inputs used to produce it remain unchanged. This will make firms, which are in business to earn profits, wish to produce more of the commodity whose price has risen.[7]

The Supply Schedule and the Supply Curve

The general relationship just discussed can be illustrated by a *supply schedule,* which shows the relationship between quantity supplied of a commodity and the price of the commodity, other things being equal. A supply schedule is analogous to a demand schedule; the former shows what producers would be willing to sell, whereas the latter shows what households would be willing to buy, at alternative prices of the commodity. Table 4-3 presents a hypothetical supply schedule for carrots.

---

[7] Notice, however, the qualifying word *many* in the hypothesis printed in green. It is used because, as we shall see in Part 4, there are exceptions to this rule. Although the rule states the usual case, a rise in price (*ceteris paribus*) is not always necessary to produce an increase in quantity supplied.

TABLE 4-3   Supply Schedule for Carrots

	Price per ton	Quantity supplied (thousands of tons per month)
u	$ 20	5.0
v	40	46.0
w	60	77.5
x	80	100.0
y	100	115.0
z	120	122.5

The table shows the quantities that producers wish to sell at various prices, *ceteris paribus.* For example, row *y* indicates that if the price were $100 per ton, producers would wish to sell 115,000 tons of carrots per month.

FIGURE 4-5
A Supply Curve for Carrots

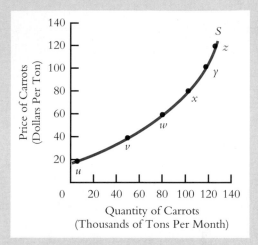

This supply curve relates quantity of carrots supplied to the price of carrots; its upward slope indicates that quantity supplied increases as price increases. The six points correspond to the price-quantity combinations shown in Table 4-3. Each row in the table defines a point on the supply curve. The smooth curve drawn through all of the points and labeled *S* is the supply curve.

A **supply curve,** the graphical representation of the supply schedule, is illustrated in Figure 4-5. Each point on the supply curve represents a specific price-quantity combination; however, the whole curve shows something more.

The supply curve represents the relationship between quantity supplied and price, other things being equal; its positive slope indicates that quantity supplied varies in the same direction as does price.

When economists speak of the conditions of supply as being given or known, they are not referring just to the particular quantity being supplied at the moment, that is, not to just one point on the supply curve. Instead, they are referring to the entire supply curve, to the complete relationship between desired sales and all possible alternative prices of the commodity.

Supply refers to the entire relationship between the quantity supplied of a commodity and the price of that commodity, other things being equal. A single point on the supply curve refers to the *quantity supplied* at that price.

Shifts in the Supply Curve

A shift in the supply curve means that at each price a different quantity will be supplied than previously. An increase in the quantity supplied at each price is shown in Table 4-4 and is graphed in Figure 4-6. This change appears as a rightward shift in the supply curve. In contrast, a decrease in the quantity supplied at each price appears as a leftward shift. A shift in the supply curve must be the result of a change in one of the factors that influence the quantity supplied other than the commodity's own price. The major possible causes of such shifts are summarized in the caption of Figure 4-7 and are considered briefly in the text.

For supply, as for demand, there is an important general rule:

A change in any of the variables (other than the commodity's own price) that affects the amount of a commodity that firms are willing to produce and sell will shift the supply curve for that commodity.

Prices of inputs. All things that a firm uses to produce its outputs, such as materials, labor, and machines, are called the firm's *inputs.* Other things

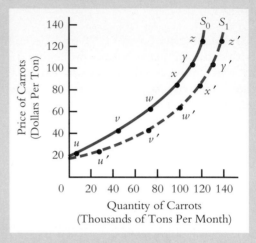

FIGURE 4-6
Two Supply Curves for Carrots

The rightward shift in the supply curve from S_0 to S_1 indicates an increase in the quantity supplied at each price. The lettered points correspond to those in Table 4-4. A rightward shift in the supply curve indicates an increase in supply such that more carrots are supplied at each price.

being equal, the higher the price of any input used to make a commodity, the less will be the profit from making that commodity. We expect, therefore, that the higher the price of any input used by a firm, the lower will be the amount that the firm will produce and offer for sale at any given price of the commodity.

A rise in the price of inputs shifts the supply curve to the left, indicating that less will be supplied at any given price; a fall in the cost of inputs shifts the supply curve to the right.

Goals of the firm. In elementary economic theory, the firm is assumed to have a single goal: profit maximization. However, a firm might have other goals, either in addition to, or as substitutes for, profit maximization; we discuss this possibility in detail in Chapter 16. However, as long as the firm prefers more profits to less, it will respond to changes in the profitabilities of alternative courses of action, and supply curves will have positive slopes.

Technology. At any time, what is produced and how it is produced depends on what is known.

TABLE 4-4   Two Alternative Supply Schedules for Carrots

Price per ton p	Quantity supplied before cost-saving innovation (thousands of tons per month) S_0		Quantity supplied after innovation (thousands of tons per month) S_1	
$ 20	5.0	u	28.0	u'
40	46.0	v	76.0	v'
60	77.5	w	102.0	w'
80	100.0	x	120.0	x'
100	115.0	y	132.0	y'
120	122.5	z	140.0	z'

A cost-saving innovation increases the quantity supplied at each price. As a result of a cost-saving innovation, the quantity that is supplied at $100 per ton rises from 115,000 to 132,000 tons per month. A similar rise occurs at every price. Thus, the supply schedule relating p and S_0 is replaced by one relating p and S_1.

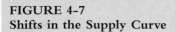

FIGURE 4-7
Shifts in the Supply Curve

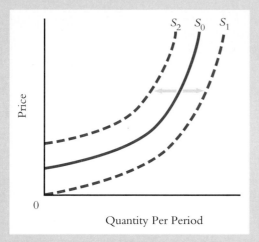

A shift in the supply curve from S_0 to S_1 indicates an increase in supply; a shift from S_0 to S_2 indicates a decrease in supply. An increase in supply means that more is supplied at each price. Such a rightward shift can be caused by certain changes in producers' goals, improvements in technology, or decreases in the costs of inputs that are important in producing the commodity.

A decrease in supply means that less is supplied at each price. Such a leftward shift can be caused by certain changes in producers' goals or increases in the costs of inputs that are important in producing the commodity.

Over time, knowledge changes; so do the quantities of individual commodities supplied. The enormous increase in production per worker that has been going on in industrial societies for about 200 years is largely due to improved methods of production. The Industrial Revolution is more than a historical event; it is a present reality. Discoveries in chemistry have led to lower costs of production for well-established products, such as paints, and to a large variety of new products made of plastics and synthetic fibers. Such inventions as transistors and silicon chips have radically changed products such as computers, audiovisual equipment, and guidance control systems, and the consequent development of smaller computers is revolutionizing the production of countless other nonelectronic products.

Any technological innovation that decreases production costs will increase the profits that can be earned at any given price of the commodity. Since

increased profitability leads to increased production, this change shifts the supply curve to the right, indicating an increased willingness to produce the commodity and offer it for sale at each possible price.

Movements Along the Supply Curve Versus Shifts of the Whole Curve

As with demand, it is important to distinguish movements along supply curves from shifts of the whole curve. Economists reserve the term **change in supply** to describe a shift of the whole supply curve, that is, a change in the quantity that will be supplied at every price. The term **change in quantity supplied** refers to a change from one point on a supply curve to another point, either on the original supply curve or on a new one. That is, an increase in supply means that the whole supply curve has shifted to the right, so that the quantity supplied at any given price has increased; a movement up and to the right along a supply curve indicates an *increase in the quantity supplied* in response to an increase in the price of the commodity.

A change in quantity supplied can result from a change in supply, with the price constant; from a movement along a given supply curve due to a change in the price; or from a combination of the two.

Determination of Price by Demand and Supply

So far demand and supply have been considered separately. Now what we really want to know is this: How do the two forces interact to determine price in a competitive market?[8] Table 4-5 brings together the demand and supply schedules from Tables 4-1 and 4-3. The quantities of carrots demanded and supplied at each price may now be compared.

There is only one price, $60 per ton, at which the quantity of carrots demanded equals the quantity supplied. At prices less than $60 per ton, there is a shortage of carrots, because the quantity demanded exceeds the quantity supplied. This is often called

[8] Roughly, a competitive market is one that has a large number of firms, each with a small share of the market; this concept, and alternative market structures that occur, are defined more precisely in later chapters.

TABLE 4-5   Demand and Supply Schedules for Carrots and Equilibrium Price

(1) Price per ton p	(2) Quantity demanded (thousands of tons per month) D	(3) Quantity supplied (thousands of tons per month) S	(4) Excess demand (+) or excess supply (−) (thousands of tons per month) D − S
$ 20	110.0	5.0	+105.0
40	90.0	46.0	+44.0
60	77.5	77.5	0.0
80	67.5	100.0	−32.5
100	62.5	115.0	−52.5
120	60.0	122.5	−62.5

Equilibrium occurs where quantity demanded equals quantity supplied—when there is neither excess demand nor excess supply. These schedules are those of Tables 4-1 and 4-3. The equilibrium price is $60. For lower prices there is excess demand; for higher prices there is excess supply.

a situation of **excess demand**. At prices greater than $60 per ton, there is a surplus of carrots, because the quantity supplied exceeds the quantity demanded. This is called a situation of **excess supply**.

To discuss the determination of market price, suppose first that the price is $100 per ton. At this price, 115,000 tons are offered for sale, but only 62,500 tons are demanded. There is an excess supply of 52,500 tons per month. We assume that sellers will then cut their prices to get rid of this surplus and that purchasers, observing the stock of unsold carrots, will pay less for what they are prepared to buy.

Excess supply causes downward pressure on price.

Next consider the price of $20 per ton. At this price there is excess demand. The 5,000 tons produced each month are snapped up quickly, and 105,000 tons of desired purchases cannot be made. Rivalry between would-be purchasers may lead them to offer more than the prevailing price in order to outbid other purchasers. Also, perceiving that they could sell their available supplies many times over, sellers may begin to ask a higher price for the quantities that they do have to sell.

Excess demand causes upward pressure on price.

Finally, consider the price of $60. At this price, producers wish to sell 77,500 tons per month, and purchasers wish to buy that quantity. There is neither a shortage nor a surplus of carrots. There are no unsatisfied buyers to bid the price up, nor are there unsatisfied sellers to force the price down. Once the price of $60 has been reached, therefore, there will be no tendency for it to change.

An equilibrium implies a state of rest, or balance, between opposing forces. The **equilibrium price** is the one toward which the actual market price will tend. It will persist, once established, unless it is disturbed by some change in market conditions.

The price at which the quantity demanded equals the quantity supplied is called the equilibrium price.

The equilibrium price is also called the *market-clearing price*. Any other price is called a **disequilibrium price**: a price at which quantity demanded does not equal quantity supplied. When there is either excess demand or excess supply in a market, that market is said to be in a state of **disequilibrium**, and the market price will be changing.

A condition that must be fulfilled if equilibrium is to be obtained in some market is called an **equilibrium condition**. The equality of quantity demanded and quantity supplied is an equilibrium condition.[6]

This same story is told in graphical terms in Figure 4-8. The quantities demanded and supplied at any price can be read off the two curves; the excess supply or excess demand is shown by the horizontal

FIGURE 4-8
Determination of the Equilibrium Price

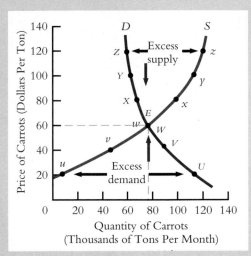

The equilibrium price corresponds to the intersection of the demand and supply curves. Equilibrium is indicated by E, which is point W on the demand curve and point w on the supply curve. At a price of $60, quantity demanded equals quantity supplied. At prices above equilibrium, there is excess supply and downward pressure on price. At prices below equilibrium, there is excess demand and upward pressure on price. The pressures on price are represented by the vertical arrows.

distance between the curves at each price. The figure makes it clear that the equilibrium price occurs where the demand and supply curves intersect. Below that price there is excess demand, and hence upward pressure on the existing price. Above that price there is excess supply, and hence downward pressure on the existing price. These pressures are represented by the vertical arrows in the figure.

The Laws of Demand and Supply

Changes in any of the variables, other than price, that influence quantity demanded or supplied will cause a shift in the supply curve, the demand curve, or both. There are four possible shifts: (1) a rise in demand (a rightward shift in the demand curve), (2) a fall in demand (a leftward shift in the demand curve), (3) a rise in supply (a rightward shift in the supply curve), and (4) a fall in supply (a leftward shift in the supply curve).

Each of these shifts causes changes that are described by one of the four "laws of demand and supply." Each of the laws summarizes what happens when an initial position of equilibrium is upset by some shift in either the demand curve or the supply curve and a new equilibrium position is then established. The sense in which it is correct to call these propositions "laws" is discussed in Box 4-2.

To discover the effects of each of the curve shifts that we wish to study, we use the method known as **comparative statics**, short for *comparative static equilibrium analysis.*[9] In this method we derive predictions by analyzing the effect on the equilibrium position of some change in which we are interested. We start from a position of equilibrium and then introduce the change to be studied. The new equilibrium position is determined and compared with the original one. The difference between the two positions of equilibrium must result from the change that was introduced, because everything else has been held constant.

The four laws of demand and supply are derived in Figure 4-9, which generalizes our specific discussion about carrots. Study the figure carefully. Previously, we had given the axes specific labels, but from here on we will simplify. Because it is intended to apply to any commodity, the horizontal axis is simply labeled *Quantity.* This should be understood to mean quantity per period in whatever units output is measured. *Price,* the vertical axis, should be understood to mean the price measured as dollars per unit of quantity for the same commodity. The four laws of demand and supply are as follows:

1. **A rise in demand causes an increase in both the equilibrium price and the equilibrium quantity exchanged.**
2. **A fall in demand causes a decrease in both the equilibrium price and the equilibrium quantity exchanged.**
3. **A rise in supply causes a decrease in the equilibrium price and an increase in the equilibrium quantity exchanged.**
4. **A fall in supply causes an increase in the equilibrium price and a decrease in the equilibrium quantity exchanged.**

---

[9] The term *statics* is used because we are not concerned with the actual path by which the market goes from the first equilibrium position to the second or with the time taken to reach the second equilibrium. Analysis of these movements would be described as dynamic analysis.

FIGURE 4-9
The Four "Laws" of Demand and Supply

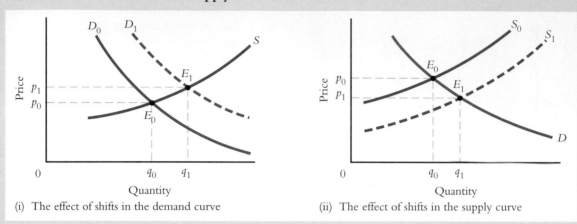

(i) The effect of shifts in the demand curve

(ii) The effect of shifts in the supply curve

The effects on equilibrium price and quantity of shifts in either demand or supply are called the laws of demand and supply. *A rise in demand.* In part (i) assume that the original demand and supply curves are D_0 and S, which intersect to produce equilibrium at E_0, with a price of p_0 and a quantity of q_0. An increase in demand shifts the demand curve to D_1, taking the new equilibrium to E_1. Price rises to p_1 and quantity to q_1.

A fall in demand. In part (i) assume that the original demand and supply curves are D_1 and S, which intersect to produce equilibrium at E_1, with a price of p_1 and a quantity of q_1. A decrease in demand shifts the demand curve to D_0, taking the new equilibrium to E_0. Price falls to p_0, and quantity falls to q_0.

A rise in supply. In part (ii) assume that the original demand and supply curves are D and S_0, which intersect to produce equilibrium at E_0, with a price of p_0 and a quantity of q_0. An increase in supply shifts the supply curve to S_1, taking the new equilibrium to E_1. Price falls to p_1, and quantity rises to q_1.

A fall in supply. In part (ii) assume that the original demand and supply curves are D and S_1, which intersect to produce equilibrium at E_1, with a price of p_1 and a quantity of q_1. A decrease in supply shifts the supply curve to S_0, taking the new equilibrium to E_0. Price rises to p_0, and quantity falls to q_0.

Demonstrations of these "laws" are given in the caption to Figure 4-9. The intuitive reasoning behind each is as follows:

1. A rise in demand creates a shortage, and the unsatisfied buyers bid up the price. This causes a larger quantity to be produced, with the result that at the new equilibrium more is bought and sold at a higher price.
2. A fall in demand creates a glut, and the unsuccessful sellers bid the price downward. As a result, less of the commodity is produced and offered for sale. At the new equilibrium, both price and quantity bought and sold are lower than they were originally.
3. An increase in supply creates a glut, and the unsuccessful suppliers force the price down. This increases the quantity demanded, and the new equilibrium is at a lower price and a higher quantity bought and sold.

4. A reduction in supply creates a shortage that causes the price to be bid up. This reduces the quantity demanded, and the new equilibrium is at a higher price and a lower quantity bought and sold.

In this chapter we have studied many forces that can cause demand or supply curves to shift. These shifts were summarized in Figures 4-3 and 4-7. By combining this analysis with the four laws of demand and supply, we can link many real-world events that cause demand or supply curves to shift with changes in market prices and quantities. For example, a rise in the price of a commodity's substitute will shift the commodity's demand curve to the right, as in Figure 4-3, thus leading to a rise in both the commodity's price and the quantity that is bought and sold, as in part (i) of Figure 4-9.

The theory of the determination of price by demand and supply is beautiful in its simplicity. Yet,

Box 4-2

Laws, Predictions, Hypotheses

In what sense can the four propositions developed for supply and demand be called "laws"? They are not like bills passed by Congress, interpreted by courts, and enforced by the police; they cannot be repealed if people do not like their effects. Nor are they, like the laws of Moses, revealed to humanity by the voice of God. Are they natural laws similar to Newton's law of gravity? In labeling them *laws,* economists clearly had in mind Newton's laws as analogies.

The term *law* is used in science to describe a theory that has stood up to substantial testing. A law of this kind is not something that has been proved to be true for all times and all circumstances, nor is it regarded as immutable. As observations accumulate, laws may be modified or the range of phenomena to which they apply may be restricted or redefined. Einstein's theory of relativity, as one example, forced such amendments and restrictions on Newton's laws.

The laws of supply and demand have stood up well to many empirical tests, but no one believes that they explain all market behavior. They are thus laws in the sense that they predict certain kinds of behavior in certain situations, and the predicted behavior occurs sufficiently often to lead people to have continued confidence in the predictions of the theory. They are not laws—any more than are the laws of natural science—that are beyond being challenged by present or future observations that may cast doubt on some of their predictions. Nor is it a heresy to question their applicability to any particular situation.

Laws, then, are hypotheses that have led to predictions that account for observed behavior. They are theories that, in some circumstances at least, have survived attempts to refute them and that have proved useful. It is possible, in economics as in the natural sciences, to be impressed both with the "laws" we do have and with their limitations: to be impressed, that is, both with the power of what we know and with the magnitude of what we have yet to understand.

as we shall see, it is powerful in its wide range of applications. The usefulness of this theory in interpreting what we see in the world around us is further discussed in Box 4-3.

Prices and Inflation

The theory we have developed explains how individual prices are determined by the forces of demand and supply. To facilitate matters, we have made *ceteris paribus* assumptions. Specifically, we have assumed the constancy of all prices except the one we are studying (and occasionally one other price, when we wish to see how a change in that price affects the market being studied). Does this mean that our theory is inapplicable to an inflationary world in which all prices are rising at the same time? Fortunately, the answer is no.

The price of a commodity is the amount of money that must be spent to acquire one unit of that commodity. This is called the **absolute price**, or *money price*. A **relative price** is the ratio of two absolute prices; it expresses the price of one good in terms of (i.e., *relative to*) another.

We have mentioned several times that what matters for demand and supply is the price of the commodity in question relative to the prices of other commodities; that is, what matters is the *relative price*.

In an inflationary world, we are often interested in the price of a given commodity as it relates to the average price of all other commodities. If, during a period when the general price level rose by 40 percent, the price of oranges rose by 60 percent, then the price of oranges rose relative to the price level as a whole. Oranges became *relatively* expensive. However, if oranges had risen in price by only 30 percent when the general price level rose by 40 percent, then the relative price of oranges would have fallen. Although the money price of oranges rose substantially, oranges became *relatively* cheap.

Box 4-3

Demand and Supply: What Really Happens

"The theory of supply and demand is neat enough," said the skeptic, "but tell me what really happens."

"What really happens," said the economist, "is that demand curves have a negative slope; supply curves have a positive slope; prices rise in response to excess demand; and prices fall in response to excess supply."

"But that's theory," insisted the skeptic. "What about reality?"

"That is reality as well," said the economist.

"Show me," said the skeptic.

The economist produced the following passages from the *New York Times*.

★★★

How deep is the art market's recession? The law of supply and demand is relentless, and in today's unforgiving economic climate, the sales of contemporary, impressionist and modern works of art took hits at this week's auctions. Sales totaled just under $100 million compared with $893 million just one year ago. Many paintings on offer went unsold, and those that did sell went for well under their predicted price.

★★★

Recession causes early peak in gas prices. "Nine times out of ten, prices will go up in June. Historically they go up about a nickel after Memorial Day," said one industry spokesman. "This summer the recession has cut into many Americans' travel plans, and gas sales are down all over the country. In some areas, gas prices have actually fallen."

★★★

Increased demand for macadamia nuts causes price to rise above competing nuts. A major producer now plans to double the size of its orchards during the next five years.

★★★

OPEC countries once again fail to agree on output quotas. Output soars and prices plummet.

★★★

Last summer, Rhode Island officials reopened the northern third of Narragansett Bay, a 9,500-acre fishing ground that had been closed since 1978 because of pollution. Suddenly clam prices dropped, thanks to an underwater population explosion that had transformed the Narragansett area into a clam harvester's dream.

★★★

The effects of [the first year of] deregulation of the nation's airlines were spectacular: cuts in air fares of up to 70 percent in some cases, record passenger jam-ups at the airports, and a spectacular increase in the average load factor [the proportion of occupied seats on the average commercial flight].

The skeptic's response is not recorded, but you should be able to tell which clippings illustrate which of the economist's four statements about "what really happens."

In Lewis Carroll's famous story *Through the Looking-Glass*, Alice finds a country where you have to run in order to stay still. So it is with inflation. A commodity's price must rise as fast as the general level of prices rises just to keep its relative price constant.

It has been convenient in this chapter to analyze changes in particular prices in the context of a constant price level. The analysis is easily extended to an inflationary period by remembering that any force that raises the price of one commodity when other prices remain constant will, given general inflation, raise the price of that commodity faster than the price level is rising. For example, a change in tastes in favor of carrots that would raise their price by 20 percent when other prices were constant would raise their price by 32 percent if, at the same time, the general price level rises by 10 percent.[10] In each case, the price of carrots rises 20 percent *relative to the average of all prices.*

---

[10] Let the price level be 100 in the first case and 110 in the second. Let the price of carrots be 120 in the first case and x in the second. To preserve the same relative price we need x such that $120/100 = x/110$, which makes $x = 132$.

In price theory, whenever we talk of a change in the price of one commodity, we mean a change relative to other prices.

If the price level is constant, this change requires only that the money price of the commodity in question rise. If the price level is itself rising, this change requires that the money price of the commodity in question rise faster than the price level.

SUMMARY

1. The amount of a commodity that households wish to purchase is called the *quantity demanded.* It is a flow expressed as so much per period of time. It is determined by tastes, average household income, the commodity's own price, the prices of related commodities, the size of the population, and the distribution of income among households.

2. Quantity demanded is assumed to increase as the price of the commodity falls, other things given. The relationship between quantity demanded and price is represented graphically by a demand curve that shows how much will be demanded at each market price. A movement along a demand curve indicates a change in the quantity demanded in response to a change in the price of the commodity.

3. A shift in a demand curve represents a change in the quantity demanded at each price and is referred to as a *change in demand.* The demand curve shifts to the right (an increase in demand) if average income rises, if population rises, if the price of a substitute rises, if the price of a complement falls, or if there is a change in tastes in favor of the product. The opposite changes shift the demand curve to the left (a decrease in demand).

4. The amount of a commodity that firms wish to sell is called the *quantity supplied.* It is a flow expressed as so much per period of time. It depends on the commodity's own price, the costs of inputs, the goals of the firm, and the state of technology.

5. Quantity supplied is assumed to increase as the price of the commodity increases, *ceteris paribus.* The relationship between quantity supplied and price is represented graphically by a supply curve that shows how much will be supplied at each market price. A movement along a supply curve indicates a change in the quantity supplied in response to a change in price.

6. A shift in the supply curve indicates a change in the quantity supplied at each price and is referred to as a *change in supply.* The supply curve shifts to the right (an increase in supply) if the costs of producing the commodity fall or if, for any reason, producers become more willing to produce the commodity. The opposite changes shift the supply curve to the left (a decrease in supply).

7. The *equilibrium price* is the one at which the quantity demanded equals the quantity supplied. At any price below equilibrium there

will be excess demand; at any price above equilibrium there will be excess supply. Graphically, equilibrium occurs where the demand and supply curves intersect.

8.   Price rises when there is excess demand and falls when there is excess supply. Thus the actual market price will be pushed toward the equilibrium price, and when it is reached, there will be neither excess demand nor excess supply, and the price will not change until either the supply curve or the demand curve shifts.

9.   Using the method of *comparative statics,* the effects of a shift in either demand or supply can be determined. A rise in demand raises both equilibrium price and equilibrium quantity; a fall in demand lowers both. A rise in supply raises equilibrium quantity but lowers equilibrium price; a fall in supply lowers equilibrium quantity but raises equilibrium price. These are called the laws of demand and supply.

10.   Price theory is most simply developed in the context of a constant price level. Price changes discussed in the theory are changes relative to the average level of all prices. The absolute price of a commodity is its price in terms of money; its relative price is its price in relation to other commodities. In an inflationary period, a rise in the *relative price* of one commodity means that its absolute price rises by more than the price level; a fall in its relative price means that its absolute price rises by less than the price level.

TOPICS FOR REVIEW

Quantity demanded and quantity actually bought

Demand schedule and demand curve

Movement along a curve and shift of a whole curve

Change in quantity demanded and change in demand

Quantity supplied and quantity actually sold

Supply schedule and supply curve

Change in quantity supplied and change in supply

Equilibrium, equilibrium price, and disequilibrium

Comparative statics

Laws of supply and demand

Relative price

DISCUSSION QUESTIONS

1.   What shifts in demand or supply curves would produce the following results? (Assume that only one of the two curves has shifted.)

   a.   The price of pocket calculators has fallen over the past few years, and the quantity exchanged has risen greatly.

   b.   As the U.S. standard of living rose, both the prices and the consumption of vintage wines rose steadily.

   c.   Summer sublets in Ann Arbor, Michigan, are at rents well below the regular rentals.

    d. Changes in styles cause the sale of jeans to decline.

    e. A potato blight causes spud prices to soar.

    f. "Gourmet food market grows as affluent shoppers indulge."

    g. Du Pont increased the price of synthetic fibers, although it acknowledged that demand was weak.

    h. The Edsel was a lemon when it was produced in 1958-1960 but is now a bestseller among cars of its vintage.

    i. Do the same for all the examples given in Box 4-3.

2. The Department of Agriculture recently predicted that this spring's excellent weather would result in larger crops of corn and wheat than farmers had expected. But its chief economist warned consumers not to expect prices to decrease because the cost of production was rising and foreign demand for U.S. crops was increasing. "The classic pattern of supply and demand won't work this time," the economist said. Discuss his observation.

3. Compact disc producers find that they are selling more at the same price than they did two years ago. Is this a shift of the demand curve or a movement along the curve? Suggest at least four reasons why this rise in sales at an unchanged price might occur.

4. What would be the effect on the equilibrium price and quantity of marijuana if its sale were legalized?

5. The relative price of personal computers has dropped drastically over time. Would you explain this falling price in terms of demand or supply changes? What factors are likely to have caused the demand or supply shifts that did occur?

6. Classify the effect of each of the following as (i) a decrease in the demand for fish, (ii) a decrease in the quantity of fish demanded, or (iii) other. Illustrate each diagrammatically.

    a. The government of Iceland bars fishermen of other nations from its waters.

    b. People buy less fish because of a rise in fish prices.

    c. The Roman Catholic Church relaxes its ban on eating meat on Fridays.

    d. The price of beef falls, and as a result households buy more beef and less fish.

    e. Fears of mercury pollution lead locals to shun fish caught in nearby lakes.

    f. It is discovered that eating fish is better for one's health than eating meat.

7. Predict the effect on the price of at least one commodity of each of the following:

    a. Winter snowfall is at a record high in Colorado, but drought continues in New England ski areas.

    b. A recession decreases employment in Detroit automobile factories.

    c. The French grape harvest is the smallest in 20 years.

    d. The state of New York cancels permission for citizens to cut firewood in state parks.

8. Are the following two observations inconsistent? (a) Rising demand for housing causes prices of new homes to soar. (b) Many families refuse to buy homes as prices become prohibitive for them.

APPENDIX TO CHAPTER

4

Foreign Trade

In Chapter 4 we discussed the determination of price in a single domestic market. But what about those goods that are traded internationally? Foreign trade is becoming increasingly important to the U.S. economy. About 11 percent of U.S. national income is currently generated by selling U.S. products in foreign markets—these are U.S. exports. About 12 percent of U.S. national income is spent on purchasing foreign-produced commodities—these are U.S. imports.

The Determination of Imports and Exports

What determines whether a single country, such as the United States, imports or exports some internationally traded commodity? If the United States produces none of the commodity at home—as with nickel, coffee, and bananas—any domestic consumption must be satisfied by imports. At the other extreme, if the United States is the only (or even the major) world producer, demand in the rest of the world must be met by exports from the United States. What of the many intermediate cases in which the United States is only one of many producers of an internationally traded commodity, as with beef, oil, and wheat? Will the United States be an exporter or an importer of such commodities, or will it just produce exactly enough to satisfy its domestic demand for the commodity?

The law of one price. Whether the United States imports or exports a commodity for which it is only one of many producers will depend to a great extent on the commodity's price.

The law of one price states that when an easily transported commodity is traded throughout the entire world, it will tend to have a single

worldwide price, which economists refer to as the "world price."

Many basic commodities, such as copper wire, steel pipe, iron ore, and coal, fall within this category. The single price for each good is the price that equates the quantity demanded worldwide with the quantity supplied worldwide.

The single world price of an internationally traded commodity may be influenced greatly, or only slightly, by the demand and supply coming from any one country. The extent of one country's influence will depend on how important its demands and supplies are in relation to the worldwide totals.

A country facing given world prices. The simplest case for us to study arises when the country, which we will take to be the United States, accounts for only a small part of the total worldwide demand and supply. In this case the United States does not itself produce enough to influence the world price significantly. Furthermore, U.S. purchasers are too small a proportion of worldwide demand to affect the world price materially. Producers and consumers in the United States thus face a world price that they cannot significantly influence by their own actions.

Notice that in this case the price that rules in the United States market must be the world price (adjusted for the exchange rate between the U.S. dollar and the foreign currency). The law of one price says that this must be so. What would happen if the U.S. domestic price diverged from the world price? If the U.S. domestic price were above the worldwide price, no buyers would buy from a U.S. source, because money could be saved by buying abroad. Conversely, if the U.S. price were below the world price, no supplier would sell in the U.S.

FIGURE 4A-1
The Determination of Exports

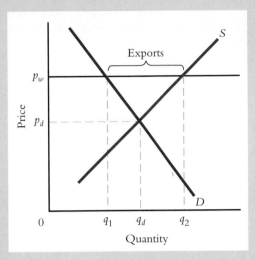

Exports occur whenever there is excess supply domestically at the world price. The domestic demand and supply curves are D and S, respectively. The domestic price in the absence of foreign trade is p_d, with q_d produced *and* consumed domestically. The world price of p_w is higher than p_d. At p_w, q_1 is demanded while q_2 is supplied domestically. The excess of the domestic supply over the domestic demand is exported.

FIGURE 4A-2
The Determination of Imports

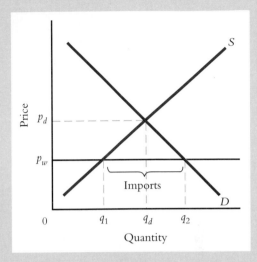

Imports occur whenever there is excess demand domestically at the world price. The domestic demand and supply curves are D and S, respectively. The domestic price in the absence of foreign trade is p_d, with q_d produced *and* consumed domestically. The world price of p_w is less than p_d. At p_w, q_2 is demanded, whereas q_1 is supplied domestically. The excess of domestic demand over domestic supply is satisfied through imports.

market, since more money could be made by selling abroad.

Now let us see what determines the pattern of U.S. foreign trade in such circumstances.

An Exported Commodity

To determine the pattern of U.S. foreign trade, we first show the U.S. domestic demand and supply curves for some commodity, say soybeans. The intersection of these two curves tells us what the price and quantity would be *if there were no foreign trade*. Now compare this "no-trade" price with the world price of that commodity.[1] If the world price is higher, then the actual price in the United States will

---

[1] If the world price is stated in U.S. dollars (as it usually is, for example, with oil), we have no problem with putting it on the diagram showing domestic demand and supply curves. If the world price is stated in terms of some foreign currency, such as Japanese yen, then the price must be converted into dollars using the current exchange rate between the foreign currency and dollars.

exceed the "no-trade" price. There will be an excess of U.S. supply over U.S. demand, and the surplus production will be exported for sale abroad.

Countries export products whose world price exceeds the price that would rule domestically if there were no foreign trade.

This result is demonstrated in Figure 4A-1.

An Imported Commodity

Now consider some other commodity: for example, oil. Once again, look first at the domestic demand and supply curves, shown this time in Figure 4A-2. The intersection of these curves determines the "no-trade" price that would rule *if there were no international trade*. The world price of oil is below the U.S. "no-trade" price, so that, at the price ruling in the United States, domestic demand is larger, and domestic supply is smaller, than if the "no-trade" price had ruled. The excess of domestic demand over domestic supply is met by imports.

Countries import products whose world price is less than the price that would rule domestically if there were no foreign trade.

This result is demonstrated in Figure 4A–2.

We have now developed the basic theory of how imports and exports are determined in competitive markets. Later in the book this theory will be used to study the effects on U.S. imports and exports of changes in the world price and of changes in U.S. domestic demand or supply.

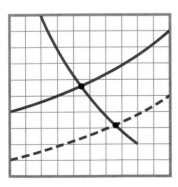

5

Elasticity

The laws of demand and supply predict the *direction* of changes in price and quantity in response to various shifts in demand and supply. However, it usually is not enough to know merely whether price and quantity each rise or fall; it is also important to know *how much* each changes.

When flood damage led to major destruction of the onion crop in the 1980s, onion prices rose sharply. Not surprisingly, overall consumption of onions fell. The press reported that many consumers stopped using onions altogether and substituted onion salt, sauerkraut, cabbage, and other products. Other consumers still bought onions but in reduced quantities. Was the dollar value (price times quantity) higher or lower? The answer is important. A government concerned with the effect of a bad crop on farm income will not be satisfied with being told that food prices will rise and quantities consumed will fall; it will need to know by approximately how much each will change if it is to assess the effects on farmers.

Measuring and describing the extent of the responsiveness of quantities to changes in prices and other variables is often essential if we are to understand the significance of these changes. This is what the concept of *elasticity* does.

Price Elasticity of Demand

Suppose that there is an increase in a farm crop, that is, a rightward shift in the supply curve. We saw in Figure 4-9 on page 74 that the equilibrium price will fall and the equilibrium quantity will rise. By how much will each change? The answer depends on a property called the *elasticity of demand*.

This is illustrated in the two parts of Figure 5-1, each of which reproduces the analysis of Figure 4-9 but using two different demand curves. The two parts of Figure 5-1 have the same initial equilibrium, and that equilibrium is disturbed by the same rightward shift in the supply curve. Because the demand curves are different in the two parts of the figure, the new equilibrium position is different, and hence the magnitude of the effects of the increase in supply on equilibrium price and quantity are different.

A shift in supply will have different quantitative effects, depending on the shape of the demand curve.

The difference may be significant for government policy. Consider what would happen if the rightward shift of the supply curve shown in Figure 5-1 occurs because the government has persuaded farmers to produce more of a certain crop. (It might, for example, have paid a subsidy to farmers for producing that crop.)

FIGURE 5-1
The Effect of the Shape of the Demand Curve

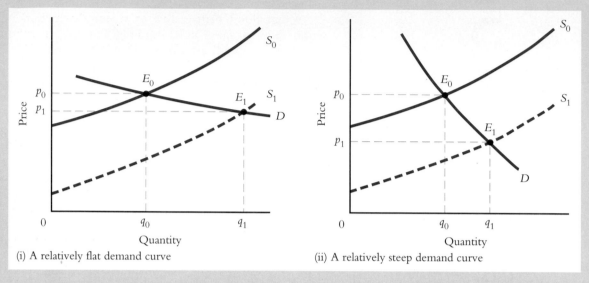

(i) A relatively flat demand curve

(ii) A relatively steep demand curve

The more responsive the quantity demanded is to changes in price, the less the change in price and the greater the change in quantity deriving from any given shift in the supply curve. Both parts of the figure are drawn to the same scale. They show the same initial equilibrium and the same shift in the supply curve. In each part, initial equilibrium is at price p_0 and output q_0 and the new equilibrium is at p_1 and q_1. In part (i) the effect of the shift in supply from S_0 to S_1 is a slight fall in the price and a large increase in quantity. In part (ii) the effect of the identical shift in the supply curve from S_0 to S_1 is a large fall in the price and a relatively small increase in quantity.

Part (i) of Figure 5-1 illustrates a case in which the quantity that consumers demand is relatively responsive to price changes. The rise in production brings down the price, but because the quantity demanded is quite responsive, only a small change in price is necessary to restore equilibrium. The effect of the government's policy, therefore, is to achieve a large increase in the production and sales of this commodity and only a small decrease in price.

Part (ii) of Figure 5-1 shows a case in which the quantity demanded is relatively unresponsive to price changes. As before, the increase in supply at the original price causes a surplus that brings the price down. However, this time the quantity demanded by consumers does not increase much in response to the fall in price. Thus the price continues to drop until, discouraged by lower and lower prices, farmers reduce the quantity supplied nearly to the level that prevailed before they received the subsidy. The effect of the government's policy is to achieve a large decrease in the price of this commodity and

only a small increase in the quantity produced and sold.

In both of the cases shown in Figure 5-1, it can be seen that the government's policy has exactly the same effectiveness as far as the farmers' willingness to supply the commodity is concerned—the supply curve shifts are identical. The magnitude of the effects on the *equilibrium* price and quantity, however, are very different because of the different degrees to which the quantity demanded by consumers responds to price changes.

If the purpose of the government's policy is to increase the quantity of this commodity produced and consumed, it will be a great success when the demand curve is similar to the one shown in part (i) of Figure 5-1, but it will be a failure when the demand curve is similar to the one shown in part (ii) of Figure 5-1. If, however, the purpose of the government's policy is to achieve a large reduction in the price of the commodity, the policy will be a failure when demand is as shown in part (i), but it will be a great success when demand is as shown in part (ii).

The Measurement of Price Elasticity

In Figure 5-1, we were able to say that the curve in part (i) showed a demand that was more responsive to price changes than the curve in part (ii) because two conditions were fulfilled. First, both curves were drawn on the same scale. Second, the initial equilibrium prices and quantities were the same in both parts of the figure. Let us see why these conditions matter.

First, by drawing both figures on the same scale, the curve that looked steeper actually did have the larger absolute slope. (The slope of a demand curve tells us the number of dollars by which price must change to cause a unit change in quantity demanded.) If we had drawn the two curves on different scales, we could have concluded nothing about the relative price changes needed to get a unit change in quantity demanded by comparing their appearances on the graph.[1]

Second, because we started from the same price-quantity equilibrium in both parts of the figure, we did not need to distinguish between percentage changes and absolute changes. If the initial prices and quantities are the same in both cases, the larger absolute change is also the larger percentage change. However, when we wish to deal with different initial price-quantity equilibria, we need to decide whether we are interested in absolute or percentage changes. To see which is relevant, assume that we have the information shown in Table 5-1. Should we conclude that the demand for radios is not as responsive to price changes as the demand for cheese? After all, price cuts of 20 cents cause quite a large increase in the quantity of cheese demanded but only a small increase in radios.

This discussion raises the issue of absolute versus percentage changes. First, a reduction in the price of 20 cents will be a large price cut for a low-priced commodity and an insignificant price cut

[1] It is misleading to infer anything about the responsiveness of quantity to a price change by inspecting the apparent steepness of a graph of a demand curve. By the same token, it can be misleading to infer anything about the relative responsiveness of two different demands by comparing the appearances of their two curves. The reason is that you can make any curve appear as steep or as flat as you wish by changing the scales. For example, a curve that looks steep when the horizontal scale is 1 inch = 100 units will look much flatter when it is drawn on a graph with the same vertical scale but when the horizontal scale is 1 inch = 1 unit.

TABLE 5-1 Price Reductions and Corresponding Increases in Quantity Demanded

Commodity	Reduction in price (cents)	Increase in quantity demanded (per month)
Cheese	20 per pound	7,500 pounds
Men's shirts	20 per shirt	5,000 shirts
Radios	20 per radio	100 radios

The data show, for each of the three commodities, the change in quantity demanded in response to the same absolute fall in price. The data are fairly uninformative about the responsiveness of demand to price because they do not tell us either the original price or the original quantity demanded.

for a high-priced commodity. The price reductions listed in Table 5-1 represent different proportions of the total prices. It is usually more revealing to know the percentage change in the prices of the various commodities. Second, by an analogous argument, knowing the quantity by which demand changes is not very revealing unless the initial level of demand is also known. An increase of 7,500 pounds is quite a significant reaction to demand if the quantity formerly bought was 15,000 pounds, but it is insignificant if the quantity formerly bought was 10 million pounds.

Table 5-2 shows the original and new levels of price and quantity. Changes in price and quantity expressed as percentages of the average prices and quantities are shown in the first two columns of Table 5-3. The **price elasticity of demand,** the measure of responsiveness of quantity of a commodity demanded to a change in market price, is symbolized by the Greek letter eta, η. It is defined as

$$\eta = \frac{\text{percentage change in quantity demanded}}{\text{percentage change in price}}$$

This measure is called the **elasticity of demand,** or simply *demand elasticity*. Because the variable causing the change in quantity demanded is the commodity's own price, the term *own price elasticity of demand* is also used. The use of *average* price and quantity is discussed further in Box 5-1. **[7]**

TABLE 5-2 Price and Quantity Information Underlying Data of Table 5-1

Commodity	Unit	Original price	New price	Average price	Original quantity	New quantity	Average quantity
Cheese	per pound	$ 1.70	$ 1.50	$ 1.60	116,250	123,750	120,000
Men's shirts	per shirt	8.10	7.90	8.00	197,500	202,500	200,000
Radios	per radio	40.10	39.90	40.00	9,950	10,050	10,000

These data provide the appropriate context for the data given in Table 5-1. The table relates the 20-cent-per-unit price reduction of each commodity to the actual prices and quantities demanded.

Interpreting Numerical Elasticities

Because demand curves have negative slopes, an *increase* in price is associated with a *decrease* in quantity demanded, and vice versa. Since the percentage changes in price and quantity have opposite signs, demand elasticity is a negative number. However, we will follow the usual practice of ignoring the negative sign and speak of the measure as a positive number, as we have done in the illustrative calculations in Table 5-3. Thus the more responsive the quantity demanded (for example, radios relative to cheese), the greater the elasticity of demand and the higher the measure (e.g., 2.0 compared to 0.5).

The numerical value of elasticity can vary from zero to infinity. Elasticity is zero when quantity demanded does not respond at all to a price change. As long as the percentage change in quantity is less than the percentage change in price, the elasticity

of demand has a value of less than unity (i.e., less than 1). When the two percentage changes are equal, elasticity is equal to unity. When the percentage change in quantity exceeds the percentage change in price, the value for the elasticity of demand is greater than unity.

When the percentage change in quantity is less than the percentage change in price (elasticity less than 1), there is said to be an **inelastic demand.** When the percentage change in quantity is greater than the percentage change in price (elasticity greater than 1), there is said to be an **elastic demand.** This terminology is important, and you should become familiar with it. It is summarized in part A of Box 5-2 on page 96.

A demand curve need not, and usually does not, have the same elasticity over every part of the curve. Figure 5-2 (page 88) shows that a negatively sloped, straight-line demand curve does not have a constant elasticity. A straight line has constant elasticity only when it is vertical or when it is horizontal. Figure 5-3 (page 89) illustrates these two cases, plus a third case of a particular *nonlinear* demand curve that also has a constant elasticity.

Price Elasticity and Changes in Total Expenditure

In the absence of sales taxes, the total amount spent by purchasers is also the total revenue received by the sellers, so we can use the terms *total (purchaser) expenditure* and *total (seller) revenue* interchangeably.[2] How does total expenditure, which is price *times* quantity, react when the price of a product

---

TABLE 5-3 Calculation of Demand Elasticities

Commodity	(1) Percentage decrease in price	(2) Percentage increase in quantity	(3) Elasticity of demand (2) ÷ (1)
Cheese	12.5	6.25	0.5
Men's shirts	2.5	2.50	1.0
Radios	0.5	1.00	2.0

Elasticity of demand is the percentage change in quantity divided by the percentage change in price. The percentage changes are based on average prices and quantities shown in Table 5-2. For example, the 20-cent-per-pound decrease in the price of cheese is 12.5 percent of $1.60. A 20-cent change in the price of radios is only 0.5 percent of the average price per radio of $40.

---

[2] Allowing for sales taxes complicates the analysis substantially and changes the conclusions in small ways but not in broad outline.

Box 5-1

Calculating Price Elasticities Using Averages

The formula in the text stresses that the changes in price and quantity are measured in terms of the *average* values of each. Averages are used in order to avoid the ambiguity caused by the fact that when a price or quantity changes, the change is a different percentage of the original value than it is of the new value. For example, the 20-cent change in the price of cheese shown in Table 5-2 is a different percentage of the original price, $1.70, than it is of the new price, $1.50 (11.8 percent versus 13.3 percent).

Using average values for price and quantity also means that the measured elasticity of demand between any two points *A* and *B* is independent of whether the movement is from *A* to *B* or from *B* to *A*. In the example of cheese in Tables 5-2 and 5-3, the 20-cent change in the price of cheese is unambiguously 12.5 percent of the average price of $1.60, and that percentage applies to a price increase from $1.50 to $1.70, as well as to the decrease discussed in the text.

The implications of using average values for price and quantity for calculating elasticity can be seen as follows. Consider a change from an initial equilibrium with a price of p_0 and an initial quantity

of q_0 to a new equilibrium following a shift in supply with a price of p_1 and a quantity of q_1. The formula for elasticity is then

$$\eta = \frac{(q_1 - q_0)/q}{(p_1 - p_0)/p} \qquad [1]$$

where p and q are the average quantity and average price, respectively. Thus $p = (p_1 + p_0)/2$, and $q = (q_1 + q_0)/2$. These expressions can be substituted for p and q in Equation 1, and canceling the 2s, we get

$$\eta = \frac{(q_1 - q_0)/(q_1 + q_0)}{(p_1 - p_0)/(p_1 + p_0)} \qquad [2]$$

which provides a very convenient formula for calculating elasticity. For example, for the case of cheese in the tables, we have

$$\eta = \frac{7,500/240,000}{0.20/3.20} = \frac{0.03125}{0.0625} = 0.5$$

which is as in Table 5-3. Further discussion of the use of averages to calculate elasticity, and of alternative methods, is found in the appendix to this chapter.

---

is changed? It turns out that the response of total expenditure depends on the price elasticity of demand.

Because price and quantity move in opposite directions—one falling when the other rises—the change in total expenditure appears to be ambiguous. It is easily shown, however, that the direction of change in total expenditure depends on the percentage change in the two variables, price and quantity. If the percentage change in price exceeds the percentage change in quantity, then the price change will dominate and total expenditure will change in the same direction as the *price* changes; this, of course, is the case of elasticity less than unity. If the percentage

change in the price is less than the percentage change in the quantity demanded (elasticity exceeds unity), then the quantity change will dominate and total expenditure will change in the same direction as *quantity* changes (that is, in the opposite direction to the change in price). If the two percentage changes are equal, then total expenditure is unchanged—this is the case of unit elasticity.

The general relationship between elasticity and change in price can be summarized as follows:

1. If demand is elastic, price and total expenditure are negatively related. A fall in price increases total expenditure, and a rise in price reduces it.

FIGURE 5-2
Elasticity Along a Straight-Line Demand Curve

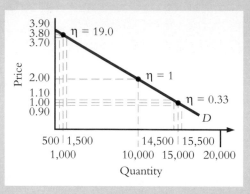

Moving down a straight–line demand curve, elasticity falls continuously. On this straight-line demand curve, a reduction in price of $0.20 always leads to the same increase (1,000 units) in quantity demanded.[a]

Near the upper end of the curve, where price is $3.80 and quantity demanded is 1,000 units, a reduction in price of $0.20 (from $3.90 to $3.70) is just slightly more than a 5 percent reduction, but the 1,000–unit increase in quantity is a 100 percent increase. Here, elasticity (η) is 19.

Near the lower end, at a price of $1.00 and a quantity of 15,000 units, a price reduction of $0.20 (from $1.10 to $0.90) leads to the same 1,000-unit increase in demand. However, the $0.20 price reduction represents a 20 percent fall, whereas the 1,000-unit increase in quantity demanded represents only a 6.67 percent increase. Here, elasticity is 0.33.

[a]The equation for the demand curve is
$$q^d = 20,000 - 5,000p$$

2. If demand is inelastic, price and total expenditure are positively related. A fall in price reduces total expenditure, and a rise in price increases it.
3. If elasticity of demand is unity, total expenditure is constant and therefore unrelated to price. A rise or a fall in price leaves total expenditure unaffected.

Table 5-4 and Figure 5-4 illustrate the relationship between elasticity of demand and total expenditure; both are based on the straight-line demand curve in Figure 5-2. Total expenditure (equal to the area under the demand curve) at each of a number of points on the demand curve are calculated in Table 5-4, and the general relationship between total expenditure and quantity demanded is shown

in Figure 5-4; there we see that expenditure reaches its maximum when elasticity is equal to one. [8]

For example, when a bumper potato crop recently sent prices down 50 percent, quantity sold increased only 15 percent. Demand was clearly inelastic, and the result of the bumper crop was that potato farmers experienced a sharp *fall* in revenues.

Another example can be constructed from Table 5-2. Calculations for what happens to total revenue when the prices of radios, men's shirts, and cheese fall are shown in Table 5-5. In the case of cheese, the demand is inelastic, and a cut in price lowers the sellers' revenue; in the case of radios, the demand is elastic, and a cut in price raises revenue. The borderline case is men's shirts; here, the elasticity is unity, and the cut in price leaves revenue unchanged.

What Determines Elasticity of Demand?

Table 5-6 shows some estimated price elasticities of demand. Evidently, elasticity can vary considerably. The main determinant of elasticity is the availability of substitutes. Some commodities, such as margarine, cabbage, lamb, and Fords, have quite close substitutes—butter, other green vegetables, beef, and Chevrolets. A change in the prices of these commodities, *with the prices of the substitutes remaining constant,* can be expected to cause much substitution. A fall in price leads consumers to buy more of the commodity and less of the substitutes, and a rise in price leads consumers to buy less of the commodity and more of the substitutes. More broadly defined commodities, such as all foods, all clothing, alcohol, and gasoline, have few, if any, satisfactory substitutes. A rise in their prices can be expected to cause a smaller fall in quantities demanded than would be the case if close substitutes were available.

A commodity with close substitutes tends to have an elastic demand; a commodity with no close substitutes tends to have an inelastic demand.

Closeness of substitutes—and thus measured elasticity—depends on both how the commodity is defined and the time period. This is explored next.

Definition of the Commodity

For food taken as a whole, demand is inelastic over a large price range. It does not follow, however,

FIGURE 5-3
Three Demand Curves

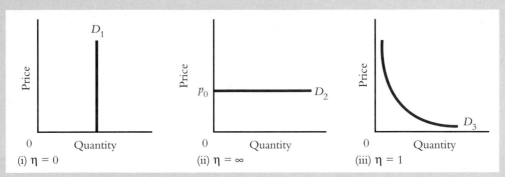

(i) $\eta = 0$　　　(ii) $\eta = \infty$　　　(iii) $\eta = 1$

Each of these demand curves has a constant elasticity. D_1 has *zero elasticity:* The quantity demanded does not change at all when price changes. D_2 has *infinite elasticity at the price p_0:* A small price increase from p_0 decreases quantity demanded from an indefinitely large amount to zero. D_3 has *unit elasticity:* A given percentage increase in price brings an equal percentage decrease in quantity demanded at all points on the curve; it is a rectangular hyperbola for which price *times* quantity is a constant.

that any one food, such as white bread or beef, is a necessity in the same sense. Individual foods can have quite elastic demands, and they frequently do.

Clothing provides a similar example. Clothing as a whole is less elastic than individual kinds of clothes.

TABLE 5-4　Changes in Total Expenditure for the Demand Curve of Figure 5-2

Price	Quantity	Expenditure
3.80	1,000	3,800
3.00	5,000	15,000
2.50	7,500	18,750
2.00	10,000	20,000
1.50	12,500	18,750
1.00	15,000	15,000

As price falls along a linear demand curve, total expenditure first rises and then falls.[a] Along the range where price is greater than 2.00, elasticity is greater than one. As a result, the percentage fall in price is smaller than the resulting percentage increase in quantity, and total expenditure rises.

Along the range where price is less than 2.00, elasticity is less than one. As a result, the percentage fall in price is greater than the resulting percentage increase in quantity, and total expenditure falls.

[a] Recall from Figure 5–2 that the equation of the demand curve is

$$q^d = 20,000 - 5,000p$$

FIGURE 5-4
Elasticity of Demand and Total Expenditure

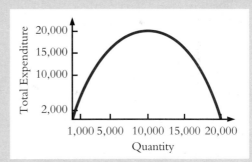

The change in total expenditure on a commodity in response to a change in price depends upon the elasticity of demand. The total expenditure for each possible quantity demanded is plotted for the demand curve in Figure 5-2. For quantities demanded that are less than 10,000, elasticity of demand is greater than one, and hence any increase in quantity demanded will be proportionately larger than the fall in price that caused it. In that range total expenditure is increasing. For quantities greater than 10,000 elasticity of demand is less than one, and hence any increase in quantity demanded will be proportionately smaller than the fall in price that caused it. In that range total expenditures is decreasing. The maximum of total expenditure occurs where the elasticity of demand equals one.

TABLE 5-5   Changes in Total Expenditure (Total Revenue) for the Example of Table 5-2

Commodity	Price × quantity (original prices and quantities)	Price × quantity (new prices and quantities)	Change in revenue (expenditure)	Elasticity of demand from Table 5-3
Cheese	$ 197,625	$ 185,625	−$12,000	0.5
Men's shirts	1,599,750	1,599,750	0	1.0
Radios	398,995	400,995	+ 2,000	2.0

Whether expenditure increases or decreases in response to a price cut depends on whether demand is elastic or inelastic. The $197,625 figure is the product of the original price of cheese ($1.70) and the original quantity (116,250 pounds); $185,625 is the product of the new price ($1.50) and quantity (123,750), and so on.

For example, when the price of wool sweaters rises, many households may buy cotton sweaters or down vests instead of buying an additional wool sweater. Thus, although purchases of wool sweaters fall, total purchases of clothing does not.

Any one of a group of related products will have a more elastic demand than the group taken as a whole.

Long-Run and Short-Run Elasticity of Demand

Because it takes time to develop satisfactory substitutes, a demand that is inelastic in the short run may prove elastic when enough time has passed. For example, at the time when cheap electric power was first brought to rural areas (long after it had come to cities), few farm households were wired for electricity. The initial measurements showed rural demand for electricity to be very inelastic. Some commentators even argued that it was foolish to invest so much money in bringing cheap electricity to farmers because they would not buy it, even at low prices. Gradually, though, farm households became electrified and, as they responded by purchasing electric appliances, measured elasticity steadily increased.

Petroleum provides a more recent example. In the early 1970s, the Organization of Petroleum Exporting Countries (OPEC) cartel shocked the world with its first sudden and large increase in the price of oil. At that time, the short-run demand for oil proved to be highly inelastic. Large price increases were met in the short run by very small reductions in quantity demanded. In this case, the short run lasted for several years. Gradually, however, the high price of petroleum products led to such adjustments as the development of smaller, more fuel-efficient cars, economizing on heating oil by installing more

efficient insulation, and replacement of fuel oil in many industrial processes with such other power sources as coal and hydroelectricity. The long-run elasticity of demand, relating the change in price to the change in quantity demanded after all adjustments were made, turned out to have an elasticity of well over 1, although the long-run adjustments took as much as a decade to work out.

TABLE 5-6   Estimated Price Elasticities of Demand[a] (selected commodities)

Demand significantly inelastic (less than 0.9)	
Potatoes	0.3
Sugar	0.3
Public transportation	0.4
All foods	0.4
Cigarettes	0.5
Gasoline	0.6
All clothing	0.6
Consumer durables	0.8
Demand of close to unit elasticity (between 0.9 and 1.1)	
Beef	
Beer	
Marijuana	
Demand significantly elastic (more than 1.1)	
Furniture	1.2
Electricity	1.3
Lamb and mutton (U.K.)	1.5
Automobiles	2.1
Millinery	3.0

[a]For the United States except where noted.

The wide range of price elasticities is illustrated by these selected measures. These elasticities, from various studies, are representative of literally hundreds of existing estimates. Explanations of some of the differences are discussed in the text.

The degree of response to a price change, and thus the measured price elasticity of demand, will tend to be greater the longer the time span considered.

Because the elasticity of demand for a commodity changes over time as consumers adjust their habits and substitutes are developed, the demand curve also changes; hence a distinction can be made between short-run and long-run demand curves. Every demand curve shows the response of consumer demand to a change in price. For such commodities as cornflakes and pillowcases, the full response occurs quickly, and there is little reason to worry about longer-term effects, but other commodities are typically used in connection with highly durable appliances or machines. A change in price of, say, electricity and gasoline may not have its major effect until the stock of appliances and machines using these commodities has been adjusted. This adjustment may take a long time to occur.

For commodities for which substitutes are developed over a period of time, it is helpful to identify two kinds of demand curves. A *short-run demand curve* shows the response of quantity demanded to a change in price for a given structure of the durable goods that use the commodity and for the existing sets of substitute commodities. A different short-run demand curve will exist for each such structure.

The *long-run demand curve* shows the response of quantity demanded to a change in price after enough time has passed to ensure that all adjustments to the changed price have occurred. The relationship between long-run and short-run demand curves is shown in Figure 5-5. The principal conclusion, already suggested in our discussion of elasticity, is this:

The long-run demand curve for a commodity will tend to have a substantially higher elasticity than the short-run demand curves for that commodity.

Other Demand Elasticities

Income Elasticity of Demand

One of the most important determinants of demand is the income of the potential customers. When the

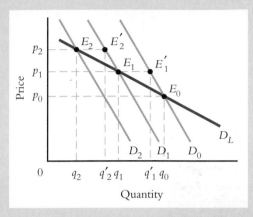

FIGURE 5-5
Short-Run and Long-Run Demand Curves

The long-run demand curve is more elastic than the short-run demand curve. D_L is a long-run demand curve. Suppose that consumers are fully adjusted to price p_0. Equilibrium is then at E_0, with quantity demanded q_0. Now suppose that price rises to p_1. In the short run, consumers will react along the short-run demand curve D_0 and adjust consumption to q_1'. Once time has permitted the full range of adjustments to price p_1, however, a new equilibrium E_1 will be reached with quantity q_1. At E_1 there is a new short-run demand curve D_1. A further rise to price p_2 would lead first to a short-run equilibrium at E_2' but eventually to a new long-run equilibrium at E_2. The long-run demand curve, D_L, is more elastic than any of the short-run curves.

Food and Agricultural Organization (FAO) of the United Nations wants to estimate the future demand for some crop, it needs to know by how much world income will grow and how much of that additional income will be spent on that particular foodstuff. As nations get richer, their consumption patterns typically change, with relatively more spent, for example, on meat and relatively less spent on staples such as rice and potatoes.

The responsiveness of demand to changes in income is termed **income elasticity of demand** and is symbolized η_Y.

$$\eta_Y = \frac{\text{percentage change in quantity demanded}}{\text{percentage change in income}}$$

For most goods, increases in income lead to increases in demand—their income elasticity is positive. These are called **normal goods.** Goods for which consumption decreases in response to a rise in income have negative income elasticities and are called **inferior goods.**

The income elasticity of normal goods may be greater than unity (elastic) or less than unity (inelastic), depending on whether the percentage change in the quantity demanded is greater or less than the percentage change in income that brought it about. It is also common to use the terms *income-elastic* and *income-inelastic* to refer to income elasticities of greater or less than unity. (See Box 5-2 for further discussion of elasticity terminology.)

The reaction of demand to changes in income is extremely important. We know that in most Western countries economic growth in the first 70 years of this century caused the level of income to double every 20 to 30 years over a sustained period of at least a century. This rise in income has been shared to some extent by most citizens. As they found their incomes increasing, they increased their demands for most commodities, but the demands for some commodities, such as food and basic clothing, did not increase much, whereas the demands for other commodities increased rapidly. In developing countries, such as Ireland and Mexico, the demand for durable goods is increasing most rapidly as household incomes rise, while in North America and Western Europe the demand for services has risen most rapidly. The uneven impact of the growth of income on the demands for different commodities has important economic effects, which are studied at several points in this book, beginning with the discussion of agriculture in Chapter 6.

What Determines Income Elasticity?

The variations in income elasticities shown in Table 5-7 suggest that the more basic or staple a commodity, the lower its income elasticity. Food as a whole has an income elasticity of 0.2, consumer durables of 1.8. In the United States, such starchy roots as potatoes are inferior goods; their quantity consumed falls as income rises.

Does the distinction between luxuries and necessities help to explain differences in income elasticities? The table suggests that it does. The case of meals eaten away from home is one example. Such meals are almost always more expensive, calorie for calorie, than meals prepared at home. It would thus be expected that at lower ranges of income, restaurant meals would be regarded as an expensive luxury, but

that the demand for them would expand substantially as households became richer. This is in fact what happens.

Does this mean that the market demand for the foodstuffs that appear on restaurant menus will also have high income elasticities? Generally, the answer is no. When a household eats out rather than preparing meals at home, the main change is not in what is eaten but in who prepares it. The additional expenditure on "food" goes mainly to pay cooks and waiters and to yield a return on the restaurateur's capital. Thus when a household expands its expenditure on restaurant food by 2.4 percent in response to a 1 percent rise in its income, most of the extra expenditure on "food" goes to workers in service industries; little, if any, finds its way into the pockets of farmers. This is a striking example of the general tendency for households to spend a rising proportion of their incomes on services and a lower proportion on foodstuffs as their incomes rise.

The more basic an item is in the consumption pattern of households, the lower is its income elasticity.

So far we have focused on differences in income elasticities among commodities. However, income elasticities for any one commodity also vary with the level of a household's income. When incomes are low, households may eat almost no green vegetables and consume lots of starchy foods such as bread and potatoes; when incomes are higher, they may eat cheap cuts of meat and more green vegetables along with their bread and potatoes; when incomes are even higher, they are likely to substitute frozen vegetables for canned, and to eat a greater variety of foods.

What is true of individual households is also true of countries. Empirical studies show that for different countries at comparable stages of economic development, income elasticities are similar. However, the countries of the world are at various stages of economic development and so have widely different income elasticities for the same products. Notice in Table 5-7 the different income elasticity of poultry in the United States, where it is a standard item of consumption, and in Sri Lanka, where it is a luxury.

Graphical Representation

Increases in income shift the demand curve to the right for a normal good and to the left for an inferior

TABLE 5-7 Estimated Income Elasticities of Demand[a] (*selected commodities*)

Inferior goods (negative income elasticities)

Whole milk	−0.5
Pig products	−0.2
Starchy roots	−0.2

Inelastic normal goods (0.0 to 1.0)

Wine (France)	0.1
All food	0.2
Poultry	0.3
Cheese	0.4

Elastic normal goods (greater than 1.0)

Gasoline	1.1
Wine	1.4
Cream (U.K.)	1.7
Consumer durables	1.8
Poultry (Sri Lanka)	2.0
Restaurant meals (U.K.)	2.4

[a]For the United States except where noted.

Income elasticities vary widely across commodities and sometimes across countries. The basic source of food estimates by country is the FAO, but many individual studies have been made. Explanations of some of the differences are discussed in the text.

good. Figure 5-6 shows a different kind of graph, an *income-consumption curve*. The curve resembles an ordinary demand curve in one respect: It shows the relationship of quantity demanded to one other variable, *ceteris paribus*. The other variable is not price, however, but household income. (An increase in the price of the commodity, incomes remaining constant, would shift the curves shown in Figure 5-6 downward.)[3]

The figure shows three different patterns of income elasticity. Goods that consumers regard as necessities will have high income elasticities at low levels of income but will show low income elasticities beyond some level. The obvious reason is that as

---

[3] In Figure 5-6, in contrast to the ordinary demand curve, quantity demanded is on the vertical axis. This follows the usual practice of putting the variable to be explained (called the *dependent variable*) on the vertical axis and the explanatory variable (called the *independent variable*) on the horizontal axis. It is the ordinary demand curve that has the axes "backward." The explanation is buried in the history of economics and dates to Alfred Marshall's *Principles of Economics* (1890), the classic that is one of the foundation stones of modern price theory. [9] For better or worse, Marshall's scheme is now used by everybody, although mathematicians never fail to wonder at this further example of the odd ways of economists.

FIGURE 5-6
Income-Consumption Curves of Different Commodities

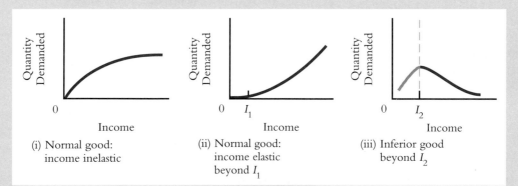

(i) Normal good: income inelastic

(ii) Normal good: income elastic beyond I_1

(iii) Inferior good beyond I_2

Different shapes of the curve relating quantity demanded to income correspond to different ranges of income elasticity. Normal goods have rising curves; inferior goods have falling curves. Many different patterns of income elasticity have been observed. The good in part (i) is a typical normal good that is a necessity. It is purchased at all levels of income; even at high levels of income, some fraction of extra income is spent on it, although this fraction steadily decreases. The good in part (ii) is a luxury good that is income-elastic beyond income I_1. The good in part (iii) is a necessity at low incomes but becomes an inferior good for incomes beyond I_2.

incomes rise, it becomes possible for households to devote a smaller proportion of their incomes to meeting basic needs and a larger proportion to buying things they have always wanted but could not afford. Some of the necessities may even become inferior goods. So-called luxury goods will not tend to be purchased at low levels of income but will have high income elasticities once incomes rise enough to permit households to sample the better things of life available to them.

Cross Elasticity of Demand

The responsiveness of demand to changes in the price of another commodity is called the **cross elasticity of demand.** It is often denoted η_{xy} and defined as follows:[4]

$$\eta_{xy} = \frac{\text{percentage change in quantity demanded of one good } (X)}{\text{percentage change in price of another good } (Y)}$$

Cross elasticity can vary from minus infinity to plus infinity. Complementary commodities, such as cars and gasoline, have negative cross elasticities. A large rise in the price of gasoline will lead (as it did in the United States in the 1970s) to a decline in the demand for cars, as some people decide to do without a car and others decide not to buy a second (or third) car. Substitute commodities, such as cars and public transport, have positive cross elasticities. A large rise in the price of cars (relative to public transport) would lead to a rise in the demand for public transport as some people shifted from cars to public transport. (See Box 5-2 for a summary of elasticity terminology.)

Measures of cross elasticity sometimes prove helpful in defining whether producers of similar products are in competition. For example, glass bottles and tin cans have a high cross elasticity of demand. The producer of bottles is thus in competition with the producer of cans. If the bottle company raises its price, it will lose substantial sales to the can

producer. Men's shoes and women's shoes have a low cross elasticity. A producer of men's shoes is not in close competition with a producer of women's shoes. If the former raises its price, it will not lose many sales to the latter. Knowledge of cross elasticities can be important in antitrust investigations in which the issue is whether a firm in one industry is or is not competing with firms in another industry. Whether waxed paper and plastic wrap or aluminum cable and copper cable are or are not substitutes may determine questions of monopoly under the law. The positive or negative sign of cross elasticities tell us whether or not goods are substitutes.

Elasticity of Supply

The concept of elasticity can be applied to supply as well as to demand. **Elasticity of supply** measures the responsiveness of the quantity supplied to a change in the commodity's price. It is denoted η_S and defined as

$$\eta_S = \frac{\text{percentage change in quantity supplied}}{\text{percentage change in price}}$$

This is often called *supply elasticity*. The supply curves considered in this chapter all have positive slopes: An increase in price causes an increase in quantity sold. Such supply curves all have positive elasticities because price and quantity both change in the same direction.

There are important special cases. If the supply curve is vertical—the quantity supplied does not change as price changes—then elasticity of supply is zero. This would be the case, for example, if suppliers produced a given quantity and dumped it on the market for whatever it would bring. A horizontal supply curve has an infinitely high elasticity of supply: A small drop in price would reduce the quantity producers are willing to supply from an indefinitely large amount to zero. Between these two extremes, elasticity of supply varies with the shape of the supply curve.[5]

---

[4] The change in price of good Y causes the *demand curve* for good X to shift. Holding the price of good X constant means that we can measure the shift in the demand curve in terms of the change in quantity demanded of good X at the given price of good X.

[5] Steepness, which is related to absolute rather than percentage changes, is not always a reliable guide. For example, as is shown in the appendix to this chapter, *any* upward-sloping straight line passing through the origin has an elasticity of +1.0 over its entire range.

Determinants of Supply Elasticity

Supply elasticities are important for many problems in economics. Much of the treatment of demand elasticity carries over to supply elasticity. For example, the ease of substitution can vary in production as well as in consumption. If the price of a commodity rises, how much more can be produced profitably? This depends in part on how easy it is for producers to shift from the production of other commodities to the one whose price has risen. If agricultural land and labor can be readily shifted from one crop to another, the supply of any one crop will be more elastic than if they cannot.

Supply elasticity depends to a great extent on how costs behave as output is varied, an issue that will be treated at length in Part 3. If the costs of producing a unit of output rise rapidly as output rises, then the stimulus to expand production in response to a rise in price will quickly be choked off by increases in costs. In this case, supply will tend to be rather inelastic. If, however, the costs of producing a unit of output rise only slowly as production increases, a rise in price that raises profits will elicit a large increase in quantity supplied before the rise in costs puts a halt to the expansion in output. In this case, supply will tend to be rather elastic.

Long-Run and Short-Run Elasticity of Supply

As with demand, length of time for response is important. It may be difficult to change quantities supplied in response to a price increase in a matter of weeks or months but easy to do so over a period of years. An obvious example is the planting cycle of crops. Also, new oil fields can be discovered, wells drilled, and pipelines built over a period of years, but not in a few months. Thus elasticity of oil supply is much greater over five years than over one year. We explore some of the implications of the distinction between short-run and long-run elasticity in the next chapter.

SUMMARY

1. *Price elasticity of demand,* also called simply *elasticity of demand,* is a measure of the extent to which the quantity demanded of a commodity responds to a change in its price. It is defined as the percentage change in quantity demanded divided by the percentage change in price that brought it about; the percentage changes are usually calculated as the change divided by the *average value.* Elasticity is defined to be a positive number, and it can vary from zero to infinity.

2. When the numerical measure of elasticity is less than unity, demand is *inelastic.* This means that the percentage change in quantity demanded is less than the percentage change in price that brought it about. When the numerical measure exceeds unity, demand is *elastic.* This means that the percentage change in quantity demanded is greater than the percentage change in price that brought it about.

3. Elasticity and total revenue of sellers are related in the following way: If elasticity is less than unity, total revenue is positively associated with price; if elasticity is greater than unity, total revenue is negatively associated with price; and if elasticity is unity, total revenue does not change as price changes.

4. The main determinant of the price elasticity of demand is the availability of substitutes for the commodity. Any one of a group of close substitutes will have a more elastic demand than the group as a whole.

5. Elasticity of demand tends to be greater the longer the time over which adjustment occurs. Items that have few substitutes in the short run may develop many substitutes when consumers and producers have time to adapt.

Box 5-2

Terminology of Elasticity

Term	Symbol	Numerical measure of elasticity	Verbal description
A. Price elasticity of demand (supply)	η (η_s)		
Perfectly or completely inelastic		Zero	Quantity demanded (supplied) does not change as price changes.
Inelastic		Greater than zero, less than one	Quantity demanded (supplied) changes by a smaller percentage than does price.
Unit elasticity		One	Quantity demanded (supplied) changes by exactly the same percentage as does price.
Perfectly, completely, or infinitely elastic		Infinity	Purchasers (sellers) are prepared to buy (sell) all they can at some price and none at all at an even higher (lower) price.
B. Income elasticity of demand	η_Y		
Inferior good		Negative	Quantity demanded decreases as income increases.
Normal good		Positive	Quantity demanded increases as income increases:
Income-inelastic		Less than one	Less than in proportion to income increase
Income-elastic		Greater than one	More than in proportion to income increase
C. Cross elasticity of demand	η_{xy}		
Substitute		Positive	Price increase of a substitute leads to an increase in quantity demanded of this good (and less of the substitute).
Complement		Negative	Price increase of a complement leads to a decrease in quantity demanded of this good (as well as less of the complement).

6. *Income elasticity of demand* is the percentage change in quantity demanded divided by the percentage change in income that brought it about. The income elasticity of demand for a commodity will usually change as income varies. For example, a commodity that has a high income elasticity at a low income (because increases in income bring it within reach of the typical household) may have a low or negative income elasticity at higher incomes (because with further rises in incomes it is gradually replaced by a superior substitute).

7. *Cross elasticity of demand* is the percentage change in quantity demanded divided by the percentage change in the price of some other commodity that brought it about. It is used to define commodities that are substitutes for one another (positive cross elasticity) and commodities that complement one another (negative cross elasticity).

8. *Elasticity of supply* is an important concept in economics. It measures the ratio of the percentage change in the quantity supplied of a commodity to the percentage change in its price. It is the analogue on the supply side to the elasticity of demand. Supply tends to be more elastic in the long run than in the short run.

TOPICS FOR REVIEW

Elasticity of demand

Inelastic and perfectly inelastic demand

Elastic and infinitely elastic demand

Relationship between demand elasticity and total expenditure

Short-run and long-run demand curves

Income elasticity of demand

Income-elastic and income-inelastic demands

Normal goods and inferior goods

Cross elasticity of demand

Substitutes and complements

Elasticity of supply

DISCUSSION QUESTIONS

1. From the following quotations, what, if anything, can you conclude about elasticity of demand?
   a. "Good weather resulted in record corn harvests and sent corn prices tumbling. For many corn farmers the result has been calamitous."
   b. "Ridership always went up when bus fares came down, but the increased patronage never was enough to prevent a decrease in overall revenue."
   c. "As the price of compact disc players fell, producers found their revenues soaring."

d. "Coffee to me is an essential—you've gotta have it no matter what the price."

e. "The soaring price of condominiums does little to curb the strong demand in Palo Alto."

2. Advocates of minimal charges for people using doctors' services in Canada (where basic medical services are now free) hope that this will greatly reduce the cost to the government while not denying essential medical services to anyone. Opponents argue that even minimal charges will deny critical services to lower-income Canadians. Use elasticity terminology to restate the views of each of these groups.

3. What would you predict about the relative price elasticity of demand of (a) food, (b) vegetables, (c) artichokes, and (d) artichokes sold at the local supermarket? What would you predict about their relative income elasticities?

4. "Avocados have a limited market, not greatly affected by price until the price falls to less than 25 cents a pound. Then they are much demanded by manufacturers of dog food." Interpret this statement in terms of price elasticity.

5. "Home computers were a leader in sales appeal through much of the 1980s. But per capita sales are much lower in Puerto Rico than in the United States and lower in Mississippi than in Illinois. Manufacturers are puzzled by the big differences." Can you offer an explanation in terms of elasticity?

6. What elasticity measure or measures would be useful in answering the following questions?
   a. Will cheaper transport into the central city help keep downtown shopping centers profitable?
   b. Will raising the bulk postage rate increase or decrease the postal deficit?
   c. Are producers of toothpaste and mouthwash in competition with each other?
   d. What effect will rising gasoline prices have on the sale of cars that use propane gas?

7. Interpret the following statements in terms of the relevant elasticity concept.
   a. "As fuel for tractors has become more expensive, many farmers have shifted from plowing their fields to no-till farming. No-till acreage increased from 30 million acres in 1972 to 95 million acres in 1982."
   b. "Fertilizer makers brace for dismal year as fertilizer prices soar."
   c. "When farmers are hurting, small towns feel the pain."

8. Suggest commodities that you think might have the following patterns of elasticity of demand.
   a. High income elasticity, high price elasticity
   b. High income elasticity, low price elasticity
   c. Low income elasticity, low price elasticity
   d. Low income elasticity, high price elasticity

9. In 1983, the new United States Football League was playing to half-empty stadiums. The Michigan Panthers averaged 22,250 people at its regular season games. When the team made the

playoffs, its owner, Alfred Taubman, *lowered* ticket prices by about 30 percent and drew a crowd of over 60,000 to the Silverdome, near Detroit. "This crowd gave us a hint," said the Panthers' general manager. "We will sit down and take that turnout into consideration. I think tickets for Panther games will be cheaper next season."

What does this tell us about price elasticity of demand? Does the fact that Detroit was suffering from 25 percent unemployment at the time have any relevance in evaluating the experience?

10. When the New York City Opera faced a growing deficit, it cut its ticket prices by 20 percent, hoping to attract more customers. At the same time, the New York Transit Authority raised subway fares to reduce its growing deficit. Was one of these two opposite approaches to reducing a deficit necessarily wrong?

APPENDIX TO CHAPTER

5

Elasticity: A Formal Analysis

The verbal definition of elasticity used in the text may be written symbolically in the following form:

$$\eta = \frac{\Delta q}{\text{average } q} \div \frac{\Delta p}{\text{average } p}$$

where the averages are over the range, or arc, of the demand curve being considered.[1] Rearranging terms, we can write

$$\eta = \frac{\Delta q}{\Delta p} \times \frac{\text{average } p}{\text{average } q}.$$

This is called **arc elasticity,** and it measures the average responsiveness of quantity to price over an interval of the demand curve.

Most theoretical treatments use a different but related concept called **point elasticity.** This is the measure of responsiveness of quantity to price at a particular point on the demand curve. The precise definition of point elasticity uses the concept of a derivative, which is drawn from differential calculus.

In this appendix we first study arc elasticity, which may be regarded as an approximation of point elasticity. Then we study point elasticity.

Before proceeding, we should notice one further change. In the text of Chapter 5, we reported our price elasticities as positive values and thus implicitly multiplied all our calculations by −1. In theoretical work it is more convenient to retain the concept's natural sign. Thus normal demand elasticities will have negative signs, and statements about "more"

or "less" elasticity must be understood to refer to the absolute, not the algebraic, value of demand elasticity.

Arc Elasticity as an Approximation of Point Elasticity

Point elasticity measures elasticity at some point (p,q). In the approximate definition, however, the responsiveness is measured over a small range starting from that point. For example, in Figure 5A-1 the elasticity at point 1 can be measured by the responsiveness of quantity demanded to a change in price that takes price and quantity from point 1 to point 2. The algebraic formula for this elasticity concept is

$$\eta = \frac{\Delta q}{\Delta p} \times \frac{p}{q} \qquad [1]$$

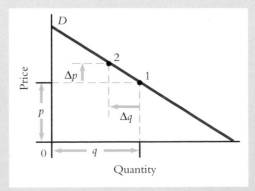

FIGURE 5A-1
A Straight-Line Demand Curve

Because p/q varies with $\Delta q/\Delta p$ constant, the elasticity varies along this demand curve; it is high at the left and low at the right.

---

[1]   The following symbols will be used throughout.

η ≡ elasticity of demand
η_s ≡ elasticity of supply
q ≡ the original quantity
Δq ≡ the change in quantity
p ≡ the original price
Δp ≡ the change in price

This is similar to the definition of arc elasticity, except that, because elasticity is being measured at a point, the p and q corresponding to that point are used (rather than the average p and q over an arc of the curve).

Equation 1 splits elasticity into two parts: $\Delta q/\Delta p$ (the ratio of the change in quantity to the change in price), which is related to the *slope* of the demand curve, and p/q, which is related to the *point* on the curve at which the measurement is made.

Figure 5A-1 shows a straight-line demand curve. To measure the elasticity at point 1, take p and q at that point and then consider a price change, say, to point 2, and measure Δp and Δq as indicated. The slope of the straight line joining points 1 and 2 is $\Delta p/\Delta q$. The term in Equation 1 is $\Delta q/\Delta p$, which is the reciprocal of $\Delta p/\Delta q$. Therefore, the first term in the elasticity formula is the reciprocal of the slope of the straight line joining the two price-quantity positions under consideration.

Although point elasticity of demand refers to a point (p,q) on the demand curve, the first term in Equation 1 still refers to changes over an arc of the curve. This is the part of the formula that involves approximation, and, as we shall see, it has some unsatisfactory results. Nonetheless, some interesting theorems can be derived by using this formula as long as we confine ourselves to straight-line demand and supply curves.

1. *The elasticity of a downward-sloping straight-line demand curve varies from zero at the quantity axis to infinity at the price axis.* First notice that a straight line has a constant slope, so the ratio $\Delta p/\Delta q$ is the same everywhere on the line. Therefore its reciprocal, $\Delta q/\Delta p$, must also be constant. The changes in η can now be inferred by inspecting the ratio p/q. Where the line cuts the quantity axis, price is zero, so the ratio p/q is zero; thus $\eta = 0$. Moving up the line, p rises and q falls, so the ratio p/q rises; thus elasticity rises. Approaching the top of the line, q approaches zero, so the ratio becomes very large. Thus elasticity increases without limit as the price axis is approached.

2. *Where there are two straight-line demand curves of the same slope, the one farther from the origin is less elastic at each price than the one closer to the origin.* Figure 5A-2 shows two parallel straight-line demand curves. Compare the elasticities of the two curves at any price, say, p_0. Because the curves are parallel, the ratio $\Delta q/\Delta p$ is the same on both curves. Because elasticities at the same price are being compared on both curves, p is the same, and the only factor left

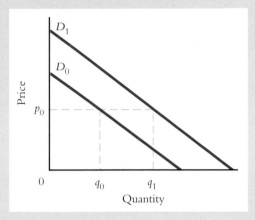

FIGURE 5A-2
Two Parallel Straight-Line Demand Curves

For any given price the quantities are different on these two parallel curves; thus the elasticities are different, being higher on D_0 than on D_1.

to vary is q. On the curve farther from the origin, quantity is larger (i.e., $q_1 > q_0$) and hence p_0/q_1 is smaller than p_0/q_0; thus η is smaller.

It follows from theorem 2 that parallel shifts of a straight-line demand curve lower elasticity (at each price) when the line shifts outward and raise elasticity when the line shifts inward.

3. *The elasticities of two intersecting straight-line demand curves can be compared at the point of intersection merely by comparing slopes, the steeper curve being the less elastic.* In Figure 5A-3 there are two intersecting curves. At the point of intersection, p and q are common to both curves and hence the ratio p/q is the same. Therefore η varies only with $\Delta q/\Delta p$. On the steeper curve, $\Delta q/\Delta p$ is smaller than on the flatter curve, so elasticity is lower.

4. *If the slope of a straight-line demand curve changes while the price intercept remains constant, elasticity at any given price is unchanged.* This is an interesting case for at least two reasons. First, when more customers having similar tastes to those already in the market enter the market, the demand curve pivots outward in this way. Second, when more firms enter a market that is shared proportionally among all firms, each firm's demand curve shifts inward in this way.

Consider in Figure 5A-4 the elasticities at point b on demand curve D_0 and at point c on demand curve D_1. We shall focus on the two triangles, abp_0 on D_0 and acp_0 on D_1, formed by the two straight-line

FIGURE 5A-3
Two Intersecting Straight-Line Demand Curves

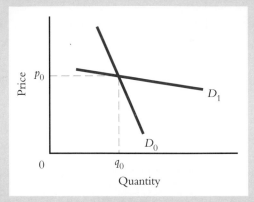

Elasticities are different at the point of intersection of these demand curves because the slopes are different, being higher on D_0 than on D_1. Therefore, D_1 is more elastic than D_0 at p_0.

demand curves emanating from point a and by the price p_0.

The price p_0 is the line segment $0p_0$. The quantities q_0 and q_1 are the line segments p_0b and p_0c,

FIGURE 5A-4
Two Straight-Line Demand Curves from the Same Price Intercept

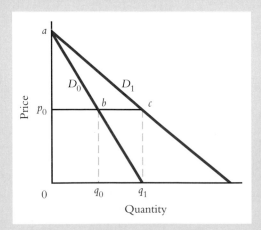

The elasticity is the same on D_0 and D_1 at any price p_0. This situation occurs because the steeper slope of D_0 is exactly offset by the smaller quantity demanded at any price.

respectively. The slope of D_0 is $\Delta p/\Delta q = ap_0/p_0b$ and the slope of D_1 is $\Delta p/\Delta q = ap_0/p_0c$. From Equation 1 we can represent the elasticities of D_0 and D_1 at the points b and c, respectively, as

η at point $b = (p_0b/ap_0) \times (0p_0/p_0b) = (0p_0/ap_0)$

η at point $c = (p_0c/ap_0) \times (0p_0/p_0c) = (0p_0/ap_0)$

The two are the same. The reason is that the distance corresponding to the quantity demanded at p_0 appears in both the numerator and the denominator and thus cancels out.

Put differently, if the straight-line demand curve D_0 is twice as steep as D_1, it has half the quantity demanded at p_0. Therefore, in the expression

$$\eta = \frac{\Delta q}{\Delta p} \times \frac{p}{q}$$

the steeper slope (a smaller Δq for the same Δp) is exactly offset by the smaller quantity demanded (a smaller q for the same p).

5. *Any straight-line supply curve through the origin has an elasticity of one.* Such a supply curve is shown in Figure 5A-5. Consider the two triangles with the sides p, q, and the S curve and Δp, Δq, and the S curve. Clearly, these are similar triangles. Therefore, the ratios of their sides are equal: that is,

$$\frac{p}{q} = \frac{\Delta p}{\Delta q} \qquad [2]$$

FIGURE 5A-5
A Straight-Line Supply Curve Through the Origin

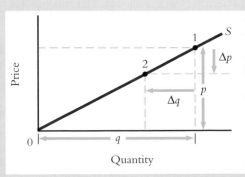

At every point on the curve, p/q equals $\Delta p/\Delta q$; thus elasticity equals unity at every point.

Elasticity of supply is defined as

$$\eta_s = \frac{\Delta q}{\Delta p} \times \frac{p}{q}$$

which, by substitution from Equation 2, gives

$$\eta_s = \frac{q}{p} \times \frac{p}{q} \equiv 1$$

6.   *The elasticity measured from any point (p,q), according to Equation 1, is dependent on the direction and magnitude of the change in price and quantity.* Except for a straight line (for which the slope does not change), the ratio $\Delta q / \Delta p$ will not be the same over different ranges of a curve. Figure 5A-6 shows a demand curve that is not a straight line. To measure the elasticity from point 1, the ratio $\Delta q / \Delta p$—and thus η—will vary according to the size and the direction of the price change.

Theorem 6 yields a result that is very inconvenient and is avoided by use of a different definition of point elasticity.

Point Elasticity According to the Precise Definition

To measure the elasticity at a point exactly, it is necessary to know the reaction of quantity to a change in price *at that point,* not over a range of the curve.

The reaction of quantity to price change at a point is called dq/dp, and this is defined to be the reciprocal of the slope of the straight line tangent to the demand curve at the point in question. In Figure 5A-7 the elasticity of demand at point 1 is the ratio p/q (as it has been in all previous measures), now multiplied by the ratio of $\Delta q / \Delta p$ measured along the straight line T, tangent to the curve at point 1, that is, by dq/dp. Thus the exact definition of point elasticity is

$$\eta = \frac{dq}{dp} \times \frac{p}{q} \qquad [3]$$

The ratio dq/dp, as defined, is in fact the differential calculus concept of the *derivative* of quantity with respect to price.

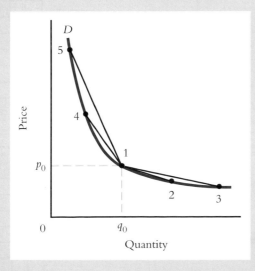

FIGURE 5A-6
Point Elasticity of Demand Measured by the Approximate Formula

When the approximation of $\eta = \frac{\Delta q}{\Delta p} \times \frac{p}{q}$ is used, many elasticities are measured from point 1 because the slope of the chord between point 1 and every other point on the curve varies.

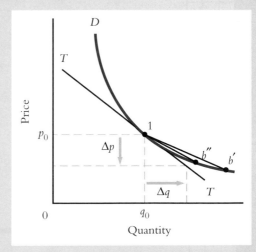

FIGURE 5A-7
Point Elasticity of Demand Measured by the Exact Formula

When the exact definition $\eta = \frac{dq}{dp} \times \frac{p}{q}$ is used, only one elasticity is measured from point 1 because there is only one tangent to the demand curve at that point.

23

An Introduction to Macroeconomics

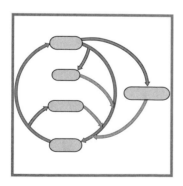

Turn on the evening news, and you will likely hear talk of unemployment, inflation, recession, international competitiveness, and economic growth. Since the adoption of the Employment Act of 1946, federal economic policy has been oriented towards preventing recessions, reducing inflation, and stimulating domestic economic growth. Almost everyone cares about the economy. Households are anxious to avoid the unemployment that comes with recessions, to protect themselves against the hazards of inflation, and to share in the rising income that is brought about by economic growth. Firms are concerned about how inflations, recessions, and foreign competition affect their profits.

Each of the concerns just mentioned plays a major role in macroeconomics.

What Is Macroeconomics?

Macroeconomics is the study of how the economy behaves in broad outline without dwelling on much of its interesting, but sometimes confusing, detail. As was noted in Chapter 3, macroeconomics is largely concerned with the behavior of economic *aggregates*, such as total consumption, total investment, and total exports, and the average price of all goods and services. These aggregates result from activities in many different markets and from the behavior of different decision makers in households, governments and firms. In contrast, *microeconomics* deals with the behavior of individual markets, such as those for wheat, coal, or strawberries, and with the detailed behavior of individual decision makers, such as firms and households.

In macroeconomics we add the value of wheat, coal, strawberries, and appendectomies to the value of all other goods and services produced and study the movement of aggregate *national product*. We also average the prices of all commodities consumed and discuss the *price level* for the entire economy. We know perfectly well that an economy that produces much wheat and few automobiles is quite different from one that produces many automobiles but little wheat. We also know that an economy with cheap wheat and expensive cars is very different from one with cheap cars and expensive wheat. Studying aggregates often means missing these important differences, but it concentrates the mind on some important issues facing the economy in general.

In return for losing valuable detail, studying aggregates allows us to view the big picture. In macroeconomics we look at the broad range of opportunities and difficulties facing the economy as a whole. When national product rises, the output of most commodities, and the incomes of most people, usually rise with it. When the price level rises, virtually everyone in the economy is forced to make adjustments. When the unemployment rate rises, workers are put at an increased risk of losing their jobs and suffering losses in their incomes. These movements in economic aggregates are strongly associated with the economic concerns of most individuals: the health of the industries in which they work and the prices of the goods that they purchase. This association is why macroeconomic aggregates get air time on the evening news, and it is one important reason why we study macroeconomics.

Major Macroeconomic Issues

Business cycles. The economy tends to move in a series of ups and downs, called *business cycles,* rather than in a steady pattern. Why did the 1930s see the greatest economic depression in the twentieth century, with almost one-fifth of the U.S. labor force unemployed and with massive unemployment in all major industrial countries? Why were the 25 years following World War II a period of sustained economic growth, with only minor interruptions caused by modest recessions? Why did the early 1980s see the onset of the worst worldwide recession since the 1930s? What fueled the recovery of the mid-1980s? Why did it falter at the end of the decade? Why did the economy fail to grow through 1990 and 1991?

Overall living standards. As we saw in Chapter 1, both total output and output per person have risen for many decades in most industrial countries. These long-term trends have meant rising average living standards. Since the early 1970s, however, average living standards have grown much less rapidly than during the preceding decades of the twentieth century. Indeed, in the United States the *real wage,* the quantity of goods and services that can be purchased in exchange for an average hour of work, was lower in 1991 than it was in 1973. Although long-term growth gets less play on the evening news than does the current inflation rate or unemployment rate, it has considerably more importance for the prospects and constraints facing a society from decade to decade and generation to generation. What caused the slowdown in worldwide growth rates that began in the 1970s? Can governments do anything about it?

Inflation and recession. Why, during the 1970s and early 1980s, did inflation in many advanced Western nations reach levels never seen before in peacetime? In the early 1970s, when inflation crept up to 4 percent, concern was so great that emergency measures were adopted by the Nixon administration. By contrast, in the mid-1980s the government claimed credit for having *reduced* inflation to 4 percent! Has our attitude toward inflation permanently changed?

Earlier in the century, alternating bouts of inflationary boom and deflationary recession caused many headaches for policymakers. Booms still tend to be accompanied by inflationary pressures, but it can no longer be assumed that recessions will bring deflations. Why were the recessions of the 1970s and early 1980s accompanied not only by their familiar companion, high unemployment, but also by an unexpected fellow traveler, rapid inflation? Will **stagflation**—simultaneous high unemployment and rapid inflation—return? Or will the relatively low inflation rates of the early 1990s persist?

Budget and trade deficits. Throughout most of the 1980s the United States was plagued with the problem of the "twin deficits." The first deficit was the enormous discrepancy between what the federal government spent and what it raised in taxes. This *budget deficit* had to be financed by borrowing funds, thus adding to the national debt. The second deficit was the *trade deficit*—the difference between the value of the goods that U.S. producers sold abroad and that U.S. purchasers bought from abroad. Did the high trade deficit reflect an underlying loss of U.S. international competitiveness, as some economists believe? Is the trade deficit primarily the consequence of the government's budget deficit, as other economists insist?

In today's globalized world economy, U.S. citizens own assets all over the world. They own shares in foreign companies, they hold bonds issued by foreign governments and firms, they have balances in foreign banks, and they possess all kinds of real estate, from hotels and apartment buildings to country cottages. Similarly, foreign citizens hold assets in the United States. In 1980 the value of foreign assets that were owned by all U.S. citizens exceeded the value of U.S. assets that were owned by foreigners. The difference was enough to make the United States the world's largest *creditor* country. By 1992, however, the United States had become, by some calculations, the world's largest *debtor* country. Its net foreign liabilities—the excess of foreign holdings of U.S. assets over U.S.

holdings of foreign assets—exceeded those of the next three largest debtor countries combined, Mexico, Brazil, and India. What caused this turnaround? What are its consequences for the well-being of U.S. citizens?

Key Macroeconomic Phenomena

The current macroeconomic state of the nation can be fairly completely described by total output and output per person, the rate of growth of output and output per person, employment and the unemployment rate, the inflation rate, the interest rate, the value of the dollar, and the balance of trade. We hear about each of these indicators on the nightly news and read about them in newspapers; politicians give campaign speeches about them; economists theorize about them. In this chapter we discuss each of these variables, with an emphasis on why and how they matter for economic welfare. In Chapter 24 we expand the discussion to consider how the macroeconomic variables are measured. The remainder of this book is largely about the causes and consequences of each of these variables, the many ways in which they interact, and the effect they have on the well-being of U.S. citizens.

Output and Income

The most comprehensive measure of a nation's overall level of economic activity is the value of its total production of goods and services, called *national product*. One of the most important ideas in macroeconomics is that national product is equal to *national income*. This equality arises from the simple observation that every expenditure is also a receipt. When you purchase a loaf of bread, a new car, or the services embodied in the cleaning and pressing of a skirt, the seller of the relevant good or service receives income exactly equal to your expenditure, less any sales taxes.[1]

Figure 23-1, which reproduces Figure 3-2, depicts national income and expenditure as a circular flow. For the nation as a whole, all of the value that is produced must ultimately belong to someone in the form of a claim on that value.[2] Thus, the national product is equal to the total income claims generated by the production of goods and services. In short, when we study national product, we are also studying national income.

There are several related measures of a nation's total output and total income. Their various definitions, and the relationships among them, are discussed in detail in the next chapter. In this chapter we use the generic term *national income* to refer to both the value of total output and the value of the income claims generated by the production of that output.

Aggregating Total Output

To measure total output, quantities of a variety of goods are *aggregated*. To construct such totals, we add up the *values* of the different products. We cannot add tons of steel to loaves of bread, but we can add the money value of steel production to the money value of bread production. Hence, by multiplying the physical output of a good by its price per unit and then summing this value for each good produced in a nation, we can calculate the quantity of total output *measured in dollars*.

Real and Nominal Values

The total that was just described gives the *money value* of national output, often called **nominal national income**. A change in this measure can be caused by a change in either the physical quantities or the prices on which it is based. To determine the extent to which any change is due to quantities or to prices, economists calculate **real national income**. This measures the value of individual outputs not at current prices, but at a set of prices that prevailed in some base period that was chosen for this purpose.

Nominal national income is often referred to as *money national income* or *current-dollar national income*. Real national income is often called *constant-dollar national income*. Denoted by the symbol Y, real national income tells us the value of current output measured at constant prices—the sum of the quantities valued at prices that prevailed in the base period. Comparing

---

[1] Of course, not all output generates receipts. Some output may be unsold, adding to inventories instead of to sales. Some sales may be sales for credit rather than for money. Generally, then, the production of output generates a *claim*, due to the producer, equal to the value of the output.

[2] Sales taxes accrue to governments and belong to the citizens whom those governments represent.

FIGURE 23-1
The Circular Flow of Expenditure and Income

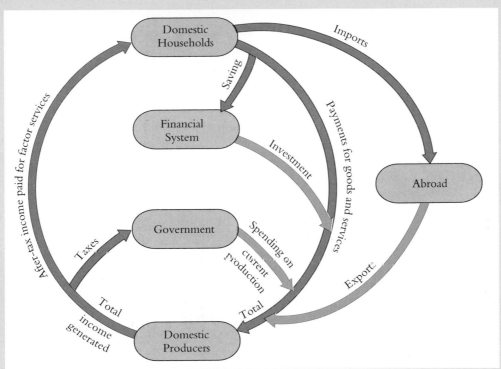

The circular flow of income and product implies that national income is equal to national product. If there were no withdrawals (imports, saving, and taxes) or injections (exports, investment, and government purchases) the flow would be a simple circle from households to producers and back to households, and the result would be obvious. Injections and withdrawals complicate the picture but do not change the basic result: Domestic production creates a claim on the value of that production. When all of the claims are added up, they must be equal to the value of all of the production.

real national incomes of different years provides a measure of the change in real output that has occurred during the intervening period.

Since its calculation holds prices constant, real national income changes only when quantities change.

Since our interest is primarily in the *real* output of goods and services, we shall use the terms *national income* and *national output* to refer to *real national income* unless otherwise specified. (An example, illustrating the important distinction between real national income and money national income, is given in Box 24-3 on page 497.)

National Income: The Historical Experience

One of the most commonly used measures of national income is called *gross domestic product*, or GDP. This can be measured in either real or nominal terms; we focus here on real GDP. The details of its calculation will be discussed in Chapter 24.[3]

Figure 23-2(i) shows real national income produced by the U.S. economy since 1929; Figure 23-2(ii) shows its annual percentage change for the same period. The GDP series in Figure 23-2(i) shows two kinds of movement. The major movement is a

_____

[3] Prior to the end of 1991, the most commonly used measure of national income in the United States was *gross national product*, or GNP. In 1991, in order to conform with the United Nations system of economic accounting, used in most other countries of the world, the official U.S. economic accounts began to emphasize GDP rather than GNP. For the purposes of the discussion in this chapter, differences between the two measures do not matter. In Chapter 24, where we show how national income is measured, we provide a detailed discussion of the differences between GDP and GNP.

FIGURE 23-2
National Income and Growth, 1929–1991

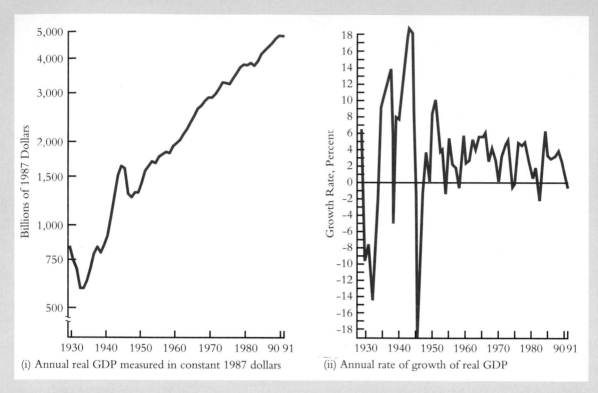

(i) Annual real GDP measured in constant 1987 dollars

(ii) Annual rate of growth of real GDP

(i) Real GDP measures the quantity of total output produced by the nation's economy over the period of a year. Real GDP is plotted in part (i) in semilog form, where equal vertical distances represent equal percentage changes. (See the Appendix to Chapter 2.) Real GDP has risen steadily since the early 1930s, with only a few interruptions. This demonstrates the growth of the U.S. economy. Short-term fluctuations are obscured by the long-term growth trend in part (i) but are highlighted in part (ii).[a]

(ii) Fluctuations in the annual rate of growth of real GDP reflect cyclical changes in the level of activity in the economy. The growth rate fluctuates considerably from year to year. High growth rates occur during war years (such as World War II in the early 1940s and the Korean War in the early 1950s). Peacetime expansions (such as the mid-1960s and the last half of the 1980s) are reflected by sustained periods of above-average growth rates. Low growth rates occur during recessions. The long-term upward trend of real GDP shows up in part (i) because most of the observations in part (ii) are positive. (*Source*: *Economic Report of the President*, various years.)

[a]For 1929 to 1959, the figure shows real GNP, because historical GDP data are not available. The differences are unimportant.

positive trend that increased real output by over 350 percent in the 50 years ending in 1989. Since the trend has generally been upward throughout U.S. economic history, it is referred to as *economic growth*.

Long-term growth in real national income is reflected in the increasing trend in real GDP.

A second feature of the real GDP series is the short-term fluctuations around the trend, often described as cyclical fluctuations. Overall growth so dominates the real GDP series that the fluctuations are hardly visible in Figure 23-2(i). However, as can be seen in Figure 23-2(ii), the growth of GDP has never been smooth. In most years GDP grows, but

**FIGURE 23-3
A Stylized Business Cycle**

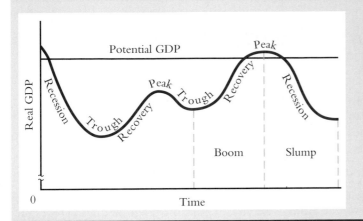

Although the phases of business fluctuations are described by a series of commonly used terms, no two cycles are the same. Starting from a lower turning point, a cycle goes through a phase of recovery, or expansion, reaches an upper turning point, and then enters a period of recession. Cycles differ from one another in the severity of their troughs and peaks and in the speed with which one phase follows another. Sometimes the entire rising half of the cycle is loosely referred to as a *boom*, and the entire falling half is called a *slump*.

in 1974–1975, 1981–1982, and 1990–1991, GDP growth was negative.

The cyclical behavior of real national income is reflected in the annual fluctuations in the growth rate of real GDP.

The business cycle.   The **business cycle** refers to the continual ebb and flow of business activity that occurs around the long-term trend after seasonal adjustments have been made.[4] Such cyclical fluctuations can be seen in many economic series; in particular, they are obvious from the continual oscillations in the growth rate of GDP that we see in Figure 23-2(ii).

Although recurrent fluctuations in economic activity are neither smooth nor regular, a vocabulary has developed to denote their different stages. Figure 23-3 shows stylized cycles that illustrate some useful terms, and Box 23-1 further discusses this terminology. It is important to realize that no two cycles are exactly the same. There are variations in duration and magnitude. Some expansions are long and drawn out, as was the one that began in 1983; others come to an end before high employment of labor and industrial capacity is reached. Nonetheless,

fluctuations are systematic enough that it still seems useful to identify common factors in the four phases, which are outlined in Box 23-1.

Potential Income and the GDP Gap

Actual national income represents what the economy does, in fact, produce. An important related concept is *potential* national income, which measures what the economy could produce if all resources—land, labor, and productive capacity—were fully employed at their normal levels of utilization. This concept is usually referred to as **potential income** but is sometimes called *high-employment income*.[5] We give it the symbol Y^* to distinguish it from actual national income, which is indicated by Y.

What is variously called the **output gap** or the **GDP gap** measures the difference between what would have been produced if potential, or high-employment, national income had been achieved and what is actually produced, as measured by the current GDP. The gap is calculated by subtracting actual national income from potential income ($Y^* - Y$).

When potential income is greater than actual income, the gap measures the market value of goods

---

[4] When economists wish to analyze monthly or quarterly data, they often make a *seasonal adjustment* to remove fluctuations that can be accounted for by the regular seasonal pattern evident in many economic series. For example, logging activity tends to be low in the winter months and high in the summer months, whereas sales of fuel oil tend to have the reverse seasonal pattern. Retail sales are highest in December.

[5] The words *real* and *actual* have similar meanings in everyday usage. In national-income theory, however, their meanings are quite distinct. *Real* national income is distinguished from *nominal* national income, and *actual* national income is distinguished from *potential* national income. The latter both refer to real measures, so that the full descriptions are, in fact, actual real national income and potential real national income.

Box 23-1

The Terminology of Business Cycles

Trough

A trough is characterized by high unemployment and a level of demand that is low in relation to the economy's capacity to produce. There is thus a substantial amount of unused productive capacity. Business profits are low; for some individual companies they are negative. Confidence about economic prospects in the immediate future is lacking, and, as a result, many firms are unwilling to risk making new investments.

Recovery

The characteristics of a recovery, or expansion, are many: Run-down equipment is replaced; employment, income, and consumer spending all begin to rise; and expectations become more favorable as a result of increases in production, sales, and profits. Investments that once seemed risky may be undertaken as the climate of business opinion starts to change from one of pessimism to one of optimism. As demand rises, production can be increased with relative ease merely by reemploying the existing unused capacity and unemployed labor.

Peak

A peak is the top of a cycle. At the peak, existing capacity is utilized to a high degree; labor shortages may develop, particularly in categories of key skills;

and shortages of essential raw materials are likely. As shortages develop in more and more markets, a situation of general excess demand develops. Costs rise, but since prices rise also, business remains profitable.

Recession

A **recession**, or contraction, is a downturn in economic activity. Common usage defines a recession as a fall in the real GDP for two quarters in succession. Demand falls off, and, as a result, production and employment also fall. As employment falls, so do households' incomes. Profits drop, and some firms encounter financial difficulties. Investments that looked profitable with the expectation of continually rising demand now appear unprofitable. It may not even be worth replacing capital goods as they wear out, because unused capacity is increasing steadily. In historical discussions, a recession that is deep and long-lasting is often called a **depression**.

Booms and Slumps

Two nontechnical but descriptive terms are often used. The whole falling half of the cycle is often called a *slump*, and the whole rising half is often called a *boom*. These are useful terms to use when we do not wish to be more specific about the economy's position in the cycle.

and services that *could have been produced* if the economy's resources had been fully employed but that actually went unproduced. The goods and services that are not produced when the economy is operating below Y^* are permanently lost to the economy. Because these losses occur when employable resources are not used, they are often called the *deadweight loss* of unemployment.

When the economy is operating below its potential level of output—that is, when Y is less than Y^*—there is a **recessionary gap**. In booms the

GDP gap may change signs, such that actual national income *exceeds* potential income. Actual GDP can exceed potential income because potential income is defined for a *normal rate of utilization* of factors of production, and there are many ways in which these normal rates can be exceeded temporarily. Labor may work longer hours than normal; factories may operate an extra shift or not close for routine repairs and maintenance. Although these expedients are only temporary, they are effective in the short term. When actual GDP exceeds potential GDP there is generally upward pressure on prices. Thus, when Y exceeds Y^*, we say there is an **inflationary gap**.

Figure 23-4(i) shows potential income for the years 1955 through 1991. The rising trend reflects the growth in the productive capacity of the U.S. economy over this period. The figure also shows actual real national income (reproduced from Figure 23-2), which has kept approximately in step with potential income. The distance between the two, which is the GDP gap, is plotted in part (ii) of Figure 23-4. Fluctuations in economic activity are apparent from fluctuations in the size of the gap. The deadweight loss from unemployment over any time span is indicated by the overall amount of the gap over that time span. It is shown in part (ii) of Figure 23-4 by the shaded area between the curve and the zero line, which represents the level at which actual output equals potential output.

Why National Income Matters

National income is an important measure of economic performance in both the short run and the long run. Short-run movements in the business cycle

---

FIGURE 23-4
Potential National Income and the GDP Gap, 1955–1991

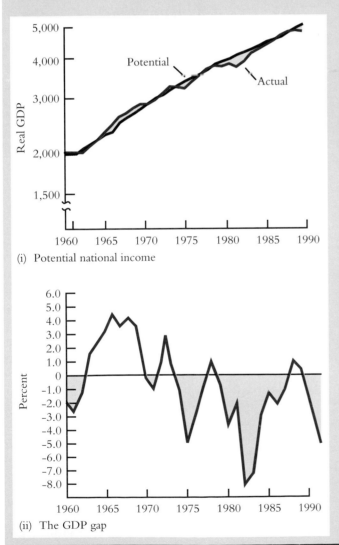

(i) Potential national income

(ii) The GDP gap

(i) Potential and actual GDP both display an upward trend over the past half decade. Growth in the economy has been such that both potential and actual GDP have more than doubled since 1960. These are plotted in part (i) in semilog form. (See the Appendix to Chapter 2.) Recall that both measures are in real terms; in the figure they are measured in 1987 dollars. The distance between the two curves represents the GDP gap. The shaded areas indicate periods when there has been a recessionary GDP gap.

(ii) The GDP gap measures the difference between an economy's potential output and its actual output; the gap is expressed here as a percentage of potential output. The cyclical behavior of the economy is clearly apparent from the behavior of the GDP gap from 1960 to 1991. Slumps in economic activity cause large gaps; booms reduce the gaps. The shaded area below the zero line, at which actual output equals potential output, represents the deadweight loss from unemployment. (*Source:* Congressional Budget Office, 1992.)

receive the most attention in politics and in the press, but most economists agree that long-term growth, the rate of change of *potential GDP*, is at least as important.

The business cycle.   Recessions cause unemployment and lost output. When actual GDP is below potential GDP, there is economic waste and human suffering as a result of a failure to use the economy's resources (including its human resources) at their normal intensity of use.

Booms, although associated with high employment and high output, can bring problems of their own. When actual national income exceeds potential income, strong inflationary pressure usually results, causing serious concern for any government that is committed to keeping the inflation rate low.

Long-term growth.   The long-run trend in real national income per capita is the principal determinant of improvements in a society's overall standard of living. When income per person grows, each generation can expect, on average, to be substantially better off than preceding ones. For example, if real income per capita grows at the relatively modest rate of 1.5 percent per year, the average person's lifetime income expectancy will be *twice* that of his or her grandparents.

In the long run, national income per person can grow for two reasons. One is growth in the amount of output produced per hour of work. It is this growth, the growth of *labor productivity*, that has generally eliminated the low living standards that prevailed at the start of the Industrial Revolution. A second source of growth in per capita income arises from changes in the amount of labor (that is, the total hours of work) supplied by a given population. If people work more hours, they will produce more output. The difference between these two sources of growth is important. When productivity increases, more output is obtained for a given amount of effort. When total hours worked increase, more output is obtained by using more resources. Income rises, but the amount of time that people have to devote to life's pleasures falls.

In the U.S. economy, much of the growth in per capita income during the 1970s and 1980s was due to increases in the number of hours worked per capita. A relatively small part of that growth, compared to the trend of the rest of the century,

could be attributed to growth in labor productivity. This reduction in productivity growth has created new interest in the sources of economic growth, a subject that is one of the major themes in our discussion of macroeconomics.

Finally, it is important to remember that although economic growth makes people better off on average, it does not necessarily make every individual better off. Additionally, national income is far from a perfect measure of economic well-being, in part because it fails to measure many things, such as leisure time, that matter to people. Chapter 24 contains a detailed discussion of how economists measure national income and an evaluation of the strengths and weaknesses of those measures.

Employment, Unemployment, and the Labor Force

National income and *employment* (and, hence, *unemployment*) are closely related. If more is to be produced, either more workers must be used in production or existing workers must produce more. The first change means a rise in employment; the second means a rise in output per person employed, which, as we have seen, is called a rise in *labor productivity*. In the short run, when the productive capacity of the economy (potential GDP) is fixed, the only way to produce more output is to employ more workers. Trend increases in productivity are a major source of economic growth, but they only occur over longer periods of time.

Employment denotes the number of adult workers (defined in the United States as workers aged 16 and over) who hold jobs. **Unemployment** denotes the number of adult workers who are not employed and are actively searching for a job. The **labor force** is the total number of people who are employed plus the number of unemployed. The **unemployment rate**, usually represented by the symbol U, is unemployment expressed as a percentage of the labor force.

$$U = \frac{\text{unemployed}}{\text{labor force}} \times 100 \text{ percent}$$

The number of unemployed persons in the United States is estimated from the Current Population Survey that is conducted each month by the

Box 23-2

How Accurate Are the Unemployment Figures?

No measurement of unemployment is completely accurate. The unemployment figures that are calculated by the Bureau of Labor Statistics, however, have a number of shortcomings that reveal much about the concept of unemployment itself.

Measured unemployment may overstate or understate the number of people who are involuntarily unemployed. On the one hand, measured unemployment overstates true unemployment by including people who are voluntarily out of work. For example, unemployment compensation provides protection against genuine hardship, but it also induces some people to stay out of work and collect unemployment benefits for as long as the benefits last. Such people have, in fact, voluntarily withdrawn from the labor force, although, in order to remain eligible for unemployment payments, they must make a show of looking for a job by registering at the local unemployment service office. Such people usually are included in the ranks of the unemployed because, for fear of losing their benefits, they tell the person who surveys them that they are actively looking for a job.

On the other hand, the measured figure understates involuntary unemployment by omitting some people who would accept a job if one were available but who did not actively look for one during the week in which the data were collected. For example, people who have not found jobs after searching for a long time may become discouraged and stop seeking work. Such people have withdrawn voluntarily from the labor force and will not be recorded as unemployed. They are, however, unemployed in the sense that they would willingly accept a job if one were available. People in this category are referred to as *discouraged workers*. They have voluntarily withdrawn from the labor market because they believe that they cannot find a job under current conditions.

In addition, there are part-time unemployed people. If some people are working 6 hours instead of 8 hours per day because there is insufficient demand for the product that they help to make, then these workers are suffering 25 percent unemployment even though none of them are reported as unemployed. Twenty-five percent of that group's potential labor resources are going unused. Involuntary part-time work is a major source of unemployment of labor resources that is not reflected in the overall unemployment figures that are reported in the press.

The official figures for unemployment are useful, particularly because they tell us the *direction* of changes in unemployment. It is unlikely, for example, that the figures will be rising when unemployment is really falling. For all of the reasons that we have just discussed, however, they can at times give under- or overestimates of the total number of persons who would be genuinely willing to work if they were offered a job at the going rate of pay.

Bureau of the Census. Persons who are currently without a job but who say they have searched actively for one during the sample period are recorded as unemployed. The total number of estimated unemployed is then expressed as a percentage of the labor force (employed plus unemployed) to obtain the figure for percentage unemployment. Some problems connected with this measurement are discussed in Box 23-2.

When the economy is at potential GDP, we call the level of employment *full employment*, or, sometimes, *high employment*. This nomenclature is confusing, however, because "full employment" does *not* mean no unemployment.[6] There are two main reasons why full employment is always accompanied by some unemployment.

First, there is a constant turnover of individuals in given jobs and a constant change in job opportunities. New members enter the work force; some people quit their jobs; others are fired. It may take some time for these people to find jobs. So, at any point in time, there is unemployment due to the normal turnover of labor. Such unemployment is called **frictional unemployment**.

Second, because the economy is constantly changing and adapting, at any moment in time there will always be some mismatch between the characteristics of the labor force and the characteristics of the available jobs. This is a mismatch between the *structure* of the supplies of labor and the *structure* of the demands for labor. The mismatch may occur, for example, because labor does not have the skills that are in demand or because labor is not in the part of the country where the demand is located. Unemployment that occurs because of a mismatch between the characteristics of the supply of labor and the demand for labor, even when the overall demand for labor is equal to the overall supply, is called **structural unemployment**.

High or **full employment** is said to occur when the only existing unemployment is frictional and structural. When this is the case, factors of production are being used at their normal intensity, and the economy is at potential GDP. At less than full employment, other types of unemployment are present as well. One major reason for lapses from full employment lies in the business cycle. During recessions, unemployment rises above the minimum avoidable amount of frictional and structural unemployment. This excess amount is called **cyclical unemployment** (or, sometimes, *deficient-demand unemployment*).

The measured unemployment rate when the economy is at potential GDP (i.e., at full employment) is often called the *natural rate of unemployment* or the **NAIRU**.[7] Although estimates of this rate are difficult to obtain, they provide a useful benchmark against which to gauge the current performance of the economy, as measured by the actual unemployment rate. Estimates indicate that the NAIRU rose throughout the 1970s, from around 4 percent to a high of around 7 percent in the early 1980s, and it has now fallen to between 5 and 6 percent. (We shall discuss the reasons for these changes in Chapter 33.)

Unemployment: The Historical Experience

Figure 23-5(i) shows the trends in the labor force, employment, and unemployment since 1929. Despite booms and slumps, employment has grown roughly in line with the growth in the labor force and in the total population. In the 1980s, however, the labor force and employment grew faster than the total population in response to the maturing of the "baby boom" generation and the increasing participation of women in the labor force.

Although the long-term growth trend dominates the employment figures, some unemployment is always present. Figure 23-5(ii) shows that the short-term fluctuations in the unemployment rate have been quite marked. The unemployment rate has been as low as 1.2 percent in 1944 and as high as 24.9 percent in 1933; in the post–World War II period, the unemployment rate fell as low as 2.9 percent in 1953 and rose as high as 9.7 percent in 1982. The high unemployment rate of the Great Depression in the early 1930s tends to dwarf the fluctuations in unemployment that have occurred since then. Nonetheless, the fluctuations in unemployment in recent decades have been neither minor nor unimportant.[8]

Unemployment can rise either because employment falls or because the labor force expands. In recent decades the number of people entering the labor force has exceeded the number leaving it. The resulting increase in the labor force has meant that unemployment has sometimes grown even in periods when employment was also growing.

---

[6] This is one reason why the concept is now more often called *high employment*, although the long history of the use of the term *full employment* in economics guarantees that it will be used for some time to come.

[7] NAIRU is an acronym for "Non Accelerating Inflation Rate of Unemployment." The association of the NAIRU with potential GDP is discussed in Chapter 32.

---

[8] In addition, changes in the details by which unemployment is defined and measured have generally made recent fluctuations appear to be somewhat smaller than they would have under the old procedures.

FIGURE 23-5
Labor Force, Employment, and Unemployment, 1929–1991

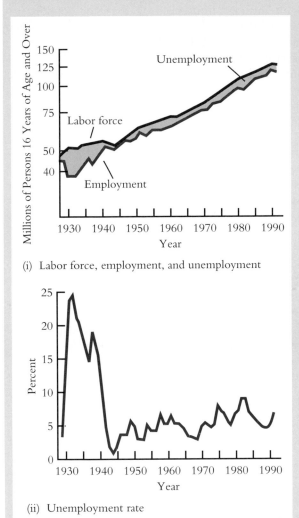

(i) Labor force, employment, and unemployment

(ii) Unemployment rate

(i) The labor force and employment have grown since the 1930s with only a few interruptions. The size of the labor force in the United States has doubled since 1930, and so has the number of the employed. These are plotted on a semilog scale. The fall in the labor force in the early 1940s occurred in the civilian labor force. The missing workers were in the military, and the Bureau of Labor Statistics' (BLS) definition of the labor force in use at the time did not include persons in the military. Unemployment, the gap between the labor force and employment, has fluctuated, but it has not again reached the peak of almost 13 million that occurred in 1933. As a fraction of the total labor force [see part (ii) for the unemployment rate], unemployment in 1933 was much higher than in any recent year.

(ii) The unemployment rate responds to the cyclical behavior of the economy. Booms are associated with low unemployment and slumps with high unemployment. The Great Depression of the 1930s produced record unemployment figures for an entire decade. During World War II unemployment rates fell to very low levels. Since 1945, however, the unemployment rate has exhibited a slight upward trend. The recession of the early 1980s produced unemployment rates second only to those of the 1930s; these rates were extremely high by the standards of the post–World War II behavior of the U.S. economy. After reaching a high of nearly 10 percent in 1982, the rate fell steadily throughout the rest of the decade, until it reached 5 percent in 1989. With the recession that began in 1990, unemployment rose again, but it has not come near its 1982 high. (*Source: Economic Report of the President*, various years.)

Why Unemployment Matters

The social and political significance of the unemployment rate is enormous. The government is blamed when it is high and takes credit when it is low. Few macroeconomic policies are planned without some consideration of how they will affect unemployment. No other summary statistic, with the possible exception of the inflation rate, carries such weight as a source of both formal and informal policy concern as does the percentage of the labor force that is unemployed.

Unemployment causes economic waste, and it causes human suffering. The economic waste is obvious. Human effort is the least durable of economic commodities. If a fully employed economy has 120 million people who are willing to work in 1993, their services must either be used in 1993 or wasted. When the services of only 108 million are used because 10 percent of the labor force is unemployed, one year's potential output of 12 million workers is lost forever. In an economy in which there is not enough output to meet everyone's needs, such a waste of potential output seems pointless and possibly tragic.

Severe hardship can be caused by prolonged periods of unemployment. A person's spirit can be broken by a long period of desiring but being unable to find work. Careful research has shown that crime, mental illness, and general social unrest tend to be positively associated with unemployment. The loss of income associated with unemployment can and does push people into poverty.

In the not-so-distant past only private charity, or help from friends and relatives, stood between the unemployed and starvation. Today welfare and unemployment insurance have softened those effects, particularly when unemployment is for short periods, as is often the case. However, when an economic slump lasts long enough, as in the mid-1970s, the early 1980s, and the early 1990s, people begin to exhaust their unemployment insurance and must fall back on savings, welfare, or charity.

Inflation and the Price Level

Everyone knows what inflation is. Most people complain about its effects when the inflation rate is high and worry that it is just around the corner when the inflation rate is low. Inflation means that prices in general are going up—not just the price of gasoline, blue jeans, or chewing gum, but the price of almost everything.

To study inflation, economists use two concepts. The first is the *price level*, which refers to the average level of all prices in the economy and is given by the symbol P. The second is the *rate of inflation*, which is the rate at which the general price level (P) is rising.

In order to measure the average price level, economists construct a *price index*, which averages the prices of different commodities according to how important they are. The best-known price index in the United States is the **Consumer Price Index (CPI)**, which measures the average cost of the goods and services that are bought by the average U.S. consumer.

The CPI expresses the price level at any time in relation to what a given bundle of commodities (those consumed by the average U.S. urban resident) cost in a base period. The base period in use in 1992 was 1982–1984, for which the average value of the index is set to 100. Thus, when we read that the CPI for March 1992 had a value of 139.4, we know that a bundle of goods and services that cost $100 during 1982–1984 would have cost $139.40 if purchased in March 1992. Generally, price indexes compare the cost of a given bundle of goods and services purchased at different times.[9]

The CPI is designed to measure changes in the cost of living for average urban households in the United States. Because it is based on consumption for the average household, it does not measure accurately the change in the cost of living for each and every household. Rich, poor, young, old, single, married, urban, and rural households typically consume goods in different proportions. An increase in air fares, for example, will raise the cost of living of a frequent traveler but not affect that of a nontraveling household.

The more an individual household's consumption pattern conforms to that of the typical pattern used to create a price index, the better the index will reflect changes in that household's cost of living.

By allowing us to compare the general price level at different times, a price index such as the CPI also allows us to measure the rate of inflation. For example, the value of the CPI in March 1992 was 139.4 and in March 1991 was 135.1. The *rate of inflation* during that one-year period, expressed in percentage terms, would be the change in the price level divided by the initial price level, times 100: $[(139.4 - 135.1)/135.1] \times 100 = 3.18$ percent.

When time periods are not exactly one year apart, changes in price levels are usually converted to *annual rates*, the average year-to-year percentage change in prices over the period measured. For example, the CPI in March 1992 was 139.4, and in December 1991 it was 138.2. During the three months separating December and March, the CPI rose by 0.87 percent. If the CPI continued to grow at 0.87 per three months for a whole year, the percentage increase over the year would be 3.5. Thus, over the period from December 1991 to March 1992 we say that the CPI was growing at an annual rate of 3.5 percent.[10] **[32]**

Inflation: The Historical Experience

Figure 23-6 shows the CPI and the inflation rate (measured by the annual rate of change in the CPI) from 1947 to 1991. What can we learn from Figure 23-6? First, we learn that the price level is constantly

---

[9] Details on how the CPI is constructed are provided in the appendix to this chapter.

[10] Notice that 3.5 is slightly more than 0.87 times 4. The reason for this is that the growth rate of 0.87 percent per quarter-year is *compounded* when the annual rate is calculated.

changing. Second, we learn that in only 2 out of the 44 observations did the price level fall; in the other 42 years the inflation rate was positive. The cumulative effect of this sequence of small, but repeated, price increases is quite dramatic; in 1991 the price level was over six times higher than it was in 1946.

Third, we learn that, although the long-term increasing trend stands out when we look at the price level, the short-term fluctuations stand out when we look at the inflation rate. From 1965 to 1974 inflation averaged 3.8 percent, whereas from 1975 to 1984 it averaged 8.5 percent! The sharp swings in the inflation rate in the late 1970s and the early 1980s were even more dramatic. The increase in the inflation rate into double-digit levels in 1974, and again in 1979, were associated with major shocks to the world prices of oil and foodstuffs, while the declines in inflation that followed were delayed responses to major recessions. (Note that even when the inflation rate *falls*, as it did in 1991, for example, the price level continues to rise as long as inflation remains *positive*.)

Why Inflation Matters

Money is the universal yardstick in our economy. We measure economic values in terms of money, and we use money to conduct our economic affairs. Things as diverse as wages, bank balances, the value of a house, and a university's endowment all are stated in terms of money. We value money, however, not for itself but for what we can purchase with it. The terms **purchasing power of money** and *real value of money* refer to the amount of goods and services that can be purchased with a given amount of money. A change in the price level affects us because it changes the real value of money.

The purchasing power of money is negatively related to the price level.

For example, if the price level doubles, a dollar will buy only one-half as much, whereas if the price level halves, a dollar will buy twice as much. Figure 23-6 shows that inflation has reduced the purchasing power of money over each of the last five decades.

If inflation reduces the real value of a given sum of money, it also reduces the real value of anything else whose price is *fixed* in money terms. Thus, the real value of a money wage, a savings and loan account, or the balance that is owed on a student loan is reduced by inflation.

FIGURE 23-6
Price Level and the Inflation Rate, 1947–1991

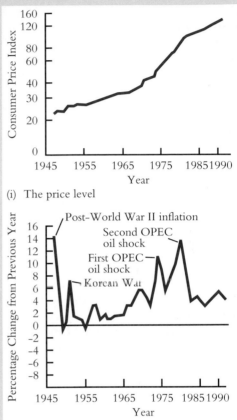

(i)   The price level

(ii)   Inflation rate

(i) The trend in the price level has been upward over the past half century. The data are for the Consumer Price Index from 1947 to 1991 with the average of 1982–1984 equal to 100. They are plotted on a semilog scale. The price level rose by 100 percent over the 25 years from 1947 to 1973. In the next 15 years, the price level rose by 250 percent.

(ii) The rate of inflation has varied from minus 1 percent to +14 percent since 1947. Prices fell dramatically during the onset of the Great Depression. They rose sharply during and after World War II and during the Korean War. The inflation rate was variable but had no discernible trend from the end of the Korean War to the mid-1960s. The period starting in the mid-1960s experienced a strong upward trend in the inflation rate. In 1983, however, the inflation rate fell to the lowest figure since the early 1970s, and it stayed in the 3–4 percent range through 1988. It rose above that range in 1990, due to the oil price increase at the onset of the war with Iraq, and then fell in 1991 due to the recession that began in 1990. (*Source*: Department of Labor, Bureau of Labor Statistics.)

The real effects of inflation depend to a great extent on whether or not the inflation comes as a surprise.

A fully anticipated inflation.   It is possible to imagine an inflation that has no real effects of any kind. What is required for this to happen is, first, that everyone who is making any sort of financial arrangement knows what the inflation rate will be over the life of the contract and, second, that *all* financial obligations be stated in real terms. The real behavior of the economy then would be exactly the same with, and without, an inflation. Say, for example, that both sides of a wage contract agree that wages should go up by 3 percent in real terms. If the inflation rate is expected to be zero, they would agree to a 3 percent increase in money wages. If a 10 percent inflation is expected, however, they would agree to a 13 percent increase in money wages. Ten percent would be needed to maintain the purchasing power of the money wages that would be paid, and 3 percent would be needed to bring about the desired increase in purchasing power.

Similarly, a loan contract would specify that the amount repaid on the loan be increased over the amount borrowed by the rate of inflation. Thus, if $100 is borrowed and the price level rises by 10 percent, then $110 would have to be returned (quite apart from any interest that might be paid on the loan). This would ensure that the real value of what is borrowed stays equal to the real value of what is returned.

Taxes would also have to be adjusted. For example, the personal exemption on the income tax (the amount of income that each person can exempt from taxation) would have to be increased by 10 percent to keep the real value of the exemption constant, given a 10 percent inflation rate.

The result of all this would be a 10 percent increase in everyone's money incomes and money assets, combined with a 10 percent increase in all money prices and all money liabilities. Nothing real would have changed. People's higher money incomes would buy the same amount as before, and the real value of their assets and liabilities would be unchanged.

Once everything has adjusted, any one price level works as well as any other price level.

This is just what we should expect, since it would indeed be magic if altering the number of zeros that we use when stating monetary values could change anything real.[11]

A completely unanticipated inflation.   At the opposite extreme from a fully anticipated inflation is a completely unanticipated inflation. No one sees it coming; no one is prepared to offset its consequences. The real value of all contracts that are specified in money terms will change unexpectedly. Who will gain and who will lose?

An unexpected inflation benefits anyone who has an obligation to pay out money and harms anyone who is entitled to receive money.

For example, consider a wage contract that specifies a wage increase of 3 percent on the assumption that the price level will remain constant. Both employers and employees expect that the purchasing power of wages paid will rise by 3 percent as a result of the new contract. Now assume, however, that the price level unexpectedly rises by 10 percent over the life of the wage contract. The 3 percent increase in money wages now means a reduction in the purchasing power of wages of about 7 percent. Employers gain because their wage payments represent a smaller part of the value of their output than they had expected. Workers lose because their wages represent a smaller receipt of purchasing power than they had expected.

People who have borrowed money will pay back a smaller real amount than they borrowed. By the same token, people who have lent money will receive back a smaller real amount than they lent. Say, for example, that Gerry lends Helen enough money to buy a medium-sized house, and the price level subsequently doubles. When Helen pays back the money that she borrowed, Gerry finds himself with only one-half of the amount now required to buy the house.

Wage earners and lenders will be able to adjust to the new price level when they make new contracts, but some people will be locked into their old money contracts for the rest of their lives. The extreme case is suffered by those who live on fixed money incomes. For example, pensions that are provided

---

11 For those of you who have studied microeconomics, this is another way of stating the point that *only relative prices matter* for resource allocation. If all prices rise by 10 percent, or by any other uniform percentage, relative prices are unchanged.

by the private sector often promise to pay a certain number of dollars per year for life. On retirement, this sum may look adequate, even generous. Twenty years later, however, inflation may have reduced its purchasing power to the poverty level. A family that retired on a fixed money income in 1971 would have found the purchasing power of that income reduced year by year, until in 1991, it would have been only 30 percent of its original value. To understand the impact of this, imagine being told that, for every dollar that you now spend, only $0.30 can be spent in the future.

Intermediate cases.   There are several reasons why virtually all real inflations fall somewhere between the two extremes (fully anticipated or complete surprise) that we have just discussed.

First, the inflation rate is usually variable and seldom foreseen exactly, even though its general course may be anticipated. Thus, the actual rate will sometimes be higher than expected—to the benefit of those who have contracted to pay money. At other times the inflation rate will be lower than expected—to the benefit of those who have contracted to receive money. Given the lack of certainty, different people will have different expectations.

Because it is hard to foresee accurately, inflation adds to the uncertainties of economic life. Highly variable inflation rates cause great uncertainty.

Second, even if the inflation rate is foreseen, all adjustments to it cannot occur at the same speed. As a result, inflation redistributes income, and it does so in a haphazard way. Those whose money incomes adjust more slowly than prices are rising will lose; those whose money incomes keep ahead of the inflation will gain.

Third, even if the inflation rate is foreseen, the full set of institutions that would be needed for everyone to avoid its consequences do not exist. For example, many private pension plans are stated in money terms. Employees have little choice but to take the only plan that their employers make available to them. Thus, even when inflation is foreseen, some people will wind up living on fixed nominal incomes and thus will see their real incomes erode over time.

Fourth, much of the tax system is defined in nominal money terms, causing its effects to vary with the price level. For example, machinery and equipment owned by businesses wear out with use. The tax code allows for this by permitting firms to deduct *depreciation allowances* from their income for tax purposes. The depreciation allowances are calculated as a certain fraction of the original purchase price of the machinery or equipment. If there has been a rapid inflation, the allowed depreciation may be much less than the real depreciation. This makes capital more expensive for firms and tends to reduce investment (and, as we shall see, economic growth) in the economy.

Indexation.   Some of the real effects of inflation can be avoided by indexing. **Indexation** means linking the payments that are made under the terms of a contract to changes in the price level. For example, a retirement pension might pay the beneficiary $15,000 per year starting in 1992, and it might specify that the amount paid will increase each year in proportion to the increase in the CPI. Thus, if the CPI rises by 10 percent between 1992 and 1993, the pension that is payable in 1991 would rise by 10 percent, to $16,500. If the CPI rose only 5 percent, the pension would also rise by 5 percent, to $15,750. In either case, indexing would hold the real purchasing power of the pension constant.

Indexing is potentially valuable as a defense against unforeseen changes in the price level, as a method of reducing uncertainty, and as a way of adapting institutions so that contracts can be made in real terms. In practice, however, indexing is used relatively little in the United States. Most of the tax code is not indexed, and the vast majority of contracts are written in nominal terms, putting them at risk for the consequences of unanticipated inflation.

The Interest Rate

If a bank lends you money, it will usually ask you to agree to a schedule for repayment. Furthermore, it will charge you interest for the privilege of borrowing the money. If, for example, you are lent $1,000 today, repayable in one year's time, you may also be asked to pay $10 per month in interest. This makes $120 in interest over the year, which can be expressed as an interest rate of 12 percent per annum [$(120/1,000) \times 100$ percent].

The **interest rate** is the price that is paid to borrow money for a stated period of time and is expressed as a percentage amount per dollar borrowed. For example, an interest rate of 12 percent per year means that the borrower must pay $0.12 per year for every dollar that is borrowed. (Unless explicitly indicated otherwise, interest rates are almost invariably expressed as the amount of interest per dollar per year.)

Just as there are many prices of goods in the economy, so there are many interest rates. The bank will lend money to an industrial customer at a lower rate than it will lend money to you—there is a lower risk of not being repaid. The rate charged on a loan that is not to be repaid for a long time will usually differ from the rate on a loan that is to be repaid quickly.

When economists speak of *the* interest rate, they mean a rate that is typical of all the various interest rates in the economy. Dealing with one interest rate suppresses much interesting detail. However, interest rates generally move together, so following the movement of one rate allows us to consider changes in the level of interest rates in general. The *prime rate* of interest, the rate that banks charge to their best business customers, may be thought of as *the* interest rate, since, when the prime rate changes, most other rates change in the same direction.

Interest Rates and Inflation

How does inflation affect the rate of interest? In order to begin developing an answer, imagine that your friend lends you $100 and that the loan is repayable in one year. The amount that you pay her for making this loan, measured in money terms, is the **nominal interest rate**. If you pay her $108 in one year's time, $100 will be repayment of the amount of the loan (which is called the *principal*) and $8 will be payment of the interest. In this case, the nominal interest rate is 8 percent $[(8/100) \times 100 \text{ percent}]$.

How much purchasing power has your friend gained or lost by making this loan? As we have already noted in our discussion of the consequences of inflation, the answer will depend on what happens to the price level during the year. Intuitively, the more the price level rises, the worse your friend will do, and the better the transaction will be for you. This result occurs because the more the price level rises, the less valuable are the dollars that you use to repay the loan. The **real rate of interest** measures the *real* return on a loan, in terms of purchasing power.

If the price level remains constant over the year, then the real rate of interest that your friend earns would also be 8 percent, because she can buy 8

percent more goods and services with the $108 that you repay her than with the $100 that she lent you. However, if the price level rises by 8 percent, the real rate of interest would be zero, because the $108 that you repay her buys the same quantity of goods as the $100 that she originally gave up. If she is unlucky enough to lend money at 8 percent in a year in which prices rise by 10 percent, the real rate of interest that she earns is minus 2 percent. The repayment of principal and nominal interest of 8 percent will purchase 2 percent *less*, in goods and services, than the original loan.

If lenders and borrowers are concerned with real costs, measured in terms of purchasing power, the nominal rate of interest will be set at the real rate to which they agree as a return on their money *plus* an amount to cover any expected rate of inflation. Consider a one-year loan that is meant to earn a real return to the lender of 5 percent. If the expected rate of inflation is zero, the nominal interest rate set for the loan will be 5 percent. If a 10 percent inflation is expected, the nominal interest rate will be 15 percent.

To provide a given expected real rate of interest, the nominal interest rate must be set at the desired real rate of interest plus the expected annual rate of inflation.

Because they often overlook this point, many people are surprised at the high nominal rates of interest that exist during periods of rapid inflation. For example, when the nominal interest rates rose drastically in 1980, many commentators expressed shock at the "unbearably" high rates. Most of them failed to notice that with inflation running at about 12 percent, an interest rate of 15 percent represented a real rate of only 3 percent. Had the Federal Reserve given in to the pressure to hold interest rates to the more "reasonable" level of 10 percent, it would have been imposing a *negative* real rate of interest. The purchasing power that lenders would get back, including interest, would be less than the purchasing power of the amount that was originally lent.

The burden of borrowing depends upon the real, not the nominal, rate of interest.

For example, a nominal interest rate of 8 percent, combined with a 2 percent rate of inflation, is a much greater real burden on borrowers than a nominal rate of 16 percent, combined with a 14 percent rate of inflation.

Figure 23-7 shows the nominal and the real rate of interest paid on short-term government borrowing since 1950. Interest rates were both high and volatile during the early part of the 1980s. During the latter part of the 1980s, rates fell somewhat and became somewhat less variable. During late 1991 and early 1992, both real and nominal interest rates fell, with real interest rates reaching their lowest levels in over a decade.

Why Interest Rates Matter

As we shall see in Chapter 30, real interest rates help to determine how much investment takes place in the economy. When real interest rates are high, it is costly to borrow, and there is less real investment than when interest rates are low. The greater is investment, the greater will be potential GDP in

the future. Thus, real interest rates, through their effect on investment, affect long-term growth and *future* living standards. Changes in investment can also cause swings in the business cycle. A slowdown in investment can trigger a slump; conversely, when investment increases sharply, GDP generally follows. Thus, via their effect on investment, real interest rates also affect unemployment and output in the short run. In addition, interest rates are an important determinant of the standard of living of many retired people who live on pensions. For them, the higher are real interest rates, the higher will be the level of their real income.

The International Economy

The two important indicators of the U.S. position in the international economy are the *exchange rate*, which measures the international value of the dollar,

FIGURE 23-7
Real and Nominal Interest Rates, 1950–1991

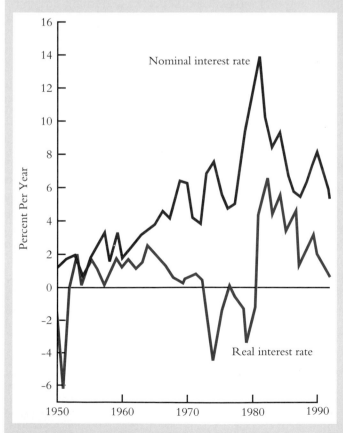

The inflationary trend over the last four decades has meant that the real interest rate has almost always been less than the nominal interest rate. The data for the nominal interest rate show the average rate of interest on three-month treasury bills in each year from 1950. The real interest is calculated in this case as the nominal interest rate minus the actual rate of inflation over the same period. With the exception of the early 1980s, the real interest rate has been below 3 percent throughout the period. Through much of the 1970s, the real interest rate was negative, indicating that the inflation rate exceeded the nominal interest rate. The 1980s saw real interest rates rise to heights that were unprecedented in the past. Later in the decade, as inflation moderated, both real and nominal interest rates fell.

and the *balance of payments*, which records virtually all international economic transactions.

The Exchange Rate

If you are going on a holiday to France, you will need French francs to pay for your purchases. Many of the larger banks, as well as any foreign exchange office, will make the necessary exchange of currencies for you; they will sell you francs in return for your dollars. If you get 5 francs for each dollar that you give up, then the two currencies are trading at a rate of 1 dollar = 5 francs or, what is the same thing, 1 franc = 0.2 dollars.

The exchange rate refers to the rate at which different national currencies are traded for each other.

As the preceding example shows, the exchange rate can be defined either as dollars per franc or francs per dollar. In this book we adopt the convention of defining the **exchange rate** between the U.S. dollar and any foreign currency as the quantity of the foreign currency that can be purchased with one U.S. dollar.[12] For example, at the beginning of April 1992, 1 U.S. dollar was worth 5.6375 francs. The value of the dollar in francs, then, was 5.6375, which we define to be the exchange rate between dollars and francs. (Put the other way, it cost 0.1774 U.S. dollars to buy 1 franc.)

The term **foreign exchange** refers to foreign currencies or claims to foreign currencies, such as bank deposits, checks, and promissory notes, that are payable in foreign money. The **foreign exchange market** is the market where foreign exchange is traded—at a price expressed by the exchange rate.

The value of the dollar. The **external value of the dollar** refers to its power to purchase foreign currencies. This is equal to the exchange rate, which measures the amount of foreign exchange that can be purchased for a dollar.[13]

Figure 23-8 shows two indicators of the external value of the U.S. dollar for the period since 1970.

The trend fall in the value of the dollar-yen exchange rate over most of the 1970s is really a reflection of the strength of the yen, which slowly rose in value against almost all of the world's currencies during the decade. From the point of view of any of these currencies (e.g., the British pound, the French franc, or the U.S. dollar), the strength of the yen appeared as a fall in the value of those currencies *relative to the yen*.

A more general indicator of the external value of the U.S. dollar is shown by the dollar's *trade-weighted exchange rate*. This measures the external value of the dollar against an average of the currencies of the major trading nations. The importance of each currency in the average is proportional to the amount of trade between the United States and the country using that currency.

Figure 23-8(ii) clearly shows the dramatic rise in the trade-weighted exchange rate in the first half of the 1980s, with the dollar rising to a high external value and then falling back again. These movements are very important to the recent economic history of the United States, as we shall see later in this book. One obvious effect was on the relative demand for imports and exports. When the external value of the dollar is high, foreign goods are relatively inexpensive for U.S. residents, and U.S. goods are relatively expensive for foreigners. Thus, the high value of the dollar in the mid-1980s was associated with a strong U.S. demand for imports, and a weak foreign demand for U.S. exports.

The Balance of Payments

In order to know what is happening to the course of international trade and international capital movements, governments keep an account of the transactions among countries. These accounts are called the **balance-of-payments accounts**. They record all international payments that are made for the buying and selling of both goods and services, as well as financial assets such as as stocks and bonds.

Figure 23-9 shows one part of the balance of payments that caused much controversy throughout the 1980s: the balance of payments on goods and services.[14] The balance, also called *net exports*, is

---

[12] Many economists define the exchange rate as the number of dollars needed to purchase a unit of the foreign currency. It is up to the student, then, to examine carefully the definition that is being used by a particular writer or speaker.

[13] The term *internal value of the dollar* is often used to refer to the dollar's purchasing power in the domestic market. We have already seen that the price level and the internal value of the dollar are negatively related. The higher is the price level, the lower is the purchasing power of a dollar.

[14] The trade balance that one hears about on the evening news is usually the *merchandise* trade account, which counts only trade in tangible goods, such as automobiles and farm products, and excludes trade in services, such as design engineering and marketing. There is no economic rationale for treating exports and imports of goods differently from trade in services, and in this book, unless otherwise specified, when we refer to the balance of trade we mean the balance on both goods and traded services.

FIGURE 23-8
Exchange Rates for the U.S. Dollar, 1970–1991

(i) Price of U.S. dollar in yen

(ii) Trade-weighted exchange rate of U.S. dollars

The trend over the past two decades has been for the U.S. dollar to fall in terms of Japanese yen while fluctuating around a more stable value in terms of an average of most important foreign currencies. Part (i) shows the number of Japanese yen needed to buy one U.S. dollar between 1970 and 1991. The fall in the value of the dollar relative to the yen is shown by the fact that one U.S. dollar could be bought for about 360 yen in 1970 and for only a little over 100 yen in 1991. Part (ii) shows the exchange rate of the U.S. dollar against all other major currencies, each being weighted by the importance of trade between the United States and expressed as an index number with 1973 equal to 100. Although interrupted by shorter-term fluctuations, the value of the dollar fell throughout the 1970s, then rose dramatically through the first half of the 1980s, and fell equally dramatically through the latter part of the decade. (*Source: Economic Report of the President*, 1992.)

the difference between the value of U.S. exports and the value of U.S. imports. As we can see from Figure 23-9, U.S. exports and imports rose fairly closely in step with each other until the second half of the 1970s, when a small, negative net export balance appeared and persisted throughout the latter half of the decade. In the 1980s the shortfall of exports below imports became enormous, exceeding $100 billion in several years. In spite of some fluctuations, these negative net exports persisted throughout the decade, although they fell somewhat starting in 1988.

As we shall see in later chapters, a negative balance of trade (imports exceed exports), which is also called a *trade deficit*, is not always undesirable. During the 1980s, however, many commentators expressed the fear that the large trade deficit indicated that there was a serious reduction in the ability of U.S. industry to compete against stiff-

ening foreign competition. Others argued that the trade deficit merely reflected the large government budget deficit that existed throughout the 1980s. The trend in the data is clear and striking. The interpretation of it must wait until we have studied macroeconomics.

Cycles and Trends

Why are the price level, national income, employment, and the value of the dollar what they are today? What causes them to change? These are some of the questions that macroeconomics seeks to answer.

Before we begin to study these questions, it is useful to emphasise a distinction that has been made repeatedly in this chapter—the distinction between *cycles* and *trends*. Both are crucial to understanding the economy and evaluating its ability to provide goods, services, and opportunities.

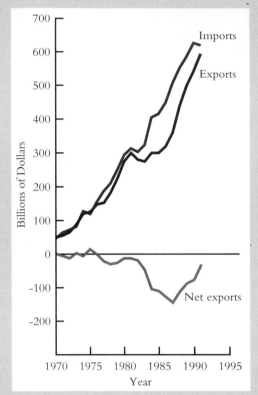

FIGURE 23-9
U.S. Imports, Exports, and Net Exports, 1970–1991

The 1980s saw an enormous increase in the U.S. trade deficit. The nominal values of imports and exports of goods and services rose greatly over the last two decades, due partly to price increases and partly to quantity increases. The world recession during the early 1980s was marked by a fall in both exports and imports. The trade deficit grew dramatically in the first half of the 1980s, when imports quickly returned to their rising trend, while exports were much slower to recover; they did not return to their 1981 level until 1987. Since 1987, the trade deficit has continued to fall. (*Source: Economic Report of the President*, 1992.)

Trends. The study of economic trends is the study of the economy over extended periods of time. Here we are primarily concerned with understanding the sources of long-term growth and the development of public policies that affect economic growth. Recent economic history has made the study of trends especially important. From the end of World War II until the late 1960s, output per hour of work in the United States grew at a rate of about 3 percent

a year. Since 1970 it has grown at a rate of about 1.3 percent a year. The rate for the 1980s is slightly lower. These differences matter: With productivity growing at 3 percent a year, living standards double in 23 years. At an annual growth of 1.3 percent a year, living standards double in 53 years. The trend in productivity and the trend in potential GDP that is determined by productivity growth and population growth are the key objects of study for the long term.

In studying long-term trends, we will simplify our task by ignoring deviations from trend.

For trend analysis, this simplification does not cost us much, because over the long haul, actual GDP moves quite closely with potential GDP. And, over long time periods, we are most interested in the evolution of the economy's *capacity* (i.e., its potential).

Cycles. While trends greatly affect economic welfare over the long haul, at any given time what matters more is how the economy is doing relative to its *current* potential. To examine this we study business cycles, shorter-term fluctuations away from trend growth. These fluctuations are important: When the economy is operating below its potential, there is generally unemployment, with its accompanying human suffering and economic waste. When the economy is operating above its potential, there are threats of inflation, with its accompanying economic distortions and (as we shall see) policy problems.

Changes in productivity and in the labor force dominate the long-term trends of output and employment, but productivity and the labor force generally change only slowly.

Our study of short-term movements in the economy is simplified by treating both the labor force and productivity as constant.

Under these assumptions, a rise in output means a rise in employment and a fall in unemployment: Output is positively associated with employment and negatively associated with unemployment. Taking productivity and the labor force as constant not only greatly simplifies our discussion but also reasonably approximates reality when we are dealing with the *short-term* behavior of the economy.

SUMMARY

1. Macroeconomics examines the behavior of such broad aggregates and averages as the price level, national income, potential national income, the GDP gap, employment, and unemployment.

2. The value of the total production of goods and services in a nation is called national product. Since production of output generates income in the form of claims on that output, the total is also referred to as *national income*. One of the most commonly used measures of national income is gross domestic product (GDP).

3. Nominal national income evaluates output in current prices. Real national income evaluates output in base period prices. Changes in real national income reflect changes in quantities of output produced.

4. Fluctuations of national income around its potential level are associated with the business cycle. Recoveries pass through peaks and turn into recessions, which in turn pass through troughs to become recoveries. Although these movements are systematic rather than random, they are by no means predictably regular.

5. Potential real national income measures the capacity of the economy to produce goods and services when factors of production are employed at their normal intensity of use. The GDP gap is the difference between potential and actual real national income.

6. The unemployment rate is the percentage of the labor force not employed but actively searching for a job. The labor force and employment have both grown steadily for the past half century. The unemployment rate fluctuates considerably from year to year. Unemployment imposes serious costs on the economy in the form of economic waste and human suffering.

7. The average price level is measured by a price index, which measures the cost of a set of goods in one year relative to their cost in an (arbitrary) base year.

8. The price level has displayed a continual upward trend since 1929. The inflation rate measures the rate of change of the price level. Although it fluctuates considerably, the inflation rate has been consistently positive.

9. Other important macroeconomic variables include nominal and real interest rates; exchange rates, which refer to the cost of U.S. dollars in terms of foreign currency; and the balance of payments, which is a record of all international transactions made by U.S. firms, households, and governments. The value of net exports is a part of the balance of payments that refers to the difference between the value of exports and the value of imports of goods and traded services. (The merchandise balance of trade refers only to the balance in traded goods.)

10. The dominant historical trends of the economy are growth of the price level, real output, and employment over the long term. This growth has never been entirely smooth; there have always been fluctuations in the price level, output, and unemployment around their trend growth rates. The study of growth is simplified by ignoring these fluctuations and focusing on the broad trends. The study of the fluctuations is simplified by assuming that the labor force and productivity do not change during the period being analyzed.

TOPICS FOR REVIEW

National product and national income

Real and nominal national income

Potential and actual national income and the GDP gap

Employment, unemployment, and labor force

The price level and rate of inflation

The exchange rate

The real and nominal interest rates

The balance of payments

The effects of anticipated and unanticipated inflation

DISCUSSION QUESTIONS

1. Classify as microeconomic or macroeconomic (or both) the issues that are raised in the following newspaper headlines.
   a. "Lettuce crop spoils as strike hits California lettuce producers."
   b. "Analysts fear rekindling of inflation as economy recovers toward full employment."
   c. "Index of Industrial Production falls by 4 points."
   d. "Price of bus rides soars in Centersville as city council withdraws transport subsidy."
   e. "A fall in the unemployment rate signals the beginning of the end of the recession in the Detroit area."
   f. "New computer technology brings falling prices and growing sales of microcomputers."
   g. "Rising costs of imported raw materials cause most U.S. manufacturers to raise prices."

2. Explain carefully what has happened to the CPI to justify each of the following newspaper headlines.
   a. "Prices on the rise again after a year of stability."
   b. "Inflation increases for three successive months."
   c. "President pleased at moderation in inflation rate."
   d. "Cost-of-living increases devastating pensioners."
   e. "Union leader warns that inflation is stabilizing at a disturbingly high level."

3. In his 1992 State of the Union Address, President Bush referred to inflation as a "thief." What might he have meant by this? How would you evaluate this view?

4. Most of the films on the list of the 10 largest money makers have been made in the recent past. Does this mean that the most successful films are the most recent ones?

5. Evaluate the following statements about unemployment.
   a. "Unemployment is a personal tragedy and a national waste."
   b. "No one needs to be unemployed these days; just look at the help wanted ads in the newspapers and the signs in the stores."
   c. "Unemployment insurance is a boondoggle for the lazy and unnecessary for the industrious."

6. How could you make a sure profit in a year in which the interest rate was 10 percent and you knew that the inflation rate was going to be 15 percent?

7. Use the current *Economic Report of the President* to discover the real interest rate in the latest year for which figures are available.

8. A friend's grandmother has just become a widow and has been left government bonds by her late husband as her only means of support. Explain to her why she cannot regard all of the interest that she receives as current income. (Hint: What will happen to her ability to purchase real goods and services each year if she does treat all of her interest receipts as current income and spends all of it each year?)

9. If you thought the inflation rate was going to be 10 percent next year, why should you be unwilling to lend money at 5 percent interest? Say 5 percent was all you could get and you had money that you did not want to spend for a year. Would you do better just to hold the money? What could you do that would be better than lending your money at 5 percent?

10. Output per hour of work fell between 1980 and 1992, but per capita GDP rose by about 1 percent a year over the same period. How could this have happened?

APPENDIX TO CHAPTER

23

How the CPI Is Constructed

Two important questions must be answered when any price index is constructed. First, what group of prices should be used? This depends on the index. The Consumer Price Index (CPI), which is calculated by the Bureau of Labor Statistics, covers prices of commodities that are commonly bought by households. Changes in the CPI are meant to measure changes in the typical household's *cost of living*. (Other indexes, such as the wholesale price index, cover the prices of different groups of commodities. The implicit deflators for GNP and GDP, as we have seen, cover all of the nation's output, not just consumer prices.)

Second, how should the movements in consumer prices be added up and summarized in one price index? If all prices change in the same proportion, this would not matter: A 10 percent rise in every price would mean a 10 percent rise in the average of all prices, no matter how the average was constructed. However, different prices usually change in different proportions. It then matters how much importance we give to each price change. Changes in the price of bread, for example, are much more important to the average consumer than changes in the price of caviar. In calculating a price index, each price is given a *weight* that reflects its importance.

Let us see how this is done for the CPI. Government statisticians periodically survey a representative group of households in what is called the Consumer Expenditure Survey. This shows how consumers spend their incomes. The average bundle of goods that is bought is determined, along with the proportion of expenditure that is devoted to each good. These proportions become the weights attached to the individual prices in calculating the CPI. As a result, the CPI weights rather heavily the prices of commodities on which consumers spend much of their income and weights rather lightly the prices of commodities on which consumers spend only a little of their income. Table 23A-1 provides a simple example of how these weights are calculated.

Once the weights are chosen, the average price can be calculated for each period. This is done, as shown in Table 23A-2, by multiplying each price by its weight and summing the resulting figures. However, a single average price is not informative. Suppose, for example, you were told that the average price of all goods that were bought by consumers last year was $89.35. "So what?" you might well ask, and the answer would be, "So, not very much; by itself, this tells you nothing useful." Now suppose you are told that this year's average price for the

---

TABLE 23A-1   Calculation of Weights for a Price Index

Commodity	Price	Quantity	Expenditure price × quantity	Proportional weight
A	$5	60	$300	0.50
B	1	200	200	0.33
C	4	25	100	0.17
Total			$600	1.00

The weights are the proportions of total expenditure that are devoted to each commodity. This simple example lists the prices of three commodities and the quantities bought by a typical household. Multiplying price by quantity gives expenditure on each, and summing these gives the total expenditure on all commodities. Dividing expenditure on each good by total expenditure gives the proportion of total expenditure that is devoted to each commodity, as shown in the last column. These proportions become the weights for the price indexes that are calculated in Table 23A-2.

TABLE 23A-2   Calculation of a Price Index

Commodity	Weight	Price 1980	Price 1985	Price 1990	Price × weight 1980	Price × weight 1985	Price × weight 1990
A	0.50	$5.00	$6.00	$14.00	$2.50	$3.00	$7.00
B	0.33	1.00	1.50	2.00	0.33	0.495	0.66
C	0.17	4.00	8.00	9.00	0.68	1.36	1.53
Total	1.00				$3.51	$4.855	$9.19

$$\text{Index} \quad 1980 \quad \frac{3.51}{3.51} \cdot 100 = 100$$

$$1985 \quad \frac{4.855}{3.51} \cdot 100 = 138.3$$

$$1990 \quad \frac{9.19}{3.51} \cdot 100 = 261.8$$

A price index expresses the weighted average of prices in the given year as a percentage of the weighted average of prices in the base year. The prices of the three commodities in each year are multiplied by the weights from Table 23A-1. Summing the weighted prices for each year gives the average price in that year. Dividing the average price in the given year by the average price in the base year and multiplying by 100 gives the price index for the given year. The index is, of course, 100 when the year is also taken as the given year, as is the case for 1980 in this example.

same set of consumers' purchases is $107.22. Now you know that, on average, prices paid by consumers have risen sharply over the year. In fact, the increase is 20 percent.[1]

The average for each period is divided by the value of the average for the base period and multiplied by 100. The resulting series is called an index number series; by construction, the base period value in this series equals 100. If prices in the next period average 20 percent higher, the index number for that period will be 120. A simple example of how these calculations are carried out is given in Table 23A-2.

Price indexes are constructed by assigning weights to reflect the importance of the individual items being combined. The value of the index is set equal to 100 in the base period.

Table 23A-2 shows the calculation of what is called a *fixed-weight index*. The weights are the proportion of income that is spent on the three goods in the base year. These weights are then applied to

the prices in each subsequent year. The value of the index in each year measures exactly how much the base-year bundle of goods would cost at that year's prices.[2] Fixed-weight indexes are easy to interpret, but problems arise with a fixed-weight index because consumption patterns change over the years. The fixed weights represent with decreasing accuracy the importance that consumers *currently* place on each of the commodities.

The CPI used to be calculated using fixed weights that were changed only every decade or so. Recently, however, there has been a change in this procedure. The Bureau of Labor Statistics now updates its Consumer Expenditure Survey continually. The weights used in the CPI are now an average of several past surveys, with the most recent one counting for 20 percent of the total weight. This avoids the problem of the fixed-weight index becoming steadily less representative of current expenditure patterns.

---

[1] The change is $17.87, which is 20 percent of the initial average price of $89.35.

[2] To verify this, calculate the total expenditure required to buy 60 units of commodity A, 200 units of commodity B and 25 units of commodity C in each of the three years for which price data are given in Table 23A-2. Divide the resulting amounts by $600, multiply by 100, and you will get exactly the index values shown in the table.

Measuring the Rate of Inflation

At the end of 1991 the CPI was 137.9 (the average of 1982–1984 = 100). This means that at the end of 1991 it cost just under 38 percent more to buy a representative bundle of goods than it did in the base period, which, in this case, is taken as the average of prices prevailing in the years 1982–1984. In other words, there was a 37.9 percent *increase* in the price level over that period as measured by the CPI. The *percentage change* in the cost of purchasing the bundle of goods that is covered by any index is thus the level of the index minus 100.

The *inflation rate* between any two periods of time is measured by the percentage increase in the relevant price index from the first period to the second period. In the rare event of a drop in the price level, we speak of a *deflation*. When the amount of the rise in the price level is being measured from the base period, all that needs to be done is to subtract the two indexes, as we have just done. When two other periods are being compared, we must be careful to express the change as a percentage of the index in the first period.

If we let P_1 indicate the value of the price index in the first period and P_2 its value in the second period, the inflation rate is merely the difference between the two, expressed as a percentage of the value of the index in the first period:

$$\textbf{Inflation rate} = \frac{(P_2 - P_1)}{P_1} \times 100$$

(When P_1 is the base period, its value is 100, and the expression shown above reduces to $P_2 - 100$.) In other cases the full calculation must be made. For example, the index went from 133.8 in December 1990 to 137.9 in December 1991, indicating a rate of inflation of 3.1 percent over the year. The rise of 4.1 points in the index is a 3.1 percent rise over its initial value of 133.8

If the two values being compared are not a year apart, it is common to convert the result to an *annual rate*. For example, the CPI was 135.2 in April 1991 and 135.6 in May 1991. This is an increase of 0.295 percent over the month $[(0.4/135.2) \times 100]$. It is also an *annual rate* of approximately 3.55 percent (0.295 percent $\times$ 12) over the year.[3] This means that *if* the rate of increase that occurred between April and May 1991 did persist for a year, the price level would rise by approximately 3.55 percent over the year.

---

[3] We say *approximately* because a 0.295 percent rise each month that is *compounded* for 12 months will give rise to an increase over the year that is greater than 3.55 percent. The appropriate procedure is to increase the index in January by 0.295 twelve times rather than just to multiply it by 12. The two results are the difference between simple and compound interest rates. (See MN 32.)

24

The Measurement of Macroeconomic Variables

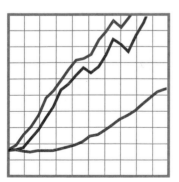

O ur goal is to understand the macroeconomic events that were outlined in the previous chapter. Our first step is to look in some detail at the measurement and interpretation of variables relating to national output and national income.[1] We need to understand these variables in some detail in order to develop the concepts used in macroeconomic theory and to interpret measures that play a prominent role in everyday discussion.

National Output Concepts

We are concerned in this chapter with measuring the nation's output and the income that is generated by its production. We start by asking what we mean by output.

Value Added as Output

It may seem strange to ask what we mean by output. Surely the town bakery knows what it produces, and if General Motors does not know its own output, what does it know? If each firm knows the value of its total output, the national income statisticians simply have to add up each separate output value to get the nation's output—or is that really all?

The reason that obtaining a total for the nation's output is not quite that simple is that one firm's output is often another firm's input. The local baker uses flour that is the output of the flour milling company, and the flour milling company, in turn, uses wheat that is the farmer's output. What is true for bread is true for most commodities.

Production occurs in stages: Some firms produce outputs that are used as inputs by other firms, and these other firms in turn produce outputs that are used as inputs by yet other firms.

If we merely added up the market values of all outputs of all firms, we would obtain a total that was greatly in excess of the value of the economy's actual output.

The local baker provides an example. If we added the total value of the sales of the wheat farmer, the flour mill, and the baker, we would be counting the value of the wheat three times, the value of the milled flour twice, and the value of the bread once.

---

[1] We saw in Chapter 23 how the important labor force variables are measured. Measurement of the other important macroeconomic phenomena discussed in that chapter follows directly from measurement of income and output, which is the main subject of this chapter. The construction of price indexes is discussed in the Appendix to Chapter 23.

The error that would arise in estimating the nation's output by adding all sales of all firms is called **double counting**. *Multiple counting* would be a better term, since if we added up the values of all sales, the same output would be counted every time that it was sold by one firm to another.

The problem of double counting is solved by distinguishing between two types of output. **Intermediate goods** are outputs of some firms that are in turn inputs for other firms. **Final goods** are goods that are not, in the period of time under consideration, used as inputs by other firms. The term **final demand** refers to the purchase of final goods for consumption, for investment (including inventory accumulation), for use by governments, and for export. It does not include goods that are purchased by firms for use as inputs during the period under consideration.

If the sales of firms could be readily disaggregated into sales for final use and sales for further processing by other firms, measuring total output would still be straightforward. It would equal the value of all *final goods* produced by firms, excluding all intermediate goods. However, when USX (formerly, U.S. Steel) sells steel to the Ford Motor Company, it does not care, and usually does not know, whether the steel is for final use (say, construction of a warehouse that will not be sold by Ford) or whether it is for use as part of an automobile that will be sold again.[2] The problem of double counting must therefore be resolved in some other manner.

To avoid double counting, statisticians use the important concept of **value added**. Each firm's value added is the value of its output minus the value of the inputs that it purchases from other firms (and which in turn were the outputs of those other firms). Thus, a steel mill's value added is the value of the steel it produces minus the value of the ore that it buys from the mining company, the value of the electricity and fuel oil that it uses, and the values of all other inputs that it buys from other firms. A bakery's value added is the value of the baking products that it produces minus the value of the flour and other inputs that it buys from other firms.

The total value of a firm's output is the gross value of its output. The firm's value added is the net value of its output. It is this latter figure that is the firm's true contribution to the nation's total output, representing the firm's own efforts to add to the value of what it takes in as inputs.

Value added is useful in avoiding the statistical problem of double counting; it is the correct measure of each firm's contribution to total output, the amount of market value that is produced by that firm.

The concept of value added is further illustrated in Box 24-1. In this simple example, as in all more complex cases, the value of the nation's total output of final goods is obtained by summing all the individual values added.

The sum of all values added in an economy is a measure of the economy's total output. This measure of total output is called gross domestic product (GDP). It is a measure of all final output that is produced by all productive activity in the economy.

Table 24-1 gives the GDP by major industry groups for the U.S. economy in 1989.

National-Income Accounting: Gross Domestic Product

The measures of national income and national product that are used in the United States derive from an accounting system called the National Income and Product Accounts (NIPA). The accounts, produced by the Bureau of Economic Analysis of the Department of Commerce, provide us with a framework for analyzing the generation of national income. The National Income and Product Accounts are not simply collections of economic data. They have a logical structure, based on the simple yet important idea that whenever money is spent on national product, it generates an equivalent amount of national income.

Look again at Figure 23-1, page 461, which shows the circular flow of expenditure and income. The right half of the figure focuses on expenditure to purchase the nation's output in product markets, and the left half focuses on factor markets through which the receipts of producers are distributed to factors of production.

---

[2] Even in our earlier example of bread, a bakery cannot be sure that its sales are for final use, since the bread may be further "processed" by a restaurant prior to its final sale to a customer for eating.

Box 24-1

Value Added Through Stages of Production

Because the output of one firm often becomes the input of other firms, the total value of goods sold by all firms greatly exceeds the value of the output of final products. This general principle is illustrated by a simple example in which firm R starts from scratch and produces goods (raw materials) valued at $100; the firm's value added is $100. Firm I purchases raw materials valued at $100 and produces semimanufactured goods that it sells for $130. Its value added is $30 because the

value of the goods is increased by $30 as a result of the firm's activities. Firm F purchases the semimanufactured goods for $130, works them into a finished state, and sells the final products for $180. Firm F's value added is $50. The value of the final goods, $180, is found either by counting only the sales of firm F or by taking the sum of the values added by each firm. This value is much smaller than the $410 that we would obtain if we merely added up the market value of the commodities sold by each firm.

	Transactions at three different stages of production				
	Firm R	*Firm I*	*Firm F*		*All firms*
A. Purchases from other firms	$ 0	$100	$130	$230	Total interfirm sales
B. Purchases of factors of production (wages, rent, interest, profits)	100	30	50	180	Total value added
A + B = value of product	$100	$130	$180	$410	Total value of all sales

Corresponding to the two halves of the circular flow are two ways of measuring national income: by determining the value of what is produced and by determining the value of the incomes generated by production. Both measures yield the same total, which is called **gross domestic product (GDP)**.[3] When it is calculated by adding up the total expenditure for each of the main components of final output, the result is called *GDP on the expenditure side*. When it is calculated by adding up all the incomes generated by the act of production, it is called *GDP on the income side*.

The conventions of double-entry bookkeeping require that all value produced must be accounted

for by a claim that someone has to that value. Thus, the two values calculated from the income and the expenditure sides are identical conceptually and differ in practice only because of errors of measurement. Any discrepancy arising from such errors is then reconciled so that one common total is given as *the* measure of GDP. Both calculations are of interest, however, because each gives a different and useful breakdown. Also, having two independent ways of measuring the same quantity, in this case the sum of values added in the economy, provides a useful check on statistical procedures and on unavoidable errors in measurement.

GDP from the Expenditure Side

GDP for a given year is calculated from the expenditure side by adding up the expenditures needed to

---

[3] Each of these totals must also equal the sum of value added in the economy, as discussed in the preceding section.

TABLE 24-1   Gross Domestic Product, 1989

	Billions of dollars	Percent of GDP
Value added by sector		
Agriculture, forestry, and fisheries	113.5	2.2
Mining	80.3	1.5
Manufacturing	966	18.7
Construction	247.7	4.8
Transportation and public utilities	460.9	8.9
Retail and wholesale trade	825.5	16.0
Financial insurance and real estate	896.7	17.3
Services	970.5	18.8
Government and government enterprises	619.3	12.0
Statistical discrepancy	−17.0	
GDP	5,163.4	100.0
Investment income received from nonresidents less investment income paid to nonresidents	37.6	
GNP	5,201.0	

Source: Survey of Current Business, 1991.

GDP measures total output produced in the United States by summing the value added by each industry. As can be seen, manufacturing and trade (retail and wholesale) are major components of GDP, contributing 18.7 and 16.0 percent, respectively. GDP measures output *produced in,* and hence income *generated in,* the United States. To obtain GNP, which is income *earned by U.S. residents,* it is necessary, as pointed out on page 492 of the text, to subtract income generated in the United States but earned by foreign residents and to add income generated abroad but earned by U.S. residents.

purchase the final output produced in that year. Total expenditure on final output is the sum of four broad categories of expenditure: consumption, investment, government, and net exports. In the following chapters we will discuss in considerable detail the causes and consequences of movements in each of these four expenditure categories. Here we define what they are and how they are measured. Throughout it is important to remember that they are exhaustive: They are defined in such a way that *all* expenditure on final output falls into one of the four categories.

Consumption Expenditure

Consumption expenditure includes expenditure on all goods and services produced and sold to their final users during the year. It includes services, such as haircuts, medical care, and legal advice; nondurable goods, such as fresh meat, clothing, cut flowers, and fresh vegetables; and durable goods, such as cars, television sets, and air conditioners. We denote actual, measured, consumption expenditure by the symbol C^a.

Investment Expenditure

Investment expenditure is expenditure on the production of goods not for present consumption, including inventories, capital goods such as factories, machines and warehouses, and residential housing. Such goods are called **investment goods**.

Inventories.   Almost all firms hold stocks of their inputs and their own outputs. These stocks are called **inventories**. Inventories of inputs and unfinished materials allow firms to maintain a steady stream of production in spite of short-term fluctuations in the deliveries of inputs bought from other firms. Inventories of outputs allow firms to meet orders in spite of temporary fluctuations in the rate of output or sales.

Inventories require an investment of the firm's money, since the firm has paid for the goods but has not sold them yet. An accumulation of inventories counts as current investment because it represents goods produced but not used for current consumption. A drawing down, often called a *decumulation,* counts as disinvestment because it represents a reduction in the stock of finished goods that are available to be sold.

Additions to inventories are a part of the economy's production of investment goods. These goods are included in the national-income accounts at market value, which includes the wages and other costs that the firm incurred in producing them and the profit that the firm will make when they are sold. Thus, in the case of inventories of a firm's own output, the expenditure approach measures what will have to be spent to purchase the inventories when they are sold rather than what has so far been spent to produce them.

Plant and equipment.   All production uses capital goods, which are manufactured aids to production, such as tools, machines, and factory buildings. The economy's total quantity of capital goods is called the **capital stock**. Creating new capital goods is an act of investment and is called *business fixed investment*, or the shortened form, **fixed investment**.

Residential investment.   A house or an apartment building is a durable asset that yields its utility over a long period of time. This meets the definition of investment that we gave earlier, so housing construction is counted as investment expenditure rather than as consumption expenditure. When a household purchases a house from the builder, an existing asset is transferred, and the transaction is not a part of national income.

Gross and net investment. The total investment that occurs in the economy is called **gross investment**. Gross investment is divided into two parts: replacement investment and net investment. **Replacement investment** is the amount of investment that just maintains the level of existing capital stock; it is called the **capital consumption allowance** or simply **depreciation**. Gross investment minus replacement investment is **net investment**. Positive net investment increases the economy's total stock of capital, while replacement investment keeps the existing stock intact by replacing what has been used up.

All of gross investment is included in the calculation of national income. This is because all investment goods are part of the nation's total output, and their production creates income (and employment) whether the goods produced are a part of net investment or are merely replacement investment. Actual total investment expenditure is denoted by the symbol I^a.

Government Purchases of Goods and Services

When governments provide goods and services that households want, such as roads and air traffic control, it is obvious that they are adding to the sum total of valuable output in the same way as do private firms that produce the trucks and airplanes that use the roads and air lanes. With other government activities, the case may not seem so clear. Should expenditures by the federal government to send a rocket to Jupiter or to pay a civil servant to refile papers from a now defunct department be regarded as contributions to national income? Some people believe that many (or even most) activities "up in Washington" or "down at City Hall" are wasteful, if not downright harmful. Others believe that it is governments, not private firms, that produce many of the important things of life, such as education and pollution control.

National-income statisticians do not speculate about which government expenditures are worthwhile. Instead they include all government purchases of goods and services as part of national income. (Government expenditure on investment goods is included as government expenditure rather than investment expenditure.) Just as the national product includes, without distinction, the outputs of both gin and Bibles, it also includes bombers and the upkeep of parks, along with the services of CIA agents, senators, and even IRS investigators. Actual government purchases of goods and services is denoted by the symbol G^a.

Government output typically is valued at cost rather than at the market value. In many cases there is really no choice. What, for example, is the market value of the services of a court of law? No one knows. We do know, however, what it costs the government to provide these services, so we value them at their cost of production.

Although valuing at cost is the only possible way to measure many government activities, it does have one curious consequence. If, due to an increase in productivity, one civil servant now does what two used to do, and the displaced worker shifts to the private sector, the government's contribution to national income will register a decline. On the other hand, if two workers now do what one worker used to do, the government's contribution will rise. Both changes could occur even though what the government actually does has not changed. This is an inevitable but curious consequence of measuring the value of the government's output by the cost of the factors, mainly labor, that are used to produce it.

It is important to recognize that only government *expenditure on currently produced goods and services* is included as part of GDP. A great deal of government expenditure does not, in fact, count as part of GDP. For example, when a government agency makes social security payments to a retired person, the government is not purchasing any currently produced goods or services from the retiree. The payment itself adds neither to employment of factors nor to total output. The same is true of payments on account of unemployment insurance, welfare, and interest on the national debt (which transfers income from taxpayers to holders of government bonds). All such payments are examples of **transfer payments**, which are government expenditures that are not made in return for currently produced goods and services. They are not a part of expenditure on the nation's total output and therefore are not included in GDP.[4]

---

[4] Of course, the recipients of transfer payments often choose to spend their money on consumption expenditure. Such expenditure then counts as consumption, and thus as part of GDP, in the same way as any other consumption expenditure.

Thus, when we refer to government purchases as part of national income or use the symbol G^a, we include all government expenditure on currently produced goods and services, and we *exclude* all government transfer payments. (The term *government outlays* is often used to describe all government spending, including transfer payments.)

Net Exports

The fourth category of aggregate expenditure, and one that is increasingly important to the U.S. economy, arises from foreign trade. How do imports and exports influence national income?

Imports. A country's national income is the total value of final commodities produced in that country. If your cousin spends $12,000 on a car that was made in Japan, only a small part of that value will represent expenditure on U.S. production. Some of it represents payment for the services of the U.S. dealers and for transportation; the rest is the output of Japanese firms and expenditure on Japanese products. If you take your next vacation in Italy, much of your expenditure will be on goods and services produced in Italy and thus will contribute to Italian GDP.

Similarly, when a U.S. firm makes an investment expenditure on a U.S.-produced machine tool that was made partly with imported raw materials, only part of the expenditure is on U.S. production; the rest is expenditure on the production by the countries that are supplying the raw materials. The same is true for government expenditure on such things as roads and dams; some of the expenditure is for imported materials, and only part of it is for domestically produced goods and services.

Consumption, investment, and government expenditures all have an import content. To arrive at total expenditure on U.S. products, we need to subtract from total U.S. expenditure any expenditure on imports, which is given the symbol IM^a.

Exports. If U.S. firms sell goods to German households, the goods are a part of German consumption expenditure but also constitute expenditure on U.S. output. Indeed, all goods and services that are produced in the United States and sold to foreigners must be counted as part of U.S. production and income; they are produced in the United States, and they create incomes for the U.S. residents who produce them. They are not purchased by U.S. residents, however, so they are not included as part of C^a, I^a, or G^a. Therefore, to arrive at the total value of expenditure on U.S. domestic product, it is necessary to add in the value of U.S. exports. Actual exports are denoted by the symbol X^a.

It is customary to group actual imports and actual exports together as **net exports**. Net exports are defined as total exports minus total imports ($X^a - IM^a$), which we will also denote NX^a. When the value of U.S. exports exceeds the value of U.S. imports, the net export term is positive. When, as in recent years, the value of imports exceeds the value of exports, the net export term becomes negative.

Total Expenditures

Gross domestic product from the expenditure side is the sum of the four expenditure categories that we have just discussed. These data are shown in Table 24-2 for the United States in 1991.

GDP, calculated from the expenditure side, is the sum of consumption, investment, government, and net export expenditures.

GDP from the Income Side

The production of a nation's output generates income. Labor must be employed, land must be rented, and capital must be used. The calculation of GDP

TABLE 24-2   Components of GDP from the Expenditure Side, 1991

Expenditure category	Billions of dollars	Percent of GDP
Consumption	3,889.1	68.5
Government	1,087.5	19.2
Investment	726.7	12.8
Net exports	−30.7	−0.5
	5,672.6	100

Source: Economic Report of the President, 1992.

GDP measured from the expenditure side of the national accounts gives the size of the major components of aggregate expenditure. Consumption was by far the largest expenditure category, equal to more than two-thirds of GDP. In 1991 net exports were negative, so that the other three expenditure categories added up to slightly *more* than the total GDP.

from the income side involves adding up factor incomes and other claims on the value of output until all of that value is accounted for. We have already noted that because all value produced must be owned by someone, the value of production must equal the value of income claims generated by that production.

Factor Payments

National-income accountants distinguish four main components of factor incomes: wages, rent, interest, and profits.

Wages. Wages and salaries (which national-income accountants call *compensation to employees*, but which are usually just called *wages*) are the payment for the services of labor. Wages include take-home pay, taxes withheld, social security, pension fund contributions, and other fringe benefits. In total, wages represent that part of the value of production that is attributable to labor.[5]

Rent. Rent is the payment for the services of land and other factors that are rented. For the purposes of national-income accounting, home owners are viewed as renting accommodations from themselves. The amount of rent in the GDP thus includes payments for rented housing plus "imputed rent" for the use of owner-occupied housing. This allows national-income measures to reflect the value of all housing services used, whether or not the housing is owned by its user.

Interest. Interest includes interest that is earned on bank deposits, interest that is earned on loans to firms, and miscellaneous other investment income.

Profits. Some profits are paid out as **dividends** to owners of firms; the rest are retained for use by firms. The former are called *distributed profits*, and the latter are called *undistributed profits* or *retained earnings*. Both distributed and undistributed profits are included in the calculation of GDP. For accounting purposes, total profits are reported in two separate categories—corporate profits and incomes of

unincorporated businesses (mainly small businesses, farmers, partnerships, and professionals).

Profits and interest together represent the payment for the use of capital—interest for borrowed capital and profits for capital contributed by the owners of firms.

Nonfactor Payments

Indirect business taxes. An important claim on the market value of output arises out of indirect business taxes, which are taxes on the production and sale of goods and services. In the United States the most important indirect business taxes are retail sales taxes.

If, for example, a good's market price of $10.00 includes $0.50 in sales taxes, only $9.50 is available as income to factors of production. Fifty cents worth of market value represents some government's claim on that value. When adding up income claims to determine GDP, it is therefore necessary to include that part of the total market value of output that is the government's claim exercised through its taxes on goods and services.

Subsidies. It is also necessary to subtract government subsidies on goods and services, since these payments allow incomes to *exceed* the market value of output. Suppose, for example, that a municipal bus company spends $150,000 producing bus rides and covers its costs by selling $140,000 in fares and obtaining a $10,000 subsidy from the local government. The total income that the company will generate from its production is $150,000, but the total market value of its output is only $140,000, with the difference made up by the subsidy. To get from total income to total output, we must subtract the amount of the subsidy.

Net domestic product. Adding indirect business taxes to the four components of factor incomes and subtracting subsidies gives **net domestic product**. Taxes and subsidies often are combined into a single term, called *indirect taxes net of subsidies*.

Net domestic product equals the sum of wages, rent, interest, profits, and indirect taxes net of subsidies.

Depreciation. Another component on the income side arises from the distinction between net and gross investment. One claim on the value of final output is depreciation, or capital consumption allowance.

---

[5] The concepts of wages, rent, interest, and profits that are used in macroeconomics do not correspond exactly to the concepts with the same names that are used in microeconomics, but the details of the differences need not detain us.

Depreciation is the value of capital that has been used up in the process of producing final output. It is part of gross profits, but, being that part needed to compensate for capital used up in the process of production, it is not part of net profits. Hence, depreciation is not income earned by any factor of production. Instead it is value that must be reinvested just to maintain the existing stock of capital equipment.

Total Product

Adding depreciation to net domestic product gives **gross domestic product**.

From the income side, GDP is the sum of the factor incomes that are generated in the process of producing final output *plus* indirect taxes net of subsidies *plus* depreciation.

The various components of the income side of the GDP in the U.S. economy in 1991 are shown in Table 24-3. Note that one of the terms in the table is called *statistical discrepancy*; this is a "fudge factor" to make sure that the independent measures of income and product come to the same total. Statistical discrepancy is a clear indication that national income and product accounting is not an error-free science. Although national income and the value of national product are conceptually identical, in practice both are measured with error.

Box 24-2 provides a further discussion of the way in which arbitrary classification decisions, inherent in any accounting scheme, affect measures of national income and national product.

GDP and GNP

Until 1991 the U.S. national-income accounts were oriented toward providing estimates of **gross national product (GNP)** rather than GDP. The change was made in the interest of international standardization (almost all of the other countries of the world, as well as the United Nations system of international accounts, use GDP to measure national income). As is shown in Table 24-3, in 1991 GNP was about $13.2 billion, or 0.2 percent, greater than GDP. However, there is good reason to believe that sometime during the decade of the 1990s GDP will surpass GNP.

The difference between GDP and GNP is the difference between *income produced* and *income received*. GDP measures the total output *produced in the United*

TABLE 24-3 Components of GDP from the Income Side, 1991

Income component	Billions of dollars	Percent of GDP
Compensation to employees	3,388.2	60
Business income	686.8	12
Capital consumption allowance	622.9	11
Indirect business taxes net of subsidies	501.6	9
Interest	480.2	8
Rental income	−12.7	—
Statistical discrepancy	+18.8	—
GNP	5,685.8	100
Investment income paid to nonresidents less investment income received from nonresidents	−13.2	
GDP	5,672.6	

Source: Economic Report of the President, 1992.

GDP measured from the income side of the accounts gives the size of the major components of the income that is generated by producing the nation's output. The largest category, equal to 60 percent of GDP, was compensation to employees, which includes wages and salaries plus employers' contributions to unemployment insurance, pensions, and other similar schemes. Business income includes incomes of both corporations and unincorporated businesses. The capital consumption allowance is that part of the earnings of businesses that is needed to replace capital used up during the year.

States and the total income generated as a result of that production. However, the total income received by U.S. residents differs from GDP for two reasons. Some U.S. production creates factor income for foreigners who have previously invested in the United States or who sell services to producers in the United States. For example, the profits generated by the Honda factory in Marysville, Ohio, are income from production in the United States (part of GDP), but these profits are not received by U.S. residents and thus are not part of GNP. (Wages earned in the Marysville plant count as both GDP and GNP. They are income earned in the United States by U.S. residents.)

At the same time, many U.S. residents earn income as a result of foreign investments and factor services sold abroad. Profits on Chrysler plants in Canada are an example, as are the incomes of U.S.

Box 24-2

The Significance of Arbitrary Decisions

National-income accounting practices contain many arbitrary decisions. Goods that are finished and held in inventories are valued at market value, thereby anticipating their sale, even though the actual sales price may not be known. In the case of a Ford in a dealer's showroom, this practice may be justified because the *value* of this Ford is perhaps virtually the same as that of an identical Ford that has just been sold to a customer. However, what is the correct market value of a half-finished house or an unfinished novel? Accountants arbitrarily treat goods in process at cost (rather than at market value) if the goods are being made by business firms. They ignore completely the value of the novel-in-progress. The arbitrary nature of these decisions is inevitable: Because people must arrive at some practical compromise between consistent definitions and measurable magnitudes, any decision will be somewhat arbitrary.

The definition of final goods provides further examples. Business investment expenditures are treated as final products, as are all government purchases. Intermediate goods purchased by business for further processing are not treated as final products. Thus, when a firm buys a machine or a truck, the purchase is treated as a final good; when it buys a ton of steel, the steel is treated as a raw material that will be used as an input into the firm's production process. If the steel sits in inventory, however, it is regarded as a business investment and thus *is* a final good.

Such arbitrary decisions surely affect the size of measured GDP. Does it matter? The surprising answer, for many purposes, is no. In any case, it is wrong to believe that just because a statistical measure falls short of perfection (as all statistical measures do), it is useless. Crude measures often give estimates to the right order of magnitude, and substantial improvements in sophistication may make only second-order improvements in these estimates.

In the third century, for example, the Alexandrian astronomer Eratosthenes measured the angle of the sun at Alexandria at the moment that it was directly overhead 500 miles south at Aswan, and he used this angle to calculate the circumference of the earth to within 15 percent of the distance as measured today by the most advanced measuring devices. For the knowledge he wanted—the approximate size of the earth—his measurement was satisfactory, even though it would have been disastrously inadequate for launching a modern earth satellite.

Absolute figures mean something in general terms, although they cannot be taken seriously to the last dollar. In 1991 U.S. GDP was measured as $5,672.6 billion. It is certain that the market value of all production in the United States in that year was neither $100 billion nor $10,000 billion, but it might well have been $6,000 billion or $5,200 billion had different measures been defined with different arbitrary decisions built in.

International and intertemporal comparisons, though tricky, may be meaningful if they are based on measures that contain roughly the same arbitrary decisions. U.S. per capita GDP is a little more than three times the Spanish per capita GDP and 22 percent higher than the Japanese per capita GDP. Other measures might differ, but it is unlikely that any measure would reveal that either the Spanish or the Japanese per capita GDP was higher than the per capita GDP in the United States. U.S. output grew at 2.8 percent per year for the 30 years following World War II; it is unlikely that another measure of output would have indicated a 6 percent increase. Further, the Japanese output grew at about 9 percent per year over the same period. It is inconceivable that another measure would change the conclusion that Japanese national output rose faster than U.S. national output in recent decades.

oilfield workers who helped to extinguish oil fires in Kuwait following the Gulf War in 1991. Income accruing to U.S. citizens from activities undertaken abroad are part of GNP but are not part of GDP.

The relative sizes of GDP and GNP depend primarily on the balance between income from U.S. investments abroad and income from foreign investments in the United States. Until the mid-1980s the United States was a net creditor country. This meant that the value of foreign-based assets owned by U.S. residents exceeded the value of U.S.-based assets owned by foreigners. As a result, the foreign-generated incomes received by U.S. residents exceeded the U.S.-generated incomes going to foreigners, making U.S. GNP exceed GDP. Income earned by U.S. residents exceeded the value of U.S. domestic output.

In the 1980s foreign investment in the United States soared. Many economists pointed to the federal government's large budget deficits as the reason for this dramatic change. Whatever the reasons—and we shall study these in a later chapter—by the end of the decade the United States had, by most standard measures, become the world's largest net debtor country in the sense that the value of U.S.-based assets owned by foreigners greatly exceeded the value of foreign-based assets owned by U.S. residents. As a result, U.S. GNP may soon fall below its GDP. U.S. residents then will earn incomes that are less than the value of U.S. output. In the meantime, U.S. assets abroad earn higher returns than foreign assets in the United States, with the result that the smaller stock of U.S.-owned foreign assets is earning more current income than the larger stock of foreign-owned U.S. assets.

Disposable Personal Income

Both GDP and GNP are important measures of overall economic activity and of national income. Most important to consumers, however, is **disposable personal income**, the part of national income that is available to households to spend or to save. The easiest way to calculate disposable personal income is to subtract from GNP the parts of the GNP that are not available to households. Thus, we must subtract capital consumption allowances, taxes net of subsidies, retained earnings, and interest paid to institutions. However, having subtracted taxes, we need to add back in transfer payments made to households, such as social security pensions. In 1990 GDP was $5,514 billion. Net factor payments from the rest of the world were $11 billion, yielding a GNP

of $5,525 billion. Capital consumption allowances, retained earnings, and other deductions added up to $959 billion. Taxes were $1,192 billion, and transfers (added back in) were $685 billion, leaving disposable income of $4,059 billion, which represented 74 percent of GDP and 82 percent of net domestic product.

Disposable personal income is GNP *minus* any part of it that is not actually paid to households *minus* personal income taxes paid by households *plus* transfer payments received by households.

Real and Nominal Measures

In Chapter 23 (page 460) we distinguished between real and nominal measures of national income and output. When we add up money values of outputs, expenditures, or incomes, we end up with what are called *nominal values*. Suppose we found that nominal GDP rose by 73 percent between 1982 and 1990. If we wanted to compare *real GDP* in 1990 to that in 1982, we would need to determine how much of that 73 percent nominal increase was due to increases in prices and how much was due to increases in quantities produced. Although there are many possible ways of doing this, the underlying principle is always the same: The value of output, expenditure, and income in each period is computed using a common set of *base period prices*. When this is done, real output, expenditure, or income is measured in *constant dollars*.

Total GDP that is valued at current prices is a nominal measure, often called nominal national income. GDP that is valued at base period prices is a real measure, often referred to as real national income.

Any *change* in nominal GDP reflects the combined effects of changes in quantities and changes in prices. However, when real income is measured over different periods by using a common set of base period prices, changes in real income reflect only changes in real output.

The Implicit Deflator

If nominal and real GDP change by different amounts over a given time period, then prices must have changed over that period. Comparing what has happened to nominal and to real GDP over the same period implies the existence of a price index measuring the change in prices over that period. We say "implies" because no price index is used in calculating either real or nominal GDP. However, an index can be inferred by comparing these two values. Such an index is called an *implicit price index* or an *implicit deflator*. It is defined as follows:

$$\text{Implicit deflator} = \frac{\text{GDP at current prices}}{\text{GDP at base period prices}} \times 100$$

The implicit GDP deflator is the most comprehensive available index of the price level because it covers all the goods and services that are produced by the entire economy. Implicit deflators use the current year's "bundle" of production to compare the current year's prices with those prevailing in the base period. The GDP deflator was 3.6 percent higher in 1991 than it was in 1990. This means that in 1991 it cost 3.6 percent more to produce the goods and services than it would have cost to produce the same goods and services in 1990. Box 24-3 illustrates the calculation of real and nominal GDP and an implicit deflator for a simple hypothetical economy that produces only wheat and steel.

A change in any nominal measure of national income can be split into a change due to prices and a change due to quantities. For example, in 1991 U.S. nominal GDP was 87 percent higher than in 1981.

This increase was due to a 48 percent increase in prices and a 26 percent increase in real GDP.[6] Table 24-4 gives nominal and real income and the implicit deflator for selected years since 1959.

Total Values, Productivity, and Per Capita Values

The rise in real GDP during this century has had two main causes: an increase in the amounts of land, labor, and capital used in production and an increase in output per unit of input. In other words, more inputs have been used, and each input has become more productive. Although we want to measure total output for some purposes, such as assessing a country's potential military strength or the total size of its market, for other purposes, such as studying changes in living standards, we can use output per person, which is called **per capita output**. Alternatively, we

---

[6] For large percentage changes in price and quantity, the nominal percentage change is not equal to the sum of the price and the quantity changes. Generally, the relationship is multiplicative. In this case, prices and quantities are 1.48 and 1.26 times their original values. This makes nominal GDP (1.48)(1.26) = 1.87 times its original value, which is an increase of 87 percent. For small percentage changes, the sum is a very good approximation of the multiplicative change. If prices grow by 4 percent and quantities by 3 percent, the nominal change is (1.04)(1.03) = 1.071, which is very close to 1.07. See MN 32.

TABLE 24-4 Nominal and Real National Income (GDP)

	Nominal national income (billions of current dollars)	Real national income (billions of 1987 dollars)	Implicit national income deflator (1987 = 100)
1959	494.2	1,931.3	28.4
1970	1,010.7	2,875.8	35.1
1980	2,708.0	3,776.3	71.7
1985	4,038.7	4,279.8	84.4
1991	5,672.6	4,848.8	117.0

Source: Economic Report of the President, various years.

Nominal national income tells us about the money value of output; real national income tells us about changes in physical output. Nominal national income (i.e., national income in current dollars) gives the total value of all final output in any year, valued in the selling prices of that year. Real national income (i.e., national income in base period constant dollars) gives the total value of all final output in any year, valued in the prices ruling in one particular year, in this case 1987. The ratio *national income in current dollars/national income in constant dollars* times 100 is the implicit deflator.

can use measures of productivity, such as ouput per worker or output per hour of work.

Until recently it didn't much matter whether we used per capita output or one of the productivity measures, because the growth in per capita output has largely been due to growth in labor productivity. Figure 24-1 shows that starting about 1975, although per capita output continued to rise, much of the increase could be accounted for by increases in the amount of labor supplied. There was a slowdown in productivity growth accompanied by a marked increase in both the number of workers and hours of work relative to the population.

The divergence between the growth of output per capita and the growth of labor productivity means the increases in output per capita overstate increases in economic welfare. When output grows while inputs stay constant, the average person will be unambiguously better off. When output grows because more people are working more, the average person may be no better off than before. Because of this, productivity measures are generally the best measures of the ability of an economy to produce goods and services for its people.

What National Income Does Not Measure

National income as measured by the statisticians at the Bureau of Economic Analysis provides an excellent measure of the flow of economic activity in organized markets in a given year. But much economic activity takes place outside of the markets that the national-income accountants survey. Although these activities are not typically included in GDP or GNP, they nevertheless use real resources and satisfy real wants and needs.

Illegal activities. GDP does not measure illegal activities, even though many of them are ordinary business activities that produce goods and services sold on the market and that generate factor incomes. The liquor industry during Prohibition (1919–1933) is an important example; it accounted for a significant part of the nation's total economic activity. Today the same is true of many forms of illegal gambling, prostitution, and drug trade. To gain an accurate measure of the *total* demand for factors of production in the economy, of *total* marketable output, or of

---

FIGURE 24-1
Output Per Capita and Productivity, 1959–1991 (1959 = 100)

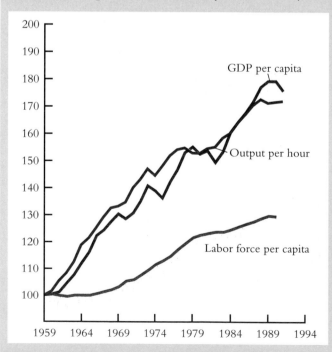

Much of the increase in output per capita during the 1980s can be accounted for by labor force growth rather than productivity growth. The top two lines are two alternative measures of economic well-being, GDP per capita and output per hour. Over the period 1959 to 1991, they have, on average, moved together. However, during the first part of the period, productivity, as measured by output per hour, rose considerably more than did GDP per capita. This relationship reversed starting in the mid-1970s. The lower line on the graph shows the labor force per capita. This started to grow in the mid-1960s, and it is the growth in labor force (and work effort) per capita that explains how output can grow more rapidly than productivity. Note that recessions show in the figure as downturns in GDP per capita. These occur in 1991, 1980–1982, 1973–1975, and 1970.

Box 24-3

Calculation of Nominal and Real National Income

To see what is involved in calculating nominal national income, real national income, and the implicit deflator, an example may be helpful. Consider a simple hypothetical economy that produces only two commodities, wheat and steel. Table 1 gives the basic data for output and prices in the economy for two years.

TABLE 1 Data for a Hypothetical Economy

	Quantity produced		Prices	
	Wheat (bushels)	Steel (tons)	Wheat (dollars per bushel)	Steel (dollars per ton)
Year 1	100	20	10	50
Year 2	110	16	12	55

Table 2 shows nominal national income, calculated by adding the money values of wheat output and of steel output for each year. In year 1 the value of both wheat and steel production was $1,000, so nominal income was $2,000. In year 2 wheat output rose, and steel output fell; the value of wheat output rose to $1,320, and that of steel fell to $880. Since the rise in value of wheat was greater than the fall in value of steel, nominal income rose by $200.

TABLE 2 Calculation of Nominal National Income

Year 1 (100 × 10) + (20 × 50) = $2,000
Year 2 (110 × 12) + (16 × 55) = $2,200

Table 3 shows real national income, calculated by valuing output in each year by year 2 prices; that is, year 2 becomes the base year for weighting purposes. In year 2 wheat output rose, but steel output fell. Using year 2 prices, the value of the fall in steel output between years 1 and 2 exceeded the value of the rise in wheat output, and real national income fell.

TABLE 3 Calculation of Real National Income Using Year 2 Prices

Year 1 (100 × 12) + (20 × 55) = $2,300
Year 2 (110 × 12) + (16 × 55) = $2,200

In Table 4 the ratio of nominal to real national income is calculated for each year and multiplied by 100. This ratio implicitly measures the change in prices over the period in question and is called the *implicit deflator* or *implicit price index*. The implicit deflator shows that the price level increased by 15 percent between year 1 and year 2.

In Table 4 we used year 2 as the base year for comparison purposes, but we could have used year 1. The implicit deflator would then have been 100 in year 1 and 115 in year 2, and the increase in price level would still have been 15 percent. Or, the base year could be some earlier year. No matter what year is picked as the year in which the index had a value of 100, however, the change in the implicit deflator between year 1 and year 2 is 15 percent.

TABLE 4 Calculation of the Implicit Deflator

Year 1 (2,000 ÷ 2,300) × 100 = 86.96
Year 2 (2,200 ÷ 2,200) × 100 = 100.00

Part Seven National Income and Fiscal Policy

incomes generated, we should include these activities, whether or not we as individuals approve of them. The omission of illegal activities is no trivial matter. The drug trade alone is a multibillion-dollar business in the United States.[7]

Unreported activities.   A significant omission from the measured GDP is the so-called underground economy. The transactions that occur in the underground economy are perfectly legal in themselves; the only illegality involved is that such transactions are not reported for tax purposes. One example of this is the carpenter who repairs a leak in your roof and takes payment in cash or in kind in order to avoid taxation. Because such transactions go unreported, they are omitted from GDP.

The growth of the underground economy is facilitated by the rising importance of services in the nation's total output. It is much easier for a carpenter to pass unnoticed by government authorities than it is for a manufacturing establishment. Estimates of the value of income earned in the U.S. underground economy run from 2 percent to 15 percent of U.S. GDP. In other countries the figures are even higher. The Italian underground economy, for example, has been estimated at close to 25 percent of that country's total GDP!

Nonmarketed activities.   If a home owner hires a firm to do some landscaping, the value of the landscaping enters into GDP; if the home owner does the landscaping herself, the value of the landscaping is omitted from GDP. Other nonmarketed activities include, for example, the services of homemakers, any do-it-yourself activity, and voluntary work such as canvassing for a political party, helping to run a volunteer day-care center, or leading a Boy Scout troop.

In most advanced industrial economies the non-market sector is relatively small, although much household maintenance, education, and child care are performed "at home." The omissions become very misleading, however, when national income measures are used to compare living standards in structurally different economies. Generally, the non-market sector of the economy is larger in rural than in urban settings and in less-developed than in more-developed economies. Be cautious, then, when interpreting data from a country with a very different climate and culture. When you hear that the per capita GDP of Nigeria is about $900 per year, you should not imagine living in Ohio on that income.

One extremely important nonmarketed activity is leisure itself. If an attorney voluntarily chooses to work 2,200 hours a year instead of 2,400 hours, measured national income will fall by the attorney's wage rate times 200 hours. Yet the value of the 200 hours of new leisure, which is enjoyed outside of the marketplace, must exceed the lost wages, so total economic welfare must rise rather than fall. Until recently, one of the most important ways in which economic growth benefited people was by permitting increased amounts of time off work. Because the time off is not marketed, its value does not show up in measures of national income.

Economic bads.   When an electric power plant sends sulfur dioxide into the atmosphere, leading to acid rain and environmental damage, the value of the electricity sold is included as part of GDP, but the value of the damage done by the acid rain is not deducted. Similarly, the gasoline that we use in our cars is part of national income, but the damage done by burning that gasoline is not deducted. To the extent that economic growth brings with it increases in pollution, congestion, and other disamenities of modern living, national income measures will overstate the value of the growth. They measure the increased economic output and income, but they fail to deduct for the increased "bads" that generally accompany economic growth.[8]

Do the Omissions Matter?

GDP does a reasonable job of measuring the flow of goods and services through the market sector of the economy. Usually, an increase in GDP implies greater opportunities for employment for those

---

[7] Some illegal activities do get included in national income measures, although they are generally misclassified by industry. The income is included because people sometimes report their earnings from illicit activities as part of their earnings from legal activities. They do this to avoid the fate of Al Capone, a famous Chicago gangster in the 1920s and 1930s, who, having avoided conviction on many counts, was finally caught for tax evasion.

[8] In a number of countries, national income accountants are developing official estimates of the "bads" that are produced in conjunction with measured national income and product. In the United States there have been intermittent private efforts along these lines, but the official National Income and Product Accounts do not provide any estimates of the costs of pollution, congestion, and the like.

households that sell their labor services in the market. Unless the importance of unmeasured economic activity changes rapidly, *changes* in GDP will do an excellent job of measuring *changes* in economic activity and economic opportunities. However, when the task at hand is measurement of the overall flow of goods and services available to satisfy people's wants, regardless of the source of the goods and services, then the omissions that we have discussed above become undesirable and potentially serious. Still, in the relatively short term changes in GDP will usually be good measures of the direction, if not the exact magnitude, of changes in economic welfare.

Is There a Best Measure of National Income?

To ask which is *the* best income measure is like asking which is *the* best carpenter's tool. The answer depends on the job to be done. The decision concerning which measure to use will depend on the problem at hand, and solving some problems may require information provided by several different measures or information not provided by any conventional measures. If we wish to predict households' consumption behavior, then disposable income may be the measure that we need to use. If we wish to account for changes in employment, then constant-dollar GDP may be the measure that we want. For an overall measure of economic welfare, we may need to supplement or modify conventional measures of national income, none of which measure *the quality of life*.

Even if economists do develop new measures for some purposes, it is unlikely that GDP (and its relatives) will be discarded. Economists and policymakers who are interested in changes in market activity and in employment opportunities for factors of production will continue to use GDP and other related measures because they are the ones that come closest to telling them what they need to know.

SUMMARY

1. Each firm's contribution to total output is equal to its value added, which is the gross value of the firm's output minus the value of all intermediate goods and services—that is, the outputs of other firms—that it uses. Goods that count as part of the economy's output are called final goods; all others are called intermediate goods. The sum of all the values added produced in an economy is the economy's total output, which is called gross domestic product (GDP).

2. Gross domestic product (GDP) can be calculated as the sum of values added, from the expenditure side, or from the income side. The expenditure side gives the total value of expenditures required to purchase a nation's output, and the income side gives the total value of incomes generated by the production of that output. By standard accounting conventions, these three aggregations define the same total.

3. From the expenditure side, GDP $= C^a + I^a + G^a + (X^a - IM^a)$. C^a comprises consumption expenditures of households. I^a is investment in plant and equipment, residential construction, and inventory accumulation. Gross investment can be split into replacement investment (necessary to keep the stock of capital intact) and net investment (net additions to the stock of capital). G^a is government purchases of goods and services. $(X^a - IM^a)$ represents net exports, or exports minus imports; it will be negative if imports exceed exports.

4. GDP measured from the income side adds up all claims to the market value of production. Wages, rent, interest, profits, depreciation (or capital consumption allowance), and indirect business taxes net of subsidies are the major categories.

5. GDP measures production that is located in the United States, and gross national product (GNP) measures income accruing to U.S. residents. The difference is due to the balance between U.S. claims to incomes that are generated abroad and foreign claims to incomes that are generated in the United States.

6. Real measures of national income are calculated to reflect changes in real quantities. Nominal measures of national income are calculated to reflect changes in both prices and quantities. Any change in nominal income can be split into a change in real income and a change due to prices. Appropriate comparisons of nominal and real measures yield implicit deflators.

7. Disposable personal income is the amount that actually is available to households to spend or to save, that is, income minus taxes.

8. GDP and related measures of national income must be interpreted with their limitations in mind. GDP excludes production resulting from activities that are illegal, that take place in the underground economy, or that do not pass through markets. Moreover, GDP does not measure everything that contributes to human welfare.

9. Notwithstanding its limitations, GDP remains a useful measure of the total economic activity that passes through the nation's markets and for accounting for changes in the employment opportunities that face households that sell their labor services on the market.

TOPICS FOR REVIEW

Value added

GDP as the sum of all values added

Intermediate and final goods

GDP from the expenditure and income sides

GNP

Disposable income

Measures of real and nominal national income

Implicit deflator

The significance of omissions from measured income

DISCUSSION QUESTIONS

1. If Canada and the United States were to join together as a single country, what would be the effect on their total GDP (assuming that output in each country is unaffected)? Would any of the components in their GDPs change significantly?

2. Residents of many U.S. cities have recently become concerned about the growing proportion of their real estate that is being bought up by foreign residents. What is the effect of this transfer of ownership on U.S. GNP and GDP?

3. "Every time you rent a U-haul, brick in a patio, grow a vegetable, fix your own car, photocopy an article, join a food co-op, develop your own film, sew a dress, purchase a frozen dinner from a local supermarket, stew fruit, or raise a child, you are performing a productive act, even though these activities are not reflected in the gross domestic product." To what extent are each of the items

listed "productive acts"? Are any of them included in GDP? Where they are excluded, does the exclusion matter?

4. In measuring U.S. GDP from the expenditure side, which of the following expenditures are included? Why?

    a. Expenditures on automobiles by consumers and by firms

    b. Expenditures on food and lodging by tourists and by business people on expense accounts

    c. Expenditures on new machinery and equipment by U.S. firms

    d. The purchase of one corporation by another corporation

    e. Increases in business inventories and decreases in business inventories

5. What would be the effect of the following events on the measured value of U.S. real GDP? Speculate on the effects of each event on the true well-being of U.S. residents.

    a. Destruction of 1,000 homes by flood waters

    b. Passage of a constitutional amendment that would make abortion illegal

    c. Outbreak of a new foreign conflict in which U.S. troops become as heavily involved as they were in Kuwait

6. Use the table that appears on the inside back cover of this book to calculate the percentage increase over the most recent two decades of each of the following magnitudes. Can you account for the relative size of these changes?

    a. GDP in current dollars

    b. GDP in constant dollars

    c. Disposable income in constant dollars

    d. Disposable income per capita in constant dollars

7. Consider the effect that each of the following has on measured GDP and on economic well-being:

    a. Reduction in the standard work week from 40 hours to 30 hours

    b. Hiring of all welfare recipients as government employees

    c. Increase in the salaries of priests and ministers as a result of increased contributions of churchgoers

8. A recent newspaper article reported that Switzerland was considered to be the "best" place in the world to live. In view of the fact that Switzerland does not have the highest per capita income in the world, how can it be ranked as the "best" place to live?

9. There is now a good deal of scientific evidence that the burning of fossil fuels is causing general "global warming," which may pose considerable long-term risk to economic and social well-being. In the current national accounts, value added in the production and use of fossil fuel adds to the GDP. What does this suggest about GDP as a measure of economic welfare?

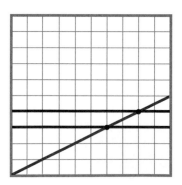

25

National Income and Aggregate Expenditure I: Consumption and Investment

In Chapters 23 and 24 we encountered a number of important macroeconomic variables. We described how they are measured and how they have behaved over the past half century or so. We now turn to a more detailed study of what *causes* these variables to behave as they do. In particular, we study the forces that determine national income (and hence employment and unemployment) and the price level.

National income and the price level are determined simultaneously. However, it is easier to study one at a time. So in this chapter and the next we deliberately oversimplify matters by studying the determination of national income *under the assumption that the price level is constant.* The simplified analysis that we explore now will be an important step toward understanding how prices *and* incomes are determined together, which is the subject of Chapters 27 and 28.

Our ability to explain the behavior of national income depends on our understanding of what determines the amount that households and firms spend, and why they change their spending. For this reason we begin with an examination of the *expenditure decisions* of households and firms. As a first step we distinguish between *desired* expenditure and *actual* expenditure.

Desired Expenditure

In Chapter 24 we discussed how national-income statisticians divide GDP, calculated from the expenditure side, into its components: consumption, C^a, investment, I^a, government, G^a, and net exports, $(X^a - IM^a)$.

In this chapter and the next we are concerned with a different concept. It is variously called *desired, planned,* or *intended* expenditure. Of course, all people would like to spend virtually unlimited amounts, if only they had the resources. Desired expenditure does not refer, however, to what people would like to do under imaginary circumstances; it refers to what people want to spend out of the resources that are at their command. The *actual* values of the various categories of expenditure are indicated by C^a, I^a, G^a, and $(X^a - IM^a)$. We use the same letters without the superscript *a* to indicate the *desired* expenditure in the same categories: $C, I, G,$ and $(X - IM)$.

Everyone with income to spend makes expenditure decisions. Fortunately, it is unnecessary for our purposes to look at each of the millions of such individual decisions. Instead, it is sufficient to consider four main groups of decision makers: domestic households, firms, governments, and foreign purchasers of domestically produced commodities. The actual purchases made by these four groups account for the four main categories of expenditure that we have studied in the previous chapter: consumption, investment, government, and net exports. Their desired expenditures, made up of desired consumption, desired investment, desired government purchases, and desired exports, account for total desired expenditure. (To allow for the fact that some of the commodities desired by each group will have an import content, we subtract expenditure on imports.) The result is total desired expenditure on domestically produced goods and services, called **aggregate expenditure,** *AE:*

$$AE = C + I + G + (X - IM)$$

Desired expenditure need not equal actual expenditure, either in total or in any individual category. For example, firms may not plan to invest in inventory accumulation this year but may do so unintentionally. If they produce goods to meet estimated sales but demand is unexpectedly low, the unsold goods that pile up on their shelves are undesired, and unintended, inventory accumulation. In this case, actual investment expenditure, I^a, will exceed desired investment expenditure, I.

National-income accounts measure actual expenditures in each of the four categories: consumption, investment, government, and net exports. National-income theory deals with desired expenditures in each of these four categories.

To develop a theory of national-income determination, we need to examine the determinants of each component of desired aggregate expenditure.

In this chapter we focus on desired consumption and desired investment. Consumption is the largest single component of aggregate expenditure, and as we will see, it provides the single most important link between desired aggregate expenditure and national income. Investment is national income that is not used either for current consumption or by governments, and it is an important determinant of potential income in the future.

We will discuss net exports and government expenditure in detail in Chapter 26. These two components of aggregate expenditure are essential to understanding how national income is determined and are important in their own right. However, our purpose here is to develop a simple (indeed, oversimplified) model of a national economy, one that shows how desired spending and actual national income are determined together.

A closed economy. The basic structure of the model is most easily seen if things are kept as simple as possible. Here we consider a **closed economy,** an economy that has no international trade. We also assume that the economy has no government and that its price level is constant. What we are left with is an economy that is about as simple as an economy can get. The principles of national income and expenditure determination that we discern from this simple model apply directly to a complete model that includes international trade and government, as we shall see in the next chapter. For now, however, imagine a remote island populated by rugged individualists.

Autonomous and induced expenditure. Before proceeding, it will be useful to distinguish between *autonomous* and *induced* expenditure. Components of aggregate expenditure that do *not* depend on national income are called **autonomous expenditures**. Autonomous expenditures can and do change, but such changes do not occur systematically in response to changes in national income. Components of aggregate expenditure that *do* change in response to changes in national income are called **induced expenditures.** As we will see, the induced response of aggregate expenditure to a change in national income plays a key role in the determination of equilibrium national income.

Desired Consumption Expenditure

Households can do one of two things with their disposable income: spend it on consumption or save it. **Saving** is all disposable income that is not consumed.

By definition there are only two possible uses of disposable income, consumption or saving. Therefore, when the household decides how much to put to one use, it has automatically decided how much to put to the other use.

What determines the division between the amount that households decide to spend on goods and services for consumption and the amount that they decide to save? The factors that influence this decision are summarized in the consumption function and the saving function.

The Consumption Function

The **consumption function** relates the total desired consumption expenditure of all households to the factors that determine it. It is, as we shall see, one of the central relationships in macroeconomics.

Although we are ultimately interested in the relationship between consumption and national income, the underlying behavior of households depends on the income that they actually have to spend—their disposable income. Under the simplifying assumptions that we have made in this chapter, there is no government and there are no taxes. Therefore, disposable income, which we denote by Y_d, is just equal to national income, Y. (Later in our discussion, Y and Y_d will diverge, because taxes are a part of national income that is not at the disposal of households.)

Consumption and Disposable Income

It should not surprise us to hear that a household's expenditure is related to the amount of income that it has at its disposal. There is, however, more than one way in which this relationship could work. To see what is involved, consider two quite different households.

The first household is headed by the proverbial prodigal son. It spends everything it receives and puts nothing aside for a rainy day. When overtime results in a large paycheck, the household goes on a binge. When it is hard to find work during periods of slack demand, the household's paycheck is small and its members cut their expenditures correspondingly. This household's expenditure each week is thus directly linked to each week's take-home pay, that is, its current disposable income.

The second household is completely different from the first. It thinks about the future as much as the present, and it makes plans that stretch over its lifetime. It puts money aside for retirement and for the occasional rainy day when disposable income may fall temporarily—it knows that it must expect alternating bouts of good and bad times. It also knows that it will need to spend extra money while the family is being raised and educated and that its income will probably be highest later in life when the children have left home and the parents have finally reached the peaks of their personal careers. This household may borrow to meet higher expenses earlier in life, paying back out of the higher income that the household expects to attain later in life. A temporary, unexpected windfall of income may be saved. A temporary, unexpected shortfall may be cushioned by spending the savings that were put aside for just such a rainy day. In short, this household's current expenditure will be closely related to its expected *lifetime income*. Fluctuations in its *current income* will have little effect on its current expenditure, unless such fluctuations also cause the household to change its expectations of lifetime income, as would be the case, for example, if an unexpected promotion came along.

John Maynard Keynes, the famous English economist who developed the basic theory of macroeconomics—and, incidentally, gave his name to "Keynesian economics"—inhabited his theory with prodigal sons. For them current consumption expenditure depended only on current income. To this day, a consumption function based on this assumption is called a *Keynesian consumption function*.

Later two U.S. economists, Franco Modigliani and Milton Friedman, both of whom were subsequently awarded the Nobel Prize in economics, analyzed the behavior of prudent households. Their theories, which Modigliani called the *life-cycle theory* and which Friedman called *the permanent-income theory*, explain some observed consumer behavior that cannot be explained by the Keynesian consumption function. (For more details, see the appendix to this chapter.)

However, the differences between the theories of Friedman and Modigliani, on the one hand, and Keynes, on the other, are not as great as it might seem at first sight. To see why this is so, let us return to our two imaginary households and see why their actual behavior may not be quite so divergent as we have described it.

Even the household that is headed by the prodigal son may be able to do some smoothing of expenditures in the face of income fluctuations. Most households have some money in the bank and some ability to borrow, even if it is just from friends and relatives. As a result, every income fluctuation will not be matched by an equivalent expenditure fluctuation.

In contrast, although the prudent household wants to smooth its pattern of consumption completely, it may not have the borrowing capacity to do so. Its bank may not be willing to lend money for consumption when the security consists of nothing more than the expectation that the household's income will be much higher in later years. This may mean that the household's consumption expenditure fluctuates more with its current income than it would wish.

This suggests that a household's consumption expenditure will fluctuate to some extent with its current disposable income and to some extent with its expectations of future disposable income. Moreover, in any economy there will be households of both types, both spendthrifts and planners, and aggregate consumption will be determined by a mix of the two types. As we develop our basic theory, we will often find it useful to make the simplifying assumption that consumption expenditure is primarily determined by current disposable income. That is, we will often use a Keynesian consumption function and then indicate how things change if we consider more sophisticated theories of consumer spending.

The term *consumption function* describes the relationship between consumption and the variables that influence it; in the simplest theory, consumption is primarily determined by current disposable income.

When a household's income is zero, it will still (via begging, borrowing, or drawing down savings) consume some minimal amount. This level of consumption expenditure is *autonomous*. The higher a household's income, the more it will want to con-

sume. This part of consumption is *induced*; that is, it varies with disposable income and hence with national income.

Consider the schedule relating disposable income to desired consumption expenditure for a hypothetical economy that appears in the first two columns of Table 25-1. In this example, autonomous consumption expenditure is $100 billion, whereas induced consumption expenditure is 80 percent of disposable income. In what follows we use this hypothetical example to illustrate the various properties of the consumption function.

Average and marginal propensities to consume.   To discuss the consumption function concisely, economists use two technical expressions.

The **average propensity to consume (APC)** is total consumption expenditure divided by total disposable income: $APC = C/Y_d$. The third column of Table 25-1 shows the APC calculated from the data in the table. Note that APC falls as disposable income rises.

The **marginal propensity to consume (MPC)** relates the *change* in consumption to the *change* in disposable income that brought it about. MPC is the change in disposable income divided into the

TABLE 25-1   The Calculation of Average Propensity to Consume (*APC*) and Marginal Propensity to Consume (*MPC*) (*billions of dollars*)

Disposable income (Y_d)	Desired consumption (C)	$APC = C/Y_d$	ΔY_d (change in Y_d)	ΔC (change in C)	$MPC = \Delta C/\Delta Y_d$
$ 0	$ 100	—			
			$ 100	$ 80	0.80
100	180	1.800			
			300	240	0.80
400	420	1.050			
			100	80	0.80
500	500	1.000			
			500	400	0.80
1,000	900	0.900			
			500	400	0.80
1,500	1,300	0.867			
			250	200	0.80
1,750	1,500	0.857			
			250	200	0.80
2,000	1,700	0.850			
			1,000	800	0.80
3,000	2,500	0.833			

APC **measures the proportion of disposable income that households desire to spend on consumption;** ***MPC*** **measures the proportion of any *increment* to disposable income that households desire to spend on consumption.** The data are hypothetical. We call the level of income at which desired consumption equals disposable income the break-even level; in this example it is $500 billion. *APC*, calculated in the third column, exceeds unity—that is, consumption exceeds income—below the break-even level. Above the break-even level, *APC* is less than unity. It is negatively related to income at all levels of income. The last three columns are set between the lines of the first three columns to indicate that they refer to changes in the levels of income and consumption. *MPC*, calculated in the last column, is constant at 0.80 at all levels of Y_d. This indicates that in this example $0.80 of *every* additional $1.00 of disposable income is spent on consumption, and $0.20 is used to increase saving.

resulting consumption change: $MPC = \Delta C / \Delta Y_d$ (where the Greek letter Δ, delta, means "a change in"). The last column of Table 25-1 shows the MPC that corresponds to the data in the table. Note that, by construction, the MPC is constant. **[33]**

The slope of the consumption function. Part (i) of Figure 25-1 shows a graph of the consumption function, derived by plotting consumption against income using data from the first two columns of Table 25-1. The consumption function has a slope of $\Delta C / \Delta Y_d$, which is, by definition, the marginal propensity to consume. The upward slope of the consumption function shows that the MPC is positive; increases in income lead to increases in expenditure.

Using the concepts of the average and marginal propensities to consume, we can summarize the prop-

erties of the short-term consumption function as follows:

1. There is a break-even level of income at which APC equals unity. Below this level, APC is greater than unity; above it, APC is less than unity.

2. MPC is greater than zero but less than unity for all levels of income.

The 45° line. Figure 25-1(i) contains a line that is constructed by connecting all points where desired consumption (measured on the vertical axis) equals disposable income (measured on the horizontal axis). Because both axes are given in the same units, this line has a positive slope of unity; that is it forms an angle of 45° with the axes. The line is therefore called the **45° line.**

FIGURE 25-1
The Consumption and Saving Functions

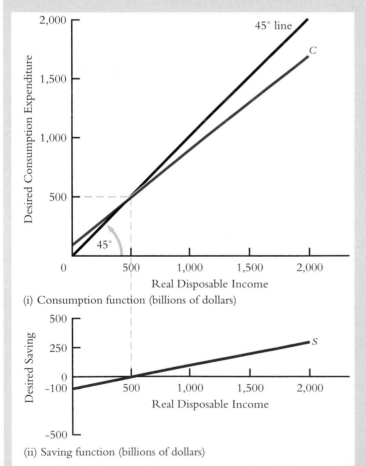

(i) Consumption function (billions of dollars)

(ii) Saving function (billions of dollars)

Both consumption and saving rise as disposable income rises. Line C in part (i) relates desired consumption expenditure to disposable income by using the hypothetical data from Table 25-1. Its slope, $\Delta C / \Delta Y_d$, is the marginal propensity to consume (MPC). The consumption line cuts the 45° line at the break-even level of disposable income, $500 billion in this case. Note that the level of autonomous consumption is $100 billion.

Saving is all disposable income that is not spent on consumption ($S = Y_d - C$). The relationship between desired saving and disposable income is derived in Table 25-2, and it is shown in part (ii) by line S. Its slope, $\Delta S / \Delta Y_d$, is the marginal propensity to save (MPS). The saving line cuts the horizontal axis at the break-even level of income. The vertical distance between C and the 45° line in part (i) is by definition the height of S in part (ii); that is, any given level of disposable income must be accounted for by the amount consumed plus the amount saved. Note that the level of autonomous saving is $-$100 billion. This means that at zero income a household will draw down existing assets by $100 a year.

The 45° line makes a handy reference line. In part (i) of Figure 25-1 it helps to locate the break-even level of income at which consumption expenditure equals disposable income. The consumption function cuts the 45° line at the break-even level of income, in this instance $500 billion. (The 45° line is steeper than the consumption function because the MPC is less than unity.)

The Saving Function

Households decide how much to consume and how much to save. As we have said, this is a single decision: how to divide disposable income between consumption and saving. It follows that, once we know the dependence of consumption on disposable income, we also automatically know the dependence of saving on disposable income. (This is illustrated in Table 25-2.)

There are two saving concepts that are exactly parallel to the consumption concepts of APC and MPC. The **average propensity to save (APS)** is the proportion of disposable income that households want to save, derived by dividing total desired saving by total disposable income, $APS = S/Y_d$. The **marginal propensity to save (MPS)** relates the change in total desired saving to the *change* in disposable income that brought it about: $MPS = \Delta S/\Delta Y_d$.

TABLE 25-2 Consumption and Saving Schedules (*billions of dollars*)

Disposable income	Desired consumption	Desired saving
$ 0	$ 100	$−100
100	180	−80
400	420	−20
500	500	0
1,000	900	+100
1,500	1,300	+200
1,750	1,500	+250
2,000	1,700	+300
3,000	2,500	+500
4,000	3,300	+700

Saving and consumption account for all household disposable income. The first two columns repeat the data from Table 25-1. The third column, desired saving, is disposable income minus desired consumption. Consumption and saving both increase steadily as disposable income rises. In this example the break-even level of disposable income is $500 billion.

There is a simple relationship between the saving and the consumption propensities. APC and APS must sum to unity, and so must MPC and MPS. Because income is either spent or saved, it follows that the fractions of incomes consumed and saved must account for all income ($APC + APS = 1$). It also follows that the fractions of any increment to income consumed and saved must account for all of that increment ($MPC + MPS = 1$). **[34]**

Calculations from Table 25-2 will allow you to confirm these relationships in the case of the example given. MPC is 0.80 and MPS is 0.20 at all levels of income, while, for example, at an income of $2,000 billion APC is 0.85 and APS is 0.15.

Figure 25-1(ii) shows the saving schedule given in Table 25-2. At the break-even level of income, where desired consumption equals disposable income, desired saving is zero. The slope of the saving line $\Delta S/\Delta Y_d$ is equal to the MPS.

Wealth and the Consumption Function

The Keynesian consumption function that we have been analyzing can easily be combined with the more recent "permanent-income" theories of consumption. According to the permanent-income theories, households save in order to accumulate wealth that they can use during their retirement. Suppose that there is an unexpected rise in wealth. This will mean that less of current disposable income needs to be saved for the future, and it will tend to cause a larger fraction of disposable income to be spent on consumption and a smaller fraction to be saved. Thus, the consumption function will be shifted upward and the saving function downward, as shown in Figure 25-2. A fall in wealth increases the incentive to save in order to restore wealth. This shifts the consumption function downward and the saving function upward.

Desired Investment Expenditure

Investment expenditure is the most volatile component of GDP, and changes in investment expenditure are strongly associated with economic fluctuations. For example, the Great Depression witnessed a dramatic fall in investment. Total investment in the U.S. economy fell from $16.2 billion in 1929 (almost double the amount that was needed to replace the capital goods that were being used up in the process of producing GDP) to just $1 billion in 1932 (less than one-sixth the amount that was needed just to keep the stock of capital intact). Less dramatically, at the

FIGURE 25-2
Wealth and the Consumption Function

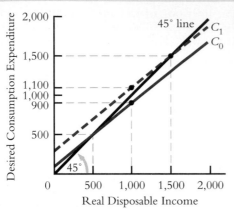

(i) The consumption function shifts upward with an increase in wealth (billions of dollars)

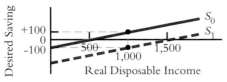

(ii) The saving function shifts downward with an increase in wealth (billions of dollars)

Changes in wealth shift consumption as a function of disposable income. In part (i) line C_0 reproduces the consumption function from Figure 25-1(i). An increase in the level of wealth raises desired consumption at each level of disposable income, thus shifting the consumption line up to C_1. In the figure the consumption function shifts up by $200, so with disposable income of $1,000, for example, desired consumption *rises* from $900 to $1,100. As a result of the rise in wealth, the break-even level of income rises to $1,500.

The saving function in part (ii) shifts down by $200, from S_0 to S_1. Thus, for example, at a disposable income of $1,000, saving *falls* from +$100 to −$100.

trough of the recession of the early 1990s, investment expenditure was only 85 percent of its average level of the previous three years.

Investment and the Real Interest Rate

Other things being equal, the higher is the real interest rate, the higher is the cost of borrowing money for investment purposes and the less is the

amount of investment expenditure. This relationship is most easily seen if we disaggregate investment into its major parts: inventories, business fixed investment, and residential housing.

Inventories. Inventory changes represent only a small percentage of private investment in a typical year, but their average size is not an adequate measure of their importance. They are one of the more volatile elements of total investment and therefore have a major influence on shifts in investment expenditure.

When a firm ties up funds in inventories, those same funds cannot be used elsewhere to earn income. As an alternative to holding inventories, the firm could lend the money out at the going rate of interest. Thus, the higher the real rate of interest, the higher will be the opportunity cost of holding an inventory of a given size; the higher that opportunity cost, the smaller are the inventories that will be desired.

The higher the real rate of interest, the lower is the desired stock of inventories. Changes in the rate of interest cause temporary bouts of investment (or disinvestment) in inventories.

Residential housing construction. Expenditure on residential housing is also volatile. Since 1970 it has varied between one-fifth and one-third of all gross private investment in the United States and between 2.5 percent and 5.5 percent of GDP. Because expenditures for housing construction are both large and variable, they exert a major impact on the economy.

Most houses are purchased with money that is borrowed by means of mortgages. Interest on the borrowed money typically accounts for over one-half of the purchaser's annual mortgage payments; the remainder is repayment of the original loan, called the principal. Because interest payments are such a large part of mortgage payments, variations in interest rates exert a substantial effect on the demand for housing.

The importance of interest rates was borne out by experiences from 1979 to 1982, when mortgage rates rose from less than 11 percent to just over 15 percent and housing starts fell from 1,194,000 units in 1979 to a mere 661,000 in 1982. (Because inflation fell from 1980, the increased nominal interest rates also meant increased real rates.) The construction industry itself and its major suppliers, such as the cement and the lumber industries, felt the blow of a dramatic fall in demand. Conversely, during the mid-1980s interest rates fell sharply, and there was a boom in the demand for new housing; that boom persisted until late 1988, when interest rates started to rise again.

Expenditure for residential construction tends to vary negatively with interest rates.

Plant and equipment. Investment in plant and equipment is the largest component of domestic investment. Over one-half is financed by firms' retained profits (profits that are *not* paid out to their shareholders). This means that current profits are an important determinant of investment.

The rate of interest is also a major determinant of investment in plant and equipment. As became abundantly clear during the early 1980s, high interest rates greatly reduce the volume of investment as more and more firms find that their expected profits from investment do not cover the interest on borrowed investment funds. Other firms who had cash on hand found that purchasing interest-earning assets provided a better return than investment in plant and equipment; for them the increase in real interest rates meant that the opportunity cost of investing had risen.

Changes in Sales

Studies show that the stock of inventories tends to rise as production and sales rise. Because the size of inventories is related to the level of sales, the *change* in inventories (which is current investment) is related to the *change* in the level of sales.

A firm may decide, for example, to hold inventories of 10 percent of its sales. Thus, if sales are $100,000, it will wish to hold inventories of $10,000. If sales increase to $110,000, it will want to hold inventories of $11,000. Over the period during which its stock of inventories is being increased, there will be a total of $1,000 new inventory investment.

The higher the level of production and sales, the larger is the desired stock of inventories. Changes in the rate of production and sales cause temporary bouts of investment (or disinvestment) in inventories.

Changes in sales have similar effects on investment in plant and equipment. If there is a rise in aggregate demand that is expected to persist and that cannot be met by existing capacity, then investment in new plant and equipment will be needed. Once the new plants have been built and put into operation, however, the rate of new investment will fall.

This further illustrates an important characteristic of investment that we have encountered already in the case of inventories:

If the desired stock of capital goods increases, there will be an investment boom that will last as long as the new capital is being produced.

However, if nothing else changes, and even if business conditions continue to look rosy enough to justify the increased stock of capital, investment in new plant and equipment will cease once the larger capital stock is achieved.[1]

Expectations and Business Confidence

Investment takes time. When a firm invests, it increases its future capacity to produce output. If the new output can be sold profitably, the investment will prove to be a good one. If the new output does not generate profits, the investment will be a bad one. When the investment is undertaken, the firm does not know if it will turn out well or badly—it is betting on a favorable future that cannot be known with certainty.

When firms see good times ahead, they will want to invest so as to reap future profits. When they see bad times, they will not invest, because, given their expectations, there will be no payoff to doing so. Often firms will project the near future based on the recent past. That is, they will tend to see good times ahead, and invest accordingly, when sales are rising and to see bad times in the future when sales are falling.

In general, investment depends in part on firms' forecasts of the future state of the economy.

---

[1] There may also be an induced increase in investment. The higher the level of national income, the larger, usually, will be the capital stock used to help produce that income. Because the capital stock wears out over time, a large capital stock will require more replacement investment than a small one. Thus, the higher the level of income, the higher will be desired investment expenditure. In the interest of simplicity, we ignore the possibility of induced investment for the remainder of this chapter.

The Aggregate Expenditure Function

The aggregate expenditure function relates the level of desired real expenditure to the level of real income. Generally, total desired expenditure on the nation's output is the sum of desired consumption, investment, government, and net export expenditures. In the simplified economy of this chapter, aggregate expenditure is just equal to $C + I$.

$$AE = C + I$$

Table 25-3 shows how the AE function can be calculated, given the consumption function of Tables 25-1 and 25-2 and a constant level of desired investment of $250 billion.[2] In this specific case, all of investment expenditure is autonomous, as is the $100 billion of consumption that would be desired at zero national income. Total autonomous expenditure is thus $350 billion—induced expenditures are just equal to induced consumption, which is equal to $0.8Y$. Thus, desired aggregate expenditure, whether thought of as $C + I$ or as autonomous plus induced expenditure, can be written as $AE = \$350$ billion $+ 0.8Y$. This aggregate expenditure function is illustrated in Figure 25-3.

The propensity to spend out of national income. The fraction of any increment to national income that will be spent on domestic production is called the economy's **marginal propensity to spend.** The marginal propensity to spend is measured by the change in aggregate expenditure divided by the change in income, or $\Delta AE/\Delta Y$, the slope of the aggregate expenditure function. In this book we will denote the marginal propensity to spend by the symbol z, which will typically be a number greater than zero and less than one.

Similarly, the **marginal propensity not to spend** is the fraction of any increment to national income that does not add to desired aggregate ex-

TABLE 25-3 The Aggregate Expenditure Function in a Closed Economy with No Government (*billions of dollars*)

National income (Y)	Desired consumption expenditure (C = 100 + 0.8Y)	Desired investment expenditure (I = 250)	Desired aggregate expenditure (AE = C + I + G + [X − IM])
$ 100	$ 180	$250	$ 430
400	420	250	670
500	500	250	750
1,000	900	250	1,150
1,500	1,300	250	1,550
1,750	1,500	250	1,750
2,000	1,700	250	1,950
3,000	2,500	250	2,750
4,000	3,300	250	3,550

The aggregate expenditure function is the sum of desired consumption, investment, government, and net export expenditures. In this table, government and net exports are assumed to be zero, investment is assumed to be constant at $250 billion, and desired consumption is based on the hypothetical data given in Table 25-2. The autonomous components of desired aggregate expenditure are desired investment and the constant term in desired consumption expenditure. The induced component is the second term in desired consumption expenditure $(0.8Y)$.

The marginal response of consumption to a change in national income is 0.8, the marginal propensity to consume. The marginal response of desired aggregate expenditure to a change in national income, $\Delta AE/\Delta Y$, is also 0.8, because all induced expenditure in this economy is consumption expenditure.

penditure. This is denoted $(1-z)$—if z is the part of a dollar of incremental income that is spent, $(1-z)$ is the part that is not spent.[3]

---

[2] For the present it is convenient to study how the level of national income adjusts to a fixed level of planned investment. So we assume that firms plan to make a constant amount of fixed business investment in plant and equipment each year and that they plan to hold their inventories constant. Later we shall drop these assumptions and study the important effects on national income that are caused by changes in the level of desired investment.

---

[3] More fully, these terms would be called the marginal propensity to spend *on national income* and the marginal propensity not to spend *on national income*. The marginal propensity not to spend $(1-z)$ is often referred to as the *marginal propensity to withdraw.* Not spending part of income amounts to a *withdrawal* from the circular flow of income, as illustrated in Figure 23-1.

FIGURE 25-3
An Aggregate Expenditure Curve

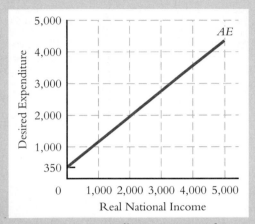

The aggregate expenditure curve relates total desired expenditure to national income. The *AE* curve in the figure plots the data from the first and the last columns of Table 25-3, which are repeated in Table 25-4. Its intercept (which in this case is $350) shows autonomous expenditure, which in this case is the sum of autonomous consumption of $100 and investment of $250. Its slope (which in this case is 0.8) shows the marginal propensity to spend.

In the example given in Table 25-3, z, the marginal propensity to spend, is 0.8. If national income increases by a dollar, 80 cents will go into increased spending. Twenty cents [one dollar times 0.2, the value of $(1-z)$] will go into increased saving and will not be spent. In the simple model of this chapter, the marginal propensity to spend is equal to the marginal propensity to consume, and the marginal propensity not to spend is equal to the marginal propensity to save. [In later chapers, when we add government and the international sector, the marginal propensity to spend differs from the marginal propensity to consume. Both here and in later chapters, it is the more general measures z and $(1-z)$ that are important for determining equilibrium national income.]

Determining Equilibrium National Income

We are now ready to see what determines the *equilibrium* level of national income. Recall from Chapter 4

TABLE 25-4   The Determination of Equilibrium National Income (*billions of dollars*)

National income (Y)	Desired aggregate expenditure (AE = C + I)	
$ 100	$ 430	Pressure on
400	670	income to
500	750	rise
1,000	1,150	↓
1,500	1,550	
1,750	1,750	Equilibrium income
2,000	1,950	
3,000	2,750	↑
4,000	3,550	Pressure on income to fall

National income is in equilibrium where aggregate desired expenditure equals national income. The data are copied from Table 25-3. When national income is below its equilibrium level, aggregate desired expenditure exceeds the value of current output. This creates an incentive for firms to increase output and hence for national income to rise. When national income is above its equilibrium level, aggregate desired expenditure is less than the value of current output. This creates an incentive for firms to reduce output and hence for national income to fall. Only at the equilibrium level of national income is aggregate desired expenditure exactly equal to the value of the current output.

that equilibrium is a state of balance between opposing forces. When something is in equilibrium, there is no tendency for it to change; forces are acting on it, but they balance out, and the net result is *no change*. Any conditions that are required for something to be in equilibrium are called its *equilibrium conditions*.

Table 25-4 illustrates the determination of equilibrium national income for our simple hypothetical economy. Suppose that firms are producing a final output of $1,000 billion, and thus national income is $1,000 billion. According to the table, at this level of income aggregate desired expenditure is $1,150 billion. If firms persist in producing a current output of only $1,000 billion in the face of an aggregate desired expenditure of $1,150 billion, one of two things must happen.[4]

---

[4] A third possibility, that prices could rise, is ruled out by assumptions in this chapter.

One possibility is that households, firms, and governments will be unable to spend the extra $150 billion that they would like to spend, so lines or waiting lists of unsatisfied customers will appear. These will send a signal to firms that they can increase their sales if they increase their production. When the firms increase production, national income rises. Of course, the individual firms are interested only in their own sales and profits, but their individual actions have as their inevitable consequence an increase in GDP.

The second possibility is that all spenders will spend everything that they wanted to spend. Then, however, expenditure will exceed current output, which can happen only when some expenditure plans are fulfilled by purchasing inventories of goods that were produced in the past. In our example the fulfillment of plans to purchase $1,150 billion worth of commodities in the face of a current output of only $1,000 billion will reduce inventories by $150 billion. As long as inventories last, more goods can be sold than are currently being produced.[5]

Eventually, inventories will run out. But in all likelihood, before this happens, firms will increase their output as they see their inventories being depleted. Extra sales can then be made without a further depletion of inventories. Once again, the consequence of each individual firm's behavior, in search of its own individual profits, is an increase in national income. Thus, the final response to an excess of aggregate desired expenditure over current output is a rise in national income.

At any level of national income at which aggregate desired expenditure exceeds total output, there will be pressure for national income to rise.

Next consider the $4,000 billion level of national income in Table 25-4. At this level desired expenditure on domestically produced goods is only $3,550 billion. If firms persist in producing $4,000 billion worth of goods, $450 billion worth must remain unsold. Therefore, inventories must rise. However,

firms will not allow inventories of unsold goods to rise indefinitely; sooner or later they will reduce the level of output to the level of sales. When they do, national income will fall.

At any level of income for which aggregate desired expenditure is less than total output, there will be a pressure for national income to fall.

Finally, look at the national-income level of $1,750 billion in Table 25-4. At this level, and only at this level, aggregate desired expenditure is exactly equal to national income. Purchasers fulfill their spending plans without causing inventories to change. There is no incentive for firms to alter output. Because total output is the same as national income, national income will remain steady; it is in equilibrium.

The equilibrium level of national income occurs where aggregate desired expenditure equals total output.

This conclusion is quite general and does not depend on the numbers that are used in the specific example. A more general derivation of equilibrium national income is given in the Appendix to Chapter 26.

Saving and Investment

We have just seen that equilibrium national income occurs where desired aggregate expenditure equals total national output. The same equilibrium can be described as the level of national income where desired saving equals desired investment.

In this chapter, the saving-investment formulation of the model is useful mostly because it adds some perspective on how equilibrium national income is determined. Later in this book, however, looking at equilibrium national income via the saving-investment balance will illuminate a key issue in economic policy—the relationship between macroeconomic policy and economic growth. Investment is one of the most important determinants of economic growth; investment adds to an economy's productive resources; investment is often the only way for new, productive technologies to improve economic performance. Because investment

---

[5] Notice that in this example, actual national income is equal to $1,000. Desired consumption is $900 and desired investment is $250, but the reduction of inventories of $150 is unplanned negative investment; thus, actual investment is only $100.

uses current national income but does not provide current consumption, investment must be financed by saving. In the *long run,* the level of a country's saving, through its effect on investment, can exert an important influence on economic growth. We are not yet ready to explore this point, but when we are, the saving-investment balance will be an important part of the story.

The Saving-Investment Balance

Table 25-5 is just Table 25-4 with two columns added: desired saving (which is disposable income minus consumption) and investment. Suppose that national income is $1,000 billion. At that level of income, desired saving will be $100 billion ($1,000 billion less $900 billion of desired consumption). Desired investment will be $250 billion. This implies that desired aggregate expenditure exceeds

national income by $150 billion. Why? Because if desired saving is $100 billion, desired consumption must account for all but $100 billion of national income. With desired investment at $250 billion, output will be $150 billion short of desired expenditure.

Suppose that national income is $4,000 billion. Here desired saving is $700 billion, and desired investment is $250 billion. This implies that desired aggregate expenditure falls short of national income by $450 billion. Desired consumption is $700 billion less than total output, and investment is only taking up $250 billion of the slack, leaving a shortfall of $450 billion.

At any level of national income, the difference between desired saving and desired investment is exactly the same as the difference between national income and desired aggregate expenditure.

Finally, notice that at the equilibrium level of national income, $1,750 billion, desired saving and desired investment are equal, at $250 billion.

When desired investment equals desired saving, there is just enough saving to finance the investment, and the economy is in equilibrium.

Equilibrium illustrated. Figure 25-4 shows the determination of the equilibrium level of national income. In panel (i) the line labeled AE graphs the aggregate expenditure function. Its slope is the marginal propensity to spend, z. The line labeled $AE = Y$ shows the equilibrium condition that desired aggregate expenditure, AE, equals national income, Y. Because the $AE = Y$ line plots points where the vertical distance equals the horizontal distance, it forms an angle of 45° with the axes. Any point on this line is a possible equilibrium.

Graphically, equilibrium occurs at the level of income at which the aggregate desired expenditure line intersects the 45° line. This is the level of income where desired expenditure is just equal to total national income and therefore is just sufficient to purchase total final output.

Exactly the same equilibrium is illustrated in panel (ii) but in terms of the saving-investment balance. The line labeled S is equal to aggregate saving.

TABLE 25-5   The Saving-Investment Balance

National income (Y)	Desired aggregate expenditure (AE = C + I)	Desired saving (S = Y_d − C)	Desired investment (I)
100	430	−80	250
400	670	−20	250
1,000	1,150	100	250
1,750	1,750	250	250
2,000	1,950	300	250
3,000	2,750	500	250
4,000	3,550	700	250

National income is in equilibrium where desired saving is equal to desired investment. The data for Y, AE, and I are copied from Table 25-3. The data for desired saving are copied from Table 25-2. When national income is below its equilibrium level, desired saving is less than desired investment, by exactly the same amount that national income is less than desired aggregate expenditure. There is upward pressure on national income, because demand exceeds firms' current production. When national income is above its equilibrium level, desired saving exceeds desired investment, by the same amount that national income exceeds desired aggregate expenditure. There is downward pressure on national income, because firms are producing more than they can sell.

Where desired saving is equal to desired investment, desired aggregate expenditure is equal to national income, and the economy is in equilibrium.

FIGURE 25-4
Equilibrium National Income

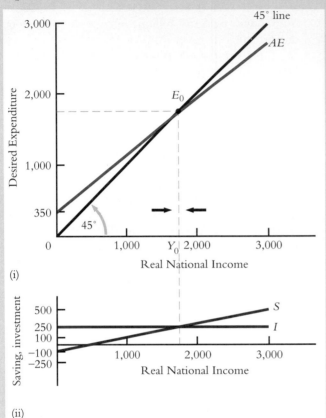

(i)

(ii)

In panel (i) equilibrium national income occurs at E_0, where the desired aggregate expenditure line intersects the 45° line. If real national income is below Y_0, desired aggregate expenditure will exceed national income, and production will rise. This is shown by the arrow to the left of Y_0. If national income is above Y_0, desired aggregate expenditure will be less than national income, and production will fall. This is shown by the arrow to the right of Y_0. Only when real national income is Y_0 will desired aggregate expenditure equal real national income.

Panel (ii) shows desired saving and desired investment on exactly the same scale as panel (i). Equilibrium national income occurs where saving equals investment. The vertical distance between saving and investment is exactly the same as the vertical distance in panel (i) between AE and the 45° line. When desired investment exceeds desired saving, AE exceeds national income by the same amount.

In an economy without government and without international trade, the case we are studying here, aggregate saving is just equal to $Y - C$, the difference between national income and consumption. The line labeled I is investment, in this case assumed to be constant at all levels of income.

Notice that the vertical distance between S and I is just equal to the distance between the 45° line and AE. When desired investment exceeds desired saving, desired aggregate expenditure exceeds national income by the same amount. When desired investment is less than desired saving, desired aggregate expenditure is less than national income by the same amount.

Now we have explained the equilibrium level of national income that arises at a *given price level*. In the next section we shall study the forces that cause equilibrium income to change. We shall see that shifts in desired consumption and investment expenditure can cause major swings in national income.

Changes in National Income

Because the AE function plays a central role in our explanation of the equilibrium value of national income, you should not be surprised to hear that shifts in the AE function play a central role in explaining why national income changes. (Remember that we continue to assume that the price level is constant.) To understand this influence, we must recall an important distinction first encountered in Chapter 4—the distinction between *shifts* in a curve and *movements along* a curve.

Suppose desired aggregate expenditure rises. This may be a response to a change in national income, or it may be the result of an increased desire to spend at each level of national income. A change in national income causes a *movement along* the aggregate expenditure function. An increased desire to spend at each level of national income causes a *shift in* the aggregate expenditure function. Figure 25-5 illustrates this important distinction.

Shifts in the Aggregate Expenditure Function

For any specific aggregate expenditure function there is a unique level of equilibrium national income. If the aggregate expenditure function shifts, the equilibrium will be disturbed and national income will change. Thus, if we wish to find the causes of changes in national income, we must understand the causes of shifts in the *AE* function.

The aggregate expenditure function shifts when one of its components shifts, that is, when there is a shift in the consumption function, in desired investment expenditure, in desired government expenditure on goods and services, or in desired net exports. In this chapter we consider only shifts in

the consumption function and in desired investment expenditure. Both of these are changes in *autonomous* aggregate expenditure.

Upward Shifts in Aggregate Expenditure Functions

What will happen if households permanently increase their levels of consumption spending at each level of disposable income, or if the Ford Motor Company increases its rate of annual investment by $2 billion in order to meet the threat from imported cars? (In considering these questions, remember that we are dealing with continuous flows measured as so much per period of time. An upward shift in the expenditure function means that the desired expenditure associated with each level of national income rises to and stays at a higher amount.)

Because any such increase shifts the entire aggregate expenditure function upward, the same analysis applies to each of the changes mentioned. Two types of shift in *AE* occur. First, if the same addition to

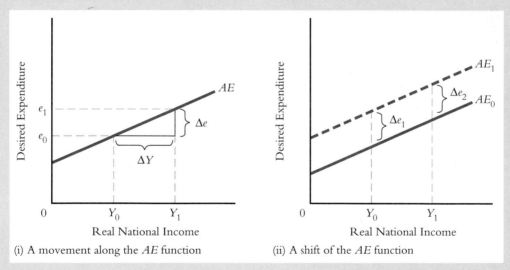

FIGURE 25-5
Movements Along and Shifts of the *AE* Function

(i) A movement along the *AE* function

(ii) A shift of the *AE* function

A movement along the aggregate expenditure function occurs in response to a change in income; a shift of the *AE* function indicates a different level of desired expenditure at each level of income. In part (i) a change in income of ΔY, from Y_0 to Y_1, changes desired expenditure by Δe, from e_0 to e_1. In part (ii) a shift in the expenditure function from AE_0 to AE_1 raises the amount of expenditure associated with *each* level of income. At Y_0, for example, desired aggregate expenditure is increased by Δe_1; at Y_1 it is increased by Δe_2. (If the aggregate expenditure line shifts parallel to itself, $\Delta e_1 = \Delta e_2$.)

expenditure occurs at all levels of income, the AE curve shifts parallel to itself, as shown in part (i) of Figure 25-6. Second, if there is a change in the propensity to spend out of national income, the slope of the AE curve changes, as shown in part (ii) of Figure 25-6. (Recall that the slope of the AE curve is z, the marginal propensity to spend.) A change such as the one illustrated would occur if consumers decided to spend more of every dollar of disposable income.

Figure 25-6 shows that upward shifts in the aggregate expenditure function increase equilibrium national income. After the shift in the AE curve, income is no longer in equilibrium at its original level because at that level desired expenditure exceeds national income. Equilibrium national income

now occurs at the higher level indicated by the intersection of the new AE curve with the 45° line, along which aggregate expenditures equal real national income.

Saving, Investment, and Changes in Equilibrium National Income

We saw earlier that at equilibrium national income, aggregate expenditure is equal to national income and saving is equal to investment. When the aggregate expenditure function shifts and equilibrium income changes, this equality must still hold true.

For a given economy, saving equals investment at exactly the same level of income at which $Y = AE$. Both approaches to determin-

---

FIGURE 25-6
Shifts in the AE Curve

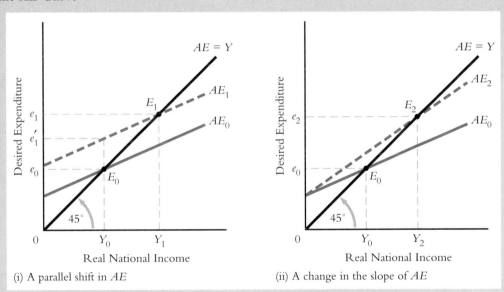

(i) A parallel shift in AE (ii) A change in the slope of AE

Upward shifts in the AE curve increase equilibrium income; downward shifts decrease equilibrium income. In parts (i) and (ii) the aggregate expenditure curve is initially AE_0 with national income Y_0.

In part (i) a parallel upward *shift* in the AE curve from AE_0 to AE_1 means that desired expenditure has increased by the same amount at each level of national income. For example, at Y_0 desired expenditure rises from e_0 to e_1' and therefore exceeds national income. Equilibrium is reached at E_1, where income is Y_1 and expenditure is e_1. The increase in desired expenditure from e_1' to e_1, represented by a *movement along* AE_1, is an induced response to the increase in income from Y_0 to Y_1.

In part (ii) a nonparallel upward shift in the AE curve, say, from AE_0 to AE_2, means that the marginal propensity to spend at each level of national income has increased. This leads to an increase in equilibrium national income. Equilibrium is reached at E_2, where the new level of expenditure e_2 is equal to income Y_2. Again, the initial *shift* in the AE curve induces a *movement along* the new AE curve.

Downward shifts in the AE curve, from AE_1 to AE_0 or from AE_2 to AE_0, lead to a fall in equilibrium income to Y_0.

ing equilibrium income must yield the same answer.

Consider the case of a shift in the aggregate expenditure function that is caused by a shift in the consumption function. As we discussed earlier (see Figure 25-2), when the consumption function shifts, the saving function shifts as well, by an equal and opposite amount. Why? Consumption plus saving must exhaust disposable income. Thus, if the consumption function shifts up by some amount at every level of income, the saving function must shift down by exactly the same amount. This is true because the sum of consumption and saving adds up to disposable income at every level of disposable income.

Figure 25-7(i) shows the effect of an upward shift in the consumption function as a *downward* shift in the saving function. Equilibrium national income occurs where desired saving equals desired investment. With desired investment fixed, a downward shift in the saving function leads to an *increase* in equilibrium national income. This is just as it should be; a downward shift in the saving function implies an upward shift in the consumption and aggregate expenditure functions.

In Figure 25-7(ii) the same increase in equilibrium national income is shown as arising from an upward shift in the investment function. Such a change might take place in response to a fall in real interest rates, which would increase the level of desired investment.

Notice that although the change in equilibrium income is the same in both panels of Figure 25-7, the composition of GDP is not. When the saving function shifts down, investment is unchanged in the new equilibrium—remember, I is constant. With Y up and I constant, consumption must have risen. When the investment function shifts up, saving, consumption, and investment are all higher at the new level of income. (The higher levels of saving and investment can be seen directly on the figure. The higher level of consumption is inferred from the fact that income has risen, the marginal propensity to consume is positive, and the consumption function has not shifted.)

Downward Shifts in Aggregate Expenditure Functions

What happens to national income if consumption or investment decreases? These changes shift the aggregate expenditure function downward. A constant

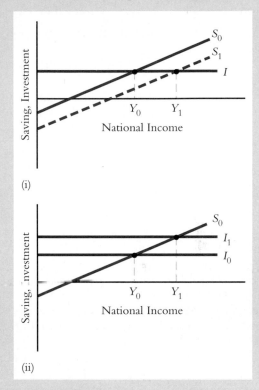

FIGURE 25-7
Shifts in Desired Saving and Investment

Upward shifts in investment and downward shifts in saving both increase equilibrium income but lead to different compositions of national product. Panel (i) shows a downward shift in desired saving (the equivalent of an upward shift in desired consumption). National income increases from Y_0 to Y_1.

In panel (ii) the economy starts at the same initial equilibrium (Y_0) and ends at the same equilibrium income (Y_1). The economy in panel (ii) differs from that of panel (i), however. At Y_1, the economy in panel (ii) has higher saving and investment than that in panel (i). This implies that in the future, the panel (ii) economy will have greater productive resources in the form of a larger capital stock.

reduction in expenditure at all levels of income shifts AE parallel to itself. A fall in the marginal propensity to spend out of national income reduces the slope of the AE function. In the saving-investment approach, a downward shift in the consumption function will cause an upward shift in the saving function, reducing the equilibrium level of income, at which saving equals investment.

The Results Restated

We have derived two important general propositions of the elementary theory of national income.

1. A rise in the amount of desired aggregate expenditure that is associated with each level of national income will increase equilibrium national income.
2. A fall in the amount of desired aggregate expenditure that is associated with each level of national income will lower equilibrium national income.

The Multiplier

We have learned how to predict the direction of the changes in national income that occur in response to various shifts in the aggregate expenditure function. We would like also to predict the *magnitude* of these changes.

Economists need to know the *size* of the effects of changes in expenditures. During a recession the government sometimes takes measures to stimulate the economy. If these measures have a larger effect than estimated, demand may rise too much and full employment may be reached with demand still rising. This outcome will have an inflationary impact on the economy. If the government greatly overestimates the effect of its measures, the recession will persist longer than is necessary. In this case there is a danger that the policy will be discredited as ineffective, even though the correct diagnosis is that too little of the right thing was done.

Definition.   A measure of the magnitude of changes in income is provided by the *multiplier*. We have just seen that a shift in the aggregate expenditure curve will cause a change in equilibrium national income. Such a shift could be caused by a change in any autonomous component of aggregate expenditure, for example, an increase or decrease in investment. An increase in desired aggregate expenditure increases equilibrium national income by a multiple of the initial increase in autonomous expenditure. The **multiplier** is the ratio of the change in income to the change in expenditure, that is, the change in national income *divided by* the change in autonomous expenditure that brought it about.

Why the multiplier is greater than unity.   What will happen to national income if Apple Computer builds a $1 billion factory? Initially the construction of the factory will create $1 billion worth of new national income and a corresponding amount of employment for households and firms on which the initial $1 billion is spent, but this is not the end of the story. The increase in national income of $1 billion will cause an increase in disposable income, which will cause an induced rise in consumption expenditure.

Electricians, masons, and carpenters—who gain new income directly from the building of the factory—will spend some of it on food, clothing, entertainment, cars, television sets, and other commodities. When output expands to meet this demand, employment will increase in all the affected industries. New incomes will then be created for workers and firms in these industries. When they, in turn, spend their newly earned incomes, output and employment will rise further. More income will be created, and more expenditure will be induced. Indeed, at this stage we might wonder whether the increases in income will ever come to an end. To deal with this concern, we need to consider the multiplier in somewhat more precise terms.

The simple multiplier defined.   Consider an increase in autonomous expenditure of ΔA, which might be, say, $1 billion per year. Remember that ΔA stands for *any* increase in autonomous expenditure; this could be an increase in investment or in the autonomous component of consumption. The new autonomous expenditure shifts the aggregate expenditure function upward by that amount. National income is no longer in equilibrium at its original level, because desired aggregate expenditure now exceeds income. Equilibrium is restored by a *movement along* the new AE curve.

The **simple multiplier** measures the change in equilibrium national income that occurs in response to a change in autonomous expenditure *at a constant price level*. We refer to it as "simple" because we have simplified the situation by assuming that the price level is fixed. Figure 25-8 illustrates the simple multiplier and makes clear that it is greater than unity. Box 25-1 provides a numerical example.

The Size of the Simple Multiplier

The size of the simple multiplier depends on the slope of the AE function, that is, on the marginal propensity to spend, z. This is illustrated in Figure 25-9.

FIGURE 25-8
The Simple Multiplier

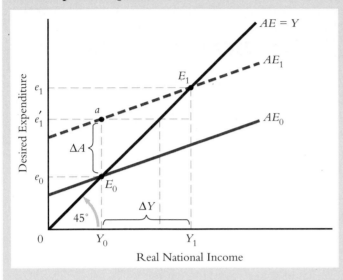

An increase in the autonomous component of desired aggregate expenditure increases equilibrium national income by a multiple of the initial increase. The initial equilibrium is at E_0, where AE_0 intersects the 45° line. At this point, desired expenditure, e_0, is equal to national income, Y_0. An increase in autonomous expenditure of ΔA then shifts the desired expenditure function upward to AE_1. If national income stays at Y_0, desired expenditure rises to e_1' (the coordinates of point a are Y_0 and e_1'). Because this level of desired expenditure is greater than national income, national income will rise.

Equilibrium occurs when income rises to Y_1. Here desired expenditure, e_1, equals income, Y_1. The extra expenditure of e_1 represents the induced increases in expenditure. It is the amount by which the final increase in income, ΔY, exceeds the initial increase in autonomous expenditure, ΔA. Because ΔY is greater than ΔA, the multiplier is greater than unity.

A high marginal propensity to spend means a steep AE curve. The expenditure induced by any initial increase in income is large, with the result that the final rise in income is correspondingly large. By contrast, a low marginal propensity to spend means a relatively flat AE curve. The expenditure induced by the initial increase in income is small, and the final rise in income is not much larger than the initial rise in autonomous expenditure that brought it about.

The larger the marginal propensity to spend, the steeper is the aggregate expenditure function and the larger is the multiplier.

The precise value of the simple multiplier can be derived by using elementary algebra. (The derivation is given in Box 25-2.) The result is that the simple multiplier, which we call K, is

$$K = \frac{\Delta Y}{\Delta A} = \frac{1}{1 - z}$$

where z is the marginal propensity to spend out of national income. (As we have seen, z is the slope of the aggregate expenditure function.)

As we saw earlier, the term $(1 - z)$ stands for the marginal propensity not to spend out of national

income. For example, if $0.80 of every $1.00 of new national income is spent ($z = 0.80$), then $0.20 is the amount not spent. The value of the multiplier is then calculated as $K = 1/0.20 = 5$.

The simple multiplier equals the reciprocal of the marginal propensity not to spend.

From this we see that, if $(1 - z)$ is small (that is, if z is large), the multiplier will be large (because extra income induces much extra spending). What if $(1 - z)$ is large? The largest possible value of $(1 - z)$ is unity, which arises when z equals zero, indicating that none of any additional national income is spent. In this case the multiplier itself has a value of unity; the increase in equilibrium national income is confined to the initial increase in autonomous expenditure. There are no induced additional effects on spending, so national income only increases by the original increase in autonomous expenditure. The relation between $(1 - z)$ and the size of the multiplier is illustrated in Figure 25-9.

To estimate the size of the multiplier in an actual economy, we need to estimate the value of the marginal propensity not to spend out of national income in that economy, that is, $(1 - z)$. Evidence suggests that the U.S. value is larger than the 0.2 that we used in our example, in large part because

Box 25-1

The Multiplier: A Numerical Example

Consider an economy that has a marginal propensity to spend out of national income of 0.80. Suppose that autonomous expenditure increases by $1 billion per year because a large corporation spends an extra $1 billion per year on new factories. National income initially rises by $1 billion, but that is not the end of it. The factors of production involved in factory building that received the first $1 billion spend $800 million. This second round of spending generates $800 million of new income. This new income, in turn, induces $640 million of third-round spending, and so it continues, with each successive round of new income generating 80 percent as much in new expenditure. Each additional round of expenditure creates new income and yet another round of expenditure.

The table carries the process through 10 rounds. Students with sufficient patience (and no faith in mathematics) may compute as many rounds in the process as they wish; they will find that the sum of the rounds of expenditures approaches a limit of $5 billion, which is five times the initial increase in expenditure.[35]

The graph of the cumulative expenditure increases shows how quickly this limit is approached. The multiplier is thus 5, given that the marginal propensity to spend is 0.8. Had the marginal propensity to spend been lower, say, 0.667, the process would have been similar, but it would have approached a limit of three instead of five times the initial increase in expenditure.

Round of spending	Increase in expenditure (millions of dollars)	Cumulative total (millions of dollars)
Initial increase	1,000.0	1,000.0
2	800.0	1,800.0
3	640.0	2,440.0
4	512.0	2,952.0
5	409.6	3,361.6
6	327.7	3,689.3
7	262.1	3,951.4
8	209.7	4,161.1
9	167.8	4,328.9
10	134.2	4,463.1
11 to 20 combined	479.3	4,942.4
All others	57.6	5,000.0

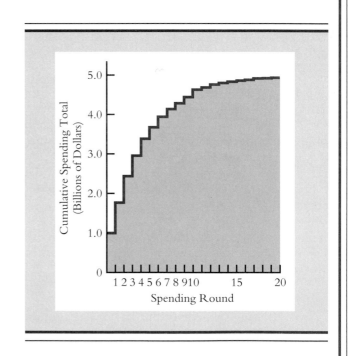

Box 25-2

The Multiplier: An Algebraic Approach

Basic algebra is all that is needed to derive the exact expression for the multiplier. Readers who feel at home with algebra may want to follow this derivation. Others can skip it and rely on the graphical and numerical arguments that have been given in the text.

First, we derive the equation for the AE curve. Aggregate expenditure is divided into autonomous expenditure, A, and induced expenditure, N. In the simple model of this chapter, A is just equal to investment plus autonomous consumption. N is just equal to induced consumption.*

Thus, we can write

$$AE = N + A \qquad [1]$$

Because N is expenditure on domestically produced output that varies with income, we can write

$$N = zY \qquad [2]$$

where z is the marginal propensity to spend out of national income. (z is a positive number between zero and unity. In the simple model of this chapter, with no government and no foreign sector, it is equal to the marginal propensity to consume.) Substituting Equation 2 into Equation 1 yields the equation of the AE curve.

$$AE = zY + A \qquad [3]$$

---

* When we add imports and government in the next chapter, N will include induced imports, and A will include government spending and exports. The derivation here is quite general, however. All that matters is that desired aggregate expenditure can be divided into one class of expenditure, N, that varies with income and another class, A, that does not.

Now we write the equation of the 45° line,

$$AE = Y \qquad [4]$$

which states the equilibrium condition that desired aggregate expenditure equals national income. Equations 3 and 4 are two equations with two unknowns, AE and Y. To solve them we substitute Equation 3 in Equation 4 to obtain

$$Y = zY + A \qquad [5]$$

Subtracting zY from both sides yields

$$Y - zY = A \qquad [6]$$

Factoring out Y yields

$$Y(1 - z) = A \qquad [7]$$

Dividing through by $1-z$ yields

$$Y = A/(1 - z) \qquad [8]$$

This tells us the equilibrium value of Y in terms of autonomous expenditures A and the propensity not to spend out of national income $(1-z)$. Now consider a one-dollar increase in A. The expression $Y = A/(1 - z)$ tells us that if A changes by one dollar, the change in Y will be $1/(1 - z)$ dollars. Generally, for a change in autonomous spending of ΔA, the change in Y, which we call ΔY, will be

$$\Delta Y = \Delta A/(1 - z) \qquad [9]$$

Dividing through by ΔA gives the value of the multiplier, which we designate by K:

$$K = \Delta Y/\Delta A = 1/(1 - z) \qquad [10]$$

FIGURE 25-9
The Size of the Simple Multiplier

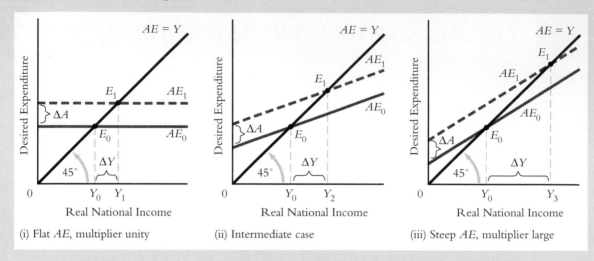

(i) Flat *AE*, multiplier unity

(ii) Intermediate case

(iii) Steep *AE*, multiplier large

The larger the marginal propensity to spend out of national income (z), the steeper is the *AE* curve and the larger is the multiplier. In each part of the figure the initial aggregate expenditure function is AE_0, equilibrium is at E_0, with income Y_0. The *AE* curve then shifts upward to AE_1 as a result of an increase in autonomous expenditure of ΔA. ΔA is the same in each part. The new equilibrium is at E_1.

In part (i) the *AE* function is horizontal, indicating a marginal propensity to spend of zero ($z = 0$). The change in income ΔY is only the increase in autonomous expenditure, because there is no induced expenditure by those who receive the initial increase in income. The simple multiplier is then unity, its minimum possible value.

In part (ii) the *AE* curve slopes upward but is still relatively flat (z is low). The increase in national income to Y_2 is only slightly greater that the increase in autonomous expenditure that brought it about.

In part (iii) the *AE* function is quite steep (z is high). Now the increase in income to Y_3 is much larger than the increase in autonomous expenditure that brought it about. The simple multiplier is quite large.

there are a number of elements of national income that are "not spent" that we have not yet discussed. In addition to saving, which we have discussed, these withdrawals from the circular flow of income include income taxes and import expenditures. For the U.S. economy in the 1990s, this leads to a realistic estimate of something that is a little more than 0.5 for $(1 - z)$.

Thus, the simple multiplier is something less than 2, not 5, as in the example.

The simple multiplier is a useful starting point for understanding the effects of expenditure shifts on national income; however, as we shall see in subsequent chapters, many complications will arise.

SUMMARY

1. Desired aggregate expenditure includes desired consumption, desired investment, and desired government expenditures, plus desired net exports. It is the amount that economic agents want to spend on purchasing the national product. In this chapter we consider only consumption and investment.

2. A change in disposable income leads to a change in consumption and saving. The responsiveness of these changes is measured by the marginal propensity to consume (*MPC*) and the marginal propensity to save (*MPS*), which are both positive and sum to one.

3. A change in wealth tends to cause a change in the allocation of disposable income between consumption and saving. The change

in consumption is positively related to the change in wealth, while the change in saving is negatively related to this change.

4. In the simple theory of this chapter, investment expenditures and the constant term in the consumption function are called autonomous expenditures. The part of consumption that responds to income is called induced expenditure.

5. At the equilibrium level of national income, purchasers wish to buy neither more nor less than what is being produced. At incomes above equilibrium, desired expenditure falls short of national income, and output will sooner or later be curtailed. At incomes below equilibrium, desired expenditure exceeds national income, and output will sooner or later be increased.

6. In a closed economy with no government, at equilibrium national income, saving equals investment.

7. Equilibrium national income is represented graphically by the point at which the aggregate expenditure curve cuts the 45° line, that is, where total desired expenditure equals total output. This is the same level of income at which the saving function cuts the investment function.

8. With a constant price level, equilibrium national income is increased by a rise in the desired consumption, investment, government, or export expenditure that is associated with each level of the national income. Equilibrium national income is decreased by a fall in desired expenditures.

9. The magnitude of the effect on national income of shifts in autonomous expenditure is given by the multiplier. It is defined as $K = \Delta Y / \Delta A$, where ΔA is the change in autonomous expenditure.

10. The simple multiplier is the multiplier when the price level is constant. It is equal to $1/(1 - z)$, where z is the marginal propensity to spend out of national income. Thus, the larger z is, the larger is the multiplier. It is a basic prediction of national income theory that the simple multiplier is greater than unity.

TOPICS FOR REVIEW

Desired expenditure

Consumption function

Average and marginal propensities to consume and to save

Aggregate expenditure function

Marginal propensities to spend and not to spend

Equilibrium national income at a given price level

Saving-investment balance

Shifts of and movements along expenditure curves

Effect on national income of changes in desired expenditures

The simple multiplier

The size of the multiplier and slope of the AE curve

DISCUSSION QUESTIONS

1. "The concept of an equilibrium level of national income is useless because the economy is never in equilibrium. If it ever got there, no economist would recognize it anyway." Discuss this quotation.

2. Interpret each of the following statements either in terms of the shape of a consumption function or the values of MPC and APC.
   a. "Tom Green has lost his job, and his family is existing on its past savings."
   b. "The Grimsby household is so rich that they used all the extra income they earned this year to invest in a wildcat oil-drilling venture."
   c. "We always thought Harris was a miser, but when his wife left him he took to wine, women, and song."
   d. "The inflation has made the Schultzes feel so poor that they are adding an extra $100 a week to their account at the savings bank."
   e. "The last stock market crash led young Ross to cancel two planned trips abroad, even though his job as a broker was never at risk."

3. Why might an individual's marginal propensity to consume be higher in the long run than in the short run? Why might it be lower? Is it possible for an individual's average propensity to consume to be greater than unity in the short run? In the long run? Can a country's average propensity to consume be greater than unity in the short run? In the long run?

4. What relationship holds along the 45° line between total expenditures and total income? In determining equilibrium graphically, are we restricted to choosing identical vertical and horizontal scales?

5. Explain carefully why national income changes when desired aggregate expenditure does not equal national income. Sketch scenarios that fit the cases of too much and too little desired expenditure.

6. Explain how a sudden unexpected fall in consumer expenditure would initially cause an increase in investment expenditure by firms.

7. Explain how an increase in desired saving would reduce equilibrium income.

8. What relationship is suggested by the following newspaper headline: "Auto sales soar as recovery booms"?

9. Locate at least two current press stories that suggest shifts in the AE curve.

APPENDIX TO CHAPTER

25

The Permanent-Income and Life-Cycle Hypotheses of Household Consumption

In the Keynesian theory of the consumption function, current consumption expenditure is related to current income—either current disposable income or current national income. As we saw in the chapter, more recent theories relate consumption to some longer term concept of income than the income that the household is currently earning.

The two most influential theories of this type are the *permanent-income theory (PIT)*, developed by Professor Friedman, and the *life-cycle theory (LCT)*, developed by Professors Modigliani, Ando, and Brumberg. Although there are differences between these, it is their similarities that are important. In particular, we note that, in both the PIT and the LCT, household behavior tends to smooth the time pattern of consumption relative to that of disposable income. Later in this appendix we consider a potentially important difference between the two hypotheses.

In discussing this "consumption-smoothing" issue, it is important to ask: What variables do these theories seek to explain? What assumptions do they make? What are the major implications of these assumptions?

Variables

Three variables need to be considered: consumption, saving, and income. Keynesian-type theories seek to explain the amounts that households spend on purchasing goods and services for consumption. This concept is called *consumption expenditure*. Permanent-income theories seek to explain the actual flows of consumption of the *services* that are provided by the commodities that households buy. This concept is called *actual consumption*.[1]

With services and nondurable goods, expenditure and actual consumption occur more or less at the same time, and the distinction between the two concepts is not important. Consumption of a haircut, for example, occurs at the time that it is purchased, and an orange or a package of corn flakes is consumed very soon after it is purchased. Thus, if we knew when purchases of such goods and services were made, say, last year, we would also know last year's consumption of those goods and services.

This, however, is not the case with durable consumer goods. An automobile is purchased at one point in time, but it yields its services over a long period of time. The same is true of a personal computer, a watch, or a stereo system. For such products, if we know last year's purchases we do not necessarily know last year's consumption of the services that the products yielded.

Thus, one important characteristic of durable goods is that *expenditure* to purchase them is not necessarily synchronized with *consumption* of the stream of services that the goods provide. If in 1988 Ms. Smith buys a car for $12,000, uses it for six years, and then discards it as worn out, her expenditure on

---

[1] Because Keynes' followers did not always distinguish carefully between the concepts of consumption expenditure and actual consumption, the word *consumption* is often used in both contexts. We follow this normal practice, but where there is any possible ambiguity in the term we will refer to *consumption expenditure* and *actual consumption*.

automobiles is $12,000 in 1988 and zero for the next five years. Her consumption of the services of automobiles, however, is spread out at an average annual rate of $2,000 for six years. If everyone followed Ms. Smith's example and bought a new car in 1988 and replaced it in 1994, the automobile industry would undergo wild booms in 1988 and 1994 with five intervening years of slump, even though the actual consumption of automobiles would be spread more or less evenly over time. This example is extreme, but it illustrates the possibilities, where consumer durable goods are concerned, of quite different time paths of *consumption expenditure*, which is the subject of Keynesian theories of consumption, and *actual consumption*, which is the subject of permanent-income theories.

Now consider saving. The change in emphasis from consumption expenditure to actual consumption implies a change in the definition of saving. Saving is no longer income minus consumption expenditure; it is now income minus the value of actual consumption. When Ms. Smith spent $12,000 on her car in 1988 but used only $2,000 worth of its services during that year, she was actually consuming $2,000 and saving $10,000. The purchase of a consumer-durable good is thus counted as saving, and only the value of its services actually consumed is counted as consumption.

The third important variable is income. Instead of using current income, the theories use a concept of long-term income. The precise definition varies from one theory to another, but basically it is related to the household's expected income stream over a fairly long planning period. In the LCT it is the income that the household expects to earn over its lifetime, called its *lifetime income*.

Every household is assumed to have a view of its lifetime income. This is not as unreasonable as it might seem. Students who are training to become doctors have a very different view of expected lifetime income than those who are training to become schoolteachers. Both expected income streams—for a doctor and for a schoolteacher—will be different from that expected by an assembly line worker or a professional athlete. One possible lifetime income stream is shown in Figure 25A-1.

The household's expected lifetime income is then converted into a single figure for annual **permanent income**. In the life-cycle theory this permanent income is the maximum amount that the household could spend on consumption each year

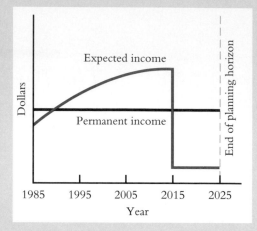

FIGURE 25-A1
Current Income and Permanent Income

Expected current income may vary greatly over a lifetime, but expected permanent income is defined to be the constant annual equivalent. The graph shows a hypothetical expected income stream from work for a household whose planning horizon was 40 years from 1985. The current income rises to a peak and falls sharply on retirement. The corresponding permanent income is the amount that the household could consume at a steady rate over its lifetime by borrowing early against future earnings (as do most newly married couples), then repaying past debts, and finally saving for retirement when income is at its peak without either incurring debt or accumulating new wealth to be passed on to future generations.

into the indefinite future without accumulating debts that are passed on to future generations. If a household were to consume a constant amount that was equal to its permanent income each year, it would add to its debts or reduce its assets in years when current income was less than permanent income, and it would reduce its debt or increase its assets in years when its current income exceeded its permanent income. Over its lifetime, however, it would just break even, leaving neither accumulated assets nor debts to its heirs. If the interest rate were zero, permanent income would be just the sum of all expected incomes divided by the number of expected years of life. With a positive interest rate, permanent income will diverge from this amount because of the cost of borrowing and the extra income that can be earned by investing savings.

Assumption

The basic assumption of this type of theory, whether it is the PIT or LCT, is that the household's actual consumption is related to its permanent rather than to its current income. Two households that have the same permanent income (and are similar in other relevant characteristics) will have similar consumption patterns, even though their current incomes may behave differently.

Implications

The major implication of these theories is that changes in a household's current income will affect its actual consumption only so far as they affect its permanent income. Consider two income changes that could occur in a household with a permanent income of $30,000 per year and an expected lifetime of 30 or more years. In the first case suppose that the household receives an unexpected extra income of $2,000 *for this year only*. The increase in the household's permanent income is small. If the rate of interest were zero, the household could consume an extra $66.66 per year for the rest of its expected life span; with a positive rate of interest, the extra annual consumption would be more because money not spent this year could be invested and would earn interest. Still, the extra annual consumption enabled by the $2,000 would be very small relative to the current level of annual consumption.[2] In the second case suppose that the household gets a totally unforeseen increase of $2,000 per year *for the rest of its life*. In this event the household's permanent income has risen by $2,000 because the household actually can consume $2,000 more every year without accumulating new debts. Although in both cases current income rises by $2,000, the effect on permanent income is very different.

In the Keynesian consumption function, *consumption expenditure* is related to current income, and therefore the same change in this year's consumption expenditure is predicted for each of the cases just discussed. Permanent-income theories relate *actual consumption* to permanent income and therefore predict different changes in actual consumption in each

case. In the first case there would be only a small increase in actual annual consumption; in the second case there would be a large increase.

In the LCT and the PIT, any change in current income that is thought to be temporary will have only a small effect on permanent income and hence on actual consumption.

Implications for the Behavior of the Economy

According to the permanent-income and the life-cycle hypotheses, actual consumption is not affected much by temporary changes in income. Does this mean that aggregate expenditure, $C + I + G + (X - IM)$, is not affected much? This is not necessarily true. Consider what happens when households get a temporary increase in their incomes. If actual consumption is not greatly affected by this, then households must be saving most of this increase. However, from the point of view of these theories, households save when they buy a durable good just as much as when they buy a financial asset, such as a stock or a bond. In both cases actual current consumption is not changed.

Thus, using a temporary increase in income either to increase savings or to buy a new car is consistent with both the PIT and the LCT, but it makes a great deal of difference to the short-run behavior of the economy which one of these choices is made. If households increase their savings, aggregate expenditure on currently produced final goods will not rise when income rises temporarily. If households buy automobiles or any other durable consumer good, aggregate expenditure on currently produced final goods will rise when income rises temporarily. Thus, the PIT and the LCT leave unsettled the question that is critical in determining the size of the multiplier: What is the reaction of household *expenditures* on currently produced goods and services, particularly durables, to short-term, temporary changes in income?

Assume, for example, that a serious recessionary gap emerges and that the government attempts to stimulate a recovery by giving tax rebates and by cutting tax rates—both on an announced, temporary basis. This will raise households' current disposable incomes by the amount of the tax cuts, but it will raise their permanent incomes by only a small amount.

---

[2] If the rate of interest were 7 percent, the household could invest the $2,000, consume an extra $161 per year, and have nothing left at the end of 30 years.

According to the PIT and the LCT, the flow of actual current consumption should not rise much. Yet it is quite consistent with the PIT and the LCT that households should spend their tax savings on durable consumer goods, the consumption of which can be spread over many years.

In this case, even though actual consumption this year would not respond much to the tax cuts, expenditure would respond a great deal. Because current output and employment depend on expenditure rather than on actual consumption, the tax cut would be effective in stimulating the economy. However, it is also consistent with the LCT and the PIT that households spend only a small part of their tax savings on consumption goods and seek to invest the rest in bonds and other financial assets. In this case the tax cuts may have only a small stimulating effect on the economy. It is important to note that the PIT and the LCT *do not predict unambiguously* that changes in taxes that are announced to be only short-lived will be ineffective in changing aggregate expenditure.

26

National Income and Aggregate Expenditure II: An Open Economy with Government

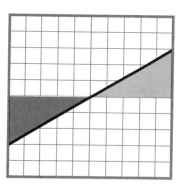

I n Chapter 25 we developed a highly simplified model of income and expenditure determination in a closed economy with fixed prices. The economy that we live in and wish to study is both more interesting and more complicated. Unlike the economy of Chapter 25, it has a government (in fact, many governments), and it engages in foreign trade. In this chapter we expand our model of national income determination to incorporate the government and foreign sectors. In Chapter 27 we will expand the model further to explain the price level as well.

Adding the government sector to the model allows us to study *fiscal policy*, the ability of the government to use its taxing and spending powers to affect the level of national income.

As we proceed, it is important to remember that the key elements of our theory of income determination are unchanged. The most important of these, which will remain true even after incorporating government and the foreign sector, are restated here.

1. Aggregate desired expenditure can be divided into autonomous expenditure and induced expenditure. Induced expenditure is expenditure that depends on the level of national income.
2. The equilibrium level of national income is the level at which the sum of autonomous and induced desired expenditure is equal to the level of national income. Graphically, this is where the aggregate expenditure line intersects the 45° line.
3. The simple multiplier measures the change in equilibrium national income that takes place in response to a unit change in autonomous expenditure, with the price level held constant.

Government: Spending and Taxes

Government spending and taxing policies affect equilibrium national income in two important ways. First, government purchases are part of autonomous expenditure. Second, taxes must be subtracted from national income (and government transfer payments must be added) in deriving disposable income. Because disposable income determines consumption expenditure, the relationship between desired consumption and national income will become somewhat more complicated.

A government's plans for taxes and spending define its *fiscal policy*, which has important effects on the level of national income in both the short and the long run. Our discussion of fiscal policy begins in this chapter and continues in Chapter 28 and in Chapter 34.

G from both sides of this equation yields $(S + T - G)$ equal to $(I + X - IM)$. In words, national saving equals national asset formation.

Graphical exposition. Figure 26-6 shows the determination of equilibrium income using the national saving and national asset formation concepts. The national saving function is taken from Figure 26-5. The national asset formation function is the sum of desired investment and desired net exports. Its downward slope is equal to (minus) the marginal propensity to import. Equilibrium occurs at the level of national income where national saving (the part of national income that the private and public sectors desire to set aside for the future) is just equal to national asset formation (the part of national product that is not used to satisfy current consumption and government purchases of goods and services).

The vertical distance between the AE function and the 45° ($AE = Y$) line in Figure 26-4 is just equal to the vertical distance between the desired national asset formation function and the desired national saving function in Figure 26-6. The level of

equilibrium income in the two figures is the same, as both are representations of exactly the same model of income determination.

Changes in Aggregate Expenditure and National Income

Changes in any of the components of planned aggregate expenditure will cause changes in equilibrium national income. In Chapter 25 we investigated the consequences of shifts in the consumption function and in the investment function. Here we take a first look at fiscal policy—the effects of government spending and taxes. We also consider shifts in the net export function. First, we take account of the fact that the simple multiplier is reduced by the presence of taxes and the marginal propensity to import.

The simple multiplier revisited. In Chapter 25 we saw that the *simple multiplier*, the amount by which equilibrium national income changes when autonomous expenditure changes by a dollar, was equal to $1/(1 - z)$. In the example considered throughout Chapter 25 z, the marginal propensity to spend, was equal to 0.8, and the multiplier was equal to 5, or $1/(0.2)$. In the example that we have developed in this chapter, with a marginal propensity to import of 0.1 and a marginal income tax rate of 0.1, the marginal propensity to spend is 0.62. (Ten percent of a dollar increase in autonomous spending goes to taxes, leaving 90 cents. With a marginal propensity to consume of 0.8, 72 cents is spent. Of this, 10 cents is spent on imports, leaving a total of 62 cents to be spent on domestically produced consumption goods.) Thus, $(1 - z)$ is (0.38), and the simple multiplier is $1/(0.38) = 2.63$.

Fiscal Variables

A reduction in tax rates or an increase in government expenditure shifts the AE curve upward, causing an increase in equilibrium GDP. An increase in tax rates or a decrease in government expenditure shifts the AE curve downward, causing a decrease in equilibrium GDP.

FIGURE 26-6
National Saving and National Asset Formation

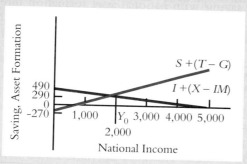

The economy is in equilibrium at Y_0, where desired national saving, $T - G + S$, equals desired national asset formation, $I + (X - IM)$. To the left of Y_0, desired national asset formation exceeds desired national saving. This implies that desired aggregate expenditure exceeds national income. Firms will respond to the imbalance by producing more, moving the economy toward equilibrium. To the right of Y_0, desired national asset formation is less than desired national saving, and aggregate expenditure is less than national income. Firms will cut back on output in order to avoid accumulating excess inventories, and the economy will move toward equilibrium.

Changes in Government Purchases

Suppose the government decides to reduce the size of the armed forces, saving $30 billion a year in spending. Planned government purchases (G) would fall by $30 billion at every level of income, shifting AE downward by the same amount. How much would equilibrium income change? This can be calculated using the multiplier. Government purchases are part of autonomous expenditure, so a *change* in government purchases of ΔG will lead to a *change* in equilibrium national income of the multiplier times ΔG. In this example, equilibrium income would fall by $30 billion times the simple multiplier.

Increases in government purchases would have the opposite effect. If the government were to spend $10 billion repairing the interstate highway system, equilibrium national income would rise by $10 billion times the simple multiplier.

Changes in Tax Rates

If tax rates change, the relationship between disposable income and national income changes. As a result, the relationship between desired consumption expenditure and national income also changes. For any given level of national income there will be a different level of disposable income and thus a different level of consumption, as illustrated in Table 26-6.

Consequently, a change in tax rates will also cause a change in z, the marginal propensity to spend out of national income.

Consider a decrease in tax rates. If the government decreases its rate of income tax so that it collects $0.05 less out of every dollar of national income, then disposable income rises in relation to national income. Thus, consumption also rises at every level of national income. This results in a (nonparallel) upward shift of the AE curve, that is, an increase in the slope of the curve, as shown in Figure 26-7. The result of this shift will be a rise in equilibrium national income, as is also shown in Figure 26-7.

A rise in taxes has the opposite effect. A rise in tax rates causes a decrease in disposable income, and hence consumption expenditure, at each level of national income. This results in a (nonparallel) downward shift of the AE curve and thus decreases the level of equilibrium national income, as illustrated in Figure 26-7.

Tax rates and the multiplier. Earlier in this chapter we recalled that the *simple multiplier* is equal to the reciprocal of one minus the marginal propensity to spend. That is, the multiplier equals $1/(1 - z)$, where z is the marginal propensity to spend out of national income. The simple multiplier tells us how

---

TABLE 26-6 Tax Changes Shift the Function Relating Consumption to National Income (*billions of dollars*)

(1) National income (Y)	Disposable income equal to 80 percent of national income (tax rate = 0.2)		Disposable income equal to 90 percent of national income (tax rate = 0.1)	
	(2) Disposable income ($Y_d = 0.8Y$)	(3) Consumption ($C = 100 + 0.8Y_d$)	(4) Disposable income ($Y_d = 0.9Y$)	(5) Consumption ($C = 100 + 0.8Y_d$)
100	80	164	90	172
500	400	420	450	460
1,000	800	740	900	820

The consumption function shifts if the relationship between disposable and national income changes. The table is based on the simplified hypothetical consumption function from Table 25-1 combined with the assumption that Y_d is a constant fraction of Y. Initially $Y_d = 0.8Y$, yielding the schedule relating consumption to national income that is given in columns 1 and 3 and is described by the equation $C = 100 + 0.64Y$. Income-tax rates are then decreased so that 90 percent of national income becomes disposable income. Column 4 indicates the Y_d that corresponds at the decreased tax rate to each level of Y shown in column 1. With an unchanged consumption function, consumption at the new tax rate is given by column 5. Columns 1 and 5 give the new schedule relating consumption to national income, described by the equation $C = 100 + 0.72Y$.

FIGURE 26-7
The Effect of Changing the Tax Rate

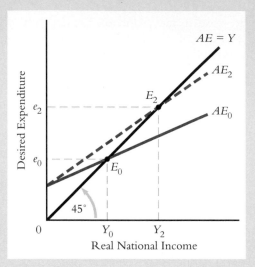

Changing the tax rate changes equilibrium income by changing the slope of the *AE* curve. A reduction in tax rates pivots the *AE* curve from AE_0 to AE_2. The new curve has a steeper slope because the lower tax rate withdraws a smaller amount of national income from the desired consumption flow. Equilibrium income rises from Y_0 to Y_2 because at every level of national income, desired consumption, and hence aggregate expenditure, is higher.

If we take AE_2 and Y_2 to be the initial equilibrium, an increase in tax rates will reduce the slope of the *AE* curve, thereby reducing equilibrium income, as shown by AE_0 and Y_0.

much equilibrium national income changes when autonomous expenditure changes by a dollar and there is no change in prices.

When tax rates change, the multiplier also changes. Suppose that the *MPC* is 0.8 and the tax rate *falls* by $0.05 per dollar of national income. This would increase the marginal propensity to spend by $0.04 per dollar of national income. (Disposable income would rise by $0.05 per dollar at each level of national income, and consumption would rise by the marginal propensity to consume, 0.8, times $0.05, which is $0.04.) The increase in the value of *z*, the marginal propensity to spend, would cause the multiplier to rise, making equilibrium income more responsive to changes in autonomous expenditure from any source.

The lower is the income tax rate, the larger is the simple multiplier.

Figure 26-7 illustrates the effect of tax rates on the multiplier and also illustrates the effect of a change in tax rates on equilibrium income: When the tax rate falls, disposable income rises at each level of income. According to the consumption function, the increase in disposable income causes desired consumption to rise as well, rotating the *AE* curve upward. The new, steeper *AE* curve intersects the 45° line at a higher level of income. Similarly, when the tax rate rises, the process is reversed.

Net Exports and Equilibrium National Income

Earlier in this chapter we discussed the determinants of net exports and of shifts in the net export function. As with the other elements of desired aggregate expenditure, if the net export function shifts upward, equilibrium national income will rise; if the net export function shifts downward, equilibrium national income will fall.

Autonomous net exports. Net exports have both an autonomous component and an induced component. Generally, exports themselves are autonomous with respect to domestic national income. Foreign demand for U.S. goods and services depends on foreign income, on foreign and U.S. prices, and on the exchange rate, but it does not depend on U.S. income. Export demand could also change because of a change in tastes. Suppose that foreign consumers develop a taste for U.S.-made breakfast cereals and desire to consume $2 billion more per year of these comestibles than they had in the past. The net export function (and the aggregate expenditure function) will shift up by $2 billion, and equilibrium national income will increase by $2 billion times the multiplier.

Induced net exports. The U.S. demand for imports depends, in part, on U.S. income. The greater is domestic income, the greater will be U.S. demand for goods and services in general, including those produced abroad. Because imports are subtracted to obtain net exports (net exports equal $X - IM$), the marginal propensity to import (*m*) is subtracted from the marginal propensity to spend, *z*. Thus, the greater is the marginal propensity to import, the lower will be the marginal propensity to spend, and the lower will be the multiplier, $1/(1 - z)$.

Fiscal Policy and the Budget Balance

Government tax revenues are related to the performance of the economy. For a given tax rate, tax revenues will rise when income rises and fall when income falls. Because government purchases are relatively insensitive to the level of national income, the budget surplus will rise (the budget deficit will fall) as income rises. This relationship is given by the *budget surplus function*. The budget surplus function is illustrated both in Figure 26-1, where the budget surplus is called by its other name, public saving, and in Figure 26-8 by the curves labeled $B = T - G$.

With a given spending and taxing policy, as national income changes, the budget surplus changes in the same direction.

When the government makes its plans for spending and taxing, it determines the position of the budget surplus function. The higher the net tax rate, the higher and steeper will be the curve in Figure 26-8. (Recall that the net tax rate includes taxes net of transfer payments. Typically, tax revenues rise *and* transfer payments fall as income rises.) The lower the level of planned government purchases, the higher will be the budget surplus function. The higher is the budget surplus function, the higher will be the surplus (the lower the deficit) at any given level of national income.

FIGURE 26-8
The Budget Surplus (Deficit) Function

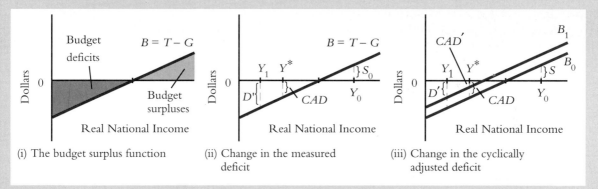

(i) The budget surplus function   (ii) Change in the measured deficit   (iii) Change in the cyclically adjusted deficit

The budget surplus can change either because of a change in fiscal policy or because of a change in national income. Parts (i) and (ii) illustrate the same budget surplus function, showing that the budget surplus increases (budget deficit falls) as national income rises.

Part (ii) defines the cyclically adjusted surplus (or deficit) (*CAS* or *CAD*) as the budget balance that obtains at potential national income, Y^*. In the example, the *CAD* is a deficit, as it is for current fiscal policy in the United States. At a sufficiently high income, Y_0, the actual budget would be in surplus by an amount S_0. At incomes lower than Y^*, such as Y_1, the actual budget would be in deficit by D', more than the amount of the *CAD*. Throughout the curve in part (ii), fiscal policy is unchanged. The deficit and surplus change only because national income changes.

Part (iii) shows how the actual deficit (or surplus) might move in a different direction from the *CAD* or *CAS*. Suppose the economy starts at Y_0, with fiscal policy given by B_0. If fiscal policy is made more restrictive, through some combination of higher taxes and lower government purchases, the budget balance will now behave according to B_1. At the same time, if income should fall to Y_1, the budget surplus of S will turn into a deficit of D'. By looking at the actual budget balance, one would see the budget move from surplus to deficit, suggesting, incorrectly, that the fiscal policy had become more stimulative of the economy. Focusing on the *CAD*, however, the level of budget balance at Y^*, makes it clear that B_1 is more restrictive than B_0—the *CAD* is smaller at Y^* (and at every level of income) with the fiscal policy given by B_1.

Fiscal policy determines the *position* of the budget surplus (or deficit) function.

The actual budget surplus (or deficit). In 1990 the president and Congress reached an agreement on fiscal policy and adopted a plan, raising *t* and reducing *G*, that was designed to reduce the budget deficit. Yet between 1990 and 1991 the budget deficit *grew* by $32 billion, and it grew further in 1992. Does this imply that the Omnibus Budget Reconciliation Act of 1990 (OBRA) failed in its stated purpose—to reduce the deficit? No. The budget deficit grew between 1990 and 1991 because the economy went into a recession. Thus, while OBRA shifted the budget surplus function up, the economy moved to the left along the new, higher curve. The net effect was an increase in the deficit. Part (iii) of Figure 26-8 illustrates how this outcome could happen.

The actual level of the budget surplus (or deficit) depends on both fiscal policy, which determines the location of the budget surplus function, *and* the level of national income, which determines a specific point on the budget surplus function.

The cyclically adjusted surplus (or deficit). Because it depends in part on the level of national income, the actual budget deficit is a poor measure of the effect of fiscal policy on the economy. For example, if national income fell by enough, the budget deficit could increase at the same time that fiscal policy became more restrictive. In order to measure fiscal policy independently of the level of national income, it is necessary to develop a measure of the budget balance that is also independent of the level of national income.

Economists have developed the concept of the **cyclically adjusted surplus (*CAS*) and cyclically adjusted deficit (*CAD*)**. These are also known as the *structural surplus (or deficit)*, defined as the budget surplus (or deficit) that *would obtain if the economy were operating at potential national income.*[8]

By fixing the level of income at which the surplus is measured, the effect of income on the actual deficit is removed. The structural surplus measures the position of the budget surplus function, which is solely determined by fiscal policy.

The behavior of the *CAD* in recent years is shown in Table 26-7. Parts (ii) and (iii) of Figure 26-8 illustrate how the *CAD* can be used to judge the stance of fiscal policy. The higher is the struc-

---

TABLE 26-7   Actual and Cyclically Adjusted Budget Balances for the Federal Government (*billions of dollars*)

Year	Actual deficit	Cyclically adjusted deficit
1970	2.8	7.6
1971	23.0	19.3
1972	23.4	20.1
1973	14.9	23.0
1974	6.1	11.4
1975	53.2	31.3
1976	73.7	47.6
1977	53.7	41.5
1978	59.2	58.3
1979	40.2	41.2
1980	73.8	47.5
1981	79.0	42.5
1982	128.0	48.9
1983	207.8	108.0
1984	185.4	134.2
1985	212.3	176.5
1986	221.2	184.8
1987	149.8	120.4
1988	155.2	158.0
1989	153.5	147.7
1990	220.5	150.4
1991	268.7	171.6

Source: Congressional Budget Office, 1992.

Wide swings in the cyclically adjusted budget deficit indicate wide swings in the stance of fiscal policy. Because the economy operated at less than full employment during most of the 1970s, actual budget deficits were larger than cyclically adjusted deficits in most years. The large actual deficits during the mid-1970s were mainly a response to low levels of national income during the recession. Variations in the cyclically adjusted deficits show the variability of the stance of fiscal policy. The sharp increases in 1975 and after 1982 indicate expansionary fiscal policy, whereas the decreases in 1974 and 1979 indicate contractionary fiscal policy.

---

[8] The concept used to be called the *full employment surplus.* The change from *full employment* to *cyclically adjusted* came during the 1970s, when the amount of unemployment that is associated with potential income rose so much that referring to it as *full employment* became embarrassing. The change from *surplus* to *deficit* in common usage took place between the 1960s, when many economists were concerned that high surpluses exerted a depressing effect on GDP, and the 1980s, when nearly everyone became concerned about large deficits.

tural surplus, the higher is public saving at potential income and the lower is the government's net contribution to aggregate expenditure at that level of income.

Lessons and Limitations of the Income-Expenditure Approach

In this and the preceding chapter we have discussed the determination of the four categories of aggregate expenditure and seen how they simultaneously determine equilibrium national income. The basic approach, which is the same no matter how many categories are considered, was first presented in Chapter 25 and has been recapitulated and extended in this chapter. The appendix to this chapter provides an algebraic exposition of the model.

Any factor that shifts one or more of the components of desired aggregate expenditure will change equilibrium national income, *at a given price level*.

In the following chapters we augment the income-expenditure model by allowing the price level to change, in both the short run and the long run. As we shall see, changes in desired aggregate expenditure generally change both prices *and* real national income. This is why the simple multiplier, derived under the assumption that prices do not change, is too simple. When prices change, real income will change by amounts different from those predicted by the simple multiplier.

However, there are three ways in which the simple income-aggregate expenditure model developed here remains useful, even when prices are incorporated. First, the simple multiplier will continue to be a valuable starting place in calculating actual changes in national income in response to changes in autonomous expenditure. Second, no matter what the price level, the components of aggregate expenditure add up to national income in equilibrium. Third, no matter what the price level, equilibrium requires that national saving be equal to national asset formation. This last point will be especially important when we consider the determinants of national income and prices in the long run.

SUMMARY

1. Government spending is part of autonomous aggregate expenditure. Taxes minus transfer payments are called net taxes and affect aggregate expenditure indirectly. Taxes reduce disposable income, whereas transfers increase disposable income. Disposable income, in turn, determines desired consumption, according to the consumption function.

2. The budget balance is defined as government revenues minus government expenditures. When the result is positive, the budget is in surplus; when it is negative, the budget is in deficit.

3. When the budget is in surplus, there is positive public saving because the government is using less national product than the amount of income that it is withdrawing from the circular flow of income and product. When the government budget is in deficit, public saving is negative.

4. Since desired imports increase as national income increases, desired net exports decrease as national income increases, other things being equal. Hence, the net export function is negatively sloped.

5. As in Chapter 25, national income is in equilibrium when desired aggregate expenditure, $C + I + G + (X - IM)$, equals national income.

6. The sum of investment and net exports is called national asset formation because investment and net exports represent the two ways in which national income that is not used in the current year can be used to generate future national income. At the equilibrium level of national income, desired national saving, $S + T - G$, is just equal to national asset formation.

7. Equilibrium national income is negatively related to the amount of tax revenue that is associated with each level of national income. The size of the multiplier is negatively associated with the income tax rate.

8. The budget surplus depends on both the level of national income and the government's plans for taxing and spending. The government's plans are summarized by the government surplus (or deficit) function, which relates the level of the surplus (or deficit) to national income. Fiscal policy determines the position of the budget surplus function.

9. The cyclically adjusted surplus (or deficit) (*CAS* or *CAD*) is the level of the budget surplus that would obtain if the economy were producing its potential output. The *CAS* or *CAD* is used to summarize fiscal policy.

TOPICS FOR REVIEW

Taxes and net taxes

The budget balance

Public saving

The net export function

Aggregate expenditure

The marginal propensity to spend

National asset formation

National saving

Calculation of the simple multiplier

Fiscal policy and equilibrium income

Actual budget deficits

Cyclically adjusted budget deficits and surpluses

DISCUSSION QUESTIONS

1. State the implied impact on the *AE* curve and hence on equilibrium national income that relates to each of the following headlines.
   a. "Pentagon announces sharp cuts."
   b. "Russia agrees to buy more U.S. wheat."
   c. "Major U.S. companies expected to cut capital outlays."
   d. "Congress considers decreasing personal income-tax rates."

2. Look at Table 26-7 and explain the rather different patterns that the actual and cyclically adjusted deficits have followed for the past decade. (*Hint:* What other economic time series would you need information about in order to be able to answer this question fully?)

3. In August 1989 the Congressional Budget Office projected a budget deficit of $127 billion for fiscal year 1991, while the White House projected a deficit of "only" $88 billion. CBO economists said that their less optimistic assumptions about the economy accounted for much of the difference. How do assumptions about the economy affect estimates of the budget deficit? Look at the data and see who

was closer to being right about the economy in August 1989 and the deficit in 1990–1991.

4. During the recession of 1990–1991 net exports rose. Is this what you would expect, given the net export function discussed in this chapter? Look at the data and see what happened to each of imports and exports during this period. Was the movement of either or both consistent with your expectations?

5. Suppose the government offered a tax credit of one dollar for every dollar that households increased their private saving. (A tax credit reduces the amount of tax that is owed.) What would be the effect on private saving? What would be the effect on national saving?

6. State and local governments are often prohibited by law from running budget deficits. What effect do such laws have on the shape of these governments' budget surplus functions?

7. Classify each of the following government activities as government purchase (G) or transfer program ($-T$).
   a. Food stamps for the poor
   b. Payments to teachers in public schools
   c. Payments to teachers at military academies
   d. Medicare (reimbursement to the elderly or disabled for medical expenses)
   e. Public Health Service vaccination programs

APPENDIX TO CHAPTER

26

An Algebraic Exposition of the Elementary Income-Expenditure Model

We start with the definition of desired aggregate expenditure:

$$AE = C + I + G + (X - IM) \qquad [1]$$

For each component of *AE*, we write down a behavioral function.

$$C = a + bY_d \text{ (consumption function)} \qquad [2]$$

where *a* is autonomous consumption spending and *b* is the marginal propensity to consume.

$$I = I_0 \qquad [3]$$
$$G = G_0 \qquad [4]$$
$$X = X_0 \qquad [5]$$
$$IM = mY \text{ (import function)} \qquad [6]$$

where *m* is the marginal propensity to import. (Obviously, the "behavioral" functions for investment, government purchases, and exports are very simple: These are all assumed to be independent of the level of national income.)

Before deriving aggregate expenditure, we need to determine the relationship between national income (*Y*) and disposable income (Y_d), because it is Y_d that determines desired consumption expenditure. Y_d is defined as income after net tax collections, where net tax collections are total tax collections minus government transfer payments. (Government transfers to households have exactly the same effect as tax reductions. They put money in the hands of the private sector without directly using goods and services.) In Chapter 26 we examined a very simple linear income tax of the form $T = tY$. More generally, we might imagine autonomous net taxes T_0 and

induced net taxes *tY*, so the tax function is given by:

$$T = T_0 + tY \qquad [7]$$

Taxes must be subtracted from national income to obtain disposable income,

$$Y_d = Y - T_0 - tY = Y(1 - t) - T_0 \qquad [8]$$

Substituting Equation 8 into the consumption function allows us to write consumption as a function of national income.

$$C = a - bT_0 + b(1 - t)Y \qquad [9]$$

Notice that autonomous consumption now has two parts, *a* and $-bT_0$, where the latter term is the effect of autonomous taxes on consumption.

Now we can add up all of the components of desired aggregate expenditure, substituting Equations 3, 4, 5, 6 and 9 into Equation 1:

$$AE = a - bT_0 + b(1 - t)Y + I_0 + G_0$$
$$+ X_0 - mY \qquad [10]$$

In equilibrium, aggregate expenditure must equal income, so, as an equilibrium condition,

$$AE = Y \qquad [11]$$

Substitute [11] into [10]:

$$Y = a - bT_0 + b(1 - t)Y + I_0$$
$$+ G_0 + X_0 - mY \qquad [12]$$

Group all the terms in *Y* on the right hand side, and subtract them from both sides:

$$Y = Y[b(1 - t) - m] + a - bT_0 + I_0 + G_0 + X_0 \ [13]$$

$$Y - Y[b(1 - t) - m] = a - bT_0 + I_0 + G_0 + X_0 \ [14]$$

Notice that $[b(1 - t) - m]$ is exactly the marginal propensity to spend out of national income, defined earlier as z. When national income goes up by a dollar, only $1 - t$ dollars go into disposable income, and only b of that gets spent on consumption. Additionally, m gets spent on imports, which are not expenditure on national income. Thus, $b(1 - t) - m$ gets spent on domestic output.

Substituting z for $b(1 - t) - m$ and solving Equation 14 for equilibrium Y yields

$$Y = \frac{a - bT_0 + I_0 + G_0 + X_0}{1 - z} \quad [15]$$

Notice that the numerator of Equation 15 is autonomous expenditure, A (see Box 25-2). Thus, Equation 15 can be rewritten as

$$Y = \frac{A}{1 - z} \quad [16]$$

Notice also that if autonomous expenditure rises by some amount ΔA , Y will rise by $\Delta A/(1 - z)$. Thus, the simple multiplier is $1/(1 - z)$.

The Algebra Illustrated

The numerical example that was carried through Chapters 25 and 26 can be used to illustrate the preceding exposition. In that example, the behavioral equations are

$$C = 100 + 0.8Y_d \quad [17]$$

$$I = 250 \quad [18]$$

$$G = 170 \quad [19]$$

$$X - IM = 240 - 0.1Y \quad [20]$$

$$T = 0.1Y \quad [21]$$

T_0 is 0, so, from Equation 8 disposable income is given by $Y(1 - t) = 0.9Y$. Substituting this into Equation 17 yields

$$C = 100 + 0.72Y_d$$

as in Equation 9.

Now, recalling that in equilibrium $AE = Y$, we add up all of the components of AE and set the sum equal to Y, as in Equation 12:

$$Y = 100 + 0.72Y + 250 + 170 + 240 - 0.1Y \quad [22]$$

Collecting terms yields

$$Y = 760 + 0.62Y \quad [23]$$

Subtracting $0.62Y$ from both sides gives

$$0.38Y = 760 \quad [24]$$

and dividing through by 0.38, we have

$$Y = 760/0.38 = 2,000 \quad [25]$$

This can also be derived by using Equation 16. Autonomous expenditure is 760, and z, the marginal propensity to spend out of national income, is 0.62. Hence, $(1 - z)$ is 0.38. Thus, from Equation 16, equilibrium income is $760/(0.38) = 2,000$, which is exactly the equilibrium we obtained in Table 26-4.

27

National Income and the Price Level in the Short Run

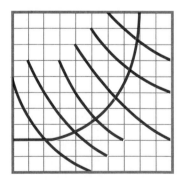

I n the preceding two chapters we have developed a model of income determination in an economy with constant prices. In a real economy, of course, prices are changing all the time. On the supply side, the prices of imported materials used by firms and households change frequently and sometimes dramatically, as when oil prices soared during 1973–1974 and 1979–1980. On the demand side, a boom in less-developed countries can increase the exports of U.S.-made goods that go to those countries, as happened during the 1970s. As we discussed in Chapter 26, a domestic tax cut can lead to an increase in spending; the event actually occurred during the 1980s.

Virtually all shocks to the economy affect *both* national income *and* the price level; that is, they have both real and nominal effects, at least initially. To understand these effects, we need to drop the assumption that the price level is constant and also to develop some further tools, called the *aggregate demand curve* and *aggregate supply curve*.

We make the transition to a variable price level in two steps. First, we study the consequences for national income of *exogenous* changes in the price level—changes that happen for reasons that are not explained by our model of the economy. Then we use our model to *explain* movements in both national income *and* the price level.

Exogenous Changes in the Price Level

What happens to equilibrium national income when the price changes for some exogenous reason, such as a rise in the price of imported raw materials? To find out, we need to understand how the change affects desired aggregate expenditure.

Shifts in the AE Curve

There is one key result that we need to establish: A rise in the price level *shifts* the aggregate expenditure curve downward, while a fall in the price level *shifts* it upward. In other words, the price level and desired aggregate expenditure are negatively related to each other. A major part of the explanation lies with how the change in the price level affects desired consumption expenditure and how it affects net exports.

Changes in Consumption

Much of the private sector's total wealth is held in the form of assets with a fixed nominal money value. One obvious example is money itself—cash and bank deposits. Other examples include many kinds of debt, such as treasury bills and bonds. When a bill or a bond matures, the owner is repaid a stated sum of money. What that money can buy—its real value—depends on the price level. The higher the price level, the less the given sum of money can purchase. For this reason, a rise in the domestic price level lowers the real value of all assets that are denominated in money units and hence lowers the wealth of their owners.

How does a fall in the real value of the private sector's wealth affect the aggregate expenditure curve?[1] As we saw in Chapter 25 (see Figure 25-2 on page 508), there is a relationship between wealth and consumption. Because households have less wealth, they increase their saving so as to restore their wealth to the level that they desire for such purposes as retirement. At any level of income, an increase in desired saving, of course, implies a reduction in desired consumption.

A rise in the domestic price level lowers the real value of total wealth, which leads to a fall in desired consumption; this, in turn, implies a downward shift in the aggregate expenditure curve. A fall in the domestic price level leads to a rise in wealth and desired consumption and thus to an upward shift in the aggregate expenditure curve.

We have concentrated here on the direct effect of the change in wealth on desired consumption expenditure. There is also an indirect effect that operates through the interest rate. Although this effect is potentially very powerful, we cannot study it until we have studied the macroeconomic role of money and interest rates. Further discussion of this point must therefore be postponed until Chapter 30.[2]

Changes In Net Exports

When the domestic price level rises, U.S. goods become more expensive relative to foreign goods. As we saw in Chapter 26, this change in relative prices causes U.S. consumers to reduce their purchases of U.S. goods, which now have become relatively more expensive, and to increase their purchases of foreign goods, which now have become relatively less expensive. At the same time, consumers in other countries reduce their purchases of the now relatively expensive U.S. goods. We saw in Chapter 26 that these changes can be summarized as a downward shift in the net export function.

A rise in the domestic price level shifts the net export function downward, which means a downward shift in the aggregate expenditure curve. A fall in the domestic price level shifts the net export function and the aggregate expenditure curves upward.

In simple language, if U.S. goods become more expensive, less of them will be bought by foreigners, so total desired expenditure on U.S. output will fall; if U.S. goods become cheaper, more will be bought, and total desired expenditure on them will rise.[3]

Changes in Equilibrium Income

Because it causes downward shifts in both the net export function and the consumption function, a rise in the price level causes a downward shift in the aggregate desired expenditure curve, as shown in Figure 27-1. Figure 27-1 also allows us to reconfirm what we already know from Chapter 26: When the *AE* curve shifts downward, the equilibrium level of national income falls.

Because a rise in the domestic price level causes the aggregate expenditure curve to shift downward, it reduces equilibrium national income.

Now suppose that there is a fall in the price level. Because this is the opposite of the case that we have just studied, we can summarize the two key effects briefly. First, U.S. goods become rela-

---

[1] It is worth noting that changes in the real value of a person's wealth do not necessarily change the total wealth of the private sector. In many cases the change in wealth of a creditor is exactly offset by the change in wealth of a debtor. For example, a rise in the price level lowers the real wealth of a bondholder but raises the real wealth of the bond issuer, who will have to part with less purchasing power when the bond is redeemed. However, many assets held by individuals are government debt, and hence any change in the price level causes a net change in the wealth of the private sector.

[2] Here is a brief summary of what is involved. When the price level rises, firms and households need to cover their increased money expenses between one payday and the next. This means that they need to hold more money on average. The increased demand for money bids up the price that must be paid to borrow money (the interest rate). Firms that borrow money to build plants and to purchase equipment and households that borrow money to buy consumer goods and housing respond to rising interest rates by choosing to spend less on a host of items such as capital goods, housing, automobiles, and many other durable goods. This means that there is a decrease in the aggregate demand for the nation's output.

---

[3] This assumes that the price elasticity of demand for traded goods exceeds unity. This standard assumption in the study of international trade is discussed further in Chapter 38.

FIGURE 27-1
Aggregate Expenditure and the Price Level

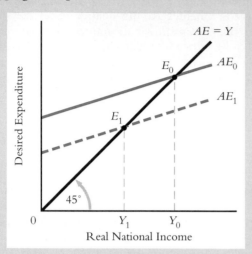

Changes in the price level cause the AE curve to shift and thus cause equilibrium national income to change. At the initial price level, the AE curve is given by the solid line AE_0, and hence equilibrium national income is Y_0. An increase in the price level reduces desired aggregate expenditure and thus causes the AE curve to shift downward to the dashed line, AE_1. As a result, equilibrium national income falls to Y_1.

Starting with the dashed line, AE_1, a fall in the price level increases desired aggregate expenditure, shifting the AE curve up to AE_0 and raising equilibrium national income to Y_1.

tively cheaper internationally, so net exports rise. Second, the purchasing power of some existing assets that are denominated in money terms is increased, so households spend more. The resulting increase in desired expenditure on U.S. goods causes the AE curve to shift upward and hence raises equilibrium national income. This is also shown in Figure 27-1.

Because a fall in the domestic price level causes the aggregate expenditure curve to shift upward, it increases equilibrium national income.

The Aggregate Demand Curve

We now know from the behavior underlying the aggregate expenditure curve that the price level and real national income are negatively related to each other; that is, a change in the price level changes equilibrium

national income in the opposite direction. This negative relationship can be shown in an important new concept, called the *aggregate demand curve*.

Recall that the AE curve relates equilibrium national income to desired expenditure for a given price level, plotting income on the horizontal axis. The **aggregate demand (AD) curve** relates equilibrium national income to the price level, again plotting income on the horizontal axis. Because the horizontal axes of both the AE and the AD curves measure real national income, the two curves can be placed one above the other so that the level of national income on each can be compared directly. This is shown in Figure 27-2.

Now let us see how the AD curve is derived. Given a value of the price level, equilibrium national income is determined in part (i) of Figure 27-2 at the point where the AE curve crosses the 45° line. In part (ii) of Figure 27-2, the combination of the equilibrium level of national income and the corresponding value of the price level is plotted, giving one point on the AD curve.

When the price level changes, the AE curve shifts, for the reasons just seen. The new position of the AE curve gives rise to a new equilibrium level of national income that is associated with the new price level. This determines a second point on the AD curve, as shown in part (ii) of Figure 27-2.

Any change in the price level leads to a new AE curve and hence to a new level of equilibrium income. Each combination of equilibrium income and its associated price level becomes a particular point on the AD curve.

Note that, because the AD curve relates equilibrium national income to the price level, changes in the price level that cause *shifts in* the AE curve cause *movements along* the AD curve. A movement along the AD curve thus traces out the response of equilibrium income to a change in the price level.

The Slope of the AD Curve

Figure 27-2 provides us with sufficient information to establish that the AD curve is negatively sloped.

1. A rise in the price level causes the aggregate expenditure curve to shift downward and hence leads to a movement upward and to the left along the AD curve, reflecting a fall in the equilibrium level of national income.
2. A fall in the price level causes the aggregate expenditure curve to shift upward and hence

FIGURE 27-2
The *AD* Curve and the *AE* Curve

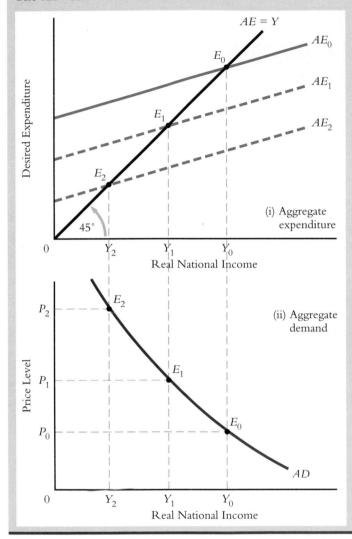

(i) Aggregate expenditure

(ii) Aggregate demand

Equilibrium income is determined by the *AE* curve for each given price level; the level of income and its associated price level are then plotted to yield a point on the *AD* curve. When the price level is P_0, the *AE* curve is AE_0, and hence equilibrium national income is Y_0, as shown in part (i). (This reproduces the initial equilibrium from Figure 27-1.) Plotting Y_0 against P_0 yields the point E_0 on the *AD* curve in part (ii).

An increase in the price level to P_1 causes AE_0 in part (i) to shift downward to AE_1 and thus causes equilibrium national income to fall to Y_1. Plotting this new, lower level of national income, Y_1, against the higher price level, P_1, yields a second point, E_1, on the *AD* curve in part (ii). A further increase in the price level to P_2 causes the *AE* curve in part (i) to shift downward further, to AE_2, and thus causes equilibrium national income to fall further, to Y_2. Plotting Y_2 yields a third point, E_2, on the *AD* curve in part (ii).

Thus, a change in the price level causes a shift in the *AE* curve in part (i) and a movement along the *AD* curve in part (ii).

leads to a movement downward and to the right along the *AD* curve, reflecting a rise in the equilibrium level of national income.

In Chapter 4 we saw that demand curves for individual goods such as carrots and automobiles are negatively sloped. However, the reasons for the negative slope of the *AD* curve are different from the reasons for the negative slope of individual demand curves that are used in microeconomics; this important point is discussed further in Box 27-1.

Points Off the *AD* Curve

The *AD* curve depicts combinations of national income and the price level that give equilibrium between aggregate desired expenditure and actual output in the sense that aggregate desired expenditure equals actual output. These points are said to be *consistent* with expenditure decisions.

The national income given by any point on the aggregate demand curve is such that, *if* that level of output is produced, aggregate desired expenditure at the *given price level* will exactly equal the output.

Points to the left of the *AD* curve show combinations of national income and the price level that cause aggregate desired expenditure to exceed output. There is thus pressure for income to rise because firms could sell more than current output. Points

Box 27-1

The Shape of the Aggregate Demand Curve

In Chapter 4 we studied the demand curves for individual products. It is tempting to think that the properties of the aggregate demand curve arise from the same behavior that gives rise to those individual demand curves. Unfortunately, life is not so simple. Let us see why we cannot take such an approach.

If we assume that we can obtain a downward sloping aggregate demand curve in the same manner that we derived downward sloping individual market demand curves, we would be committing the fallacy of composition. This is to assume that what is correct for the parts must be correct for the whole.

Consider a simple example of the fallacy. An art collector can go into the market and add to her private collection of nineteenth-century French paintings provided only that she has enough money. However, the fact that any one person can do this does not mean that everyone could do so simultaneously. The world's stock of nineteenth-century French paintings is fixed. All of us cannot do what any one of us with enough money can do.

How does the fallacy of composition relate to demand curves? An individual demand curve describes a situation in which the price of one commodity changes while the prices of all other commodities and consumers' money incomes are constant. Such an individual demand curve is negatively sloped for two reasons. First, as the price of the commodity rises, each consumer's given money income will buy a smaller *total* amount of goods, so a smaller quantity of each commodity will be bought, other things being equal. Second, as the price of the commodity rises, consumers buy less of it and more of the now relatively cheaper substitutes.

The first reason has no application to the aggregate demand curve, which relates the total demand for all output to the price level. All prices and total output are changing as we move along the *AD* curve. Because the value of output determines income, consumers' money incomes will also be changing along this curve.

The second reason does apply, but in a limited way, to the aggregate demand curve. A rise in the price level entails a rise in *all* domestic commodity prices. Thus, there is no incentive to substitute among domestic commodities whose prices do not change relative to each other. However, it does give rise, as we saw earlier in this chapter, to some substitution between domestic and foreign goods. Domestic goods rise in price relative to imported goods, and the switch in expenditure will lower desired aggregate expenditure on domestic output and hence will lower equilibrium national income.

to the right of the *AD* curve show combinations of national income and the price level for which aggregate desired expenditure is less than current income. There is thus pressure for income to fall because firms will not be able to sell all of their current output. These relationships are illustrated in Figure 27-3.

Shifts in the *AD* Curve

Because the *AD* curve plots equilibrium national income as a function of the price level, anything that alters equilibrium national income *at a given price level* must shift the *AD* curve. In other words, any change (other than a change in the price level) that causes the *aggregate expenditure curve* to shift will also cause the *AD* curve to shift. (Recall that a change in the price level causes *a movement along* the *AD* curve.) Such a shift is called an *aggregate demand shock*. For example, in the early 1980s changes in the tax laws led to an increase in the amount of consumption expenditure associated with each level of national income. This was an expansionary demand shock that shifted the *AD* curve to the right.

Using our new concepts, the conclusions on page 518 now can be restated as follows:

FIGURE 27-3
The Relationship Between the AE and AD Curves

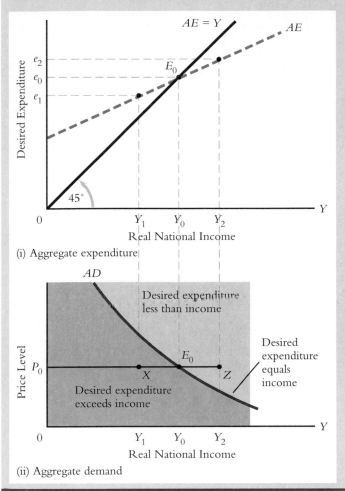

(i) Aggregate expenditure

(ii) Aggregate demand

The AD curve plots the price level against the level of national income consistent with expenditure decisions at that price level. With the price level P_0, equilibrium national income is Y_0, shown by the intersection of AE and the 45° line at E_0 in part (i) and by the point E_0 on the AD curve in part (ii).

With the price level constant at P_0, consider a level of national income of Y_1, which is less than Y_0. As can be seen in part (i), if national income were equal to Y_1, desired aggregate expenditure would be e_1, which is greater than Y_1. Hence, Y_1 is not an equilibrium level of national income when the price level is P_0, and the combination (P_0, Y_1) is not a point on the AD curve in part (ii), as shown by point X.

Now consider a level of national income of Y_2, which is greater than Y_0. As can be seen in part (i), if national income were equal to Y_2, desired aggregate expenditure would be e_2, which is less than Y_2. Hence, Y_2 is not an equilibrium level of national income when the price level is P_0, and the combination (P_0, Y_2) is not a point on the AD curve in part (ii), as shown by point Z.

Repeating the same analysis for each given price level tells us that, for all points to the left of the AD curve (dark-shaded area), income is tending to rise because desired expenditure exceeds income, whereas, for all points to the right of the AD curve (light-shaded area), income is tending to fall because desired aggregate expenditure is less than income.

A rise in the amount of desired consumption, investment, government, or net export expenditure that is associated with each level of national income shifts the AD curve to the right. A fall in any of these expenditures shifts the AD curve to the left.

The Simple Multiplier and the AD Curve

We saw in Chapter 26 that the simple multiplier measures the magnitude of the *change* in equilibrium national income in response to a change in autonomous expenditure when the price level is constant. It follows that this multiplier gives the magnitude of the *horizontal* shift in the AD curve in response to a change in autonomous expenditure. This is shown in Figure 27-4.

The simple multiplier measures the horizontal shift in the AD curve in response to a change in autonomous expenditure.

If the price level remains constant and firms are willing to supply everything that is demanded at that price level, the simple multiplier will also show the change in equilibrium income that will occur in response to a change in autonomous expenditure.

Equilibrium National Income and Price Level

So far we have explained how the equilibrium level of national income is determined *when the price*

FIGURE 27-4
The Simple Multiplier and Shifts in the *AD* Curve

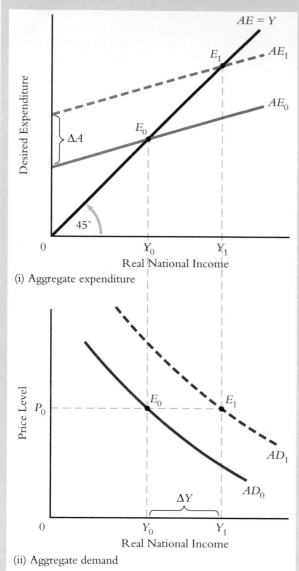

(i) Aggregate expenditure

(ii) Aggregate demand

A change in autonomous expenditure changes equilibrium national income for any given price level, and the simple multiplier measures the resulting horizontal shift in the aggregate demand curve. The original desired expenditure curve is AE_0 in part (i). Equilibrium is at E_0, with national income Y_0 at price level P_0. This yields point E_0 on the curve AD_0 in part (ii).

The AE curve in part (i) then shifts upward from AE_0 to AE_1, due to an increase in autonomous expenditure of ΔA. Equilibrium income now rises to Y_1, with the price level still constant at P_0. Thus, the AD curve in part (ii) shifts to the right to point E_1, indicating the higher equilibrium income Y_1, associated with the same price level P_0. The magnitude of the shift, ΔY, is given by the simple multiplier.

A fall in autonomous expenditure can be analyzed by shifting the AE curve from AE_1 to AE_0, which shifts the AD curve from AD_1 to AD_0 at the price level of P_0. The equilibrium value of national income falls from Y_1 to Y_0.

level is taken as given and how that equilibrium changes as the price level is changed exogenously. We are now ready to take an important further step: adding an *explanation* for the behavior of the price level. To do this, we need to take account of the supply decisions of firms.

The Aggregate Supply Curve

Aggregate supply refers to the total output of goods and services that firms wish to produce, assuming that they can sell all that they wish to sell. Aggregate supply thus depends on the decisions of firms to use workers and all other inputs in order to produce goods and services to sell to households, governments, and other firms, as well as for export.

An *aggregate supply curve* relates aggregate supply to the price level. It is necessary to define two types of such curves. The **short-run aggregate supply (SRAS) curve** relates the price level to the quantity that firms would like to produce and to sell *on the assumption that the prices of all factors of production* remain constant. The *long-run aggregate supply (LRAS) curve*, which we will define more fully in the next chapter, relates the price level to desired sales after the economy has fully adjusted to that price level. For the remainder of this chapter we confine our attention to the *SRAS* curve.

The Slope of the Short-Run Aggregate Supply Curve

To study the slope of the *SRAS* curve, we need to see how costs are related to output and then how prices and outputs are related.

Costs and output. Suppose that firms wish to increase their outputs above current levels. What will this do to their costs per unit of output—often called their **unit costs**? The short-run aggregate supply curve assumes that the prices of all factors of production that firms use, such as labor, remain constant. This does not, however, mean that unit costs will be constant. As output increases, less efficient standby plants may have to be used, and less efficient workers may have to be hired, while existing workers may have to be paid overtime rates for additional work. For these and other similar reasons unit costs will tend to rise as output rises, even when input prices are constant.[4]

Unit costs and output are positively related.

Prices and output. To consider the relationship between price and output, we need to consider firms that sell in two distinct types of markets: those in which firms are price takers and those in which firms are price setters. Some industries, including those that produce most basic industrial materials and some energy products, contain many individual firms. In these cases each one is too small to influence the market price, which is set by the overall forces of demand and supply. Each firm must accept whatever price is set on the open market and adjust its output to that price. The firms are said to be *price takers* and *quantity adjusters*. When the market price changes, these firms will react by altering their production.

Because their unit costs rise with output, price-taking firms produce more when price rises and less when price falls.

Many other industries, including most of those that produce manufactured products, contain so few firms that each can influence market prices. Most such firms sell products that differ from one another, although all are similar enough to be thought of as the single commodity produced by one industry. For example, no two kinds of automobiles are the same, but all automobiles are sufficiently alike so that we have no trouble talking about the automobile industry and the commodity, automobiles. In such cases each firm must quote a price at which it is prepared to sell each of its products; that is, the firm is a price setter. If the demand for the output of price-setting firms increases sufficiently to take their outputs into the range in which their unit costs rise (e.g., because overtime is worked and standby plants are brought into production), these firms will not increase their outputs unless they can pass at least some of these extra costs on through higher prices. When the demand falls, they will reduce output, and competition among them will tend to cause a reduction in prices whenever their unit costs fall.

Price-setting firms will increase their prices when they expand output into the range in which unit costs are rising.

This is the basic behavior of firms in response to the changes in demand and prices when factor prices are constant, and it explains the slope of the *SRAS* curve, such as the one shown in Figure 27-5.

The actions of both price-taking and price-setting firms cause the price level and total output to be positively associated with each other; the graphical expression of this relationship is the positively sloped, short-run aggregate supply curve.

Shifts in the *SRAS* Curve

Shifts in the *SRAS* curve, which are shown in Figure 27-6, are called *aggregate supply shocks*. Two sources of aggregate supply shocks are of particular importance: changes in the price of inputs and increases in productivity.

Changes in input prices. Factor prices are held constant along the *SRAS* curve, and when they change, the curve shifts. If factor prices rise, firms will find the profitability of their current production reduced. For any given level of output to be produced, an increase in the price level will be required. If prices

---

[4] Readers who have studied microeconomics will recognize the law of diminishing returns as one reason why costs rise in the short run as firms squeeze more output out of a fixed quantity of capital equipment.

FIGURE 27-5
A Short-Run Aggregate Supply Curve

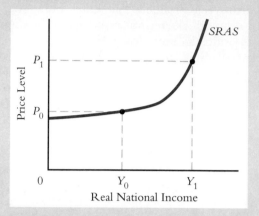

The SRAS curve is positively sloped. The positive slope of the SRAS curve shows that with the prices of labor and other inputs given, total desired output and the price level will be positively associated. Thus, a rise in the price level from P_0 to P_1 will be associated with a rise in the quantity of total output supplied, from Y_0 to Y_1.

Notice that the slope of the SRAS curve is fairly flat at low levels of income and very steep at higher levels. Box 27-3 provides a detailed explanation of this characteristic shape. Briefly, at low levels of income, where there is excess capacity in the economy, output can be increased with little change in cost. As the economy approaches potential income (somewhere between Y_0 and Y_1 in the figure), it becomes very difficult to increase real output in response to demand changes, and increased demand will mainly generate higher prices.

FIGURE 27-6
Shifts in the SRAS Curve

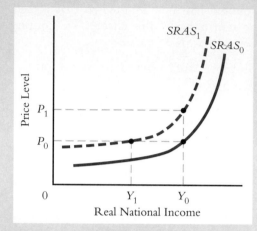

A shift to the left of the SRAS curve reflects a decrease in supply; a shift to the right reflects an increase in supply. Starting from P_0, Y_0 on $SRAS_0$, suppose there is an increase in input prices. At price level P_0 only Y_1 would be produced. Alternatively, to get output Y_0 would require a rise to price level P_1. The new supply curve is $SRAS_1$, which may be viewed as being above and to the left of $SRAS_0$. An increase in supply, caused, say, by a decrease in input prices, would shift the SRAS curve downward and to the right, from $SRAS_1$ to $SRAS_0$.

do not rise, firms will react by decreasing production. For the economy as a whole, this means that there will be less output at each price level than before the increase in factor prices. Thus, if factor prices rise, the SRAS curve shifts upward. (Notice that when a positively sloped curve shifts upward, it also shifts to the left.)

Similarly, a fall in factor prices causes the SRAS curve to shift downward (and to the right). This increase in supply means that more will be produced and offered for sale at each price level.[5]

Increases in productivity. If labor productivity rises, meaning that each worker can produce more, the unit costs of production will fall as long as wage rates do not rise sufficiently to offset the productivity rise fully. Lower costs generally lead to lower prices. Competing firms cut prices in attempts to raise their market shares, and the net result of such competition is that the fall in production costs is accompanied by a fall in prices.

Because the same output is sold at a lower price, this causes a downward shift in the SRAS curve. This shift is an increase in supply, as illustrated in Figure 27-6.

A rightward shift in the SRAS curve, brought about, for example, by an increase in productivity with no increase in factor prices, means that firms will be willing to produce more national income with no increase in the price level. This result has been the object of many government policies that seek to encourage increases in productivity.

A change in either factor prices or productivity will shift the SRAS curve, because any given

---

[5] Note that, for either the AD or the SRAS curve, a shift to the right means an increase, and a shift to the left means a decrease. Upward and downward shifts, however, have different meanings for the two curves. An upward shift of the AD curve reflects an increase in aggregate demand, but an upward shift in the SRAS curve reflects a decrease in aggregate supply.

output will be supplied at a different price level than previously. **An increase in factor prices shifts the** *SRAS* **curve to the left; an increase in productivity or a decrease in factor prices shifts it to the right.**

Macroeconomic Equilibrium

We have now reached our objective: We are ready to see how both real national income and the price level are simultaneously determined by the interaction of aggregate demand and aggregate supply.

The equilibrium values of national output and the price level occur at the intersection of the *AD* and *SRAS* curves, as shown by the pair Y_0 and P_0 that arise at point E_0 in Figure 27-7. We describe the combination of national income and price level that is on both the *AD* and the *SRAS* curves as a *macroeconomic equilibrium*.

To see why this pair of points is the only macroeconomic equilibrium, first consider what Figure 27-7 shows would happen if the price level were below P_0. At this lower price level, the desired output of firms, as given by the *SRAS* curve, is less than desired aggregate expenditure at that level of output. The excess desired aggregate expenditure will cause prices to be bid up, and national income will increase along the *SRAS* curve. Hence, there can be no macroeconomic *equilibrium* when the price level is below P_0.

Similarly, Figure 27-7 shows that, when the price level is above P_0, the behavior underlying the *SRAS* and *AD* curves is not consistent. In this case producers will wish to supply more than the level of output that is demanded at that price level. If firms were to produce their desired levels of output, desired expenditure would not be large enough to purchase everything that would be produced.

Only at the combination of national income and price level given by the intersection of the *SRAS* **and** *AD* **curves are spending (demand) behavior and supply behavior consistent.**

When the price level is less than its equilibrium value, expenditure behavior is consistent with a level of national income that is greater than the desired output of firms. When the price level is greater than its equilibrium value, expenditure behavior is consistent with a level of national income that is less than the desired output of firms.

FIGURE 27-7
Macroeconomic Equilibrium

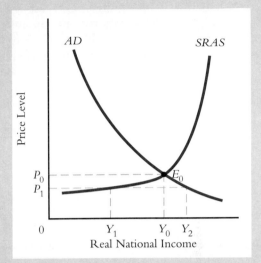

Macroeconomic equilibrium occurs at the intersection of the *AD* **and** *SRAS* **curves and determines the equilibrium values for national income and the price level.** Given the *AD* and *SRAS* curves in the figure, macroeconomic equilibrium occurs at E_0, with national income equal to Y_0 and the price level equal to P_0. At P_0 the desired output of firms, as given by the *SRAS* curve, is equal to the level of national income that is consistent with expenditure decisions, as given by the *AD* curve.

If the price level were equal to P_1, less than P_0, the desired output of firms, given by the *SRAS* curve, would be Y_1. However, at P_1 the level of output that is consistent with expenditure decisions, given by the *AD* curve, would be Y_2, greater than Y_1. Hence, when the price level is P_1, or any other level less than P_0, the desired output of firms will be less than the level of national income that is consistent with expenditure decisions.

Similarly, for any price level above P_0 the desired output of firms, given by the *SRAS* curve, would exceed the level of output that is consistent with expenditure decisions, given by the *AD* curve.

The only price level where the supply decisions of firms are consistent with desired expenditure is at macroeconomic equilibrium. At P_0 firms wish to produce Y_0. When they do so, they generate a national income of Y_0; when income is Y_0, decision makers wish to spend exactly Y_0, thus purchasing the nation's output. Hence, all decisions are consistent with each other.

Macroeconomic equilibrium thus requires that two conditions be satisfied. The first is familiar to us because it comes from Chapters 25 and 26: At the prevailing price level, desired aggregate expenditure must be equal to national income, which means that households are just willing to buy all that is produced. This condition holds everywhere on the *AD* curve. The second requirement for equilibrium is introduced by consideration of aggregate supply: At the prevailing price level, firms must wish to produce the prevailing level of national income, no more and no less. This condition is fulfilled everywhere on the *SRAS* curve. Only where the two curves intersect are both conditions fulfilled simultaneously.

Changes in National Income and the Price Level

The aggregate demand and aggregate supply curves now can be used to understand how various shocks to the economy change both national income and the price level.

A shift in the *AD* curve is called an **aggregate demand shock**. A *rightward* shift in the *AD* curve is an *increase* in aggregate demand; it means that, at all price levels, expenditure decisions will now be consistent with a *higher* level of real national income. Similarly, a *leftward* shift in the *AD* curve is a *decrease* in aggregate demand; it means that, at all price levels, expenditure decisions will now be consistent with a *lower* level of real national income.

A shift in the *SRAS* curve is called an **aggregate supply shock**. A *rightward* shift in the *SRAS* curve is an *increase* in aggregate supply; at any given price level, *more* real national income will be supplied. A *leftward* shift in the *SRAS* curve is a *decrease* in aggregate supply; at any given price level, *less* real national income will be supplied.[6]

What happens to real national income and to the price level when one of the aggregate curves shifts?

---

[6] The distinction between movements along and shifts of curves that we encountered in Chapter 4 and again in Chapter 26 is also relevant here. A *movement along* a demand curve is called a "change in the quantity demanded," whereas a *shift* in a demand curve is called a "change in demand." A similar distinction applies to the supply curve.

A shift in either the *AD* or the *SRAS* curve leads to changes in the equilibrium values of the price level and real national income.

Box 27-2 deals with the special case of a perfectly elastic *SRAS* curve. In that case the aggregate supply curve determines the price level by itself, while the aggregate demand curve then determines real national income by itself.

Aggregate Demand Shocks

Figure 27-8 shows the effects of an increase in aggregate demand. This increase could have occurred because of, say, increased investment or government spending; it means that more national output would be demanded at any given price level. For now we are not concerned with the source of the shock; we are interested in its implications for the price level and real national income. As is shown in the figure, following an increase in aggregate demand, both the price level and real national income rise.

Figure 27-8 also shows that both the price level and real national income fall as the result of a decrease in demand.

Aggregate demand shocks cause the price level and real national income to change in the same direction; both rise with an increase in aggregate demand, and both fall with a decrease in aggregate demand.

An aggregate demand shock means that there is a shift in the *AD* curve (for example, from AD_0 to AD_1 in Figure 27-8). Adjustment to the new equilibrium following an aggregate demand shock involves a movement along the *SRAS* curve (for example, from point E_0 to point E_1).

The Multiplier When the Price Level Varies

We saw earlier in this chapter that the simple multiplier gives the extent of the horizontal shift in the *AD* curve in response to a change in autonomous expenditure. If the price level remains constant and *if* firms are willing to supply all that is demanded at the existing price level, then the simple multiplier gives the increase in equilibrium national income.

Now that we can use aggregate demand and aggregate supply curves, we can answer a more interesting question: What happens in the more usual case in which the aggregate supply curve slopes upward?

Box 27-2

The Keynesian SRAS *Curve*

In this box we consider an extreme version of the *SRAS* curve that is horizontal over some range of national income. It is called the Keynesian short-run aggregate supply curve, after John Maynard Keynes, who in his famous book *The General Theory of Employment, Interest and Money* (1936) pioneered the study of the behavior of economies under conditions of high unemployment.

The behavior that gives rise to the Keynesian *SRAS* curve can be described as follows. When real national income is below potential national income, individual firms are operating at less than normal-capacity output, and they hold their prices constant at the level that would maximize profits if production were at normal capacity. They then respond to demand variations below that capacity by altering output. In other words, they will supply whatever they can sell at their existing prices as long as they are producing below their normal capacity. This means that the firms have horizontal supply curves and that their output is *demand determined.**

Under these circumstances, the economy has a horizontal aggregate supply curve, indicating that

any output up to potential output will be supplied at the going price level. The amount that is actually produced is then determined by the position of the aggregate demand curve, as shown in the figure. Thus, we say that real national income is demand determined. If demand rises enough so that firms are trying to squeeze more than normal output out of their plants, their costs will rise, and so will their prices. Thus, the horizontal Keynesian *SRAS* curve applies only to national incomes below potential income.

---

* The evidence is strong that firms, particularly in the manufacturing sector, do behave like this in the short run. One possible explanation for this is that changing prices frequently is too costly, so firms set the best possible (profit-maximizing) prices when output is at normal capacity and then do not change prices in the face of short-term fluctuations in demand.

In this case a rise in national income caused by an increase in aggregate demand will be associated with a rise in the price level. However, we have seen that a rise in the price level (by reducing net exports and by lowering the real value of household wealth) shifts the *AE* curve downward, which lowers equilibrium national income, other things being equal. The outcome of these conflicting forces is easily seen using aggregate demand and aggregate supply curves.

As can be seen in Figure 27-8, when the *SRAS* curve is positively sloped, the change in national income that has been caused by a change in autonomous expenditure is no longer equal to the size of the horizontal shift in the *AD* curve. A rightward shift of the *AD* curve causes the price level to rise, which in turn causes the rise in national income to be less than the horizontal shift of the *AD* curve. Part of the expansionary impact of an increase in demand

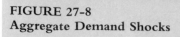

FIGURE 27-8
Aggregate Demand Shocks

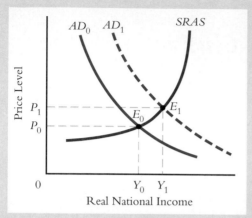

Shifts in aggregate demand cause the price level and real national income to move in the same direction. An increase in aggregate demand shifts the AD curve to the right, say, from AD_0 to AD_1. Macroeconomic equilibrium moves from E_0 to E_1. The price level rises from P_0 to P_1, and real national income rises from Y_0 to Y_1, reflecting a movement along the $SRAS$ curve.

A decrease in aggregate demand shifts the AD curve to the left, say, from AD_1 to AD_0. Equilibrium moves from E_1 to E_0. Prices fall from P_1 to P_0, and real national income falls from Y_1 to Y_0, again reflecting a movement along the $SRAS$ curve.

is dissipated by a rise in the price level, and only part is transmitted to a rise in real output. Of course, there still is an increase in output, so a multiplier still may be calculated, but its value is not the same as that of the simple multiplier.

When the $SRAS$ curve is positively sloped, the multiplier is smaller than the simple multiplier.

Why is the multiplier smaller when the $SRAS$ curve is positively sloped? The answer lies in the behavior that is summarized by the AE curve. To understand this, it is useful to think of the final change in national income as occurring in two stages, as shown in Figure 27-9.

First, with prices remaining constant, an increase in autonomous expenditure shifts the AE curve upward and therefore shifts the AD curve to the right. This is shown by a shift upward of the AE curve in part (i) of the figure and a shift to the right of the

AD curve in part (ii). The horizontal shift in the AD curve is measured by the simple multiplier, but this cannot be the final equilibrium position because firms are unwilling to produce enough to satisfy the extra demand at the existing price level.

Second, we take account of the rise in the price level that occurs owing to the positive slope of the $SRAS$ curve. As we have seen, a rise in the price level, via its effect on net exports and on wealth, leads to a downward shift in the AE curve. This second shift of the AE curve partially counteracts the initial rise in national income and so reduces the size of the multiplier. The second stage shows up as a downward shift of the AE curve in part (i) of Figure 27-9 and a movement upward and to the left along the AD curve in part (ii).

The Importance of the Shape of the $SRAS$ Curve

We now have seen that the shape of the $SRAS$ curve has important implications for how the effects of an aggregate demand shock are divided between changes in real national output and changes in the price level. Figure 27-10 highlights this by considering AD shocks in the presence of an $SRAS$ curve that exhibits three distinct ranges. Box 27-3 explores some possible reasons for such an increasing slope of the $SRAS$ curve.

Over the *flat* range, from 0 to Y_0, any change in aggregate demand leads to no change in prices and, as seen earlier, a response of output nearly equal to that predicted by the simple multiplier.

Over the *intermediate* range, along which the $SRAS$ curve is positively sloped, from Y_1 to Y_4, a shift in the AD curve gives rise to appreciable changes in both real income and the price level. As we saw earlier in this chapter, the change in the price level means that real income will change by less in response to a change in autonomous expenditure than it would if the price level were constant.

Over the *steep* range, for output above Y_4, virtually nothing more can be produced, however large the demand is. This range deals with an economy near its capacity constraints. Any change in aggregate demand leads to a sharp change in the price level and to virtually no change in real national income. The multiplier in this case is nearly zero.

How do we reconcile what we have just discovered with the analysis of Chapters 25 and 26, where shifts in AE *always* change national income?

FIGURE 27-9
The *AE* Curve and the Multiplier When the Price Level Varies

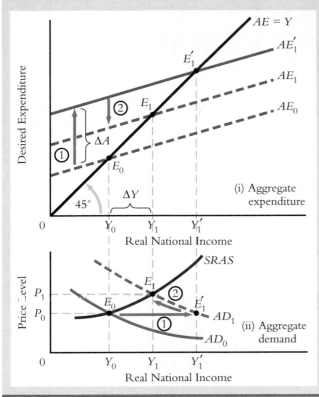

(i) Aggregate expenditure

(ii) Aggregate demand

An increase in autonomous expenditure causes the *AE* curve to shift upward, but the rise in the price level causes it to shift part of the way down again. Hence, the multiplier effect on income is smaller than when the price level is constant. Originally, equilibrium is at point E_0 in both part (i) and part (ii), with real national income at Y_0 and price level at P_0. Desired aggregate expenditure then shifts by ΔA to AE_1', taking the aggregate demand curve to AD_1. These shifts are shown by arrow 1 in both parts. If the price level had remained constant at P_0, the new equilibrium would have been E_1' and real income would have risen to Y_1'. The amount $Y_0 Y_1'$ is the change called for by the simple multiplier.

Instead, however, the shift in the *AD* curve raises the price level to P_1 because the *SRAS* curve is positively sloped. The rise in the price level shifts the aggregate expenditure curve down to AE_1, as shown by arrow 2 in part (i). This is shown as a movement along the *AD* curve, as indicated by arrow 2 in part (ii). The new equilibrium is thus at E_1. The amount $Y_0 Y_1$ is ΔY, the actual increase in real income, whereas the amount $Y_1 Y_1'$ is the shortfall relative to the simple multiplier due to the rise in the price level.

The multiplier, adjusted for the effect of the price increase, is the ratio of $\Delta Y / \Delta A$ in part (i).

FIGURE 27-10
The Effects of Increases in Aggregate Demand

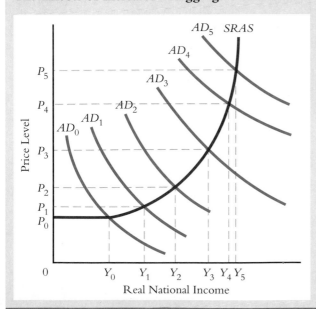

The effect of increases in aggregate demand is divided between increases in real income and increases in prices, depending on the shape of the *SRAS* curve. Because of the increasing slope of the *SRAS* curve, increases in aggregate demand up to AD_0 have virtually no impact on the price level. When aggregate demand increases from AD_0 to AD_1, there is a relatively small increase in the price level, from P_0 to P_1, and a relatively large increase in output, from Y_0 to Y_1. Successive further increases bring larger price increases and relatively smaller output increases. By the time aggregate demand is at AD_4 or AD_5, virtually all of the effect is on the price level.

Box 27-3

More on the Shape of the SRAS Curve

The *SRAS* curve relates the price level to the quantity of output that producers are willing to sell. Notice two things about the shape of the *SRAS* curve that is reproduced in Figure 27-3: It has a positive slope, and the slope increases as output rises.

Positive Slope

The most obvious feature of the *SRAS* curve is its positive slope, indicating that a higher price level is associated with a higher volume of real output, other things being equal. Because the prices of all of the factors of production are being held constant along the *SRAS* curve, why is the curve not horizontal, indicating that firms would be willing to supply as much output as might be demanded with no increase in the price level?

The answer is that, even though *input prices* are constant, *unit costs of production* eventually rise as output increases. Thus, a higher price level for increasing output—rising short-run aggregate supply—is necessary to compensate firms for rising costs.

The preceding paragraph addresses this question: What has to happen to the price level if national output increases, with the price of factors of production remaining constant? Alternatively, one could ask: What will happen to firms' willingness to supply output if product prices rise with no increase in factor prices? Production becomes more profitable, and since firms are interested in making profits, they will usually produce more.* Thus, when the price level of final output rises while factor prices are held constant,

firms are motivated to increase their outputs. This is true for the individual firm and also for firms in the aggregate. This increase in the amount produced leads to an upward slope of the *SRAS* curve.

Thus, whether we look at how the price level will respond in the short run to increases in output or how the level of output will respond to an increase in the price level with input prices being held constant, we find that the *SRAS* curve has a positive slope.

Increasing Slope

A less obvious but in many ways more important property of a typical *SRAS* curve is that its slope *increases* as output rises. It is rather flat to the left of potential output and rather steep to the right. Why? Below potential output, firms typically have unused capacity—some plant and equipment are idle. When firms are faced with unused capacity, only a small increase in the price of their output may be needed to induce them to expand production—at least up to normal capacity.

Once output is pushed far beyond normal capacity, however, unit costs tend to rise quite rapidly. Many higher-cost expedients may have to be adopted. Standby capacity, overtime, and extra shifts may have to be used. Such expedients raise the cost of producing a unit of output. These higher-cost methods will not be used unless the selling price of the output has risen enough to cover them. The further output is expanded beyond normal capacity, the more rapidly unit costs rise and hence the larger is the rise in price that is needed to induce firms to increase output even further.

This increasing slope is sometimes called the *first important asymmetry* in the behavior of aggregate supply. (The second, "sticky wages," will be discussed in the next chapter.)

---

* Those who have studied microeconomics already can understand this in terms of perfectly competitive firms being faced with higher prices and thus expanding output *along* their marginal cost curves until marginal cost is once again equal to price.

The answer is that each *AE* curve is drawn on the assumption that there is a constant price level. A rise in *AE* shifts the *AD* curve to the right. However, a steep *SRAS* curve means that the price level rises significantly, and this shifts the *AE* curve downward, offsetting some of its initial rise.

This interaction is seen most easily if we study the extreme case, shown in Figure 27-11, in which the *SRAS* curve is vertical. An increase in autonomous expenditure shifts the *AE* curve upward, thus raising the amount demanded. However, a vertical *SRAS* curve means that output cannot be expanded to satisfy the increased demand. Instead, the extra demand merely forces prices up, and, as prices rise, the *AE* curve shifts downward once again. The rise in prices continues until the *AE* curve is back to where it started. Thus, the rise in prices offsets the expansionary effect of the original shift and, as a result, leaves both real aggregate expenditure and equilibrium real income unchanged.

The discussion of Figures 27-10 and 27-11 illustrates a general proposition.

The effect of any given shift in aggregate demand will be divided between a change in real output and a change in the price level, depending on the conditions of aggregate supply. The steeper the *SRAS* curve, the greater is the price effect, and the smaller is the output effect.

For reasons discussed in Boxes 27-2 and 27-3, many economists think that the *SRAS* curve is shaped like that in Figure 27-10, that is, relatively flat for low levels of income and becoming steeper as the level of national income increases. This shape of the *SRAS* curve implies that at low levels of national income (well below potential), shifts in aggregate demand primarily affect output, and at high levels of national income (above potential), shifts in aggregate demand primarily affect prices.

Of course, as we have noted already, treating wages and other factor prices as constant is appropriate only when the time period under consideration is short. Hence, the *SRAS* curve is used only to analyze short-run, or *impact*, effects. In the next chapter we shall see what happens in the *long run* when factor prices respond to changes in national income and the price level. First, however, our analysis of the short run needs to be rounded out with a study of aggregate supply shocks.

FIGURE 27-11
Demand Shocks When the *SRAS* Curve Is Vertical

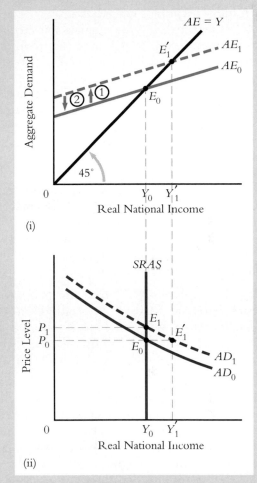

(i)

(ii)

If the *SRAS* curve were vertical, the effect of an increase in autonomous expenditure would be solely a rise in the price level. An increase in autonomous expenditure shifts the *AE* curve upward from AE_0 to AE_1, as shown by arrow 1 in part (i). Given the intitial price level P_0, equilibrium would shift from E_0 to E_1' and real national income would rise from Y_0 to Y_1' (Primes are used on these variables because these results cannot persist; real national income cannot rise to Y_1'.) However, the price level does not remain constant. This is shown by the *SRAS* curve in part (ii). Instead, the price level rises to P_1. This causes the *AE* curve to shift back down all the way to AE_0, as shown by arrow 2 in part (i), and equilibrium income stays at Y_0. In part (ii) the new equilibrium is at E_1 with income at Y_0, which is associated with the new price level, P_1.

Aggregate Supply Shocks

A decrease in aggregate supply is reflected in a shift to the left in the *SRAS* curve and means that less national output will be supplied at any given price level. An increase in aggregate supply is reflected in a shift to the right in the *SRAS* curve and means that more national output will be produced at any given price level.

Figure 27-12 illustrates the effects on the price level and real national income of aggregate supply shocks. As can be seen from the figure, following the decrease in aggregate supply, the price level rises and real national income falls. This combination of events is called *stagflation*, a rather inelegant word that has been derived by combining *stagnation* (a term that is sometimes used to mean less than full employment) and *inflation*.

Figure 27-12 also shows that an increase in aggregate supply leads to an increase in real national income and a decrease in the price level.

Aggregate supply shocks cause the price level and real national income to change in opposite directions: With an increase in supply, the price level falls and income rises; with a decrease in supply, the price level rises and income falls.

An aggregate supply shock means that there is a shift in the *SRAS* curve (for example, from $SRAS_0$ to $SRAS_1$ in Figure 27-12). Adjustment to the new equilibrium following the shock involves a movement along the *AD* curve (for example, from E_0 to E_1).

Oil prices have provided three major examples of aggregate supply shocks in recent decades. The economy is especially responsive to changes in the market for oil, because, in addition to being used to produce energy, oil is an input into plastics and many other materials that are widely used in the economy. Massive increases in oil prices during 1973–1974 and 1979–1980 caused leftward shifts in the *SRAS* curve. National income fell while the price level rose, causing stagflation. During the mid-1980s oil prices fell substantially. This shifted the *SRAS* curve to the right, increasing national income and putting downward pressure on the price level.

We can see now how a rightward shift in the *SRAS* curve, which is brought about by an increase in productivity without a fully offsetting increase in factor prices, raises real national income and lowers the price level.

FIGURE 27-12
Aggregate Supply Shocks

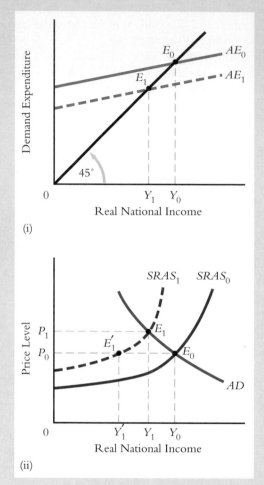

(i)

(ii)

Shifts in aggregate supply cause the price level and real national income to move in opposite directions. The orginal equilibrium is at E_0, with national income of Y_0 appearing in both parts of the figure. The price level is P_0 in part (ii), and, at that price level, the desired aggregate expenditure curve is AE_0 in part (i).

An aggregate supply shock now shifts the *SRAS* curve in part (ii) to $SRAS_1$. At the original price level of P_0, firms are now only willing to supply Y_1'. The fall in supply, with no corresponding fall in demand, causes a shortage that leads to a rise in the price level along $SRAS_1$. The new equilibrium is reached at E_1, where the *AD* curve intersects $SRAS_1$. At the new, and higher, equilibrium price level of P_1, the *AE* curve has fallen to AE_1, as shown in part (i), which is consistent with equilibrium national income of Y_1.

Supply-side economics. The happy state of affairs that takes place when the *SRAS* curve is shifted to the right has led many a policymaker to look for ways to cause such shifts. Generally, such policies are more microeconomic than macroeconomic—they involve improving the efficiency with which markets operate, thereby lowering unit costs and shifting the *SRAS* curve to the right. President Ronald Reagan (in office 1981–1989) used the promise of enhanced supply to justify the large tax cuts that took place from 1981 to 1983. (During this time, the top income tax rate fell from 70 percent to 50 percent; in 1986 it was cut to 28 percent. In 1991 it was increased to 31 percent.) On some occasions Rea-

gan and his advisers argued that the tax cuts would generate so much increased supply that tax revenues would actually increase. This would be possible if income increased by a higher percentage than the reduction in tax rates. These predictions did not materialize.

By increasing disposable income and consumption, the Reagan tax cuts shifted the *AD* curve to the right. There is little clear evidence that there was much effect on supply either in the short or the long run. Thus, the net effect was inflationary, due to the rightward shift of aggregate demand. The ability of economic policy to shift aggregate supply to the right is discussed further in Chapters 34 and 35.

SUMMARY

1. The *AE* curve shows desired aggregate expenditure for each level of income at a particular price level. Its intersection with the 45° line determines equilibrium national income for that price level, on the assumption that firms will produce everything that they can sell at the going price level. Equilibrium income then occurs where desired aggregate expenditure equals national income (output). A change in the price level is shown by a *shift* in the *AE* curve: upward when the price level falls and downward when the price level rises. This leads to a new equilibrium level of national income.

2. The *AD* curve plots the equilibrium level of national income that corresponds to each possible price level. A change in equilibrium national income following a change in the price level is shown by a *movement along* the *AD* curve.

3. A rise in the price level lowers exports and lowers consumers' spending (because it decreases consumers' wealth). Both of these changes lower equilibrium national income and cause the aggregate demand curve to have a negative slope.

4. The *AD* curve shifts when any element of autonomous expenditure changes, and the simple multiplier measures the magnitude of the shift. This multiplier also measures the size of the change in real equilibrium national income when the price level remains constant *and* firms produce everything that is demanded at that price level.

5. The short-run aggregate supply (*SRAS*) curve, drawn for given factor prices, is positively sloped because unit costs rise with increasing output and because rising product prices make it profitable to increase output. An increase in productivity or a decrease in factor prices shifts the curve to the right. A decrease in productivity or an increase in factor prices has the opposite effect.

6. Macroeconomic equilibrium refers to equilibrium values of national income and the price level, as determined by the intersection of the *AD* and *SRAS* curves. Shifts in the *AD* and *SRAS* curves, called aggregate demand shocks and aggregate supply shocks, change the equilibrium values of national income and the price level.

7. When the *SRAS* curve is positively sloped, an aggregate demand shock causes the price level and national income to move in the same direction. The division of the effects between a change in national income and a change in the price level depends on the shape of the *SRAS* curve. When the *SRAS* curve is flat, shifts in the *AD* curve primarily affect real national income. When the *SRAS* curve is steep, shifts in the *AD* curve primarily affect the price level.

8. An aggregate supply shock moves equilibrium national income along the *AD* curve, causing the price level and national income to move in opposite directions. A leftward shift in the *SRAS* curve causes a stagflation—rising prices and falling national income. A rightward shift causes an increase in real national income and a fall in the price level. The division of the effects of a shift in *SRAS* between a change in national income and a change in the price level depends on the shape of the *AD* curve.

TOPICS FOR REVIEW

Effects of a change in the price level

Relationship between the *AE* and *AD* curves

Negative slope of the *AD* curve

Positive slope of the *SRAS* curve

Macroeconomic equilibrium

Aggregate demand shocks

The multiplier when the price level varies

Aggregate supply shocks

Stagflation

Supply-side economics

DISCUSSION QUESTIONS

1. Explain the following by shifts in either the aggregate demand curve or the aggregate supply curves, or both. Pay attention to the initial position before the shift(s) occur.
   a. Output and unemployment rise while prices hold steady.
   b. Prices soar, but employment and output hold steady.
   c. Inflation accelerates even as the recession in business activity deepens.

2. A survey of private economic forecasters in mid-1989 showed that the consensus economic outlook for 1990 was cautiously optimistic—most thought that real growth would remain roughly constant while unemployment would fall slightly; more worry was expressed that inflation might rise well above the 5 percent level. Explain what factors underlying the *AD* and *SRAS* curves would give rise to such a forecast. In retrospect, how accurate were these forecasts? What happened to the underlying determinants to cause actual events to differ from the forecasts?

3. During 1979 through 1980 the British government greatly reduced income taxes but restored the lost government revenue by raising excise and sales taxes. This led to a short burst of extra inflation and

a fall in employment. Explain this in terms of shifts in the aggregate demand or aggregate supply curves, or both.

4. Indicate whether each of the following events is the cause or the consequence of a shift in aggregate demand or supply. If it is a cause, what do you predict will be the effect on the price level and on real national income?

   a. Unemployment decreases in 1989.
   b. OPEC raises oil prices in 1980.
   c. OPEC is forced to accept lower oil prices in 1985.
   d. In the late 1960s and early 1970s the United States experiences a rapid inflation under conditions of approximately full employment.
   e. In France in 1981 income and employment continue to fall while the price level is quite stable.
   f. The Bush administration implements a large decrease in defense spending.
   g. U.S. exports fall in response to a high value of the U.S. dollar and intense competition from foreign suppliers.
   h. Congress slashes personal income tax rates.
   i. Inflationary pressures recede during the recession of 1990–1991.
   j. The Bush administration and Congress finally agree on measures to cut the federal budget deficit.

5. What would happen to employment and income if, in an attempt to lower American unemployment, Congress enacted large increases in American tariff rates? What would happen if all countries did the same?

6. Show the effects on the price level and output of income tax cuts that make people work more in an economy that is experiencing an inflationary gap.

7. Following are the combinations of output and price level, given by indexes for GDP and the CPI, respectively, for some recent years. Treat each pair as if it is the intersection of an *AD* and an *SRAS* curve. Plot these and indicate in each case the direction of shift of the *SRAS* or *AD* curve that could have caused them. Why might you be uncertain about some of the shifts?

	CPI (1982–1984 = 100)	GDP (billions of 1987 dollars)
1979	72.6	3,797
1980	82.4	3,776
1981	90.9	3,843
1982	96.5	3,760
1983	99.6	3,907
1984	103.9	4,149
1985	107.6	4,280
1986	109.6	4,405
1987	113.6	4,540
1988	118.3	4,719
1989	124.0	4,837
1990	130.7	4,885
1991	136.2	4,849

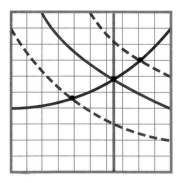

28

National Income and the Price Level in the Long Run

Every worker knows that the best time to ask for a raise is during a boom, when the demand for labor is high. Workers also know that it is difficult to get significant wage increases during a recession, when high unemployment signals a low demand for labor. Every businessperson knows that the cost of needed materials tends to rise rapidly during business expansions and to fall—often dramatically—during recessions. In short, factor prices change with economic conditions, and we need to understand how and why. It is high time, therefore, to go beyond the assumption of fixed factor prices that we used to study the initial effects of aggregate demand and aggregate supply shocks in Chapter 27. To do this we need to see what happens in a longer-term setting, when changes in national income *induce* changes in factor prices. Once we have completed this task, we can use our model of the macroeconomy to investigate the causes and consequences of business cycles and continue our exploration of fiscal policy.

Induced Changes in Factor Prices

We must begin by reconsidering two key concepts that we first encountered in Chapter 23: potential income and the output (or GDP) gap.

Another Look at Potential Income and the Output Gap

Recall that potential income is the total output that can be produced when all productive resources—labor and capital equipment in particular—are being used at their *normal rates of utilization*. When a nation's actual national income diverges from its potential income, the difference is called the output gap. (See Figure 23-4 on page 465.)

Although growth in potential income has powerful effects from one decade to another, its change from one year to another is small enough to be ignored when studying the year-to-year behavior of national income and the price level. Therefore, in this discussion we continue with the assumption, first made in Chapter 23, that potential income is constant. This means that variations in the output gap are determined solely by variations in actual national income around a given potential national income.

Figure 28-1 shows actual national income being determined by the intersection of the *AD* and *SRAS* curves. Potential income is constant, and it is shown by identical vertical lines in the two parts of the figure. In part (i) the *AD* and *SRAS* curves intersect to produce an equilibrium national income that falls short of potential income. The result is called a *recessionary gap* because recessions often begin when actual income falls below potential income. In part (ii)

FIGURE 28-1
Actual Income, Potential Income, and the Output Gap

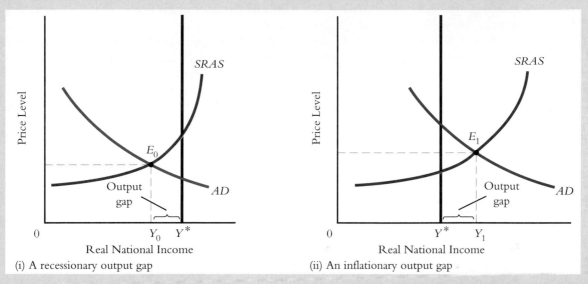

(i) A recessionary output gap

(ii) An inflationary output gap

The output gap is the difference between potential national income, Y^*, and the actual national income, Y. Potential national income is shown by a vertical line because it refers to a given, constant level of real national income. Actual national income is determined by the intersection of the aggregate demand (AD) and short-run aggregate supply ($SRAS$) curves.

In part (i) the positions of the AD and $SRAS$ curves result in a recessionary gap: Equilibrium is at E_0, so actual national income is given by Y_0, which is less than potential income. The output gap is thus $Y^* - Y_0$.

In part (ii) the positions of the AD and $SRAS$ curves result in an inflationary gap. Although potential income is unchanged at Y^*, equilibrium is now at E_1, so actual national income is given by Y_1, which is greater than potential income. The output gap is $Y^* - Y_1$.

the AD and $SRAS$ curves intersect to produce an equilibrium national income that exceeds potential income, resulting in an *inflationary gap*. The way in which an inflationary output gap puts upward pressure on prices will become clear in the following discussion.

Factor Prices and the Output Gap

The output gap provides a convenient measure of the pressure of demand on factor prices. When national income is high relative to potential income, demand for factors will also be high. When national income is low relative to potential income, demand for factors will be correspondingly low. This relationship is true of all factors. The discussion that follows is simplified, however, by focusing on one key factor, labor, and on its price, the wage rate.

When there is an inflationary gap, actual income exceeds potential, so that the demand for labor services will be relatively high. When there is a recessionary gap, the demand for labor services will be relatively low.

Each of these situations will have implications for wages. Before turning to a detailed analysis, we first consider a benchmark for the behavior of wages. Earlier we referred to average costs per unit of output as *unit costs*; to focus on labor costs, we now use average wage costs per unit of output, which we refer to as *unit labor costs*.

Upward and downward wage pressures. In this section we consider the *upward* and *downward* pressures on wages that are associated with various output gaps. Inflationary gaps will exert upward pressure on wages, and recessionary gaps will exert downward pressure on wages. To what do the upward and downward pressures relate? One answer would be that upward pressure means that wages would rise, and downward pressure means that wages would fall. However, most wage bargaining starts from the assumption that, other things being equal, workers should get the benefit of increases in their own productivity by receiving higher wages. Thus, when national income is at its potential level, so that there are neither upward nor downward pressures on wages caused by output gaps, wages will tend to be rising at the same rate as productivity is rising.[1] When wages and productivity change proportionately, *unit labor costs* remain unchanged. For example, if each worker produces 4 percent more and earns 4 percent more, unit labor costs will remain constant. This, then, is the benchmark:

When there is neither excess demand nor excess supply in the labor market, wages will tend to be rising at the same rate as labor productivity; as a result, unit labor costs will remain constant.

Note that, with unit labor costs remaining constant, there is no pressure coming from the labor market for the *SRAS* curve to shift and hence no pressure for the price level to rise or to fall.

In comparison with this benchmark, upward pressure on wages means that there is pressure for wages to rise faster than productivity is rising. Thus, unit labor costs will also be rising. For example, if money wages rise by 8 percent while productivity rises by only 4 percent, labor cost per unit of output will be rising by about 4 percent. In this case, the *SRAS* curve will be shifting to the left, reflecting upward pressure on wages coming from the labor market.

Downward pressure on wages means that there is pressure for wages to rise less fast than productivity. When this occurs, unit labor costs will be falling. For example, if productivity rises by 4 percent while money wages rise by only 2 percent, labor costs

per unit of output will be falling by about 2 percent. In this case, the *SRAS* curve will be shifting to the right, reflecting downward pressure on wages coming from the labor market.

Actual GDP exceeds potential GDP. Sometimes the *AD* and *SRAS* curves intersect where actual output exceeds potential, as illustrated in part (ii) of Figure 28-1. Firms are producing beyond their normal capacity output, so there is an unusually large demand for all factor inputs, including labor. Labor shortages will emerge in some industries and among many groups of workers, particularly skilled workers. Firms will try to bid workers away from other firms in order to maintain the high levels of output and sales made possible by the boom conditions.

As a result of these tight labor-market conditions, workers will find that they have considerable bargaining power with their employers, and they will put upward pressure on wages. Firms, recognizing that demand for their goods is strong, will be anxious to maintain a high level of output. Thus, to prevent their workers from either striking or quitting and moving to other employers, firms will be willing to accede to some of these upward pressures.

The boom that is associated with an inflationary gap generates a set of conditions—high profits for firms and unusually large demand for labor—that exerts upward pressure on wages.

Potential GDP exceeds actual GDP. Sometimes the *AD* and *SRAS* curves intersect where actual output is less than potential, as illustrated in part (i) of Figure 28-1. In this situation firms are producing below their normal capacity output, so there is an unusually low demand for all factor inputs, including labor. The general conditions in the market for labor will be the opposite of those that occur when actual output exceeds potential. There will be labor surpluses in some industries and among some groups of workers. Firms will have below-normal sales and not only will resist upward pressures on wages but also will tend to offer wage increases below productivity increases and may even seek reductions in money wages.

The slump that is associated with a recessionary gap generates a set of conditions—low profits for firms, unusually low demand for labor, and a desire on the part of firms to

---

[1] Ongoing inflation would also influence the normal pattern of wage changes. Wage contracts often allow for changes in prices that are expected to occur during the life of the contract. (Of course, if wages merely rise to keep pace with product prices, there is no effect on unit labor costs; labor cost per dollar's worth of output will be constant.) For now we make the simplifying assumption that the price level is expected to be constant; hence, changes in money wages also are expected to be changes in real wages. The distinction between changes in money wages and real wages, and the important role played by expectations of price level changes, will be discussed in Chapter 32.

resist wage demands and even to push for wage concessions—that exerts downward pressure on wages.

Adjustment asymmetry. At this stage we encounter an important asymmetry in the economy's aggregate supply behavior. Boom conditions, along with severe labor shortages, cause wages, unit labor costs, and the price level to rise rapidly. When there is a large excess demand for labor, wage (and price) increases often run well ahead of productivity increases. Money wages might be rising by 10 or 15 percent, while productivity might be rising at only 2 or 3 percent. Under such conditions, unit labor costs will be rising rapidly.

The experience of many developed economies suggests, however, that the downward pressures on wages during slumps often do not operate as quickly as do the upward pressures during booms. Even in quite severe recessions, when the price level is fairly stable, money wages may continue to rise, although their rate of increase tends to fall below that of productivity. For example, productivity might be rising at, say, 1.5 percent per year while money wages are rising at 0.5 percent. In this case, unit labor costs are falling, but only at about 1 percent per year, so the leftward shift in the *SRAS* curve and the downward pressure on the price level are correspondingly slight. Money wages may actually fall, reducing unit wage costs even more, but the reduction in unit labor costs in times of the deepest recession has never been as fast as the increases that have occurred during several of the strongest booms.

Both upward and downward adjustments to unit wage costs do occur, but there are differences in the speed at which they typically operate. Excess demand can cause unit labor costs to rise very rapidly; excess supply often causes unit labor costs to fall more slowly.

In Chapters 32 and 33, we explore the consequences of this asymmetry for the relationship between unemployment and inflation, which is one of the most important relationships in macroeconomics.[2]

---

[2] This is the second asymmetry in aggregate supply that we have encountered. The first refers to the changing slope of the *SRAS* curve, as discussed in Box 27-3.

Inflationary and recessionary gaps. Now it should be clear why we have named the output gaps the way we have. When actual national income exceeds potential national income, there will normally be rising unit costs, and the *SRAS* curve will be shifting upward. This, in turn, will push the price level up. Indeed, the most obvious event accompanying these conditions is likely to be a significant inflation. The larger is the excess of actual income over potential income, the greater will be the inflationary pressure. To emphasize this salient feature, when output exceeds potential output we say that there is an *inflationary gap*.

When actual output is less than potential output, as we have seen, there will be unemployment of labor and other productive resources. Unit labor costs will fall only slowly, leading to a slow downward shift in the *SRAS* curve. Hence, the price level will be falling only slowly, so that unemployment will be the output gap's most obvious result. Large, *recessionary gaps* will be accompanied by high rates of unemployment.

The induced effects of output gaps on unit labor costs and the consequent shifts in the *SRAS* curve play an important role in our analysis of the long-run consequences of aggregate demand shocks, to which we now turn.

The Long-Run Consequences of Aggregate Demand Shocks

We can now extend our study to cover the longer-run consequences of aggregate demand shocks, when incorporating changes in factor prices. We need to examine separately the effect of aggregate demand shocks on factor prices for expansionary and for contractionary shocks, since the behavior of unit costs is not symmetrical for the two cases. In the following discussion we make the simplifying assumption that labor productivity is constant, so that all changes in wages are also changes in unit labor costs and hence cause the *SRAS* curve to shift. Do not forget, however, that the more general result is that the *SRAS* curve shifts upward whenever money wages rise faster than productivity and downward whenever they rise more slowly than productivity.

Expansionary Shocks

Suppose that the economy starts with a stable price level at full employment, so actual income equals potential income, as shown by the initial equilibrium in part (i) of Figure 28-2.

Now suppose that this happy situation is disturbed by an increase in autonomous expenditure, perhaps caused by a sudden boom in investment spending. Figure 28-2(i) shows the effects of this aggregate demand shock in raising both the price level and national income. Now actual national income exceeds potential income, and there is an inflationary gap.

We have seen that an inflationary gap leads to increases in wages, which cause unit costs to rise. The SRAS curve shifts to the left as firms seek to pass on their increases in input costs by increasing their output prices. For this reason, the initial increases in the price level and in real national income shown in part (i) Figure 28-2 are *not* the final effects of the demand shock. As seen in part (ii) of the figure, the upward shift of the SRAS curve causes a further

rise in the price level, but this time the price rise is associated with a fall in output.

The cost increases (and the consequent upward shifts of the SRAS curve) continue until the inflationary gap has been removed, that is, until income returns to Y^*, its potential level. Only then is there no abnormal demand for labor, and only then do wages and unit costs, and hence the SRAS curve, stabilize.

This important expansionary demand-shock sequence can be summarized as follows:

1. Starting from full employment, a rise in aggregate demand raises the price level and raises income above its potential level as the economy expands along a given SRAS curve.

2. The expansion of income beyond its normal capacity level puts pressure on factor markets; factor prices begin to rise, shifting the SRAS

FIGURE 28-2
Demand-Shock Inflation

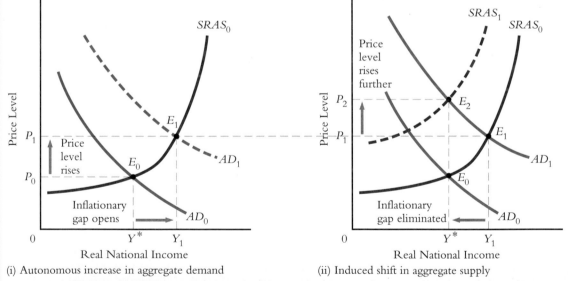

(i) Autonomous increase in aggregate demand

(ii) Induced shift in aggregate supply

A rightward shift of the AD curve first raises prices and output along the SRAS curve. It then induces a shift of the SRAS curve that further raises prices but lowers output along the AD curve. In part (i) the economy is in equilibrium at E_0, at its level of potential output, Y^*, and price level P_0. The AD curve then shifts to AD_1. This moves equilibrium to E_1, with income Y_1 and price level P_1, and opens up an inflationary gap of $Y^* - Y_1$.

In part (ii) the inflationary gap results in an increase in wages and other input costs, shifting the SRAS curve leftward. As this happens, income falls and the price level rises along AD_1. Eventually, when the SRAS curve has shifted to $SRAS_1$, income is back to Y^* and the inflationary gap has been eliminated. However, the price level has risen to P_2.

curve upward, such that prices are higher at every level of output.

3. The shift of the *SRAS* curve causes national income to fall along the *AD* curve. This process continues *as long as* actual income exceeds potential income. Therefore, actual income eventually falls back to its potential level. The price level is, however, now higher than it was after the initial impact of the increased aggregate demand, but inflation will have come to a halt.

The ability to wring more output and income from the economy than its underlying potential output (as in point 2) is only a short-term possibility. National income greater than Y^* sets into motion inflationary pressures that tend to push national income back to Y^*.

There is an adjustment mechanism that eventually eliminates any inflation caused by a one-time demand shock by returning output to its potential level and thus removing the inflationary gap.

Contractionary Shocks

Let us return to that fortunate economy with full employment and stable prices. It appears again in part (i) of Figure 28-3, which is similar to part (i) of Figure 28-2. Now assume that there is a *decline* in aggregate demand, perhaps due to a major reduction in investment expenditure.

The first effects of the decline are a fall in output and some downward adjustment of prices, as shown in part (i) of the figure. As output falls, unemployment rises. The difference between potential output and actual output is the recessionary gap that is shown in Figure 28-3.

FIGURE 28-3
Demand-Shock Deflation with Flexible Wages

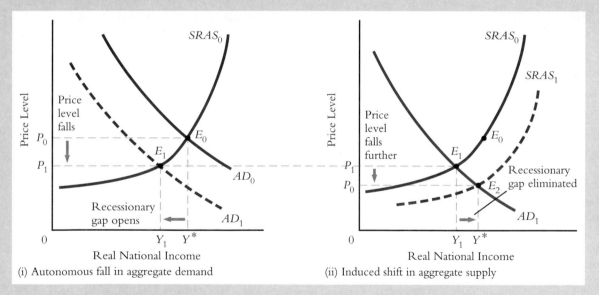

(i) Autonomous fall in aggregate demand

(ii) Induced shift in aggregate supply

A leftward shift of the *AD* curve first lowers price and output along the *SRAS* curve and then induces a (slow) shift of the *SRAS* curve that further lowers prices but raises output along the *AD* curve. In part (i) the economy is in equilibrium at E_0, at its level of potential output, Y^*, and price level P_0. The *AD* curve then shifts to AD_1, moving equilibrium to E_1, with income Y_1 and price level P_1, and opens up a recessionary gap of $Y^* - Y_1$.

Part (ii) shows the adjustment back to full employment that occurs from the supply side of the economy. The fall in wages shifts the *SRAS* curve to the right. Real national income rises, and the price level falls further along the *AD* curve. Eventually, the *SRAS* curve reaches $SRAS_1$, with equilibrium at E_2. The price level stabilizes at P_2 when income returns to Y^*, eliminating the recessionary gap.

Flexible wages. What would happen if severe unemployment did cause wage rates to fall rapidly? Falling wage rates would lower unit costs, causing a rightward shift of the *SRAS* curve. As shown in part (ii) of Figure 28-3, the economy would move along its fixed *AD* curve, with falling prices and rising output until full employment was restored at potential national income Y^*. We conclude that if wages were to fall whenever there was unemployment, the resulting fall in the *SRAS* curve would restore full employment.

Flexible wages that fell during periods of unemployment would provide an automatic adjustment mechanism that would push the economy back toward full employment whenever output fell below potential.[3]

Box 28-1 takes up the interesting case of how the adjustment mechanism might work if the aggregate demand shock were anticipated in advance.

Sticky wages. Boom conditions, along with severe labor shortages, do cause wages to rise rapidly, shifting the *SRAS* curve upward. However, as we noted earlier when we encountered the second asymmetry of aggregate supply behavior, the experience of many economies suggests that wages typically do not fall rapidly in response to recessionary gaps and their accompanying unemployment. It is sometimes said that wages are "sticky" in a downward direction. This does not mean that wages never fall. They do. Typically, however, they do not fall as fast in response to recessionary gaps as they rise in response to inflationary gaps. If wages are sluggish in their response to recessionary gaps, unit labor costs will fall only slowly. This, in turn, means that the downward shifts in the *SRAS* curve occur slowly, and the adjustment mechanism that depends on these shifts will act sluggishly.

The weakness of the adjustment mechanism does not mean that slumps must always be prolonged. Rather, this weakness means that speedy recovery back to full employment must be generated mainly from the demand side. If the economy is to avoid a lengthy period of recession or stagnation, the force leading to recovery usually must be a rightward shift of the *AD* curve rather than a downward drift of the *SRAS* curve. The possibility that government *stabilization policy* might accomplish this is one of the most important and contentious issues in macroeconomics, one that we will return to often throughout the remainder of this book.

The *SRAS* curve shifts to the left fairly rapidly when national income exceeds Y^*, but it shifts to the right only slowly when national income is less than Y^*.

The asymmetry. This difference in speed of adjustment is a consequence of the important asymmetry in the behavior of aggregate supply that was noted earlier in this chapter. This asymmetry helps to explain two key facts about our economy. First, unemployment can persist for quite long periods without causing decreases in unit costs and prices of sufficient magnitude to remove the unemployment. Second, booms, along with labor shortages and production beyond normal capacity, do not persist for long periods without causing increases in unit costs and prices.

The Long-Run Aggregate Supply (LRAS) Curve

The adjustment mechanism leads us to an important concept: the **long-run aggregate supply (*LRAS*) curve**. This curve relates the price level to real national income after wage rates and all other input costs have been fully adjusted to eliminate any unemployment or overall labor shortages.[4]

Shape of the LRAS curve. Once all the adjustments that are required have occurred, the economy will

---

[3] Recall that what determines unit costs is how money wages behave relative to productivity. Since we are assuming productivity to be constant, we can talk about increases or decreases in wages. However, this should always be understood to mean increases or decreases relative to the change in productivity.

[4] Students who have studied microeconomics will notice that this use of the term *long run* is different from its meaning in microeconomics. Note, however, the key similarity that the long run has more flexibility for adjustment than does the short run.

Box 28-1

Anticipated Demand Shocks

Suppose that the increase in aggregate demand that is illustrated in Figure 28-2 was widely anticipated well before it occurred. For example, as an election approached it might become widely believed that the administration would stimulate the economy in order to improve its electoral chances (as the Nixon administration did in 1972, and as the Bush administration tried to do in 1992).

Further, suppose that most employers and employees believe that one of the effects of the demand stimulation will be an inflation. Workers might press for wage increases to prevent the purchasing power of their earnings from being eroded by the coming price increases. Firms would know that demand for their products was likely to rise, enabling them to raise their selling prices. They might therefore be persuaded to grant wage increases now and pass these on to consumers in terms of higher prices.

A demand stimulus that was widely expected to occur and whose inflationary effects were widely understood could lead to upward pressure on wages, even without the opening of any inflationary gap.

If this were to occur, the leftward shift in the *SRAS* curve that is depicted in part (ii) of Figure 28-2 could occur quickly, perhaps accompanying, or even preceding, the rightward shift in the *AD* curve in part (i). Given *perfect* anticipation of the effects of the demand stimulus, and *full* adjustment to it in advance, the equilibrium would go straight from E_0 to E_2. The intermediate position, E_1, with its

accompanying inflationary gap (with national income in excess of potential income), would be completely bypassed.

A similar story might be told for an anticipated fall in aggregate demand. The effects of an unanticipated fall are shown in the two parts of Figure 28-3. However, if the fall were widely anticipated and its effects were generally understood, firms might reduce their wage offers and workers might accept the decreases because they expect prices to fall as well. In this case, it is conceivable that the economy could bypass the recessionary stage and go straight to a lower price level at an unchanged level of real national income.

This possibility, that anticipated demand shocks might have no real effects on real national income and hence on unemployment, plays a key role in some important controversies concerning the effectiveness of government policies. We shall study these in detail in Chapter 33.

In the meantime, we may notice that the complete absence of real effects in the transitionary period, with the only change being in the price level, requires that everyone has full knowledge both of the exact amount of the stimulus that the government will induce and of the new equilibrium values of the relevant prices and wages. In other words, everyone knows what the new equilibrium will be and goes directly to it. Generally, people do not have such perfect knowledge and foresight, so there is some groping toward the equilibrium, and hence some real effects, until the final equilibrium set of wages and prices is reached.

have eliminated any excess demand or excess supply of labor. In other words, full employment will prevail, and output will necessarily be at its potential level, Y^*. It follows that the aggregate supply curve becomes a vertical line at Y^*, as shown in Figure 28-4. The *LRAS* curve is sometimes called the clas-

sical aggregate supply curve because the classical economists were mainly concerned with the behavior of the economy in long-run equilibrium.

Notice that the vertical *LRAS* curve does not represent the same thing as the vertical portion of the *SRAS* curve (see Figure 27-10). Over the

FIGURE 28-4
The Long-Run Aggregate Supply (LRAS) Curve

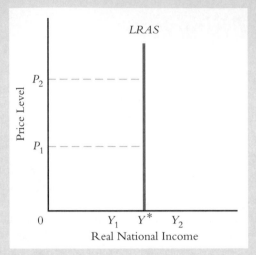

The long-run aggregate supply curve is a vertical line drawn at the level of national income that is equal to potential income, Y^*. It is a vertical line because the total amount of goods that the economy produces when all factors are efficiently used at their normal rate of utilization does not vary with the price level. If the price level were to rise from P_1 to P_2 *and* wages and all other factor prices were to rise by the same proportion, the desired output of firms would remain at Y^*.

If income were Y_1, which is less than Y^*, wages would be falling and the *SRAS* curve would be shifting rightward; hence, the economy would not be on its *LRAS* curve. If income were Y_2, which is greater than Y^*, wages would be rising and the *SRAS* curve would be shifting leftward; hence, again, the economy would not be on its *LRAS* curve.

vertical range of the *SRAS* curve, the economy is at its utmost limit of productive capacity, when no more can be squeezed out, as might occur in an all-out war effort. The vertical shape of the *LRAS* curve is due to the workings of an adjustment mechanism that brings the economy back to its potential output, even though it may move away for considerable periods of time. It is called the long-run aggregate supply curve because it arises as a result of adjustments that take a substantial amount of time.

Along the *LRAS* curve all the prices of all outputs and all inputs have been fully adjusted to

eliminate any excess demands or supplies. Proportionate changes in money wages and the price level (which, by definition, will leave real wages unaltered) will also leave equilibrium employment and output unchanged. The key concept is this: If the price of absolutely everything (including labor) doubles, nothing real changes. When the price of everything bought and sold doubles, neither workers nor firms gain any advantage, and hence neither has any incentive to alter their behavior. Output, therefore, is unchanged. The level of output will be what can be produced in the economy when all factors of production, including labor, are utilized at "normal capacity."

The vertical *LRAS* curve shows that, given full adjustment of input prices, potential income, Y^*, is compatible with any price level.

Long-Run Equilibrium

Figure 28-5 shows the equilibrium output and the price level as they are determined by the intersection of the *AD* curve and the vertical *LRAS* curve. Because the *LRAS* curve is vertical, shifts in aggregate demand change the price level but not the level of equilibrium output, as shown in part (i). By contrast, a shift in aggregate supply changes both output and the price level, as shown in part (ii). For example, a rightward shift of the *LRAS* curve increases national income and leads to a fall in the price level.

With a vertical *LRAS* curve, in the long run, output is determined solely by conditions of supply, and the role of aggregate demand is simply to determine the price level.

National Income in the Short and Long Run

We have now identified two distinct equilibrium conditions for the economy.

1. In the short run, the economy is in equilibrium at the level of income and prices where the *SRAS* curve intersects the *AD* curve.

FIGURE 28-5
Long-Run Equilibrium and Aggregate Supply

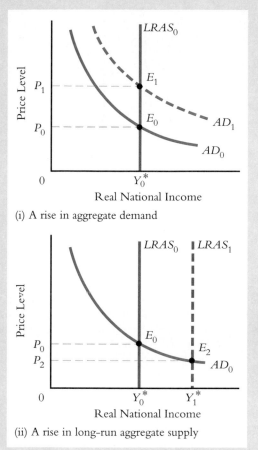

(i) A rise in aggregate demand

(ii) A rise in long-run aggregate supply

When the LRAS curve is vertical, aggregate supply determines the long-run equilibrium value of national income at Y^*. Given Y^*, aggregate demand determines the long-run equilibrium value of the price level. In both parts of the figure the initial long-run equilibrium is at E_0, so the price level is P_0 and national income is Y_0^*.

In part (i) a shift in the AD curve from AD_0 to AD_1, with the $LRAS$ curve remaining unchanged, moves the long-run equilibrium from E_0 to E_1. This raises the price level from P_0 to P_1 but leaves national income unchanged at Y_0^* in the long run.

In part (ii) a shift in the $LRAS$ curve from $LRAS_0$ to $LRAS_1$, with the aggregate demand curve remaining constant at AD_0, moves the long-run equilibrium from E_0 to E_2. This raises national income from Y_0^* to Y_1^* but lowers the price level from P_0 to P_2.

2. In the long run, the economy is in equilibrium at potential income, the position of the vertical $LRAS$ curve. The price level is that at which AD curve intersects the $LRAS$ curve.

When the economy is in long-run equilibrium, it is also in short-run equilibrium.

The *position* of the $LRAS$ curve is at Y^*, which is determined by past economic growth. Deviations of actual income from potential income—output gaps—are generally associated with business cycles. Changes in total real output (and hence in employment, unemployment, and living standards) may take place due either to growth or to the business cycle.

Cycles and Growth

Figure 28-6 illustrates three ways in which GDP can be increased.

Increases in aggregate demand. As shown in part (i) of Figure 28-6, an increase in aggregate demand will yield a one-time increase in real GDP. If that increase occurs when there is a recessionary gap, it pushes GDP toward potential income and thus short-circuits the working of the automatic adjustment mechanism that eventually would have achieved the same outcome by depressing wages and other costs. (The operation of this adjustment mechanism is discussed in detail earlier in this chapter; see especially pages 572–573.)

If the demand shock pushes GDP beyond potential income, the rise in GDP above potential income will only be temporary; the inflationary gap will cause wages and other costs to rise, shifting the $SRAS$ curve to the left. This drives GDP back toward potential so that the only lasting effect is on the price level. Box 28-2 gives a number of reasons why we might expect the effect of demand shocks on GDP to be cyclical, that is, to cause GDP to move first one way, then the other.

Increases in aggregate supply. Increases in aggregate supply will also lead to an increase in GDP. Here it is useful to distinguish between two possible kinds of increases that might occur—those that leave the $LRAS$ curve unchanged and those that shift it.

Part (ii) of Figure 28-6 shows the effects of a temporary increase in aggregate supply. This will shift

FIGURE 28-6
Three Ways of Increasing National Income

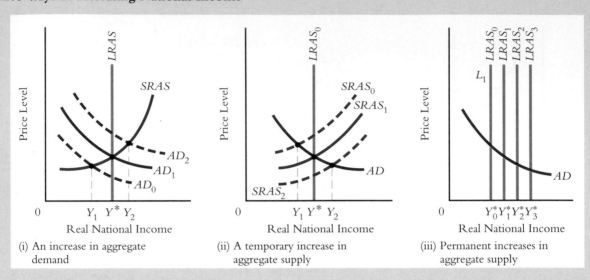

National income will increase in response to an increase in aggregate demand or an increase in aggregate supply. The increase will be permanent if the *LRAS* curve shifts, but if the *LRAS* curve does not shift, any divergences of GDP from potential will be only temporary; the output gap that is created will set in motion the wage adjustments that we studied earlier in this chapter. In part (i) of the figure the *AD* curve shifts to the right. If the initial level of income is Y_1, then the shift from AD_0 to AD_1 eliminates the recessionary gap and raises national income to Y^*. If the initial level of income is Y^*, then the shift from AD_1 to AD_2 raises national income to Y_2 and thereby opens up an inflationary gap.

In part (ii) the *SRAS* curve shifts to the right. If the initial level of income is Y_1, then the shift from $SRAS_0$ to $SRAS_1$ eliminates the recessionary gap and raises national income to Y^*. If the initial level of income is Y^*, then the shift from $SRAS_1$ to $SRAS_2$ raises national income to Y_2 and thereby opens up an inflationary gap.

In the cases shown in parts (i) and (ii), any increase in GDP beyond potential is temporary, since, in the absence of any additional shocks, the inflationary gap will cause wages and other factor prices to rise; this will cause the *SRAS* curve to shift upward and, hence, national income to converge to Y^*.

In part (iii) the *LRAS* curve shifts to the right, causing potential income to increase. Whether or not actual income increases immediately depends on what happens to the *AD* and *SRAS* curves. Since, in the absence of other shocks, actual income eventually converges to potential income, a rightward shift in the *LRAS* curve eventually leads to an increase in actual GDP. If the shift in the *LRAS* curve is recurring, then national income will grow continually.

the *SRAS* curve to the right but will have no effect on the *LRAS* curve or, hence, on potential income. The shock will thus cause GDP to rise relative to potential, but the increase will be soon reversed—in this case, possibly even before any significant impact on wages and other costs can be detected.

Part (iii) of Figure 28-6 shows the effects of permanent increases in aggregate supply that shift the *LRAS* curve. A once-and-for-all increase due, say, to a labor-market policy that reduces the level of structural unemployment will lead to a one-time increase in potential GDP. A recurring increase that is due, say, to population growth, capital accumula-

tion, or ongoing improvements in productivity causes a continual rightward shift in the *LRAS* curve, giving rise to a continual increase in the level of potential GDP.

Economic Growth

A gradual but continual rise in potential GDP, or what we have called *economic growth*, contributes significantly to improvements in the standard of living.

Eliminating a severe recessionary gap will cause a once-and-for-all increase in national income of perhaps 4 percent, while eliminating structural unemployment will raise it by somewhat less. However,

Box 28-2

Demand Shocks and Business Cycles

Aggregate demand shocks are a major source of fluctuations in GDP around Y^*. As we have seen, an expansionary demand shock, starting from a position of full employment, will lead to an increase in output, followed by a fall in output accompanied by an increase in prices as the adjustment mechanism restores the economy to equilibrium. Depending on the nature and magnitude of the shock, the adjustment will take many months, often stretching into one or two years.

Suppose that the government increases spending on roads or that economic growth in Europe leads to an increase in demand for U.S. exports. No matter what the source of growth in demand, the economy will not respond instantaneously. In many industries it takes weeks or months, or even longer, to bring new or mothballed capacity into production and to hire and train new workers. The multiplier process itself also takes time, as households and firms respond to the change in income that results from an initial increase in autonomous spending.

Because of these lags in the economy's response, changes in demand give rise to changes in output that are spread out over a substantial period of time. An increase in demand may lead to a gradual increase

in output that builds up over several months. Then, as output does change, the adjustment mechanism comes into play. As an inflationary gap opens up, wages and costs start to rise, shifting the $SRAS$ curve to the left.

Thus, a once-and-for-all positive demand shock gives rise to a *cyclical* output response, with GDP first rising because of the rightward shift in the AD curve, and then falling because of the upward shift in the $SRAS$ curve. A negative demand shock is likely to play out even more slowly because of the asymmetry of response. Again, however, the behavior of output will be cyclical: Starting from potential output, GDP will fall over a period of time, because of a leftward shift in the AD curve, and then rise slowly as the adjustment mechanism shifts $SRAS$ to the right.

Each major component of aggregate expenditure, consumption, investment, net exports, and government purchases is subject to continual random shifts, which are sometimes large enough to disturb the economy significantly. Adjustment lags convert such shifts into cyclical oscillations in national income.

---

a growth rate of 3 percent per year raises national income by 10 percent in 3 years and *doubles* it in about 24 years.

In any given year, the position of the $LRAS$ curve is at potential GDP, Y^*. The "long run" to which the $LRAS$ curve refers is thus one in which the resources available to the economy do not change, but in which all markets reach equilibrium. Economic growth moves the $LRAS$ curve to the right, year by year. Here, there is no "long run" in which everything settles down, because growth is a continuing process. Rather, the movement in $LRAS$ is a continuing movement in Y^*. '

National saving and economic growth. One important determinant of economic growth is the level of national saving at potential GDP.[5]

We can now use the concepts of national saving and national asset formation, which we introduced in Chapter 26, to show the effect of national saving on economic growth.

---

[5] In Chapter 35 we present a detailed discussion of the determinants of long-term economic growth and of policies that can affect economic growth.

Consider two economies, both of which are currently in long-run (and short-run) equilibrium at the same level of income, Y^*. One of these economies, Futuria, has a relatively high level of national saving and national asset accumulation. The other economy, The Now Republic, has a relatively low level of national saving and national asset accumulation. (Recall from Chapter 26, pages 537–540, that in equilibrium national saving must equal national asset accumulation.) The position of these two economies is depicted in Figure 28-7.

Although the two economies have the same level of national income in the current period, next year the *LRAS* curve of Futuria will be further to the right than that of The Now Republic. This difference will occur because current asset accumulation generates future income, and Futuria is accumulating more assets than is The Now Republic.

Cyclical Fluctuations

Figure 28-6 allows us to distinguish the causes of trend growth in potential GDP, which is the gradual rightward shifting of the *LRAS* curve, from the causes of cyclical fluctuations, which are deviations from that trend.

Cyclical fluctuations in GDP are caused by shifts in the *AD* and *SRAS* curves that cause actual GDP to deviate temporarily from potential GDP.

These shifts, in turn, are caused by changes in a variety of factors, including interest rates, exchange rates, consumer and business confidence, and government policy. Although the resulting deviations of actual from potential GDP are described as "temporary," recall from the discussion above that the automatic adjustment mechanism may work slowly enough that the deviations can persist for some time, perhaps several years.

Figure 28-8 shows graphically the extent to which business cycles (in GDP) have been the norm in U.S. economic history. Figure 28-9 shows three different economic series. Each of these, as well as dozens of others that might be studied, tells us something about the general variability of the economy. Some move more than others, and no two move exactly together; yet all exhibit a cyclical pattern, and they tend to move approximately together.

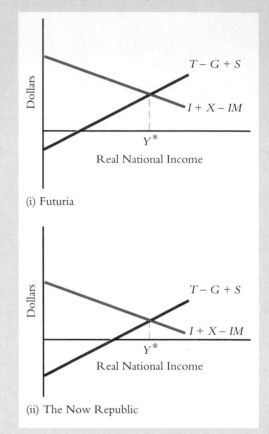

FIGURE 28-7
National Saving and Long-Run Growth

(i) Futuria

(ii) The Now Republic

At a given level of equilibrium income, the higher the level of national saving, the greater the level of national asset accumulation and economic growth. Part (i) depicts an economy, Futuria, with a high level of saving and asset accumulation, in equilibrium at Y^*. (Recall from Chapter 26 that national asset formation equals national saving at the equilibrium level of income.) Part (ii) depicts an economy, The Now Republic, with a low level of saving and asset accumulation, also in equilibrium at the same level of income, Y^*.

The economy of Futuria will grow more rapidly than the economy of The Now Republic. Although both have the same potential income today, the economy that accumulates more assets today will have a higher potential income next year, since those assets will become part of its productive capacity.

Fiscal Policy and the Business Cycle

As we have seen, national income fluctuates continually, primarily due to shifts in aggregate demand and short-run aggregate supply. Any policy that attempts to stabilize national income at or near a desired level (usually potential national income) is called **stabilization policy**. In the remainder of this chapter we conduct a preliminary investigation of *fiscal policy*, taxing and spending, as a tool of stabilization policy. In Chapter 34, after we have discussed money and the banking system, we will return to the subject in more detail.

Since government expenditure increases aggregate demand and taxation decreases it, the *direction* of the required changes in spending and taxation is generally easy to determine once we know the direction of the desired change in national income. However, the *timing*, *magnitude*, and *mixture* of the changes pose more difficult issues.

There is no doubt that the government can exert a major influence on national income. Prime examples are the massive increases in military spending during major wars. U.S. federal expenditure during World War II rose from 7.7 percent of GDP in 1940 to 47.3 percent of GDP in 1944. At the same time, the unemployment rate fell from 14.6 percent to 1.2 percent. Economists agree that the increase in government spending helped to bring about the rise in GDP and the associated fall in unemployment. Similar experiences occurred during the rearmament of most European countries before, or just following, the outbreak of World War II in 1939 and in the United States during the Vietnam War in the late 1960s and early 1970s.

When used appropriately, fiscal policy can be an important tool for stabilizing the economy. In the heyday of fiscal policy, from about 1945 to about 1970, many economists were convinced that the economy could be stabilized adequately just by varying the size of the government's taxes and expenditures. That day is past. Today most economists are aware of the many limitations of fiscal policy.

The Basic Theory of Fiscal Stabilization

A reduction in tax rates or an increase in government expenditure will shift the *AD* curve to the right, causing an increase in GDP. An increase in tax rates or a cut in government expenditure will shift the *AD* curve to the left, causing a decrease in GDP. (See Figures 27-7 and 27-9 for detailed discussions.)

A more detailed look at how fiscal stabilization works will provide a useful review. It will also help to show some of the complications that arise in making fiscal policy.

A recessionary gap. The removal of a recessionary gap is illustrated in Figure 28-10. There are two possible ways in which the gap may be removed.

First, the recessionary gap may eventually drive wages and other factor prices down by enough to shift the *SRAS* curve to the right and thereby reinstate full employment and potential income (at a lower price level). The evidence, however, is that this process takes a substantial period of time.

Second, the *AD* curve could shift to the right, restoring the economy to full employment and potential income (at a higher price level). The government can cause such a shift by using expansionary fiscal policy. The advantage of using fiscal policy is that it may substantially shorten what would otherwise be a long recession. One disadvantage is that the use of fiscal policy may stimulate the economy just before private-sector spending recovers on its own. As a result, the economy may overshoot its potential output, and an inflationary gap may open up. In this case, fiscal policy that is intended to promote economic stability can actually cause instability.

An inflationary gap. Figure 28-11 (page 586) shows the ways in which an inflationary gap can be removed.

First, wages and other factor prices may be pushed up by the excess demand. The *SRAS* curve will therefore shift to the left, eventually eliminating the gap, reducing income to its potential level, and raising the price level.

Second, the *AD* curve can shift to the left, restoring equilibrium GDP. The government, by raising taxes or cutting spending, can induce such a shift, reducing aggregate demand sufficiently to remove the inflationary gap. The advantage of this approach is that it avoids the inflationary increase in prices that accompanies the first method. One disadvantage is that if private-sector expenditures fall due to natural causes, national income may be pushed below potential, thus opening up a recessionary gap.

FIGURE 28-8
U.S. Business Activity Since 1870

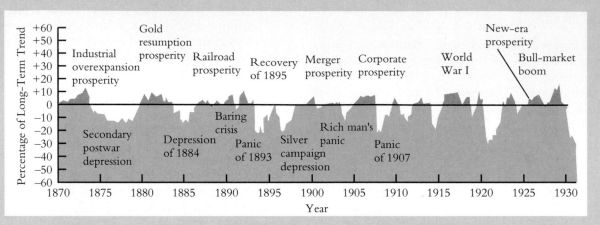

Cyclical ups and downs have dominated the short-term behavior of the U.S. economy since at least 1870. This chart is constructed by selecting one index of general economic activity, fitting a trend line to it, and plotting the deviations of the index from its trend value. It clearly shows the tendency for an economy to fluctuate. Major

FIGURE 28-9
Fluctuations in Output, Selected Series, 1950–1991

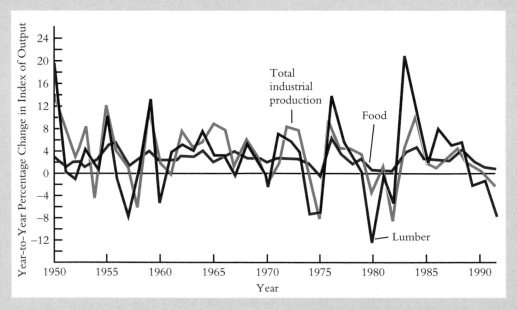

Fluctuations follow similar, but by no means identical, paths for various output series. Fluctuations are easily seen in these series. Food tends to fluctuate much less than, and lumber fluctuates somewhat more than, the overall series for industrial production. (*Source: Economic Report of the President,* various issues.)

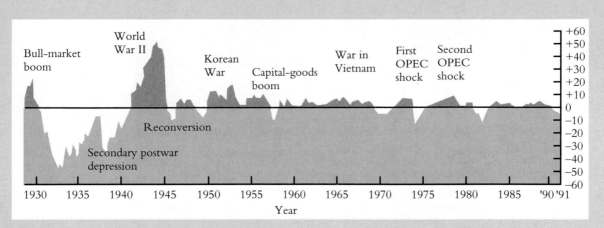

booms and slumps are unmistakable. (*Source:* The AmeriTrust Company, Cleveland, Ohio; and *Economic Report of the President,* 1992.)

FIGURE 28-10
Removal of a Recessionary Gap

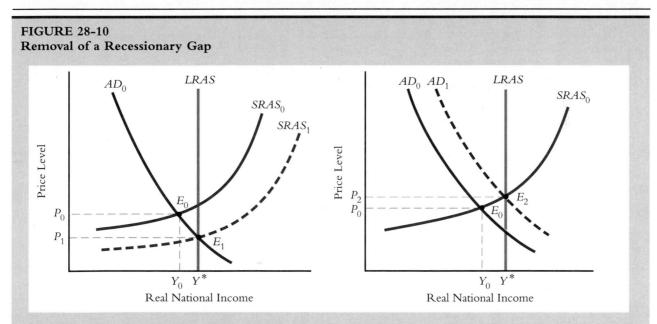

A recessionary gap may be removed by a (slow) rightward shift of the *SRAS* curve, a natural revival of private-sector demand, or a fiscal policy–induced increase in aggregate demand. Initially, equilibrium is at E_0, with national income at Y_0 and the price level at P_0. The recessionary gap is $Y_0 Y^*$.

As shown in part (i), the gap might be removed by a shift in the *SRAS* curve to $SRAS_1$. This increase in aggregate supply could occur as a result of reductions in wage rates and other input prices. The shift in the *SRAS* curve causes a movement down and to the right along AD_0. This movement establishes a new equilibrium at E_1, achieving potential income, Y^*, and lowering the price level to P_1.

As shown in part (ii), the gap might also be removed by a shift of the *AD* curve to AD_1. This increase in aggregate demand could occur either because of a natural revival of private-sector expenditure or because of a fiscal policy-induced increase in expenditure. The shift in the *AD* curve causes a movement up and to the right along $SRAS_0$. This movement shifts the equilibrium to E_2, raising income to Y^* and the price level to P_2.

FIGURE 28-11
Removal of an Inflationary Gap

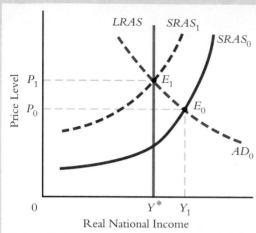

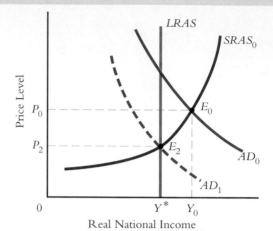

(i) An inflationary gap removed by a leftward shift in *SRAS*

(ii) An inflationary gap removed by a leftward shift in *AD*

An inflationary gap may be removed by a leftward shift of the *SRAS* curve, a reduction in private-sector demand, or a policy-induced reduction in aggregate demand. Initially, equilibrium is at E_0, with national income at Y_0 and the price level at P_0. The inflationary gap is Y^*Y_0.

As shown in part (i), the gap might be removed by a shift in the *SRAS* curve to $SRAS_1$. This decrease in aggregate supply could occur as a result of increases in wage rates and other input prices. The shift in the *SRAS* curve causes a movement up and to the left along AD_0. This movement establishes a new equilibrium at E_1, reducing income to its potential level, Y^*, and raising the price level to P_1.

As shown in part (ii), the gap might also be removed by a shift in the *AD* curve to AD_1. This decrease in aggregate demand could occur either because of a natural fall in private spending or because of contractionary fiscal policy. The shift in the *AD* curve causes a movement down and to the left along $SRAS_0$. This movement shifts the equilibrium to E_2, lowering income to Y^* and the price level to P_2.

A key proposition. This discussion suggests that, in circumstances in which the automatic adjustment mechanisms either fail to operate quickly enough or give rise to undesirable side effects such as rising prices, there is a potential stabilizing role for fiscal policy.

Government taxes and expenditure shift the *AD* curve and hence can be used to remove persistent GDP gaps.

The Paradox of Thrift

As we discovered in Chapter 26, government tax revenues are related to the performance of the economy; they are high during booms and low during slumps. Thus, if a government follows a balanced budget policy, its fiscal policy becomes **procyclical.** It will restrict its spending during a recession because its tax revenue is low, and it will increase its spending during a recovery when its tax revenue is rising.

In other words, it rolls with the economy, raising and lowering its spending in step with everyone else, exactly counter to the theory of fiscal stabilization that we just discussed.

The theory of national income determination predicts that an increase in national saving will shift the *AD* curve to the left and hence *reduce* the equilibrium level of income in the short run. The contrary case, a general decrease in thrift and increase in expenditure, shifts the *AD* curve to the right and hence increases national income in the short run. This prediction is known as the *paradox of thrift*.[6]

---

[6] The prediction is not actually a paradox. Rather, the prediction is a straightforward implication of the theory of income determination. The expectations that lead to the "paradox" are based on the fallacy of composition: the belief that what is true for the parts is necessarily true for the whole.

The policy implication of this prediction is that substantial unemployment can be combatted by encouraging governments, firms, and households to spend more, *not* to save more. In times of unemployment and depression, frugality will only make things worse. This prediction goes directly against the idea that we should tighten our belts when times are tough. The notion that it is not only possible but also acceptable to spend one's way out of a depression touches a sensitive point with people raised on the belief that success is based on hard work and frugality and not on prodigality; as a result, the idea often arouses great hostility.

Applications. As is discussed in Box 28-3, the implications of the paradox of thrift were not generally understood during the Great Depression, and most governments followed procyclical spending policies in order to balance their budgets. When Milton Friedman said, "We are all Keynesians now," he was referring to (among other things) the general acceptance of the view that the government's budget is much more than just the revenue and expenditure statement of a very large organization. Whether we like it or not, the sheer size of the government's budget inevitably makes it a powerful tool for influencing the economy.

State and local government have fiscal policies, too. If there is no change in policy, their tax revenues tend to rise and fall with income. Like the federal government, their budget surplus functions are upward sloping in income. Unlike the federal government, however, most state and local governments are required by their constitutions to balance their budgets every year, with the result that their fiscal policies are procyclical. During the recession that began in 1990, state and local governments increased taxes and cut spending by tens of billions of dollars, moving the *AD* curve to the left when there was already a recessionary gap, tending to deepen the recession.

Limitations. The paradox of thrift concentrates on shifts in aggregate demand that have been caused by changes in saving (and hence spending) behavior. Hence, it applies only in the short run, when the *AD* curve plays an important role in the determination of national income.

In the long run, when the economy is on its *LRAS* curve and hence aggregate demand is not important for the determination of real national income (see Figure 28-5), the paradox of thrift does

not apply. The more people and governments save, the larger is the supply of funds available for investment.

The more people invest, the greater is the growth of potential income. Increased potential income causes the *LRAS* curve to shift to the right.

These longer-term effects were discussed briefly earlier in this chapter (pages 581–582) and are taken up in detail in Chapter 35 in the discussion of economic growth. In the meantime, we concentrate on the short-run demand effects of saving and spending.

The paradox of thrift is based on the short-run effects of changes in saving and investment on aggregate demand.

Automatic Stabilizers

In Chapter 26 we introduced the *budget surplus function*. The *discretionary* fiscal policy that we have been discussing in this chapter involves *shifts* in the budget surplus function. Expansionary policies, whether increases in purchases or decreases in net taxes, reduce the budget surplus (increase the deficit) at every level of national income, shifting the *AD* curve to the right. Contractionary policies increase the surplus (reduce the deficit) at every level of income, shifting the *AD* curve to the left.

Even when the government does not undertake to stabilize the economy via discretionary fiscal policy, the upward slope of the budget surplus function means that there are fiscal effects that cause the budget to act as an *automatic stabilizer* for the economy.

The budget surplus increases as income increases because tax revenues rise, and some transfer payments, especially unemployment insurance, fall. Thus, net taxes move in the same direction as national income. (Unless there are changes in policy, government purchases are generally unaffected by cyclical movements in the economy.) With procyclical net tax revenues, disposable income moves in the same direction as national income but does not move by as much. The government keeps a share of the increased national income when national income rises. When national income falls, the fall in net taxes makes disposable income fall by less.

In Chapter 26, for example, we assumed that the net income tax rate was 0.1. This implies that a \$1 rise in autonomous spending would increase

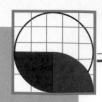

Box 28-3

Fiscal Policy and the Great Depression

Failure to understand the implication of the paradox of thrift led many countries to adopt disastrous policies during the Great Depression. In addition, failure to understand the role of built-in stabilizers has led many observers to conclude, erroneously, that fiscal expansion was tried in the Great Depression but failed. Let us see how these two misperceptions are related.

The Paradox of Thrift in Action

In 1932 Franklin Roosevelt was elected president on a platform of fighting the Great Depression with government policies. His actual policies did not, however, lead to an increase in aggregate demand. They were based instead on the notion that in a recession it is necessary to "tighten our belts." In his inaugural address he urged, "Our great primary task is to put people to work.... [This task] can be helped by insistence that the Federal, State and local governments act forthwith on the demand that their costs be drastically reduced. . . . There must be a strict supervision of all banking and credits and investments."

Across the Atlantic, King George V told the British House of Commons in 1931, "The present condition of the national finances, in the opinion of His Majesty's Ministers, calls for the imposition of additional taxation and for the effecting of economies in public expenditure."

As the paradox of thrift predicts, these policies tended to worsen, rather than cure, the depression.

Interpreting the Deficit in the 1930s

The deficits that occurred following Roosevelt's election were not the result of a program of deficit-financed public expenditure. Instead, they were the result of the fall in tax yields, brought about by the fall in national income as the economy sank into depression. President Roosevelt and his advisers did not advocate a program of massive deficit-financed spending to shift the AD curve to the right. Instead, they hoped that a small amount of government spending plus numerous policies, designed to stabilize prices and to restore confidence, would lead to a recovery of private-investment expenditure that would substantially shift the AD curve. To have expected a massive revival of private-investment expenditure as a result of the puny increase in aggregate demand that was instituted by the federal government now seems hopelessly naive.

When we judge Roosevelt's policies from the viewpoint of modern multiplier theory, their failure is no mystery. Indeed, Professor E. Cary Brown of MIT, after a careful study, concluded, "Fiscal policy seems to have been an unsuccessful recovery device in the 'thirties—not because it did not work, but because it was not tried." In 1933 the federal government was spending $2 billion for purchases of goods and services, compared to $1.3 billion that it spent in 1929. This increase was a small drop in a very large bucket, considering that GNP fell from $103 billion in 1929 to $46 billion in 1933! Given the deficits achieved, it would have taken a multiplier of 25 for the U.S. economy to have approached full employment; in fact, the multiplier in the 1930s was closer to 2. Expenditures were wastefully small, not (as many people thought at the time) wastefully large.

Once the massive, war-geared expenditure of the 1940s began, income responded sharply and unemployment evaporated. Government expenditures on goods and services, which had been running at under 15 percent of GNP during the 1930s, jumped to 46 percent by 1944, while unemployment reached the incredible low of 1.2 percent of the civilian labor force.

The performance of the American economy from 1930 to 1945 is quite well explained by national income theory. It is clear that the government did not effectively use fiscal measures to stabilize the economy. War cured the Depression, because war demands made acceptable a level of government expenditure sufficient to remove the deflationary gap. Had the first Roosevelt administration been able to do the same, it might have ended the waste of the Great Depression many years sooner.

disposable income by only $0.90, dampening the multiplier effect of the initial increase. Generally, the wedge that income taxes place between national income and disposable income reduces the marginal propensity to spend out of national income, thereby reducing the size of the multiplier. The lower the multiplier, the less will equilibrium national income tend to change for a given change in autonomous expenditure. The effect is to stabilize the economy, reducing the fluctuations in national income that are caused by changes in autonomous expenditure. Because no policies need to be changed in order to achieve this result, the properties of the government budget that cause the multiplier to be reduced are called **automatic fiscal stabilizers.**

The Council of Economic Advisers estimated that during the 1970s a decrease in GDP automatically produced a reduction in government receipts and an increase in unemployment benefits of roughly $0.35 for every $1 reduction in GDP. Thus, these two stabilizers reduced the movement of disposable income to about two-thirds of the movement of national income. Because taxes are now somewhat less responsive to national income following the tax cuts of the 1980s, the power of automatic stabilizers is currently somewhat lower than it was in the 1970s.

Limitations of Discretionary Fiscal Policy

At the end of 1991 and the beginning of 1992, when these words were written, the United States was experiencing a recessionary gap; the unemployment rate was about two percentage points above its high-employment level. Many politicians and other public figures were calling upon the government to engage in expansionary fiscal policy, in order to eliminate the recessionary gap. There was also a good deal of resistance to these calls. Indeed, the *New York Times* opined that "It's no secret that many of the President's economists, along with much of the economics establishment, fear that economic stimulus of any kind is as likely to harm as help."[7]

According to the discussion of the previous few pages, returning the economy to high employment would simply be a matter of cutting taxes and raising government spending, in some combination. Why did so many economists believe that such policies would be "as likely to harm as help"? Part of the

answer is that the execution of discretionary fiscal policy is anything but simple.[8]

Lags. To change fiscal policy requires making changes in taxes and government expenditures. The changes must be agreed upon by the president and Congress. The political stakes in such changes are generally very large; taxes and spending are called "bread and butter issues" precisely because they affect the economic well-being of almost everyone. Thus, even if economists agreed that the economy would be helped by, say, a tax cut, politicians would likely spend a good deal of time debating *whose* taxes should be cut by *how much*. The delay between the initial recognition of a recession or inflation and the enactment of legislation to change fiscal policy is called a **decision lag**. In the United States the decision lag for fiscal changes is quite long, especially in comparison with countries that have parliamentary systems.

Once policy changes are agreed upon, there is still an **execution lag**, adding time between the enactment and the implementation of the change. Furthermore, once policies are in place, it will usually take still more time for their economic consequences to be felt. Because of these lags, it is quite possible that by the time a given policy decision has any impact on the economy, circumstances will have changed such that the policy is no longer appropriate. Figure 28-12 illustrates the problems that can arise in these circumstances.

To make matters even more frustrating, tax measures that are known to be temporary are generally less effective than measures that are expected to be permanent. If households know that a given tax cut will only last for a year, they will recognize that the effect on their long-run consumption possibilities is small and will adjust their short-run consumption relatively little.

The more closely household consumption expenditure is related to lifetime income rather than to current income, the smaller will be the effects on current consumption of tax changes that are known to be of short duration.

---

[7] *New York Times*, December 11, 1991, p. 1.

[8] Another part of the answer has to do with the long-term consequences of budget deficits. This subject is taken up in Chapter 34. Also, as we shall see in Chapter 39, international considerations may reduce (but not eliminate) fiscal policy's effectiveness as a stabilization tool.

FIGURE 28-12
Effects of Fiscal Policies That Are Not Reversed

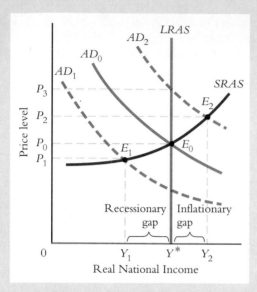

Fiscal policies that are initially appropriate may become inappropriate when private expenditure shifts. The normal level of the aggregate demand function is assumed to be AD_0, leaving income normally at Y^* and the price level at P_0. Suppose a slump in private investment shifts aggregate demand to AD_1, lowering national income to Y_1 and causing a recessionary gap of Y^*Y_1.

The government now introduces fiscal expansion to restore aggregate demand to AD_0 and national income to Y^*. Suppose that private investment then recovers, raising aggregate demand to AD_2. If fiscal policy can be quickly reversed, aggregate demand can be returned to AD_0 and income stabilized at Y^*. If the policy is not quickly reversed, equilibrium will be at E_2 and an inflationary gap Y^*Y_2 will open up. This gap will cause wages to rise and thus shift the $SRAS$ curve leftward and eventually restore Y^* at price level P_3.

Now suppose that starting from equilibrium E_0 a persistent investment boom takes AD_0 to AD_2. In order to stop the price level from rising in the face of the newly opened inflationary gap, the government introduces fiscal restraint, thereby shifting aggregate demand back to AD_0. Further assume, however, that the investment boom then comes to a halt, so that the aggregate demand curve shifts downward to AD_1. Unless the fiscal policy can be rapidly reversed, a recessionary gap will open up and equilibrium income will fall to Y_1.

The role of discretionary fiscal policy. All of these difficulties suggest that attempts to use discretionary fiscal policy to **fine tune** the economy are likely to fail. Neither economic nor political science has yet advanced far enough to allow policymakers to undo the consequences of every aggregate demand shock. On the other hand, many economists would still argue that when a recessionary gap is large enough and persists for long enough, **gross tuning** may be appropriate: Fiscal policy can and should then be used to return the economy to full employment. Other economists believe that fiscal policy should not be used for economic stabilization at all. Rather, they would argue, tax and spending behavior should be the outcome of public choices regarding the size and financing of the public sector. We return to these debates in Chapters 34 and 35.

Economic Policy, Economic Stability, and Economic Growth

To get ahead of our story, the desirability of using fiscal policy to stabilize the economy depends a great deal on the speed with which the adjustment mechanism returns the economy to potential income. If the adjustment mechanism works quickly, there is no role for discretionary fiscal policy. If the adjustment mechanism works slowly, there may well be a role for policies that can be used to shift aggregate demand. Fiscal policy is one such policy. Monetary policy, which we take up in the next three chapters, is another. Only when we have completed our study of the way in which money and monetary institutions fit into the overall macroeconomy can we fully articulate the choices available to governments wishing to stabilize their economies.

Stabilization policy will generally have consequences for economic growth—for the movement of the $LRAS$ curve over time. Given that an economy is at or near potential GDP, the more expansive is its fiscal policy, the lower will be national saving and national asset formation. Thus, the lower will be economic growth. (See Figure 28-7.) Of course, if the economy would otherwise stay in recession for a period of years, the gain in output in the near term could easily outweigh the longer-term consequences of a smaller stock of assets at full employment. (After all, and this was part of Keynes' message, the state of the world at full employment is not very interesting to members of a society who are a long way from it.)

Stability, growth, and the effect of economic policy on both are among the key subjects of this book.

With the tools that we have developed thus far, we can begin to see how they fit together. Once we add a better understanding of money and monetary policy, presented in the next three chapters, we will be able to complete the story.

SUMMARY

1. Potential income is treated as given and is represented by a vertical line at Y^*. The output gap is equal to the horizontal distance between Y^* and the actual level of income, as determined by the intersection of the AD and $SRAS$ curves.

2. An inflationary gap means that Y is greater than Y^*, and hence demand in the labor market is relatively high. As a result, wages rise faster than productivity, causing unit costs to rise. The $SRAS$ curve shifts leftward, and the price level rises.

3. A recessionary gap means that Y is less than Y^*, and hence demand in the labor market is relatively low. Although there is some resulting tendency for wages to fall relative to productivity, asymmetrical behavior means that the strength of this force will be much weaker than that indicated in summary point 2. Unit costs will only fall slowly, so the output gap will persist.

4. An expansionary demand shock creates an inflationary gap that causes wages to rise faster than productivity. Unit costs rise, shifting the $SRAS$ curve to the left and resulting in a higher level of prices, with output eventually falling back to its potential level.

5. A contractionary demand shock works in the opposite direction. If, however, factor prices are sticky, the automatic adjustment process may be slow, and a recessionary gap may not be quickly eliminated.

6. The long-run aggregate supply ($LRAS$) curve relates the price level and national income after all wages and other costs have been adjusted fully to long-run equilibrium. The $LRAS$ curve is vertical at the level of potential income, Y^*.

7. Because the $LRAS$ curve is vertical, output in the long run is determined by the position of the $LRAS$ curve, and the only long-run role of the AD curve is to determine the price level. Economic growth determines the position of the $LRAS$ curve.

8. GDP can increase (or decrease) for any of three reasons: a change in aggregate demand, a change in short-run aggregate supply, or economic growth, a change in long-run aggregate supply. The first two changes are typically associated with business cycles.

9. Demand shocks are an important source of business cycles. As the shock works its way through the economy and the adjustment mechanism comes into play, GDP will often exhibit a cyclical (up and down, or down and up) pattern.

10. In the long run, when the level of GDP is equal to Y^*, the higher is the level of national saving, the higher will be the level of national

Definitions of the Money Supply

Different definitions of the money supply include different types of deposits. The narrowly defined money supply, called **M1,** includes currency and those deposits that are themselves usable as media of exchange. Broader definitions include other deposits as well.

Prior to 1980, when the distinction between demand and time deposits was quite clear, *narrow money* was defined simply as the sum of currency plus demand deposits. The growth in ATS and NOW accounts has led to an expanded definition of M1 that includes them and similar accounts at credit unions and mutual savings banks.

Broader definitions include M2 and M3. **M2** is M1 plus savings and smaller time deposits of all kinds, including money market accounts and overnight loans. **M3** is M2 with the addition of several components, the most important of which are large-denomination savings deposits called **certificates of deposit (CDs).**

M1 concentrates on the medium-of-exchange function of money, and to a great extent so does M2. M3 and other, even broader definitions include assets that serve the temporary store-of-value function and in practice are quickly convertible into a medium of exchange at a known price ($1 on deposit in a savings account is always convertible into a $1 demand deposit or $1 in cash). Table 29-1 shows the principal components in the money supply.

Near Money and Money Substitutes

Over the past two centuries, what has been accepted by the public as money has expanded from gold and silver coins to include, first, bank notes and, later, bank deposits subject to transfer by check. Until recently, most economists would have agreed that money stopped at that point. Today an active debate centers on the definition of money that is appropriate to present circumstances.

If we concentrate only on the medium-of-exchange function of money, money certainly consists of the assets included in M1, and most economists argue that it extends to those included in M2 as it is currently measured. Some of these media of exchange—currency (which earns no interest) and demand deposits (which earn only very low

TABLE 29-1   Money Supply in the United States, 1991 (*billions of dollars*) (*annual averages of daily figures*)

Currency	$ 267
Demand deposits	289
Traveler's checks	8
Other checkable deposits	333
M1	$ 897
Overnight repurchase agreements (RPs) and Eurodollars	$ 76
Money market mutual balances	352
Money market deposit accounts and savings deposits	1,037
Small-denomination time deposits	1,061
M2	$3,425
Large-denomination time deposits	$ 457
Term repurchase agreements	73
Term Eurodollars	61
Institutional money market mutual funds	167
M3	$4,172

Source: Economic Report of the President, 1992; totals may not add up due to rounding.

The three widely used measures of the money supply are M1, M2, and M3. The narrow definition of the money supply concentrates on what can be used directly as a medium of exchange. The broader definitions add in deposits that serve the store-of-value function and can be readily, and sometimes automatically, converted to a medium of exchange on a dollar-for-dollar basis.

Note that M1 includes traveler's checks held by the public, which clearly are a medium of exchange. Within M2, RPs are funds lent out on the overnight money market, and Eurodollars are U.S. dollar–denominated deposits in U.S. banks located outside of the United States. M2 and M3 include similar items, with the difference in most cases being that the term deposits are in M3 and the demand deposits in M2.

interest)—are poor stores of value. Assets that earn a higher interest return will do a better job of meeting this function than will currency or demand deposits. At the same time, however, these other assets are less capable of fulfilling the medium-of-exchange function.

Assets that adequately fulfill the store-of-value function and are readily converted into a medium of exchange but are not themselves a medium of exchange are sometimes called **near money.** There is a wide spectrum of assets in the economy that pay interest and also serve as reasonably satisfactory temporary stores of value. For example, you may elect to hold a treasury bill that matures in 30 days; although it is less liquid than a demand deposit (because there is the risk that its market value may change between the time you buy it and the time you want to sell it, say, 10 days later), such a security is a reasonably satisfactory short-run store of purchasing power.

In general, whether or not it pays to convert cash and demand deposits into higher-interest *near money* for a given period of time will depend on the inconvenience and other transaction costs of shifting funds and on the amount of interest that can be earned.

Things that serve as temporary media of exchange but are not a store of value are sometimes called **money substitutes.** Credit cards are a prime example of a money substitute. The credit card serves the short-run function of a medium of exchange by allowing you to make purchases even though you may have no cash or bank deposit currently in your possession. However, this is only temporary; money remains the final medium of exchange for these transactions when the credit account is settled.

Choosing a Measure

Since the eighteenth century, economists have known that the amount of money in circulation is an important economic variable. For theories to be useful, however, we must be able to identify real-world counterparts of these theoretical magnitudes.

What is included in the definition of *money* has changed and will continue to change over time. New monetary assets are continually being developed to serve some, if not all, the functions of money, and they are more or less readily convertible into money. There is no single, timeless definition of what is money and what is only near money or a money substitute.

For the purposes of this book we will focus on the medium of exchange function of money, and thus define it to include currency plus deposits that can be withdrawn or transferred on very short notice—that is, money will mean M2.

The Banking System

Many types of institutions make up a modern banking system such as exists in the United States today. The **central bank** is the government institution that serves to control the banking system and is the sole money-issuing authority. Through it, the government's monetary policy is conducted. In the United States the central bank is the Federal Reserve System, nicknamed "the Fed."

Financial intermediaries are privately owned institutions that serve the general public. They are called *intermediaries* because they stand between savers, from whom they accept deposits, and investors, to whom they make loans. In this chapter we focus on the *commercial banks,* although, as discussed in footnote 3 on page 603, much of the analysis applies as well to other intermediaries.

Central Banks

All advanced free-market economies have, in addition to commercial banks, a central bank. Many of the world's early central banks were private, profit-making institutions that provided services to ordinary banks. Their importance, however, led to their developing close ties with government. Central banks soon became instruments of the government, though not all of them were publicly owned. The Bank of England, one of the world's oldest and most famous central banks, began to operate as the central bank of England in the seventeenth century, but it was not formally taken over by the government until 1947.

The Federal Reserve System

The Federal Reserve System (the Fed) began operation in 1914, following the passage of the Federal Reserve Act in 1913. Although the Fed appears, at first glance, to consist of a number of privately owned banks, controlled by the commercial banks, it actually functions as the country's central bank. The most important thing about the Fed is this:

In its role as the central bank of the United States, the Federal Reserve System is responsible for the U.S. government's monetary policy.

The basic elements in the Federal Reserve System are described in Box 29-3.

Box 29-3

The Federal Reserve System

The basic elements of the Federal Reserve System are: (1) the board of governors; (2) the Federal Advisory Council, which has no real power but whose 12 members advise the board of the views of commercial bankers; (3) the 12 Federal Reserve banks; (4) the Federal Open Market Committee (FOMC); and (5) the more than 25,000 member commercial banks.

The Board of Governors

The board of governors consists of seven members who are appointed by the president of the United States and confirmed by the Senate. Members serve for 14 years. The length of term is important, for it means that each member of the board serves beyond the term of the president who is making the appointment. Board members are top-level public servants who often come from the world of business or banking.

The board is responsible to Congress but works closely with the Department of the Treasury. It supervises the entire Federal Reserve System and exercises general policy control over the 12 Federal Reserve banks. The chairman of the board (Allan Greenspan in 1992) is in a powerful position to influence the country's monetary policies. The chairman's term is four years, although historically most chairmen have served more than one term.

The Federal Reserve Banks

The 12 Federal Reserve banks serve the 12 districts into which the country is divided. The banks are located in Boston, New York, Philadelphia, Cleveland, Richmond, Atlanta, Chicago, St. Louis, Minneapolis, Kansas City, Dallas, and San Francisco. Each bank is nominally owned by the member banks in its district. A commercial bank that is a member of the system is required to purchase a specific amount of Federal Reserve bank stock on which it receives a flat dividend. Each Federal Reserve bank has nine directors: three bankers elected by the member banks; three representatives of business, agriculture, or industry; and three public members appointed by the board of governors.

Although technically privately owned and operated, the Federal Reserve banks are actually operated under guidelines set down by the board of governors in what it deems to be the public interest.

The Federal Reserve banks have a strong tradition of service to the banking community within the policy guidelines laid down by the board of governors. Revenues that they have earned in excess of expenses and of fixed minimum profits that they can retain for their own use must be turned over to the U.S. Treasury. Most Federal Reserve banks, along with the office of the board of governors, engage in research and publish many bulletins of interest to the financial communities that they serve.

The Federal Open Market Committee

The FOMC has 12 members: the 7 members of the board of governors, the president of the Federal Reserve Bank of New York, plus presidents of four other Federal Reserve banks (who serve on a rotating basis). This committee determines the open market policy of the system, which deals principally with how many government securities the Federal Reserve banks should buy or sell on the open market.

This FOMC determines the country's monetary policy. Its decisions are made independently of the wishes of either the president or Congress, because neither have any formal authority to set monetary policy. Many critics argue that it is undemocratic to have 12 people setting monetary policy without any formal review by elected representatives of the people. However, those who defend the Fed's independence argue that it allows the Fed to act quickly and with a long-term view of the consequences of its actions, free of the constraints imposed by short-term political considerations.

TABLE 29-2 Federal Reserve Banks, Consolidated Balance Sheet, January 1992 (*billions of dollars*)

Assets	
Gold certificates and other cash	11.1
U.S. government securities	267.0
Loans to commercial banks	0.1
Other assets	54.3
	332.5
Liabilities	
Federal Reserve notes outstanding	283.1
Deposits of member bank reserves	31.8
Deposits of U.S. Treasury	4.6
Other liabilities	13.0
	332.5

Source: Federal Reserve Bulletin, June 1992.

The balance sheet of the Fed shows that it serves as banker to the commercial banks and to the U.S. Treasury and as issuer of our currency; it also suggests the Fed's role as regulator of money markets and the money supply. Federal Reserve notes are currency, and the deposits of member banks give commercial banks the reserves that they use to create deposit money. The Fed's principal assets, holdings of U.S. government securities, arise from its open-market operations that are designed to regulate the money supply and also from direct purchases from the Treasury.

Basic Functions of a Central Bank

A central bank serves four main functions. It is a banker for commercial banks, a banker for the government, the controller of the nation's supply of money, and a regulator of money markets. The first three functions are reflected by the Fed's balance sheet, which lists its assets and its liabilities, as shown in Table 29-2.

Banker to commercial banks. The central bank accepts deposits from commercial banks and will, on order, transfer them to the account of another bank. In this way the central bank provides each commercial bank with the equivalent of a checking account and with a means of settling debts to other banks. The deposits made by the commercial banks with the central bank appear in Table 29-2 as *liabilities* (its promises to pay) of the central bank. These deposits are liabilities of the central bank because they are owned by the commercial banks, and the central bank must pay the commercial banks on demand.

Central banks provide temporary liquidity to such commercial banks by making short-term loans to them. Loans made by the Fed to commercial banks are said to be made available through the Fed's "discount window." The rate of interest that the Fed charges on such loans is called the **discount rate.**

Bank for the government. Governments, too, need to hold their funds in an account into which they can make deposits and against which they can write checks. The U.S. Treasury keeps its checking deposits at the Federal Reserve banks, replenishing them from much larger "tax and loan" accounts kept at commercial banks. When the government requires more money than it collects in taxes, it, too, needs to borrow, and it does so by selling securities. Most are sold directly to the public, but when the central bank buys a new government bond on the open market, it is indirectly lending to the government.

Controller of the money supply. One of the most important functions of a central bank is to control the money supply. From Table 29-2 it is clear that the overwhelming proportion of a central bank's liabilities (its promises to pay) are either Federal Reserve notes or the deposits of commercial banks, which provide reserves for demand deposits that are owned by households and firms. Later in this chapter we shall study how the Fed can control the money supply, and in Chapter 31 we will see how it uses this ability to conduct monetary policy.

Regulator of money markets. The central bank frequently enters money markets for purposes other than controlling the money supply.

Financial institutions are in the business of borrowing on a short-term basis (i.e., accepting deposits) and lending on a long-term basis. Large, unanticipated increases in interest rates tend to squeeze these institutions. The average rate that they earn on their investments rises only slowly as old contracts mature and new ones are made, but they must either pay higher rates to hold on to their deposits or accept wide-scale withdrawals that could easily bring about their insolvency. The Fed sometimes helps such institutions by moderating rapid swings in interest rates.

Central banks assume responsibility for supporting the country's financial system and for preventing serious disruption by wide-scale panic and the resulting bank failures. From their very beginnings, central banks have acted as "lenders of last resort"

Box 29-4

The Globalization of Financial Markets

Technological innovations in communication and the desire to avoid onerous government regulations have led to a globalization of the financial service industry over the past two decades. Computers, satellite communication systems, reliable telephones with direct worldwide dialing, electronic mail, and fax machines—all coming into widespread use only within the past decade—have put people in instantaneous contact anywhere in the world.

As a result of these new technologies, borrowers and lenders can learn about market conditions and then move their funds instantly in search of the best loan rates. Large firms need transaction balances only while banks in their area are open. Once banks close for the day in each center, the firms will not need these balances until tomorrow's reopening; thus, the funds can be moved to another market, where they are used until it closes. They are then moved to yet another market. Funds are thus free to move from London to New York to Tokyo and back to London on a daily rotation. This is a degree of global sophistication that was inconceivable before the advent of the computer, when international communication was much slower and costlier than it now is. To facilitate the movement in and out

of various national currencies, increasing amounts of bank deposits are denominated in foreign rather than domestic currencies.

One of the first developments in this movement toward globalization was the growth of the foreign currency markets in Europe in the 1960s. At first the main currency involved was the U.S. dollar, and hence *Eurodollar* markets were the first to develop. Today the *Eurobond* market is an international market where bonds of various types, denominated in various national currencies, are issued and sold to customers located throughout the world. The customers are mainly public corporations, international organizations, and multinational enterprises. The *Eurocurrency* market is a market for short-term bank deposits and bank loans denominated in various currencies.

The original attraction of the Eurodollar market was the freedom from the restrictions placed by the Federal Reserve on American commercial banks. By operating in offshore markets, banks were able to cut unit costs by dealing in large volume at the wholesale level. They could then offer rates that were higher for lenders and lower for borrowers than those prevailing in the United States.

to the commercial banking system. Commercial banks with sound investments sometimes find themselves in urgent need of cash to meet the demands of their depositors. If such banks cannot obtain ready cash, they may be forced into insolvency, despite their being in a basically sound financial position.

Conflicts among functions. The several functions of the central bank are not always compatible. For example, we shall see in Chapter 31 that an antiinflationary policy requires the Fed to cause interest rates to rise. The resulting squeeze makes life uncomfortable for banks and other financial institutions and makes borrowing expensive for the government. If the Fed chooses to ease those problems, say, by

lending money to banks, we will see that this means relaxing its antiinflationary policy.

The Fed must strive to balance conflicting objectives. We shall discuss a number of aspects of this conflict in Chapter 31. However, at this stage we note that many critics think that the Fed does not always succeed in finding the right balance among its conflicting objectives.

The Commercial Banks

Modern commercial banking systems are of two main types: One type has a small number of banks, each with a large number of branch offices; the other consists of many independent banks. The banking

The progressive worldwide lifting of interest-rate ceilings and other capital market restrictions that occurred in the 1980s led to a further globalization of financial markets. Although this removed some of the original reasons for their growth, the Euro-markets prospered. First, they allowed banks to avoid the remaining domestic regulations. Second, the advantage of having an international market dealing in many different national currencies was sufficient to sustain the markets.

The increasing sophistication of information transfer also led to a breakdown of the high degree of specialization that had characterized financial markets in earlier decades. When information was difficult to obtain and analyze, an efficient division of labor called for a host of specialist institutions, each with expertise in a narrow range of transactions. As a result of the new developments in communication technology, economies of large scale led to the integration of various financial operations within one firm. For example, in many countries banks have moved into the markets where securities are traded, while many security-trading firms have begun to offer a range of banking services. As the scale of such integrated firms increases, they find it easier to extend their operations geographically as well as functionally.

It has often been difficult for government regulations to keep up with these rapid changes. Governments that relaxed their regulations first in face of the evolving realities often allowed their financial institutions to gain important advantages in international competition. The UK government has been quick to react to these developments, and as a result London has retained its strong position in the international financial world. In contrast, the U.S. government has been slow to adapt. For example, it still limits interstate banking and prevents U.S. banks from extending their operations beyond the ones traditionally reserved for banks. As a result, the U.S. banks have lost out heavily to European and Japanese banks.

The kinds of government intervention into domestic capital markets and government control over international capital flows that characterized the 1950s and 1960s is no longer possible. International markets are just too sophisticated. Globalization is here to stay, and by removing domestic restrictions and exchange controls, governments in advanced countries are only bowing to the inevitable.

systems of the United Kingdom and Canada are of the first type, with only a few banks accounting for the overwhelming bulk of the business. The U.S. system is of the second type.

Branch banking in the United States is governed by state law. In some states banks are permitted to branch statewide; in other so-called unit-bank states, no branching at all is permitted; and some states permit limited branching into areas near the home office. Many of these prohibitions are under pressure and are disappearing as regulations are relaxed. Sweeping changes in banking have been occurring internationally; these developments and their interaction with domestic regulation are discussed in Box 29-4.

There is a wide variety of banking systems in existence, but they all function in essentially the same manner.

The basic unit of the U.S. banking system is the **commercial bank,** which is a privately owned, profit-seeking institution. Commercial banks use invested funds to "earn money" in the same sense as do firms that make neckties or bicycles. A commercial bank provides a variety of services to its customers: a relatively safe and convenient place to store money and to earn a modest but secure return, the convenience of demand deposits that can be transferred by personal check, and often financial advice and estate management services. The bank earns some revenue by charging for these services, but such fees are only a part of its total earnings. A larger portion of a bank's earnings is derived from using the funds placed with it to make loans to households and firms and to invest in government securities.

It is the variety of functions performed, and in particular the holding of demand deposits, that traditionally has distinguished commercial banks from other financial institutions, each of which performed some but not all of these functions. Although the various types of financial institutions continue to specialize to some extent, sweeping deregulation over the past decade has made the distinction between the various financial institutions much less sharp.

Commercial banks differ from one another in many ways. Some are large, and others are small; some are located in big cities, and others are located in small towns; some hold charters from the federal government (national banks), and others hold charters from state governments (state banks). Nearly 40 percent of the commercial banks, including most of the larger ones, are members of the Federal Reserve System. All national banks must be members, and any state bank may join the system by agreeing to abide by its regulations. However, nonmember banks are indirectly tied into the system, because they are invariably *correspondents* of larger member banks; that is, they have regular commercial relations with the member banks.

In practice, all commercial banks—members and nonmembers alike—have always come under the regulatory influence of the Fed.

Interbank Activities

Commercial banks have a number of interbank cooperative relationships. These are encouraged by special banking laws because they facilitate the smooth functioning of money and credit markets.

For example, banks often share loans. Even the biggest bank cannot meet all of the credit needs of an industrial giant such as General Motors, and often a group of banks will offer a "pool loan." On a different scale, a small bank, when it is approached for a loan that is larger than it can safely handle, will often ask a larger bank to "participate" in the loan. Another form of interbank cooperation is the bank credit card—VISA and MasterCard are each operated by a large group of banks.

Probably the most important form of interbank cooperation is check clearing and collection. Bank deposits are an effective medium of exchange only because banks accept each other's checks. If a depositor in bank A writes a check to someone who deposits it in bank B, bank A owes money to bank B. This, of course, creates a need for the banks to present checks to each other for payment.

There are millions of such transactions in the course of a day, and they result in an enormous sorting and bookkeeping job. Multibank systems make use of a **clearing house** where interbank debts are settled. At the end of the day, all the checks drawn by bank A's customers and deposited in bank B are totaled and set against the total of all the checks drawn by bank B's customers and deposited in bank A. The actual checks are passed through the clearing house back to the bank on which they were drawn. For member banks, this clearing function is performed by the Federal Reserve System, and much of it is done electronically by a system operated by the Fed called *Fedwire*.

Principal Assets and Liabilities

Table 29-3 shows the combined balance sheet of the commercial banks in the United States. The bulk of a bank's liabilities are deposits that are owed to its depositors. The principal assets of a bank are the

---

TABLE 29-3 Consolidated Balance Sheet of U.S. Commercial Banks, March 1992 *(billions of dollars)*

Assets		Liabilities	
Reserves (cash assets including deposits with Federal Reserve banks)	$ 205.0	Deposits Demand Savings Time	663.6 691.1 999.2
Loans	2,256.3	Borrowings	495.4
U.S. government securities	557.3	Other liabilities	290.7
Other securities	162.7	Capital and	
Other assets	310.6	residual	351.9
	$3,491.9		$3,491.9

Source: Federal Reserve Bulletin, June 1992.

Reserves are only a small fraction of deposit liabilities. If all of the banks' customers who held demand deposits tried to withdraw them in cash, the banks could not meet this demand without liquidating $458.6 billion of other assets. This would be impossible without assistance from the Fed.

securities that it owns (including government bonds), which pay interest or dividends, and the *loans* that it makes to individuals and to businesses. A bank loan is a liability to the borrower (who must pay it back) but an asset to the bank. The bank expects not only to have the loan repaid but also to receive interest that more than compensates for the paperwork involved and the risk of nonpayment.

Banks attract deposits by paying interest to depositors and by providing them, for a fee that does not cover the banks' full cost, with services such as clearing checks and issuing regular monthly statements. Banks earn profits by lending and investing money that is deposited with them for more than they pay their depositors in terms of interest and other services provided.

Competition for Deposits

Competition for deposits is active among banks and between banks and other financial institutions. Financial deregulation that removed many restrictions on the activities of various financial institutions has contributed to this competition.

Banks offer different types of deposits, each offering different services and having different restrictions. Interest paid on demand, as well as savings deposits, money market funds, high-interest certificates of deposit (CDs), advertising, personal solicitation of accounts, giveaway programs for new deposits to existing accounts, and improved services are all forms of competition for funds. Among the special services are payroll-accounting and pension-accounting schemes for industrial customers. Banks also establish locked post office boxes to which retail customers of large companies send their payments, with the bank then crediting them to the company's account. All of these services are costly to the bank, but they serve as inducements for customers to make deposits.

Reserves

The Need for Reserves

All bankers would prefer, as a matter of convenience and prudence, to keep sufficient cash on hand to be able to meet depositors' day-to-day requirements for cash. However, just as the goldsmiths of old discovered that only a fraction of the gold that they held was ever withdrawn at any given time, and just as banks of old discovered that only a fraction of convertible bank notes was actually converted,

so, too, have modern banks discovered that only a fraction of their deposits will be withdrawn in cash at any one time. Most deposits of any individual bank remain on deposit with it; thus, an individual bank need keep only fractional reserves against its deposits.

The reserves that are needed to ensure that depositors can withdraw their deposits on demand will be quite small in normal times.

In abnormal times, however, nothing short of 100 percent would do the job if the commercial banking system had to stand alone. When a few bank failures cause a general loss of confidence in banks' ability to redeem their deposits, the results can be devastating. Until relatively recent times, such an event—or even the rumor of it—could lead to a "run" on banks, as depositors rushed to withdraw their money. Faced with such a panic, banks would have to close until they had borrowed enough funds or sold enough assets to meet the demand or until the demand subsided. However, banks could not instantly turn their loans into cash, because the borrowers would have the money tied up in such things as real estate or business enterprises. Neither could the banks obtain cash by selling their securities to the public, because payments would be made by checks, which would not provide cash to pay off depositors.

The difficulty of providing sufficient reserves to meet abnormal situations can be alleviated by the central bank. Most importantly, because it controls the supply of bank reserves, the central bank can provide all the reserves that are needed to meet any abnormal situation. It can do this in two ways. First, it can lend reserves directly to commercial banks on the security of assets that are sound but not easy to liquidate quickly. Second, it can enter the open market and buy all the securities that commercial banks need to sell. Once the public finds that deposits can be turned into cash, the panic usually will subside and any further drain of cash out of banks will cease.

The possibility of panic withdrawals is also greatly diminished by the provision of Federal Deposit Insurance, which guarantees that depositors will get their money back, even if a bank fails completely. Most depositors will not withdraw their money as long as they are *sure* they can get it when they need it; thus, the existence of deposit insurance serves as a deterrent to bank runs.

Although deposit insurance confers a number of benefits to the operation of the financial system, it has

Box 29-5

The Crisis in the Savings and Loan Industry

As the 1990s began, attention was focused on some U.S. financial institutions—the so-called thrifts, primarily savings and loan institutions (or S&Ls)—that were suffering staggering losses. Analysis suggests that the problem arose because of a combination of economic and regulatory events—in particular, because of "a fatal flaw" in the deposit insurance system.

Economic, Regulatory, and International Events

S&Ls make most of their loans in the form of long-term mortgages; because of their long-term nature, the return on these assets is very slow to adjust to current economic conditions. Their deposit liabilities are, however, relatively short-term. The general level of interest rates rose steadily throughout most of 1988; as a result, the interest costs paid by the S&Ls on deposits rose quite sharply while their interest return on assets did not. This placed the S&Ls in a profit squeeze.

These problems were intensified by the fact that real estate values had been falling in certain areas of the country—especially in the oil-producing states of the Southwest—and S&Ls that were holding mortgages for property concentrated in these areas suffered unusually poor collections and unusually high default rates.

The conflicting pressures on deposit and asset rates were intensified by increased competition resulting from two, not unrelated sources—one international and one domestic. First, in the market for deposits, S&Ls faced increased competition from foreign institutions as a result of the ongoing "globalization" of financial markets, as discussed in Box 29-4; as a result, S&Ls had to pay more to hold or to attract deposits. Second, as a result of ongoing deregulation of domestic financial markets, other domestic financial intermediaries were not only competing directly with S&Ls for deposits, but also were becoming major suppliers of home mortgages; as a result, S&Ls were not able to raise mortgage rates as much as they previously would have done.*

The Flaw in Deposit Insurance

Deposit insurance assures depositors that their deposits are secure, independent of the losses of the institution. The text describes the role that this plays in stabilizing the economic system in times of financial panic. However, economists have long stressed that such insurance also creates an incentive for financial intermediaries to pursue riskier investments than they otherwise would; the existence of deposit insurance means that depositors are not deterred from depositing in a given institution, even if that institution is widely perceived to hold very risky assets.†

---

* Deregulation also allowed the S&Ls to expand into a new area, commercial lending, where they lacked expertise and (probably inevitably) made a disproportionate number of poor loans as they learned while they loaned.

† Those who have studied microeconomics will recognize this incentive as an example of *moral hazard*.

---

also been subject to considerable criticism in recent years. This is discussed in Box 29-5.

Actual and Required Reserves

Look again at Table 29-3 and observe that, as we said earlier, the banking system's cash reserves are just a fraction of its deposits. If the holders of even one-third of its demand deposits had demanded cash sometime in March 1992, the commercial banking system would have been unable (without outside help) to meet the demand.

The U.S. banking system is thus a **fractional reserve system,** with commercial banks holding reserves—either as cash or as deposits with the

What the recent experience of the S&L industry has shown is that this incentive to pursue risky investment strategies increases dramatically as an institution approaches insolvency. After a period of sustained losses, such as many S&Ls experienced during the late 1980s, liabilities were as large as assets, and owner equity had been reduced to virtually zero. As a result, the owners had a powerful incentive to take risks. If a high-risk investment succeeded, the owners would reap large profits. If it failed, they lost little of their own capital, and depositors were repaid by deposit insurance—in this case, the Federal Savings and Loan Insurance Corporation. As one commentator put it, these owners faced a "heads I win, tails you lose" situation.

Who Pays?

The Congressional Budget Office has estimated the total losses (as of 1991) to be over $200 billion. Some of these represent losses sustained due to normal operations in the face of adverse circumstances, and some represent abnormal losses arising from risky strategies that were taken by decision makers who did not bear the losses themselves.[‡]

If the owner-managers and the depositors do not

bear the losses, then who does? Ultimately, they are borne by the taxpayers.

Raising taxes by over $200 billion to pay the total cost in one year would mean a one-year tax increase of over $800 for every man, woman, and child in the United States. This is neither politically feasible nor economically desirable. Hence, the government will borrow the money by selling bonds.

Issuing bonds merely defers the taxes that must be paid; it does not replace them. Further, it means that taxes must also eventually be levied to pay the interest on the bonds. As the CBO reports, issuing $200 billion in debt would increase the national debt of the United States by about 8.5 percent, with a similar effect on the annual debt-service obligations of the federal government.

What Can Be Done?

The implications of deposit insurance for the investment behavior of financial intermediaries suggests that, if deposit insurance is to be maintained, then other regulations concerning capital requirements and investment standards should be considered. In addition, the deposit insurance system might be reformed to relate the cost of insurance for a particular institution to the risks implied by that institution's asset position.

Whatever is done, it is important to ensure that in the future the risks from investment decisions made by financial institutions are borne by their owners, not by taxpayers.

[‡] A number of economists also argue that the costs would have been significantly lower had policymakers acted to correct the industry's problems, rather than cover them up, when the issue first emerged.

---

central bank—of much less than 100 percent of their deposits. The size of the reserves reflects not only the judgment of bankers but also the legal requirements imposed on the banks by the Fed.

A bank's **reserve ratio** is the fraction of its deposits that it holds as reserves. Those reserves that the Federal Reserve System requires the bank

to hold are called **required reserves.** Any reserves held over and above required reserves are called **excess reserves.** Reserves are required by the Fed both to ensure the stability of the banking system and as part of its policy arsenal for controlling the money supply, as we shall discuss at the end of this chapter.

Money Creation by the Banking System

The fractional reserve system provides the leverage that permits commercial banks and other financial institutions to create new money. The process is important, so it is worth examining in some detail.

Some Simplifying Assumptions

To focus on the essential aspects of how banks create money, assume that banks can invest in only one kind of asset, loans, and that there is only one kind of deposit, a demand deposit.

Three other assumptions, listed below, are provisional. When we have developed the basic ideas concerning the banks' creation of money, these assumptions will be relaxed.

1. *Fixed required reserve ratio.* It is assumed that all banks have the same required reserve ratio, which does not change. In our numerical illustration we shall assume that the required reserve ratio is 20 percent (i.e., 0.20); that is, at least $1 of reserves must be held for every $5 of deposits.
2. *No excess reserves.* It is assumed that all banks want to invest any reserves that they have in excess of the legally required amount. This implies that they always believe that there are safe investments—loans, in our example—to be made when they have excess reserves.
3. *No cash drain from the banking system.* It is assumed that the public holds a fixed amount of currency in circulation. This means that any transfers of funds between individuals will not cause changes in the total amount of currency available for the banks to hold as reserves. Changes in the money supply thus will take the form of changes in deposits held at the commercial banks.

The Creation of Deposit Money

A simplified bank balance sheet is shown in Table 29-4. The Incidental Bank and Trust Co. (IB&T Co.) has assets of $200 of reserves (all figures

---

TABLE 29-4   The Initial Balance Sheet of the Incidental Bank and Trust Company (*thousands of dollars*)

Assets		Liabilities	
Cash and other reserves	$ 200	Deposits	$1,000
Loans	900	Capital	100
	$1,100		$1,100

The IB&T Co. has a reserve of 20 percent of its deposit liabilities. The commercial bank earns money by finding profitable investments for much of the money deposited with it. In this balance sheet, loans are its earning assets.

---

are in thousands of dollars), held partly as cash on hand and partly as deposits with the central bank, and $900 of loans outstanding to its customers. Its liabilities are $100 to those who initially contributed capital to start the bank, and $1,000 to current depositors. The bank's ratio of reserves to deposits is 0.20 (200/1,000), exactly equal to its minimum requirement.

A Single New Deposit

Suppose that the Fed now buys $100 worth of securities on the open market, and that the individual or firm who sells the securities to the Fed opens an account with the IB&T Co. and deposits the $100. This is a wholly new deposit for the bank, and it results in a revised balance sheet (Table 29-5). As

---

TABLE 29-5   The Balance Sheet of the IB&T Co. After an Initial Deposit of $100 (*thousands of dollars*)

Assets		Liabilities	
Cash and other reserves	$ 300	Deposits	$1,100
Loans	900	Capital	100
	$1,200		$1,200

The deposit raises deposit liabilities and cash assets by the same amount. Because both cash and deposits rise by $100, the cash reserve ratio, formerly 0.20, increases to 0.27. The bank has more cash than it needs to provide a 20 percent reserve against its deposit liabilities.

TABLE 29-6   The IB&T Co. Balance Sheet After a New Loan and Cash Drain of $80 (*thousands of dollars*)

Assets		Liabilities	
Cash and other reserves	$ 220	Deposits	$1,100
Loans	980	Capital	100
	$1,200		$1,200

The bank lends it surplus cash and suffers a cash drain. The bank keeps $20 as a reserve against the initial new deposit of $100. It lends $80 to a customer, who writes a check to someone who deals with another bank. When the check is cleared, the IB&T Co. suffers an $80 cash drain. Comparing Tables 29-4 and 29-6 shows that the bank has increased its deposit liabilities by the $100 initially deposited and has increased its assets by $20 of cash reserves and $80 of new loans. It has also restored its reserve ratio of 0.20.

a result of the new deposit, the IB&T's cash assets and deposit liabilities have both risen by $100. More important, the IB&T's ratio of reserves to deposits has increased from 0.20 to 0.27 (300/1,100). The bank now has $80 in excess reserves; with $1,100 in deposits, its required reserves are only $220.

The IB&T Co. will now lend the $80 in excess reserves that it is holding. Table 29-6 shows the position after this has been done and after the proceeds of the loan have been withdrawn to be deposited to the account of a customer of another bank. The IB&T Co. once again has a 20 percent reserve ratio.

So far, of the $100 initial deposit in the IB&T Co., $20 is held by the IB&T Co. as reserves against the deposit and $80 has been lent out in the system. As a result, other banks have received new deposits of $80 stemming from the loans made by the IB&T Co.; persons receiving payment from those who borrowed the $80 from the IB&T Co. will have deposited those payments in their own banks.[5]

The banks that receive deposits from the proceeds of the IB&T Co.'s loan are sometimes called *next-generation banks* or, more specifically according to the situation, *second-generation, third-generation,* and so on. In this case the second-generation banks receive new deposits of $80, and when the checks clear, they have new reserves of $80. Because they require only $16 in additional reserves to support the new deposits, they have $64 of excess reserves. They now increase their loans by $64. After this money has been spent by the borrowers and has been deposited in other, third-generation banks, the balance sheets of the second-generation banks will have changed, as in Table 29-7.

The third-generation banks now find themselves with $64.00 of new deposits. Against these they need to hold only $12.80 in cash, so they have excess reserves of $51.20 that they can immediately lend out. Thus, there begins a long sequence of new deposits, new loans, new deposits, and new loans. These stages are shown in Table 29-8. The series in the table should look familiar, for it is the same convergent process that we saw when we were dealing with the multiplier in Chapter 25.

The banking system has created new deposits and thus new money, although each banker can honestly say, "All I did was invest my excess reserves. I can do no more than manage wisely the money that I receive."

TABLE 29-7   Changes in the Balance Sheets of Second-Generation Banks (*thousands of dollars*)

Assets		Liabilities	
Cash and other reserves	+$16	Deposits	+$80
Loans	+ 64		
	+$80		+$80

Second-generation banks receive cash deposits and expand loans. The second-generation banks gain new deposits of $80 as a result of the loan granted by the IB&T Co., which is used to make payments to customers of the second-generation banks. These banks keep 20 percent of the cash that they acquire as their reserve against the new deposit, and they can make new loans using the other 80 percent. When the customers who borrowed the money make payments to the customers of third-generation banks, a cash drain occurs.

---

[5] Note that, although the *banking system* suffers no cash drain (i.e., all the money that has been lent out is returned to the banking system as deposits), the IB&T Co. does suffer a cash drain (i.e., most of the $80 goes to other banks and is not redeposited at the IB&T Co.).

TABLE 29–8 The Sequence of Loans and Deposits After a Single Initial Deposit of $100.00

Bank	New deposits	New loans	Addition to reserves
IB&T Co.	$100.00	$ 80.00	$20.00
Second-generation bank	80.00	64.00	16.00
Third-generation bank	64.00	51.20	12.80
Fourth-generation bank	51.20	40.96	10.24
Fifth-generation bank	40.96	32.77	8.19
Sixth-generation bank	32.77	26.22	6.55
Seventh-generation bank	26.22	20.98	5.24
Eighth-generation bank	20.98	16.78	4.20
Ninth-generation bank	16.78	13.42	3.36
Tenth-generation bank	13.42	10.74	2.68
Total for first 10 generations	446.33	357.07	89.26
All remaining generations	53.67	42.93	10.74
Total for banking system	$500.00	$400.00	$100.00

The banking system as a whole can create deposit money whenever it receives new reserves. The table shows the process of the creation of deposit money on the assumptions that all the loans made by one set of banks end up as deposits in another set of banks (the next-generation banks), that the required reserve ratio (v) is 0.20, and that there are no excess reserves. Although each bank suffers a cash drain whenever it grants a new loan, the system as a whole does not, and the system ends up doing in a series of steps what a monopoly bank would do all at once; that is, it increases deposit money by $1/v$, which, in this example, is five times the amount of any increase in reserves that it obtains.

If v is the reserve ratio, the ultimate effect on the deposits of the banking system of a new deposit will be $1/v$ times the new deposit. [37]

At the end of the process that is depicted in Table 29–8, the change in the combined balance sheets of all the banks in the system is shown in Table 29–9.[6]

Many Deposits

A more realistic picture of deposit creation is one in which new deposits accrue simultaneously to all

TABLE 29–9 The Combined Balance Sheets of All the Banks in the System Following the Multiple Expansion of Deposits

Assets		Liabilities	
Cash and other reserves	+$100	Deposits	+$500
Loans	+ 400		
	+$500		+$500

The reserve ratio is returned to 0.20. The entire initial deposit of $100 ends up as reserves of the banking system. Therefore, deposits rise by $(1/0.2)$ times the initial deposit, that is, by $500.

banks, perhaps because of changes in the monetary policy of the Fed. (We shall study monetary policy in detail in Chapter 31.)

Suppose, for example, that a community contains 10 banks of equal size and that, as a result of a purchase by the Fed of $1,000 worth of securities, each receives new deposits of $100 in cash. Now each bank is in the position shown in Table 29–5, and each can begin to expand deposits based on the $100 of excess reserves. (Each bank does this by granting loans to customers.)

Because each bank does one-tenth of the total banking business, an average of 90 percent of any newly created deposit will find its way into other banks as the customer pays other people in the community by check. This will represent a cash drain from the lending bank to the other banks. However, roughly 10 percent of each new deposit created by every other bank should find its way into any particular bank. All banks receive new cash, and all begin creating deposits simultaneously.

The expansion can go on, with each bank watching its own ratio of cash reserves to deposits, expanding deposits as long as the ratio exceeds $1/5$, and ceasing when it reaches that figure. The process will come to a halt when each bank has created $400 in additional deposits, so that for each initial $100 cash deposit, there is now $500 in deposits backed by $100 in cash.

The general rule, if there is no cash drain, is that a banking system with a reserve ratio of v can change its deposits by $1/v$ times any change in reserves.

---

[6] The "multiple expansion of deposits" that has just been worked through applies in reverse to a withdrawal of funds. Deposits of the banking system will fall by $1/v$ times any amount withdrawn from the bank and not redeposited at another.

Excess Reserves and Cash Drains

Two of the simplifying assumptions that were made earlier can now be relaxed.

Excess reserves. If banks do not choose to invest their excess reserves, the multiple expansion that we discussed will not occur. Go back to Table 29-5. If the IB&T Co. had been content to hold 27 percent in reserves, it might well have done nothing more. Other things being equal, banks will choose to invest their excess reserves because of the profit motive, but there may be times when they believe that the risk is too great. It is one thing to be offered a good rate of interest on a loan, but if the borrower defaults on the payment of interest and principal, the bank will be the loser. Similarly, if the bank expects interest rates to rise in the future, it may hold off making loans now so that it will have reserves available to make more profitable loans after the interest rate has risen.

Deposit creation does not happen automatically; it depends on the decisions of bankers. If banks do not choose to use their excess reserves to expand their investments, there will not be an expansion of deposits.

The money supply is thus at least partially determined by the commercial banks in response to such forces as changes in national income and interest rates. However, the upper limit of deposits is determined by the required reserve ratio and by the reserves available to the banks, both of which are under the influence of the central bank.

Cash drain. Suppose that firms and households find it convenient to keep a fixed *fraction* of their money holding in cash (say, 5 percent) instead of a fixed *number* of dollars. In that case, an extra $100 in money supply will not all stay in the banking system; only $95 will remain on deposit, while the rest will be added to currency in circulation. In such a situation, any multiple expansion of bank deposits will be accompanied by a cash drain to the public that will substantially reduce the maximum expansion below what it was when the public was content to hold all its new money as bank deposits.

TABLE 29-10   The Combined Balance Sheets of All the Banks in the System Following the Multiple Expansion of Deposits with a Cash Drain

Assets		Liabilities	
Cash and other reserves	+$ 80	Deposits	+$400
Loans	+ 320		
	+$400		+$400

The reserve ratio is 0.20, and cash drain is 0.05. Only $80 of the initial deposit of $100 ends up as reserves of the banking system. Therefore, deposits rise by (1/0.2) times the $80, that is, by $400.

The story of deposit creation when all banks receive new deposits and there is a cash drain to the public, happens as follows: Each bank starts creating deposits and suffers no significant cash drain to other banks. However, because 5 percent of newly created deposits is now withdrawn to be held as cash, each bank suffers a cash drain to the public. The expansion continues, each bank watching its own ratio of cash reserves to deposits, expanding deposits as long as the ratio exceeds 1/5 and ceasing when it reaches that figure. Because the expansion is accompanied by a cash drain, it will come to a halt with a smaller deposit expansion than in the case of no cash drain.[7]

Table 29-10 shows the consolidated balance sheets of the banking system after the deposit expansion, arising from an initial deposit of $100 when there is a cash drain. As shown, because there is a cash drain of $20, reserves rise by only $80 and deposits rise by only $400.

The Fed and the Money Supply

In this chapter we have seen that the Fed can exert control over the reserves of the banking system and that the reserves of the banking system are systematically related to the money supply. Together, these provide the basis for assuming throughout the rest of this book that the Fed controls the money supply.

---

[7] It can be shown algebraically that the percentage of cash drain must be added to the reserve ratio to determine the maximum possible expansion of deposits. **[38]**

SUMMARY

1. Early economists regarded the economy as being divided into a real sector and a monetary sector. The real sector is concerned with production, allocation of resources, and distribution of income, determined by relative prices. The level of prices at which all transactions take place is determined by the monetary sector, that is, by the demand for and supply of money. With the demand for money being constant, an increase in the money supply would cause all equilibrium money prices to increase, but relative prices, and hence everything in the real sector, would be left unaffected.

2. Traditionally in economics, money has referred to any generally accepted medium of exchange. A number of functions of money may, however, be distinguished. The major ones are that it acts as a medium of exchange, a store of value, and a unit of account.

3. Money arose because of the inconvenience of barter, and it developed in stages from precious metal, to metal coinage, to paper money convertible to precious metal, to token coinage and paper money fractionally backed by precious metals, to fiat money, and to deposit money. Societies have shown great sophistication in developing monetary instruments to meet their needs.

4. The money supply—the stock of money in an economy at a specific moment—can be defined in various ways. M1, the narrowest definition, includes currency, traveler's checks, and demand and other checkable deposits. M2 includes M1 plus savings deposits and smaller time deposits. M3, the widest definition, includes a number of assets, such as money market funds and overnight loans, that are readily convertible into M1 on a dollar-for-dollar basis, with or without notice.

5. Near money includes interest-earning assets that are convertible into money on a dollar-for-dollar basis but that are not currently included in the definition of money. Money substitutes are things such as credit cards that temporarily serve as a medium of exchange but are not money.

6. The banking system in the United States consists of two main elements: the Federal Reserve System (which is the central bank) and the commercial banks. Each has an important effect on the money supply.

7. The central bank of the United States is the set of Federal Reserve banks and its board of governors. Although they are technically private, the Federal Reserve banks, in fact, belong to a system that functions as a central bank that administers the nation's monetary policy. Effective power is exercised by the board of governors, whose seven members are appointed by the president of the United States for 14-year terms.

8. Commercial banks are profit-seeking institutions that allow their customers to transfer demand deposits from one bank to another by means of checks. They create money as a by-product of their commercial operations by making or liquidating loans and various other investments.

9. Because most customers are content to pay their accounts by check rather than by cash, banks need only small reserves to back their

deposit liabilities. Consequently, banks are able to create deposit money. When the banking system receives a new cash deposit, it can create new deposits to some multiple of this amount. The amount of new deposits created depends on the legal minimum reserves that the Federal Reserve enforces on the banks, the amount of cash drain to the public, and whether the banks choose to hold excess reserves.

TOPICS FOR REVIEW

Real and monetary sectors of the economy

Medium of exchange, store of value, and unit of account

Fully backed, fractionally backed, and fiat money

Demand and time deposits

The money supply

Near money and money substitutes

The banking system and the central bank (the Federal Reserve System)

Reserve ratio, required reserves, and excess reserves

Creation of deposit money

DISCUSSION QUESTIONS

1. "For the love of money is the root of all evil" (I Timothy 6:10). If a nation were to become a theocracy in which money was illegal, would you expect the level of national income to be affected? How about the productivity of labor?

2. Consider each of the following with respect to its potential use as a medium of exchange, a store of value, and a unit of account. Which would you think might be regarded as money?
   a. A $100 Federal Reserve note
   b. An American Express charge card
   c. A painting by Picasso
   d. A NOW account
   e. A U.S. Treasury bill payable in three months
   f. A savings account at a savings and loan association in Las Vegas, Nevada
   g. One share of General Motors stock
   h. A lifetime pass to Pittsburgh Steelers football games

3. When the Austrian government minted a new 1,000-shilling gold coin, worth $59 at face value, the 1-inch diameter coin came into great demand among jewelers and coin collectors. By law, the number of such coins to be minted each year is limited. Lines of people eager to get the coins formed outside the government mint and local banks.

   "There is exceptional interest in the new coin," said a Viennese banker. "It's a numismatic hit and a financial success." However, it has disappeared from circulation. Explain why.

4. A Canadian who receives a U.S. coin has the option of spending it at face value or taking it to the bank and converting it to Canadian money at the going rate of exchange. When the rate of exchange was near par, so that $1 Canadian was within plus or minus $0.03 of $1 American, American and Canadian coins circulated side by side, exchanged at their face values. Use Gresham's law to predict which coinage disappeared from circulation in Canada when the Canadian dollar fell to $0.75 American. Why did a $0.03 differential not produce this result?

5. Some years ago a strike closed all banks in Ireland for several months. What do you think happened during that period?

6. During hyperinflations in several foreign countries after World War II, American cigarettes were sometimes used in place of money. What made them suitable?

7. Assume that on January 1, 1992, a couple had $100,000, which they wished to hold for use 1 year later. Calculate, using library sources, which of the following would have been the best store of value over that period. Will the best store of value over that period necessarily be the best over the next 24 months?
    a. The dollar
    b. Stocks whose prices moved with the Dow-Jones industrial average
    c. A Georgia Power 11 ¾ percent 2005 bond
    d. Gold
    e. Silver

8. If all depositors tried to turn their deposits into cash at once, they would find that there are not sufficient reserves in the system to allow all of them to do this at the same time. Why then do we not still have panicky runs on the banks? Would a 100 percent reserve requirement be safer? What effect would such a reserve requirement have on the banking system's ability to create money? Would it preclude any possibility of a panic?

9. What would be the effect on the money supply of each of the following?
    a. Declining public confidence in the banks
    b. A desire on the part of banks to increase their levels of excess reserves
    c. Monopolizing of the banking system into a single superbank
    d. Increased use of credit cards
    e. Transfer of deposits from banks to new nonbank institutions

30

The Role of Money in Macroeconomics

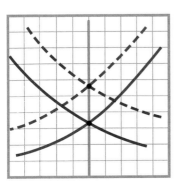

A t one time or another, most of us have known the surprise of opening our wallets and discovering that we had either more or less money than we thought. There can be pleasure in deciding how to spend an unexpected windfall in the first case, just as there can be pain in deciding what expenditure to eliminate in the second.

What determines how much money people hold in their wallets and in the bank? What happens when people discover that they are holding more, or less, money than they wish to? These turn out to be key questions for our study of the influence of money on output and prices.

Financial Assets

At any moment, households have a stock of wealth that they hold in many forms. Some of it is money in the bank or in the wallet; some may be in treasury bills and bonds; and some may be in stocks and shares.[1]

To simplify our discussion, we will group wealth into just two categories, which we will call money and bonds. By *money* we mean M2, as defined in Chapter 29; it includes all assets that serve as a medium of exchange, that is, paper money, coins, and deposits on which checks may be drawn. By *bonds* we mean all other forms of wealth; they include interest-earning financial assets *plus* claims on real capital.[2]

The Rate of Interest and Present Value

Recall from Box 29-2 that a bond is a financial asset that promises to make one or more specified payments at specified dates in the future. The **present value (PV)** of a bond, or of any asset, refers to the value now of the future payment or payments to which the asset represents a claim.

Present value depends on the rate of interest because when we calculate present value, the interest rate is used to *discount* the future payments. This relationship between the rate of interest and present value can be seen by considering two extreme examples.

A single payment one year hence. We start with the simplest case. How much would someone be prepared to pay *now* to purchase a bond that will produce a single payment of $100 in one year's time?

Suppose that the interest rate is 5 percent, which means that $1.00 invested today will be worth $1.05 in one year's

---

[1] At this time you may find it helpful to review the discussion of the various types of financial assets in Box 29-2 on pages 604–605.

[2] This simplification can take us quite a long way. However, for some problems it is necessary to treat debt and claims on capital as distinct assets, in which case at least three categories—money, debt (bonds), and equity (stocks)—are used.

Box 30-1

Calculating Present Value

An asset held now will generate returns in the future. What that stream of future income is worth now is called the asset's *present value*. In general, present value *(PV)* refers to the value *now* of one or more payments to be received in the future.

This box provides some details concerning the calculation of present value that will prove helpful for understanding the material in the text. If you have studied microeconomics first, some of this material will be familiar from Chapter 18.

Present Value of a Single Future Payment

One period hence. The numerical examples given in the text are easy to generalize. In calculating the present value of a payment one year hence, we divided the sum that is receivable in the future by 1 plus the rate of interest. In general, the present value of R dollars one year hence at an interest rate of *i* per year is

$$PV = \frac{R}{(1 + i)}$$

Several periods hence. What happens to our calculation if the bond still offered a single future payment but the payment were receivable at a later date than one year from now? What, for example, is the present value of $100 to be received *two* years hence if the interest rate is 5 percent? This

is $100/(1.05)(1.05) = $90.70.* We can check this by seeing what would happen if $90.70 were lent out for two years. In the first year the loan would earn an interest of (0.05)($90.70) = $4.54, and hence after one year the lender would receive $95.24. In the second year the interest would be earned on this entire amount; interest earned in the second year would thus equal (0.05)($95.24) = $4.76. Hence, in two years the lender would have $100. (Payment of interest in the second year on the interest income earned in the first year is called *compound interest*.)

In general, the present value of R dollars after *t* years at *i* percent is

$$PV = \frac{R}{(1 + i)^t}$$

This formula simply discounts the sum, R, by the interest rate, *i*, repeatedly—once for each of the *t* periods that pass until the sum becomes available. If we look at the formula, we see that the higher *i* or *t* is, the higher the whole term $(1 + i)^t$. This term, however, appears in the denominator, so that *PV* is *negatively* related to both *i* and *t*.

---

* As noted in the text, in this type of formula the interest rate is expressed as a decimal fraction. For example, 5 percent is expressed as 0.05, so $(1 + i)$ equals 1.05.

---

time. Now ask how much someone would have to lend out in order to have $100 a year from now. If we use *PV* to stand for this unknown amount, we can write *PV*(1.05) = $100 (which means *PV* *multiplied by* 1.05). Thus *PV* = $100/1.05 = $95.24.[3] This tells us that the present value of $100 receivable in one year's time is $95.24; anyone who lends out $95.24 for one year at 5 percent interest will get

back the $95.24 plus $4.76 in interest, which makes $100.

What if the interest rate had been 7 percent? At that interest rate, the present value of the $100 receivable in one year's time would be $100/1.07 = $93.46, which is less than the present value when the interest rate was 5 percent.

A perpetuity. Now consider another extreme case— a perpetuity that promises to pay $100 per year to its holder *forever*. The *present value* of the perpetuity depends on how much $100 per year is worth, and this again depends on the rate of interest.

---

[3] Notice that in this type of formula the interest rate is expressed as a decimal fraction where, for example, 5 percent is expressed as 0.05, so $(1 + i)$ equals 1.05.

The formula $PV = R/(1 + i)^t$ shows that the present value of a given sum payable in the future will be smaller the more distant the payment date and the higher the rate of interest.

Present Value of a Sequence of Payments

Suppose now that we wish to calculate the present value of a bond that promises a sequence of payments for a given number of periods. Let R_1, R_2, R_3, and so on represent the payment promised after period 1, period 2, period 3, and so on, and let the last period for which a payment is promised be period T.

The present value of a bond that produces a sequence of payments is just the sum of the present values of each of the payments.

If we also suppose that the interest rate remains constant at i percent, this can be written as follows:

$$PV = \frac{R_1}{(1 + i)} + \frac{R_2}{(1 + i)^2} + \frac{R_3}{(1 + i)^3} + \cdots + \frac{R_T}{(1 + i)^T}$$

Present Value of a Perpetual Stream of Payments

Now consider the value that a buyer would place on a $100 perpetuity, that is, on a bond that produces a stream of payments of $100 a year forever. To find the present value of $100 payable every year in the future, we ask how much money would have to be invested now at an interest rate of 10 percent per year to obtain $100 every year in the future. This present value is simply $0.1(PV) = \$100$, where PV is the sum required. In other words, $PV = \$100/0.1 = \$1,000$. This tells us that $1,000 invested at 10 percent interest forever would yield a constant stream of income of $100 per year; put the other way around, when the interest rate is 10 percent, the present value of $100 per year forever is $1,000.

To generalize for any interest rate, we merely write i for the interest rate and R for the revenue to be received each year. Now we wish to find the amount PV that, invested at i, will yield R per year forever. This is $i(PV) = R$, or

$$PV = \frac{R}{i}$$

Here, as before, PV is related to the rate of interest: The higher the interest rate, the less the (present) value of any stream of future receipts will be, and hence the lower the price that anyone would be prepared to pay to purchase the bond.

A bond that will produce a stream of income of $100 per year forever is worth $1,000 at 10 percent interest because $1,000 invested at 10 percent per year will yield $100 interest per year forever. However, the same bond is worth $2,000 when the interest rate is 5 percent per year, because it takes $2,000 invested at 5 percent per year to yield $100 interest per year. The lower the rate of interest obtainable on the market, the more valuable is a bond paying a fixed amount of interest.

A general statement. Similar relations apply to bonds that are more complicated than single payments but that are not perpetuities. Although in such cases the calculation of present value is more complicated, the same negative relationship between the interest rate and present value still holds.

The present value of any asset that yields a given stream of money over time is negatively related to the interest rate.

Further details on the calculation of present value are given in Box 30-1.

Present Value and Market Price

Present value is important because it establishes the market price for an asset.

The present value of an asset is also the amount that someone would be willing to pay now to secure the right to the future stream of payments conferred by ownership of the asset.

To see this, return to our example of a bond that promises to pay $100 one year hence.

When the interest rate is 5 percent, the present value is $95.24. To see why this is the maximum that anyone would pay for this bond, suppose that some sellers offer to sell the bond at some other price, say, $98. If, instead of paying this amount for the bond, a potential buyer lends its $98 out at 5 percent interest, it would have at the end of one year more than the $100 that the bond will produce. (At 5 percent interest, $98 yields $4.90 in interest, which when added to the principal makes $102.90.) Clearly, no well-informed individual would pay $98—or by the same reasoning any sum in excess of $95.24—for the bond.

Now suppose that the bond is offered for sale at a price less than $95.24, say, $90. A potential buyer could borrow $90 to buy the bond and would pay $4.50 in interest on the loan. At the end of the year, the bond yields $100. When this is used to repay the $90 loan and the $4.50 in interest, $5.50 is left as profit. Clearly, it would be worthwhile for someone to buy the bond at the price of $90 or, by the same argument, at any price less than $95.24.

This discussion should make clear that the present value of an asset determines its market price. If the market price of any asset is greater than the present value of the income stream that it produces, no one will want to buy it, and the market price will fall. If the market value is below its present value, there will be a rush to buy it, and the market price will rise. These facts lead to the following conclusion:

In a free market, the equilibrium price of any asset will be the present value of the income stream that it produces.

The Rate of Interest and Market Price

The discussion above leads us to three important propositions. The first two stress the negative relationship between interest rates and asset prices:

1. If the rate of interest falls, the value of an asset producing a given income stream will rise.

2. A rise in the market price of an asset producing a given income stream is equivalent to a decrease in the rate of interest earned by the asset.

Thus, a promise to pay $100.00 one year from now is worth $92.59 when the interest rate is 8 percent and only $89.29 when the interest rate is 12 percent: $92.59 at 8 percent interest ($92.59 × 1.08) and $89.29 at 12 percent interest ($89.29 × 1.12) are both worth $100.00 in one year's time.

The third proposition focuses on the term to maturity of the bond:

3. The sooner the maturity date of a bond, the less the bond's value will change with a change in the rate of interest.

To see this, consider an extreme case. The present value of a bond that is redeemable for $1,000 in one week's time will be very close to $1,000 no matter what the interest rate is. Thus, its value will not change much, even if the rate of interest leaps from 5 percent to 10 percent during that week. Note that the interest-earning assets included in our definition of money are so short-term that their values remain unchanged when the interest rate changes.

As a second example, consider two bonds, one that promises to pay $100 next year and one that promises to pay $100 in 10 years. A rise in the interest rate from 8 to 12 percent will lower the value of $100 payable in one year's time by 3.6 percent, but it will lower the value of $100 payable in 10 years' time by 37.9 percent.[4]

---

[4] The example assumes annual compounding. The first case is calculated from the numbers of the previous example: (92.58 − 89.29)/92.58. The 10-year case uses the formula

$$\text{Present value} = \frac{\text{principal}}{(1 + r)^n}$$

which gives $46.30 at 8 percent and $28.75 at 12 percent. The percentage fall in value is thus (46.30 − 28.75)/46.30 = 0.379.

Supply of Money and Demand for Money

The Supply of Money

The money supply is a stock. (It is so many billions of dollars, *not* a flow of so much per unit of time; the distinction was discussed in Box 4-1 on page 61.) In January 1992, M2 was approximately $3,425 billion.

We saw in Chapter 29 that deposit money is created by the commercial banking system, but only within limits set by their reserves. Because, as we also saw in Chapter 29 and as will be discussed in more detail in Chapter 31, the reserves of the banking system are under the control of the Fed, ultimate control of the money supply is also in the hands of the Fed. In this chapter we simply assume that the money supply can be controlled by the Fed.

The Demand for Money

The amount of wealth that everyone in the economy wishes to hold in the form of money balances is called the **demand for money.** Because households are choosing how to divide their given stock of wealth between money and bonds, it follows that if we know the demand for money, we also know the demand for bonds. With a *given level of wealth,* a rise in the demand for money necessarily implies a fall in the demand for bonds; if people wish to hold $1 billion more money, they must wish to hold $1 billion less of bonds. It also follows that if households are in equilibrium with respect to their money holdings, they are in equilibrium with respect to their bond holdings.

When we say that on January 1, 1992, the quantity of money demanded was $3,425 billion, we mean that on that date the public wished to hold money balances that totaled $3,425 billion, but why do firms and households wish to hold money balances at all? There is a cost to holding any money balance. The money could have been used to purchase bonds, which earn higher interest than does money.[5]

The opportunity cost of holding any money balance is the extra interest that could have been earned if the money had been used instead to purchase bonds.

In terms of the distinction between the real and nominal rates of interest that were noted in Chapter 23, the nominal rate of interest is the opportunity cost of holding money. However, because in this chapter we make the simplifying assumption that there is no ongoing inflation, the nominal and real rates of interest are the same; both are measured by the market rate of interest.

Clearly, money will be held only when it provides services that are valued at least as highly as the opportunity cost of holding it. Three important services that are provided by money balances give rise to three motives for holding money: the transactions, precautionary, and speculative motives. We examine each of these in detail.

The Transactions Motive

Most transactions require money. Money passes from households to firms to pay for the goods and services produced by firms; money passes from firms to households to pay for the factor services supplied by households to firms. Money balances that are held to finance such flows are called **transactions balances.**

In an imaginary world in which the receipts and disbursements of households and firms are perfectly synchronized, it would be unnecessary to hold transactions balances. If every time a household spent $10 it received $10 as part payment of its income, no

---

[5] As we saw in Chapter 29 (see especially Table 29-1), M2 includes some interest-bearing deposits. This complicates, but does not fundamentally alter, the analysis of the demand for money. In particular, it means that the opportunity cost of holding those interest-bearing components of M2 is not the *level* of interest rates paid on bonds but the *difference* between that rate and the rate paid on M2 assets. Because the interest earned on deposits tends to fluctuate less than rates on marketable securities, the difference tends to move with the level of interest rates in the economy, rising when rates rise and falling when rates fall. For simplicity, we talk of the demand for money responding to the *level* of interest rates, although in reality it is the *difference* that is the opportunity cost of money.

transactions balances would be needed. In the real world, however, receipts and disbursements are not perfectly synchronized.

Consider the balances that are held because of wage payments. Suppose, for purposes of illustration, that firms pay wages every Friday and that households spend all their wages on the purchase of goods and services, with the expenditure spread out evenly over the week. Thus, on Friday morning firms must hold balances equal to the weekly wage bill; on Friday afternoon households will hold these balances.

Over the week, households' balances will be drawn down as a result of purchasing goods and services. Over the same period, the balances held by firms will build up as a result of selling goods and services until, on the following Friday morning, firms will again have amassed balances equal to the wage bill that must be met on that day.

The transactions motive arises because payments and receipts are not synchronized.

What determines the size of the transactions balances to be held? It is clear that in our example total transactions balances vary with the value of the wage bill. If the wage bill doubles for any reason, the transactions balances held by firms and households for this purpose will also double. As it is with wages, so it is with all other transactions: The size of the balances held is positively related to the value of the transactions.

Next we ask how the total value of transactions is related to national income. Because of the double counting problem, which we first discussed in Chapter 24, the value of all transactions exceeds the value of the economy's final output. When the miller buys wheat from the farmer and when the baker buys flour from the miller, both are transactions against which money balances must be held, although only the value added at each stage is part of national income.

Generally, there will be a stable, positive relationship between transactions and national income. A rise in national income also leads to a rise in the total value of all transactions and hence to an associated rise in the demand for transactions balances. This allows us to relate transactions balances to national income. [39]

The larger the value of national income, the larger is the value of transactions balances that will be held.

The Precautionary Motive

Many goods and services are sold on credit. The seller can never be certain when payment will be made, and the buyer can never be certain of the day of delivery and thus when payment will fall due. As a precaution against cash crises, when receipts are abnormally low or disbursements are abnormally high, firms and households carry money balances. **Precautionary balances** provide a cushion against uncertainty about the timing of cash flows. The larger such balances are, the greater is the protection against running out of money because of temporary fluctuations in cash flows.

The seriousness of the risk of a cash crisis depends on the penalties for being caught without sufficient money balances. A firm is unlikely to be pushed into insolvency, but it may incur considerable costs if it is forced to borrow money at high interest rates in order to meet a temporary cash crisis.

The precautionary motive arises because households and firms are uncertain about the degree to which payments and receipts will be synchronized.

The protection provided by a given quantity of precautionary balances depends on the volume of payments and receipts. A $100 precautionary balance provides a large cushion for a household whose volume of payments per month is $800 and a small cushion for a firm whose monthly volume is $25,000. Fluctuations of the sort that create the need for precautionary balances tend to vary directly with the size of the firm's cash flow. To provide the same degree of protection as the value of transactions rises, more money is necessary.[6]

The precautionary motive, like the transactions motive, causes the demand for money to vary positively with the money value of national income.

The Speculative Motive

Firms and households hold some money in order to provide a hedge against the uncertainty inherent in fluctuating prices of other financial assets. Money

---

[6] Institutional arrangements affect precautionary demands. In the past, for example, a traveler would have carried a substantial precautionary balance in cash, but today a credit card covers most unforeseen expenses that may arise during traveling.

balances held for this purpose are called **speculative balances.** This motive was first analyzed by Keynes, and the classic modern analysis was made by Professor James Tobin, the 1981 Nobel Laureate in Economics.

When a household or a firm holds money balances, it forgoes the extra interest income that it could earn if it held bonds instead. However, market interest rates fluctuate, and so do the market prices of existing bonds (their present values depend on the interest rate). Because their prices fluctuate, bonds are a risky asset. Many households and firms do not like risk; they are said to be *risk-averse*.[7]

In choosing between holding money or holding bonds, wealth holders must balance the extra interest income that they could earn by holding bonds against the risk that bonds carry. At one extreme, if a household or a firm holds all its wealth in the form of bonds, it earns extra interest on its entire wealth, but it also exposes its entire wealth to the risk of changes in the price of bonds. At the other extreme, if the household or firm holds all its wealth in the form of money, it earns less interest income, but it does not face the risk of unexpected changes in the price of bonds. Wealth holders usually do not take either extreme position. They hold part of their wealth as money and part of it as bonds; that is, they *diversify* their holdings.

Influence of wealth.   Suppose that Ms. B. Smart elects to diversify her wealth by holding 5 percent of her wealth in money and the other 95 percent in bonds. If her wealth is $50,000, her demand for money will be $2,500. If her wealth increases to $60,000, her demand for money will rise to $3,000.

The speculative motive implies that the demand for money varies positively with wealth.

Although an individual's wealth may rise or fall rapidly, the total wealth of a society changes only slowly. For the analysis of short-term fluctuations in national income, the effects of changes in wealth are fairly small, and we shall ignore them for the present. Over the long term, however, variations in wealth can have a major effect on the demand for money.

Influence of interest rates.   Wealth that is held in cash or deposits earns little or no interest; hence, the reduction in risk involved in holding money carries a cost in terms of forgone interest earnings. The speculative motive leads households and firms to add to their money holdings until the reduction in risk obtained by the last dollar added is just balanced (in each wealth holder's view) by the cost in terms of the interest forgone on that dollar.

When the rate of interest falls, the opportunity cost of holding money falls. This leads to more money being held both for the precautionary motive (to reduce risks caused by uncertainty about the flows of payments and receipts) and for the speculative motive (to reduce risks associated with fluctuations in the market price of bonds). When the rate of interest rises, the cost of holding money rises. This leads to less money being held for speculative and precautionary motives.

The precautionary and speculative motives both cause the demand for money to be negatively related to the rate of interest.

Real and Nominal Money Balances

In referring to the demand for money, it is important to distinguish real from nominal values. Real values are measured in purchasing power units; nominal values are measured in money units.

First, consider the demand for money in real terms. This demand is the number of units of purchasing power that the public wishes to hold in the form of money balances. For example, in an imaginary one-product wheat economy, this would be measured by the number of bushels of wheat that could be purchased with the money balances held. In a more complex economy, it could be measured in terms of the number of "baskets of goods" represented by a price index, such as the CPI, that could be purchased with the money balances held. When we speak of the demand for money in real terms, we speak of the amount demanded in constant dollars:

The real demand for money is the nominal quantity demanded divided by the price level.

For example, in the decade from 1980 to 1990, the nominal quantity of M1 balances held in the United States roughly doubled, from almost $400

---

[7] For those who have studied microeconomics, recall that a person is risk-averse when he or she prefers a certain sum of money to an uncertain outcome in which the expected value is the same.

billion to almost $800 billion. Over the same period, however, the price level, as measured by the CPI, rose by about 80 percent. This tells us that the real quantity of M1 rose only slightly, from $400 billion to about $440 billion, measured in constant 1980 dollars.

From real demand to nominal demand. Our discussion has identified the determinants of the demand for real money balances as real national income, real wealth, and the interest rate. Notice that the real demand for money depends on, among other things, real national income; it is not influenced by the price level.

Now suppose that with the interest rate, real wealth, and real national income being held constant, the price level doubles. Because the demand for real money balances will be unchanged, the demand for nominal balances must double. If the public previously demanded $30 billion in nominal money balances, it will now demand $60 billion. This keeps the real demand unchanged at $60/2 = $30 billion.

The money balances of $60 billion at the new, higher price level represents exactly the same purchasing power as $30 billion at the old price level.

Other things being equal, the nominal demand for money balances varies in proportion to the price level; when the price level doubles, desired nominal money balances also double.

This is a central proposition of the quantity theory of money, which is discussed further in Box 30-2.

Total Demand for Money

Figure 30-1 summarizes the influences of national income, the nominal rate of interest, and the price level, the three variables that account for most of the short-term variations in the nominal quantity of money demanded. The function relating money demanded to the rate of interest is often called the **liquidity preference (LP) function.** It is also called the **demand for money function.**

FIGURE 30-1
The Demand for Money as a Function of Interest Rates, Income, and the Price Level

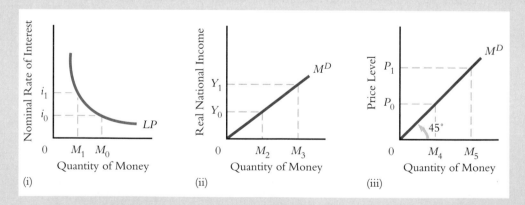

The quantity of money demanded varies negatively with the nominal rate of interest and positively with both real national income and the price level. In part (i) the demand for money is shown varying negatively with the interest rate along the liquidity preference function. When the interest rate rises from i_0 to i_1, households and firms reduce the quantity of money demanded from M_0 to M_1.

In part (ii) the demand for money varies positively with national income. When national income rises from Y_0 to Y_1, households and firms increase the quantity of money demanded from M_2 to M_3.

In part (iii) the demand for money varies in proportion to the price level. When the price level doubles from P_0 to P_1, households and firms double the quantity of money demanded fom M_4 to M_5.

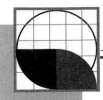

Box 30-2

The Quantity Theory of Money

The quantity theory of money can be set out in terms of four equations. Equation 1 states that the demand for money balances depends on the value of transactions as measured by nominal income, which is real income multiplied by the price level:

$$M^D = kPY \qquad [1]$$

Equation 2 states that the supply of money, *M*, is set by the central bank:

$$M^S = M \qquad [2]$$

Equation 3 states the equilibrium condition that the demand for money must equal the supply:

$$M^D = M^S \qquad [3]$$

Substitution from Equations 2 and 3 into Equation 1 yields:

$$M = kPY \qquad [4]$$

The original classical quantity theory assumes that *k* is a constant given by the transactions demand for money and that *Y* is constant because full employment is maintained. Thus, increases or decreases in the money supply lead to proportional increases or decreases in prices.

Often the quantity theory is presented by using the *equation of exchange:*

$$MV = PY \qquad [5]$$

where *V* is the **velocity of circulation,** defined as national income divided by the quantity of money:

$$V = \frac{PY}{M} \qquad [6]$$

Velocity may be interpreted as showing the average amount of "work" done by a unit of money. If annual national income is $400 billion and the stock of money is $100 billion, on average, each dollar's worth of money is used four times to create the values added that compose the national income.

There is a simple relationship between *k* and *V*. One is the reciprocal of the other, as may be seen immediately by comparing Equations 4 and 6. Thus, it makes no difference whether we choose to work with *k* or *V*. Further, if *k* is assumed to be constant, this implies that *V* must also be treated as being constant.

An example may help to illustrate the interpretation of each. Suppose the stock of money that people wish to hold equals one-fifth of the value of total transactions. Thus, *k* is 0.2 and *V,* the reciprocal of *k,* is 5. If the money supply is to be one-fifth of the value of annual transactions, each dollar must be "used" on average five times.

The modern version of the quantity theory does not assume that *k* and *V* are exogenously fixed. However, it does argue that they will not change in response to a change in the quantity of money.

Monetary Forces and National Income

We are now in a position to examine the relationship between monetary forces, on the one hand, and the equilibrium values of national income and the price level, on the other. The first step in explaining this relationship is a new one: the link between monetary equilibrium and aggregate demand. The second is familiar from earlier chapters: the effects of shifts in aggregate demand on equilibrium values of national income and the price level.

Monetary Equilibrium and Aggregate Demand

Monetary equilibrium occurs when the demand for money equals the supply of money. In Chapter 4

Box 30-3

The Transmission Mechanism in an Open Economy

The text focuses on the interest rate as the channel through which the effects of monetary policy are transmitted to the economy. However, as we have observed in earlier chapters, the "openness" of the economy to international trade and to capital flows means that two additional complications must be allowed for.* First, the effects of monetary contraction or expansion are weakened because U.S. interest rates are closely linked to interest rates in the rest of the world; this restricts the scope for domestic interest rates to change in response to monetary policy. Second, there is an added channel through which the effects of monetary policy are transmitted to real aggregate demand. This is through changes in the external value of the dollar on the foreign exchange market.

The Link Between Interest Rates and the External Value of the Dollar

If U.S. interest rates rise relative to those in other countries, the demand for dollar assets will also rise. U.S. residents will be less inclined to invest in assets of other countries, and foreign demand for high-yielding U.S. assets will increase. In order to invest in these assets, foreigners need to buy dollars, and their demand for these dollars on the foreign exchange rate will cause the dollar to appreciate.

Low U.S. interest rates have the opposite effect. U.S. citizens will want to invest in foreign assets, and foreigners will be less anxious to invest in U.S. assets. Foreigners will demand fewer dollars, and people in the United States will be selling more dollars in order to obtain foreign currencies to invest in higher-yielding foreign assets. This will cause a depreciation of the dollar on the foreign exchange market.

Other things being equal, the higher U.S. interest rates are, the higher will be the external value of the dollar, and the lower U.S. interest rates are, the lower will be the external value of the dollar.

This *positive* relationship between the interest rate and the external value of the dollar is shown in the figure. It is this relationship that is often featured in newspaper and television discussions about movements in the exchange rate. For example, an appreciation of the dollar, say, from 1.80 pounds sterling to 1.85, will often be the result of a rise in U.S. interest rates relative to those in the United Kingdom.

The Impact of Changes in the Money Supply

Suppose that in order to stimulate the economy, the Fed increases the money supply. The initial effects will be exactly the same as in the closed economy analyzed in the text. Banks will find that they have excess reserves and will want to make more loans and expand their deposits; households and firms will want to add to their holdings of interest-earning assets. Their combined actions will cause U.S. interest rates to fall.

It is at this point that open economy forces come into play. As U.S. interest rates fall, foreigners and U.S. citizens will start to sell U.S. assets in order to purchase foreign assets that now earn interest rates higher than those prevailing in the United States.

Because people are selling dollar assets, the fall in U.S. interest rates is mitigated. In this way U.S. interest rates are constrained by those abroad; the availability of interest-earning assets in foreign currencies that investors think are substitutes for U.S. securities implies that U.S. interest rates do not move as much in response to changes in the money supply as they would in a closed economy.

---

* These issues are discussed in more detail in Chapter 39.

People who have sold their dollar assets will now wish to sell dollars in order to buy foreign exchange, which they will use to purchase foreign assets. This causes a depreciation of the dollar on the foreign exchange market.[†]

These effects of an increase in the money supply can be shown in terms of the figure as a movement from point A, with the interest rate of i_0 and the value of the dollar of v_0, to point B, with a lower interest rate of i_1 and a lower value of the dollar of v_1.

An increase in the money supply will lead to a fall in domestic interest rates and a depreciation of the dollar. A decrease in the money supply will have the opposite effects, resulting in an increase in interest rates and an appreciation of the dollar.

The Transmission Mechanism

How are impacts on the interest rate and the external value of the dollar transmitted into changes in the level of economic activity? The reduced response of interest rates to monetary policy implies less effect, for a given change in the money supply, on interest-sensitive expenditures. However, the induced changes in the value of the dollar add a new channel by which monetary policy is transmitted to the economy. As we saw in Chapter 26, a depreciation of the dollar, other things being equal, makes U.S.-produced goods more competitive on world markets and thus increases exports and decreases imports.

Because an increase in the money supply leads to a depreciation of the dollar, it stimulates net

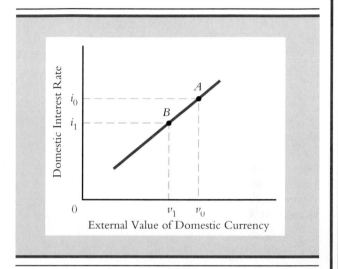

exports and thereby raises aggregate demand. Similarly, a decrease in the money supply will lower aggregate demand because it leads to an appreciation of the dollar and hence to a fall in net exports.

The operation of this channel of the transmission mechanism can be seen in terms of the definition of aggregate demand:

$$AD = C + I + G + (X - IM)$$

In a closed economy, monetary policy operates through changes in the interest rate influencing investment expenditure (I) as well as any interest-sensitive consumption expenditures (C); in the open economy, that channel is weakened, but the effects on aggregate demand are reinforced through the effects of changes in the exchange rate on net exports ($X - IM$).

Though the channels are different, the ability of monetary policy to affect national income remains. In the rest of this chapter, we maintain the closed economy analysis for simplicity; we return to the open economy issues in Chapters 38 and 39.

[†] Equilibrium will occur when the dollar has depreciated so much that people expect it to appreciate later (i.e., the exchange rate "overshoots" its long-run value), and that expected appreciation compensates investors for the lower nominal interest rate on U.S. bonds. This theory is discussed in more detail later in Chapter 39.

Inflation is said to be *validated* when the money supply is increased as fast as the price level so that the adjustment mechanism is frustrated. Validated inflation can go on indefinitely, although, as we shall see in Chapter 32, not at a constant rate.

A recessionary gap. In principle, the adjustment mechanism will also operate to eliminate a recessionary gap. If the recessionary gap were to lead to a fall in wages and other factor prices, the *SRAS* curve would shift to the right, causing the price level to fall and national income to rise. However, as we saw in Chapter 28, many economists argue that wages are slow to fall in the face of a recessionary gap. (This was referred to as the second asymmetry of aggregate supply; see the discussion surrounding Figure 28-3.) In this circumstance the adjustment mechanism will not be effective in causing national income to return quickly to its potential level. This is one reason why many economists argue that aggregate demand should be stimulated in the face of a persistent recessionary gap, either through fiscal policy, which we studied in Chapter 28, or through monetary policy. However, this view is challenged by other economists; we will study this debate in Chapter 31.

The Strength of Monetary Forces

How much will a given change in the money supply cause national income to change? Because a change in the money supply affects national income by causing the *AD* curve to shift, we know from the analysis developed earlier in this chapter (which in turn built on that in Chapter 28) that it is important to distinguish between the effects on national income in the long run and in the short run.

Long-Run Effects on National Income

We have seen that the adjustment mechanism operates to ensure that, regardless of the size of the money supply, real national income eventually converges to its potential level. The operation of this adjustment mechanism following an increase in the money supply is illustrated in Figure 30-9.

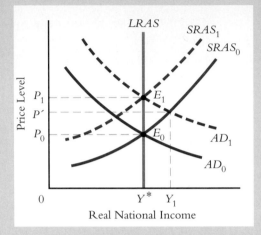

FIGURE 30-9
Long-Run Effect of an Increase in the Money Supply

An increase in the money supply leads to a rightward shift in the *AD* curve, but because it has no effect on potential income, in the long run it has no effect on national income and results only in a change in the price level. The economy is initially in equilibrium at E_0, with price level P_0 and real national income Y^*. An increase in the money supply causes the *AD* curve to shift rightward from AD_0 to AD_1. National income rises to Y_1, and the price level rises to P'. The inflationary gap of $Y_1 Y^*$ sets the adjustment mechanism in action, driving up wages and causing the *SRAS* curve to shift up and to the left. The process comes to a halt when national income has returned to its potential level, Y^*, thus eliminating the inflationary gap, and the price level has risen to P_1.

Although a change in the money supply causes the *AD* curve to shift, it has no effect on the level of national income in the long run.

Figure 30-9, which essentially reproduces the analysis of part (i) of Figure 28-5 on page 579, also shows that the only long-run effect of a shift in the *AD* curve following a change in the money supply is a change in the price level. This result is often referred to as the *neutrality of money*, as discussed at the beginning of Chapter 29, and it is at the heart of the quantity theory of money, discussed in Box 30-2.

Short-Run Effects on National Income

We now focus on the effects of a change in the money supply on the short-run equilibrium level of national income. As shown in Figure 30-7, this will depend on both aggregate demand and aggregate supply.

The Role of Aggregate Demand

The size of the shift in the *AD* curve in response to an increase in the money supply depends on the size of the increase in investment expenditure that is stimulated. This in turn depends on the strength of the two key linkages that make up the transmission mechanism.

The first consideration is how much interest rates fall in response to the increase in the money supply. *The more interest-sensitive the demand for money, the less interest rates will have to fall to induce firms and households to hold the increase in the money supply.*

The second consideration is how much investment expenditure increases in response to the fall in interest rates. *The more interest-sensitive investment expenditure is, the more it will increase in response to any given fall in the interest rate.*

It follows that the size of the shift in aggregate demand in response to a change in the money supply depends on the shapes of the demand for money and marginal efficiency of investment curves. The influence of the shapes of the two curves is shown in Figure 30-10 and may be summarized as follows:

**1. The steeper (less interest-sensitive) the *LP* function, the greater the effect a change in the money supply will have on interest rates.
2. The flatter (more interest-sensitive) the *MEI* function, the greater the effect a change in the interest rate will have on investment expenditure and hence the larger will be the shift in the *AD* curve.**

The combination that produces the largest shift in the *AD* curve for a given change in the money supply is a steep *LP* function and a flat *MEI* function. This combination is illustrated in Figure 30-10(i). It accords with the view that monetary policy is relatively effective as a means of influencing the economy—a view associated with the so-called monetarists. The combination that produces the smallest shift in the *AD* curve is a flat *LP* function

and a steep *MEI* function. This combination is illustrated in Figure 30-10(ii). It accords with the view that monetary policy is relatively ineffective—a view associated with some so-called Keynesians. (We shall encounter the differences between monetarists and Keynesians again in Chapter 31.)

The Role of Aggregate Supply

As we saw in Chapter 28, the response of real national income and the price level to any given shift in the *AD* curve depends on the behavior of aggregate supply. Two aspects of this behavior are relevant.

The slope of the SRAS curve. As shown in Figure 27-10 on page 563, the steeper the *SRAS* curve is, the larger will be the change in the price level and the smaller will be the change in real national income following a shift in the *AD* curve. Many economists think that when the level of real national income is near (or above) its capacity level, the *SRAS* curve is very steep.

When the economy is operating near or above its capacity level of output, increases in aggregate demand (including those caused by increases in the money supply) will lead to small increases in real national income but will have a substantial effect on the price level.

Shifts in the SRAS curve. As we saw in Figure 28-2, shifts in the *SRAS* curve can offset the expansionary effects of an increase in aggregate demand. In that figure, such shifts were induced by changes in factor prices that occurred in response to an inflationary gap. However, many economists think that such offsetting shifts in the *SRAS* curve can occur even without the emergence of an inflationary gap if the *AD* shock was caused by an increase in the money supply that was *anticipated*. (This view is related to the views discussed in Box 28-1 on page 577, where we examined the possibility that expectations effects can cause the *SRAS* curve to shift following an anticipated shift in the *AD* curve.)

Figure 30-9 can also be used to illustrate the case of an increase in the money supply that is perfectly foreseen by workers and employers alike. The monetary disturbance shifts the *AD* curve rightward. Workers, knowing that the prices of goods that they buy are going to rise, demand increases in wages to

FIGURE 30-10
Two Views on the Strength of Monetary Changes

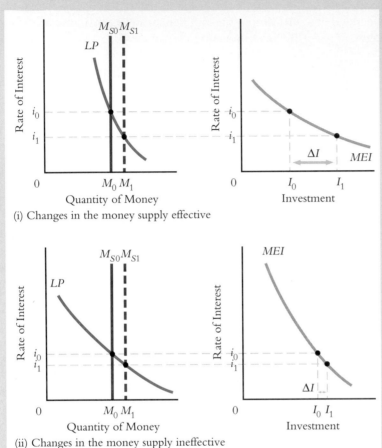

(i) Changes in the money supply effective

(ii) Changes in the money supply ineffective

The strength of the effect of a change in the money supply on investment and hence on aggregate demand depends on the interest elasticity of both the demand for money and desired investment expenditure. Initially, the money supply is M_{S0}, and the economy is in equilibrium, with an interest rate of i_0 and investment expenditure of I_0.

In both parts of the figure the central bank expands the money supply from M_{S0} to M_{S1}. The rate of interest thus falls from i_0 to i_1, as shown in each of the left panels. This causes an increase in investment expenditure of ΔI, from I_0 to I_1, as shown in each of the right panels.

In part (i) the demand for money is highly interest-inelastic, so the increase in the money supply leads to a large fall in the interest rate. Further, desired investment expenditure is highly interest-elastic, so the large fall in interest rates also leads to a large increase in investment expenditure. Hence, in this case the change in the money supply will be effective in stimulating aggregate demand.

In part (ii) the demand for money is more interest-elastic, so the increase in the money supply leads to only a small fall in the interest rate. Further, desired investment expenditure is interest-inelastic, so the small fall in interest rates also leads to only a small increase in investment expenditure. Hence, in this case the change in the money supply will not be effective in stimulating aggregate demand.

compensate. Employers, knowing that the price of their output is going to rise, grant the wage increases. Thus, the *SRAS* curve immediately shifts leftward; this *expectations effect* means that the adjustment mechanism operates very quickly, thus reducing the effect of a monetary disturbance on real national income.

How far does the *SRAS* curve shift in anticipation of a future shock? In the extreme case where there is no disagreement about the extent or the implications of the initial monetary disturbance and no contractual or institutional forces that would cause wages to adjust slowly to changes in the economy,

wages would rise immediately to offset the price increase completely. Real wages would thus remain unchanged, as would real output. Hence, the *SRAS* curve must shift enough to offset completely the expansionary effects on real national income, as shown in the figure.

It is conceivable that in the case of a perfectly anticipated monetary disturbance, all the effects fall immediately on money wages and prices anticipated, and none fall on real wages or real national output.

Of course, most monetary disturbances are, at best, imperfectly foreseen, and typically there is considerable uncertainty about the exact nature and implications of any particular disturbance. Further, responses take time. Hence, an outcome in which the effects on real national income are completely offset is extreme, and any monetary disturbance can be expected to have at least some temporary effects. However, the expectations effects complicate the analysis of monetary disturbances and create problems for economists who are trying to understand the implications of current monetary events or to advise governments on the use of monetary policy. We will encounter this issue repeatedly in the next few chapters as we study monetary policy and other macroeconomic problems and controversies.

SUMMARY

1. For simplicity, we divide all forms in which wealth is held into money, which is a medium of exchange, and bonds, which earn a higher interest return than money and can be turned into money by being sold at a price that is determined on the open market.

2. The price of bonds varies negatively with the rate of interest. A rise in the interest rate lowers the prices of all bonds. The longer its term to maturity, the greater the change in the price of a bond will be for a given change in the interest rate.

3. The value of money balances that the public wishes to hold is called the *demand for money*. It is a stock (not a flow), measured as so many billions of dollars.

4. Money balances are held, despite the opportunity cost of bond interest forgone, because of the transactions, precautionary, and speculative motives. They have the effect of making the demand for money vary positively with real national income, the price level, and wealth, and negatively with the nominal rate of interest. The nominal demand for money varies proportionally with the price level.

5. When there is an excess demand for money balances, people try to sell bonds. This pushes the price of bonds down and the interest rate up. When there is an excess supply of money balances, people try to buy bonds. This pushes the price of bonds up and the rate of interest down. Monetary equilibrium is established when people are willing to hold the fixed stocks of money and bonds at the current rate of interest. The liquidity preference (*LP*) function is the relationship between money demand and the nominal interest rate.

6. With given inflationary expectations, changes in the nominal interest rate translate into changes in the real interest rate. A change in the real interest rate causes desired investment to change along the marginal efficiency of investment (*MEI*) function. This shifts the aggregate desired expenditure function and causes equilibrium national income to change. This means that the aggregate demand curve shifts.

7. Points 5 and 6 together describe the transmission mechanism that links money to national income. A decrease in the supply of money tends to reduce aggregate demand. An increase in the supply of money tends to increase aggregate demand.

8. The negatively sloped aggregate demand curve indicates that the higher the price level, the lower the equilibrium national income. The explanation lies in part with the effect of money on the adjustment mechanism: Other things being equal, the higher the price level, the higher the demand for money and the rate of interest, the lower the aggregate expenditure function, and thus the lower the equilibrium income.

9. The adjustment mechanism that causes the aggregate demand curve to have a negative slope means that a sufficiently large rise in the price level will eliminate any inflationary gap. However, this mechanism can be frustrated if the Fed validates the price rise by increasing the money supply.

10. Changes in the money supply affect national income via shifts in the *AD* curve; hence, they have no effect on national income in the long run.

11. The steeper the *LP* curve and the flatter the marginal efficiency of investment curve, the greater the effect a given change in the money supply will have on aggregate demand. The steeper the *SRAS* curve or the faster wages adjust, the smaller the transitory effect of a given shift in the *AD* curve on national income. If the change in the money supply were widely foreseen and its effects understood, the *SRAS* curve might shift very quickly so as to reduce any effects on national income.

TOPICS FOR REVIEW

Interest rates and bond prices

Transactions, precautionary, and speculative motives for holding money

Liquidity preference (*LP*) function

Monetary equilibrium

Transmission mechanism

Marginal efficiency of investment (*MEI*) function

Money and the adjustment mechanism

The strength of monetary forces

DISCUSSION QUESTIONS

1. "Central banker says using monetary policy to lower interest rates now would only cause inflation to rise and lead to higher interest rates in the future." Explain how this might be so.

2. "Bond prices pressed downward by news of M1's sharp rise, economy's rebound." Does this *Wall Street Journal* headline necessarily contradict our theory about the postulated positive relationship between money supply and bond prices?

3. Historically, construction of new houses has been one of the most interest-sensitive categories of spending. In 1989 the financial press carried a number of stories suggesting that because of financial deregulation and innovations in housing finance, this interest

sensitivity had apparently decreased. If this were true, what would be the implications for monetary policy?

4. Describing a possible future "cashless society," a public report recently said, "In the cashless society of the future, a customer could insert a plastic card into a machine at a store and the amount of the purchase would be deducted from his 'bank account' in the computer automatically and transferred to the store's account. No cash or checks would ever change hands." What would such a "debit card" do to the various motives for holding money balances? What functions would remain for commercial banks and for the central bank if money, as we now know it, disappeared in this fashion? What benefits and disadvantages can you see in such a scheme?

5. What motives do you think explain the following holdings?

   a. Currency and coins in the cash register of the local supermarket at the start of each working day

   b. The payroll account of the Ford Motor Company in the local bank

   c. Term deposits that mature after one's retirement

   d. Government bonds held by private individuals

6. What would be the effects on the economy if Congress were to vote a once-and-for-all universal social dividend of $5,000 paid to every American over the age of 15, to be financed by the creation of new money?

7. In 1989 economists Christina and David Romer produced a study of post–World War II policies of the U.S. Federal Reserve Board. They examined six episodes in which the Fed tightened monetary policy to reduce inflation and found that each time, following the tightening of monetary policy, the unemployment rate rose sharply and industrial production fell. Further, they estimated that these effects persist, so that unemployment is at its peak $2\frac{1}{2}$ years after the policy is initiated, and "there is only a limited tendency for economic activity to return to its previous path subsequently." Interpret these results in terms of the theoretical framework developed in this chapter.

8. Suppose that you alone know that the Fed is going to engage in policies that will decrease the money supply sharply, starting next month. How might you make speculative profits by purchases or sales of bonds now?

9. What would happen if, starting from a situation of a 10 percent rate of inflation and of monetary expansion, the Fed cut the rate of monetary expansion to 5 percent?

10. Trace the full sequence of events by which the adjustment mechanism would work if, in the face of a constant money supply, workers and firms insisted on actions that raised prices continually at a rate of 10 percent per year. "Sooner or later in this situation, something would have to give." What possible things could "give"? What would be the consequence of each "giving"?

APPENDIX TO CHAPTER

30

The Slope of the Aggregate Demand Curve

The *AD* curve relates the price level to the equilibrium level of real national income. Its negative slope means that the higher the price level, the lower is the equilibrium national income. A major reason for this negative slope is the transmission mechanism.

Let us look at this process in detail. Although the argument contains nothing new, it does require that you follow carefully through several steps.

We start with an initial equilibrium position, corresponding to a given price level P_0, shown by the 0 subscripts in the two figures. Figure 30A-1, which reproduces the relationships depicted in Figure 30-4, shows the determination of the interest

rate by the conditions of monetary equilibrium in part (i); that in turn determines the level of desired investment spending by the marginal efficiency of investment schedule in part (ii). Figure 30A-2, which reproduces the relationships depicted in Figure 30-5, shows the *AE* curve, drawn for that level of investment spending, and the determination of equilibrium national income in part (i); that level of national income is then plotted against the price level to give point *A* on the *AD* curve in part (ii).

A rise in the price level raises the money value of transactions and increases the quantity of money

---

FIGURE 30A-1
Changes in the Price Level: Interest Rates and Investment

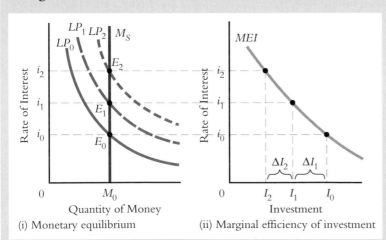

(i) Monetary equilibrium   (ii) Marginal efficiency of investment

Changes in the price level influence the demand for money and hence cause the level of interest rates and desired investment spending to change. In part (i) the money supply is fixed at M_0. Initially money demand is given by LP_0, equilibrium is at E_0, and the interest rate is i_0. Given that interest rate, desired investment spending is I_0, as shown in part (ii) by the *MEI* schedule.

An increase in the price level causes an increase in the demand for money, and hence the *LP* curve shifts upward to LP_1. Equilibrium is at E_1, the interest rate rises to i_1, and desired investment spending falls by ΔI_1 to I_1. A further increase in the price level causes a further increase in the demand for money, to LP_2. Equilibrium is at E_2, the interest rate rises to i_2, and desired investment spending falls by ΔI_2 to I_2.

FIGURE 30A-2
Changes in the Price Level: Aggregate Expenditure and National Income

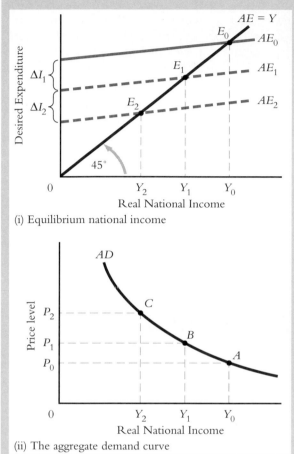

(i) Equilibrium national income

(ii) The aggregate demand curve

Changes in the price level lead to changes in desired aggregate expenditure and hence in the equilibrium level of national income. Equilibrium national income is determined in part (i). At a given initial price level—hence with an initial level of desired investment spending of I_0 from Figure 30A-1—desired aggregate expenditure is shown by AE_0. Equilibrium is at E_0, and equilibrium national income is Y_0. In part (ii) Y_0 is plotted against P_0 to give point A on the AD curve.

An increase in the price level causes a decrease of ΔI_1 in the level of desired investment spending, as determined in Figure 30A-1 and shown in part (i) here. Thus, the AE curve shifts down to AE_1. Equilibrium is at E_1, and equilibrium national income falls to Y_1. In part (ii) the higher price level P_1 is plotted against the lower equilibrium level of income Y_1 as point B on the AD curve.

A further increase in the price level causes a further decrease of ΔI_2 in desired investment spending, as determined in Figure 30A-1 and shown in part (i) here. Thus, the AE curve shifts downward to AE_2. Equilibrium is at E_2, and equilibrium national income falls to Y_2. In part (ii) the higher price level P_2 is plotted against the lower equilibrium level of income Y_2 as point C on the AD curve.

demanded at each possible value of the interest rate. As a result, the liquidity preference function shifts upward, raising the interest rate and reducing the level of desired investment expenditure, as shown in Figure 30A-1. The reduction in investment spending in turn causes the AE curve to shift downward, leading to a reduction in the equilibrium level of national income, as shown in part (i) of Figure 30A-2. The combination of the higher price level and the lower equilibrium level of national income can be plotted as another point, say, point B, on the AD curve in part (ii).

Changes in the price level lead to changes in the interest rate and hence in desired aggregate expenditure and the equilibrium level of national income; other things being equal, the higher the price level, the lower is the equilibrium level of national income.

The negative relationship between the price level and equilibrium real income shown by the AD curve occurs because, other things being equal, a rise in the price level raises the quantity of money demanded. Notice the qualification "other things being equal." It is important for this process that the nominal money *supply* remain constant. The adjustment mechanism operates because the demand for money increases when the price level rises while the money supply remains constant. The attempt to add to money balances by selling bonds is what drives the interest rate up and reduces desired expenditure, thereby reducing equilibrium national income. (This argument is conducted in terms of the nominal supply of and demand for money. Arguing in terms of the real demand and supply of money leads to identical results.) **[40]**

31

Monetary Policy

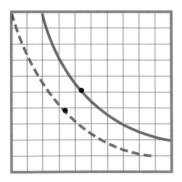

The Fed conducts monetary policy in order to influence key macroeconomic variables. Regardless of what variables it targets, the Fed's policies will influence real national income, employment and unemployment, inflation, interest rates, and the exchange rate. Later in this chapter we study in detail how the Fed conducts monetary policy and what is involved in choosing among different operating procedures and policy goals. We begin by examining how the Fed controls the money supply.

Control of the Money Supply

Deposit money is an important part of the money supply. It accounts for over 75 percent of M1, the narrowest definition of money, and roughly 15 percent of M3, the broadest measure in widespread use (see Table 29-1). As we saw in Chapter 29, the ability of banks to create deposit money depends on their reserves.[1]

The ability of the central bank to affect the money supply is critically related to its ability to affect the size and adequacy of the reserves of the banking system.

Open Market Operations

The most important tool that the Fed uses to influence the supply of money is its purchase or sale of government securities in financial markets. These are known as **open market operations**. Just as there are stock markets, there are active and well-organized markets for government securities—as discussed in Box 29-2, these consist of treasury bills (which are quite short-term) and bonds of various maturities. You or I, General Motors, the Chase Manhattan Bank, or the Fed can enter this market and buy or sell government securities at the market price established by supply and demand.

At the start of 1992 the Federal Reserve held more than $267 billion in government securities. This was $30 billion more than at the start of 1989; the Fed had added that amount to its holdings as a result of net purchases on the open market, and during the three-year period its gross purchases and sales amounted to many times this amount. What is the effect of these purchases and sales?

---

[1] Recall from Chapter 29 that the terms *bank* and *banking system* include commercial banks *and* other financial intermediaries such as savings banks, credit unions, and savings and loan associations.

Purchases on the Open Market

When a Federal Reserve bank buys a bond from a household or firm, it pays for the bond with a check drawn on the central bank and payable to the seller. The seller deposits this check in its own bank. The bank presents the check to the Fed for payment, and the central bank makes a book entry, increasing the deposit of the bank at the central bank.

Table 31-1 shows the changes in the balance sheets of the several parties involved in a Federal Reserve bank purchase of $10,000 in government securities from a household. At the end of these transactions, the Fed has acquired a new asset in the form of a security and a new liability in the form of a deposit by the bank. The household has reduced its security holdings and increased its deposits. The bank has increased its deposit liabilities and its reserves by the amount of the transaction.

Given a constant required reserve ratio, the banks have excess reserves after these transactions are completed, and they are thus in a position to expand their loans and deposits. Indeed, after the household deposits the proceeds of its sale of the security in its bank account, its bank is in the same position as was the bank in Table 29-5 that received the new deposit.[2]

When the central bank buys securities, the reserves of the banks are increased. These banks can then expand deposits, thereby increasing the money supply.

However, this expansion of the money supply is not automatic. Banks often hold excess reserves as a matter of policy, and the amount that they hold varies with economic conditions. Changes in the banks' desired excess reserves can lead to a change in the money supply without any actions on the part of the central bank. Further, if the central bank increases excess reserves through open market purchases at the same time that the banks decide to hold more excess reserves, the increase will not lead to an increase in the money supply.

Voluntary holding of excess reserves weakens the link between the creation of excess reserves and the creation of money.

---

[2] The Fed sometimes buys government securities from banks, thus directly increasing their reserves by the amount of the purchase.

TABLE 31-1 Balance Sheet Changes Caused by an Open Market Purchase from a Household (*thousands of dollars*)

Private household		
Assets		Liabilities
Bonds	−$10	No change
Deposits	+ 10	
Commercial banks		
Assets		Liabilities
Reserves (deposits with central bank)	+$10	Demand deposits +$10
Central bank		
Assets		Liabilities
Bonds	+$10	Deposits of commercial banks +$10

The money supply is increased when the Fed makes an open market purchase from a household. When the Fed buys a $10,000 bond from a household, the household gains money and gives up a bond. The commercial banks gain a new deposit of $10,000 and thus new reserves of $10,000. Commercial banks can now engage in a multiple expansion of deposit money of the sort that was analyzed in Chapter 29.

However, voluntary excess reserve holding does not destroy the link. Excess reserves make it *possible* for the banks to expand the money supply, and an increase in excess reserves due to an open market purchase by the Fed will generally lead to some undesired excess reserves and hence to some deposit creation.

Sales on the Open Market

When the Fed sells a $10,000 security to a household or a firm, it receives the buyer's check, drawn against a bank. The central bank presents the check to the bank for payment, which is made by a book entry that reduces the bank's deposit at the Fed.

The changes in this case are opposite to those shown in Table 31-1. The Fed has reduced its assets by the value of the security it sold and has reduced its liabilities in the form of the deposits of banks. The household or firm has increased its holdings of securities and reduced its cash on deposit with a bank. The bank has reduced its deposit liability to the household or firm and has reduced its reserves (on deposit with the central bank) by the same amount. Each of the asset changes is balanced by a liability change.

The bank, however, finds that, by suffering an equal change in its reserves and deposit liabilities, its ratio of reserves to deposits falls.[3] Banks whose reserve ratios are pushed below the minimum requirement must take immediate steps to restore their reserve ratios. The necessary reduction in deposits can be accomplished by not making new investments when old ones are redeemed (e.g., by not granting new loans when old ones are repaid) or by selling (liquidating) existing investments.

When the Fed sells securities on the open market, bank reserves are decreased. These banks, in turn, may contract deposits, thereby decreasing the money supply.

Although the process just described reflects the mechanics of an open market sale, it does not accurately portray some of the subtleties involved in how the Fed pursues a tight monetary policy. These are discussed further in Box 31-1.

---

[3] Consider, for example, a bank with $10 million in deposits, backed by $2 million in cash, in fulfillment of a 20 percent cash reserve ratio. As a result of the Fed's open market sales of $100,000 worth of bonds, the bank loses $100,000 of deposits and reserves. Reserves are now $1.9 million, while deposits are $9.9 million, making a reserve ratio of only 19.19 percent.

Implications for the Money Supply

Notice in Table 29-2 that the Fed's holdings of government securities are large relative to the reserves of banks. If it chooses, it can sell securities and thus reduce those reserves sharply. Similarly, it can buy securities and thereby expand bank reserves.

Open market operations give the Fed a potent weapon for affecting the size of bank reserves, and thus for affecting the money supply.

Other Tools for Influencing the Money Supply

The major tool that the Fed uses in conducting monetary policy is its open market operations, but other tools are available and on occasion have been used extensively.

Reserve Requirements

One way that the Fed can control the money supply is by altering the required minimum reserve ratios. Suppose the banking system is "loaned-up"; that is, it has no excess reserves. If the Fed were to increase the required reserve ratio (say, from 20 percent to 25 percent), the dollar amount of reserves held by the banks would no longer be adequate to support their outstanding deposits. Banks would then be forced to reduce their deposits until they achieve the

---

TABLE 31-2(a)	Balance Sheet for a Loaned-up Banking System with a 20 Percent Reserve Ratio

Assets		Liabilities	
Reserves	$1,000	Deposits	$5,000
Loans	4,100	Capital	100
	$5,100		$5,100

TABLE 31-2(b)	Balance Sheet for a Loaned-up Banking System After Responding to a Change in Its Reserve Ratio to 25 Percent

Assets		Liabilities	
Reserves	$1,000	Deposits	$4,000
Loans	3,100	Capital	100
	$4,100		$4,100

Increasing the required reserve ratio forces a loaned-up bank to reduce its deposits and thus decreases the supply of deposit money. The banking system in part (a) has a ratio of reserves to deposits of 0.20. If the Fed raises the required reserve ratio to 0.25, the reserves of $1,000 will support deposits of only $4,000. As shown in part (b), the banking system can reduce its deposits by reducing its loans. A reduction in reserve requirements from 0.25 to 0.20 would permit a banking system in the position of (b) to expand its loans and deposits to those of (a) even though there is no increase in the reserves held by its member banks.

Box 31-1

More on Contractionary Monetary Policy

This box looks at two additional issues that arise with a contractionary monetary policy.

Can the Fed Always Find Buyers for Securities?

One way in which the Fed pursues a contractionary monetary policy is to sell government securities, thus reducing the reserves available to the banking system. What if the public does not wish to buy the securities that the Fed wishes to sell? Can the Fed force them to do so?

The answer is that there is always a price at which the public will buy. The Fed must be prepared in its open market operations to lower the price of securities as far as necessary in order to sell them. This fall in price is, as we have seen, the same thing as an increase in the interest rate. If the Fed wishes to pursue a contractionary policy by selling government securities, it will have to accept that it is necessary for interest rates to rise.

Do Reserves and the Money Supply Actually Fall?

In every year since 1950, real growth and inflation have ensured that nominal national income has risen. As a result, the demand for money has grown. As a result, in every year in the period the nominal money supply has grown, reflecting the Fed's decision to supply additional reserves to the banking system to meet the growing demand for money. Does this mean that the Fed has never followed a contractionary monetary policy?

The answer is no. When real income growth and inflation result in a continually growing nominal national income, the stance of monetary policy depends upon the rate at which the money supply is allowed to grow *relative* to the rate of growth of the demand for money. A contractionary monetary policy occurs when the growth in the money supply is held below the rate of growth in the demand for money; it does not require a fall in the absolute size of the money supply.

For example, if nominal national income and the demand for money are both growing at 10 percent per year, the Fed can follow a contractionary policy if it limits the rate of growth of reserves and the money supply to 7 percent. This would create an excess demand for money, causing interest rates to rise. The higher interest rates, in turn, would feed through the transmission mechanism to slow the growth in spending and, hence, slow the growth in real income or inflation, or both.

---

new, higher required reserve ratio.[4] This decrease in demand deposits is a decrease in the money supply. The process is illustrated in Table 31-2.

The effect of a reduction in required reserve ratios is also shown in Table 31-2. The reduction first creates excess reserves. Of course, if banks choose not to increase their loans, they will not respond to this increase in excess reserves. Normally, however, the profit motive will lead most banks to respond by increasing loans and deposits and will thus lead to an increase in the money supply.

Increases in required reserve ratios force banks with no excess reserves to decrease deposits and thus reduce the money supply. Decreases in required reserve ratios permit banks to expand deposits and thus increase the money supply.

In 1934 the Federal Reserve Board was given authority by Congress to set, within limits, required reserve ratios for both demand and time deposits. The Fed has changed reserve requirements (even as recently as 1992, when some reserve ratios were reduced slightly), and Congress from time to time has changed the limits. However, such changes are

---

[4] They would do this by gradually decreasing their loans or by selling some of their securities. In the short term they may borrow from the Fed to give themselves time to meet the increased reserve requirements without disrupting financial markets.

not relied upon for the day-to-day executions of monetary policy, primarily because open market operations provide a much more flexible way of achieving the same effects.

The Discount Rate

The *discount rate* is the interest rate at which the Fed will lend funds to member banks whose reserves are temporarily below the required level. Such loans play an important role in helping banks meet their reserve requirements when open market sales by the Fed cause a sudden contraction of bank reserves. The banks often need this temporary help to bridge the gap until they can make longer-term adjustments in their portfolios. As a matter of policy, the Fed discourages long-term borrowing from it by banks and accommodates requests at the "discount window" only on a short-term basis. Hence, the discount rate plays a relatively minor role as a policy tool. However:

A change in the discount rate is important because it is a signal of the Fed's intentions.

Changes in the discount rate are usually associated with like changes in other interest rates. It is not always clear whether the discount rate follows or leads changes in other interest rates. One reason the discount rate sometimes follows other developments is that open market operations that apply the monetary brakes by selling bonds tend to push up interest rates. To discourage banks from turning to its discount window, the Fed must then raise the discount rate. One reason the discount rate sometimes leads other rates is that sharp changes in the discount rate often create expectations about future Fed policy in providing reserves to the system.

Net unborrowed reserves, often also called **free reserves**, are the total reserves of the banking system minus required reserves minus the reserves that have been borrowed from the Fed—that is, excess reserves minus borrowed reserves. Net unborrowed reserves indicate the long-term ability of the banking system to support deposit money. If these free reserves are below the level of required reserves, it follows that the banks are meeting their reserve requirements by using temporary borrowings from the Fed. Thus the banks will be exerting contractionary pressure on the money supply. They will be trying to reduce their deposits in order to bring their unborrowed reserves up to the legal requirements so that they will be able to pay off their loans from the Fed. If, on the other hand, the banks have an excess of net unborrowed reserves over required reserves, they are in a position to expand the supply of deposit money.

Selective Credit Controls

Monetary policy seeks to make money and credit *generally* scarce or *generally* plentiful. **Selective credit controls**, on the other hand, allow the Fed to decide where the initial impact of tight or plentiful credit will be felt. Margin requirements, installment-credit controls, mortgage controls, and maximum interest rates are all examples of selective credit controls that have been used since World War II. These controls can be powerful. Increasing the down payment that is required for an installment-plan purchase, for example, can cause a major fall in demand until households accumulate enough money to make the new, larger down payments.

Although all of these selective credit controls have at some time been used somewhere in the Western world, their use has been steadily declining. For example, installment-credit controls were dropped after World War II, mortgage controls after 1953, and interest rate ceilings during the 1980s.

Margin requirements. Stock market speculation can be controlled to some extent by the Federal Reserve Board through its power to regulate the **margin requirement**, which is the fraction of the price of a stock that must be put up in cash by the purchaser. (The balance may be borrowed from the brokerage firm through which the purchaser buys the security.) Since 1960 the margin requirement has varied between 50 percent and 90 percent. Such variations can have a substantial selective effect on stock market activity that is independent of the general credit picture. Thus, if the Federal Reserve Board wishes to impose moderate credit restraint but is particularly apprehensive about stock market speculation, it may combine a moderate amount of open market selling with a sharp increase in margin requirements.

Moral Suasion

If the banking system is prepared to cooperate, the Federal Reserve banks can attempt to tighten monetary policy merely by asking banks to be conservative in granting loans. When the need for restriction is over, the bankers then can be told that it is all right to grant loans and to extend deposits up to the legal maximum.

The use of moral suasion does not depend on pure "jawboning." Member banks depend on the Federal Reserve banks for loans, and in the long term noncooperation with the Fed's "suggestions" can prove to be costly to a bank.

Changing Regulation of the Banking System

In 1980 many of the legal restrictions on the U.S. banking system were relaxed under the Depository Institutions Deregulation and Monetary Control Act. The main purpose of this *deregulation* was "to facilitate the implementation of monetary policy, to provide for a gradual elimination of all limitations on the rates of interest payable on deposits and accounts, and to authorize interest-bearing transactions accounts."

The act initiated a phase-out of the interest rate ceilings that had existed for certain types of deposits. This increased the competitiveness of the banking system. Many economists also argued that removing the ceilings removed distortions in the system and thus made it more efficient.

The act also set the same reserve requirements for all banks, large or small, whether they are members of the Federal Reserve System or not. This eliminated the preferential treatment that was given previously to small banks, which faced lower reserve requirements. A bank's reserve requirements were set at 3 percent against its first $25 million in demand deposits (and other accounts subject to direct or indirect transfer by check) and at a ratio to be determined by the Fed (between the limits of 8 percent and 14 percent) on demand deposits in excess of $25 million. The ratio on time deposits is set by the Fed between the limits of 3 percent and 9 percent.

The Fed was also given the power to require that all banks hold up to 4 percent in additional reserves, provided that "the sole purpose of such requirements is to increase the amount of reserves maintained to a level essential for the conduct of monetary policy." This instrument is copied from one used at one time by the Bank of England to prevent deposit expansion in the case where banks unexpectedly find themselves with excess reserves at a time when the central bank does not deem monetary expansion desirable.

Instruments and Objectives of Monetary Policy

The Fed conducts monetary policy in order to influence real national income and the price level. These ultimate objectives of the Fed's policy are called **policy variables**. The variables that it controls *directly* in order to achieve these objectives are called its **policy instruments**. Variables that are neither policy variables nor policy instruments but that nevertheless can play a key role in the execution of monetary policy are called **intermediate targets**; their importance lies in their close relationship to policy variables.

Policy Variables

The Fed's twin policy variables are real national income and the price level. Recall from Chapter 30 that monetary policy operates by influencing aggregate demand; the resulting link between the Fed's monetary actions and the determination of the price level and real national income is summarized in Figure 31-1.

Nominal national income as a policy variable in the short run. We also saw in Chapter 30 that the short-run effects of a shift in the *AD* curve are divided between the price level and real output in a manner determined by the slope of the *SRAS* curve. However, the Fed has no control over this slope. Thus, although the Fed cares about the separate reactions of the price level and of real output, there is little that it can do in the short run to control them independently. For any price level response that is achieved, the real output consequence must be accepted. Alternatively, for any real output response that is achieved, the price level consequence must be accepted.

Monetary policy is not capable of pursuing two objectives of pushing the price level (P) and national income (Y) toward independently determined targets.

For this reason central banks often focus on nominal national income (PY) as the target for monetary policy in the short run.

FIGURE 31-1
Monetary Policy and Macroeconomic Equilibrium

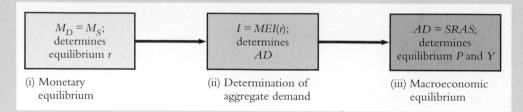

| $M_D = M_S$; determines equilibrium r | $I = MEI(r)$; determines AD | $AD = SRAS$; determines equilibrium P and Y |

(i) Monetary equilibrium   (ii) Determination of aggregate demand   (iii) Macroeconomic equilibrium

Monetary policy influences aggregate demand through the transmission mechanism, and macroeconomic equilibrium determines the price level P and the level of real output Y. Monetary equilibrium requires that the interest rate be such that the money supply equal the quantity of money demanded; for a given money supply this gives rise to the liquidity preference theory of interest, as illustrated in Figure 30-2.

Monetary equilibrium is linked to the determination of aggregate demand via the transmission mechanism, as illustrated in Figure 30-6: Changes in the money market give rise to the changes in interest rates and hence, via the transmission mechanism, to changes in desired aggregate expenditure.

Aggregate demand and short-run aggregate supply together determine the equilibrium values for the price level P and real national income Y. Changes in aggregate demand thus give rise to changes in P and Y; the exact combination of changes in P and Y depends on the slope of the $SRAS$ curve, as shown in Figure 27-10.

The price level as the policy variable in the long run. We have seen that in the long run, when the level of wages is fully adjusted and any inflationary or recessionary gap has been eliminated, the major impact of monetary policy will be on the price level.

Although monetary policy influences both real output and the price level in the short run, its main effects in the long run are on the price level.

Policy Instruments

Having selected its policy variables and formulated targets for them, the Fed must decide how to reach these targets. How can the policy variables be made to behave in the way that the Fed wishes? Because the Fed cannot control national income directly, it must employ its *policy instruments*, which it does control directly, to influence aggregate demand in the desired manner.

The primary instrument used by the Fed to conduct monetary policy is open market operations.

Open market operations change the size of the Fed's monetary liabilities, which are the sum of currency in circulation plus reserves of the banks. Bank reserves are held on deposit with the Fed and can be redeemed on demand. These monetary liabilities of the Fed, as we saw in Chapter 29, form the *base* on which banks can expand and create deposits. For this reason the Fed's liabilities are often referred to as the monetary base. The deposit expansion process that we studied in Chapter 29 means that changes in the *monetary base* lead to changes in the same direction in the money supply.

Intermediate Targets

Major changes in the direction or the method of monetary policy usually are made only infrequently. Policy decisions must, however, be made almost daily. Given the values that the Fed wishes its policy variables to take on, and given the current state of the economy, is a purchase or a sale in the open market called for? How big a purchase? Or how big a sale? At what interest rate? Such questions must be answered continually by the Fed in its day-to-day operations.

Daily information about the policy variables, however, is rarely available. Inflation and unemployment rates are available only on a monthly basis and with a considerable time lag. National income figures are available even less frequently; they appear on a quarterly basis. Thus, the policymakers do not know exactly what is happening to the policy variables when they make decisions regarding their policy instruments.

How, then, does the Fed make decisions? Central banks typically use *intermediate targets* to guide them when implementing monetary policy in the very short run. To serve as an intermediate target, a policy variable must satisfy two criteria. First, information about it must be available on a frequent basis—daily if possible. Second, its movements must be closely correlated with those of the policy variable so that changes in it can reasonably be expected to indicate that the policy variable is also changing.

The two most commonly used intermediate targets have been the money supply and the interest rate. However, these two variables are not independent of each other; recall that liquidity preference relates the quantity of money demanded to the rate of interest. This relationship and its implications for the Fed's choice of intermediate targets are reviewed in Figure 31-2.

The Fed cannot expect to be able to use its open market operations to influence both the interest rate and the money supply independently.

Hence it is important that the Fed not choose a target for one that is inconsistent with the other. By the same token, because the two are closely related, it might appear not to matter much which one is used.

For example, if the Fed wishes to remove an inflationary gap by reducing aggregate demand, it will sell securities and thus drive their prices down and interest rates up. These open market sales will also contract the money supply. It is largely immaterial whether the Fed seeks to force interest rates up or to contract the money supply; doing one accomplishes the other. Similarly, driving interest rates down by means of open market purchases of government securities will tend to expand the money supply as the public gains money in return for the securities that it sells to the Fed.

In spite of what we have just said, whether the Fed uses interest rates or the money supply as its intermediate target can have some important effects in the short run.

FIGURE 31-2
Alternative Intermediate Targets

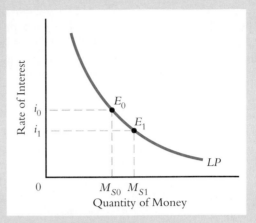

The liquidity preference function relates the money supply to the interest rate, and hence the central bank cannot choose independent targets for the two. The demand for money is given by the negatively sloped liquidity preference function, LP, reproduced from Figure 30-2.

If the Fed chooses a target of M_{S0} for the money supply, it must accept that the interest rate will be i_0 because that is the interest rate consistent with the chosen target for the money supply; it cannot expect to be able to achieve a money supply of M_{S0} and an interest rate of i_1.

If the Fed chooses a target of i_0 for the interest rate, it must accept that the money supply will be M_{S0} because that is the money supply consistent with the chosen target for the interest rate; it cannot expect to be able to achieve an interest rate of i_0 and a money supply of M_{S1}.

Changes in intermediate targets. Prior to 1970 the Fed's policy was generally couched in terms of the net unborrowed reserve position of member banks and short-term interest rates. (Together these were referred to as money market conditions.)

Many economists, and particularly monetarists, criticized this practice of using interest rates as intermediate targets. They argued that because interest rates tended to vary directly with the business cycle, rising in booms and falling in slumps, it was often difficult for the Fed to determine the impact of its monetary policy by observing the interest rate alone. Historical examples were pointed to in which the Fed wished to restrain a boom and was convinced that it was doing so because interest rates were rising sharply, only to later determine that the high demand for money due to the strong expansion was pushing up interest rates. During such periods the money supply grew substantially, so that contrary to the signals from the rising interest rate, monetary policy had been stimulative—resulting in a cumulative inflationary impact.

These criticisms, and the experience with focusing on interest rates, led to changes in intermediate targets.

In the 1970s many central banks, including the Fed, turned to focusing on the money supply as their intermediate target.

At the outset the measure that was used for this purpose was the narrowly defined money supply, M1. However, it soon became clear that problems also arose when the Fed focused exclusively on M1 as its intermediate target.[5]

Changes in the money supply are reliable indicators of the direction of monetary policy *only* if the demand for money is relatively stable. Experience of the past two decades suggests that the demand for any particular monetary aggregate can change quite substantially and that the Fed often discovers this only after a considerable period of time. Very often the shifts are out of one type of financial instrument into another; if only the former is included in the monetary aggregate being monitored, then it appears that monetary policy is becoming tighter when, in fact, all that is happening is a substitution of one type of asset for another. The Fed's response to the problems caused by shifts of this type was to again change its intermediate targets.

In the early 1980s dissatisfaction with M1 as an intermediate target led the Fed, and many other central banks, to monitor several monetary aggregates rather than just one.

Indeed, the Fed temporarily abandoned explicit targets for monetary aggregates in late 1982. When they were reinstated early in 1983, there was a change from M1 to M2 as the main target.

Other experience suggests that there are times when the current state of monetary policy needs to be gauged by measures other than money supply magnitudes. For example, slow growth in all measures of the money supply suggested that monetary policy was fairly tight during the last half of the 1970s. However, decreases in the demand for money that were not fully appreciated at the time meant that the money supply was growing quite rapidly relative to demand, and hence monetary policy was much more expansionary than was thought at the time. More attention to interest rates would have given an important signal of this because throughout this period interest rates were quite low; in fact, short-term real interest rates were negative.[6] Figure 31-3 illustrates the general lesson.

As we have seen, the exclusive use of interest rates as the intermediate target can be misleading. However, to ignore the information that can be obtained from the behavior of interest rates can also lead to errors.

Recent developments have also led to increased focus on the external value of the dollar in assessing monetary policy. The value of the dollar in terms of foreign currencies fluctuated a great deal during the 1980s, rising steadily throughout the first part of the decade and then falling dramatically during the period 1985 through 1988, and then fluctuating around a more moderate cycle, rising a bit in 1988 and 1989 and falling steadily through 1991. We shall study more about the causes and the effects of these movements in later chapters. For the moment we merely note that the movements in the exchange rate have been of increasing interest to those who study developments in the economy and in economic policy.

It has often been suggested that the Fed should try to stabilize the exchange rate, and, indeed, the

---

[5] One consequence of the focus on the money supply is that interest rates are free to find their own level. However, many economists did not expect the degree of interest rate volatility that occurred when this new policy was adopted. In response to the unprecedented variability of short-term interest rates, the Fed in late 1982 modified its operating procedures, although it did not return to using the interest rate as its intermediate target.

---

[6] This means that the rate of inflation exceeded short-term interest rates, so that in terms of purchasing power, lenders were paying borrowers for the privilege of lending money to them! The distinction between nominal and real interest rates is stressed in Chapter 23; see Figure 23-7 on page 475.

Lags and the Controversy over Monetary Policy

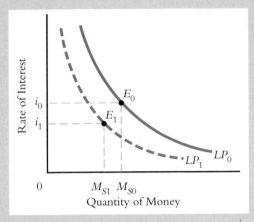

FIGURE 31-3
Intermediate Targets When the Demand for Money Shifts

Shifts in the liquidity preference function change the relationship between the money supply and the interest rate. The demand for money is initially given by the negatively sloped liquidity preference function, LP_0, reproduced from Figure 31-2. It then shifts to the left to the dashed liquidity preference function LP_1.

Suppose that, following the shift, equilibrium moves from E_0 to E_1 so the money supply falls from M_{S0} to M_{S1} and the interest rate falls from i_0 to i_1. If the Fed focuses on the fall in the money supply, it will draw the conclusion that monetary policy has tightened. If it focuses on the fall in the interest rate, it will draw the conclusion that monetary policy has eased. In effect, the money supply has fallen less than the demand for money.

Fed itself has on occasion expressed concern about developments in the exchange rate. However, most economists believe that, although movements in the exchange rate can provide information that can be of use in guiding policy, a particular value for the exchange rate should not itself be a policy objective. Thus, in this sense, the exchange rate has become an intermediate target.

Today most central banks—including the Fed—assess their monetary stance by looking at interest rates, various money supply measures, and other intermediate targets, including the exchange rate.

In Chapter 30 (see the discussion surrounding Figure 30-10) we encountered one difference between two groups of macroeconomists who were involved in a debate that was prominent in the 1960s and 1970s. *Monetarists* argued that monetary policy was potentially very powerful in the sense that a given change in the money supply would give rise to a substantial increase in aggregate demand, whereas *Keynesians* were associated with the view that monetary policy was much less powerful. This debate had some of its roots in differing interpretations of one of the most dramatic episodes in the history of the American economy, the Great Depression, as discussed in Box 31-2.

However, the debate between the monetarists and the Keynesians involved more than just the size of the effect of a change in the money supply on national income; it also focused on the question of whether active use of monetary policy in an attempt to stabilize output and the price level was likely to be successful, or whether it would instead lead to an increase in fluctuations in those variables. This aspect of the debate centers on the role of *lags*.

Experience has shown that lags in the operation of policy can cause stabilization policy to be destabilizing. In Chapter 28 we discussed how decision and implementation lags might limit the extent to which active use of fiscal policy can be relied upon to stabilize the economy. Although both of these sources of lags are much less relevant for monetary policy, the full effects of monetary policy nevertheless occur only after quite long-time lags. *Execution lags*, lags that occur after the decision has been made to implement the policy, can have important implications for the conduct of monetary policy.

Sources of Execution Lags

1. Open market operations affect the reserves of the banks. The full increase in the money supply occurs only when the banks have granted enough new loans and made enough investments to expand the money supply by the full amount that is permitted by existing reserve ratios. This process can take quite a long time.

Box 31-2

Two Views on the Great Depression

The stock market crash of 1929, and other factors associated with a moderate downswing in business activity during the late 1920s, caused the public to wish to hold more cash and less demand deposits. The banking system could not, however, meet this increased demand for liquidity without help from the Federal Reserve System. (As we saw in Chapter 29, banks are never able to meet from their own reserves a sudden demand to withdraw currency on the part of a large fraction of their depositors. Their reserves are always inadequate to meet such a demand.)

The Fed had been set up to provide just such emergency assistance to banks that were basically sound, but that were unable to meet sudden demands by depositors to withdraw cash. However, the Fed refused to extend the necessary help, and successive waves of bank failures followed as a direct result. During each wave, hundreds of banks failed, ruining many depositors and thereby worsening an already severe depression. In the last half of 1931 almost 2,000 U.S. banks were forced to suspend operations. One consequence of this was a sharp drop in the money supply; by 1932 the money supply was 35 percent below the level of 1929.

To monetarists these facts seem decisive: The fall in the money supply was clearly the major cause of the fall in output and employment that occurred during the Great Depression.

Although Keynesians accept the argument that the Fed's behavior was perverse, they argue that the cyclical behavior of investment and consumption expenditure was the major cause of the Great Depression. In support of this view, they point out that in Canada and the United Kingdom, where the central bank came to the aid of the banking system, bank failures were trivial during the Great Depression, and as a consequence the money supply did *not* shrink drastically as it did in the United States.

Despite these markedly different monetary histories, the behavior of the recessionary gap, investment expenditure, and unemployment was very similar in the three countries. Thus, Keynesians conclude that changes in the money supply were not necessary for the fall in output and employment.

2. Dividing all assets into just two categories, money and bonds, is useful for showing the underlying forces at work in determining the demand for money. In fact, however, there is a whole series of assets, including currency and demand deposits, term deposits, treasury bills, short-term bonds, long-term bonds, and equities. When households find themselves with larger money balances than they require, a chain of substitution occurs, and households try to hold less money and more interest-earning assets. The resulting fall in interest rates, in turn, affects interest-sensitive expenditures. These adjustments can take considerable time to work out.

3. It takes time for new investment plans to be drawn up, approved, and put into effect. It may take a year or more before the full increase in investment expenditure occurs in response to a fall in interest rates.

4. The increased investment expenditures set off the multiplier process that increases national income. This, too, takes some time to work out.

Furthermore, although the end result is fairly predictable, the speed with which the entire expansionary or contractionary process works itself out can vary in ways that are hard to predict. Similar considerations apply to contractionary monetary policies that seek to shift the aggregate expenditure function downward.

Monetary policy is capable of exerting expansionary and contractionary forces on the economy, but it operates with a time lag that is unpredictably long.

Implications of Execution Lags

To see the significance of execution lags for the conduct of monetary policy, assume that the lag is 18 months. If on December 1 the Fed decides that the economy needs a stimulus, it can increase the money supply within days, and by the end of the year a significant increase may be registered.

However, because the full effects of this policy take time to work out, the policy may prove to be destabilizing. By the fall, a substantial inflationary gap may have developed because of cyclical forces unrelated to the Fed's monetary policy. However, the full effects of the monetary expansion that was initiated nine months earlier are just being felt, so an expansionary monetary stimulus is adding to the existing inflationary gap.

If the Fed now applies the monetary brakes by contracting the money supply, the full effects of this move will not be felt for another 18 months. By that time a contraction may have already set in because of the natural cyclical forces of the economy. If this is so, the delayed effects of the monetary policy may turn a minor downturn into a major recession.

The long execution lag of monetary policy makes monetary fine tuning difficult; the policy may have a destabilizing effect.

If the execution lag were known with certainty, it could be built into the Fed's calculations, but the fact that the lag is highly variable makes this nearly impossible. Of course, when a persistent gap has existed and is predicted to continue for a long time, monetary policy may be stabilizing even when its effects occur after a long time lag.

A Monetary Rule?

Monetarists have persistently criticized the Fed for fine tuning, and the poor record of monetary policy as a short-run stabilizer has lent force to their criticisms. Monetarists argue that (1) monetary policy is a potent force of expansionary and contractionary pressures; (2) monetary policy works with lags that are both long and variable; and (3) the Fed is, in fact, given to sudden and sharp reversals of its policy stance. Consequently, (4) monetary policy has sometimes had a destabilizing effect on the economy, the policy itself accentuating rather than dampening the economy's natural cyclical swings.

Monetarists argue from this position that the stability of the economy would be much improved if the Fed stopped trying to stabilize it. What then should the Fed do? Because growth of population and of productivity leads to a rising level of output, the Fed ought to expand the money supply year in and year out at a constant rate that is equal to the rate of growth of real income. When the growth rate shows signs of long-term change, the Fed can adjust its rate of monetary expansion. It should not, however, alter this rate with a view to stabilizing the economy against short-term fluctuations.

Many other economists think that an appropriate monetary fine-tuning policy can, *in principle*, reduce cyclical fluctuations below what they would have been under a constant-rate rule. However:

The experience of the 1970s convinced many that whatever may be true of *the best conceivable monetary policy*, the Fed's *actual* policy made cyclical fluctuations larger than they would have been under a constant-rate rule.

Subsequent experience has shown, however, that the demand for money sometimes can shift quite substantially. A stable money supply rule in the face of demand instability guarantees monetary shocks, rather than monetary stability. This undermines confidence in the appropriateness of a monetary rule. The daunting challenge that faces central banks in this situation is to offset such shifts in the demand for money while not overreacting and thereby destabilizing the economy. It is also recognized that attempts to use monetary policy to *fine tune* the economy remain fraught with dangers.

Monetary Policy in Action

The Federal Open Market Committee generally meets every 4 weeks. Its decisions are embodied in a directive, issued to the Federal Reserve Bank of New York, in which open market operations are conducted by the manager of the system's Open Market Account. In order to put current debates about monetary policy in perspective, we now turn to a review of the issues surrounding the use of monetary policy over the past 40 years. We look first at the historic accord of 1951 that dramatically altered the framework in which the Fed conducts monetary policy, and we then review the interaction of policy actions and the performance of the economy.

The Treasury–Federal Reserve Accord

The use of monetary policy as a tool of stabilization policy in the post–World War II period began in 1951 with the Treasury–Federal Reserve accord.

During the war, the Fed had followed a practice of supporting the prices of treasury securities so as to hold down interest rates. This served to reduce the interest that had to be paid on the enormous amounts of government borrowing that was needed to finance the war effort. This practice meant that the Fed had to supply new money to buy that part of newly issued government debt that the public would not buy at the fixed rate of interest. Thus the interest rate was the Fed's main policy variable, and as a result the Fed had no control over the money supply—recall the discussion surrounding Figure 31-2.

The accord reestablished a potential for the Fed to control the money supply, and to establish policy goals in terms of macroeconomic performance.

The basic concern of monetary policy since the accord has been the achievement of full employment and price stability; this makes real national income and the price level the Fed's policy variables.

Monetary Policy Since the Accord

Figure 31-4 shows the behavior of M1 and of M2 from 1960 to 1991. Although the two measures differ sharply in behavior in any given year, two things stand out. First, by either measure monetary growth has shown sharp, short-term changes. Second, by either measure in the 1960s there was a steady upward trend in the rate of monetary expansion, which continued through the 1970s but was reversed in the first half of the 1980s. As we shall see in Chapter 33, the tight monetary policy of the early 1980s led to a sharp decline in inflation, but also contributed to a serious recession. The latter half of the 1980s is characterized by highly variable growth in both aggregates, but especially in M1, and by the tightening of monetary policy that many commentators feel contributed to the recession in the early 1990s. In 1991 growth in M2 accelerated, but that of M1 did not, creating a debate about whether monetary policy was contributing to the persistence of the recession or to the forces that would lead to recovery.

The Lessons for Monetary Policy

The experience over the last quarter century suggests a number of important lessons about the conduct of monetary policy.

FIGURE 31-4
Monetary Growth, 1960–1988

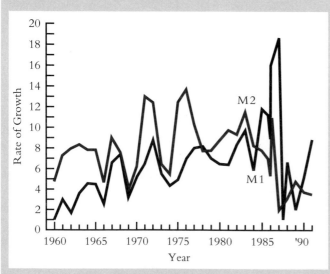

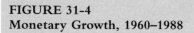

The rate of monetary expansion has shown substantial short-term variability combined with a strong long-term upward trend. The annual growth rate is shown for money narrowly defined, M1, and the broader monetary aggregate, M2. Although for any given year fluctuations in the two are not closely related, both exhibit the same general pattern.

The tight monetary policy at the start of the 1980s, the accommodation of the growth in the demand for money during the recovery in the middle of the decade, and the gradual tightening of monetary policy toward the end of the decade are all evident in both series. *(Source: Monetary Trends, Federal Reserve Bank of St. Louis, various issues.)*

The variability of monetary policy.   From the accord through the late 1960s, sharp variations in the rate of growth of the money supply occurred primarily as a result of the Fed's attempt to use monetary policy to fine tune the economy. Monetary policy typically oscillated from "full ahead" to "hard astern." The recessions of 1954–1955, 1957–1958, 1960–1961, and 1969–1970 caused the Fed to respond with expansionary monetary policies. Then, when inflation increased during the later recovery phases, monetary policy typically turned sharply contractionary. Given the lags in the effects of monetary policy, it appears that what the Fed thought was a stabilizing policy actually helped to destabilize the economy, accentuating the upswings and then contributing to the downswings of the business cycle.

Some economists attributed this destabilizing tendency of monetary policy to the Fed's use of interest rates as its intermediate target, as discussed earlier. However, in the mid-1970s the Fed had begun to focus on monetary aggregates as its intermediate target, but monetary policy nevertheless continued to be highly variable. In 1976–1977 the Fed pursued an expansionary monetary policy but then became worried about renewed inflation and turned to a severely contractionary policy in 1979.

Monetary policy appears often to have been inadvertently perverse throughout the period from 1950 to 1980. A series of alternating expansionary and contractionary policies augmented the economy's natural cyclical swings.

Several economists have spoken of "this incredible series of self-inflicted wounds." In a detailed study of the mid-1970s, Professor Alan Blinder of Princeton University says that monetary policy in the period "bears eloquent witness to the monetarists' incessant complaint that policy is too variable, too apt to swing from one extreme to another. It is true that whenever monetary policy departed notably from what a fixed rule would have called for, it did so in the wrong direction and made things worse than they need to have been."[7]

Inflation and monetary growth.   The relationship between monetary growth and inflation is not so tight as to be viewed as automatic or mechanical, nor does it appear to resolve the issue of causality; however, there is a close relationship exhibited.

For example, as shown in Figure 31-4, fluctuations in monetary expansion from 1960 to 1979 occurred around a rising trend, and over the same period inflation also rose steadily.

The rising trend in monetary growth over the period 1960–1979 accompanied a similar rising trend in prices, indicating an unmistakable connection between the rate of monetary growth and the rate of inflation.

Many economists, and certainly most monetarists, believe that monetary expansion was the main cause of inflation in the 1970s. Others believe that the monetary expansion was mainly a passive reaction to price increases caused by aggregate supply shocks in 1974 and 1979. Either way, there is no doubt that the inflation of the 1970s was accompanied by monetary expansion. Most economists also agreed that there was little chance of reducing inflation to the relatively modest levels of previous decades until the rate of monetary expansion was reduced to the more modest annual rates of those years.[8]

By 1979 inflation had reached double-digit levels, and in response to increasing concern over the acceleration of inflation, the Fed tightened monetary policy. The rate of growth of M1 fell sharply, and interest rates climbed to unprecedented levels. For example, the *prime rate*, which is closely related to the rate charged by banks to favored customers, topped 20 percent in December 1980 and stayed over that figure for most of 1981. Because the inflation rate was about 9 percent, this represented a real rate of over 11 percent. This served to depress aggregate demand sharply, leading to the most severe recession since the 1930s; this in turn caused inflation to come down dramatically.

A sharp reduction in monetary growth led to high interest rates, a severe recession, and a dramatic reduction in inflation in the early 1980s.

By 1983, the recession appeared to have ended and inflation had returned to the more "normal"

---

[7] Alan S. Blinder, *Economic Policy and the Great Stagflation* (New York: Academic Press, 1979), p. 201.

[8] These issues, and the analysis and evidence surrounding them, are discussed in detail in Chapter 33.

level of 3.2 percent. During the rest of the decade money growth fluctuated quite sharply, but there was no strong rising trend; over this period inflation fluctuated around a fairly narrow trend, rising towards the 5 percent range by the end of the decade. A combination of factors, including a tightening of monetary policy, led to a recession in 1990, and inflation fell to about 4 percent in 1991. Interest rates fell sharply in late 1991 and through the first half of 1992, but only a very weak recovery occurred. By mid-1992 there were strong pressures on the Fed to ease monetary policy further in order to sustain the recovery, but critics argued that the Fed had already eased too much and thereby sown the seed for increased inflation down the road.

Implementation problems. The episodes reviewed above confirm the role of money and monetary policy in the economy spelled out in this and the preceding chapters—with monetary policy influencing economic activity via the transmission mechanism, and the price level in turn responding to the output gap in a manner that led to inflation being quite closely correlated with monetary growth. However, the experience also highlights a number of problems that arise in implementing monetary policy.

For example, it seems that in 1979–1980 monetary policy was somewhat more contractionary than the Fed had intended. Part of the reason was the unprecedented variations in the rate of growth of demand for M1 balances. The Fed used past experience to estimate how fast this demand would grow as national income grew, and then it set its target for the growth in the supply of M1 at a level sufficient to meet this demand at a steadily rising level of income. However, there was an unexpected surge in the growth of demand for M1 that created a severe excess demand for money, even though the Fed met its money supply targets, resulting in rapid increases in interest rates and severe contractionary pressures on national income.[9] Although most observers agreed that it was desirable to stop inflation, many thought that monetary policy had been too contractionary and that the resulting recession was more severe than necessary.

Similar problems had arisen in earlier years. Indeed, several times during the 1970s institutional innovations caused major shifts between the demands for some of the assets that are included in the wider definitions of money but not in the narrow definition. For example, various types of money management techniques and the development of overnight markets for funds made it profitable for firms to transfer transactions balances that were unneeded, even for a matter of hours, out of demand deposits and into other highly liquid interest-earning assets. This led to major reductions in the demand for M1. In these circumstances, the growth of M1 balances became a poor indicator of the expansionary or contractionary force of current monetary policy; maintaining constant growth of M1 in the face of this declining demand would have been expansionary. Recall, as we saw in Chapter 30 (see Figure 30-6), that a fall in the demand for money can start the transmission mechanism working in an expansionary direction, just as can an increase in the supply of money.

Exclusive concentration on rigid targets for M1 can lead to changes in monetary policy that are contractionary when the demand for M1 increases and expansionary when the demand for M1 diminishes.

The reentry problem. A related problem for monetary policy arises when the quantity of money demanded changes as a result of changes in the level of income and interest rates rather than as a result of shifts in the liquidity preference function. For example, in late 1982 the economy began a long period of recovery that by mid-1986 had taken national income much of the way back toward its potential level. During the same period, interest rates fell, responding to falling inflation. As a result, the quantity of money demanded grew sharply, leading to what is often referred to as a *reentry problem* for monetary policy.

Some economists advocated that the Fed stick rigidly to long-range money growth targets even during the recovery period. Other economists argued that a policy of meeting rigid M1 targets would have put major contractionary pressure on the economy, because the observed growth in M1 was a response to an increase in demand for such balances and hence was not, in fact, expansionary. These economists called for an accommodating monetary

---

[9] As we saw earlier, this led the Fed to expand its set of intermediate targets to include M2.

policy that would allow M1 to expand to meet the new demand. This, they argued, would put neither contractionary nor expansionary pressure on the economy. In the event, the Fed accepted the counsel of these critics and allowed the money supply to expand to accommodate the increase in demand. In spite of dire predictions of an inflationary expansion from some advocates of a rigid monetary target, no inflationary increase in aggregate demand ensued.

Accommodating shocks. A recurring problem for monetary policy is how to respond to major unexpected shocks that buffet the economy and disrupt the relationship between the Fed's policy instruments and its policy variables. We have already encountered the issues that arose in the context of the major supply-side shocks associated with OPEC and rising commodity prices in 1974 and again in 1979. A second source of important shocks is the stock market. (The stock market is discussed in more detail in the appendix to this chapter, and one important historical episode is discussed in Box 31-2.)

On October 19, 1987, the stock market fell dramatically. A number of commentators argued that this, combined with rising interest rates, would serve to slow the expansion. However, throughout 1988 and early in 1989 growth remained strong, and inflationary pressures continued to build; the stock market crash had a smaller effect on the economy than many expected. In retrospect this was in large part because of the strong infusion of liquidity into the economy by the Fed immediately after the crash.

After the "blip" in response to the stock market crash, monetary policy continued to tighten gradually, but by mid-1989 the question remained whether, in terms of containing inflation, this was a case of "too little, too late." Could sustained growth, with steady moderate inflation, be maintained, or would inflation continue to grow, eventually evoking stronger monetary restraints that would risk throwing the economy into a policy-induced recession?

As we saw earlier in this chapter, it was the latter that occurred. A combination of factors, including tight monetary policy that was responding to fears about rising inflation, pushed the economy into recession in mid-1990. By mid-1992, despite sharp reductions in interest rates, only a modest recovery had occurred, and there were no signs of renewed inflation. With a weak economy and low inflation, there was increased pressure on the Fed (some of it from those worried about President Bush's reelection prospects) for the Fed to stimulate the economy by easing monetary policy.

Some Tentative Conclusions

The experience of the last two decades has led to the general acceptance of a number of views.

The role of intermediate targets. Although it is now widely acknowledged that a broad monetary aggregate such as M2 is the most useful as an intermediate target, the search for a single monetary aggregate to be *the* correct intermediate target has slowly been abandoned. The high degree of substitutability among M1, M2, and M3 means that all three magnitudes need to be surveyed for the information that they can give to the Fed. It has also come to be generally accepted that the behavior of interest rates conveys information that might not be available from monetary aggregates alone. For example, in the mid-1980s real interest rates were high by historical standards—this served to counter the view that monetary policy was loose based on the fact that growth in monetary aggregates was also high.

The exchange rate also became a more important variable for the Fed in the mid-1980s as the Fed became concerned with the effect of the exchange rate on the competitive position of the U.S. economy. The behavior of the exchange rate influences the health of American industries that either export or compete with imports and therefore has an important influence on domestic economic performance. (This issue is further discussed in Chapter 39.)

The role of policy variables. The Fed seems to have come more and more to take nominal national income as its policy target. Although the Fed cares about the twin goals of real national income and the price level, the understanding has spread that the Fed can, at best, influence the *AD* curve; how this influence divides itself between income and the price level depends on the shape of the *SRAS* curve, which is beyond the Fed's control. The Fed is still concerned with the long-term trend in the price level as its most important goal, but in the shorter term it seems to accept that it should adjust its policies in response to the behavior of nominal national income—a composite of changes in real income and the price level.

Other issues. Two other key issues have had an important impact on monetary policy in the past few years—the sustained high government deficits and the health of the financial system.

Government deficits. The Fed has been increasingly concerned about the implications of the large and persistent government budget deficit. As the bank for the government, the Fed has to monitor the effects of the continuing massive flow of new government securities onto financial markets. If and when the deficit starts to be reduced, there may be a need for the Fed to adopt a compensating monetary policy. The reduction in the deficit means some combination of tax increases and expenditure decreases on the part of the government. As we saw in Chapter 28, both of these changes reduce aggregate demand and tend to contract economic activity. To offset these forces, the Fed can engage in a once-and-for-all monetary expansion. As we saw in Chapter 30, this increases aggregate demand. There is no reason in theory why a change in the *mix* of macroeconomic policy to a more restrictive fiscal policy and a more expansionary monetary policy cannot leave the level of aggregate demand unchanged. This would mean that the policy changes would not significantly affect either national income or the price level, although, as discussed in Chapter 34 (see pages 731–732), the change in mix could have important implications for economic growth.

The financial system. During the 1970s a number of third-world countries piled up enormous debt that became unsustainable during the 1980s.

(See the further discussion in Chapter 40.) Much of this debt was owed to banks in the developed countries, with the United States being the most important single creditor country. The Fed realized that a sudden default of these debtor countries could cause a crisis in the banking system. This meant that the Fed, along with key international organizations such as the IMF, had to concern itself with the efforts of the banks to delay the final day of reckoning by rescheduling some of the loans and by lending some of the money needed to repay the remaining interest until the major banks could adjust their portfolios sufficiently to write off some of their loans without going into insolvency. The Fed also had to conduct monetary policy with one eye on the state of the banking system. For example, it was aware that every time the interest rate rose 1 percent, the burden on these debtor countries was measured in billions of dollars of extra payments, and hence the risk of default increased.

Although the international debt crisis has currently subsided, the banking system remains quite fragile. Capital bases of many financial institutions were eroded by the losses suffered on loans to third-world countries, and more recently the widespread failures of savings and loan associations and the loan defaults and write-downs suffered in the face of the fall in real estate prices in many parts of the United States (see Box 29-5) have served to make it necessary for the Fed to continue to conduct monetary policy with one eye on the implications for the health of the financial system.

SUMMARY

1. The Fed can affect the reserves of the banking system in many ways. Its major instrument is open market operations. It can also, among other things, change required reserves, change the rate of interest at which it will lend to banks, and apply moral suasion.
2. The major policy instrument that is used by the Fed is open market operations. The purchase of bonds on the open market increases reserves, permitting (but not forcing) a multiple expansion of bank deposits and hence of the money supply. The sale of bonds on the open market reduces bank reserves, forcing a multiple contraction of bank deposits on the part of all banks that do not have excess reserves.
3. The ultimate objectives of the Fed's monetary policy are called its *policy variables.* In principle, these include real national income and the rate of change of the price level. However, in practice

nominal national income is often taken to be the policy variable in the short term, because the Fed cannot expect to be able to influence the composition of changes in nominal income between real growth and inflation.

4. Because the Fed cannot influence its policy variables directly, it must work through policy instruments that it can control and that will, in turn, influence its policy variables. Intermediate targets are used to guide decisions about how to change policy instruments. Both the money supply and the interest rate are often used as intermediate targets, although the liquidity preference function means that they cannot be used independently.

5. National income can be influenced by open market operations. Because it cannot control both independently, the Fed must choose between the interest rate and the money supply as the intermediate target of such operations. When the Fed pursues a contractionary policy, it sells bonds on the open market, thereby reducing bank reserves and the money supply while driving up the rate of interest. When the Fed pursues an expansionary policy, it buys bonds on the open market, thereby increasing bank reserves and the money supply while driving down the rate of interest.

6. The modern use of monetary policy in the United States dates from the 1951 accord between the Treasury and the Fed, by which the Fed's main policy objective ceased to be minimizing the cost of financing the government's debt by controlling interest rates. During the 1950s and 1960s, the rate of interest was the main intermediate target through which the Fed sought to influence national income. During the 1970s the emphasis shifted to influencing national income by targeting the money supply.

7. Exclusive concentration on rigid targets for M1 risks misassessing the effects of active monetary policy as the public merely shifts funds between M1 and M2 or M3. It also risks leading the Fed inadvertently into an expansionary or contractionary policy when the demand for money function shifts.

8. The Fed has been criticized for alternating too quickly between an expansionary and a contractionary policy, thereby contributing to cyclical swings in the economy. During the 1960s and 1970s a series of strong and abrupt changes in monetary policy exerted a destabilizing force on the economy.

9. During the early 1980s the Fed pursued a target of reducing the inflation rate. Monetary tightness caused high interest rates, leading to a severe recession and eventually to a sharp fall in inflation. During the sustained recovery from that recession, the demand for M1 increased in response to the fall in the inflation rate and the growth in national income; this increase in demand was by and large accommodated by the Fed.

10. It is generally agreed that rapid changes in the money supply and interest rates can have large effects on the economy. There is disagreement, however, on how much monetary policy can and should be used as a device for stabilizing national income at its potential level or coping with temporary bouts of rising prices.

TOPICS FOR REVIEW

Open market operations and the money supply

The discount rate

Policy variables, policy instruments, and intermediate targets

Nominal income as a policy variable

Interest rates and monetary aggregates as intermediate targets

Lags in the effect of monetary policy

Variability of monetary policy and monetary rules

Rising inflation

Shifts in the demand for money

The mix of monetary and fiscal policies

DISCUSSION QUESTIONS

1. In the study of banking history, we often see the term *elastic currency*. For example, to provide an elastic currency was a purpose behind the creation of the Federal Reserve System. What do you think this term might mean, and why might it be emphasized?

2. In mid–1989 many observers forecast that the economy was moving into recession. At the same time, the cumulative effect of several years of high growth was causing inflationary forces to grow. This combination was perceived as posing a dilemma for the Fed, and a common question found in the financial press was whether the Fed could "engineer a soft landing." Discuss the dilemma posed for the Fed, and, using the benefit of hindsight (that is, the evidence on what the Fed did and how the economy responded), evaluate the Fed's performance.

3. Compare the reaction of the Fed to the stock market crash of 1929 with that of October 19, 1987.

4. During the recovery of the American economy from 1983 to 1985, two different views were often expressed. Some said that the adherence to a long-run constant-rate rule for monetary growth was particularly important lest inflationary expectations be rekindled by an overly fast rate of monetary expansion. Others said that encouraging the recovery required a temporary burst of monetary expansion. Discuss these two views.

5. The Federal Reserve Board runs a facility in Culpeper, Virginia, that costs $1.8 million per year to maintain and to guard against robbery, according to former Senator William Proxmire of Wisconsin. Inside this "Culpeper switch," a dugout in the side of a mountain, the government has hidden $4 billion in new currency for the purpose, it says, of "providing a hedge against any nuclear attack that would wipe out the nation's money supply." Comment on the sense of this policy.

6. Describe the chief weapons of monetary policy that are available to the Federal Reserve Board and indicate whether and, if so, how they might be used for the following purposes:
   a. To create a mild tightening of bank credit
   b. To signal that the Fed favors a sharp curtailment of bank lending

  c. To permit an expansion of bank credit with existing reserves

  d. To supply banks and the public with a temporary increase of currency for Christmas shopping

7. It is often said that an expansionary monetary policy is like "pushing on a string." What is meant by such a statement? How does this contrast with a contractionary monetary policy?

8. In what situations might the following pairs of objectives come into conflict?

  a. Lowering the cost of government debt and using monetary policy to change aggregate demand

  b. Ending a deep recession and maintaining a currently achieved target for monetary growth

  c. Maintaining stable interest rates and controlling inflation

  d. Stimulating the economy and supporting the value of the dollar on foreign-exchange markets

9. Writing in 1979, Nobel Laureate Milton Friedman accused the Fed of following "an unstable monetary policy," arguing that although the Fed "has given lip service to controlling the quantity of money...it has given its heart to controlling interest rates." Why might the desire to stabilize interest rates create an "unstable" monetary policy?

APPENDIX TO CHAPTER

31

Securities Markets (Stock Markets)

Stock market values sometimes display cumulative upward movements or cumulative downward movements. The first are called *bull markets,* and the second are called *bear markets.* Most people also know that the Great Depression of the 1930s was preceded by the stock market crash of 1929, which caused what is still the largest percentage loss of stock values ever to be suffered by U.S. investors.

There is clearly some association between fluctuations in the stock market and those in the economy, but is there a causal connection? Do stock market booms help to cause business cycle booms, and do stock market slumps help to cause business cycle slumps? Before we can answer these questions, we need to learn a bit about such markets.

The Function of Securities Markets

When a household buys shares that have been newly issued by a company, it becomes one of the firm's owners. If, at some future date, the household wishes to cease being a shareholder in the firm, the firm will generally *not* repurchase the shares, except in the rare event that the firm is liquidated. If the household wishes to get its money back, it can do so only by persuading someone else to buy its shares in the company.

When a household buys a bond from a company, it becomes one of the firm's creditors. It cannot get its money back from the company before a specified date. For example, if you bought a 2010 bond in 1990, the bond would be redeemed by the company (i.e., the loan would be paid back) only in 2010. If you wished to get your money back sooner, all you could do would be to sell the bond to someone who was willing to become one of the company's creditors.

An organized market in which stocks and bonds are bought and sold is called a *securities market.* Securities markets that deal in shares, or equities, are known as **stock markets**. Two of the best-known stock markets are the New York Stock Exchange and the American Stock Exchange. The trading of *existing* shares on the stock market indicates that ownership is being transferred; it does not indicate that companies are raising new money from the public, although firms also do raise funds by issuing new shares.

Securities markets are important because they allow people to put their savings into stocks and bonds that are not directly or quickly redeemable by their issuer.

For example, if I want to invest in a particular stock that I think will earn an attractive yield, I may do so, even though I know that I will want my money back after only a year. I can be confident that I will be able to sell the security a year from now. Nevertheless, although securities markets provide for the quick sale of stocks and bonds, they do not guarantee the price at which stocks and bonds can be sold. The price at any time is the one that equates the demand and supply for a particular security, and rapid fluctuations in stock prices are common.

Prices on the Stock Market

Figure 31A-1 shows the wide swings in a well-known index of stock market prices, the Dow-Jones industrial average. The most recent swing in the period covered in the figure began from a trough in May 1984, when the Dow was about 1,100. The index then rose steadily until September to 1,738. It then climbed fairly steadily, and by early 1989 it had almost reattained its August 1987 peak.[1] It continued to rise steadily through September 1990, when it again fell, although this time by much less than in 1987. From then until early 1992, the Dow rose steadily, reaching over 4,000; once again, many commentators were predicting that the Dow was overvalued and were anticipating a downward correction.

From September 1986 to mid-1992, the Dow went through a series of sharp swings, first rising by almost 40 percent in 12 months, then falling by almost 40 percent in the next 2 months, and then rising again by over 50 percent in the next 16 months.

Causes of Stock Market Swings

What causes such rapid gains and losses, and what do they have to do with business cycles?

When investors buy a company's stocks, they are buying rights to share in the stream of dividends to be paid out by that company. They are also buying an asset that they can sell in the future for a gain or a loss.

The value of that stock thus depends on two factors: first, what people expect the stream of future dividend payments to be, and, second, what price people expect to receive when the stocks are sold. (If the price rises, the owner earns a *capital gain*; if the price falls, the owner suffers a *capital loss*.) Both influences make dealing in stocks an inherently risky operation. Will the company in which people are

---

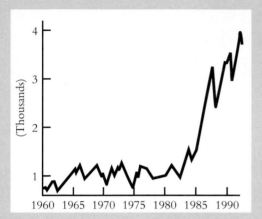

FIGURE 31A-1
Fluctuations in the Dow-Jones Index of Stock Prices, 1960–1991

Stock market fluctuations are very sharp and irregular, and the decade has witnessed a sharp net increase. The figure shows quarterly variations in the Dow-Jones industrial average of 30 industrial stocks. The index grew steadily from 1962 to 1966 and then displayed very little trend over the next 15 years. Over that period the index did, however, fluctuate sharply; it is these fluctuations that make large speculative gains and losses possible. Three notable falls in the index occurred during the economic downturns in 1969, 1974, and 1981. Although the index was at approximately the same level in 1980 as it was in 1965, the Consumer Price Index had risen by a factor of about 2.6, causing many commentators to believe that the market was "undervalued."

The market fell during the 1981 recession, but the economic recovery that started in 1982 was accompanied by a dramatic sustained increase in the Dow-Jones. From mid-1986 through mid-1992, the index roughly doubled, although that period also witnessed three significant downturns—a relatively minor one in September 1986, a dramatic one in October 1987, and one in September 1990.

1986, when it reached a value of 1,919, a rise of 75 percent in just 28 months. After a significant fall of about 8 percent in September 1986, it then rose spectacularly, reaching 2,722 in August 1987. It then started to fall, gradually at first, and then on October 19, 1987—Black Monday—it fell by over 20 percent

---

[1] Commentators are often careless about making the key distinction between the *number of points* by which the index changes over some period and the *percentage* change in that index over the same period. For example, the fall of 984 points from August to October 1987 is the largest fall ever in terms of points. This represented a fall of 36 percent from the August peak of 2,722 points. Although this number is significant, it remains dwarfed by the loss that everyone hopes never will be repeated: Over 80 percent of the value of stocks was lost over the 4-year period from 1929 to 1933!

Box 31A-1

Speculative Booms

In addition to responding to a host of factors that reasonably can be expected to influence the earnings of companies, stock prices often develop an upward or downward movement of their own, propelled by little more than speculation that feeds on itself.

In major stock market booms, people begin to expect rising stock prices and hurry to buy while stocks are cheap. This action bids up the prices of shares and creates the capital gains that justify the original expectations. Such a situation is an example of *self-realizing expectations*. Investors get rich on paper, in the sense that the market value of their holdings rises. Money making now looks easy to others, who also rush in to buy stocks, and new purchases push up prices still further. At this stage attention to current earnings all but ceases. If a stock can yield, say, a 50 percent capital gain in one year, it does not matter much if the current earnings represent only a small percentage yield on the purchase price of the stocks. Everyone is "making money," so more people become attracted to the get-rich-quick opportunities. Their attempts to buy pushed prices up still further. In such speculative booms, current earnings represent an ever-diminishing percentage yield on the current price of the stocks.

Capital gains can be so attractive that investors may buy stocks on margin, that is, borrow money to buy them, using the stocks themselves as security for the loans. In doing this, many investors may be borrowing money at a rate of interest that is considerably in excess of the yield from current dividends. Even if $50,000 is borrowed at 10 percent (interest payments are $5,000 per year) to buy stocks and yields a current dividend return of only 4 percent (dividend receipts are $2,000 per year), the investor's logic

says "never mind," for the stocks can be sold in a year or so for a handsome capital gain that will more than repay the $3,000 of interest not covered by dividends. Some people have the luck or good judgment to sell out near the top of the market, and they actually make money. Others wait eagerly for ever greater capital gains, and in the meantime they get richer and richer—on paper.

Eventually, something breaks the period of unrestrained optimism. Some investors may begin to worry about the very high prices of stocks in relation not only to current yields but also to possible future yields, even when generous allowances for growth are made. Or it may be that the prices of stocks become depressed slightly when a sufficiently large number of persons try to sell out in order to realize their capital gains. As they offer their securities on the market, they cannot find purchasers without some fall in prices. Even a modest price fall may be sufficient to persuade others that it is time to sell. However, every share that is sold must be bought by someone. A wave of sellers may not find new buyers at existing prices, causing prices to fall. Panic selling may now occur.

A household that borrowed $50,000 to buy stocks near the top of the market may find the paper value of its holdings sliding below $50,000. How will it repay its loan? Even if it does not worry about the loan, its broker will. The household may sell now before it loses too much, or its broker may "sell the customer out" to liquidate the loan. All this causes prices to fall even further and provides another example of self-realizing expectations. If enough people think that prices are going to come down, their attempt to sell out at the present high

investing pay high dividends in future years? Will the company's value rise so that these people can sell their shares for more than what they bought them for? Although dividend policies of most established companies tend to be fairly stable, stock prices are subject to wide swings.

The Influence of Present and Future Business Conditions

Many influences affect stock market prices; these include the state of the business cycle and the stance prices will create the fall in prices, the expectations of which caused the selling.

This is a very simple and stylized description of a speculative cycle, yet it describes the basic elements of market booms and busts that many believe have recurred throughout stock market history. It happened in the Jay Cooke panic of 1873 and in the Grover Cleveland panic of 1893. The biggest boom of all began in the mid-1920s and ended on Black Tuesday, October 29, 1929. The collapse was dramatic, with stocks losing about one-half of their value in about two months. Nor did it stop there. For 4 years stock prices continued to decline, until the average value of stock sold on the New York Stock Exchange had fallen from its 1929 high of $89.10 per share to $17.35 per share by late 1933. It also happened, although less dramatically, in the booms and busts of the 1970s and 1980s, discussed earlier in this section.

Speculative behavior means that stock market prices do not always just reflect the fundamentals that underlie the expected profitability of companies; in this sense, the stock market is sometimes said to be over- or undervalued. However, the extent of the over- or undervaluation is difficult to determine, and hence it is hard to predict when, and by how much, prices will "correct." For example, consider the long upswing that more than doubled stock prices in just over three years between early 1984 and October 1987. At the time the United States enjoyed a very strong recovery, and the rising stock prices no doubt reflected the resulting favorable profit outlook of companies. However, many doubted that the full increase was justified by underlying business opportunities and hence felt that

there may have been a speculative component to the rise in stock values. These people argued that the dramatic fall that occurred on Black Monday represented a "correction" that removed much of the speculative component from the prices. Of course, this is easy to say after the fact. If any of us had known in advance when and by how much prices would correct, we would have been able to make a huge profit.

Stock Markets: Investment Marketplaces or Gambling Casinos?

Stock markets fulfill many important functions. It is doubtful that the great aggregations of capital that are needed to finance modern firms could be raised under a private-ownership system without them. There is no doubt, however, that they also provide an unfortunate attraction for many naive investors, whose get-rich-quick dreams are more often than not destroyed by the fall in prices that follows the occasional speculative booms that they help to create.

To some extent public policy has sought to curb the excesses of stock market speculation through supervision of security issues. Public policy seeks, among other things, to prevent both fraudulent or misleading information and trading by "insiders" (those in a company who have confidential information). Moreover, the regulators can limit the ability of speculators to trade on margin.

All in all, the stock market is both a real marketplace and a place to gamble. As in all gambling situations, players who are less well informed and less clever than the average player tend to be losers in the long term.

of government policies. Box 31A-1 examines the interesting possibility of self-reinforcing speculative booms.

Cyclical forces. If investors expect a firm's earnings to increase, the firm will become more valuable

and the price of its stock will rise. Such influences cause stock prices to move with the business cycle, being high when current profits are high and low when current profits are low. These influences also cause stock prices to vary with a host of factors that influence expectations of future profits. A poor crop, destruction of trees by acid rain, an announcement of new defense spending, a change in the foreign-exchange value of the dollar, and a change in the political complexion of the administration can all affect profit expectations and hence stock prices.

Policy factors.   We shall see later in this book that changes in monetary policy can cause changes in interest rates. Such changes, or just the expectation of them, will have effects on stock prices. Say, for example, that interest rates rise rapidly. Investors will see that they can now earn an increased amount by holding government bonds. As a result, they will wish to alter their investment portfolios to hold more bonds and fewer stocks. Everyone cannot do this, however, because only so many stocks and bonds are available to be held at any given time. As all investors try to sell their stocks, prices fall. The fall will stop only when the expected rate of return to investment in stocks, based on their lower purchase price, makes stocks as attractive as bonds. Then investors will no longer try to shift out of stocks *en masse*.

Stock Market Swings: Cause or Effect of Business Cycles?

Stock markets tend often to lead, and sometimes to follow, booms and slumps in business activity. In both cases the causes usually run from real business conditions, whether actual or anticipated, to stock market prices. This is the dominant theme: the stock market as a reflector.

Stock market fluctuations are more typically a consequence than a cause of the business cycle.

It is also possible for the stock market to be a causal factor in the business cycle. The value of the stock market influences the wealth of households, which ultimately own the market, either directly or through their pension funds. Thus, stock prices can be expected to influence their consumption spending. (Recall the wealth effect from Chapter 25; see Figure 25-2.) Firms also use the stock market to issue new shares in order to finance investment spending; when stock market prices are low, they find this an unattractive way to raise new money and thus may choose to cancel, or at least postpone, investments. As a result, many people believed that the dramatic fall in stock values in the October 1987 crash would cause households to curtail their consumption spending in response to their perceived fall in wealth. On this basis many forecasters predicted that the stock market fall of Black Monday would lead to a serious downturn in the economy. After the event, such gloom-and-doom forecasts turned out to be inaccurate; apparently, people did not perceive the fall in the stock market as an indication that their permanent incomes or wealth had fallen dramatically, and hence they did not reduce their consumption spending.

In many cases the stock market and the business cycle both reflect the common influence of other factors. For example, stock markets often react to changes in interest rates that may be caused by government policy; as we have seen, such interest rate changes can also play a causal role in cyclical fluctuations in the economy. Typically, the stock market responds more quickly than does the economy to such influences, and for this reason many observers look to it as a "leading indicator" of likely future economic developments.

The relationship between the stock market and the economy is further complicated by the existence of occasional speculative booms and busts. There are often real economic forces influencing expectations of stock prices, but, at least for a while, the prices may become dominated by speculative psychology. (This is discussed in Box 31A-1.) Unfortunately, speculative behavior causes the stock market to react to many events that turn out to have little or no enduring implications for the economy. As one wag put it, the stock market has predicted seven out of the last two recessions!

MACROECONOMIC PROBLEMS AND POLICIES

32

Inflation

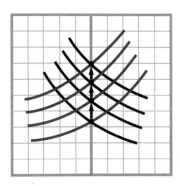

I f you look again at Figure 23-1 on page 461 you will see that inflation remained low for 20 years following World War II. The only exceptions were the "bubbles" immediately following World War II and during the Korean War. Starting in the late 1960s, the inflation rate slowly rose, reaching the double-digit range by the mid-1970s. It fell only slightly during the late 1970s, in spite of a concerted antiinflationary policy, and rose again to the double-digit level in 1979 and 1980. It remained quite high during the recession of 1981, fell dramatically to 4 percent in 1982, and remained near that figure through 1987. Inflation slowly crept up again in 1989 and rose to an average of over 6 percent in 1990. Then it fell sharply to around 3 percent in 1991 under the impact of the prolonged recession that began in 1990 and the slow recovery that extended beyond 1992.

In Chapter 23 we examined the costs of inflation. We now need to ask further questions about inflation. What are its causes? What are the costs of reducing it? Can inflation be prevented from rising into the double-digit range again? Can inflation ever be eliminated altogether?

Causes and Consequences of Inflation

An inflationary shock is anything that tends to increase the price level; a deflationary shock is anything that tends to decrease it. We start by making three important distinctions concerning these shocks.

1. Inflations or deflations that are caused by shifts in aggregate demand—which are referred to as demand shocks—must be distinguished from inflations or deflations that are caused by shifts in aggregate supply—which are referred to as supply shocks.
2. Isolated, once-and-for-all shocks must be distinguished from repeated shocks. The former cause temporary bouts of inflation as the price level moves from one equilibrium level to another. The latter cause continuous, or sustained, inflations.
3. Increases in the price level that occur even though the money supply is constant must be distinguished from those that take place when the money supply is increasing. When an increase in the money supply accompanies inflationary shocks, the resulting inflation is said to be *validated* by the monetary expansion.

In this book we use the term *inflation* as it is commonly used in ordinary speech to mean any rise in the price level. We then make the distinction between once-and-for-all and continuing rises in the price level (discussed in point 2 above) by referring to temporary or once-and-for-all inflation on the one hand and to continuing or sustained inflation on the other.[1]

We first studied inflationary shocks in Part 7. At that time it was enough to say that an inflationary gap implies excess demand for labor, low unemployment, upward pressure on wages, and hence an upward-shifting *SRAS* curve. Understanding the forces that cause wage rates to change, and knowing when these changes do and do not cause the *SRAS* curve to shift, are keys to understanding inflation.

Why Wages Change

We saw in Chapter 28 that increases in wage rates do not necessarily cause unit costs to rise because these costs depend on the relationship between the price of labor and labor productivity (i.e., output per unit of labor input). For example, if wage rates and productivity both rise by 3 percent, each unit of labor costs 3 percent more but also produces 3 percent more. As a result, labor costs per unit of output remain unchanged. What matters then is the relation between changes in money wages and changes in productivity. We use the words "changes in money wages *relative to productivity*" to refer to *the percentage change in money wages minus the percentage change in productivity*; the result measures the change in unit costs of production.

Two main forces that can cause unit wage costs to change systematically are demand for labor and expectations.[2] Much of what we say in the case of demand is a recapitulation of material first presented in Chapter 28, but the points are important enough to bear repeating.

---

[1] Some economists reserve the term *inflation* for sustained changes in the price level, using other words, such as a rise in the price level, to refer to once-and-for-all changes. As long as one understands the distinction, the choice of words is not a substantial matter.

[2] Changes in wages relative to productivity may be affected by other forces that are associated with neither excess demand nor expectations of inflation—such as government guidelines, union power, and employers' optimism. These forces can be positive, pushing wages higher than they otherwise would go, or negative, pushing wages lower than they otherwise would go. Since there are many such forces that tend to act independently of one another, they may be regarded as *random shocks*. Although they may occasionally have significant effects in any one year, over a longer period of time positive shocks in some years will tend to be offset by negative shocks in other years so that, in total, they contribute little to the long-term trend of the price level. For this reason, they can be ignored in an introductory study.

Labor Demand

In Chapter 28 we stated three propositions about how changes in money wages relative to productivity were influenced by the relation between aggregate demand and aggregate supply:

1. The excess demand for labor that is associated with an inflationary gap puts upward pressure on money wages relative to productivity. Money wages rise more rapidly than productivity is rising.
2. The excess supply of labor associated with a recessionary gap puts downward pressure on money wages relative to productivity. Money wages rise more slowly than productivity is rising, and they may even fall.
3. The absence of either an inflationary or a recessionary gap means that demand forces do not exert any pressure on money wages either to rise or to fall relative to productivity.

The NAIRU. We saw in Chapter 23 that when current national income is at its potential level ($Y = Y^*$), unemployment is not zero. Instead, there may be a substantial amount of frictional and structural unemployment caused, for example, by the movement of people between jobs. Recall that the rate of unemployment that exists when national income is at its potential level is called the *NAIRU* (and is designated by the symbol U^*).[3] It follows from this definition that when current national income exceeds full-employment income ($Y > Y^*$), current unemployment will be less than the NAIRU ($U < U^*$). When current national income is less than full-employment income ($Y < Y^*$), current unemployment will exceed the NAIRU ($U > U^*$).[4]

We have seen that wages and unit costs react to various pressures of demand. These demand pressures can now be stated either in terms of the relation between actual and potential income or the relation between actual unemployment and the NAIRU. This is done in Table 32-1.

---

[3] As we have noted earlier, these initials stand for *nonaccelerating inflationary rate of unemployment*. The reason for using this mouthful to describe the amount of unemployment associated with Y^* will be explained later in the chapter.

[4] The NAIRU is sometimes called the *natural rate of unemployment*, but NAIRU is now the more common usage.

TABLE 32-1   The Characteristics of Various Output Gaps

Recessionary gaps	Potential income	Inflationary gaps
$Y < Y^*$	$Y = Y^*$	$Y > Y^*$
$U > \text{NAIRU } (U^*)$	$U = \text{NAIRU } (U^*)$	$U < \text{NAIRU } (U^*)$
$\dot{W} < \dot{g}$	$\dot{W} = \dot{g}$	$\dot{W} > \dot{g}$
$\dot{c} < 0$	$\dot{c} = 0$	$\dot{c} > 0$

Unit costs fall during recessionary gaps and rise during inflationary gaps. During a recessionary gap, income is less than potential, the unemployment rate exceeds the NAIRU (U^*), money wages rise at a lower rate (indicated by $\dot{W}$) than does productivity (indicated by $\dot{g}$), and the change in unit costs (which we indicate by $\dot{c}$) is negative—i.e., unit costs fall. During an inflationary gap, income exceeds potential, the unemployment rate is less than the NAIRU, money wages rise at a faster rate than productivity, and unit costs rise. When income is at its potential level, unemployment is at the NAIRU, money wages change at the same rate as productivity, and unit costs remain constant.

The effect of the demand for labor on wages can be shown by what is called a *Phillips curve*, which is discussed in Box 32-1.

Expectational Forces

A second force that can influence wages is *expectations*. Suppose, for example, that both employers and employees expect a 4 percent inflation next year. Workers will start negotiations from a base of a 4 percent increase in money wages, which would hold their *real wages* constant. Firms also may be inclined to begin bargaining by conceding at least a 4 percent increase in money wages relative to productivity, because they expect that the prices at which they sell their products will rise by 4 percent. *Starting from that base*, workers will attempt to obtain some desired increase in their real wages. At this point such factors as profits and bargaining power become important.

The general expectation of some specific inflation rate creates pressure for wages to rise by that rate relative to productivity and, hence, for unit costs to rise at that rate.

The key point is that money wages can be rising relative to productivity even if no inflationary gap is present. As long as people expect prices to rise, their behavior will put upward pressure on money wages, causing unit costs to rise, thus shifting the *SRAS* curve upward.

The formation of expectations. The foregoing discussion suggests that the manner in which people form their expectations about the future course of inflation may have an important effect on that inflation. Generally, we can distinguish two main patterns: One is to look backward to past experience; the other is to look at current circumstances for a clue as to what may happen in the near future.

The first type of expectations can be called *backward-looking*. People look to the past to predict what will happen in the future. The simplest possible form of such expectations is to expect the past to be repeated in the future. According to this view, if inflation has been 10 percent over the last two years, people will expect it to be 10 percent next year. This expectation, however, is excessively naive. Everyone knows that the inflation rate does change, and therefore the past cannot be a perfectly accurate guide to the future.

A less naive version would have people revise their expectations in light of the mistakes that they made in estimating inflation in the past. For example, if you thought that this year's inflation rate was going to be 10 percent but it turned out to be only 6 percent, you might revise your estimate of next year's rate down somewhat from 10 percent. Perhaps you might not go all the way to 6 percent; you might split the difference and estimate next year's rate to be 8 percent.

These are just simple illustrations of the many ways in which people can base their predictions of the future on the immediate past.

Backward-looking expectations tend to change slowly because some time must pass before a change in the actual rate of inflation provides enough past experience to cause expectations to adjust.

The second main type of expectations are those that look to current conditions to estimate what is likely to happen in the future. One version of this type assumes that people look to the government's current macroeconomic policy to form their expectations of future inflation. They are assumed to understand how the economy works, and they form their expectations by predicting the outcome of the policies now being followed. In an obvious sense, such expectations are *forward-looking*.

A strong version of forward-looking expectations is called **rational expectations**. Rational expectations are not necessarily always correct; instead, *the rational expectations hypothesis assumes that people make the best possible use of all the available information, which implies that they will not continue to make persistent, systematic errors in forming their expectations.* Thus, if the economic system about which they are forming expectations remains stable, their expectations will be correct *on average*. Sometimes next year's inflation rate will turn out to be above what people expected it to be; at other times it will turn out to be below what people expected it to be. On average over many years, however, the actual rate will not, according to the rational expectations theory, be consistently under- or overestimated.

Rational expectations have the effect of speeding up the adjustment of expectations. Instead of being based on past inflation rates, expected inflation is based on the anticipation of the outcome of existing and expected economic conditions and government policies.

Assuming that expectations are solely backward-looking seems overly naive. People do look ahead and assess future possibilities rather than just blindly reacting to what has gone before. Yet the assumption of "rational" forward-looking expectations that predict the expected inflation rate correctly, or nearly correctly, much of the time requires that workers and firms have a degree of understanding about the effects of government policy on inflation that few economists would claim to have.

Of course, people will not make the same error of consistently underpredicting (or overpredicting) the inflation rate for decades, but evidence suggests that they can do so for substantial periods, especially when they do not fully understand the causes of current inflation. Every past period of inflation has led to intense debate among economists about its causes, cures, and probable future course. If professionals are uncertain, it would be surprising if wage and price setters made correct predictions on average over any short period of time.

Many observers suspect that the process of wage setting combines rational, forward-looking behavior with expectations based on the experience of the recent past. Depending on the circumstances, expectations will sometimes tend to rely more on past experience and at other times more on present events whose effects are expected to influence the future.

Overall Effect

The overall change in wage costs is a result of the two basic forces that we have just studied:

Percentage increase in money wages =
Demand effect + Expectational effect

It is important to realize that what happens to wage costs is the net effect of both of these forces. Consider two examples.

First, suppose that, with productivity unchanged, both labor and management expect 3 percent inflation next year and are willing on this account to allow money wages to increase by 3 percent. Doing so would leave the relationship between wages and other prices unaltered. Suppose as well that at the current level of national income there is a significant inflationary gap with an associated labor shortage. The demand pressure causes wages to rise by an additional 2 percentage points. The final outcome is that wages rise by 5 percent, the net effect of a 3 percent increase due to expectations and a 2 percent increase due to demand forces.

For the second example, assume again that, with productivity constant, expected inflation is 3 percent but that this time there is a recessionary gap at the current level of national income. The associated heavy unemployment exerts downward pressure on wage bargains. Hence the demand effect now works to moderate wage increases, say, to the extent of 2 percentage points. Wages rise by 1 percent, the net effect of a 3 percent increase due to expectations and a 2 percent decrease due to demand forces.

Box 32-1

The Phillips Curve and the Shifting SRAS Curve

In the early 1950s Professor A. W. Phillips of the London School of Economics was conducting path-breaking research on macroeconomic policy. In his early models he related the rate of inflation to the difference between actual and potential income, Y^*. Later he investigated the empirical underpinnings of this equation by studying the relationship between the rate of increase of wage costs and the level of unemployment. He studied these variables because unemployment data were available as far back as the mid-nineteenth century, whereas very little data on output gaps were available when he did his empirical work. In 1958 he reported that a stable relationship had existed between these two variables for 100 years in the United Kingdom. This relationship came to be known as the Phillips curve. The **Phillips curve**

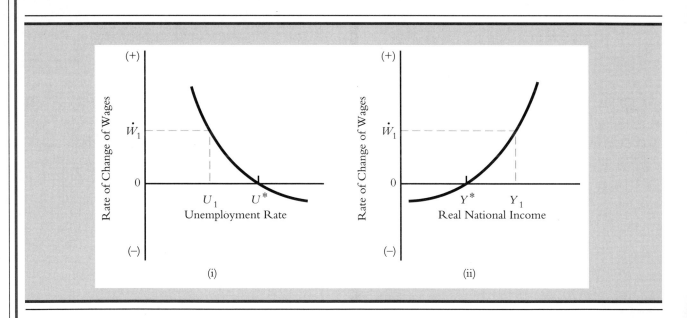

From Wages to the SRAS Curve

We have already established in Chapter 28 that shifts in the SRAS curve depend on what happens to unit costs. (Recall that for movements along a given SRAS curve, wage rates and other input prices are constant.)

We have just seen that inflationary gaps and expectations of inflation put pressure on wage rates to rise relative to productivity and, hence, on the SRAS curve to shift upward. Recessionary gaps and expectations of deflation put pressure on wage rates to fall relative to productivity and, hence, on the SRAS curve to shift downward. What happens to the SRAS curve in any one year is the net effect of these two forces.

provided an explanation, rooted in empirical data, of the speed with which wage changes shifted the *SRAS* curve by changing unit labor costs.

The Phillips curve can be translated into one that relates wage changes to output gaps by noting that unemployment and the gaps are negatively related. A recessionary gap is associated with high unemployment, and an inflationary gap is associated with low unemployment. Thus the Phillips curve can also be drawn with national income on the horizontal axis, as in the accompanying figures.

Both figures show the same information. Inflationary gaps (which correspond to low unemployment rates) are associated with *increases* in wages relative to productivity, whereas recessionary gaps (which correspond to high unemployment rates) are associated with *decreases* in wages relative to productivity. (For simplicity, we assume zero productivity growth in this box.)

The Phillips curve must be clearly distinguished from the *SRAS* curve. The *SRAS* curve has the *price level* on the vertical axis, whereas the Phillips curve has the *rate of wage inflation* on the vertical axis. Therefore, the Phillips curve tells us how fast the *SRAS* curve is shifting when actual income does not equal potential income.

Only when $Y = Y^*$ is the *SRAS* curve not shifting because of demand pressures. Aggregate demand

for labor then equals aggregate supply; the only unemployment is thus frictional and structural. There is then neither upward nor downward pressure of demand on wages. Thus the Phillips curve cuts the axis at potential income Y^* and at the corresponding level of unemployment U^*. This is how Phillips drew his curve.

The Phillips curve soon became famous. It provided a link between national-income models and labor markets. This link allowed macroeconomists to drop the uncomfortable assumption, which they had often been forced to use in many of their earlier formal models, that money wages were rigidly fixed and neither rose nor fell as national income varied. By relating money wages to national income, the Phillips curve determines (in conjunction with productivity changes) the speed at which the *SRAS* curve shifts.

Consider, for example, the situation that is shown in Figure 32-2, where the level of income determined by the *AD* and *SRAS* curves is Y_1. Plotting Y_1 on the Phillips curve in part (i) of the accompanying figure tells us that wage costs will be rising at $\dot{W}_1$. Then the *SRAS* curve in Figure 32-2 will be shifting upward by that amount. The same information can be seen in part (ii) of the accompanying figure, where a national income of Y_1 in part (ii) corresponds to unemployment of U_1 in part (i).

The net effect of the two forces acting on unit costs—demand and expectations—determines what happens to the *SRAS* curve.

We are now ready to examine the causes and consequences of inflationary shocks. We begin with an economy in long-run equilibrium: The price level is stable, and national income is at its potential level. We then study the economy as it is buffeted

by different types of shocks. Figure 32-1 provides a guide to the various cases that we will consider; it should be used as a reference as the discussion proceeds.

Demand Shocks

An inflation that is caused by general excess demand in the markets for final output and for factors of production is variously called a *demand-shock infla-tion*, a *demand-side inflation*, or more simply, *demand inflation*. Demand inflation occurs when a rightward shift in the *AD* curve causes aggregate demand to exceed aggregate supply at full-employment income. The initial shift in the *AD* curve could have been caused by a reduction in taxes; by an increase in such autonomous expenditure items as investment, government, and net exports; or by an increase in the money supply.[5]

Demand shock inflations accompanied or fol-lowed the Revolutionary War, the Civil War, and the First and Second World Wars. In these cases, large increases in government expenditure without fully offsetting increases in taxes led to expansions in the money supply and general excess demand. During the Second World War, inflation was held in check by price controls. These postponed the inflation until the immediate post-war years, when the controls were removed. During the Korean War, heavy stockpiling of material by firms in anticipation of shortages led to a demand inflation. Demand inflation also occurred during the period of the buildup of the Vietnam War in the late 1960s and early 1970s. Government expenditure on arms rose rapidly, again without a fully offsetting increase in taxes. Demand inflations sometimes occur at the end of strong peacetime upswings, as rising output causes excess demand to develop simultaneously in the markets for labor, intermediate goods, and final output.

To begin our study of demand inflation, suppose that an initial equilibrium is disturbed by a rightward shift in the aggregate demand curve. This shift causes the price level and output to rise, as shown in Figure 27-8 on page 562 and summarized under "initial effects" of a demand shock in Figure 32-1.

It is important next to distinguish between the case in which the Fed validates the demand shock and the case in which it does not.

No monetary validation. The case of no monetary validation is also covered in Figure 28-2 on page 574, and its results are summarized as Case 1 in Figure

32-1. Because the initial rise in *AD* takes output above the full-employment level, an inflationary gap opens up. The pressure of excess demand soon causes wages to rise relative to productivity, shifting the *SRAS* curve upward and to the left. As long as the Fed holds the money supply constant, the rise in the price level moves the economy upward and to the left along the fixed *AD* curve, reducing the inflationary gap. Eventually, the gap is eliminated, and equilibrium is established at a higher but stable price level, with income at its potential level. In this case, the initial period of inflation is followed by further inflation that lasts only until the new equilibrium is reached.

Monetary validation. Next, suppose that after the demand shock has created an inflationary gap, the Fed increases the money supply whenever output starts to fall. This case takes us beyond our discussions in earlier chapters. It is analyzed in Figure 32-2, and its results are summarized as Case 2 in Figure 32-1.

Two forces are now brought into play. Spurred by the inflationary gap, the increases in wages relative to productivity cause the *SRAS* curve to shift to the left. Fueled by the expansionary monetary policy, the *AD* curve shifts to the right. As a result of both of these shifts, the price level rises, but national income need not fall. Indeed, if the shift in the *AD* curve exactly offsets the shift in the *SRAS* curve, national income and the inflationary gap will remain constant.

Validation of an initial demand shock turns what would have been a transitory inflation into a sustained inflation fueled by monetary expansion. The subsequent shifts in the *AD* curve that perpetuate the inflation are caused by monetary forces.

Supply Shocks

Any rise in the price level originating from increases in costs *that are not caused by excess demands in the markets for factors of production* is variously called a *supply-shock inflation*, a *supply-side inflation,* or some-times a *cost-push inflation*.

An example of a supply-side shock is a rise in the costs of imported raw materials or a rise in

---

[5] As we saw in Chapter 30, an increase in the money supply works through the transmission mechanism—higher price of bonds, lower interest rates, increased investment expenditure—to shift the *AD* curve to the right.

FIGURE 32-1
The Effects of Inflationary Shocks

Initial shock	Initial effects	Alternative possibilities			Final effects
Demand Shock (*AD* curve shifts rightward)	*P* rises *Y* rises above Y^* (inflationary gap) *SRAS* curve starts to shift upwards	Isolated shock Not validated →			**Case 1** *P* rises further *Y* falls back to Y^*
		Sustained shock Validated →			**Case 2** *P* rises continuously *Y* remains above Y^*
Supply Shock (*SRAS* curve shifts leftward)	*P* rises *Y* falls below Y^* (recessionary gap)	Isolated shock	Not validated →		**Case 3** *P* falls *Y* returns to Y^*
			Validated →		**Case 4** *P* rises further *Y* returns to Y^*
		Repeated shock Validated →			**Case 5** *P* continues to rise *Y* remains at, or below, Y^*

Demand and supply shocks have different final effects, depending on whether or not they are isolated or sustained and are validated or nonvalidated. This figure summarizes the analysis of each of the five cases given in the text. It should be referred to after reading the text discussion of each of the cases. All comparisons assume that income is initially at its potential level and that the price level is stable.

The initial effects of a demand shock are to raise national income and the price level. If the shock is isolated, the price level continues to rise until income falls back to its potential level (Case 1). If the shock is sustained and validated (validation turns an isolated shock into a sustained shock), the price level continues to rise while income stays above its potential level (Case 2).

The initial effects of a supply shock are to raise the price level but to reduce national income. Once the shock is over, income will return to its potential level, with a lowered price level if there is no validation (Case 3) and with a higher price level if there is validation (Case 4). If the shock is sustained and validated, the price level can continue to rise with or without a persistent recessionary gap (Case 5).

domestic wage costs per unit of output.[6] The rise in wage costs may occur, as we saw above, because of generally held expectations of inflation. If both employers and employees expect an inflation, money wages are likely to rise in relation to productivity in anticipation of that inflation.

These shocks cause the *SRAS* curve to shift upward. They may or may not also shift the *LRAS* curve. Suppose, for example, that the shock takes the form of a large increase in money wages relative to productivity. This shock will raise costs of production, and hence the price level needed to sustain any given output will be higher. As a result, the *SRAS* curve will shift upward. However, this price change will not affect the economy's capacity to produce output when all resources are fully employed at normal levels of capacity. This type of shock, called

---

[6] Many advanced industrial countries have national sales taxes (called the VAT in Europe and the GST in Canada). A rise in the rate at which this tax is levied shifts the *SRAS* curve upward, causing a once-and-for-all increase in the price level.

FIGURE 32-2
A Validated Demand-Shock Inflation

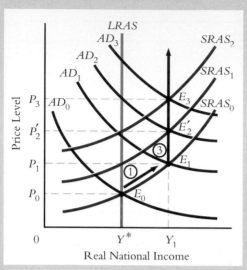

Monetary validation causes the AD curve to shift rightward, offsetting the leftward shift in the SRAS curve and thereby leaving an inflationary gap in spite of the ever-rising price level. As in Figure 28-2, an initial demand shock shifts equilibrium from E_0 to E_1, taking income to Y_1 and the price level to P_1. The resulting inflationary gap then causes the SRAS curve to shift to the left. This time, however, the money supply is increased, shifting the AD curve to the right. By the time the aggregate supply curve has reached $SRAS_1$, the aggregate demand curve has reached AD_2. Now instead of being at E_2 as in Figure 28-2, equilibrium is at E_2'. Income remains constant at Y_1, leaving the inflationary gap constant at Y^*Y_1, while the price level rises to P_2'.

The persistent inflationary gap continues to push the SRAS curve to the left, while the continued monetary validation continues to push the AD curve to the right. By the time the aggregate supply reaches $SRAS_2$, the aggregate demand has reached AD_3. The price level has risen still further to P_3, but because of the frustration of the adjustment mechanism, the inflationary gap remains unchanged at Y^*Y_1. As long as this monetary validation continues, the economy moves along the vertical path of arrow 3.

raw materials brought about because more and more labor and capital are needed to produce a given output from depleting stocks. This is an example of a *real shock*. Firms are not just paying more money for the same inputs and outputs; instead more real inputs are required to produce the same domestic outputs. Shocks of this sort reduce the economy's capacity to produce—potential output is reduced, causing the LRAS curve to shift to the left.[7]

Adverse aggregate supply shocks always shift the SRAS curve to the left; if they are real shocks, they will also tend to shift the LRAS curve to the left.

In the following discussion, we deal with supply-side shocks that shift the SRAS curve to the left but leave the LRAS curve unchanged.[8]

Initial Effects

The initial effects of any leftward shift in the SRAS curve are that the equilibrium price level rises while the equilibrium output falls. The rise in the price level shows up as a temporary burst of inflation. These effects were first discussed in Figure 27-12 on page 566. Although we now wish to go beyond that earlier discussion, we will begin by repeating it in Figure 32-3, which compares the original equilibrium with the equilibrium after the supply shock. (Figure 32-1 summarizes these results as the initial effects of a supply shock.)

What happens next depends both on whether the shock curve is an isolated event or one of a series of recurring shocks, and on how the Fed reacts. If the Fed responds by increasing the money supply, it validates the supply shock; if it holds the money supply constant, the shock is not validated.

Isolated Supply Shocks

Suppose that the leftward shift in the SRAS curve is an isolated event, perhaps caused by a once-and-for-all increase in the cost of imported raw materials.

a *nominal shock*, tends to leave the economy's potential income unchanged and therefore does not shift the LRAS curve.

Now suppose, in contrast, that the shock comes in the form of rising prices of energy and other

---

[7] Other real supply-side shocks, such as improvements in technology, shift the LRAS and the SRAS curves to the right. Since this chapter is concerned with inflation, we do not consider such shocks until Chapter 35.

[8] Other cases can be handled easily by shifting the LRAS curve to the left. In such cases, when the analysis in the text tells us that the long-run position is restored, it will not be at its pre-shock level of income but, rather, at a lower one that is consistent with the new leftward-shifted LRAS curve.

FIGURE 32-3
Supply Shocks with and without Monetary Validation

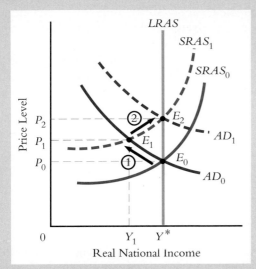

Inflationary supply shocks initially raise prices while lowering income. A supply shock causes the $SRAS$ curve to shift leftward from $SRAS_0$ to $SRAS_1$, as shown by arrow 1. Equilibrium is established at E_1.

If there is no monetary validation, the unemployment would put downward pressure on wages and other costs, causing the $SRAS$ curve to shift slowly back to the right, to $SRAS_0$. Prices would fall and output would rise until the original equilibrium was restored.

If there is monetary validation, the AD curve shifts from AD_0 to AD_1, as shown by arrow 2. This reestablishes full-employment equilibrium at E_2 but with a higher price level, P_2.

How does monetary policy affect the economy's response to such an isolated supply shock?

No monetary validation. The possibility of a nonvalidated isolated supply shock is summarized as Case 3 under "final effects" in Figure 32-1. The leftward shift in the $SRAS$ curve in Figure 32-3 causes the price level to rise and pushes income below its full-employment level, opening up a recessionary gap. Pressure mounts for money wages and other factor costs to fall relative to productivity.

As long as money wages rise less rapidly than productivity is rising, unit costs will fall. Conse-

quently, the $SRAS$ curve shifts rightward, increasing equilibrium income while reducing the price level. The $SRAS$ curve will continue to shift, stopping only when national income is returned to its potential level. If potential income is unaffected by the shock, then the $SRAS$ curve will shift back to its initial position (i.e., $SRAS_0$ in Figure 32-3). Equilibrium income is returned to Y^*, and the price level is returned to its initial value of P_0. Thus, the period of inflation accompanying the original supply shock is eventually followed by a period of deflation that continues until long-run equilibrium is reestablished at the intersection of the AD and $LRAS$ curves.

A major concern in this case is the speed of the adjustment, which in earlier chapters we referred to as the second asymmetry of aggregate supply. If unit labor costs do not fall rapidly in the face of excess supply in the labor market, the adjustment back to full employment can take a very long time. Assume, for example, that the original shock raised prices and money costs by 10 percent. To reverse this shock, unit costs must fall by 10 percent. If money wages stay constant while productivity rises by 2 percent each year, it will take nearly 5 years to complete the adjustment.

Whenever unit costs fall only slowly in the face of excess supply, the recovery back to full employment from a nonvalidated supply-shock inflation will take a long time.

Concern that such a lengthy adjustment will occur is the motive that often lies behind the strong pressure on the Fed to validate supply shocks.

Monetary validation. Now let us see what happens if the money supply is changed in response to the isolated supply shock. Suppose that the monetary authorities decide to validate the supply shock because they believe that relying on cost deflation to restore full employment would force the economy to suffer an extended slump. The monetary validation shifts the aggregate demand curve to the right and causes both the price level and output to *rise*. As the recessionary gap is eliminated, the price level rises further, rather than falling back to its original value as it did when the supply shock was not validated. These effects are also illustrated in Figure 32-3, and they are summarized under Case 4 in Figure 32-1.

Monetary validation of an isolated supply shock causes the initial rise in the price level to be followed by a further rise, resulting in a higher price level than would occur if the recessionary gap were relied on to reduce costs and prices.

The most dramatic example of an isolated supply-shock inflation came in the wake of the first OPEC oil-price shock. In 1974 the countries who were members of the Organization of Petroleum Exporting Countries (OPEC) agreed to restrict output. Their action caused a dramatic increase in the prices of petroleum and many petroleum-related products such as fertilizer and chemicals. The resulting increase in industrial costs shifted *SRAS* curves upward in all industrial countries. At this time, the Canadian central bank validated the supply shock with large increases in the money supply, while the Fed did not. As the theory predicts, Canada experienced a large increase in its price level but almost no recession, while the United States experienced a much smaller increase in its price level but a severe recession.

Repeated Supply Shocks

Now assume that the economy is buffeted by a series of repeated supply shocks. One example would be a repeated rise in the prices of all imported raw materials and energy products for several successive years. A second example could come from wages in the case studied earlier, where persistent expectations of continued inflation cause wages to rise period by period. Since it turns out to be important to our later analysis, we take the second case, in which wages rise relative to productivity because both employers and employees expect further inflation. This rise in wages shifts the *SRAS* curve upward.

No monetary validation.   Suppose that the Fed does not validate these repeated supply shocks and instead holds the money supply constant. The initial effect of the leftward shift in the *SRAS* curve is to open up a recessionary gap, as shown by arrow 1 in Figure 32-3. If wages continue to rise, subjecting the economy to further supply shocks, prices continue to rise and output continues to fall. Eventually, the trade-off between higher wages and unemployment will become obvious to everyone. On the one hand, workers will realize that higher wages come at the cost of falling employment, and they will cease pressing for wage increases. On the other hand, employers will realize that they cannot simply pass on increased wages in

the form of increased prices without suffering further decreases in sales, and they will become less willing to grant such increases in wages even if they expect the inflation to continue for some time. Thus, a nonvalidated supply-shock inflation is self-limiting because the rising recessionary gap that it causes tends to restrain further wage increases.

Because repeated nonvalidated supply shocks must come to an end, their results are identical to those of a single, isolated supply shock. Whether the recessionary position shown by E_1 in Figure 32-3 is the result of a single, isolated supply-side shock or of a series of repeated shocks, the end result is the same: the price level is higher and national income is lower than in the economy's initial, preshock equilibrium.

What happens next is also just a repeat of what we have already studied for an isolated shock. When the persistent unemployment eventually erodes inflationary expectations, wages will fall relative to productivity, thus reversing the supply shock. Eventually, full employment will be restored, and the price level will return to its original value. This is Case 3 in Figure 32-1.

Nonvalidated supply-shock inflations caused by expectations of further inflation have natural correctives created by the rising recessionary gap. But these correctives may take a long time to operate, and hence a wage-cost push can cause a long and sustained stagflation, combining inflation with rising unemployment.

Monetary validation.   Now suppose that the Fed validates the initial supply shock with an increase in the money supply, thus shifting the aggregate demand curve to the right, as shown in Figure 32-4.

In the new full-employment equilibrium, both money wages and prices have risen. Workers are no better off than they were originally, although those who remained in jobs were temporarily better off in the transition after wages had risen (taking equilibrium to E_1 in Figure 32-4) but before the price level had risen (taking equilibrium to E_2). The rise in wages has been offset by a rise in prices.

There is no reason for employers and employees to expect that the inflation will stop here. Insofar as expectations are backward-looking, people have the experience of past inflation to go on. Insofar as expectations are forward-looking, there is no reason for people to see current monetary policy stopping

FIGURE 32-4
Monetary Validation of a Repeated Supply Shock

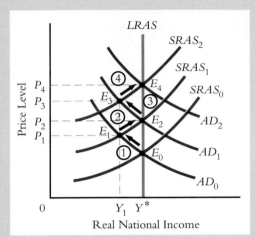

Monetary validation of a repeated supply shock causes continuous inflation in the absence of excess demand. The initial equilibrium is at E_0. A supply shock then takes equilibrium to E_1, just as in Figure 32-3. This is the stagflation phase of rising prices and falling output; it is indicated by arrow 1.

The Fed then validates the supply shock by increasing the money supply, taking the AD curve to AD_1 and equilibrium to E_2. This is the expansionary phase of rising prices and output (arrow 2).

A second supply shock, followed by monetary validation, takes equilibrium to E_3 (arrow 3) and then to E_4 (arrow 4). As long as the supply shocks and monetary validation continue, inflation continues.

inflation unless, first, the Fed emphasizes that what it has just done is a once-and-for-all monetary accommodation and, second, the Fed is believed by wage and price setters.

The stage is now set for wages and prices to rise further when the economy is hit with another supply shock. If the Fed again validates the shock with an appropriate increase in the money supply, full employment is restored, but at the cost of a further round of inflation. If this process goes on repeatedly, it causes a continual supply-shock inflation. The wage-cost push tends to cause stagflation, with rising prices and falling output. Monetary validation tends to reinforce the rise in prices but to offset the fall in output. The results are summarized as Case 5 in Figure 32-1.

Two things are required for this type of supply-shock inflation to be sustained over a long time. First, continued increases in money wages must occur, even in the absence of excess demand for labor and goods. In some countries powerful unions can cause such increases, but this occurrence is not a real possibility in the United States today (although about 15 years ago this possibility worried some prominent U.S. economists in ways discussed in Box 32-2). What can cause continued wage increases today, however, is expectations of continued inflation. As discussed earlier, if everyone expects, say, 4 percent inflation, workers may ask for a 4 percent increase in money wages just to hold their own against the expected inflation, and employers may grant the increases, expecting to be able to pass the extra costs on through increased prices. The result is self-fulfilling expectations. Because everyone expects the inflation rate, their actions in expectation of that rate bring that rate about.

Second, the central bank must validate the resulting inflation by increasing the money supply, thereby preventing the unemployment that would otherwise occur. The process set up by this sequence of wage-cost increases and monetary validation is often called a *wage-price spiral.*

Is Monetary Validation of Supply Shocks Desirable?

Once started, a wage-price spiral can be halted only if the Fed stops validating the supply shocks that are causing the inflation. The longer it waits to do so, the more firmly held will be the expectations that it will continue its policy of validating the shocks. These entrenched expectations may cause wages to continue rising even after validation has ceased. Because employers expect prices to rise, they go on granting wage increases. If expectations are entrenched firmly enough, the wage push can continue for quite some time, in spite of the downward pressure caused by the rising unemployment associated with the growing recessionary gap.

Because of this possibility, many economists argue that the wage-price spiral should not be allowed to begin. One way to ensure that it does not is to refuse to validate any supply shock whatsoever.

To some economists, caution dictates that no supply shocks should be validated, lest a wage-price spiral be set up. Other economists are willing to risk validating obviously isolated

Box 32-2

Is Wage-Cost Push a Possibility?

As far back as the 1940s, early Keynesians were worried that, once the government was committed to maintaining full employment, much of the discipline of the market would be removed from wage bargains. They felt that the scramble of every group trying to get ahead of other groups would lead to a wage-cost-push inflation. The government's commitment to full employment would then lead it to validate the resulting inflation through increases in the money supply. In these circumstances, cost-push inflation could go on indefinitely without any market mechanism to bring it to a halt.

The possibility of a sustained wage-cost-push inflation has been greatly reduced over the years. For one thing, the governments of many advanced countries have abandoned their commitment to maintain continuous full employment under any circumstances. For another, in many countries, including the United States and the United Kingdom, there has

been a steady decline in the membership and power of unions.

Although few people worry about wage-cost-push inflation in the United States today, it was taken seriously only 15 years ago by some U.S. economists. It was also regarded as a serious threat in Western Europe throughout most of the period from 1945 to 1990 because strong unions seemed to have arbitrary power over wages.

Those who worried about this type of inflation often looked to nonmarket methods of controlling it. These methods went under the general name of *incomes policies*. A proposal commonly made by U.S. economists who worried about wage-push inflation in the late 1970s and early 1980s was for a **tax-related incomes policy (TIP)**, which would operate through the tax system to provide penalties for "excessive" wage and price hikes and rewards for moderate ones.

---

shocks in order to avoid the severe, though transitory, recessions that otherwise accompany them.

Inflation as a Monetary Phenomenon

A long-standing debate among economists concerns the extent to which inflation is a monetary phenomenon. Does it have purely monetary causes—changes in the demand or the supply of money? Does it have purely monetary consequences—only the price level is affected? One slogan that states an extreme position on this issue was made popular many years ago by Milton Friedman: "Inflation is *everywhere* and *always* a monetary phenomenon." To consider these issues, let us summarize what we have learned already. First, look at the causes:

1. On the demand side, anything that shifts the *AD* curve to the right will cause the price level to rise. This includes such expenditure changes as upward shifts in the consumption, investment, government expenditure, or net export functions, and such monetary changes as an increase in the money supply or a decrease in money demand. On the supply side, anything that increases costs of production will shift the *SRAS* curve to the left and cause the price level to rise.
2. Such inflations can continue for some time without being validated by increases in the money supply.
3. The price level increases must *eventually* come to a halt, unless monetary expansion occurs.

Points 1 and 2 provide the sense in which, looking at causes, a temporary burst of inflation need not be a monetary phenomenon. It need not have monetary causes, and it need not be accompanied by monetary expansion. Point 3 provides the sense in which, looking at causes, *sustained* inflation must be a monetary phenomenon. If a rise in prices is to continue indefinitely, it must be accompanied by continuing increases in the money supply (or decreases in money demand). This is true regardless of the cause that set the inflation in motion.[9] Of course, something that cannot continue indefinitely might continue for a very long time, so there is still plenty of room for disagreement over the mix of monetary and nonmonetary causes in any observed inflation.

Second, let us summarize the consequences of inflation, assuming that actual national income was initially at its potential level.

4. In the short run, demand-shock inflation tends to be accompanied by an increase in national income above its potential level.
5. In the short run, supply-shock inflation tends to be accompanied by a decrease in national income below its potential level.
6. When all costs and prices are adjusted *fully* (so that the relevant supply-side curve is the *LRAS* curve), shifts in either the *AD* or *SRAS* curve leave national income unchanged and affect only the price level.

Points 4 and 5 provide a sense in which, looking at consequences, inflation is not, in the short run, a purely monetary phenomenon. Point 6 provides the sense in which, looking at consequences, inflation is a purely monetary phenomenon from the point of view of long-run equilibrium.

There is still plenty of room for debate, however, on how long the short run will last. Most economists believe that the short run can be long enough for inflation to have major real effects. Indeed, if the inflation is sustained, many of its real effects may persist indefinitely. For example, distortions caused

by many aspects of the tax system being defined in money rather than real terms will persist as long as inflation continues, even if it proceeds at a steady and fully expected rate.

We have now reached three important conclusions:

1. Without monetary validation, demand shocks cause temporary bursts of inflation that are accompanied by inflationary gaps. The gaps are removed as rising costs push the *SRAS* curve to the left, returning national income to its potential level, but at a higher price level.
2. Without monetary validation, supply shocks cause temporary bursts of inflation that are accompanied by recessionary gaps. The gaps are removed as wages fall relative to productivity, restoring equilibrium at potential income and at the initial price level.
3. With continuing validation, inflation initiated by either supply or demand shocks can continue indefinitely; an ever-increasing money supply is necessary for sustained inflation.

Sustained Inflation[10]

Why has the U.S. economy undergone several periods of sustained inflation—sometimes rapid, as in the 1970s and early 1980s, and sometimes more gradual, as in the late 1980s and early 1990s? Can sustained inflation continue indefinitely at a more or less constant rate? What are the costs and benefits of reducing or eliminating a sustained inflation?

Accelerating Inflation

To study one of the most serious problems associated with a sustained inflation, we take up the story where we left it on page 680 at the end of the section discussing the monetary validation of a demand shock inflation. When the Fed engages

---

[9] The statement that inflation is everywhere and always a monetary phenomenon depends on a restricted and specific definition of the term *inflation*. To justify the statement, a temporary burst of inflation with nonmonetary causes must be called *a rise in the price level*, and the term *inflation* must be reserved for increases in the price level that are sustained long enough so that they must be accompanied by monetary expansion.

---

[10] The rest of this chapter can be omitted without loss of continuity.

in such validation, the *AD* and *SRAS* curves will both be shifting upward, allowing the price level to rise with no necessary reduction in the inflationary gap. This is the situation shown in Figure 32-2 on page 682.

What now happens to the rate of inflation is predicted by the **acceleration hypothesis**, which holds that when the central bank engages in whatever rate of monetary expansion is needed to hold the inflationary gap constant, the actual inflation rate will accelerate. The Fed may start by validating a 3 percent inflation, but soon 3 percent will become 4 percent, and if the Fed insists on validating 4 percent, the rate will become 5 percent, and so on without limit, until the Fed finally stops its validation.

There are several steps in the reasoning behind this acceleration hypothesis. The first concerns the development of inflationary expectations.

Expectational effects. To illustrate the importance of expectations in accelerating a sustained inflation, assume that the inflationary gap shown in Figure 32-2 creates sufficient excess demand to push up wages 2 percent per year faster than productivity is rising. The demand effect in the equation on page 677 is thus 2 percent. As a result, unit costs and hence the *SRAS* curve will also tend to be rising at 2 percent per year.

When the inflation has persisted for some time, however, people will come to expect that the monetary validation, and hence inflation, will continue. Once this happens, the expectation of 2 percent inflation will tend to push up wages and unit costs by that amount *in addition to* the demand pressure. As the demand effect on wages is augmented by the expectational effect, the *SRAS* curve will begin to shift upward more rapidly. When expectations are for a 2 percent inflation and demand pressure is also pushing wages up by 2 percent, the overall effect will be a 4 percent increase in wages, unit costs, and the *SRAS* curve. Sooner or later, however, the 4 percent inflation will come to be expected, and the expectational effect will rise to 4 percent. This, added to the demand component, will create an inflation rate of 6 percent. And so this cycle will go on. As long as there is a demand effect arising from an inflationary gap, and as long as actual inflation is equal to the demand effect plus the expectational effect, the inflation rate cannot stay constant because expectations will always be revised upward toward the actual inflation rate.[11]

More rapid monetary validation required. The second step in the argument is that, if the Fed still wishes to hold the level of output constant, it must increase the rate at which the money supply is growing. This action is necessary because in order to hold national income constant, the *AD* curve must be shifted at an increasingly rapid pace to offset the increasingly rapid shifts in the *SRAS* curve, which are driven by the continually rising rate of expected inflation.

An increasing rate of inflation. The third step in the argument is that the rate of inflation must now be increasing because of the increasingly rapid upward shifts in both the *AD* and *SRAS* curves. The rise in the actual inflation rate will in turn cause an increase in the expected inflation rate. This will then cause the actual inflation rate to increase, which will in turn increase the expected inflation rate, and so on. The net result is a *continually increasing rate of inflation.*[12] The tendency for inflation to accelerate is discussed further in Box 32-3 on pages 690–691.

According to the acceleration hypothesis, as long as an inflationary gap persists, expectations of inflation will be rising, which will lead to increases in the actual rate of inflation.

A Sustained, Constant Rate of Inflation

The discussion of accelerating inflation implies that a sustained inflation at a constant rate is possible

---

[11] This can easily be seen if we write the actual inflation rate (which we call A) as the sum of the demand effect (which we call D) and the expectations effect (which we call E): $A = D + E$. If we have a positive actual rate, A, and a positive demand rate, D, the expected rate cannot equal the actual rate. Instead, it must be less than the actual rate by the amount of the demand effect: $E = A - D$. Thus, it is not possible to find a steady inflation rate in which expectations are fulfilled in the face of an inflationary gap. Correct expectations means $E = A$, and this is inconsistent with any positive D.

[12] Now we see the reason for the name *NAIRU*. At any level of unemployment less than the NAIRU, national income is above Y^*, and the inflation rate tends to accelerate. So the NAIRU is the lowest level of unemployment consistent with a nonaccelerating rate of inflation.

only when national income is at its potential level, so that there is no demand component to inflation. In that case, all inflation is expectational. If the inflation is fully expected, the actual and the expected rates must be equal. Provided that there is no demand component, the inflation can go on forever at a constant rate, validated by a constant rate of monetary expansion.[13] This case is considered in more detail in Box 32-4 on page 692.

Breaking a Sustained Inflation

An economy may be undergoing a sustained inflation in either of two situations. First, income may exceed its potential level, producing an inflationary gap with the resulting demand inflation fully validated by the Fed. Such a situation is shown in Figure 32-2. Second, there may be a validated pure expectational inflation with the income at or a bit below its potential income.

Costs

In either situation, reducing the inflation takes time and involves major costs. The technique is for the Fed to stop validating the inflation. It does this by lowering the rate of growth of the money supply below the rate of growth of money demand, thus creating an excess demand for money. This action forces up interest rates and lowers real aggregate demand, reducing any existing inflationary gap. We shall soon see that it is usually necessary for the Fed to go further, creating a substantial recessionary gap that persists until the inflation is eliminated.

The process involves many costs. The recessionary gap hurts all those who suffer from recessions, including the unemployed and the owners of firms who lose profits and risk bankruptcy. Unemployed resources mean lost output and, hence, lower real national income than would otherwise be produced. The temporary rise in interest rates hurts borrowers, including people with mortgages and firms with large loans. Among these groups who are most exposed, and may lose their wealth, are young households with large mortgages and small firms that have taken on large debts to finance expansions.

Reducing a sustained inflation is thus a classic case of a policy that brings short-term pain for long-term gain. Inevitably the question arises: Are the future benefits worth the immediate costs?

Reducing a sustained inflation quickly incurs high costs for a short period of time; reducing it slowly incurs lower costs but for a longer period of time.

The process of reducing a sustained inflation can be divided into three phases.

Phase 1: Removing the Monetary Validation

The first phase consists of slowing the rate of monetary expansion below the current rate of inflation, thereby slowing the rate at which the *AD* curve is shifting upward. The simplest case is when the Fed adopts a "cold turkey approach," in which the rate of monetary expansion is cut to zero so that the upward shift in the *AD* curve is halted abruptly. This case implies a large and rapid increase in both nominal and real interest rates.

At this point a controversy often breaks out—as it did in the early 1980s—over the effects that the increase in the interest rate has on inflation. One group will point out that the rise in the interest rate increases business costs and that passing on the extra costs through higher prices adds to inflation. They will condemn the Fed's tight monetary policy as inflationary. A second group will argue that the rising interest rate signifies a slowdown in the rate of monetary expansion without which inflation cannot be curbed.

The first group is correct in pointing out that the rise in interest rates may cause a one-time increase in the price level. The rise in interest costs may shift the *SRAS* curve upward, just as a rise in wage costs does. This rise in interest costs, however, has only a one-time effect on the price level. The first group is wrong, therefore, in asserting that the Fed's

---

[13] The relation developed in the previous footnote can be used to explain why a constant rate of inflation that persists must be a purely expectational inflation. Actual inflation is the sum of expected and demand inflation: $A = D + E$. If the rate of inflation is to be constant, expected inflation must not be changing. This will only happen when expectations are being fulfilled—which means that expected and actual inflation are equal, so $E = A$. This can only be true when D is zero. But D can only be zero at potential income, where there is neither an inflationary nor a deflationary gap.

Box 32-3

The Phillips Curve and Accelerating Inflation

As discussed in Box 32-1, Phillips was interested in studying the short-run behavior of an economy subjected to cyclical fluctuations. Other economists, however, treated the curve as establishing a long-term trade-off between inflation and unemployment.

Let the government stabilize income at Y_1 (and thus unemployment at U_1), as shown in the accompanying figures. To do this it must validate the ensuing wage inflation, which is indicated by $\dot{W}_1$

in the figure. The government thus seems to be able to choose among particular combinations of inflation and unemployment, with lower levels of unemployment being attained at the cost of higher rates of inflation.

In the 1960s Phillips curves were fitted to the data for many countries, and governments made decisions about where they wished to be on the trade-off between inflation and unemployment. Then in the late 1960s, in country after country,

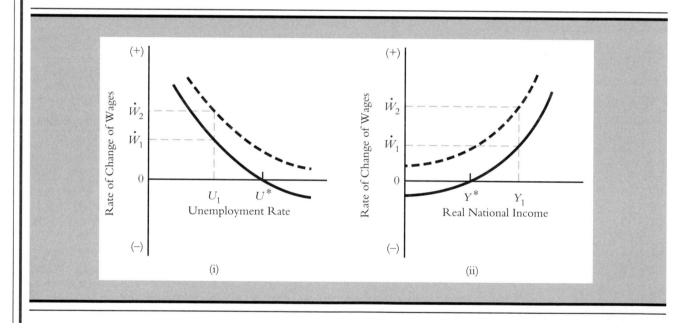

(i)

(ii)

policy of driving up interest rates is contributing to a long-term increase in the rate of inflation.

The second group is correct in saying that the rise in the interest rate is a necessary part of an antiinflationary policy. As long as the price level continues to rise, the rise in the interest rate

reduces aggregate desired expenditure, taking equilibrium national income upward along a fixed *AD* curve.

Now suppose that the Fed resists the pleas to hold down interest rates. It continues with its "no validation" policy. The *AD* curve stops shifting, but, under the rate of wage and price inflation associated with any given level of unemployment began to rise. Instead of being stable, the Phillips curves began to shift upward. The explanation lay primarily in a shifting relationship between the pressure of demand and wage increases due to expectations, as discussed in the text.

It was gradually understood that the original Phillips curve concerned only the influence of demand and left out inflationary expectations. This omission proved to be important and unfortunate. An increase in expected inflation shows up as an upward shift in the original Phillips curve that was drawn in Box 32-1. The importance of expectations can be shown by drawing what is called an **expectations-augmented Phillips curve**, as shown here. The heights of the Phillips curves above the axis at Y^* and at U^* show the expected inflation rate. These distances represent the amount that wages will rise when neither excess-demand nor excess-supply pressures are being felt in labor markets. The actual wage increase is shown by the augmented curve, with the increase in wages exceeding expected inflation whenever $Y > Y^*$ ($U < U^*$) and falling short of expected inflation whenever $Y < Y^*$ ($U > U^*$).

The demand component shown by the simple Phillips curve tells us by how much wage changes will deviate from the expected inflation rate.

Now we can see what was wrong with the idea of a stable inflation-unemployment trade-off. Targeting a particular income Y_1 or unemployment U_1 in the figures is fine as long as no inflation is *expected*, but once some particular rate of inflation comes to be expected, people will demand that much just to hold their own. The Phillips curve will shift upward to the position shown in the figures. Now there is inflation $\dot{W}_2$ because of the combined effects of expectations and excess demand.

However, this higher rate is above the expected rate. Once this higher rate comes to be expected, the Phillips curve will shift upward once again.

The expectations-augmented Phillips curve shows that the actual rate of inflation exceeds the expected rate whenever there is an inflationary gap.

Sooner or later such a situation will cause inflationary expectations to be shifted upward. As a result, the inflation rate associated with any given level of Y or U rises over time. This is the phenomenon of accelerating inflation that is discussed in the text.

The shifts in the Phillips curve are such that most economists agree that in the long run, when inflationary expectations have fully adjusted to actual inflation, there is no trade-off between inflation and unemployment. That is, they believe that the long-run Phillips curve is a vertical line at the NAIRU.

the combined influence of the present inflationary gap and expectations of continued inflation, wages continue to rise. Thus the *SRAS* curve continues to shift upward. Eventually, the inflationary gap will be removed, as shown in part (i) of Figure 32-5.

If demand were the only influence on wages, that would be the end of the story. At $Y = Y^*$ there would be no upward demand pressure on wages and other costs. Unit costs would stop rising, the *SRAS* curve would be stabilized, and the economy would remain at full employment with a stable price level.

Box 32-4

Constant Inflation

When national income is at its potential level, there is neither an inflationary nor a recessionary gap. In this case there is no demand effect operating on wage changes. Leaving random shocks aside, the only force operating on wages is expectations. Say, for example, that both workers and employers expect 4 percent inflation and that employers are prepared to raise wages by 4 percent per year to keep wages in line with everything else. Wages will rise by 4 percent per year, and the *SRAS* curve will shift upward by that amount each year. If the Fed validates the resulting inflation, the *AD* curve will also shift upward by that amount.

This case is illustrated in the accompanying figure. Expectations of a constant rate of inflation cause wages, unit costs, and the *SRAS* curve to shift upward at a uniform rate from $SRAS_0$ to $SRAS_1$, to $SRAS_2$, and so on. Monetary validation is causing the *AD* curve to shift upward at the same time from AD_0 to

AD_1, to AD_2, and so on. As a result, national income remains at Y^*, with unemployment at the NAIRU and a steady inflation rate which takes the price level from P_0 to P_1, to P_2, and so on. Equilibrium follows the arrow from E_0 to E_1, to E_2, and so on. In this situation, wage costs are rising due to expectations of inflation, and these expectations are being fulfilled.

Steady inflation at potential income results when the rate of monetary growth, the rate of wage increase, and the expected rate of inflation are all consistent with the actual inflation rate.

The key point about a pure expectational inflation at a constant rate is that there is no demand effect operating on wage bargains. Wages rise at the expected rate of inflation, just enough to preserve the existing relationship between wages and all other prices. The labor shortages that accompany an inflationary gap are absent, as are the labor surpluses that accompany a recessionary gap.

If all forces worked precisely as described in the simple theoretical model, steady inflation would occur only when income was exactly at its potential level. In practice, however, stable inflation rates also seem to be compatible with modest recessionary gaps.

In such circumstances, there is a tendency for wages to fall (relative to productivity), forcing the *SRAS* curve downward. However, the negative demand effect of a recessionary gap seems to be weak. Thus, when the gap is relatively small, the demand effect may be swamped by the expectational effect and random shocks, so that an approximately stable inflation rate is the net result.

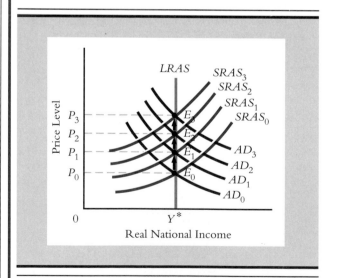

Phase 2: Stagflation[14]

Governments around the world have often wished that things were really so simple. However, wages depend not only on current excess demand but also on inflationary expectations. Once inflationary expectations have been established, it is not always easy to get people to revise them downward, even in the face of announced changes in monetary policies. Thus the *SRAS* curve continues to shift upward, causing the price level to continue to rise and income to fall.

Expectations can cause inflation to persist after its original causes have been removed. What was initially a demand and expectational inflation due to an inflationary gap becomes a pure expectational inflation.

This is Phase 2, shown in part (ii) of Figure 32-5.

The ease with which the Fed can end such an inflation, and the costs of doing so, both depend on how easy it is to change these expectations of continued inflation. This change is more difficult to the extent that expectations are backward-looking and easier to the extent that expectations are forward-looking.

To the extent that people look mainly to past inflation rates to determine their expectations of the future, they will be slow to change their expectations. As the actual rate falls below their expected rate, a long time will be required for the downward adjustment to take place. The longer a given rate has persisted, the more firmly will expectations that the rate will persist be built into people's behavior. An inflation that has persisted long enough to create firmly established expectations that it will continue is sometimes called an *entrenched inflation.*

To the extent that expectations are adjusted to current events, people will take notice of the Fed's changed behavior and revise their expectations of future inflation downward in the light of the new monetary policy. If people fully understand the Fed's policies as soon as they are implemented, if they have full confidence that the Fed will stick to its policies, if they know exactly how much time will be required for the Fed's policies to have effect, and if they adjust their expectations exactly in line with this knowledge, then there is little need for any recessionary gap to develop. Once the inflationary gap has been removed, expectations will immediately be revised downward, so there will then be no pressure on unit costs to rise because of either demand or expectational forces. The inflation will be eliminated at almost no cost.

How long the inflation persists after the inflationary gap has been removed depends on how quickly expectations of continued inflation are revised downward. This revision will be faster the more are expectations based on a rational understanding of the Fed's current policies, the stronger is the belief that these policies will be adhered to in the future, and the better is the public's knowledge of how the economy will react to the antiinflationary policies.

The emerging recessionary gap has two effects. First, there is rising unemployment. Thus the demand influence on wages becomes negative. Second, as the recession deepens and monetary restraint continues, people revise their expectations of inflation downward. When they have no further expectations of inflation, there are no further increases in wages relative to productivity, and the *SRAS* curve stops shifting. The stagflation phase is over. Inflation has come to a halt, but a large recessionary gap now exists. At this point nominal interest rates will fall because they no longer need to include an inflationary premium. Furthermore, the Fed can allow real interest rates to fall, since it no longer wishes to exert contractionary pressure on the economy.

As we note later in this chapter, the evidence from the U.S. economy is that Phase 2 can be accompanied by large recessionary gaps and significant amounts of lost output before the inflation is checked.

Phase 3: Recovery

The final phase is the return to full employment. When the economy comes to rest at the end of the stagflation, the situation is exactly the same as when the economy is hit by an isolated supply shock (see Figure 32-3). The move back to full employment can be accomplished in either of two ways. First, the recessionary gap can be relied on to reduce unit costs,

---

[14] If the economy began with a purely expectational inflation with national income at or below full employment, what we call Phase 2 would be the first phase. However, the rest of the story is the same whether the starting point is a demand inflation or a pure expectational inflation.

FIGURE 32-5
Eliminating Entrenched Inflation

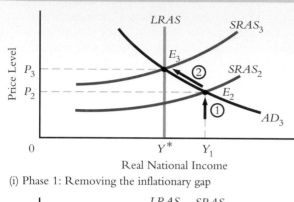

(i) Phase 1: Removing the inflationary gap

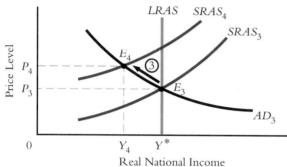

(ii) Phase 2: Stagflation

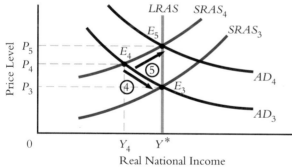

(iii) Phase 3: Recovery

(i) Phase 1: The elimination of entrenched inflation begins with a demand contraction to remove the inflationary gap. Fully validated inflation of the type shown in Figure 32-2 is taking the economy along the path shown by arrow 1 here. When the curves reach $SRAS_2$ and AD_3, the Fed stops expanding the money supply, thus stabilizing aggregate demand at AD_3. Wages continue to rise, taking the $SRAS$ curve leftward. The economy moves along arrow 2, with income falling and the price level rising. When aggregate supply reaches $SRAS_3$, the inflationary gap is removed, income is Y^*, and the price level is P_3.

(ii) Phase 2: Expectations and wage momentum lead to stagflation, with falling output and continuing inflation. The economy moves along the path shown by arrow 3. The driving force is now the $SRAS$ curve, which continues to shift because inflationary expectations cause wages to continue to rise. The recessionary gap grows as income falls. Inflation continues, but at a diminishing rate. If wages stop rising when income has reached Y_4 and the price level has reached P_4, the stagflation phase is over, with equilibrium at E_4.

(iii) Phase 3: After expectations are reversed, recovery takes income to Y^*, and the price level is stabilized. There are two possible scenarios for recovery. In the first the recessionary gap causes wages to fall (slowly), taking the $SRAS$ curve back to $SRAS_3$ (slowly), as shown by arrow 4. The economy retraces the path originally followed in part (ii) back to E_3. In the second scenario, the Fed increases the money supply sufficiently to shift the AD curve to AD_4. The economy then moves along the path shown by arrow 5. This restores potential income at the cost of further temporary inflation that takes the price level to P_5. Full employment and a stable price level are now achieved.

thus shifting the $SRAS$ curve downward. Second, the money supply can be increased to shift the AD curve to a level that is consistent with full employment. These two possibilities are illustrated in part (iii) of Figure 32-5.

Some economists worry about waiting for costs and prices to fall because they fear that the process will take a very long time. Others worry about a temporary burst of monetary expansion because they fear that expectations of inflation may be rekindled when the Fed increases the money supply. If inflationary expectations are revived, the Fed will then have an unenviable choice. Either it must let another severe recession develop to break these new inflationary expectations or it must validate the inflation in order to reduce unemployment. In the latter case the

Fed is back where it started, with validated inflation on its hands and with diminished credibility.[15]

Inflationary Experience

The experience of inflation since World War II is shown in Figure 23-6 on page 471. This concluding section focuses on the experience of inflation starting with the historically high rates that prevailed at the end of the 1970s.

As noted in Chapter 31, the 1970s witnessed steady expansion of the money supply as well as a number of inflationary supply shocks. As a result, inflation rose steadily, especially during the second half of the decade. In 1976 inflation was 4.9 percent, and in 1979 it was 13.3 percent (both measured by the December-to-December percentage change in the CPI). Briefly, the key subsequent developments were:

1. The high inflation in 1979 led to the adoption of restrictive monetary policies, which in turn led to a severe recession and a substantial reduction in inflation over the period from 1980 to 1982. By 1983 inflation had fallen to 3.8 percent.
2. The recession was followed by a sustained recovery over the period from 1983 to 1989, during which time the inflation rate remained in the 3 percent to 4 percent range. Inflation then started to creep up, reaching 4.8 percent in 1989 and 5.4 percent in 1990.
3. A combination of factors, including a restrictive monetary policy, brought the recovery to an end by late 1990, and the economy entered into a recession while inflation fell to 4.2 percent by 1991.

We now look at each of these three periods in a little more detail.

Inflation Reduction: 1979–1982

At the end of the 1970s there was some controversy about how much of the prevailing double-digit inflation was due to demand forces, how much was due to entrenched expectations, and how much was due to the supply shock of massive OPEC-induced increases in oil prices. Nevertheless, there was widespread agreement on the desirability of reducing inflation. However, there was substantial disagreement as to the best means of achieving the goal of lower inflation.[16]

Monetarists advocated breaking the inflation with monetary restraint in the manner that we analyzed earlier in this chapter. They believed that inflation and inflationary expectations would fall quickly once the Fed adopted a restrictive monetary policy. The actual inflation would also fall quickly, without the need for a major recession. In terms of the discussion earlier in this chapter, they felt that Phase 2 would be short. Accordingly, they advocated exclusive use of monetary restraint to reduce inflation.

Keynesians agreed that a low rate of monetary growth was a necessary condition for returning to a low rate of inflation. However, they believed that expectations were backward-looking and would not be quickly revised downward. Thus Phase 2 would be long—some talked in terms of 5 to 10 years. As a result they were reluctant to use monetary policy alone during the transition and often advocated using **incomes policies**, a term that includes any direct government intervention that is used to affect wage and price setting. They hoped that such intervention would shorten Phase 2 by helping to break inflationary expectations.

The effects of monetary restraint. After some initial vacillation, the Fed adopted a contractionary monetary policy. As noted in Chapter 31, the monetary squeeze led to increases in interest rates, reductions in expenditure, a recessionary gap, and moderation of inflation. By 1983 the policy had succeeded in reducing inflation to 3.8 percent (lower than in all but two years since the mid-1960s), but it also produced a major recession with all of its attendant costs, including unemployment, lost output, business bankruptcies, and foreclosed mortgages.

The results came out somewhere between the extremes that had been predicted by monetarists and Keynesians. On the one hand, Keynesians were right in predicting that the antiinflationary policies would induce a severe recession, but the inflation rate came down much faster than they had predicted. (Not only

---

[15] This is the so-called reentry problem that was discussed in Chapter 31.

[16] This same disagreement no doubt would occur again if the Fed advocated a policy of substantially reducing the current rate of inflation to, say, as close to zero as possible.

were new wage agreements moderated in response to the excess supply of labor, but also a significant number of existing contracts were reopened and lower wages agreed upon.) On the other hand, although the monetarists' prediction that inflation would fall sharply proved correct, the recession was much more severe than most of them predicted. Economists still argue about why the results turned out the way they did.

Monetarists have to explain why there was a significant stagflation phase at all. They do so by claiming that the Fed did not take a consistently tough line on reducing the rate of monetary accommodation, which left people uncertain as to whether or not inflation really was going to fall. Because of this uncertainty, inflationary expectations remained high, sustaining the stagflation phase of the adjustment. The fault, according to this view, was not with the tight monetary policy but in the Fed's lack of credibility. People did not think the Fed would sustain its tough policy and so were slow to revise their expectations of inflation downward.

Keynesians have to explain why the stagflation phase was so much shorter than they expected. One of their main explanations lies in the weakness of the steel and automobile industries at the time. These industries always have had strong unions, which the Keynesians claim were a major cause of the wage-price spiral. However, during the early 1980s both of these industries were in deep trouble, and no matter how hard their unions pushed for wage increases, the profits out of which extra wages would have to be paid did not exist as they had in the past. Because of rising foreign competition, the firms could not assume that money wage increases could be easily passed on by increasing their prices. Thus, the Keynesians say that for quite fortuitous reasons the wage push was much weaker than usual, and the stagflation phase was correspondingly shortened. Interestingly, union power has continued to weaken in the United States. Therefore the Keynesian explanation of the early 1980s implies that Phase 2 will be even shorter if a sustained inflation ever needs to be broken in the future.

Whatever the reasons, during the early 1980s inflation fell faster than many Keynesians had expected, and the recession was deeper and more prolonged than many monetarists had expected.

The costs and benefits of monetary restraint. An important policy question arises in light of the outcome mentioned above: Were the benefits of reduced inflation worth the cost of the recession? Reasonable people will differ in their answer to this question, depending on their evaluation of the benefits and costs involved.

In Chapter 23 we discussed a number of reasons why a high inflation rate is harmful to economic performance, a conclusion that leads most economists to accept that, everything else equal, a lower inflation rate is better than a higher one. However, it is very difficult to provide quantitative measures of the extent of the benefits produced by any given reduction in inflation.

The benefits from a lower inflation rate are ongoing in that they accrue each year that the lower inflation rate is maintained.

The costs of a recession are somewhat easier to quantify (although there remains plenty of scope for disagreement). The costs are measured by the cumulative loss of output that occurs while national income remains below potential.

A major cost of reducing inflation is a one-time loss of output that accrues as long as the recession persists.

Some economists have measured the cost-benefit ratio of a disinflation by the amount of output that must be given up in order to reduce the inflation rate by a given amount. The evidence from the 1980–1982 recession is that it took about a 4 percent loss of GDP in order to reduce inflation by 1 percent.

Many economists, and certainly many critics of the Fed's policies, feel that this was too high a price to pay. Others argue that maintaining inflation at double-digit levels would have seriously eroded economic performance, and they speculate that inflation at such high rates is unstable, leading to pressures for continued increases in the rate. They argue that, sooner or later, the Fed had to act to reduce the inflation.

This debate leaves open the questions of whether a more gradualist policy might have led to a permanent reduction in inflation at a smaller cumulative cost and whether employing other policies (such as

incomes policies) in conjunction with monetary restraint could have reduced the costs of attaining the
desired goal of lower inflation.

Perhaps the most important lesson that arises
from recognition of the high costs of reducing inflation is, that "an ounce of prevention is worth a
pound of cure":

**Given the benefits that arise from low inflation
and the high costs involved in reducing inflation, policymakers are well advised to avoid
any major increases in the inflation rate whenever possible.**

Relatively Stable Inflation: 1983–1989

After falling to 3.2 percent in 1983, the U.S. inflation
rate stabilized at around 4 percent for a number of
years. This was also a time of low inflation worldwide. How is it that a relatively steady inflation rate
persisted for several years with no clear tendency
toward acceleration or deceleration?

During most of this period there was a recessionary gap, significant in the early stages and
declining as the period progressed. Why then did
inflation not decelerate further? The answer seems
to be that the weak demand forces that worked
toward deceleration were swamped by the forces
of expectational inflation and random supply-side
shocks. Since demand forces were not very important, the conditions for achieving a stable, rather
than an accelerating or decelerating, rate were fulfilled. (The deflationary pressures arising from the
recessionary gap in the early part of the period
were apparently not strong enough to induce further
falls in the inflation rate, confirming our discussion
in Chapter 28 about the asymmetry in the pressures arising from positive output gaps and negative
ones.)

In 1986 the OPEC oil cartel collapsed, and oil
prices tumbled, as did the costs of all oil-related
products, including gasoline, fuel oil, plastics, and
fertilizers. As a result, inflation also fell sharply. The
recovery continued, and by 1987 the recessionary
gap had shrunk substantially; by some estimates it
had, in fact, become an inflationary gap. Money
supply growth had been very high in 1985 and
1986, and concern about an outbreak of demand
inflation was becoming widespread. The inflation
rate, which was close to 4.5 percent in both 1987
and 1988, rose slightly in 1989, and in 1990 it reached

6.1 percent, partly due to a brief oil-price shock
associated with Iraq's invasion of Kuwait. Although
not nearly so high as the peaks reached in the 1979–
1980 episode, this increase in inflation was widely
held to be unacceptable.

Disinflation and Recession: 1990–1992

The rising inflationary pressures that resulted in
the 6.1 percent inflation in 1990 elicited a tighter
monetary policy on the part of the Fed. In 1989
and 1990, monetary growth was quite low, and
through late 1989 and early 1990 interest rates rose.
These events served to restrict spending. This effect was reinforced by the loss of consumer confidence that was associated with hostilities in the
Middle East in 1990, and the economy went into
recession. Inflation fell sharply to 3.1 percent in
1991.

Once again restrictive policies worked in the
manner expected, and once again the debate about
the relative benefits and costs of reducing inflation
emerged. Although the fall in inflation was not nearly
so dramatic as the one that occurred in the 1980–
1982 period, neither was the recession as deep—
for example, the unemployment rate reached 10.8
percent in late 1982, and in early 1992 it was only
7.8 percent.

In 1992 the debate was intensified by two fears
stressed by critics of government policy. First, the
slow and halting recovery in 1991 and 1992 raised
worries that the recessionary gap would persist for
much longer than could be reasonably justified in
terms of the modest reductions in inflation that
were achieved. Second, the Fed's actions (accelerating growth of M1 and cuts in interest rates) in
early 1992 ignited fears that inflation would rise
if the recovery did occur, so that the costs of the
recession would have achieved little in terms of a
sustained reduction in inflation.

Those who defended the Fed's action in accelerating M1 growth argued that this action was
needed to nurture the recovery. They argued that
the situation was simply a reenactment of the reentry
problem discussed earlier (see pages 694–695 in this
chapter and also pages 662–663 in Chapter 31). The
gist of their argument was that the growth in real
income brought about by the recovery would also
lead to a growth in the demand for money balances,
and hence the growth in the money supply that was
occurring would not be so excessive as to be inflationary.

Inflation in the Future

In mid–1992 the Fed's immediate problem was to provide enough monetary ease to ensure that the fragile recovery that was underway would prove sustainable while avoiding any acceleration of inflation beyond the 4 percent to 5 percent range. Its longer-term policy remains, however, to reduce the existing inflation rate slowly so as to achieve "price stability."[17] This objective raises a number of important policy issues on which the future behavior of the economy will cast further evidence.

Can an inflation of 4 percent that is entrenched in people's expectations through a decade of inflationary experience be slowly reduced by gradually cutting the rate of monetary expansion? The advantage of such "gradualism" is that, if it can be made to work, it would largely avoid the stagflationary Phase 2 that accompanies any more dramatic attack on inflation. If gradualism does not work, so that a more drastic reduction in the rate of monetary expansion seems necessary to break entrenched expectations, how long will the stagflation phase of high unemployment and lost output last?

Is a Zero Inflation Rate Attainable?

In a static world there is no reason why the goal of price level stability should not mean just that: an unchanging price level. In a dynamic world, where relative prices are continually adjusting, a stable price

level requires that some individual prices rise while others fall.

Some economists believe that they have identified an asymmetry in price adjustments—prices seem to rise faster in the face of excess demand than they fall in the face of excess supply. (Note that this observation says nothing about equilibrium, only that the speeds of adjustment vary with the market and the direction of change.) As relative prices adjust continually to the forces of change, if prices rise faster in markets with excess demand than they fall in markets with excess supply, then the average level of all prices will drift upward. Under these circumstances the structure of the economy causes an inflationary bias on the order of 1 to 2 percent per year. This bias takes the form of a slowly shifting *SRAS* curve. In these circumstances the Fed has two choices: It can validate the inflation to hold income at its potential level, or it can refuse to validate the inflation and allow the recessionary gap to slowly open up.

Other economists, however, feel that in today's world of relatively flexible wages with declining union power, there is no reason why a fully stable price level could not be established at Y^*.

Throughout the history of economics, inflation has been recognized as a harmful phenomenon. This view was given renewed strength as a result of the worldwide experiences of high inflation rates during the 1970s and early 1980s. The resolve is there, at least in advanced industrial countries, to prevent another outbreak of rapid inflation, and, should one occur for reasons of unavoidable supply-side shocks, to prevent the inflation from continuing long enough to become firmly entrenched in people's expectations. The resolve is a matter that has been settled in the last decade; the success in continuing to fulfill this resolve is a matter to be tested in the coming decade.

---

[17] As the 1992 *Economic Report of the President* (page 47) stated, "Price stability need not literally mean a zero change in the price level, but a change that is low enough so that inflation no longer is an important factor in the economic decisions of consumers and businesses."

SUMMARY

1. Sustained price inflation will be accompanied by a closely related growth in wages and other factor costs, so that the *SRAS* curve is shifting upward. Factors that influence shifts in the *SRAS* curve can be divided into two main components: demand and expectations. Random supply-side shocks will also exert an influence.

2. The influence of demand can be expressed in terms of inflationary and recessionary gaps, which relate national income to potential income, or in terms of the difference between the actual rate of unemployment and the NAIRU.

3. With constant productivity, expectations of inflation tend to cause wage settlements that preserve the expected real wage and hence lead to nominal wage increases equal to the expected price level increases. Expectations can be based on past experience of inflation and/or on expectations of the outcome of current economic policies.

4. The initial effects of inflationary demand shocks are a rise in the price level and a rise in national income. If the inflation is unvalidated, income returns to its potential level while the price level rises further. Monetary validation allows a demand inflation to proceed without reducing the inflationary gap.

5. If the Fed validates a continuing demand inflation, seeking to hold the inflationary gap constant, the actual rate of inflation will tend to accelerate.

6. The initial effects of inflationary supply shocks are a rise in the price level and a fall in national income. If the inflation is unvalidated, national income will slowly return to its potential level as the price level slowly falls to its pre-shock level. Monetary validation allows a sustained cost-push inflation to continue in spite of a persistent recessionary gap.

7. If the Fed wishes to stop a sustained inflation, it must reduce its rate of monetary expansion. This reduction will raise interest rates and reduce aggregate desired expenditure, eventually eliminating any inflationary gap. Although the rise in interest rates may cause a once-and-for-all upward shift in the *SRAS* curve, the rise is a necessary part of an antiinflationary policy that slows the rate of growth of the money supply, thereby stopping the outward shift of the *AD* curve.

8. The process of stopping a sustained inflation can be divided into three phases. Phase 1 consists of ending monetary validation and allowing the upward shift in the *SRAS* curve to remove any inflationary gap that does exist. In Phase 2 a recessionary gap develops as expectations of further inflation cause the *SRAS* curve to continue to shift upward even after the inflationary gap is removed. The recession that characterizes this phase will be deeper and last longer when there is a large backward-looking component to expectations than when expectations are mainly forward-looking. In Phase 3 the economy returns to full employment, sometimes aided by a once-and-for-all monetary expansion that raises the *AD* curve to the level consistent with potential income at the present price level.

TOPICS FOR REVIEW

Temporary and sustained inflation

Monetary validation of demand and supply shocks

Expectational inflation

The NAIRU

Accelerating inflation

Breaking a sustained inflation

DISCUSSION QUESTIONS

1. On what source or sources of inflation do the following statements focus attention?
   a. "Rapid growth in M2 raises fears of renewed inflation."
   b. "Wage bargains currently being negotiated in several key industries by strong British unions may cause British inflation to accelerate."
   c. "Americans have become so accustomed to 4 percent inflation that it would be difficult for the Fed to induce the transition to 1 percent inflation."
   d. "As the U.S. recovery continued, inflationary pressures seemed to be building up across the country."
   e. "Heavy borrowing by the German government to finance investment in former East Germany fuels inflation, causing the Bundesbank (the German central bank) to push up interest rates in response."

2. It has been estimated that reducing inflation by 1 percentage point in the early 1980s required a 4-percentage-point reduction of national income for one year. Use *AD* and *SRAS* curves to show why this might be so. Why might the cost in terms of lost income vary from one inflationary period to another? Are there reasons to think that the cost might be higher the longer the inflation has persisted? What might the Fed do to reduce the cost?

3. Use the *Economic Report of the President* to plot the rate of inflation and the level of unemployment since 1986. Is there any obvious relation between reductions in inflation and temporary rises in unemployment? (*Warning:* Although looking at the data is always instructive, important relations between two variables are often not revealed by simple inspection since many influencing forces are usually changing at once and because causes take time to bring their full effects.)

4. When the persistent worldwide inflation of the early 1980s was broken, the economies of many industrial countries came to rest with a relatively low inflation rate and high unemployment. People who feared the outbreak of inflation opposed even a temporary increase in the rate of monetary expansion. Use aggregate demand and aggregate supply analysis to show why some people felt that a *temporary* burst of monetary expansion might bring increases in employment without increases in inflation.

5. Look at the rates of increases of M2 and the CPI over the past three years and decide whether or not current inflation is being validated.

6. What theory or theories of inflation are suggested by each of the following quotations?
   a. Newspaper headline in 1986: "February producer prices steady—Fall in energy costs largest in 6 years."
   b. Newspaper editorial in Manchester, England: "If American unions were as strong as those in Britain, American inflationary experience would have been as disastrous as Britain's."
   c. A study issued in 1980 by the Worldwatch Institute: "The nation's spiraling inflation reflects a global depletion of physical resources and therefore cannot be cured by traditional fiscal

and monetary tools." Has the prediction in this quotation been borne out since then?

d. Article in the London *Economist*: "Oil price collapse will reduce today's inflation rate."

e. A newspaper article in October 1990: "The combination of the Kuwaiti crisis and an emerging recession is a sure recipe for worldwide stagflation."

f. A newspaper headline in May 1992: "Fed's move to cut interest rates spurs concerns about renewed inflation."

7. In an article on the harmful effects of inflation written early in the 1980s, a reporter wrote, "With the rise in mortgage interest rates to 11 percent, heaven only knows the price of what was once idealized as 'the $100,000 house.'" At the time, the inflation rate was 8 percent. Did the 11 percent interest rate represent a heavy burden of inflation on the new homeowner? What do you think the mortgage interest rate would have been if the inflation rate had been zero? Which situation would have meant a heavier real burden on the purchaser of a new house?

8. Discuss the apparent conflict between the following views. Can you suggest how they might be reconciled using aggregate demand and aggregate supply analysis?

a. "A rise in interest rates is deflationary, since breaking entrenched inflation with a tight monetary policy usually requires that interest rates rise steeply."

b. "A rise in interest rates is inflationary, since interest is a major business cost and, as with other costs, a rise in interest will be passed on by firms in terms of higher prices."

9. Whatever its initiating causes, inflation cannot persist indefinitely unless it is validated by increases in the money supply. Why is this so? Does it not imply that control of inflation is merely a matter of not allowing the money supply to rise faster than the rate of increase of real national income?

33

Employment and Unemployment

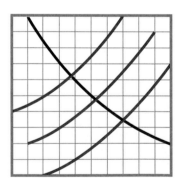

When national income changes, the volume of employment and that of unemployment change as well. Figure 23-5 on page 469 shows the course of employment and unemployment in the United States. Unemployment, which is the main subject of this chapter, follows a cyclical path, rising during periods of recession and falling in periods of business expansion. The unemployment rate does not, however, show any significant long-term trend over time.

In macroeconomics, we distinguish between the NAIRU, which you will recall is the rate of unemployment that occurs when national income is at its potential (Y^*), and the rate of cyclical unemployment, which is the unemployment associated with fluctuations of national income around its potential. The unemployed are those who are without jobs and are actively searching for jobs. We sometimes measure the unemployed as numbers of persons and sometimes as *rates,* expressed as percentages of the total labor force.

After a preliminary look at employment, we study cyclical unemployment. Then we consider the NAIRU in much more detail, asking such questions as: What types of unemployment make up the NAIRU? Why does the NAIRU change? Can government policy do anything to reduce the NAIRU?

Employment and Unemployment in the United States

Considered over the long term, the most striking features revealed by Figure 23-5 are trend increases in both total employment and the total labor force. Over the decades, the economy has generated a net increase in new jobs fast enough to employ the rising number of potential workers. As a result the unemployment *rate*—which is the difference between the labor force and employment, expressed as a percentage of the labor force—has not risen decade by decade.

The unemployment rate does fluctuate from year to year, because changes in the labor force are not exactly matched by changes in employment.

Changes in Total Employment

On the supply side, the labor force has expanded virtually every year since the end of the Second World War in 1945. The causes have included a rising population, which causes increased entry into the labor force of people born in the United States 15 to 25 years previously; increased labor force participation by various groups, especially women; and immigration of working-age persons.

On the demand side, many existing jobs are destroyed every year, and many new jobs are created. Economic growth causes some sectors of the economy to decline and others to expand. Jobs are lost in the sectors that are contracting. Jobs are created in the expanding sectors. Additionally, even in stable industries, many firms die and many new firms are born. The net increase in employment is the difference between all the jobs that are lost and all those that are created.

In most years, enough new jobs have been created both to replace the old jobs that are destroyed and to provide jobs for the increased numbers in the labor force. The result has been a net increase in employment in almost all years.

In mild recessions, often called "growth recessions," the unemployment rate increases because the net creation of new jobs, though positive, falls below the net increase in the size of the labor force. Only in relatively severe recessions does the actual number of jobs decrease.

Changes in Unemployment

In the early 1980s worldwide unemployment rose to high levels. The unemployment rate remained high in many advanced industrial countries and only began to come down, and then very slowly, during the latter half of the decade. U.S. experience reflected these international developments rather closely. From a high of 9.5 percent in 1982–1983, the U.S. unemployment rate fell to 5.2 percent in 1989, a point very close to the NAIRU. It then rose through most of 1990 and 1991, reaching nearly 8 percent by mid-1992.

Consequences of Unemployment

Unemployment is a social "bad" just as much as output is a social "good." The harm caused by unemployment is measured in terms of the output lost to the whole economy and the harm done to the individuals who are unemployed.

Lost output. Every unemployed person is someone willing and able to work but unable to find a job. The unemployed are valuable resources whose potential output is wasted. The physical counterpart

of unemployment is the recessionary gap—potential GDP that is not produced. According to an empirical relation sometimes called "Okun's law," for every percentage point that unemployment rises above the NAIRU, output falls by about 2.5 percentage points below potential. In a world of scarcity with many unsatisfied wants, this loss represents a serious waste.

Personal costs. Many social policies designed to alleviate the short-term economic consequences of unemployment have been instituted since the 1930s. Being unemployed, even for some substantial period of time, is no longer the economic disaster that it once was. But the longer-term effects of high unemployment rates, in terms of the disillusioned who have given up trying to make it within the system and who contribute to social unrest, should be a matter of serious concern to the haves as well as the have-nots. The case for concern about high unemployment has been eloquently put by Princeton economist Alan Blinder:

> A high-pressure economy provides opportunities, facilitates structural change, encourages inventiveness and innovation, *and* opens doors for society's underdogs. . . . All these promote the social cohesion and economic progress that make democratic mixed capitalism such a wonderful system when it works well. A low-pressure economy slams the doors shut, breeds a bunker mentality that resists change, stifles productivity growth, and fosters both inequality and mean-spirited public policy. All this makes reducing high unemployment a political, economic, and moral challenge of the highest order.[1]

Kinds of Unemployment

For purposes of study, the unemployed are classified in various ways. They can be grouped by personal characteristics, such as age, sex, degree of skill or education, or ethnic group. They can also be classified by geographical location, by occupation, by the duration of unemployment, or by the reasons for their unemployment.

In this chapter we are concerned mainly with the reasons for unemployment. Although it is not always possible to say why a particular person does not

---

[1] Alan S. Blinder, "The Challenge of High Unemployment," *American Economic Review,* 78, 2 (1988), p. 1.

have a job, it is often possible to gain some idea of the total number of people unemployed for each major cause.

In Chapter 23 (see Box 23-2) we noted that the recorded figures for unemployment may significantly understate or overstate the numbers who are actually willing to work at the existing set of wage rates. We noted that overstatement arises because the measured figure for unemployment includes people who are not interested in work but who say they are in order to collect unemployment benefits. We also noted that understatement arises because people who would like to work but have ceased to believe that suitable jobs are available voluntarily withdraw from the labor force. Although these people are not measured in the survey of unemployment (which requires that people actively look for work), they are unemployed in the sense that they would accept a job if one were available at going wage rates. People in this category are referred to as **discouraged workers**. They have voluntarily withdrawn from the labor market, not because they do not want to work, but because they believe that they cannot find a job given current labor market conditions.

In Chapter 23 we also distinguished three types of unemployment: *cyclical, frictional,* and *structural.* Both frictional and structural unemployment exist even when national income is at its potential level, and hence there is neither a recessionary gap nor an inflationary gap. Together these two types of unemployment make up the NAIRU. We first study cyclical unemployment and then the NAIRU.

Cyclical Unemployment

As we saw in Chapter 23, the term *cyclical unemployment* refers to unemployment that occurs whenever total demand is insufficient to purchase all of the economy's potential output, causing a recessionary gap in which actual output is less than potential. Cyclical unemployment can be measured as the number of persons currently employed minus the number of persons who would be employed at potential income. *When cyclical unemployment is zero, the number of unfilled jobs currently available is equal to the number of persons unemployed.* In this situation, all existing unemployment is either structural or frictional, and the rate of unemployment is the NAIRU.

National income theory seeks to explain cyclical unemployment.

People who are cyclically unemployed are normally presumed to be **involuntarily unemployed** in the sense that they are willing to work at the going wage rate, but jobs are not available. The persistence of cyclical unemployment poses a challenge to economic theory.

To see what is involved in this challenge, suppose that aggregate demand is fluctuating, causing national income to fluctuate around its potential level. This fluctuation will cause the demands for labor in each of the economy's labor markets to fluctuate as well, rising in booms and falling in slumps. If all of the labor markets had fully flexible wage rates, wages would fluctuate to keep quantity demanded in each individual market equal to quantity supplied in that market. We would observe cyclical fluctuations in employment, and in the wage rate, but no changes in unemployment. Again, if labor markets had fully flexible wage rates, in recessions the demand for labor would fall, and wage rates would fall as well. On the one hand, some people would withdraw from the labor force, being unwilling to work at the lower wage. On the other hand, firms would cut the number they employ by less than they would have if the wage rate had not changed. The labor market would then reach equilibrium at a lower wage and a lower volume of employment but with no involuntary unemployment. In booms the demand for labor would rise, causing the wage rate to rise. This would attract more workers into the labor force while reducing the quantity of labor demanded by firms below what it would have been if wage rates had not changed.

Employment and the labor force would vary procyclically (i.e., rising in booms and falling in slumps), but there would be no significant amounts of involuntary unemployment. The behavior just outlined is shown for a typical labor market in Figure 33-1.

The hypothetical situation we have just described is not what we actually observe. Instead, we see cyclical fluctuations, not only in employment, but also in unemployment. Furthermore, the changes in wage rates that do occur are insufficient to equate demand and supply, as is shown in Figure 33-2. Unemployment exceeds the NAIRU in slumps and is below it in booms. Although wages do tend to vary over the cycle, the fluctuations are not sufficient to remove all cyclical variations in unemployment. Why is this so?

FIGURE 33-1
Employment and Wages in a Single Competitive Labor Market

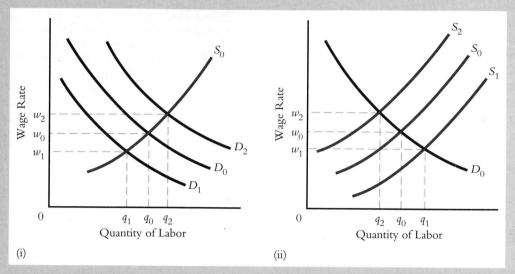

In a perfectly competitive labor market, wages and employment fluctuate in the same direction when demand fluctuates and in opposite directions when supply fluctuates; in both cases there is no involuntary unemployment. The figure shows a single perfectly competitive market for one type of labor. In part (i), the demand curves D_1, D_2, and D_0 are the demands for this market when there is a slump, a boom, and when aggregate income is at its potential level. As demand rises from D_1 to D_0 to D_2, wages rise from w_1 to w_0 to w_2, and employment rises from q_1 to q_0 to q_2. At no time, however, is there any involuntary unemployment.

In part (ii), the supply of labor fluctuates from S_1 to S_0 to S_2, and wages fluctuate from w_1 to w_0 to w_2. In this case, wages fall when employment rises, and vice versa, but again there is no involuntary unemployment.

Two types of explanation have been advanced over the years. The line of explanation that we consider first is associated with those who are sometimes called *new classical* economists. The explanation assumes that labor markets are always in equilibrium in the sense that quantity demanded is continually equated with quantity supplied.

New Classical Theories

One new classical explanation of cyclical fluctuations in employment assumes that they are caused by fluctuations in the willingness of people to supply their labor, as shown in part (ii) of Figure 33-1. If the supply curves of labor fluctuate cyclically, this will lead to cyclical variations in employment. This explanation of cyclical behavior in the labor market has two problems. First, the wage will tend to rise in slumps and fall in booms, which is not what we observe. Second, there will still be no systematic cyclical *unemployment,* since labor markets always clear, leaving everyone who wishes to work actually working. Supply-induced fluctuations in employment form

part of the basis of what is called real business cycle theory, which is discussed in Box 33-1 (pages 708–709).

A second line of explanation lies in errors on the part of workers and employers in predicting the course of the price level over the business cycle. To see the argument, start by assuming that each of the economy's markets is in equilibrium, that there is full employment, that prices are stable, and that the actual and the expected rates of inflation are zero. Now suppose the government increases the money supply by 5 percent. People find themselves with unwanted money balances, which they seek to spend. For simplicity, assume that the increased money supply leads to an increase in desired expenditure on all commodities; the demand for each commodity shifts to the right, and all prices, being competitively determined, rise. Individual decision makers see their selling prices go up and mistakenly interpret the increase as a rise in their own relative price. The reason is that they expect the overall inflation rate to be zero. Firms will produce more,

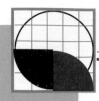

Box 33-1

Real Business Cycle Theory

As Professor Alan Stockman of the University of Rochester states, "The purpose of real business cycle (RBC) theory is to explain aggregate fluctuations in business cycles without reference to monetary policy."*

Real business cycle research has evolved from an attempt to explain cyclical fluctuations in the context of models in which equilibrium prevails at all times. In this sense, the models can be seen as a further extension of the traditional monetarist and new classical approaches. The researchers' desire to model *equilibrium* outcomes reflects their belief that the channels through which monetary policy affects real outcomes in the traditional macro model are not clearly understood. The focus on *real* disturbances reflects their skepticism about the evidence on the strength of those monetary effects in both the traditional macro model and in the new classical models.

The view of the business cycle found in RBC models is that fluctuations in national income are caused by fluctuations in the vertical *LRAS* curve.

---

* Alan C. Stockman, "Real Business Cycle Theory: A Guide, an Evaluation, and New Directions," *Federal Reserve Bank of Cleveland Monthly Review*, 1988, pp. 24–47.

In contrast, the traditional theory of fluctuations is based on fluctuations in the *AD* curve.

The explanation of cyclical fluctuations that arises in RBC models is based on the role of supply shocks originating from sources such as oil price changes, technical progress, and changes in tastes.

In this view, unemployment is always equal to the NAIRU, and it is the NAIRU itself that fluctuates.

Key Propositions and Criticisms

The RBC approach is controversial. The major claims in favor of it include the following:

1. It has been able to explain the recent behavior of the U.S. economy quite well statistically, while disavowing any role for aggregate demand fluctuations in the business cycle.

2. It suggests that an integrated approach to understanding cycles and growth may be appropriate, since both reflect forces that affect the *LRAS* curve. The distinction it makes is that some shocks are temporary (and thus have cyclical effects) and that some are permanent (and therefore affect the economy's growth).

---

being laid off. This will improve the quality of workers' output without firms' having to spend heavily to monitor workers' performance.

Economists such as George Akerlof of the University of California have observed that workers who believe that they are well treated work harder than those who believe that they are treated badly. This gives a reason for paying an efficiency wage—provided that the increased output from treating workers well covers the increased cost of doing so.

A variant of efficiency wage theory seeks to explain why firms do not cut wages during recessions. If workers feel unfairly treated when their wages are

reduced, wage reductions (at least in response to moderate recessions) may cost firms more (in lost output from unhappy employees) than they save in reduced wages.[5] If so, real wages may not fall rapidly enough to eliminate cyclical and real-wage unemployment.

The basic message of new Keynesian theories of unemployment is that competitive labor

---

[5] See Daniel Kahneman, Jack Knetsch, and Richard Thaler, "Fairness as a Constraint on Profit Seeking," *American Economic Review*, 76 (1986), pp. 728–741, for an interesting discussion, by a psychologist and two economists, of ways in which notions of fairness can influence decisions on economic matters.

3. It provides valuable insights into how shocks, regardless of their origin, spread over time to the different sectors of the economy. By abstracting from monetary issues, it is possible to address more details concerning technology and household choice involving intertemporal trade-offs between consumption, labor supply, and leisure.

4. It has focused on integrating the explanation of a number of facts that other approaches have ignored, such as seasonal and cyclical fluctuations, consumption varying less than output over the business cycle, and procyclical movements of hours worked and of average labor productivity.

Critics of the approach focus on some implausible results, express concern about its assumed underlying behavior, and argue that the phenomena mentioned in point 4 have already been given satisfactory explanations. More importantly, they are skeptical about a model in which monetary issues are completely ignored. For example, they point out that RBC models are unable to provide insights into the correlation between money and output that is at the heart of the traditional macro model. Furthermore, RBC models are unable to provide insights into empirical regularities involving nominal variables, such as prices that apparently vary less than quantities and nominal prices that vary procyclically.

Policy Implications

Because the approach gives no role to aggregate demand in influencing business cycles, it provides no role for stabilization operating through monetary and fiscal policies. However, the models predict that the use of such demand management policies can be harmful.

The basis for this prediction is the proposition in RBC models that cycles represent *efficient* responses to the shocks that are hitting the economy. Policymakers may mistakenly interpret cyclical fluctuations as deviations from full-employment equilibrium that are caused by fluctuations in aggregate demand. The policymakers may try to stabilize output and thereby distort the maximizing decisions made by households and firms. In turn, this distortion will cause the responses to the real shocks (as opposed to nominal, monetary shocks) to be inefficient.

Although only a minority of economists espouse these models as complete or even reasonable descriptions of the business cycle, and thus only a minority take seriously the strict implications for policy, many accept the view that real disturbances can play an important role in business cycles.

markets cannot be relied on to eliminate unemployment by equating current demand for labor with current supply, and, as a result, unemployment will rise and fall as the demand for labor rises and falls over the cycle.

The NAIRU

We now turn to a consideration of the NAIRU which, as we have seen, is composed of frictional and structural unemployment.

Frictional Unemployment

As we saw in Chapter 23, *frictional unemployment* results from the normal turnover of labor. An important source of frictional unemployment is young people who enter the labor force and look for jobs. Another source is people who leave their jobs. Some may quit because they are dissatisfied with the type of work or their working conditions; others may be fired. Whatever the reason, they must search for new jobs, which takes time. Persons who are unemployed while searching for jobs are said to be frictionally unemployed, or, alternatively, in *search unemployment*.

The normal turnover of labor would cause frictional unemployment to persist, even if the economy were at potential income and the structure of jobs in terms of skills, industries, occupations, and location were unchanging.

Box 33-2, which discusses search unemployment in more detail, shows that the distinction between voluntary and involuntary unemployment is not always as clear as it might at first seem.

Is Frictional Unemployment Voluntary?

Some frictional unemployment is clearly voluntary. For example, a worker may know of an available job but may not accept it so she can search for a better one. The new classical view regards all frictional unemployment as voluntary. Critics of that view argue that many frictionally unemployed workers are involuntarily unemployed because they lost their jobs through no fault of their own (e.g., their factories may have closed down) and because they have not yet located a specific case of jobs they believe to be available *somewhere* and for which they believe they are qualified.

Structural Unemployment

Structural adjustments can cause unemployment. When the pattern of demand for goods changes, the pattern of the demand for labor changes. Until labor adjusts fully, *structural unemployment* develops. Such unemployment may be defined as unemployment caused by a mismatch between the structure of the labor force—in terms of skills, occupations, industries, or geographical locations—and the structure of the demand for labor.

Natural Causes

Changes that accompany economic growth shift the structure of the demand for labor. Demand rises in such expanding areas as North Carolina and falls in declining areas such as Michigan and parts of New England. Demand rises for workers with certain skills, such as computer programming and electronics engineering, and falls for workers with other skills, such as stenography, assembly line work, and middle management. According to the 1992 *Economic Report of the President:* "... a gradual but significant shift toward high-skilled jobs has taken place. The evolutionary shift toward service-sector employment and the restructuring within all industries in response to technological change has favored workers with more years of schooling." To meet changing demands, the structure of the labor force must change. Some existing workers can retrain and some new entrants can acquire fresh skills, but the transition is often difficult, especially for experienced workers whose skills become economically obsolete. Structural unemployment occurs when such adjustments are slow enough that severe pockets of unemployment develop in areas, industries, and occupations in which the demand for factors of production is falling faster than the supply.

One of the more dramatic recent structural changes in the economy has been in the organization of the firm. Manufacturing firms used to be organized much like an army, with a pyramidal command structure. Most key strategic decisions were made near the top and lesser ones concerning implementation at lower levels. This structure required an array of middle-level managers who passed information upward to the top level and downward to the production level and who made various secondary decisions themselves. Recent changes pioneered among Japanese firms have led to a much looser organization with much more local autonomy among the subsections of the firm. As a result, large numbers of middle managers' jobs have been made redundant. They find themselves on the labor market at middle age and with many of their skills rendered obsolete.[6]

Increases in international competition can have effects similar to those of economic growth and change. As the geographical distribution of world production changes, so does the composition of production and of labor demand in any one country. Labor adapts to such shifts by changing jobs, skills, and locations, but until the transition is complete, structural unemployment exists.

Structural unemployment will increase if there is either an increase in the speed at which the

---

[6] These changes are discussed in detail in such books as Robert Reich, *The Work of Nations* (New York: Knopf, 1991) and J. Womack, D. Jones, and D. Roos, *The Machine That Changed the World* (New York: Maxwell MacMillan, 1990), both of which can be read without an in-depth knowledge of economic theory.

Box 33-2

Search Unemployment

Frictional unemployment is clearly involuntary if the job seeker has not yet found a job for which his or her training and experience are suitable. Frictional unemployment is voluntary if the unemployed person is aware of available jobs for which she is suited but is searching for better options. But how should we classify an unemployed woman who refuses to accept a job at a lower skill level than the one for which she feels she is qualified? What if she turns down a job for which she is trained because she hopes to get a higher wage offer for a similar job from another employer?

In one sense people in search unemployment are voluntarily unemployed, because they could almost always find some job; in another sense they are involuntarily unemployed, because they have not yet succeeded in finding the job for which they feel they are suited at a rate of pay that they believe is attainable.

Workers do not have perfect knowledge of all available jobs and rates of pay, and they may be able to gain information only by searching the market. Faced with this uncertainty, it may be sensible for them to refuse a first job offer, for the offer may prove to be a poor one in light of further market information. Too much search—for example, holding off while being supported by others in the hope of finding a job better than a job for which one is really suited—is an economic waste. Thus, search unemployment is a grey area: Some of it is useful, and some of it is wasteful.

It is socially desirable for there to be sufficient search unemployment to give unemployed people time to find an available job that makes the best use of their skills.

How long it pays for people to remain in search unemployment depends on the economic costs of being unemployed. By lowering the costs of being unemployed, unemployment insurance tends to increase the amount of search unemployment. This may or may not increase economic efficiency, depending on whether or not it induces people to search beyond the point at which they acquire new and valuable information about the labor market.

---

structure of the demand for labor is changing or a decrease in the speed at which labor is adapting to these changes.

Policy Causes

Government policies can influence the speed with which labor markets adapt to changes. Some countries, such as the United Kingdom and Canada, have adopted policies that discourage movement among regions, industries, and occupations. These policies tend to raise structural unemployment. Others, such as Sweden, have done the reverse and have encouraged workers to adapt to change. Partly for this reason, Sweden's unemployment rates were well below the European and North American norms during the 1980s.

Policies that discourage firms from replacing labor with machines may protect employment over the short term. If, however, such policies lead to the decline of an industry because it cannot compete effectively with innovative foreign competitors, serious structural unemployment can result in the long run.

Minimum-wage laws can cause structural unemployment by pricing low-skilled labor out of the market. As explained in Chapter 18, effective minimum-wage laws have two effects when they are imposed on competitive markets: They reduce employment of the unskilled, and they raise the wages of the unskilled who retain their jobs. In the United States today, however, minimum wages are so low in most states that they probably have little effect on wage rates and employment.

Is Structural Unemployment Voluntary?

According to the new classical view, all structural unemployment is voluntary. Say, for example, that there is an excess supply of skilled autoworkers and an excess demand for unskilled dishwashers. If an unemployed autoworker does not take one of the available jobs as a dishwasher, he is voluntarily deciding to stay unemployed in the hopes of finding a job that uses his skills.

Critics reply: "But what if it is the other way around?" What if, as is often the case, there is an excess supply of unskilled workers and an excess demand for those with skills? The unemployed dishwasher cannot accept a job as a computer programmer; his skills do not equip him for this. This mismatching between the skills of those unemployed and the skills required by the available jobs cannot easily be removed by individual actions of the unemployed dishwashers, nor can it be blamed on their union, since they have none.

The Relationship Between Frictional and Structural Unemployment

As with many distinctions, the one between structural and frictional unemployment becomes blurred at the margin. In a sense, structural unemployment is really long-term frictional unemployment. Consider a change that requires labor to move from one sector to another. If the reallocation occurs quickly, we call the unemployment *frictional;* if the reallocation occurs slowly, we call the unemployment *structural.*

The major characteristic of both frictional and structural unemployment is that there are as many unfilled vacancies as there are unemployed persons.

In the case of pure frictional unemployment, the job vacancy and the searcher are matched. The only problem is that the searcher has not yet located the vacancy. In the case of structural unemployment, the job vacancy and the searcher are mismatched in one or more relevant characteristics, such as occupation, industry, location, or skill requirements.

Experience

In practice, structural and fractional unemployment cannot be separated, and they are shown together by the amount and nature of unemployment when income is at its potential level.

As of 1993, the last year for which income was close to potential was 1989. Although data for later years are available, this peak year of the economic expansion represents the best one in which to find characteristics of structural plus frictional unemployment.

Figure 33-3 shows that education confers a twin advantage. As we saw earlier, not only does one's income expectancy rise with education, but the probability of suffering unemployment falls dramatically. Among both men and women, high school dropouts have the highest unemployment rates, high school graduates the next highest, and college graduates the lowest.

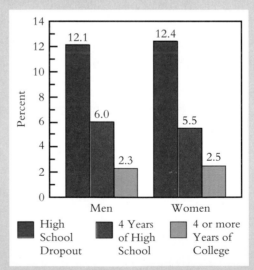

FIGURE 33-3
Unemployment Rate by Educational Attainment, 1989

Unemployment rates are lower among people with higher levels of education. Among both men and women unemployment rates for high school dropouts are over twice as high as the rates for high school graduates, which in turn are over twice as high as rates for college graduates. (*Source: Economic Report of the President,* 1992.)

Figure 33-4 shows that unemployment is very high among the young. This unemployment is partly frictional in that young people tend to change jobs more often than older people, and partly structural in that the demand for less experienced and less trained workers has been falling relative to the demand for more experienced and better trained workers. Married men tend to have the best experience with respect to unemployment, whereas women who maintain families fare relatively poorly—in contrast to women in general, who do about as well as men in general.

Why Does the NAIRU Change?

We have noted that structural unemployment can increase because the pace of change accelerates or the pace of adjustment to change slows down. An increase in the rate of growth, for example, usually speeds up the rate at which the structure of the demand for labor is changing. The adaptation of labor to the changing structure of demand may be slowed by such diverse factors as a decline in education and

new regulations that make it harder for workers in a given occupation to take new jobs in other areas or occupations. Any of these changes will cause the NAIRU to rise. Changes in the opposite direction will cause the NAIRU to fall.

Demographic Changes

Because people usually try several jobs before settling into one for a longer period of time, young or inexperienced workers have higher unemployment rates than experienced workers. The proportion of inexperienced workers in the labor force rose significantly as the baby boom generation of the 1950s entered the labor force in the 1970s and 1980s, along with an unprecedented number of women who elected to work outside the home. It is estimated that these demographic changes added nearly a percentage point to the NAIRU. Since birthrates were low in the 1960s and a further increase in the percentage of women entering the labor force is unlikely, some demographically induced fall in this type of unemployment has been occurring recently and will continue over the 1990s.

FIGURE 33-4
Variations in Unemployment Rates, 1989

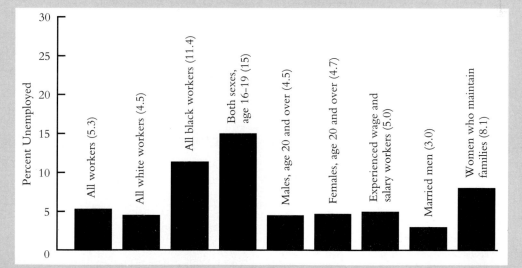

Unemployment is unevenly divided among sex, race, and skill groups. The overall rate of 5.3 percent concealed large variations among the unemployment rates for different groups. Blacks and women who maintain families had unemployment rates well above the national average, whereas married men were well below the national average. (*Source: Economic Report of the President, 1992.*)

Although the NAIRU, and youth unemployment in particular, should fall as the baby boom generation passes on to middle age, many observers worry about the long-term consequences for some individuals. Learning through on-the-job experience is a critical part of developing marketable labor skills, and those who suffered prolonged unemployment during their teens and twenties have been denied that experience early in their working careers. These workers may have little option later in life but to take temporary jobs at low pay and with little future job security.

The large increase in female participation rates and the related increase in the number of households with more than one income earner have also affected the NAIRU. In 1950 only 34 percent of women 16 years and older were in the labor force; in 1970 the figure was 43 percent; by 1990 it had jumped to 57 percent. When both husband and wife work, it is possible for one to support both while the other looks for "a really good job" rather than accepting the first job offer that comes along. This can increase recorded unemployment while not inflicting hardship on those involved.

Wage and Price Rigidity

Some research suggests that the speed with which wages and prices adjust to changing market conditions may have slowed in the 1970s and 1980s. Anything that slows the speed of adjustment to the economy's ever-changing conditions will create a larger pool of structural unemployment. The decline of unions and the willingness of many workers to accept wage cuts when their employers get into serious difficulties may increase wage flexibility in the future—particularly compared to many European countries, where wage structures are relatively insensitive to shorter-term fluctuations in business conditions. If so, this should reduce the NAIRU.

Hysteresis

Recent models of unemployment show that the size of the NAIRU can be influenced by the *size* of the actual current rate of unemployment.[7] Such models get their name from the Greek word *hysteresis,* implying "lagged effect."

One mechanism that can lead to hysteresis in labor markets has already been noted. It arises from the importance of experience and on-the-job training. Suppose, for example, that a period of recession causes a significant group of new entrants to the labor force to have unusual difficulty in obtaining their first jobs. As a result, the unlucky group will be slow to acquire the important skills that workers generally learn in their first jobs. When demand increases again, this group of workers will be at a disadvantage relative to workers with normal histories of experience, and the unlucky group may have unemployment rates that will be higher than average. Thus, the NAIRU will be higher than it would have been, had there been no recession.

Another force that can cause such effects is emphasized by commentators in Western Europe, which has a heavily unionized labor force. In times of high unemployment people who are currently employed (insiders) may use their bargaining power to ensure that their own status is maintained and prevent new entrants to the labor force (outsiders) from competing effectively. In an *insider-outsider* model of this type, a period of prolonged, high unemployment—whatever its initial cause—will tend to become "locked in." If outsiders are denied access to the labor market, their unemployment will fail to exert downward pressure on wages, and the NAIRU will tend to rise.

The empirical importance of hysteresis in the United States has not been established. In some countries in Western Europe, however, there is evidence that hysteresis may be quite important.

Increasing Structural Change

The amount of resource reallocation across industries and areas increased in the mid-1970s and appears to be carrying on through the 1980s and 1990s. In part, this is the result of the increasing integration of the U.S. economy with the rest of the world and the globalization of world markets. Most observers feel that this integration has been beneficial overall. One less fortunate consequence, however, is that U.S. labor markets are increasingly affected by changes in demand and supply conditions anywhere in the world—changes that require adjustments throughout the world's trading nations.

---

[7] See, for example, Olivier Blanchard and Lawrence Summers, "Hysteresis and the European Unemployment Problem," *NBER Macroeconomics Annual* (1986), pp. 15–78.

The following numerous structural changes have created a continuing need for rapid adjustments over the past few decades: increases in the demand for food because of the failure of agricultural industries in Eastern Europe; increases in the supply of agricultural products owing to the green revolution in less-developed countries and heavy agricultural subsidization in the European Community (EC) of Western Europe; enormous OPEC-induced increases in the price of oil in the 1970s and early 1980s, followed by almost equally precipitous declines in the mid-1980s that carried through into the 1990s; the rise of Japanese industrial power, including its challenge to the integrated U.S.-Canada auto industry; the communications revolution, leading to the decentralization of industry, with components produced in various countries and assembled in others; robotization, which increased industrial productivity and reduced the demand for assembly line workers; the growth of knowledge-intensive industries that require highly educated work forces and that can be freely movable geographically; the globalization of competition, with fewer and fewer domestic markets that are sheltered by natural or artificial barriers; the changes in the organization of firms; the decline of employment in manufacturing; and the enormous growth in service employment. Although evidence is difficult to obtain, some observers argue that the increasing pace and the changing nature of technological change since the mid-1970s has contributed to an increase in the level of structural unemployment.

Future Outlook

Certain factors may work to reduce NAIRU in the future. First, the proportion of youths and women newly entering the labor force will diminish as the baby boom generation ages and the female participation rate stabilizes. Second, educational systems in some or all states may be revamped to give students better job-related training. Third, governments may become more aware of the importance of structural changes in the economy and of the need for policies to encourage rather than inhibit adaptability and flexibility in the economy. In spite of these favorable tendencies, however, structural unemployment could rise if the demand for unskilled workers declines fast enough as a result of ongoing technological change. This could lead to increased structural unemployment among the young, the unskilled, and those with only high school educations.

Reducing Unemployment

Other things being equal, all governments would like to reduce unemployment. The questions are: "Can it be done?" and "If so, at what cost?" Some points of caution concerning policies directed at structural unemployment and other consequences of structural change are given in Box 33-3.

Cyclical Unemployment

We do not need to say much more about cyclical unemployment, because its control is the subject of stabilization policy, which we have studied in several earlier chapters. A major recession that occurs because of natural causes can be countered by monetary and fiscal policy to reduce cyclical unemployment.

There is controversy about how much the government can and should do in this respect. Advocates of stabilization policy call for expansionary fiscal and monetary policies to reduce such gaps, at least when they last for sustained periods of time. Advocates of a hands-off policy say that normal market adjustments can be relied on to remove such gaps and that well-intentioned government policy will only make things worse. They call for setting simple rules for monetary and fiscal policy that would make discretionary stabilization policy impossible. This matter was discussed in detail at the end of Chapter 28.

Whatever may be argued in principle, policymakers have not yet totally abandoned such stabilization measures in practice. Persistent slumps such as the one that beset the U.S. economy in 1990–1992 still result in changes in monetary and fiscal policy designed to provide stimulus for the recovery phase.

The mid-1970s and late 1980s saw the emergence of *policy-induced* cyclical unemployment. It occurred when the government's anti-inflation policy led to drastic contractionary policies that opened up large recessionary gaps. As we saw in Chapter 32, a temporary bout of cyclical unemployment was the price of reducing inflation.

Frictional Unemployment

The turnover that causes frictional unemployment is an inevitable part of the functioning of the economy.

Box 33-3

Industrial Change: An Economist's Cautionary Tale *

The audience hushed as the members of the government's investigating commission filed into the room. The chief forecasting wizard (behind his back, some called him the economic soothsayer) began his report: "I have identified beyond reasonable doubt the underlying trends now operating," he declared to the expectant audience. "The nation's leading industry, industry X, is in a state of decline. From its current position of employing close to 50 percent of our work force, it will, within the duration of one lifetime, employ only 3 percent."

"Over 40 percent of the nation's jobs destroyed within one lifetime!" proclaimed the newspaper headlines.

"Where can new jobs possibly come from at so rapid a pace?" asked a labor leader.

"The government must protect industry X; we just cannot let all these jobs go down the tubes," argued an employer.

"Perhaps we should identify and promote new 'sunrise industries,'" said a senior bureaucrat. Indeed, it had been widely believed that a new high-tech product, product Z, would become the wave of a future new transportation revolution. A call went out for subsidies and tax breaks to back its development.

"Is there any hope that the private sector might provide the new jobs?" someone asked.

"Possibly," said a junior economist, more out of desperation than hope, "the new product Y that is being produced by a few people in backyard sheds might grow to be a significant employer."

He was immediately pounced on by a pride of self-proclaimed realistic thinkers. "Product Y! It's noisy, it's smelly, and it's a plaything for the rich. Surely *it* will never provide significant employment."

All of the economic facts in the above tale are true; only the government commission and the policy initiatives are fictitious.

The country was the United States. The time was 1900. Industry X, the employer of close to 50 percent of the work force, was agriculture. Product Z, the sunrise industry, was the large, powered, lighter-than-air craft known as the zeppelin. Product Y, the scorned plaything of the rich, was the automobile.

The decline of some traditional industries is always a cause for concern. Some of them are suffering a temporary decline, and some are declining permanently. In either event, the hardships on those losing their jobs are severe. The tale just told has a serious message. Here are a few of the lessons that can be gained from comparing the U.S. economy in 1900 and in 1990.

First, the economy is constantly changing. Indeed, the motto of any market economy could be that "nothing is permanent." New products appear continually; others disappear. At the early stage of a

---

* Copyright 1984 by R. G. Lipsey and D. D. Purvis. Reprinted and adapted by permission of the *Financial Post*.

To the extent that it is caused by ignorance, increasing the knowledge of workers about market opportunities may help. But such measures have a cost, and that cost has to be balanced against the benefits.

Some frictional unemployment is an inevitable part of the learning process. New entrants have to try jobs to see which are suitable, and that leads to a high turnover rate among the young and hence high frictional unemployment.

Unemployment insurance is one method of helping people cope with unemployment. Certainly, it has reduced significantly the human costs of the bouts with unemployment that are inevitable in a changing society. Nothing, however, is without cost.

new product, total demand is low, costs of production are high, and many small firms are each trying to get ahead of their competitors by finding the twist that appeals to consumers or finding the technique that slashes costs. Sometimes new products never get beyond that phase; they prove to be passing fads. Others, however, do become items of mass consumption.

Successful firms in growing industries buy up, merge with, or otherwise eliminate their less successful rivals. Simultaneously, their costs fall, owing to scale economies. Competition drives prices down along with costs. Eventually, at the mature stage, a few giant firms often control the industry. They become large, conspicuous, and important parts of the nation's economy. Sooner or later, new products arise to erode the position of the established giants. Demand falls off, and unemployment occurs as the few firms run into financial difficulties.

A large, sick, declining industry may appear to many as a national failure and a disgrace. At any moment, however, firms can be found in all phases—from small firms in new industries to giant firms in declining industries. Large, declining industries are as much a natural part of a healthy, changing economy as large, stable industries and small, growing ones.

Second, the policy of shoring up the declining industries of the 1990s could be just as destructive of our living standards as the policy of protecting the agricultural sector from decline in 1900 would

have been. (Policies that ease the human cost of the adjustment are not, however, in this category.)

Third, to tell where the new employment will come from requires the kind of crystal ball that our young economist would have needed in 1900 to stick by his wild guess of identifying the new plaything of the rich as the massive automobile industry 30 years later. Economists are continually being asked: "Where will the new employment come from?" The answer "we don't know" is *wrongly* taken to mean "it won't come." In the past, the new jobs have come, and we see no new, identifiable forces that would prevent their coming in the future. For example, in the course of the current recovery, many people gaining employment are starting in *new* jobs—jobs with firms and in locations that did not exist or would not have been predicted even 5 years ago.

Fourth, picking winners and backing them with government policy is a likely way to waste public funds and inhibit the development of the real winners. People risking their own money and diversifying risks over many ventures are probably a better route to employment creation than governments that risk taxpayers' money, mesmerized by fads and fashion.

Fifth, the industrial policy that is needed is one that encourages private initiatives and risk taking. Small businesses are often, if not always, the route to the creation of new employment. Risk taking and the growth of small firms should not be discouraged by such things as complicated regulatory rules and tax laws.

Although unemployment insurance alleviates the suffering caused by some kinds of unemployment, it can itself contribute to unemployment in that it encourages search unemployment, as we have already observed.

Supporters of unemployment insurance emphasize its benefits. Critics emphasize its costs. As with

any policy, a rational assessment of the value of unemployment insurance requires a balancing of its undoubted benefits against its undoubted costs. Many U.S. citizens believe that when this calculation is made, the benefits greatly exceed the costs, although many also recognize the scope for reform of certain aspects of the program.

Reforming unemployment insurance. Many provisions have been added over the years to the unemployment insurance (UI) scheme to focus it more on those in general need and to reduce its effect of raising the unemployment rate. For example, workers must have lost their job through no fault of their own to be eligible for UI. They must also be actively seeking employment and must not turn down a suitable offer.

More recently, *experience rating* has sought to distribute the costs more in proportion to the benefits. The old system, under which all firms paid the same UI tax, implicitly subsidized those who caused most unemployment and taxed most heavily those who caused least unemployment. Under experience rating, firms with histories of sizable layoffs pay more than those with better layoff records.

The United States has held the period over which UI benefits are paid below that of most other industrial companies. Although doing so reduces the benefit to those in genuine need, the evidence suggests that increasing the period of time over which benefits are paid tends to increase the period of time over which people typically remain unemployed. Evidence quoted in the 1992 *Economic Report of the President* (page 107) suggests, first, that an additional week of available benefits will increase the expected duration of unemployment by "up to half a week" and, second, that the longer the benefit period, the less is the likelihood that workers will shift to other industries while they are unemployed.

Structural Unemployment

The reallocation of labor among occupations, industries, skill categories, and regions that gives rise to structural unemployment is an inevitable part of growth. There are two basic approaches to reducing structural unemployment: First, try to arrest the changes that accompany growth, and, second, accept the changes and try to speed up the adjustments. Throughout history, labor and management have advocated, and governments have tried, both approaches.

Resisting change. Since the beginning of the Industrial Revolution, workers have often resisted the introduction of new techniques to replace the older techniques at which they were skilled. This is understandable. New techniques often destroy the value of the knowledge and experience of workers skilled in the displaced techniques. Older workers may not even get a chance to start over with the new technique. Employers may prefer to hire younger persons who will learn the new skills faster than older workers who are set in their ways of thinking. From society's point of view, new techniques are beneficial because they are a major source of economic growth. From the point of view of the workers they displace, new techniques can be an unmitigated disaster.

Here are two characteristic ways in which economic change has been resisted. First, a declining industry may be supported with public funds. If the market would support an output of X, but subsidies are used to support an output of $2X$, jobs are provided for, say, half the industry's labor force, who would otherwise become unemployed and have to find jobs elsewhere. Second, change may be accepted but agreement reached to continue to employ workers who would otherwise be made redundant by the new technology. Both these policies are attractive to the people who would otherwise become unemployed. It may be a long time before they can find other jobs, and when they do, their skills may not turn out to be highly valued in their new occupations.

Over the long term, however, such policies run into increasing difficulties. Agreements to hire unneeded workers raise costs and can hasten the decline of an industry threatened by competitive products. An industry that is declining because of economic change becomes an increasingly large burden on the public purse as economic forces become less and less favorable to its success. Sooner or later, public support is withdrawn, and an often precipitous decline then ensues.

In assessing the remedies for structural unemployment, it is important to realize that although they are not viable in the long run for the entire economy, they may be the best alternatives for the affected workers during their lifetimes.

There is often a genuine conflict between the private interest of workers threatened by structural unemployment, whose interests lie in preserving existing jobs, and the social interest served by economic growth, which raises living standards.

Aiding adjustments to change. Another policy to deal with structural change is to accept the decline of industries and the loss of specific jobs that go with it, and try to reduce the cost of adjustment for those affected. Retraining and relocation grants make movement easier and reduce structural unemployment without inhibiting economic change and growth.

Several federal schemes seek to have some impact, although the extent to which they help is debated. The Economic Dislocation and Worker Adjustment Assistance program assists displaced workers to retrain. Another program, called the Job Opportunities and Basic Skills Training program (JOBS), seeks to provide education, training, and employment to families receiving assistance for dependent children. A new program, called Jobs Training 2000, uses market-based approaches to facilitate vocational training and the transition from welfare to work and from school to work.

Conclusion

Over the years, unemployment has been regarded in many different ways. Harsh critics see it as proof that the market system is badly flawed. Reformers regard it as a necessary evil of the market system and a suitable object for government policy to reduce its incidence and its harmful effects. Others see it as overblown in importance and believe that it does not reflect any real inability of workers to obtain jobs if they really want to work.

Most government policy has followed a middle route. Fiscal and monetary policies have sought to reduce at least the most persistent of recessionary gaps, and a host of labor market policies have sought to reduce the incidence of frictional and structural unemployment. Such social policies as unemployment insurance have sought to reduce the sting of unemployment for the many who were thought to suffer from it for reasons beyond their control.

SUMMARY

1. U.S. employment and the U.S. labor force have increased along a strong upward trend throughout all of this century. The rate of unemployment has varied cyclically while showing no strong upward trend.
2. Looking at causes, it is useful to distinguish among several kinds of unemployment: (a) cyclical unemployment, which is caused by too low a level of aggregate demand; (b) frictional unemployment, which is caused by the length of time that it takes to find a first job and to move from job to job as a result of normal labor turnover; and (c) structural unemployment, which is caused by the need to reallocate resources among occupations, regions, and industries as the structure of demands and supplies change. Together, frictional unemployment and structural unemployment make up the NAIRU, which is then expressed as a percentage of the total labor force.
3. There is debate among economists regarding the causes of cyclical unemployment.
4. New classical theories look to explanations that allow the labor market to be cleared continuously. Such theories can explain cyclical variations in employment but do not predict a large group of workers who would like to work at the going wage rates but for whom jobs are not available.
5. Recent neo-Keynesian theories have focused on the long-term nature of employer-worker relationships and on the possibility that it is efficient for employers to pay wages that are above the level that would clear the labor market.

6. The NAIRU will always be positive because it takes time for labor to move between jobs both in normal turnover and in response to changes in the structure of the demand for labor. Government policies can also influence the NAIRU.

7. Unemployment insurance helps to alleviate the human suffering that is associated with inevitable unemployment. It also increases unemployment by encouraging voluntary, search unemployment.

8. Cyclical unemployment can be reduced by raising aggregate demand. Frictional and structural unemployment can be reduced by making it easier to move between jobs, by slowing down the rate of change in the economy, and by raising the cost of staying unemployed. However, in a growing, changing, economy populated by people who wish to change jobs for many reasons, it is neither possible nor desirable to reduce unemployment to zero.

TOPICS FOR REVIEW

Cyclical unemployment

Frictional unemployment

Structural unemployment

Efficiency wages

Hysteresis

The components of the NAIRU

Determinants of the size of the NAIRU

Policies to reduce the NAIRU

Policies to reduce cyclical unemployment

DISCUSSION QUESTIONS

1. Interpret the following statements from newspapers in terms of types of unemployment:
   a. "Recession hits local factory; 2,000 laid off."
   b. "A job? I've given up trying," says a mother of three.
   c. "We closed down because we could not meet the competition from Taiwan," says a local manager.
   d. "When they raised the minimum wage, I just could not afford to keep all of these retired policemen on my payroll as security guards," says the owner of a local shopping center.
   e. "What do I pay kids in my fast-food store? I pay them the minimum wage; that's what I do, and that's what all my competitors do," says the proprietor of a hamburger outlet.
   f. "Slack sales put local foundry on short time."
   g. "Of course, I could take a job as a dishwasher, but I'm trying to find something that makes use of my high school training," says a local teenager in our survey of the unemployed.
   h. "Retraining is the best reaction to the increased use of robots."

    i. "Modernization and tariff cuts may reduce textile employment."

    j. "Uneven upturn: Signs of recovery in the sunbelt, but New England is still in depression."

2. Comment on the following statements from the 1992 *Economic Report of the President:*

    a. "Service workers are less likely than manufacturing workers to become unemployed during an economic downturn."

    b. "Present projections of Federal Government defense expenditure imply substantial job dislocation over the coming years for many highly trained engineers and others employed in the defense industries...."

    c. "Workers with more classroom education often possess knowledge that is more general and can be applied to a variety of jobs...."

    d. "Low-skilled workers are more likely to work only part time and are more frequently unemployed."

    e. "Some economists have proposed that training be linked directly to the UI program."

    f. "Another option...currently being tested...offers UI recipients...their benefit entitlement on a lump-sum payment as seed capital once they have started their own business."

Is it possible to say which type of unemployment is involved in each case? Can you suggest reasons that might account for statements made about unemployment? What do you think about those statements that suggest policy changes?

3. Discuss the following views:

    a. "U.S. workers should resist automation, which is destroying their jobs," says a labor leader.

    b. "Given the fierce foreign competition, it's a case of automate or die," says an industrialist.

4. "No one needs to be out of work if he or she really wants a job; just look at the help wanted signs in many fast-food businesses and retail shops." Does the existence of the unfilled vacancies suggested in the above quotation imply that there need be no cyclical unemployment as long as workers are not excessively fussy about the kind of job they will take?

5. What theories can you suggest to explain why unemployment rates stay persistently above average for youths and below average for males over 25?

6. It is often argued that the true unemployment figure for the United States is much higher than the officially reported figure. What are possible sources of "hidden unemployment"? On the other side, are there reasons for expecting some exaggeration of the number of people who are reported as unemployed? Would the relative strength of these opposing forces change over the course of the business cycle? What would you expect if a short recession turned into a long and deep depression?

7. At a time when the U.S. unemployment rate stood at close to 9 percent, the press reported: "Skilled labor shortages plague many

firms—newspaper ads often draw few qualified workers; wages and overtime are up." What type of unemployment does this suggest is important?

8. What differences in approach toward the problem of unemployment are suggested by the following facts?

   a. In the 1960s and 1970s, Britain spent billions of dollars on subsidizing firms that would otherwise have gone out of business, in order to protect the jobs of the employees.

   b. Sweden has been a pioneer in spending large sums to retrain and to relocate displaced workers.

34

Government Budget Deficits

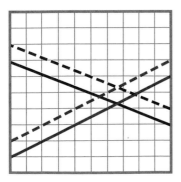

F ederal budget deficits are hardly new. Since 1940 the federal budget has been in surplus in only eight years, most recently in 1969. The budget deficits of the 1980s and early 1990s, however, were of unprecedented size for peacetime. In 1989, with the economy at potential income, the deficit was $154 billion, or 3.0 percent of GDP. In 1992 the deficit is estimated to reach $350 billion, about 5 percent of GDP. The Congressional Budget Office projects that, unless there are significant changes in policy, the budget deficit will continue to exceed 3 percent of GDP throughout the 1990s.

No single measure associated with the government has ever been the focus of so much attention and controversy in the media, on the campaign trail, and in coffeehouses and bars across the nation. Extreme views about the deficit and its potential effects are not hard to come by. At one extreme is the view that the deficit is a ticking time bomb that, if unchecked, threatens the jobs and prosperity of all U.S. citizens. At the other extreme is the view that the deficit itself is not a problem at all, and that the only threat it poses to the population arises from the possible effects of severe policy actions that might be taken on the misguided advice of deficit alarmists.

The Economics of Budget Deficits

In order to evaluate budget deficits and the policies that might be undertaken to reduce them, we need first to measure the deficit accurately and then to consider its economic effects.

Facts About the Deficit

To put the growth of the deficit in perspective, it is useful to measure it *relative* to the size of the economy, as measured by GDP. Clearly, a $200 billion deficit will have different implications in an economy in which GDP is also $200 billion than it will in an economy in which GDP is, say, $5 trillion.

The recent emergence of record federal budget deficits is shown in Figure 34-1. Part (i) shows total federal spending and total federal revenues since 1964, each as a share of GDP. The steady trend of increase in expenditures through 1983 is readily apparent. Starting in 1983 there was a marked decrease in spending as a share of GDP, a trend that was partially reversed during the recession that began in 1990. The lowest spending shares realized during the 1980s (22.1 percent in both 1988 and 1989) are larger than the *highest* shares realized during the 1960s and 1970s. Revenues, which are more sensitive to the business cycle than are expenditures, display more annual variation and only a slight upward trend over the period.

FIGURE 34-1
Federal Revenues, Expenditures, and Deficits, 1964–1991 (*as a share of GDP*)

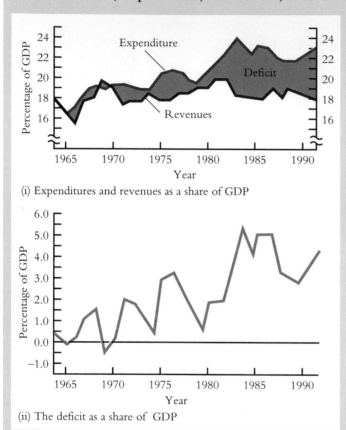

(i) Expenditures and revenues as a share of GDP

(ii) The deficit as a share of GDP

Since 1964 expenditure has grown as a fraction of GDP, while revenues have fluctuated but have shown little trend. Over the period 1965 to 1970, expenditures and revenues both grew steadily. From 1970 to 1979 expenditures grew gradually, while revenues remained roughly constant. Persistent deficits emerged. Since 1979 expenditures have grown dramatically, and revenues have fallen slightly. Over that period the deficit has increased sharply, although it fell somewhat in the three years prior to the recession that began in 1990. (*Source:* Congressional Budget Office: *The Economic and Fiscal Outlook;* and *Economic Report of the President,* various years.)

Part (ii) of Figure 34-1 shows the deficit, which is the shaded area between the two lines in part (i), also measured as a share of GDP. Prior to 1982 the deficit was not unusually large by historical standards. After 1982, however, the deficit increased dramatically as a share of GDP. By 1989 the deficit had fallen somewhat from its peak levels in the mid-1980s, but it was still 3 percent of GDP, a level that was unprecedented with the economy at high employment. In 1992, the deficit had risen to about 5 percent of GDP.

The increase in the deficit's share of GDP after 1989 can be attributed to the recession that began in 1990 and to the temporary effect of the savings and loan bailout.

The savings and loan bailout. Prior to 1988, the system that insured deposits in federally chartered banks and in savings and loan associations had virtually no effect on the federal budget. The two main deposit insurance systems [the Federal Deposit Insurance Corporation (FDIC) and the Federal Savings and Loan Insurance Corporation (FSLIC)] would usually about break even. However, as a result of the savings and loan crisis of the middle and late 1980s (see Chapter 29, especially Box 29-5 on pages 614–615), FSLIC ran out of assets in 1988, and Congress appropriated the funds necessary to cover FSLIC's obligations to insured depositors. By 1990 and 1991, federal outlays to cover such obligations were between 1.1 and 1.2 percent of GDP. Many of these outlays are in the form of loans to help solvent financial institutions to purchase bankrupt ones. Starting in 1995 these loans will start to be repaid, causing a temporary *reduction* in the size of the federal deficit.

Neither the temporary outlays nor the temporary revenues that arise from the savings and loan debacle have a significant effect on the long-term stance of U.S. fiscal policy.

Cyclical adjustment. In Chapter 26 we introduced the cyclically adjusted deficit (CAD), which we defined as the level of the deficit that would obtain if the economy were at potential income. Recall that when national income rises, tax receipts rise and transfer payments fall, which increases the budget surplus. Similarly, when national income falls, as it did in 1990 and 1991, tax receipts fall and transfer payments increase, and so too does the budget deficit. These changes in the deficit arise because of changes in the economy, rather than from changes in fiscal policy. The cyclically adjusted deficit allows us to measure fiscal policy independent of the current state of the economy. Thus, when our interest is the measurement of fiscal policy, the CAD does a better job than does the current deficit, which is influenced by current economic conditions.

Much of the growth in the deficit between 1989 and 1991 (from 3.0 percent of GDP to 4.8 percent of GDP) is due to the recession that began in 1990, and much is also due to the increase in outlays for deposit insurance. Indeed, the cyclically adjusted deficit, excluding outlays for federal deposit insurance, hardly changed; it was about 3 percent of GDP in 1988 and was 2.9 percent of GDP in 1991.

In every year since the mid-1980s, the cyclically adjusted deficit has reached shares of GDP that are unprecedented (except during World War II) in twentieth century U.S. economic history. The deficits of the 1980s and 1990s are indeed something new. The question is whether they are also something dangerous.[1]

---

[1] Some economists have argued that deficits and public debt have no important effects on the economy. The logic underlying this *Ricardian neutrality proposition* position is discussed in the appendix to this chapter, where we show that the conditions required for deficits to be irrelevant are very stringent. Briefly, the argument is that the government's decision of whether to finance current expenditure by levying current taxes or by issuing debt is irrelevant for the economy, because all that the latter decision does is postpone the taxes. Issuing bonds raises current government deficits and raises current household disposable income. However, according to this theory, neither has any implications for the performance of the economy. Forward-looking consumers will know that they have to pay higher taxes later and hence will not increase their current consumption expenditures. Thus, the theory holds that there will be no stimulus to the economy from the deficit.

Inflation adjustment. A number of economists have argued that the usual definition of the deficit (outlays minus revenues) overstates the size of the deficit when there is inflation. Their reasoning is based on the straightforward observation that inflation erodes the value of the *national debt* (first discussed in Chapter 26), just as it erodes the value of any other asset that is denominated in money terms. For example, if the national debt is $2,000 billion and there is a 5 percent inflation rate, the real value of the national debt will fall by $100 billion; that is, the real value of the goods and services needed to pay off the national debt will have fallen by $100 billion. Thus, $100 billion should be subtracted from the conventional measure of the deficit to take account of this reduction in the value of the national debt that is caused by inflation.

Box 34-1 presents and evaluates this argument in some detail. An important conclusion of that discussion, which we use later in this chapter, is that focusing on the ratio (and changes in the ratio) of the national debt to GDP solves the measurement problems created by inflation. Both the value of the debt and GDP are affected in exactly the same way by inflation, so no further adjustment for inflation needs to be made.

Economic Stabilization—The Effects of Deficits in the Short Run

Effects on national income. As we first saw in Chapter 26, policies that increase G, government purchases, or decrease T, tax revenues less transfer payments, will shift the AD curve rightward, leading to an increase in short-run equilibrium GDP. Of course, policies that increase G or decrease T will increase $G - T$, which is the budget deficit. Thus (see Chapter 28), when the economy is in recession, an increase in the budget deficit can speed the economy's return to potential income. Similarly, an inflationary gap can be removed by reducing aggregate demand through reducing the size of the deficit. Putting the point another way, discretionary fiscal policy can be used to affect the level of equilibrium national income in the short run.

Recall that changes in the budget deficit that arise from changes in fiscal policy are best measured by the cyclically adjusted deficit. The actual deficit can also change even if there is no change in fiscal policy. When national income rises, the budget deficit will tend to fall, because tax revenues rise and transfer payments fall. When national income falls, the same mechanism, operating in reverse, leads

Box 34-1

How Big Is the Deficit?

One issue in measuring the size of the government budget deficit arises from what is called *the inflation adjustment*. As we have seen (pages 474–475), nominal interest rates can be divided into a real interest component and an inflation premium. The inflation adjustment involves making the same distinction when assessing the government's debt service payments—which constitute a significant part of total government expenditures.

Debt service payments that are made by the government also have a real interest component and an inflation premium. While the real interest component constitutes a payment from the government to holders of the government debt for use of the principal, the inflation premium does not, because the inflation premium is exactly offset by a reduction in the real value of the principal.

Suppose that the current value of the government's debt is $1,000 billion. Suppose also that in the current year the government runs a deficit of $100 billion and that the current inflation rate is 10 percent. On crude measures the government has a deficit of $100 billion; this corresponds to the increase in the *nominal value* of the government's indebtedness. On an inflation-adjusted basis, the deficit is zero. This is because the *real value*—or purchasing power—of the

debt is unchanged, even though the nominal stock of debt has risen by 10 percent from $1,000 billion to $1,100 billion. Because the real value of the government's indebtedness is unchanged, the "effective," or inflation-adjusted, deficit is zero.

The inflation adjustment is made by subtracting the inflation premium of government debt service payments from the measured deficit.

The inflation-adjusted deficit directly measures the effect of the current deficit on the real national debt. It is uncertain, however, whether the inflation adjustment is appropriate for assessing the impact of the deficit on aggregate demand. This depends upon the response of households' consumption spending to inflation-induced changes in their real wealth. Those who argue for using the adjusted deficit hold that payment of the inflation premium to holders of the national debt has approximately no effect on aggregate demand. The government's outlay will be offset by an increase in private saving as wealth holders attempt to recoup the inflation-induced fall in their real wealth. Those who argue against making the adjustment hold that private-sector saving will not rise by enough to offset the inflation component

the budget deficit to rise. These changes in deficits, which are induced by changes in the overall level of economic activity, act as *automatic stabilizers,* reducing the magnitude of economic fluctuations (see Chapter 28).

As we also saw in Chapter 28, there is a good deal of controversy about the use of discretionary fiscal policy for economic stabilization. Many economists have argued that such policy does more harm than good (that is, causes more instability than stability); others attribute the relative economic stability of the past four decades to the use of discretionary fiscal (and monetary) policy. This dispute, however, turns on differences of opinion regarding the ability of

policymakers to implement discretionary fiscal policy in a way that enhances economic stability.

Almost all economists would agree that trying to eliminate or reduce a budget deficit when the economy is experiencing a recessionary gap would delay the economy's return to potential income.

Effects on inflation.   Neither economic theory nor the available evidence suggests that deficits by themselves are sufficient to cause inflation. The worry that persistent deficits may cause inflation arises out of the fear that a persistent deficit will lead to a completely.* Although the magnitude of the short-run response of household spending is a source of some controversy among economists, most economists hold that household spending will adjust completely in the long run and hence that, if one's concern is with the long-run effects of persistent deficits, the adjustment should be made.

Professor Robert Eisner of Northwestern University has led a small but vocal group of economists who argue, on the basis of this line of reasoning, that the deficit is not so large as to be considered a major problem. Indeed, Eisner and Paul Pieper have argued that, once the inflation adjustment is made and once allowance is made for the increases in the value of government assets (including gold), the *deficits*

recorded for the years 1978–1980 are, in fact, *surpluses*.† The deficits for the years after 1980 remain deficits. Even with the inflation adjustment, the Congressional Budget Office projects that deficits will exceed 1 percent of GDP throughout the remainder of the 1990s. This is still high by historical standards.

Many economists argue that long-run concerns are best captured by the evolution of the debt-to-GDP ratio. Because both real growth in the economy and inflation cause the denominator, nominal GDP, to increase, the debt-to-GDP ratio automatically allows for their effects. If the ratio increases, then the deficit was so large that it caused the stock of debt to increase faster than nominal GDP. If the ratio falls, then the deficit was small enough that the stock of debt grew slower than nominal GDP. On this basis many economists thus view the rapid run-up in the debt-to-GDP ratio that began in the 1980s (see Figure 34-2) and that is projected to continue through the 1990s as evidence that the deficit is large enough to constitute a serious problem.

---

* The difference between the tax and expenditure multipliers is another reason for adjusting the measured deficit in order to assess its impact on the economy. Because some tax revenue comes from reduced private saving, $1 of government purchases will increase aggregate demand by more than $1 of tax revenue will decrease it. Therefore, in order to properly measure the effect of fiscal actions on aggregate demand, a more sophisticated measure, which takes account of these differential effects, is required. Such a measure, called the *weighted, cyclically adjusted deficit,* is often used by economists in detailed empirical work that assesses fiscal policy.

† Robert Eisner and Paul J. Pieper, "A New View of the Federal Debt and Budget Deficits," *American Economic Review,* 74 (March 1984), pp. 11–29.

---

continuous expansion of the money supply. This, as we saw in Chapter 32, is a necessary condition for a sustained inflation to occur. To date this has not been a problem, as the deficit has been financed by government borrowing in capital markets; only if it were financed by "borrowing" from the Fed would the money supply be steadily increased. (In effect the Fed would *create* the money to finance the deficit.) If this increase were too rapid, then—as we saw in Chapter 32—it would cause inflation.

Deficits financed by the continual creation of new money may cause inflation. No one believes that such financing is desirable, nor has

it been important in recent U.S. economic history.[2]

Deficits and the National Debt

When the government runs a deficit, it borrows money to cover the difference between expenditures and revenue. As we first saw in Chapter 26,

---

[2] Although this has not been a problem in the United States, it has been a problem in other countries, and it remains one in many poorer countries, which are often unable to finance their deficits by borrowing on capital markets.

the sum of past borrowings (net of repayments of principal) is called the **national debt**. Persistent deficits lead to increases in the national debt, and hence to the amount of interest that must be paid on the national debt.

The interest bill on the national debt puts a strain on the budget process. For example, in 1991 almost 20 percent of all tax revenues went to pay interest on the national debt! The government's freedom of fiscal maneuvering is obviously hampered by such a large claim on the national tax revenues. When the government's interest obligations grow, it can, of course, incur an even larger deficit, at least for a while, but eventually interest on the stock of debt must be paid from new revenues. Eventually, the government must either reduce its expenditure on other programs, or it must raise taxes.

As it happened, interest on the national debt during the late 1980s and early 1990s was approximately the same size as the cyclically adjusted deficit itself. Had there been no interest payments, no recession, and no savings and loan crisis, the government would have run a small surplus over this period. Instead, largely because past deficits led to the accumulation of a large national debt, much government spending took the form of interest payments, which contributed to further increases in the national debt.

Much of the concern about government budget deficits arises from their *cumulative* effect on the national debt, and thus on the government's interest obligations.

It is therefore useful to examine the recent patterns in the growth of the national debt.

Facts About the Debt

The national debt in September 1992 was estimated at $4.05 trillion, more than $16,000 for every man, woman, and child in the country. About 25 percent of the debt was held by the government itself and by Federal Reserve banks; interest payments on this part of the debt are only bookkeeping transactions.[3]

The debt held by the private sector at the end of 1992 was about $3 trillion.

The figures for debt per person, which are often quoted in an attempt to shock the reader, require interpretation. For a government, as for a household, the significance of debt depends on what it represents and on whether the income is available to pay the interest. No one would be shocked, for example, to find that a family of four in the United States, earning $60,000 per year, had a mortgage of $50,000 on a $120,000 home.

As with the deficit, in evaluating the national debt and the government's interest payments on it, it is useful to consider them *relative* to the size of the economy. A national debt of $4 trillion clearly has different implications when GDP is $500 billion and when it is $5 trillion.

Figure 34-2 shows historical data for the debt and interest payments on it as a proportion of GDP. Figure 34-2(i) shows that the national debt as a proportion of GDP started to fall at the end of World War II and continued to fall until 1976. The debt then rose relative to GDP after 1977, and by 1991 the debt reached almost 64 percent of GDP. This figure is still much less than the more-than-100-percent figure at the postwar peak. Nevertheless, the trend is worrisome, and medium-term projections suggest that the debt-to-GDP ratio will continue to rise.

Consider next the interest payments on the debt, often called *debt service payments,* shown in part (ii) of Figure 34-2. Clearly, there is genuine cause for worry here. The current ratio of 3.5 percent is very high by historical standards. As we pointed out earlier, in 1991 interest payments were somewhat larger than the CAD itself (after accounting for temporary outlays due to deposit insurance) and limited the government's room for fiscal maneuvering. If interest payments as a share of GDP continue their upward trend, they will become an increasing burden on the government's taxing capacity. Either ever bigger deficits would occur and, with them, even more borrowing, or taxes would have to rise and expenditures to fall in some combination.

The rising debt-to-GDP ratio imposes costs of two kinds. First, it creates a large and potentially growing "fixed charge" (interest payments) in the budget, reducing the ability of the government to use the budget either for economic stabilization or to pursue traditional governmental functions. Second, it reduces the stock of wealth that will be available to U.S. citizens in the future. This second point requires further elaboration.

---

[3] Federal Reserve banks buy government bonds in the course of operating monetary policy (see Chapter 31). Government departments sometimes acquire government bonds when they have funds that they do not need for short, or even long, periods of time.

FIGURE 34-2
The Relative Importance of the National Debt

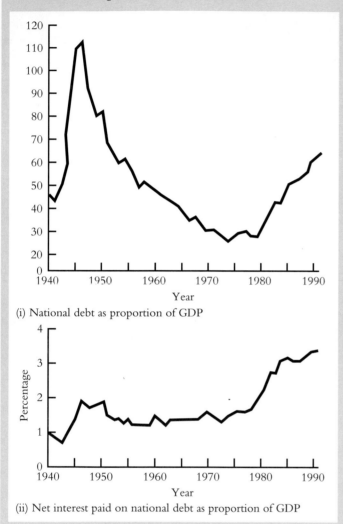

(i) National debt as proportion of GDP

(ii) Net interest paid on national debt as proportion of GDP

The national debt has not reached alarming proportions in relation to GDP, but both the debt and interest payments on it have been growing rapidly in recent years. Stated as a proportion of the country's national income in part (i), the national debt rose dramatically during World War II and again, slightly, during the major slump of 1974 to 1976. It has been growing steadily since 1977.

Part (ii) shows that net interest payments on the national debt have been a rising proportion of GDP since 1973. The different trends in debt and debt servicing between 1973 and 1981 are accounted for by the rising cost of servicing the debt owing to rising interest rates. (*Sources:* Historical tables, budget of the United States government, fiscal year 1989; *Economic Report of the President,* various years.)

Effects of Deficits on National Wealth and Economic Growth

Critics of budget deficits often assert that the burden of deficits falls on future generations. When the economy is in long-run equilibrium at potential GDP, the assertion is true.[4] *When the economy is at Y^*,* deficits reduce national saving and national asset formation, reducing the levels of income available to

future generations. The way in which this happens is most easily understood by first looking at the effects of deficits in an economy that has no international trade.

Crowding Out of Private Investment

Consider a closed economy that is in both long-run and short-run equilibrium. That is, the SRAS curve and the AD curve intersect at Y^*. Now suppose that this economy increased its budget deficit, say, by increasing G. In the short run, there would be a higher level of both GDP and prices, as the fiscal

---

[4] If there were perfect Ricardian equivalence, as discussed in the appendix to this chapter, there would be no burden on future generations.

stimulus shifted *AD* rightward along the *SRAS* curve. Assuming no monetary validation, the adjustment mechanism would then come into play, shifting the *SRAS* curve upward. The new long-run equilibrium would be at the same level of income (*Y**) and at a higher price level. All of this is illustrated in part (i) of Figure 34-3.

In the new equilibrium, with real income unchanged but with a higher price level, the demand for money will have increased because the nominal volume of transactions *PY** will have increased. This brings the transmission mechanism (see Chapter 30, pages 633–635) into play. The increase in nominal money demand, with a fixed money supply, will raise the interest rate, reducing investment according to the *MEI* schedule. Thus, the new equilibrium will have lower investment demand and lower national saving at *Y**. The deficit will have **crowded out** investment. (See the discussion of the transmission mechanism in Chapter 30. All of the steps discussed here are explained in detail there.) Figure 34-3(ii) shows the crowding out as a reduction in national saving and a reduction in investment demand at long-run equilibrium *Y*.[5]

If government borrowing to finance the deficit drives up the interest rate, some private investment expenditure will be crowded out.

Notice that when there is a large recessionary gap, crowding out will be much less important. This is because the increase in the deficit will lead an increase in real income, which in turn will raise the volume of private savings (as households move along their savings functions, as shown in Figure 25-1 on page 506). In this case the new savings generated by the rise in income helps to finance the deficit so that less crowding out of investment need occur.

To the extent that government borrowing to finance current expenditures crowds out private investment, there will be a smaller stock of capital to pass on to future generations. Less

capital means less output; this is the long-term burden of the debt.**

Crowding Out in an Open Economy

Despite large deficits, investment has been sustained at high levels in the past few years. Does this mean that we do not need to worry about a burden arising from the large deficits? Unfortunately, the answer is no. Although private investment has been maintained and deficits have had relatively little effect on interest rates, foreign lenders have supplied much of the funds.[6] Thus, although future generations of U.S. citizens may well inherit a capital stock that is not significantly reduced as a result of the deficit, their incomes will be affected. Some of the capital stock will be owned by foreigners, who will receive the income that it generates. Some of the capital will have been financed by borrowing from abroad, and U.S. citizens will owe interest and principal on any foreign debt that has been used to finance investment in the United States.

The large deficits of the 1980s have reduced U.S. citizens' wealth relative to what it would have been without the deficits.

Payments of interest and dividends on liabilities owed abroad will lower GNP (income that accrues to U.S. citizens) in relation to GDP (output produced in the United States), because some income generated by the output produced in the United States will accrue to foreigners. These payments will also lower GNP (income earned by U.S. citizens) relative to what it would have been in the absence of the deficits.

Obtaining funds from abroad entails a transfer of purchasing power to domestic residents when the funds are acquired and a transfer back to foreigners when interest payments, payments of dividends, and repayments of principal occur.

The United States slowly built up a net creditor position over the six decades before 1980. This position was completely dissipated as a result of the enormous volume of foreign borrowing that occurred during Ronald Reagan's presidency. Most economists attribute this foreign borrowing to the

---

[5] The increase in the price level will also reduce consumption demand somewhat, because it will lead to a reduction in private wealth, and hence to an increase in desired saving. This is explained in Chapter 27, where we first derive the *AD* curve. Thus, the national saving function in part (ii) of Figure 34-3 will not shift down by as much as the increased deficit, and some of the deficit will crowd out consumption rather than investment. As a practical matter, however, the reduction in investment will be virtually the same size as the increase in the deficit.

---

[6] As we shall see in Chapter 38, the capital inflows from abroad are matched by a deficit on the current account, and the association of the current account deficit with the government budget deficit has become known as the *twin deficits problem*.

FIGURE 34-3
Crowding Out of Investment

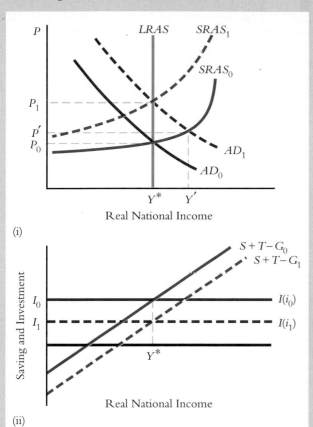

(i)

(ii)

For a closed economy whose income equals potential income, an increase in the deficit will cause a reduction in national saving and investment. Consider a closed economy that is in long-run and short-run equilibrium at Y^* and P_0, in part (i). The same position is shown in part (ii) as saving equal to investment at Y^* and I_0. Suppose that the government increases government purchases from G_0 to G_1. This raises desired aggregate expenditure (and lowers desired national saving) at all levels of income. In part (i), the new short-run equilibrium is at Y' and P'. Assuming that the demand shock is not validated by monetary expansion, the adjustment mechanism will eventually cause factor prices to rise, shifting the SRAS curve from $SRAS_0$ to $SRAS_1$. The new long-run equilibrium will be at Y^* and P_1.

The effect of this change on saving and investment can be seen in part (ii). At the new long-run equilibrium, real income is unchanged (it is still at Y^*), but the price level has risen. This implies that the demand for money will have risen, causing a rise in both the nominal and real interest rates. According to the marginal efficiency of investment curve, at the higher interest rates, there will be reduced investment demand, shown in the figure as a reduction from I_0 to I_1. The increase in G directly shifts the national saving function downward, as shown. Thus, in the long run, the increase in government purchases has no effect on national income but "crowds out" investment.

government budget deficits of the 1980s. According to many measures, by 1988 the United States had become the world's largest debtor nation, a position that it continued to hold in 1992.[7]

Implications for Economic Policy

We have seen that budget deficits (at Y^*) crowd out national asset formation, reducing the growth of real

income available to U.S. citizens. Why, then, has the government not eliminated or reduced the deficit already? There are two reasons: The first involves short-term stabilization policy and, as we shall show, can be straightforwardly dealt with if monetary and fiscal policy are coordinated. The second is much more serious—reducing the deficit involves real costs today, in higher taxes and lower government services, in exchange for benefits in the future. Such an exchange does not appeal to everyone.

A Growth-Oriented Mix of Fiscal and Monetary Policy

If the government were to reduce or eliminate the deficit, there would be a leftward shift in AD and, until the adjustment mechanism corrected the problem, a recessionary gap. If, however, monetary policy were loosened at the same time that the budget was

---

[7] The term *debtor nation* is widely used in this context, even though the assets and liabilities involved are not just debt instruments, such as bonds, but also include ownership of physical resources, such as real estate and factories. Thus, the United States is a debtor nation to the extent that the value of all assets within the United States that are owned by foreigners exceeds the value of all assets outside of the United States that are owned by U.S. citizens. Similarly, borrowing in this context means obtaining funds from foreign sources, whether via debt, stocks, or direct ownership of physical assets.

FIGURE 34-4
National Asset Formation and the Mix of Fiscal and Monetary Policy

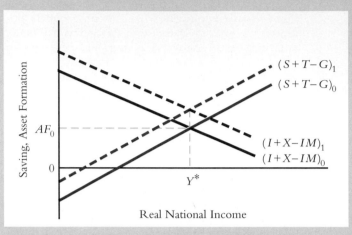

An economy at potential income can increase national saving and asset formation by changing fiscal and monetary policies. Suppose that the economy is initially in equilibrium at AF_0. More restrictive fiscal policy would raise the national saving function from $(S + T - G)_0$ to $(S + T - G)_1$. At the same time, monetary policy could be made more expansionary, reducing interest rates and increasing investment demand (and also net exports, for reasons discussed in Chapter 39). This would shift the national asset formation schedule from $(I + X - IM)_0$ to $(I + X - IM)_1$. If the fiscal and monetary policy shifts were well coordinated, there would be no change in aggregate demand. Rather, the composition of demand would be shifted away from G and C (current expenditures) toward I and NX (asset formation).

tightened, the leftward move in AD could be counteracted by the transmission mechanism, leaving the economy at Y^* but with a higher level of national saving and national asset formation. This "twist" in the policy mix affecting aggregate demand is illustrated in Figure 34-4, which depicts the national saving–national asset formation balance first developed in Chapter 26.

Note that a growth-oriented aggregate demand policy requires coordination of both fiscal and monetary policy. Fiscal policy is used to shift the national saving function upward, while monetary policy simultaneously counteracts the contractionary effect of tighter fiscal policy and shifts the composition of aggregate expenditure toward investment and net exports, that is, toward national asset formation.[8] An increase in national asset formation would

increase income in the future; relative to what it would otherwise be.

The Congressional Budget Office estimates that a permanent reduction in the deficit of 1 percent of GDP could raise the standard of living in the United States by between 1 percent and 7 percent by the middle of the twenty-first century. Chapter 35 provides an example (Table 35-2) of the long-term effects on consumption of a permanent increase in national saving, which is what a reduction in the federal deficit would be.

Government Investment

Implicit in our analysis thus far is that all of government purchases, G, is considered government *consumption*. Thus, we have measured public saving as net tax revenue (T) minus government purchases G. Some government purchases, however, are really investment and contribute to national asset formation and to economic growth. When the government builds roads, bridges, sewers, and school buildings, it is adding to the nation's capital stock, just as General Electric does when it builds a new factory. Indeed, a number of economists have taken the position that, following years of neglect, investment in the nation's *infrastructure* of transportation systems and water and sewage facilities would yield a higher

---

[8] As we shall see in Chapter 39, expansionary monetary policy, in addition to reducing interest rates and hence stimulating desired investment expenditure, tends to reduce the external value of the domestic currency. This, in turn, increases export demand (U.S. goods become relatively cheap) and reduces import demand (foreign goods become relatively expensive). Thus, both parts of national asset formation, I and NX, are stimulated by monetary expansion.

rate of economic growth than private investment of the same size. Similarly, public investment in education can yield very high returns, as we discuss in Chapter 35.

Although the U.S. system of National Income and Product Accounts does not yet distinguish between government investment and government consumption, it soon will, as part of the effort to make the U.S. system of accounts conform to the accounts used in the rest of the world. It will then be possible to separate government purchases into government consumption, G_C, and government investment, G_I. Once this separation is made, public saving can be measured more accurately, as $T - G_C$, and national investment can also be more accurately measured, as the sum of private investment, I, and public investment, G_I.[9]

A budget deficit that is used to finance productive investments may well enhance economic growth, rather than retard it.

During the 1980s many of the government's efforts to reduce the measured deficit ($G - T$) involved reductions in expenditure on government investment. Because of this, the government's net contribution to national saving fell by *more* than the increase in the size of the measured deficit. By the early 1990s, many economists who were concerned with economic growth were calling for an increase in government investment in infrastructure, arguing that even if such an increase were deficit-financed, the wealth-enhancing consequences of the investment itself would exceed the wealth-reducing consequences of the increase in the deficit.

Tax Incentives

Different types of taxes will have different effects on national saving and investment. One of the arguments for moving toward a tax system in which consumption is taxed more heavily, and income is taxed less heavily, is that doing so would stimulate private saving. If total tax revenues were unchanged, this

would also increase national saving, leading to higher national asset formation and economic growth.

In practice, most tax incentives that are purported to stimulate saving and investment involve reductions in taxes on specific activities, without increases in taxes on other activities. For example, President Bush has been a consistent proponent of reducing taxes on capital gains, arguing that this would stimulate investment demand. *Individual retirement accounts* (IRAs) allow people who save for retirement to avoid taxation of part of their income, and to avoid taxation of the interest in their retirement accounts as it accumulates. IRAs, favorable tax treatment of capital gains, and other incentives for saving and investment clearly increase *private* saving, but it is not at all clear that they increase *national* saving.

The problem with tax incentives for saving is that they operate by reducing tax revenues, thereby reducing public saving. In order for the net effect to be an increase in national saving (and hence, at Y^*, national asset formation), private saving has to increase by more than a dollar for every dollar that taxes are cut. The overwhelming weight of the empirical evidence on this subject is that this condition is rarely attained.

The net effect of tax incentives designed to increase private saving has been to reduce national saving, because the incentives directly reduce public saving.

Supply-Side Economics

During the early 1980s the idea of supply-side economics became popular, and it was the basis of much of President Reagan's economic policy. The theory of supply-side economics called for adopting measures that would shift the *LRAS* and *SRAS* curves to the right, increasing economic growth and reducing inflationary pressures.

A major part of supply-side economics was the provision of tax incentives that would increase potential national income by increasing the nation's supplies of labor and capital. Incentives were given to firms to increase their investment, which, it was hoped, would increase national productive capacity. Personal taxes were cut across the board to give everyone an incentive to work and to save more. It was argued that people who were already employed would be more inclined to work longer and harder when they were able to keep a larger percentage of their pretax earnings, and

---

[9] National saving will still be equal to national asset formation. With government purchases divided into those for consumption and those for investment, the relationship is: $S + T - G_C = I + G_I + X - IM$. Compared to the saving-asset formation balance derived in Chapter 26 (page 539), this formulation adds government investment to both sides of the equation, increasing measured national saving and measured national asset formation by the amount of government investment.

people outside of the labor force would be drawn in as a result of the higher after-tax wages. Extra tax incentives were given to persons at high income levels to increase the incentives for work and risk taking on the part of the most productive people. Many argued that the resulting increases in productive capacity and in productivity would shift the *LRAS* curve to the right, thus raising equilibrium national income and further reducing inflationary pressure.

Supply-siders also argued that the cuts in tax rates and increases in tax exemptions would not increase the federal government's budget deficit. They believed that the increase in national income would create an increase in the tax base that would be sufficient to generate larger tax *revenues* in spite of the lower tax *rates*. For example, if a 10 percent cut in tax rates were followed by a 10 percent increase in real national income, it would leave tax revenues approximately the same.

As we have seen, the budget deficits that followed the implementation of President Reagan's fiscal policies were the largest peacetime deficits in the history of the country. Whatever the supply-side effects of supply-side economics, they were plainly not large enough to prevent the deficit from increasing.

Most economists agree that the net effect of the fiscal policies associated with supply-side economics was to reduce national saving and national asset formation.

Proposals to Control the Deficit

As we have seen, government deficits contribute to aggregate demand and hence can play a useful role in damping cyclical fluctuations in the economy. As we have seen also, government deficits at high employment generally reduce national saving and national asset formation and hence lead to a reduction in future living standards of the average U.S. resident. This conflict between the short-term stabilization role of deficits and the long-term adverse effects of low national saving has been a subject of constant debate among economists and others who are concerned with government policy. Views range from those who dismiss the long-run costs of deficits to those who believe that deficits should never be used for short-term stabilization. We now look at some of the specific proposals that have been put forward; some of the general options are illustrated in Figure 34-5.

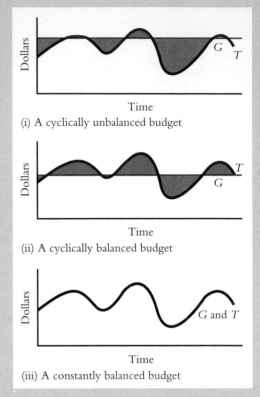

FIGURE 34-5
Balanced and Unbalanced Budgets

(i) A cyclically unbalanced budget

(ii) A cyclically balanced budget

(iii) A constantly balanced budget

An annually (constantly) balanced budget is a destabilizer; a cyclically balanced budget is a stabilizer. The flow of tax receipts, *T*, is shown varying over the business cycle; in parts (i) and (ii), government expenditure, *G*, is shown at a constant rate.

In part (i) deficits (red areas) are common and surpluses (blue areas) are rare because the average level of expenditure exceeds the average level of taxes. Such a policy will tend to stabilize the economy against cyclical fluctuations, but public saving is negative, on average. This has been the characteristic U.S. budgetary position over the last several decades.

In part (ii) government expenditure has been reduced until it is approximately equal to the average level of tax receipts. The budget is now balanced cyclically. The policy still tends to stabilize the economy against cyclical fluctuations because of deficits in slumps and surpluses in booms. However, public saving is higher than in part (i).

In part (iii) a balanced budget has been imposed. Deficits have been prevented, but government expenditure now varies over the business cycle, which tends to destabilize the economy by accentuating the cyclical swings in aggregate expenditure.

An Annually Balanced Budget

Much current rhetoric of fiscal restraint, including a constitutional amendment proposed during 1992, calls for a balanced budget. The Gramm-Rudman-Hollings bill, passed in late 1985 and discussed further in Box 34-2, mandated an elimination of the federal deficit by 1993. (Originally, the deficit was to have been eliminated by 1991. In 1987 Congress decided that the original goal could not be met and revised the schedule.) The discussion earlier in this chapter suggests that an annually balanced budget would be extremely difficult, perhaps impossible, to achieve. With fixed tax rates, tax revenues fluctuate as national income fluctuates. Much government expenditure is fixed by past commitments, and most of the rest is hard to change quickly.

Yet suppose an annually balanced budget, or something approaching it, were feasible. What would its effects be? Would it be desirable?

We saw earlier that a government sector whose expenditures on goods and services are not very sensitive to the cyclical variations in national income acts as a built-in stabilizer for the economy. To insist that annual government expenditure be tied to annual tax receipts would be to abandon the present built-in stability provided by the government. Government expenditure would then become a major *destabilizing* force. Tax revenues necessarily rise in booms and fall in slumps; an annually balanced budget would force government expenditure to do the same. Changes in national income would then cause induced changes, not only in household consumption expenditure but also in government expenditure. This would greatly increase the economy's marginal propensity to spend and hence increase the value of the multiplier. In the terminology of Chapter 28, this would serve as a *built-in destabilizer!*

An annually balanced budget would accentuate the swings in national income that accompany changes in such autonomous expenditure flows as investment and exports.

A Cyclically Balanced Budget

An alternative policy—one that would prevent continual deficits (and could also inhibit the growth in the size of the government sector)—would be to balance the budget over the business cycle. This would be more feasible than the annually balanced budget,

and it would not make government expenditure a destabilizing force.

Although more attractive in principle than the annually balanced budget, a cyclically balanced budget would carry problems of its own. Congress might well spend in excess of revenue in one year, leaving the next Congress the obligation to spend less than current revenue in following years. Could such an obligation to balance over a period of several years be made binding? It could be made a legal requirement through an act of Congress. Indeed, this is the direction taken by the Budget Enforcement Act of 1990 (see Box 34-2). That act does not require *balance* over the cycle, but it does limit overall spending while still allowing automatic stabilizers to operate. However, what Congress does, Congress can undo.[10]

Perhaps even more of a problem is that there is always room for some disagreement about the current state of the business cycle. A requirement to balance the budget over the business cycle can only be implemented based on some forecast of future economic conditions. Forecasting of the level of economic activity is imperfect, to say the least, and there will be genuine disagreement among economists about what stage of the business cycle the economy is in and about where the economy is headed. Compounding the difficulty that arises from such uncertainty is the fact that politicians will have a stake in the economic forecast. Those who favor increased government spending will tend to argue that *this* year is an unusually bad one and that the deficits of this year can be made up by the surpluses in (better) years to come. On the other side, some will always tend to find *this* year to be unusually good—a time to run surpluses against the hard times to follow.

Although a budget balanced over the course of the business cycle is in principle an acceptable way of reconciling short-term stabilization and long-term concerns with national saving, the business cycle may not be defined well enough in practice to make the proposal operational.

Allowing for growth. A further problem is that the goal of budget *balance,* whether it is applied annually

---

[10] For example, attempts to limit the size of the national debt by legal restriction never had much effect. Every time the national debt approaches the "debt ceiling," fixed in some prior year, Congress raises the ceiling and the president signs the new ceiling into law.

Box 34-2

Congress' Efforts to Impose Budget Balance on Itself

In December 1985 the U.S. Congress passed the Balanced Budget and Emergency Deficit Control Act of 1985. This potentially far-reaching bill reflected both Congress' growing frustration with its own inability to reach a satisfactory compromise with the president on budget policy and the growing perception that unchecked deficit growth will have harmful economic and political effects. Congress' frustration is easy to understand. In 1985 it had struggled to cut one program after another, only to wind up with yet another huge deficit. The act was a response to its prevailing mood of concern.

Referred to as Gramm-Rudman-Hollings (G-R-H), after the three legislators who sponsored it, the bill initially promised to balance the budget by 1991. A revised version of the act, passed in 1987, extended the deadline to 1993. In 1990 Gramm-Rudman-Hollings was scrapped in favor of the "Budget Enforcement Act" of 1990 (BEA).

G-R-H is now primarily of historical interest, but its sad history provides some insight into the difficulties that arise in trying to balance the budget by passing a law (or a constitutional amendment) that requires the budget to be balanced.

In both its original and its revised versions, G-R-H mandated a five-year schedule of deficit targets, year by year, ending with a deficit of zero. The penalty for failure to agree on a plan that would meet the targets was to be automatic expenditure

reductions in a large number of programs. (Notably, social security and interest on the national debt were exempt from the automatic budget cuts.) The idea was to force Congress to bind its own hands regarding the size of the deficit, giving it the incentive to achieve that size in the most beneficial (least harmful) way possible. For all its appeal, G-R-H suffered from a number of flaws.

The first flaw is that aiming at a zero deficit is arbitrary, perhaps dangerously so. Forcing a balanced budget could, depending on economic conditions, start a recession or stifle a healthy recovery. There was provision in the act to waive the deficit reduction schedule in the event of an economic emergency, but getting agreement on an "emergency" was not easy. As it happened, by the time recession loomed in 1990, G-R-H had been repealed.

A further flaw concerns credibility. Credibility was compromised by the fact that G-R-H did not formally require that its targets be met. Rather, it required that each summer the Office of Management and Budget (OMB) publish an economic and budgetary *forecast* that the deficit would be not more than $10 billion above the target in the fiscal year to follow. Two kinds of chicanery flowed from the form of this requirement. First, there was pressure on OMB to generate very optimistic forecasts. Second, there was the use of accounting gimmickry. The government could meet a technical requirement that next year's budget have a deficit within range of the

or over the cycle, is, in fact, stricter than is required to avoid a rising debt-to-GDP ratio. Growth in GDP (due either to growth in real output or to inflation) means that some growth in the debt, and hence a (small) deficit, is consistent with a stable debt-to-GDP ratio.

For those who think of a stable debt-to-GDP ratio as the appropriate indicator of budget balance, deficits such that the debt grows at the

same rate as nominal GDP would be perfectly acceptable.

The Political Economy of Deficits and the Debt

Almost all economists accept that, if the debt got so large that it could not be serviced without either putting a crushing burden on taxpayers or forcing the government to create new money to service it, there target by claiming that some source of revenue (e.g., proceeds from the sale of Amtrak) would become available next year. Once the forecast was made, the required sale could be postponed and used, once again, to enhance the revenue forecast in the following year. As it happens, this trick was performed with Amtrak at least three times, and, as of this writing, Amtrak is still firmly in government hands!

The Budget Enforcement Act

In the fall of 1990 G-R-H was replaced by the Budget Enforcement Act of 1990, which differed from G-R-H in a number of ways. First, the BEA directly cut government spending and increased taxes, with a net effect of about $500 billion for the period 1991 through 1995. Second, the BEA dropped the specific deficit targets of G-R-H. Rather, it set spending limits for three types of spending (defense spending, domestic discretionary spending, and international discretionary spending) and imposed a "pay-as-you-go" requirement for taxes and entitlement programs.

Within each of the three areas of discretionary spending, BEA requires Congress to stay under a pre-determined limit. The limits, usually called "caps," are adjusted for inflation.

For the fourth area, entitlement programs and taxes, the BEA imposes a requirement that increases in transfer programs must be balanced by equivalent increases in taxes. The BEA also permits reallocation among transfer programs. Thus, Congress can increase, say, social security benefits if it also increases taxes, or taxes can be cut if some entitlement program (such as Medicare, veterans' benefits, or welfare) is reduced by a similar amount. By tying entitlement programs and taxes together in this way, the Budget Enforcement Act permits automatic stabilizers to function. When GDP fell, as it did in late 1990 and early 1991, taxes fell and transfers rose, without any change in law. This was permissible under the BEA; it would have required declaration of an emergency under G-R-H.

After fiscal year 1993 the three categories of discretionary spending in the Budget Enforcement Act will be merged into one large category. Meeting the spending targets that were agreed upon in 1990 will require cuts in government programs starting in 1993. Whether these cuts will be made, or whether the BEA will be revised or scrapped, remains to be seen.

For all of the difficulties with G-R-H, and the uncertainty surrounding the Budget Enforcement Act, most observers agree that without these efforts the federal budget deficit would be even larger than it now is.

The straightforward implication of this is that Congress and the White House, while decrying budget deficits, prefer them to the alternative of cutting spending and increasing taxes in sufficient amounts to eliminate the deficit.

would be serious problems. However, most agree that we are still a long way from that point.

This does not mean that the deficit is nothing to worry about. As we have seen, persistent deficits at high employment reduce national saving and asset formation, and thus reduce the growth of national income over time. Aside from a fairly small minority who believe that deficits have no effect on the economy at all (see the appendix to this chapter), most economists agree that the large deficits of recent

years, and in prospect for the forseeable future, will reduce economic growth relative to what it would otherwise be. Why, then, are the deficits such an intractable political problem?

Reducing the deficit involves, in some combination, increasing taxes and reducing transfer payments (thereby reducing private consumption) and cutting government purchases (thereby reducing government provision of goods and services). Either one of these actions will immediately reduce the

current taxes to finance the government expenditure, thus leaving the next generation with a liability to pay the taxes that will have to be levied when the government redeems the bonds. If the recipients behave in this manner, the fiscal authority's decision to rely on deficit financing will have stimulated the economy by inducing an increase in spending.

However, this behavior would reduce the net value of the bequest that the typical household would be leaving to its heirs, because the heirs now face an increased tax liability. This violates the notion that the members of a typical household make a rational plan that includes targets for its own consumption and for the bequest that it wishes to leave to its heirs, because the government action does not change the options open to current households. The current household could have achieved this redistribution away from future generations toward itself without the government action simply by increasing its own consumption and reducing the value of the estate that it leaves to its heirs.

If the current household wishes to preserve its initial plan, all that it needs to do is maintain its spending plans and increase saving by the full amount of the increase in its disposable income, that is, by the increase in the government budget deficit. The resulting increase in the value of the next generation's inheritance will exactly offset the increase in tax liabilities that it faces. Thus, a government deficit that issues bonds now and "promises" taxes in the future would have no effect even if the taxes were expected only after the current generation were dead.

Note that the level of government expenditure is still important in this model—only the method of financing is irrelevant. However, there are a number of reasons to believe that future taxes that have a present value of $1 are not equivalent to present taxes of $1, and thus that this debt-neutral Ricardian model does not provide an accurate description of the working of a modern economy. (Ricardo himself rejected it.) We cite only three reasons.

The private sector borrows on different terms than the government sector.   This is perhaps the most important reason why deficit financing is not neutral in practice. In many circumstances households and, to some extent, firms face constraints that prevent them from borrowing all that they would like to at the prevailing market interest rate. Alternatively, they may be able to borrow, but at a much higher interest rate than that facing the government. Consequently, when the government substitutes future taxes for present taxes by running a deficit, these "constrained" private-sector agents will feel wealthier and, consequently, will spend more.

Myopic perception.   If some households imperfectly perceive the future tax liabilities implied by the government deficit, they will not offset government dissaving with private saving.

Finite lifetimes.   Another reason why households might view future taxes as not equivalent to current taxes is that future taxes may extend beyond the expected lifetime of the household. Thus, the household may anticipate escaping taxes by dying! As Barro points out, this would make no difference if households "care about their heirs"; in this case living households would simply alter any bequests that they had planned to leave to their heirs by an amount equal to the expected increase in future taxes borne by their heirs. However, if households that currently are alive do not care or are unable to alter their bequests (perhaps because such bequests cannot be reduced below their current zero level), living households will, in fact, react to a change in the deficit in a manner that does not completely offset it.

Conclusions

The basic feature of the economy that makes government deficits and the public debt matter is that, to a significant extent, current private-sector expenditure is tied to current private-sector income. The government deficit influences the current income of the private sector, because for a given level of government expenditure a larger deficit means lower current taxes and hence larger current private disposable income. In the first instance, this debt finance simply causes an intertemporal rearrangement of private-sector income. However, for the reasons noted, the private sector is not indifferent to this rearrangement of its income receipts. In particular, current private-sector expenditure rises in response to the increase in current income. This influence of government deficits on private spending not only creates the potential for a stabilization role for deficits over the business cycle but also creates the mechanism by which persistent deficits become costly and undesirable in the longer run.

35

Economic Growth

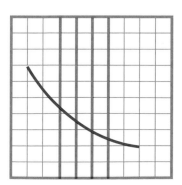

E conomic growth is the single most powerful engine for generating long-term increases in living standards. What happens to our material living standards depends on the growth in national income (as measured, for example, by the GDP) in relation to the growth in population.

The Nature of Economic Growth

We saw in Chapter 1 that in the first seven decades of the twentieth century, per capita GDP rose steadily while its distribution became somewhat less unequal. As a result most U.S. citizens found themselves better off decade by decade, and children were typically substantially better off materially than their parents had been at the same age. In the 1970s, however, the engine of growth faltered. Growth rates of GDP fell, and the distribution of income began to get more unequal. As a result, the real incomes of many U.S. families remained relatively constant. Although they still live in one of the richest societies in all of human history, many spoke of the end of the American dream that each generation could expect to be much better off than its predecessors. The change in attitudes and perceptions brought about in the minds of ordinary, middle-class citizens by the mere slowdown of rapid growth shows how important was the part that steady growth had played in people's minds, hearts, and dreams over the decades.

Shifts in Aggregate Demand and Aggregate Supply

In earlier chapters we outlined the effects of shifts in aggregate demand and aggregate supply. Economic growth concerns sustained shifts in aggregate supply; hence, many of the points made in earlier chapters in the context of one-time shifts bear repeating in this new context.

Figure 35-1, which is similar to Figure 28-6, illustrates some important causes of rising national income.[1] If there is a recessionary gap, policies that increase aggregate demand will yield a once-and-for-all increase in national income. Once potential income is achieved, however, further increases in aggregate demand yield only transitory increases in real income but lasting increases in the price level.

Policies that reduce structural unemployment can also increase the employed labor force and thus increase potential income. The resulting increase in income might not be very large, but social benefits would result from the reduction in unemployment, especially in the long-term unemployment that occurs when people are trapped in

---

[1] The figures are not identical because they emphasize slightly different points.

FIGURE 35-1
Ways of Increasing National Income

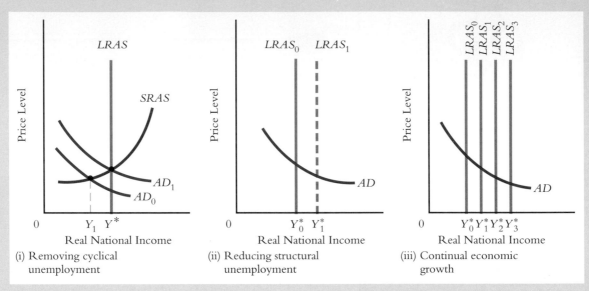

(i) Removing cyclical unemployment

(ii) Reducing structural unemployment

(iii) Continual economic growth

A once-and-for-all increase in national income can be obtained by raising aggregate demand to remove a recessionary gap or by shifting the *LRAS* curve, say, by cutting structural unemployment. Continual increases in national income are possible through continued economic growth, which shifts the *LRAS* curve. In part (i), with the aggregate demand curve at AD_0, there is a recessionary gap of $Y_1 Y^*$. An increase in aggregate demand from AD_0 to AD_1 achieves a once-and-for-all increase in national income from Y_1 to Y^*.

In part (ii) potential output rises from Y_0^* to Y_1^* due to measures that reduce structural unemployment. The *LRAS* curve shifts from $LRAS_0$ to $LRAS_1$ because people who were formerly unemployed due to having the wrong skills or being in the wrong place are now better suited for employment.

In part (iii) increases in factor supplies and productivity lead to increases in potential income. This *continually* shifts the long-run aggregate supply curve outward. In successive periods it moves from $LRAS_0$ to $LRAS_3$, taking potential income from Y_0^* to Y_1^* to Y_2^*, and so on, as long as growth continues.

declining areas, industries, or occupations. The increase, however, is once-and-for-all, as the total number of unemployed falls to a new, lower level. Similar results come from measures that increase economic efficiency. A once-and-for-all increase in potential output occurs as a given employed labor force works more efficiently.

Over the long haul, the main cause of rising national income is *economic growth*—the increase in potential income due to changes in factor supplies (labor and capital) and in the productivity of factors (output per unit of factor input). As we observed in Chapter 28, the removal of a serious recessionary gap or the elimination of all structural unemployment might cause a once-and-for-all increase in national income by, at the very most, 6 percent. However, a growth rate of 3 percent per year raises national income by 6 percent in 2 years and *doubles* it

in about 24 years. Even a 1 percent growth rate doubles income over one normal lifetime of about 70 years.

Growth is a much more powerful method of raising living standards than is the removal of recessionary gaps, structural unemployment, or inefficiencies, *because growth can go on indefinitely.*

Table 35-1 illustrates the cumulative effect of what seem to be very small differences in growth rates. Notice that if one country grows faster than another, the gap in their respective living standards will widen progressively. If, for example, countries A and B start from the same level of income and if country A grows at 3 percent per year while country B grows at 2 percent per year, A's per capita income will be twice B's in 72 years. You may not think

TABLE 35-1	The Cumulative Effect of Growth				
	Rate of growth per year				
Year	*1%*	*2%*	*3%*	*5%*	*7%*
0	100	100	100	100	100
10	111	122	135	165	201
30	135	182	246	448	817
50	165	272	448	1,218	3,312
70	201	406	817	3,312	13,429
100	272	739	2,009	14,841	109,660

Small differences in growth rates make enormous differences in levels of potential national income over a few decades. Let potential national income be 100 in year 0. At a rate of growth of 3 percent per year, it will be 135 in 10 years, 448 after 50 years, and over 2,000 in a century. The compounding of sustained rates of growth is a powerful force!

that it matters much whether the economy grows at 2 percent or 3 percent per year, but your children and grandchildren will! **[41]**

Economic Growth, Efficiency, and Redistribution

Observing that economic growth is the most important force for raising living standards over the long term in no way implies that policies designed to increase economic efficiency or to redistribute income are unimportant.

Reducing inefficiency. If, at any moment in time, national income could be increased by removing certain inefficiencies, such gains would be valuable. After all, any increase in national income is welcome in a world where many wants go unsatisfied. Furthermore, inefficiencies may themselves serve to reduce the growth rate. For example, the policy of import quotas on foreign sugar, which can be criticized for violating efficiency conditions in the food market, can also be criticized for hurting the international competitiveness of such sugar-using industries as fruit and vegetable canning by raising the cost of one of their major imports.

Redistribution. Economic growth has made the poor vastly better off than they would have been

if they had lived 100 years ago. Yet that is little consolation when they see that they can afford neither the basic medical treatment for themselves nor the schooling for their children that is currently available to citizens with higher incomes. After all, people compare themselves with others in their own society, not with their counterparts at other times or in other places. Because many people care about relative differences among individuals, governments continue to have policies to redistribute income and to make such basic services as education available to everyone, at least to some minimum acceptable degree.

Interrelations among the goals. Economists once assumed that the goals of redistributing income, increasing efficiency, and ensuring growth could each be treated independently of each other. It is now understood that income distribution, efficiency, and growth are interrelated. For example, policies that create extreme inefficiencies or a distribution of income unrelated to the market value of work can adversely affect the growth rate. It follows that policies designed to reduce inefficiencies or redistribute income need to be examined carefully for any effects that they may have on growth. A policy that reduces growth *may* be a bad bargain, even if it increases the immediate efficiency of the economy or creates a more equitable distribution of income.

Consider a hypothetical redistributive policy that raises the share of GDP going to poorer people by 5 percent but lowers the rate of economic growth from 2 to 1 percent. In 10 years those who gained from the policy would be no better off than if they had not received the redistribution of income while the growth rate had remained at 2 percent (and, of course, everyone who did not gain from the redistribution would be worse off). After 20 years, those who had gained from the redistribution would have 5 percent more of a national income that was 12 percent smaller than it would have been if the growth rate had remained at 2 percent.

Conversely, a policy that creates a more equitable distribution of income at only a small cost in terms of a lower growth rate may be judged an acceptable trade-off. Deciding among such competing policy goals requires value judgments that take us beyond economics. Economists play an important part, however, in establishing these interrelationships. Misguided policies are likely to be followed if policymakers think that measures adopted to get closer to any one of these goals will have no effect on the others.

Of course, not all redistribution policies have unfavorable effects on the growth rate. Some may have no effect, and others—by raising the health and educational standards of ordinary workers—may raise the growth rate.

Saving, Investment and Growth

Both saving and investment affect real national income. To understand their influence, it is critical to distinguish between their short-run and long-run effects.

Short-Run and Long-Run Effects of Investment

The theory of income determination that we studied in Part 7 is a short-run theory. It takes potential income as constant and concentrates on the effects of shifts in aggregate demand brought about by changes in various types of expenditure, including investment. These shifts cause actual national income to fluctuate around a given potential income. This short-term viewpoint is the focus of Figure 35-1(i).

In the long run, by adding to the nation's capital stock, investment raises potential income. This effect is shown by the continuing shift of the *LRAS* curve in Figure 35-1(iii).

The theory of economic growth is a long-run theory. It concentrates on the effects of investment in raising potential national income and ignores short-run fluctuations of actual national income around potential income.

The contrast between the short- and long-run aspects of investment is worth emphasizing. In the short run, any activity that puts income into people's hands will raise aggregate demand. Thus, the short-run effect on national income is the same whether a firm "invests" in digging holes and refilling them or in building a new factory. The long-run growth of potential income, however, is affected only by the part of investment that adds to a nation's productive capacity, that is, by the factory but not by the refilled hole.

Similar observations hold for public-sector expenditure. Any expenditure will add to aggregate demand and raise national income if there are un-employed resources, but only some expenditures increase potential income. Although public investment expenditure on such things as roads and health may increase potential national income, expenditure that shores up a declining industry in order to create employment may have an adverse effect on growth of potential income. The latter expenditure may prevent the reallocation of resources in response to shifts both in the pattern of world demand and in the country's comparative advantage. Thus, in the long run the country's capacity to produce commodities that are demanded on world markets may be diminished.

Short-Run and Long-Run Effects of Saving

The short-run effect of an increase in saving is to reduce aggregate demand. If, for example, households elect to save more, then they spend less. The resulting downward shift in the consumption function lowers aggregate demand and thus lowers equilibrium national income.

In the longer term, however, higher savings are necessary for higher investment. Firms usually reinvest their own savings, and the savings of households pass to firms, either directly through the purchase of stocks and bonds or indirectly through financial intermediaries. In the long run, the higher the level of savings, the higher the level of investment—and, due to the accumulation of more and better capital equipment, the higher the level of investment, the higher the level of real income. In Chapter 28 we saw that a high-saving economy accumulates assets faster, and thus grows faster, than does a low-saving economy.

In the long run, there is no paradox of thrift; societies with high savings rates have high investment rates and, other things being equal, high growth rates of real income.

When we refer to saving we refer, of course, to national saving: what the government saves or dissaves plus what the private sector saves. The amount of national saving available for private-sector investment is saving plus or minus the government's budget surplus or deficit: $S + (T - G)$, where, as we saw in Chapter 26, T is tax revenues net of transfer payments. This expression tells us that if the government spends more than it raises in taxes, then it diminishes the pool of savings available for private investment. In contrast, if the government spends less than it raises in taxes, then it adds to the pool.[2]

Benefits and Costs of Growth

We start by looking at the benefits of growth, and then we consider the costs. Boxes 35-1 and 35-2 outline some of the popular arguments on both sides of the growth debate.

Benefits of Growth

Growth and Living Standards

We have already observed that in the long term economic growth is the primary engine for raising general living standards. For those who share in it, growth is a powerful weapon against poverty. A family that is earning $25,000 today can expect an income of about $30,500 within 10 years (in constant dollars) if it shares in a 2 percent growth rate, and $37,000 if that rate is 4 percent.

The transformation of the life-style of ordinary workers in the United States and Canada between 1870 and 1970 (as well as in Europe and Japan) provides a notable example of the escape from poverty that growth makes possible. Much of the concern today over economic problems facing U.S. families stems from the decline of growth that occurred after 1970. Partly because growth has slowed and partly because the distribution of income has changed unfavorably to them, the incomes of the many working families have remained nearly constant over the last two decades.

Growth and Income Redistribution

Not everyone benefits equally from growth. Many of the poorest are not even in the labor force and thus are unlikely to share in the higher wages that, along with profits, are the primary means by which the gains from growth are distributed. For this reason, even in a growing economy, redistribution policies will be needed if poverty is to be averted.

A rapid growth rate makes the alleviation of poverty easier politically. If existing income is to be redistributed, someone's standard of living will actually have to be lowered. However, when there is economic growth and when the increment in income is redistributed (through government intervention), it is possible to reduce income inequalities without actually having to lower anyone's income. It is much easier for a rapidly growing economy to be generous toward its less fortunate citizens—or neighbors—than it is for a static economy.

Growth and Life-Style

A family often finds that a big increase in its income can lead to a major change in the pattern of its consumption—that extra money buys important amenities of life. In the same way, the members of society as a whole may change their consumption patterns as their average income rises. Not only do markets in a country that is growing rapidly make it profitable to produce more cars, but also the government is led to construct more highways and to provide more recreational areas for its newly affluent and mobile citizens. At yet a later stage, a concern about litter, pollution, and ugliness may become important, and their correction may then begin to account for a significant fraction of GDP. Such "amenities" usually become matters of social concern only when growth has ensured the provision of the basic requirements for food, clothing, and housing of a substantial majority of the population.

Costs of Growth

Other things being equal, most people would probably regard a fast rate of growth as preferable to a slow one, but other things are seldom equal.

The Opportunity Cost of Growth

In a world of scarcity, almost nothing is free. Growth requires heavy investments of resources in capital goods, as well as in activities such as education. Often these investments yield no immediate return in terms of goods and services for consumption; thus, they imply that sacrifices have been made by the current generation of consumers.

Growth, which promises more goods tomorrow, is achieved by consuming fewer goods today. For the economy as a whole, this sacrifice of current consumption is the primary cost of growth.

---

[2] It does this by paying off some of its debt and leaving these funds in the hands of private wealth holders.

Box 35-1

An Open Letter to the Ordinary Citizen from a Supporter of the "Growth Is Good" School

Dear Ordinary Citizen:

You live in the world's first civilization that is devoted principally to satisfying *your* needs rather than those of a privileged minority. Past civilizations have always been based on leisure and high consumption for a tiny upper class, a reasonable living standard for a small middle class, and hard work with little more than subsistence consumption for the great mass of people.

The continuing Industrial Revolution is based on mass-produced goods for you, the ordinary citizen. It ushered in a period of sustained economic growth that has dramatically raised consumption standards of ordinary citizens. Reflect on a few examples: travel, live and recorded music, art, good food, inexpensive books, universal literacy, and a genuine chance to be educated. Most important, there is leisure to provide time and energy to enjoy these and thousands of other products of the modern industrial economy.

Would any ordinary family seriously prefer to go back to the world of 150 or 500 years ago in its same relative social and economic position? Surely the answer is no. However, for those with incomes in the top 1 or 2 percent of the income distribution, economic growth has destroyed much of their privileged consumption position. They must now vie with the masses when they visit the world's beauty spots and be annoyed, while lounging on the terrace of a palatial mansion, by the sound of charter flights carrying ordinary people to inexpensive holidays in far places. Many of the rich complain bitterly about the loss of exclusive rights to luxury consumption, and it is not surprising that they find their intellectual apologists. Whether they know it or not, the anti-growth economists are not the social revolutionaries that they think they are. They say that growth has produced pollution and wasteful consumption of all kinds of frivolous products that add nothing to human happiness. However, the democratic solution to pollution is not to go back to where so few people consume luxuries that pollution is trivial but rather to learn to control the pollution that mass consumption tends to create.

It is only through further growth that the average citizen can enjoy consumption standards (of travel, culture, medical and health care, etc.) now available only to people in the top 25 percent of the income distribution—which includes the intellectuals who earn large royalties from the books that they write in which they denounce growth. If you think that extra income confers little real benefit, just ask those in the top 25 percent to trade incomes with average citizens.

Ordinary citizens, do not be deceived by disguised elitist doctrines. Remember that the very rich and the elite have much to gain by stopping growth and even more by rolling it back, but you have everything to gain by letting it go forward.

Onward!

A. N. Optimist

An example will suggest the magnitude of this cost. Suppose that a hypothetical economy has full employment and is experiencing growth at the rate of 2 percent per year. Its citizens consume 85 percent of the GDP and invest 15 percent. They know that, if they immediately decrease their consumption to 77 percent of GDP, they will produce more capital and thus shift at once to a 3 percent growth rate.

Box 35-2

An Open Letter to the Ordinary Citizen from a Supporter of the "Growth Is Bad" School

Dear Ordinary Citizen:

You live in a world that is being despoiled by a mindless search for ever-higher levels of material consumption at the cost of all other values. Once upon a time, men and women knew how to enjoy creative work and to derive satisfaction from simple activities. Today the ordinary worker is a mindless cog in an assembly line that turns out more and more goods that the advertisers must work overtime to persuade the worker to consume.

Statisticians count the increasing flow of material output as a triumph of modern civilization. You arise from your electric-blanketed bed, clean your teeth with an electric toothbrush, open a can of the sad remnants of a once-proud orange with an electric can opener, and eat your bread baked from superrefined and chemically refortified flour; you climb into your car to sit in vast traffic jams on exhaust-polluted highways.

Television commercials tell you that by consuming more you are happier, but happiness lies not in increasing consumption but in increasing the ratio of *satisfaction of wants* to *total wants*. Since the more you consume, the more the advertisers persuade you that you want to consume, you are almost certainly less happy than the average citizen in a small town in 1900, whom we can visualize sitting on the family porch, sipping lemonade, and enjoying the antics of the children as they jump rope with pieces of old clothesline.

Today the landscape is dotted with endless factories that produce the plastic trivia of the modern industrial society. They drown you in a cloud of noise, air, and water pollution. The countryside is despoiled by strip mines, petroleum refineries, acid rain, and dangerous nuclear power stations, producing energy that is devoured insatiably by modern factories and motor vehicles. Worse, our precious heritage of natural resources is being rapidly depleted.

Now is the time to stop this madness. We must stabilize production, reduce pollution, conserve our natural resources, and seek justice through a more equitable distribution of existing total income.

A long time ago, Malthus taught us that if we do not limit population voluntarily, nature will do it for us in a cruel and savage manner. Today the same is true of output: If we do not halt its growth voluntarily, the halt will be imposed on us by a disastrous increase in pollution and a rapid exhaustion of natural resources.

Citizens, awake! Shake off the worship of growth, learn to enjoy the bounty that is yours already, and reject the endless, self-defeating search for increased happiness through ever-increasing consumption.

Upward!

I. Realvalues

The new rate can be maintained as long as they keep saving and investing 23 percent of the national income. Should they do it?

Table 35-2 illustrates the choice in terms of time paths of consumption. Using the assumed figures, it takes 10 years for the actual amount of consumption to catch up to what it would have been had no reallocation been made. In the intervening 10 years, a good deal of consumption is lost, and the cumulative losses in consumption must be made up before society can really be said to have broken even. It takes an additional 9 years before total consumption over

TABLE 35-2 The Opportunity Cost of Growth

Year	(1) Level of consumption at 2% growth rate	(2) Level of consumption at 3% growth rate	(3) Cumulative gain (loss) in consumption
0	85.0	77.0	(8.0)
1	86.7	79.3	(15.4)
2	88.5	81.8	(22.1)
3	90.3	84.2	(28.2)
4	92.1	86.8	(33.5)
5	93.9	89.5	(37.9)
6	95.8	92.9	(40.8)
7	97.8	95.0	(43.6)
8	99.7	97.9	(45.4)
9	101.8	100.9	(46.3)
10	103.8	103.9	(46.2)
15	114.7	120.8	(28.6)
20	126.8	140.3	19.6
30	154.9	189.4	251.0
40	189.2	255.6	745.9

Transferring resources from consumption to investment goods lowers current income but raises future income. The example assumes that income in year zero is 100 and that consumption of 85 percent of national income is possible with a 2 percent growth rate. It is further assumed that to achieve a 3 percent growth rate, consumption must fall to 77 percent of income. A shift from column 1 to column 2 decreases consumption for 10 years but increases it thereafter. The cumulative effect on consumption is shown in column 3; the gains eventually become very large.

the whole period is as large is it would have been if the economy had remained on the 2 percent path. **[42]**

Over a longer period, however, the payoff from the progrowth policy becomes enormous. Forty years on, the national income in the more rapidly growing economy is 35 percent higher than in the slower growing economy. The total difference in consumption over those 40 years has become three times the annual amount of consumption in the faster growing society at year 40.

Social and Personal Costs of Growth

A growing economy is a changing economy. Innovation renders some machines obsolete and also leaves some people partly obsolete. No matter how well trained workers are at age 25, in another 25

years many will find that their skills are at least partly obsolete. A rapid growth rate requires rapid adjustments, which can cause much upset and misery to the people who are affected by it.

It is often argued that costs of this kind are a small price to pay for the great benefits that growth can bring. Even if this is true in the aggregate, these personal costs are very unevenly borne. Indeed, many of those for whom growth is most costly (in terms of lost jobs) share least in the fruits that growth brings.

Theories of Economic Growth

In this section we study some of the new theories that seek to explain economic growth. This is an exciting area. Ideas are changing rapidly as research of both a theoretical and an empirical nature expands our knowledge of the growth process.

Research suggests that four of the most important determinants of growth of total output are:

1. *Growth in the labor force* such as occurs when the population grows or participation rates[3] rise
2. *Investment in human capital* such as comes from formal education and on-the-job experience
3. *Investment in physical capital* such as factories, machines, and transportation and communications facilities
4. *Technological change* brought about by innovation that introduces new products, new ways of producing existing products, and new forms of business organization

The Aggregate Production Function

To study how these four forces operate, we first write a simple expression for the relation between the total amounts of labor (L) and capital (K) employed and the nation's total output, its GDP:

$$GDP = f(L, K)$$

This is called the **aggregate production function.** It is aggregate because it relates the economy's total output, its GDP, to the total amount of the two

---

[3] Recall that the participation rate is the proportion of the total population that is in the labor force.

main factors that are used to produce that output.[4] (A microproduction function, such as is discussed in Chapters 10 and 11, relates the output of one firm or one industry to the factors of production employed by that firm or industry.) The function, indicated by the letter f, shows the relation between the inputs of L and K and the output of GDP. The production function tells us how much GDP will be produced for given amounts of labor and capital employed. For example, the function may tell us that when 200 million units of labor and 300 million units of capital are used, the GDP will be 2,450 million. **[43]**

We may now use this aggregate production function to discuss some theories of economic growth.

Neoclassical Growth Theory

One branch of neoclassical theory deals with growth when the stock of technological knowledge remains

---

[4] Basic growth theory emphasizes the production of manufactured goods and services where, in contrast to agriculture, land is rarely a limiting factor. All the relatively small amounts of land that are needed can be obtained and, hence, nothing significant is lost by ignoring land in the analysis of an industrialized economy—although this could not be done for a agricultural economy.

unchanged. There are no innovations: no new ways of making things, and no new products. As a result, the relation between inputs and output, as shown by the production function, does not change. The key aspects of what is called the neoclassical model are that the aggregate production function displays *decreasing returns* when either factor is increased on its own, and *constant returns* when both factors are increased together (and in the same proportion).

Decreasing Returns to a Single Factor

To start with, suppose that the population of the country grows while the stock of capital remains constant. More and more people go to work using a fixed quantity of capital. The amount that each new unit of input adds to total output is called its *marginal product*. The operation of the famous **law of diminishing returns** tells us that the employment of equal additional amounts of labor will eventually add less to total output than the previous unit. In other words, sooner or later each additional unit of labor will encounter a diminishing marginal product. Table 35-3 and Figure 35-2 illustrate this famous relation, which is referred to as *diminishing returns to a single factor*.

The law of diminishing returns applies to any factor that is varied while the other factors are held

TABLE 35-3   Diminishing Returns Illustrated

(1) Units of fixed factor	(2) Units of variable factor	(3) Units of total output	Average product of labor (column 3 ÷ column 2)	Marginal product of labor (change in column 3)
9	1	12.0	12	12.0
9	2	17.0	8.5	5.0
9	3	20.8	6.9	3.8
9	4	24.0	6.0	3.2
9	5	26.8	5.4	2.8
9	6	29.4	4.9	2.6
9	7	31.9	4.6	2.5
9	8	34.0	4.2	2.1
9	9	36.0	4.0	2.0
9	10	37.9	3.8	1.9

With one input held constant, the marginal and average products of the variable input eventually decline. Column 3 shows total output as more and more of the variable factor is used in combination with a fixed quantity of a fixed factor. **[44]** The average product, which is total product divided by the number of units of the variable factor, declines continuously. The marginal product, which is the increase in total product as successive units of the variable factor are added, also declines continuously.

FIGURE 35-2
The Average and Marginal Products of a Variable Factor

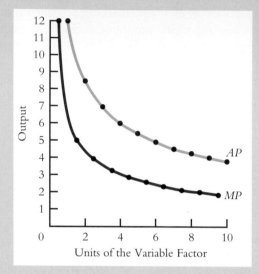

The average and marginal products of any variable factor decline as successive units of that factor are added to a fixed amount of another factor. This figure plots the data from Table 35-3. It shows the marginal and average products of variable factor declining as more and more units of that factor are used. The marginal products are plotted between the units of the variable factor since they apply to a change from one amount to the next.

constant. Thus, successive amounts of capital added to *a fixed supply of labor* will also eventually add less and less to GDP.

According to the law of diminishing returns, the increment to total production will eventually fall steadily whenever equal increases of a variable factor of production are combined with another factor of production whose quantity is fixed.[5]

Constant Returns to Scale

The other main property of the neoclassical aggregate production function is called **constant returns to scale**. This rule says that if the amounts of both labor and capital are both changed in equal proportion, the total output will also change in that proportion. For example, 10 percent increases in the amounts of both labor and capital used will lead to a 10 percent increase in GDP.

Sources of Growth in the Neoclassical Model

Now consider each of the sources of growth listed above. To begin with, we let each source operate with the others held constant.

Labor force growth. In the long term we can associate labor force growth with population growth (although in the short term the labor force can grow if participation rates rise even though the population remains constant). As more labor is used, there will be more output and, consequently, growth in total GDP. The law of diminishing returns tells us that, sooner or later, each further unit of labor to be employed will cause smaller and smaller additions to GDP. Eventually, not only will the marginal product of labor be falling, but the average product will fall as well. Beyond that point, although economic growth continues in the sense that total output is growing, living standards are falling in the sense that average GDP per head of population is falling. If we are interested in growth in living standards, we are concerned with increasing GDP *per person*. Whenever diminishing returns applies, increases in population on their own are accompanied by falling living standards.[6]

Human capital. Capital often means physical capital, the plants and equipment that embody current technological knowledge. Another kind of capital is also of great importance to the growth process. This is human capital, the knowledge and skills embodied in people.

---

[5] In some production functions, marginal product may rise at first and only begin to decline after a certain critical amount of the variable factor is used. In the neoclassical, constant-returns function, however, marginal product declines from the outset as shown in the figures.

[6] In the neoclassical model, diminishing returns sets in from the outset, so that there is no range over which population increases cause rising marginal or average product of labor. The issue of when diminishing returns sets in need not concern us here, since all that matters for the text discussion is that increases in any one factor, other things held constant, must encounter diminishing returns sooner or later.

Human capital has several aspects. One involves improvements in the health and longevity of the population. Of course, these are desired as ends in themselves, but they also have consequences for both the size and the productivity of the labor force. There is no doubt that improvements in the health of workers have increased productivity per worker-hour by cutting down on illness, accidents, and absenteeism.

A second aspect of the quality of human capital concerns technical training—from learning to operate a machine to learning how to be a scientist. This training depends on the current state of knowledge, and advances in knowledge allow us not only to build more productive physical capital but also to create more effective human capital. Training is clearly required if a person is to operate, repair, manage, or invent complex machines. More subtly, there may be general social advantages to an educated population. Productivity improves with literacy. The longer a person has been educated, the more adaptable, and thus the more productive in the long run, that person is in the face of new and changing challenges.

A third aspect of human capital is its contribution to growth and innovation. Not only can current human capital embody in people the best current technological knowledge, but, by training potential innovators, it leads to advances in our knowledge and hence contributes to growth.

Physical capital. Increases in the amount of capital on their own affect GDP in a manner similar to population growth alone. Eventually, each successive unit of capital will add less to total output than each previous unit of capital.

There is, however, a major contrast with the case of labor growth because it is output per person that determines living standards, not output per unit of capital. Thus, as capital increases, living standards increase because output is rising while the population is constant. Indeed, per capita output can be increased by adding more capital as long as its marginal product exceeds zero. However, since the increases in output are subject to diminishing returns, successive additions to the economy's capital stock bring smaller and smaller increases in per capita output.

In the neoclassical model, the operation of diminishing returns means that capital accumulation on its own brings smaller and smaller increases in per capita GDP.

Balanced growth. Now consider what happens if labor and capital grow at the same rate. In this case, the neoclassical assumption of constant returns to scale means that GDP grows in proportion to the increases in inputs. As a result, per capita output (GDP/L) remains constant. Thus, growth in labor and capital leads to growth in total GDP but unchanged per capita GDP.

This "balanced growth path" is not, however, the kind of growth that concerns those interested in living standards. It is just more of the same: larger and larger economies, with more capital and more labor doing exactly what the existing capital and the existing labor was already doing. There is nothing new.

Growth and living standards. In this neoclassical model with constant technology, the only way for growth to add to living standards is for the per capita capital stock to increase. The law of diminishing returns dictates, however, that the rise in living standards brought about by successive equal increases in capital will inexorably diminish. Raising living standards becomes more and more difficult as capital accumulation continues.

The Solow Residual

In 1957 Robert Solow, who subsequently won the Nobel Prize in economics for his path-breaking work in growth and other fields of economics, decided to see what the data could tell him about the type of growth model we have just been discussing.

He took U.S. data from 1909 to 1949, using measures of the total labor force, the total capital stock, and GDP, and applied it to the neoclassical production function given earlier in this section.[7] He made two important discoveries.

First, only about half of the growth in *total GDP* could be accounted for by growth in the inputs of labor and capital. Second, less than 20 percent of the growth in *GDP per person employed* could be accounted for by the growth in the capital stock. The growth in GDP that could *not* be accounted for by increased use of capital and labor came to be called the *Solow residual*. It was assumed to be caused by technical change coming from innovation, (although other influences on labor and capital not

---

[7] This was done by using standard statistical techniques to fit the production function to the data.

FIGURE 35-3
Shifts in the Marginal Products of Labor and Capital

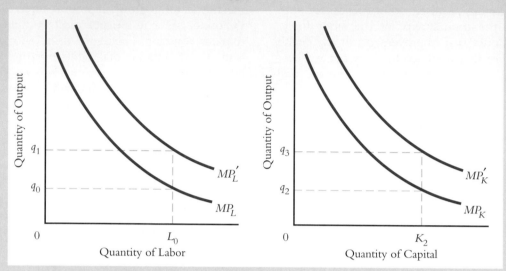

Technological change shifts the marginal product curves such that each unit of the factor adds more to the total product than previously. The original marginal product curves are MP_L and MP_K. Technological change then alters the production function to allow any given amount of labor and capital to produce more. The marginal product of labor for a given amount of capital shifts to MP_L'. The marginal product of each unit of labor therefore rises. For example, whereas the unit L_0 previously had a marginal product of q_0, its marginal product is now q_1. Likewise, the marginal product curve of capital for a given amount of labor shifts from MP_K to MP_K'. Now each quantity of capital has a higher marginal product than it had previously. For example, the unit K_2, which formerly had a marginal product of q_2, now has a marginal product of q_3.

incorporated in Solow's measurements also turned out to have significant effects).

In the neoclassical model, technological change can be regarded as shifting the production function so that the same amount of labor and capital produce more GDP. This result is depicted in Figure 35-3 by rightward shifts in the MP curves of labor and capital: The same amount of input produces more output. **[45]**

Technological Change

New knowledge and inventions can contribute markedly to the growth of potential national income, even without capital accumulation. To illustrate this point, assume that the proportion of a society's resources that is devoted to the production of capital goods is just sufficient to replace capital as it wears out. Thus, if the old capital is merely replaced in the same form, the capital stock will be constant, and there will be no increase in the capacity to produce.

However, if there is a growth of knowledge, so that, as old equipment wears out, it is replaced by different, more productive equipment, national income will be growing.

Increases in productive capacity that are created by installing new and better capital goods are called **embodied technical change.** The historical importance of embodied technical change is clear: The assembly line and automation transformed most manufacturing industries, the airplane revolutionized transportation, and electronic devices now dominate the information-technology industries. These innovations, plus less well-known but no less profound ones—for example, improvements in the strength of metals, the productivity of seeds, and the techniques for recovering basic raw materials from the ground—create new investment opportunities.

Less obvious but nonetheless important changes occur through **disembodied technical change**, that is, changes in the organization of production that are not embodied in particular capital goods. Examples are improved techniques of management, design, marketing, and feedback from user experience to product improvement.

Most innovations involve both embodied and disembodied changes. They cause continual changes in the techniques of production and in the nature of what is produced. Looking back over the past century, firms produce very few products today in the same way that they did in the past, and much of what is produced and consumed is in the form of new or vastly improved products. Major innovations of the twentieth century include the development of such key products as the telephone, the automobile, the airplane, plastics, coaxial cable, xerography, the electron microscope, the computer, the transistor, and the silicon chip. It is hard for us to imagine life without them.

The modern understanding that technological innovation is at the heart of the growth process has led to two important developments in many economists' views on growth. The first is that technological change is largely endogenous to the economic system. The second is that investment that increases the capital stock may encounter increasing rather than diminishing returns. These insights have led to new growth theories that go far beyond the neoclassical growth model.

Endogenous Growth

In the neoclassical model, innovation shifts the production function but is itself unexplained (it is assumed to be measured by the unexplained residual—the amount of income growth that cannot be accounted for by anything else). This view holds that technological change is *exogenous*. It has profound effects on economic variables, such as GDP, but it is not influenced by economic causes. It just happens.

Yet microeconomic research by many scholars over the last several decades has established that technological change is responsive to such economic "signals" as prices and profits; in other words, it is *endogenous* to the economic system. Much of the earliest work on this issue was done in Europe by scholars associated with the Science Policy Research Unit (SPRU) in Sussex, England. The most influential overall single study, however, was by the American professor Nathan Rosenberg, whose path-breaking

book *Inside the Black Box* argued this case in great detail.

Technological change stems from research and development and from innovating activities that put the results of R&D into practice. These are costly and highly risky activities, undertaken largely by firms and usually in pursuit of profit. Not surprisingly, these activities respond to economic incentives. If the price of some particular input, such as petroleum or skilled labor, goes up, R&D and innovating activities will work to alter the production function to economize on these inputs. This process is not a substitution of less expensive inputs for more expensive ones within the confines of known technologies; rather, it is the development of new technologies in response to changes in relative prices. Not only does Rosenberg show that R&D that applies known basic principles is responsive to economic signals, but he also shows that basic research itself is responsive. One reason for the latter is that the basic research agenda is strongly influenced by practical issues of the day. For example, basic research in metallurgy became popular, and was heavily funded, when the development of jet aircraft and space vehicles required the ability to cope with stresses and heat far greater than anything encountered by propeller aircraft.

There are many important implications of this new understanding that, to a great extent, growth is achieved through costly, risky, innovative activity that occurs in response to economic signals. We will now discuss some of these implications.

The Complexity of the Innovation Process

The pioneering theorist of innovation, Joseph Schumpeter, developed a model in which innovation flowed in one direction, from a pure discovery, to more applied R&D, then to working machines, and finally to output.

In contrast, modern research shows that innovation involves a large amount of "learning by doing" at all of its stages.[8] What is learned "downstream" then modifies what must be done "upstream." The best innovation-managing systems encourage feedback from the more applied steps to the purer researchers and from users to designers.

---

[8] This phenomenon, whereby costs per unit of output fall steadily over time as firms learn how to manage new technologies, is discussed in more detail in Chapter 36.

This interaction is illustrated by the differences between the Japanese automobile manufacturers and their U.S. competitors in the handling of new models. U.S. design has traditionally been centralized: Design production teams develop the overall design and then instruct their production sections what to do, as well as asking for bids from parts manufacturers to produce according to specific blueprints. As a result, defects in the original design are often not discovered until production is under way, causing many costly delays and rejection of parts already supplied. Japanese firms involve their design and production departments and their parts manufacturers in all stages of the design process. Parts manufacturers are not given specific blueprints for production but, rather, are given general specifications and asked to develop their own detailed designs. As they do so, they learn and feed information about the problems they are encountering back to the main designers while the general outlines are not yet finalized. As a result, the Japanese usually design a new product faster, at less cost, and with far fewer problems when production is finally put into place.[9]

The Location of Innovation

Innovation typically takes place in different parts of the producer-user chain in different industries—as shown, for example, by the research of Eric von Hippel of Harvard University. In some industries, manufacturers make most of the product innovations. In other industries, users make most of them.

Unless these differences are appreciated, public policy designed to encourage innovation can go seriously astray. An example is provided by von Hippel in the following words:

> [C]onsider the current concern of U.S. policymakers that the products of U.S. semiconductor process equipment firms are falling behind the leading edge. The conventional assessment of this problem is that these firms should somehow be strengthened and helped to innovate so that U.S. semiconductor equipment users (makers of semiconductors) will not also fall behind. But investigation shows that most process equipment innovations in this field are, in fact, de-

veloped by equipment *users*. Therefore, the causality is probably reversed: U.S. equipment builders are falling behind because the U.S. user community they deal with is falling behind. If this is so, the policy prescription should change: Perhaps U.S. equipment builders can best be helped by helping U.S. equipment users to innovate at the leading edge once more.[10]

The message for policymakers is important: An understanding of the details of the innovating process in each industry is needed if successful innovation-encouraging policies are to be developed.

Costly Diffusion

The *diffusion* of technological knowledge from those who have it to those who want it is not costless (as it was assumed to be in Schumpeter's model). Firms need research capacity just to adopt the technologies developed by others. Some of the knowledge needed to use a new technology can only be learned through experience by plant managers, technicians, and operators (such knowledge is called *tacit*). We often tend to think that once a production process is developed, it can easily be copied by others. Indeed, some advanced economic theories use the hypothesis of replication, which holds that any known process can be replicated in any new location by using the same factor inputs and management as are used in the old location. In practice, however, the diffusion of new technological knowledge is not so simple.

For example, Richard Nelson of Columbia University and Sidney Winter of the General Accounting Office in Washington, D.C., have argued that most industrial technologies require technology-specific organizational skills that can be "embodied" neither in the machines themselves, nor in instruction books, nor in blueprints. Acquiring tacit knowledge requires a deliberate process of building up new skills, work practices, knowledge, and experience:

> As an initial perspective on the problem, we would not recommend the [hypothesis of replication]... but the following account from Polayni: "...even in modern industries the indefinable knowledge is still an essential part of technology. I have myself watched in Hungary a new, imported machine for blowing electric lamp bulbs, the exact counterpart of which was

---

[9] A detailed account of this issue can be found in J. Womack, D. Jones, and D. Roos, *The Machine That Changed the World* (New York: Ransom Associates, 1990). U.S. firms have recently begun to adopt some of these Japanese practices.

[10] Eric von Hippel, *The Sources of Innovation* (New York: Oxford University Press, 1988), pp. 9–10.

operating successfully in Germany, failing for a whole year to produce a single flawless bulb[!]" ...[T]he creation of productive organizations is *not* a matter of implementing fully explicit blueprints by purchasing homogeneous inputs on anonymous markets, a firm that is already successful in a given activity is a particularly good candidate for being successful with new capacity of the same sort.[11]

The fact that diffusion is a costly, risky, and time-consuming business explains why new technologies take considerable time to diffuse, first through the economy of the originating country and then through the rest of the world. If diffusion were simple and virtually costless, the puzzle would be why technological knowledge, and best industrial practices, did not diffuse very quickly. As it is, decades can pass before a new technological process is diffused everywhere that it could be employed.

Market Structure and Innovation

Because it is highly risky, innovation is encouraged by a strongly competitive environment and discouraged by monopoly practices. Competition among three or four large firms often produces much innovation, but a single firm, especially if it serves a secure homemarket protected by trade barriers, seems much less inclined to innovate.[12]

---

[11] R. Nelson and S. Winter, *An Evolutionary Theory of Economic Change* (Cambridge, MA: Harvard University Press, 1982), p. 119.

[12] This is an important theme in much contemporary research, supported by evidence from such authors as Alfred D. Chandler, Jr. (*Scale and Scope: The Dynamics of Industrial Capitalism,* Cambridge, MA: Harvard University Press, 1990), David Mowrey and Nathan Rosenberg (*Technology and the Pursuit of Economic Growth*, Cambridge, England: Cambridge University Press, 1989), and Michael Porter (*The Competitive Advantage of Nations,* New York: Free Press, 1990). Although the ideas of Joseph Schumpeter lie behind much of modern growth theory, this emphasis on competition seems on the surface to conflict with his ideas. The apparent conflict arises because the theories available to Schumpeter offered only two market structures, perfect competition and monopoly. He chose monopoly as the structure more conducive to growth on the grounds that monopoly profits would provide the incentive to innovate, and innovation itself would provide the mechanism whereby new entrants could compete with established monopolies. (He called this latter process "creative destruction.") Modern economists, faced with a richer variety of theoretical market structures, find that competition among oligopolists is usually more conducive to growth-enhancing, technological change than is monopoly.

Government interventions that are designed to encourage innovation often allow the firms in an industry to work together as one. Unless great care is exercised, and unless sufficient foreign competition exists, the result may be a national monopoly that will discourage risk taking rather than encourage it, as is the intention of the policy.

The United Kingdom provides many examples of this mistaken view of policy. For example, British policy in the 1960s:

> ...operated under the faulty theory that encouraging British companies to merge would create world-class competitors. Consolidation of steel, automobiles, machine tools, and computers all led to notable failures. A program of research support for industry...proved disastrous. The British government tried to choose promising technologies and gave direct grants to firms to develop them. Most of the choices were failures. [In constrast]...unusually low levels of regulation in some service industries have avoided disadvantages faced by other nations and allowed innovation and change...in auctioneering...trading and insurance. British firms in these industries have been among the most innovative in the world.[13]

Culture and Innovation

Innovation is a highly risky business with results that are very hard to predict. One researcher called innovators "maniacs with a vision." In other words, although innovation does respond to economic incentives, it is not such a simple matter as calculating which of several established techniques to adopt when building a new factory. The nature of innovation may therefore be influenced by many forces, such as national character, religion, and the country's social attitude toward failure. For example, in English-speaking countries, a failure or two on the way to becoming a millionaire is usually taken to be one of the normal risks of business. In other countries, such as Germany and Japan, however, failure in business has serious adverse social consequences. As a result, the climate for new, start-up businesses seems to be more favorable in the United States than in Germany and Japan.

Shocks and Innovation

One interesting consequence of endogenous technical change is that shocks that would be unambigu-

---

[13] Porter, *The Competitive Advantage of Nations,* p. 507.

ously adverse to an economy operating with fixed technology can sometimes provide a spur to innovation that proves a blessing in disguise. A sharp rise in the price of one input can raise costs and lower the value of output per person for some time. But it may lead to a wave of innovations that reduce the need for this expensive input and, as a side effect, greatly raise the productivity of labor.[14]

Sometimes individual firms will respond differently to the same economic signal. Sometimes those who respond by altering technology will do better than those who concentrate their efforts on substituting within the confines of known technology. For example, in *The Competitive Advantage of Nations*, Michael Porter tells the story of the consumer electronics industry, in which U.S. firms moved their operations abroad to avoid high, and rigid, labor costs. They continued to use their existing technology and went where labor costs were low enough to make that technology pay. Their Japanese competitors, however, stayed at home. They innovated away most of their labor costs and then built factories in the United States to replace the factories of U.S. firms that had gone abroad!

Innovation as a Competitive Strategy

Managing innovation better than one's competitors is one of the most important objectives of modern firms that wish to survive. Firms often fail because they do not keep up with their competitors in the race to develop new and improved products and techniques of production and distribution.[15] Success in real-world competition often depends more on success in managing innovation than on success in adopting the right pricing policies or in making the right capacity decisions from already-known technological possibilities.

Increasing Returns Theories

We saw earlier that neoclassical theories assume that investment is always subject to diminishing returns. New growth theories emphasize the possibility of *increasing returns to investment*. A number of sources of increasing returns have been noted. These fall under the general categories of fixed costs and ideas.

Fixed Costs

1. Investment in the early stages of development of a country, state, or town may create new skills and attitudes in the work force that are then available to all subsequent investors, whose costs are therefore lower than those encountered by the initial investors.
2. Each new investor may find the environment more and more favorable to its investment because of the infrastructure that has been created by those who came before.
3. The first investment in a new product will encounter countless problems both of production and of product acceptance among customers that, once overcome, cause fewer problems to subsequent investors.

All of these cases, and many more that could be mentioned, are examples of a single phenomenon:

Many investments require fixed costs, the advantages of which are then available to subsequent investors; hence, the investment costs for "followers" can be substantially less than the investment costs for "pioneers."[16]

More generally, many of the sources of increasing returns are variations on the following general theme: Doing something really new is difficult, both technically and in terms of customer acceptance, whereas making further variations on an accepted and developed new idea becomes progressively easier.

We have already seen one reason for this rule: The costly knowledge developed by early pioneers often becomes available to followers at a much lower cost. A second reason concerns customers. When a new product is developed, customers will often resist

---

[14] This is why in microeconomics we study three runs: the short run, the long run, and the very long run. Often, the very-long-run response to a change in relative prices is much more important than either the short-run response, limited by fixed capital, or the long-run response, limited by existing technology.

[15] The book *Made in America: Regaining the Competitive Edge*, by M. Dertouzous, R. Lester, and R. Solow (Cambridge, MA: MIT Press, 1989), gives a series of case studies where these are the reasons why U.S. firms have lost out to the Japanese and why in other cases U.S. firms have done better than their Japanese competitors.

[16] The general phenomenon discussed here has been the subject of intense study since the early 1970s.

adopting it, both because they may be conservative and because they know that new products usually have teething troubles. Customers also need time to learn how best to use the new product—they need to do what is called "learning by using." The first firms in the field with a truly new idea, such as personal computers, usually meet strong customer resistance, but this resistance erodes over time.

Slow acceptance of new products by customers is not necessarily irrational. When a sophisticated new product comes on the market, no one is sure if it will be a success, and the first customers to buy it take the risk that the product may subsequently turn out to be a failure. They also incur the costs of learning how to use it effectively. Many potential users take the not unreasonable attitude of letting others try a new product, following only after the product's success has been demonstrated. This makes the early stages of innovation especially costly and risky.

These points lead to the following overall result:

For many reasons, successive increments of investment associated with a new set of innovations often yield a range of increasing returns, as costs that are incurred in earlier investment expenditure provide publicly available knowledge and experience and as customer attitudes and abilities become more receptive to new products.

The implications of these ideas have been the subject of intense study ever since they were first embedded in modern growth models by Paul Romer of the University of California and Robert Lucas of the University of Chicago.[17] Probably the most important contrast between these new theories and the neoclassical theory concerns investment and income. In the neoclassical model, diminishing returns to capital implies a limit to the possible increase of per capita GDP. In the new models, investment alone can leave a constant population on a "sustained growth path" in which per capita GDP increases without limit, provided that the investment embodies the results of continual advances in technological knowledge.

Ideas

An even more fundamental change in the new theories is the shift from the economics of goods to the economics of ideas. The economics of ideas is profoundly different from the economics of physical goods, and the differences are only just beginning to be appreciated.

Physical goods, such as factories and machines, exist in one place at one time. The nature of this existence has two consequences. First, when physical goods are used by someone, they cannot be used by someone else. Second, if a given labor force is provided with more and more physical objects to use in production, sooner or later diminishing returns will be encountered.

Ideas have different characteristics. First, once someone develops ideas, they are available for use by everyone. Ideas can be used by one person without reducing their use by others. For example, if one firm uses a truck, another firm cannot use it at the same time, but one firm's use of a revolutionary design for a new suspension on a truck does not prevent other firms from using that design as well. Ideas are not subject to the same use restrictions as goods.

Second, ideas are not necessarily subject to decreasing returns. As our knowledge increases, each increment of new knowledge does not inevitably add less to our productive ability as did each previous increment. A year spent improving the operation of semiconductors may be more productive than a year spent improving the operation of vacuum tubes (the technology used before semiconductors).

The evidence from modern research is that new technologies are usually absolutely factor saving—in other words, they use less of all inputs per unit of output. Furthermore, there is no evidence that from decade to decade the factor saving associated with increments of new knowledge is diminishing.

Modern growth theories stress the importance of ideas in producing what can be called knowledge-driven growth. New knowledge provides the input that allows investment to produce increasing rather than diminishing returns. Since there are no practical boundaries to human knowledge, there need be no immediate boundaries to finding new ways to produce more output using less of all inputs.[18]

---

[17] As with so many innovations, these new views have many historical antecedents, including a classic article in the 1960s by Nobel Prize winner Kenneth Arrow of Stanford University.

[18] Possibly, at some distant date, we may know everything there is to know, but if it ever comes, that date is clearly a long, long way in the future.

Classical and neoclassical growth theories gave economics the name "dismal science" by emphasizing diminishing returns under conditions of given technology. The modern growth theories are more optimistic because they emphasize the unlimited potential of knowledge-driven technological change to economize on all resource inputs and because they display increasing returns to investment with constant population.

Insofar as these new ideas are true, however, they refer to long-term trends. The dynamics of market systems cause growth rates to vary from decade to decade for reasons that are not fully understood. Over the long haul, however, there seems no reason to believe that equal increments of human effort must inevitably be rewarded by ever diminishing increments to material output.

Convergence or Divergence of Growth Rates

A lively current debate concerns whether growth rates will converge or diverge across nations. What does theory predict, and what do we observe?

The neoclassical model predicts that growth rates in each country will converge to a steady state that will leave the ratios of real per capita incomes constant across countries. The new theories of endogenous growth predict that per capita incomes will diverge over time as those countries that are ahead gain progressively more from the scale economies compared with those that are currently behind. The evidence is not clear on these predictions, since some groups of countries seem to be converging toward the levels of income achieved by the advanced countries, while others seem to be falling steadily behind.

Those who look to microeconomic explanations of growth based on historical situations argue that there can be no simple prediction of either convergence or divergence. If economies were all converging, the question arises: Why did they diverge in the first place? If they are all diverging steadily, the question arises: What happened before they were all at the same position (which is what a divergent model predicts if things were pushed backward in time)? Those who study historically based growth argue that at various stages of the process of introducing new technologies, leaders will pull away from the pack, and at other stages followers will catch up. They argue that both convergence and divergence should be observed, depending on the particular circumstances of the time.

Further Causes of Growth

So far we have looked at increases in labor and capital and at innovation as causes of growth. Contemporary studies suggest that other causes of growth are also important. The influence of these other causes appears as shifts in the production function, so that any given number of hours of labor operating with a given amount of capital produce more and more output as time passes.

Institutions

Almost all aspects of a country's institutions can foster or deter the efficient use of a society's natural and human resources. Social and religious habits, legal institutions, and traditional patterns of national and international trade are all important. So, too, is the political climate.

Historians of economic growth, such as Paul David and Nathan Rosenberg, attribute much of the growth of Western economies in the postmedieval world to the development of *new institutions*, such as the joint-stock company and limited liability. Many students of modern growth suggest that institutions are as important today as they were in the past. They suggest that the societies that are most successful in developing the new institutions that are needed in today's knowledge-intensive world of globalized competition will be the ones at the forefront of new economic growth.

The Role of the Government

Governments play an important role in the growth process.

First, the government needs to provide the framework for the market economy that is given by such things as well-defined property rights secure from arbitrary confiscation, security and enforcement of contracts, law and order, a sound money, and the basic rights of the individual to locate, sell, and invest where and how he or she decides.

Second, governments need to provide infrastructure. For example, transporation and communications networks are critical to growth in the modern globalized economy. Some of the facilities, such as roads, bridges, and harbors, are usually provided directly by governments. Others, such as telecommunications, rail, and air services, can be provided by private firms, but government regulations and competition policy may be needed to prevent the emergence of growth-inhibiting monopolies in these areas.

Education and health (especially for the disadvantaged) are important forms of expenditure. Creating the appropriate factors of production is critical to creating comparative advantages in products that can be exported. This requires general education, trade schools, and other appropriate institutions for formal education as well as policies to increase on-the-job training within firms.

Other possible government policies include favorable tax treatment of saving and investment and capital gains, R&D tax incentives and funding, and policies to encourage some fraction of the large pools of financial capital held by pension funds and insurance companies to be used to finance innovation.

Finally, emphasis can be placed on poverty reduction for at least two reasons. First, poverty can exert powerful antigrowth effects. People in poverty will not develop the skills to provide a productive labor force, and they may not even respond to incentives that are provided. Malnutrition in early childhood can affect a person's capacities for life. Second, although economic growth tends to reduce the incidence of poverty, it does not eliminate it.·

Growth and Competitiveness in Advanced Industrial Economies

Recent shifts in apparent competitive advantage among industrial nations have aroused an active debate about the sources of continued growth in advanced industrial countries. In particular, many U.S. industries worry about losing their competitive edge to firms in Japan and the newly industrialized countries of East Asia. An entire new field of study has developed, focusing on competitiveness in advanced industrial countries and the relation between competitiveness and economic growth.

The modern industrial world is dominated by a number of characteristics.

1. Transnational corporations control much of the world's productive capacity and most international investment flows. They can locate their production of individual components of any one commodity wherever costs are lowest.[19]
2. This leads to globalized competition among transnational firms whereby firms owned in one country compete with firms owned in many other countries.
3. In contrast, significant amounts of innovative activity are undertaken by individual entrepreneurs. As their firms succeed, they look to becoming globally competitive. At this point, it is often more profitable to sell the firm, with its ideas, to an established transnational rather than to incur the enormous cost of developing a global marketing organization to sell the firm's product.
4. Much modern production—both in transnational corporations and in small, innovating firms—is knowledge-intensive; it will go where the human capital is and where that capital is supplied at the lowest cost. Traditional natural resource motivations for industrial location are becoming less and less important in many lines of production.
5. In today's rapidly changing, globally competitive world, each firm's competitive advantage increasingly depends on its ability to innovate at a rate sufficiently rapid to stay on the cutting edge of product and production process development.[20]

For these and many more reasons, governments of many advanced nations, including the United States, are asking themselves what is needed to sustain competitive advantage and thereby sustain economic growth in a rapidly evolving world. Some consensus views have emerged:

1. Market incentives must be stressed—subsidization and other traditional supports too often end up supporting industries that cannot compete over the long term.
2. Government policies that inhibit competitiveness need to be revised. For example, protection of domestic firms against competition coming from highly innovative foreign firms can slow down the domestic rate of innovation and cause domestic firms to fall further and further behind their foreign rivals.
3. "Climate-type" encouragement to innovative activity is valuable. These include broad incentives, such as encouraging both R&D and overall savings, as well as altering education to produce more people trained to provide a compar-

---

[19] See Box 9-2 and Chapter 16, pages 312–316, for further discussions of the importance of transnationals.

[20] This last point is documented in many books. One of the most accessible to nonspecialists is *Made in America,* already cited.

the world's population was 1 billion people can easily be exhausted unless they are consciously conserved now that the world's population exceeds 5 billion. This enormous increase in population has similar effects on pollution: The earth's environment could cope naturally with much of human pollution 200 years ago, but the present population is so large that pollution has outstripped nature's coping mechanisms.

TOPICS FOR REVIEW

Short-run and long-run effects of investment and saving

Cumulative nature of growth

Benefits and costs of growth

The neoclassical aggregate production function

Balanced growth

Endogenous technical change

Increasing returns to investment

Embodied and disembodied technical change

The economics of goods and of ideas

Resource depletion and pollution

DISCUSSION QUESTIONS

1. Economic growth is often studied in macroeconomic terms, but in a market economy, who makes the decisions that lead to growth? What kinds of decisions and what kinds of actions cause growth to occur? How might a detailed study of individual markets be relevant to understanding economic growth?

2. Discuss the following quote from a newspaper article that appeared in the summer of 1989: "Economics and the environment are not strange bedfellows. Environment-oriented tourism is one creative way to resolve the conflict between our desire for a higher standard of living and the realization that nature cannot absorb everything we throw at it. The growing demand for eco-tourism has placed a premium on the remaining rain forests, undisturbed flora and fauna, and endangered species of the world."

3. Use a UN publication to discover the per capita GDP in the world today. If growth were stopped everywhere, could output be redistributed to raise living standards in the poorer countries near to those currently enjoyed in the developed countries? Would a massive redistribution of income among nations be politically and economically feasible?

4. *Family Weekly* recently listed among "inventions that have changed our lives" microwave ovens, digital clocks, bank credit cards, freeze-dried coffee, tape cassettes, climate-controlled shopping malls, automatic toll collectors, soft contact lenses, tubeless tires,

and electronic word processors. Which of these would you hate to do without? Which, if any, will have a major impact on life in the twenty-first century? If there are any that you believe will not, does this mean that they are frivolous and unimportant?

5. The Overseas Development Council recently introduced "a new measure of economic development based on the physical quality of life." Its index, called PQLI, gives one-third weight to each of the following indicators: literacy, life expectancy, and infant mortality. While countries such as the United States and Canada rank high on either the PQLI or on an index of per capita real national income, some relatively poor countries, such as Sri Lanka, rank much higher on the PQLI index than much richer countries such as Algeria and Kuwait. Discuss the merits or deficiencies of this measure.

6. "The case for economic growth is that it gives man greater control over his environment, and consequently increases his freedom." Explain why you agree or disagree with this statement by Nobel Laureate W. Arthur Lewis.

7. Consider a developed economy that decides to achieve a zero rate of growth for the future. What implications would such a "stationary state" have for the processes of production and consumption and for human inventive activity?

8. Suppose that solar energy becomes the dominant form of energy in the twenty-first century. What effects will this have on the growth rates of Africa and Northern Europe?

9. Discuss the following newspaper headlines in terms of the sources, costs, and benefits of growth.
   a. "Stress addiction: 'Life in the fast lane' may have its benefits"
   b. "Education: An expert urges multiple reforms"
   c. "Industrial radiation risk higher than thought"
   d. "Developments in the field of management design are looking ahead"
   e. "Ford urged by federal safety officials to recall several hundred thousand of its 1981–1982 front-drive vehicles because of alleged fire hazards"

10. Dr. David Suzuki, an opponent of further economic growth, has recently argued that, despite the fact that "in the twentieth century the list of scientific and technological achievements has been absolutely dazzling, the costs of such progress are so large that negative economic growth may be right for the future." Policies to achieve this include "rigorous reduction of waste, a questioning and distrustful attitude towards technological progress, and braking demands on the globe's resources." Identify some of the benefits and costs of economic growth, and evaluate Dr. Suzuki's position. What government policies would be needed to achieve his ends?

PART TEN

INTERNATIONAL ECONOMICS

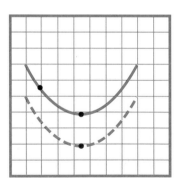

36

The Gains from Trade

United States consumers buy Volkswagens, Germans take holidays in Italy, Italians buy spices from Tanzania, Africans import oil from Saudi Arabia, Arabs buy Japanese cameras, and the Japanese buy U.S. soybeans. *International trade* refers to exchanges of goods and services that take place across international boundaries.

The founders of modern economics were concerned with international trade problems. The great eighteenth-century British philosopher and economist David Hume, one of the first to work out the theory of the price system as a control mechanism, developed his concepts primarily in terms of prices in foreign trade. Adam Smith in *The Wealth of Nations* attacked government restriction of trade. David Ricardo in 1817 developed the basic theory of the gains from trade that is presented in this chapter. The repeal of the Corn Laws—tariffs on the importation of grains into Great Britain—and the transformation of that country during the nineteenth century from a country of high tariffs to one of completely free trade were, to a significant extent, the result of agitation by economists whose theories of the gains from trade led them to condemn tariffs.

In this chapter we explore the fundamental question of what is gained by international trade; in Chapter 37 we will deal with the pros and cons of interfering with the free flow of such trade.

Sources of the Gains from Trade

The increased output as a result of trade is called the **gains from trade.** The source of such gains is most easily visualized by considering the differences between a world with trade and a world without it. Although politicians often regard foreign trade as different from domestic trade, economists from Adam Smith on have argued that the causes and consequences of international trade are simply an extension of the principles governing domestic trade. What is the advantage of trade among individuals, among groups, among regions, or among countries?

Interpersonal, Interregional, and International Trade

Consider trade among individuals. Without trade, each person would have to be self-sufficient and would have to produce all the food, clothing, shelter, medical services, entertainment, and luxuries that he or she consumed. A world of individual self-sufficiency would be a world with extremely low living standards.

Trade among individuals allows them to specialize in activities that they can do well and to buy from others the goods and services that they cannot easily produce. A good doctor who is a bad carpenter can provide medical services not only for her own family but also for an excellent carpenter who does not possess either the training or the ability to practice medicine. Thus trade and specialization are intimately connected. Without trade, individuals must be self-sufficient. With trade, individuals can specialize in what they do well and satisfy other needs by trading.

The same principles apply to regions. Without interregional trade, each region would have to be self-sufficient. With trade, each region can specialize in producing commodities for which it has some natural or acquired advantage. Plains regions can specialize in growing grain; mountain regions can specialize in mining and forest products; regions with abundant power can specialize in heavy manufacturing; and regions with highly skilled labor can specialize in knowledge-intensive, high-tech goods. Cool regions can produce wheat and other crops that thrive in temperate climates, and hot regions can grow such tropical crops as bananas, sugar, and coffee. The living standards of the inhabitants of all regions will be enhanced when each region specializes in products in which it has some natural or acquired advantage and obtains other products by trade.

The same principle also applies to nations. A national boundary seldom delimits an area that is naturally self-sufficient. Nations, like regions or persons, can gain from specialization and from the international trade that must accompany it. Specialization means that each country produces more of some goods than its residents wish to consume and less of others.

Trade is necessary to achieve the gains that specialization in production makes possible.

This relationship, which is illustrated in Figure 36-1, suggests one important possible gain from trade:

By engaging in trade, each individual, region, or nation is able to concentrate on producing goods and services that it produces efficiently while trading to obtain goods and services that it does not produce.

Specialization and trade go hand in hand because there is no motivation to achieve the gains from specialization without being able to trade the goods that are produced for other goods that are desired. Economists use the term *gains from trade* to embrace the results of both specialization and trade. Although the analysis that follows applies equally well to interpersonal and interregional trade, it is couched in terms of international trade.

We shall examine two sources of the gains from trade. The first source consists of differences among countries of the world in climate and resource endowment that lead to advantages in producing certain goods and disadvantages in producing others. These gains occur even though each country's costs of production are unchanged when the countries engage in international trade. The second source is the reduction in each country's costs of production

FIGURE 36-1
Efficiency, Specialization, and Trade

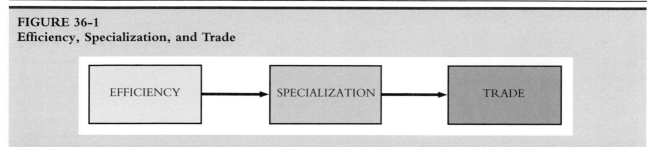

International trade and the resulting gains from trade arise in response to specialization in production undertaken to increase efficiency. The first arrow shows the link between efficiency and specialization in production; an economy can achieve increased efficiency by specializing in the production of those goods and services that it is relatively good at producing.

The second arrow shows the link between specialization in production and the need to engage in international trade. When an economy specializes in production, its production of most goods and services will not match the desired consumption of its citizens. In order to obtain the desired goods and services for consumption, it must engage in international trade, exporting those goods and services that it produces in excess of desired consumption, and importing those for which desired consumption exceeds domestic production.

that results from the greater scale of production that specialization brings.

Gains from Trade with Given Costs

In order to focus on differences in production conditions, suppose that there are no advantages arising from either economies of large-scale production or cost reductions that result from learning new skills. In these circumstances, what leads to gains from trade? To examine this question, we use an example involving only two countries and two commodities, but the general principles apply as well to the cases of many countries and many commodities.

A Special Case: Absolute Advantage

The gains from trade are clear when there is a simple situation involving absolute advantage. **Absolute advantage** concerns the quantities of a single product that can be produced using the same quantity of resources in two different countries. One country is said to have an absolute advantage over another in the production of a particular commodity when an equal quantity of resources can produce more of that commodity in that country than in another.

Suppose that country A has an absolute advantage over country B in one commodity, and that country B has an absolute advantage over A in another. This is a case of *reciprocal absolute advantage:* Each country has an absolute advantage in some commodity. In such a situation, the total production of both countries can be increased (relative to a situation of self-sufficiency) if each specializes in the commodity in which it has the absolute advantage.

Table 36-1 provides a simple example. Total world production of both wheat and cloth increases when each country produces more of the good in which it has an absolute advantage. A rise in the production of all commodities entails a rise in average living standards.

The gains from specialization make the gains from trade possible. When specialization occurs, England produces more cloth and the United States more wheat than if they were self-sufficient. The United States is producing more wheat and less cloth than U.S. consumers wish to buy, and England is producing more cloth and less wheat than English consumers wish to buy. If consumers in both countries are to

TABLE 36-1 Gains from Specialization with Absolute Advantage

Part A: Amounts of wheat and cloth that can be produced with one unit of resources in the United States and England

	Wheat (bushels)	Cloth (yards)
United States	10	6
England	5	10

Part B: Changes resulting from the transfer of one unit of U.S. resources into wheat and one unit of English resources into cloth

	Wheat (bushels)	Cloth (yards)
United States	+10	− 6
England	− 5	+10
World	+ 5	+ 4

When there is a reciprocal absolute advantage, specialization makes it possible to produce more of both commodities. Part A shows the production of wheat and cloth that can be achieved in each country by using one unit of resources. The United States can produce 10 bushels of wheat or 6 yards of cloth; England can produce 5 bushels of wheat or 10 yards of cloth. The United States has an absolute advantage in producing wheat, and England, in producing cloth. Part B shows the changes in production caused by moving one unit of resources out of cloth and into wheat production in the United States and moving one unit of resources in the opposite direction in England. There is an increase in world production of 5 bushels of wheat and 4 yards of cloth; worldwide, there are gains from specialization. In this example the more resources are transferred into wheat production in the United States and cloth production in England, the larger the gains will be.

get cloth and wheat in the desired proportions, the United States must export wheat to England and import cloth from England.

A First General Statement: Comparative Advantage

When each country has an absolute advantage over the other in the production of one commodity, the gains from trade are obvious. What, however, if the United States can produce both wheat and cloth more efficiently than England? This, in essence, was the question posed by David Ricardo nearly 200 years ago. His answer underlies the theory of comparative advantage and is still accepted by economists as a valid statement of the potential gains from trade.

To start with, suppose that U.S. efficiency increases tenfold above the levels recorded in the example, so that one unit of U.S. resources can produce either 100 bushels of wheat or 60 yards of cloth. English efficiency remains unchanged (see Table 36–2). It might appear that the United States, which is now better at producing both wheat and cloth than England, has nothing to gain by trading

with such an inefficient foreign country, but it *does* have something to gain, as shown in Table 36–2. Even though the United States is 10 times as efficient as in the situation of Table 36–1, it is still possible to increase world production of both wheat and cloth by having the United States produce more wheat and less cloth and by having England produce more cloth and less wheat.

What is the source of this gain? Although the United States has an *absolute* advantage over England in the production of both wheat and cloth, the *margin* of advantage differs in the two commodities. The United States can produce 20 times as much wheat as England by using the same quantity of resources, but only 6 times as much cloth. The United States is said to have a **comparative advantage** in the production of wheat and a comparative disadvantage in the production of cloth. (This statement implies another: England has a comparative *dis*advantage in the production of wheat, in which it is one-twentieth as efficient as the United States, and a comparative advantage in the production of cloth, in which it is only one-sixth as efficient.)

A key proposition in the theory of international trade is this:

The gains from trade depend on the pattern of comparative, not absolute, advantage.

A comparison of Tables 36–1 and 36–2 refutes the notion that the absolute *levels* of efficiency of two areas determine the gains from specialization. The key is that the margin of advantage that one area has over the other must differ between commodities. As long as this margin differs, total world production can be increased when each area specializes in the production of that commodity in which it has a comparative advantage.

Comparative advantage is necessary, as well as sufficient, for gains from trade. This is illustrated in Table 36–3, which shows a case in which the United States has an absolute advantage in both commodities but neither country has a comparative advantage in the production of either commodity. The United States is 10 times as efficient as England in the production of wheat and in the production of cloth. Now there is no way to increase the production of both wheat and cloth by reallocating resources.

Absolute advantage without comparative advantage does not lead to gains from trade.

TABLE 36-2   Gains from Specialization with Comparative Advantage

Part A: Amounts of wheat and cloth that can be produced with one unit of resources in the United States and England

	Wheat (bushels)	Cloth (yards)
United States	100	60
England	5	10

Part B: Changes resulting from the transfer of one-tenth of one unit of U.S. resources into wheat and one unit of English resources into cloth

	Wheat (bushels)	Cloth (yards)
United States	+10	− 6
England	− 5	+10
World	+ 5	+ 4

When there is comparative advantage, specialization makes it possible to produce more of both commodities. The productivity of English resources is left unchanged from Table 36–1; that of the U.S. resources is increased tenfold. England no longer has an absolute advantage in producing either commodity. Total production of both commodities can nonetheless be increased by specialization. Moving one-tenth of one unit of U.S. resources out of cloth and into wheat and moving one unit of resources in the opposite direction in England causes world production of wheat to rise by 5 bushels and cloth by 4 yards.

TABLE 36-3 Absence of Gains from Specialization When There Is No Comparative Advantage

Part A: Amounts of wheat and cloth that can be produced with one unit of resources in the United States and England

	Wheat (bushels)	Cloth (yards)
United States	100	60
England	10	6

Part B: Changes resulting from the transfer of 1 unit of U.S. resources into wheat and 10 units of English resources into cloth

	Wheat (bushels)	Cloth (yards)
United States	+100	−60
England	−100	+60
World	0	0

Where there is no comparative advantage, no reallocation of resources within each country can increase the production of both commodities. In this example the United States has the same absolute advantage over England in each commodity (tenfold). There is no comparative advantage, and world production cannot be increased by reallocating resources in both countries. Therefore, specialization does not increase total output.

A Second General Statement: Opportunity Costs

Much of the foregoing argument uses the concept of a unit of resources. It assumes that units of resources can be equated across countries, so that statements such as "The United States can produce 10 times as much wheat with the same quantity of resources as England" are meaningful. Measurement of the real resource cost of producing commodities poses many difficulties. If, for example, England uses land, labor, and capital in proportions that are different from those used in the United States, it may not be clear which country gets more output per unit of resource input. Fortunately, the proposition about the gains from trade can be restated without reference to so fuzzy a concept as units of resources.

To do this, go back to the examples of Tables 36-1 and 36-2. Calculate the *opportunity cost* of wheat and cloth in the two countries. When resources are fully employed, the only way to produce more of one commodity is to reallocate resources and produce less of the other commodity. Table 36-1 shows that one unit of resources in the United States can produce 10 bushels of wheat *or* 6 yards of cloth. From this it follows that the opportunity cost of producing one unit of wheat is 0.60 unit of cloth, whereas the opportunity cost of producing one unit of cloth is 1.67 units of wheat. These data are summarized in Table 36-4. The table also shows that in England the opportunity cost of one unit of wheat is 2.0 units of cloth forgone, whereas the opportunity cost of one unit of cloth is 0.50 unit of wheat. Table 36-2 also gives rise to the opportunity costs in Table 36-4.

The sacrifice of cloth involved in producing wheat is much lower in the United States than in England. World wheat production can be increased if the United States rather than England produces it. Looking at cloth production, we can see that the loss of wheat involved in producing one unit of cloth is lower in England than in the United States. England has the lower (opportunity) cost as a producer of cloth. World cloth production can be increased if England, rather than the United States, produces it. This situation is shown in Table 36-5.

The gains from trade arise from differing opportunity costs in the two countries.

TABLE 36-4 Opportunity Cost of Wheat and Cloth in the United States and England

	Wheat (bushels)	Cloth (yards)
United States	0.60 yards cloth	1.67 bushels wheat
England	2.00 yards cloth	0.50 bushels wheat

Comparative advantages can be expressed in terms of opportunity costs that differ between countries. These opportunity costs can be obtained from Table 36-1 or Table 36-2. The English opportunity cost of one unit of wheat is obtained by dividing the cloth output of one unit of English resources by the wheat output. The result shows that 2 yards of cloth must be sacrificed for every extra unit of wheat produced by transferring English resources out of cloth production and into wheat. The other three cost figures are obtained in a similar manner.

TABLE 36-5   Gains from Specialization with Differing Opportunity Costs

Changes resulting from each country's producing one more unit of a commodity in which it has the lower opportunity cost

	Wheat (bushels)	Cloth (yards)
United States	+1.0	−0.6
England	−0.5	+1.0
World	+0.5	+0.4

Whenever opportunity costs differ between countries, specialization can increase the production of both commodities. These calculations show that there are gains from specialization, given the opportunity costs of Table 36-4. To produce one more bushel of wheat, the United States must sacrifice 0.6 yards of cloth. To produce one more yard of cloth, England must sacrifice 0.5 bushels of wheat. Making both changes raises world production of both wheat and cloth.

The conclusions about the gains from trade arising from international differences may be summarized as follows:

1. Country A has a comparative advantage over country B in producing a commodity when the opportunity cost (in terms of some other commodity) of producing that commodity in country A is lower than in country B. This implies, however, that country A has a comparative disadvantage in the other commodity.
2. Opportunity costs depend on the relative costs of producing two commodities, not on absolute costs. (Notice that the examples in Tables 36-1 and 36-2 each give rise to the opportunity costs in Table 36-4.)
3. When opportunity costs are the same in all countries, there is no comparative advantage and hence no possibility of gains from specialization and trade. (You can illustrate this for yourself by calculating the opportunity costs implied by the data in Table 36-3.)
4. When opportunity costs differ in any two countries and both countries are producing both commodities, it is always possible to increase total world production of both commodities by a suitable reallocation of resources within each country. (This proposition is illustrated in Table 36-5.)

Market Forces and the Gains from Trade

We have seen that when opportunity costs differ between countries, total world production of both goods can be increased and hence each country can experience gains from trade—if each chooses to specialize in the production of the good in which it has a *comparative advantage*. Can market forces be relied on to generate the appropriate specialization in production? Will firms, responding to market signals, increase their production of the good in which the country has a comparative advantage?

In order to answer these questions, we first need to consider the implications of differences in opportunity costs for the *relative prices* of the goods that would prevail in the two countries prior to the establishment of trade between them.

The opportunity costs in Table 36-4 reflect the underlying production conditions in the two countries. The black lines in Figure 36-2 show the *production possibility boundaries* for the United States and England. The slopes of the production possibility boundaries give the opportunity costs of producing more of one good in terms of the output. Because the United States has a comparative advantage in producing wheat, its production possibility curve is steeper than England's, indicating that less cloth has to be given up in order to produce an extra bushel of wheat in the United States than in England.

Relative Prices When There Is No Trade

Suppose that in the United States the price of wheat is $12 per bushel. We also know from Table 36-4 that, in the United States, the opportunity cost of a bushel of wheat is 0.6 yards of cloth. Therefore 0.6 yards of cloth are worth 1 bushel of wheat. Because a bushel of wheat has a price of $12, cloth must therefore cost ($12/0.6), or $20 per yard. The relative price of cloth in terms of wheat is ($20 per yard/$12 per bushel), or 1.67, which, as can be seen from Table 36-4, is equal to the opportunity cost of cloth in terms of wheat in the United States.

Suppose that the price of wheat in England is £8 per bushel. We also know from Table 36-4 that, in England, the opportunity cost of a bushel of wheat is 2 yards of cloth. Therefore 2 yards of cloth are worth 1 bushel of wheat. Because a bushel of wheat has a price of £8, cloth must therefore cost (£8/2), or £4 per yard. The relative price of cloth in terms of wheat is (£4 per yard/£8 per bushel), or 0.5;

FIGURE 36-2
Production, Trade, and Consumption Possibilities

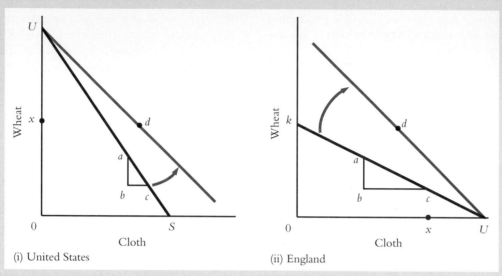

(i) United States

(ii) England

International trade leads to specialization in production and increased consumption possibilities. The black line in each part represents the production possibility boundary for the United States and England. In the absence of any international trade, these also represent each country's consumption possibilities.

The difference in the slopes of the production possibility boundaries reflects differences in comparative advantage. In each part, the opportunity cost of increasing production of wheat by the same amount (measured by the distance *ba*) is the amount by which the production of cloth must be reduced (measured by the distance *bc*). The relatively steep production possibility boundary for the United States thus indicates that the opportunity cost of producing wheat in the United States is less than that in England.

If trade is possible at some terms of trade between the two countries' opportunity costs of production, each country will specialize in the production of the good in which it has a comparative advantage. In each part of the figure, production occurs at *U*; the United States produces only wheat, and England produces only cloth.

Consumption possibilities are given by the red line that passes through *U* and has a slope equal to the terms of trade. Consumption possibilities are increased in both countries; consumption may occur at some point such as *d* that involves a combination of wheat and cloth that was not obtainable in the absence of trade.

as can be seen from Table 36-4, this is equal to the opportunity cost of cloth in terms of wheat in England.

In each country, the relative price of cloth in terms of wheat is equal to its opportunity cost in terms of wheat. Because the opportunity cost of cloth in England is lower than the opportunity cost in the United States, its relative price is also lower.[1] Therefore:

When a country has a comparative advantage in one good, in the absence of trade its relative price of that good will be lower than in its trading partner.

---

[1] Equivalently, we could have said that the relative price of wheat is lower in the United States than in England.

In the absence of trade, both countries have to produce what they consume, and hence their production possibility boundaries also indicate all possible consumption opportunities for each of the two countries.

International Trade

Now consider the implications of the two countries' being able to trade with each other.

Specialization in production. Consider first the implications for producers in the United States. The pretrade relative price of cloth in terms of wheat is 1.67, which reflects the opportunity cost of producing cloth. However, cloth can now be obtained by a method other than producing it; it can be obtained by producing wheat instead and then exchanging the wheat for cloth through trade with England. At the pretrade relative price of cloth in terms of wheat in England, a yard of cloth can be obtained for only 0.5 bushels of wheat, which is clearly much cheaper than producing cloth.[2]

The ability to engage in international trade alters the opportunity costs of production and as a result will create incentives for resources to be allocated into the production of goods in which the country has a comparative advantage. Some entrepreneurs will buy U.S. wheat, which they will then export to England, and then use the proceeds to buy English cloth for import into the United States. Because they can obtain a yard of cloth for every 0.5 bushels of wheat, they will be able to undercut domestic cloth producers who, in order to produce a yard of cloth, use resources that could produce 1.67 bushels of wheat. This will bid up the price of U.S. wheat and bid down the price of U.S. cloth; above-normal profits will arise in the wheat sector and below-normal profits will occur in the U.S. textile sector. In turn, these profits will create an incentive for resources to flow into wheat production and out of cloth production.

Some of the resource flow will reflect the decisions of existing producers to change their volumes of production—wheat farmers will increase production and textile manufacturers will decrease production. Some of the resource flow will reflect the new entrants attracted by the excess profits in the wheat sector and the exit of firms from the textile sector as equipment is not replaced when it depreciates and exiting plants are mothballed. Domestic textile firms may go out of business, and multinationals will relocate their textile production from the United States to England.

As a result, production in the United States will become more specialized in wheat; in the extreme, as long as cloth can be obtained more cheaply by importing it than by producing it, all resources in the United States will be engaged in wheat production.[3]

---

[2] For simplicity, we ignore any costs of transactions and shipping; these complicate the analysis without affecting the basic results.

[3] The conclusion that there would be complete specialization results from our simple case of a linear production possibility boundary. As discussed in Chapter 1, it is more realistic to assume that the production possibility boundary is "bowed out" from the origin, in which case trade would still create incentives for increased production of the good in which there is a comparative advantage, but specialization would not necessarily be complete.

The situation in England is exactly the opposite. There it becomes cheaper to obtain wheat by exporting cloth and using the proceeds to import wheat than by producing the wheat in England. As a result, the textile sector will expand and the agricultural sector will contract.

The ability to trade at relative prices that differ from domestic opportunity costs in production creates incentives to shift resources into those sectors in which the country has a comparative advantage and out of those in which it does not.

The terms of trade.   U.S. citizens will wish to export wheat and import cloth as long as they can obtain more than 0.6 yards of cloth for every bushel of wheat exported—that is, as long as they obtain cloth more cheaply by importing it than by producing it. The amount of cloth imports that U.S. citizens can obtain in return for their exports depends on the *relative price* of cloth in terms of wheat, also called the United States' *terms of trade*. The **terms of trade** measure the quantity of imported goods that can be obtained per unit of goods exported and are measured by the ratio of the price of exports to the price of imports.

Similarly, England will wish to export cloth and import wheat as long as it receives at least 0.5 bushels of wheat for every yard of cloth exported.   .

As long as trade occurs at some terms of trade between the two countries' opportunity costs of production, both countries will willingly engage in trade.

Consumption opportunities.   Prior to trade, we noted that consumption opportunities were limited to the goods and services that the country itself produced; that is, they were limited to the production possibility boundary. What happens to consumption possibilities when there is international trade?

First, consider the United States. In terms of part (i) of Figure 36-2, production is specialized in wheat, but consumption can now occur anywhere along the colored line. We call this the *consumption possibilities line;* it is just like a budget line, as it represents all possible combinations of cloth and wheat that can be consumed. It passes through the production point and has a slope given by the terms at which cloth can be obtained for wheat on international markets—that is, by the terms of trade. Because the United States can obtain cloth more cheaply by importing it than by producing it, the consumption possibilities line is flatter than the production possibility boundary.

In England, production is specialized in cloth, and the consumption possibilities line passes through that point. Because England can obtain wheat more cheaply by importing it than by producing it, its consumption possibility line is steeper than its production possibilities boundary.

For both countries, the posttrade consumption possibility boundary is at every point above the production possibility boundary, which is also the pretrade consumption possibility line. This means that consumption opportunities are increased by the possibility of engaging in international trade.

The gains from trade result in an expansion of the set of goods and services available for consumption.

This expansion of the consumption opportunities occurs as long as the terms of trade are different from the slope of the production possibility boundary. The determination and importance of the terms of trade are discussed further in Box 36-1.

Why Opportunity Costs Differ

We have seen that the sources of the gains from trade are comparative advantages, which themselves arise from differences in opportunity costs among nations. Why do different countries have different opportunity costs?

Different factor proportions. What is now the traditional answer to this question was provided early in the twentieth century by two Swedish economists, Eli Heckscher and Bertil Ohlin. According to their theory, differences in factor endowments among nations result in different opportunity costs. For example, a country that is well endowed with fertile land but has a small population will find that land is cheap but labor is expensive. It will therefore produce land-intensive goods (such as wheat and corn) cheaply and labor-intensive, manufactured goods (such as watches and silicon chips) only at a high cost. The reverse will be true for a second country that is small in size but has abundant and efficient labor. As a result, the first country will have a comparative advantage in land-intensive goods, the second in labor-intensive goods.

Another country that is unusually well endowed with energy will have low energy prices and will thus have a comparative advantage in energy-intensive goods, such as chemicals and aluminum.

According to the Heckscher-Ohlin theory, countries have comparative advantages in the production of commodities that are intensive in the use of the factors of production with which their endowments are relatively abundant.

This is often called the *factor endowment theory of comparative advantage.* It assumes that all countries have the same production functions (which means that equal inputs of factor services will produce equal outputs in all countries), but that the supplies of factors, and hence relative factor prices, differ among nations.

Research suggests that the factor endowment theory explains much, but by no means all, of observed comparative advantages.

Different climates. One obvious additional influence comes from all the natural factors that can be called *climate* in the broadest sense. If we combine land, labor, and capital in the same way in Nicaragua and in Iceland, we will not get the same output of most agricultural goods. Sunshine, rainfall, and average temperature also matter. If we seek to work with wool or cotton in dry and damp climates, we will get different results. (We can, of course, artificially create any climate that we wish in a factory, but it costs money to create what is freely provided elsewhere.)

Climate, interpreted in the broadest sense, undoubtedly helps to determine comparative advantages.

This explanation assumes that climatic conditions cause nations to have different production functions so that the same inputs of factor services will produce different outputs in different climates. Countries will tend to have comparative advantages in goods for whose production their climates are particularly favorable.

Different technology. Another influence arises from the fact that technology is constantly changing, and that some countries have earlier access to new technology than do others. Although new production techniques are often transferable to other countries, research has shown that such *diffusion* of technology can often be quite slow and costly, so that at any time a country in which the new technology is first developed and implemented might have a substantial cost advantage over other countries that still rely on old technology. This is often cited as a major determinant of trade between "North," or industrialized, countries, where much new technological development occurs, and "South," or less-developed, economies, which rely on the gradual diffusion of those developments to their own production techniques.

Gains from Specialization with Variable Costs[4]

So far we have assumed that unit costs are the same, whatever the scale of output, and we have seen that there are gains from specialization and trade as long as there are international differences in opportunity costs. If costs vary with the level of output or as experience is acquired via specialization, *additional* sources of gain are possible.

Economies of Scale

Over some range of outputs, unit costs of production usually fall as the scale of output increases. The larger a firm's output, the greater are its opportunities to employ efficient, large-scale machinery and to effect a detailed division of tasks among its workers. Economies of scale are illustrated in part (i) of Figure 36-3. Countries such as Canada, Sweden, and Israel, whose domestic markets are not large enough to exploit all available economies of scale, would find it prohibitively expensive to become self-sufficient. They would have to produce a little bit of everything at very high cost.[5]

---

[4] The material in this section is more accessible to students who have already studied microeconomics.

[5] Economies of scale are discussed in Chapter 11. The classic discussion of this effect is quoted in Box 3-2 on page 46.

Trade allows smaller countries to specialize in producing a limited range of commodities at high enough levels of output that they will reap the available economies of scale.

Big countries such as the United States and Germany have markets that are large enough to allow the production of most items at home at a scale of output that is great enough to obtain the available economies of scale. For them the gains from international trade arise mainly from specializing in commodities in which they have a comparative advantage. Yet even for such countries, a broadening of their markets permits achieving economies of scale in subproduct lines, such as specialty steels or blue jeans.

The importance of product diversity and specialization in specific subproduct lines has been one of the lessons learned from changing patterns of world trade since World War II. When the European Common Market (now called the European Community) was set up in the 1950s, economists expected that specialization would occur according to the classical theory of comparative advantage, with one country specializing in cars, another in refrigerators, another in fashion clothes, another in shoes, and so on. This is not the way it has worked out. Today one can buy French, English, Italian, and German fashion goods, cars, shoes, appliances, and a host of other goods in London, Paris, Bonn, and Rome. Ships loaded with Swedish furniture bound for London pass ships loaded with English furniture bound for Stockholm, and so on.

What European free trade did was allow a proliferation of differentiated products, with different countries each specializing in different subproduct lines. Consumers have shown by their expenditures that they value this enormous increase in the range of choice among differentiated products. As Asian countries have expanded into North American markets with textiles, cars, and electronic goods, North American manufacturers have increasingly specialized their production, and we now export textiles, cars, and electronics equipment to Japan while importing similar but differentiated products from Japan.

One implication of economies of scale is that they provide a barrier to entry for new firms; if scale economies are sufficiently strong, existing firms can earn large profits that new firms cannot expect to capture should they enter, at least for considerable periods of time. In existing industries this often

FIGURE 36-3
Scale and Learning Effects

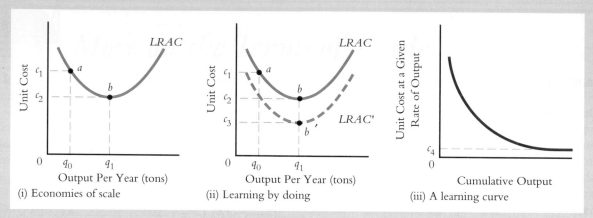

(i) Economies of scale

(ii) Learning by doing

(iii) A learning curve

Specialization may lead to gains from trade either by permitting economies of scale or by leading to downward shifts of cost curves, or both. Consider a country that wishes to consume the quantity q_0 of some product. Suppose that it can produce that quantity at a unit cost of c_1. Suppose further that the country has a comparative advantage in producing this commodity and can export the quantity q_0q_1 if it produces q_1. This may lead to cost savings in two ways. In part (i), the increased level of production of q_1 compared to q_0 permits it to *move along* its cost curve, *LRAC*, from a to b, thus reaching the *MES* and reducing unit cost to c_2. This is an economy of scale. In part (ii), as workers and management become more experienced, they may discover means of increasing productivity that lead to a downward shift of the cost curve from *LRAC* to *LRAC'*, thus learning by doing. The downward *shift* lowers the cost of producing any rate of output. At output q_1, costs per unit fall to c_3. The movement from a to b' incorporates both economies of scale and learning by doing.

Part (iii) shows a learning curve, which is another way of showing the effects of learning by doing. This curve shows the relation between the costs of *producing a given output per period* and the total output over the whole time during which production has taken place, called *cumulative output*. Growing experience with making the product causes costs to fall as more and more is produced. When all learning possibilities have been exploited, costs reach a minimum level, shown by c_4 in the figure. Moving the rate of output from q_0 to q_1 in part (i) causes the firm to move faster along its learning curve in part (iii).

---

acquire expertise, costs tend to fall. There is substantial evidence that such learning by doing does occur in a wide range of industries. It is particularly important in many of today's knowledge-intensive, high-tech products.

Learning by doing is a phenomenon quite unlike anything we have studied so far in this book. Care must be taken to distinguish it from the familiar cost curves that relate a firm's costs to its current rate of output.

When learning by doing occurs, the *LRAC* curve shifts downward.

This shift, which is shown in part (ii) of Figure 36–3, means that any given rate of output is associated with a lower average total cost than before. The shift occurs because of increased productivity due

to learning from experience gained over all past production. As a result, costs fall as the total of all cumulative *past* output rises.

This important phenomenon can be illustrated by a **learning curve.** A learning curve, as shown in part (iii) of Figure 36–3, illustrates how the cost of producing a *given rate of output* falls as the total output accumulates.

An example may help to illustrate learning by doing. Suppose that a firm starts operations on January 1, 1990, producing at a rate of 10,000 units per month. On January 1, 1991, the total of all past output is 120,000 units, and by January 1, 1992, the total is 240,000 units. Now suppose that the unit cost associated with the monthly production of 10,000 units was $5.00 on January 1, 1990, $4.00 on January 1, 1991, and $3.50 on January 1, 1992. This sequence of events allows us to identify three points on the firm's learning curve: The unit cost of producing the given rate of output is $5.00 when past output is zero, $4.00 when past output is 120,000 units, and $3.50 when past output is 240,000 units. The firm has moved along its learning curve. The costs associated with producing 10,000 units a month have fallen as its labor and management have learned from the accumulated experience of producing more and more output.

Now suppose that the firm had been producing at a faster rate, say, 20,000 units per month from the beginning of 1990. Its unit costs as of January 1, 1991, will be lower because it would have moved further along its learning curve. To illustrate the learning effect, suppose that the average total cost curve is flat for outputs between 12,000 and 24,000 units per month. Thus unit costs of producing at the higher rate of 24,000 units per month are $5.00 per unit when the firm starts operations on January 1, 1990. However, the firm will move down its learning curve faster as a result of having a higher rate of output. By January 1, 1991, it will have a cumulative past output of 240,000, and its unit costs will have fallen to $3.50, the level it took two years to reach when the firm was producing only 10,000 units a month.

Where learning by doing is important, the higher a firm's current rate of output, the faster its unit costs associated with a *given* rate of output will fall.

This tendency for costs to fall as the total of all past output accumulates confers large advantages on firms that are first into the market with a new product as well as on firms that have a large domestic market that will support a high initial rate of output.

The distinction between economies of large-scale production, which are associated with the *current rate of output,* and learning by doing, which is associated with the *total of all past output,* is illustrated in Figure 36–3. The distinction provides one more example of the difference between a movement along a curve and a shift of a curve.

Recognition of the opportunities for learning by doing leads to an important implication: Policymakers need not accept *current* comparative advantages as given. Through such means as education and tax incentives, they can seek to develop new comparative

advantages.[6] Moreover, countries cannot complacently assume that an existing comparative advantage will persist. Misguided education policies, the wrong tax incentives, or policies that discourage risk taking can lead to the rapid erosion of a country's comparative advantage in a particular product. So, too, can competitive developments elsewhere in the world.

A Changing View of Comparative Advantage

The classical theory of the gains from trade assumes that there are given cost structures, based largely on a country's natural endowments. This leads to a given pattern of international comparative advantage. It leads to the policy advice that a government, interested in maximizing its citizens' material standard of living, should encourage production to be specialized in goods in which it currently has a comparative advantage.

Today there is a competing view. In extreme form, it says that comparative advantages certainly exist but are typically acquired, not nature-given— and they change. This view of comparative advantage is *dynamic* rather than static. New industries are seen as depending more on human capital than on fixed physical capital or natural resources. The skills of a computer designer, a videogame programmer, a sound mix technician, or a rock star are acquired by education and on-the-job training (which contribute to the negative slope of their industries' learning curves). Natural endowments of energy and raw materials cannot account for Britain's prominence in modern pop music, the United States' leadership in computer software, or Japan's success in the automobile and silicon-chip industries. When a country such as the United States finds its former dominance (based on comparative advantage) declining in such smokestack industries as automobiles and steel, its firms need not sit idly by. Instead, they can begin to adapt by developing new areas of comparative advantage.

There are surely elements of truth in both extreme views. It would be unwise to neglect resource endowments, climate, culture, and social and institutional arrangements. However, it also would

---

[6] Of course, they might foolishly use the same policies to develop industries in which they do not have, and will never achieve, comparative advantage. See the discussion in Chapter 37.

be unwise to assume that all sources of comparative advantage are innate and immutable.

To some extent these views are reconciled in the theory of human capital that we discussed in Chapter 18. Comparative advantages that depend on human capital are consistent with the traditional Heckscher-Ohlin theory. The difference is that human capital is acquired by making conscious decisions relating to such matters as education and technical training.

Is comparative advantage obsolete?   Some opponents of trade liberalization argue that the case for free trade relies on an outdated view of the gains from trade based on comparative advantage. The theory of comparative advantage is sometimes said to have been made obsolete by the new theories that we have just discussed.

In spite of such assertions, comparative advantage remains an important economic concept. At any one time, the operation of the price system will result in trade that follows the current pattern of comparative advantage. This is true because comparative advantage is reflected in international relative prices, and these relative prices determine what goods a country will import and what it will export. For example, if U.S. costs of producing steel are particularly low, the U.S. price of steel will be low by international standards, and steel will be a U.S. export (which it is). If the U.S. costs of producing textiles are particularly high, the U.S. price of textiles will be high by international standards, and the United States will import textiles (which it does—as much

as U.S. tariffs and quotas permit). So there is no reason to change the view that Ricardo long ago expounded: Current comparative advantage is a major determinant of trade under free-market conditions.

However, economists' views about the *determinants* of comparative advantage have changed. It now seems that current comparative advantage may be more open to change by private entrepreneurial activities and by government policy than was previously thought. Thus what is obsolete is the belief (to the extent that it was ever held) that a country's current comparative advantages, and hence its current pattern of imports and exports, must be accepted as given by nature.

The theory that comparative advantage determines trade flows is not obsolete, but the theory that comparative advantage is completely determined by forces beyond the reach of public policy has been discredited.

It is one thing to observe that governments may be able to influence comparative advantage. It is another thing to conclude that it is advisable for them to try. The case for a specific government intervention requires that (1) there is scope for governments to improve on the results achieved by the free market, (2) the costs of the intervention be less than the value of the improvement to be achieved, and (3) governments will actually be able to carry out the required interventionist policies (without, for example, being sidetracked by considerations of electoral advantage).

SUMMARY

1. One country (or region or individual) has an absolute advantage over another country (or region or individual) in the production of a commodity when it can produce more of the commodity than the other can with the same input of resources.

2. In a situation of absolute advantage, total production of both commodities will be raised if each country specializes in the production of the commodity in which it has the absolute advantage. However, this increased output, called the gains from trade, does not require absolute advantage on the part of each country, only comparative advantage.

3. Comparative advantage is the relative advantage that one country enjoys over another in the production of various commodities. World production of all commodities can be increased if each country specializes in the production of the commodities in which it has a comparative advantage.

4. Comparative advantage arises because countries have different opportunity costs of producing particular goods. This creates the opportunity for all nations to gain from trade.

5. The most important proposition in the theory of the gains from trade is that trade allows all countries to obtain the goods in which they do not have a comparative advantage at a lower opportunity cost than they would face if they were to produce all commodities for themselves. This allows all countries to have more of all commodities than they could have if they tried to be self-sufficient.

6. In addition to gaining the advantages of specialization arising from comparative advantage, a nation that engages in trade and specialization may realize the benefits of the economies of large-scale production and of learning by doing.

7. When a country has a comparative advantage in one good, in the absence of trade its relative price of that good will be lower than that in countries that do not have a comparative advantage in the good. Trade will raise the relative price of the good, thus creating incentives for firms in the country with the comparative advantage to increase their production of the good. This increased specialization allows the country to share in the gains from trade.

8. The ratio of the prices of goods exported to the prices of goods imported is called the terms of trade. This ratio determines the quantities of exports needed to pay for imports. The terms of trade determine how the gains from trade are shared. A favorable change in terms of trade, that is, a rise in export prices relative to import prices, means that a country can acquire more imports per unit of exports.

9. Classical theory regarded comparative advantage as largely determined by natural resource endowments and climatic factors and thus difficult to change. Economists now believe that comparative advantage can be acquired and thus can be changed either by private entrepreneurial activity or by government policy.

TOPICS FOR REVIEW

Interpersonal, interregional, and international specialization

Gains from trade

Absolute advantage and comparative advantage

Opportunity cost and comparative advantage

Terms of trade

Dynamic comparative advantage

Scale economies, learning by doing, and learning curves

DISCUSSION QUESTIONS

1. Adam Smith saw a close connection between the wealth of a nation and its willingness "freely to engage" in foreign trade. What is the connection?

2. One U.S. critic of the North American Free Trade Agreement that was being negotiated between the United States, Mexico, and Canada in 1992 argued that "It can't be in our interest to sign this deal; Mexico gains too much from it." What does the theory of the gains from trade have to say about that criticism?

3. Does the fact that Canada, the United States, and Mexico are separate countries lead to a lower standard of living in the three countries than if they were united into a new country called Northica?

4. One product innovation that appears imminent is the electric car. However, development costs are high, and economies of scale and learning by doing are both likely to be operative. As a result, there will be a substantial competitive advantage for those who develop a marketable product early. What implications might this have for government policies toward U.S. automobile manufacturers' activities in this area? Should the government encourage joint efforts by the big three, even if this appears to violate antitrust regulations? Should environmental standards on emissions from internal combustion engines be changed so as to encourage development of this technology?

5. Studies of U.S. trade patterns have shown that high-wage sectors of industry are among the largest and fastest-growing export sectors. Does this contradict the principle of comparative advantage?

6. Predict what each of the following events would do to the terms of trade of the importing country and the exporting country, other things being equal.
   a. A blight destroys a large part of the coffee beans produced in the world.
   b. The Koreans cut the price of the steel they sell to the United States.
   c. General inflation of 10 percent occurs around the world.
   d. Violation of OPEC output quotas leads to a sharp fall in the price of oil.

7. Heavy U.S. borrowing abroad has several times led to a high value of the dollar and thus a rise in the ratio of export prices to import prices. Although this is called a favorable change in the terms of trade, are there any reasons why it may not have been a good thing for the U.S. economy?

8. Suppose that the situation described in the accompanying table exists. Assume that there are no tariffs and no government intervention and that labor is the only factor of production. Let X take different values—say, $10, $20, $40, and $60. In each case, in what direction will trade have to flow in order for the gains from trade to be exploited?

| Country | Labor cost of producing one unit of | |
	Artichokes	Bathtubs
Inland	$20	$40
Outland	$15	$X

37

Barriers to Free Trade

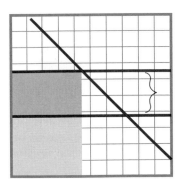

Conducting business in a foreign country can be difficult. Differences in language, in local laws and customs, and in currency all complicate transactions. Our concern in this chapter, however, is not with these difficulties but with government policy toward international trade, which is called **commercial policy.** At one extreme is **free trade,** which means an absence of any form of government interference with the free flow of international trade. **Protectionism** refers to any departure from free trade designed to give some protection to domestic industries from foreign competition.

The Theory of Commercial Policy

Today debates over commercial policy are as heated as they were 200 years ago, when economists were still working out the theory of the gains from trade that we presented in Chapter 36. Should a country permit the free flow of international trade, or should it seek to protect its local producers from foreign competition? Such protection may be achieved either by **tariffs,** which are taxes designed to raise the prices of foreign goods, or by **nontariff barriers,** which are devices other than tariffs designed to reduce the flow of imported goods. Examples include quotas and customs procedures that are deliberately made to be unnecessarily cumbersome.

The Case for Free Trade

The case for free trade is based on the analysis presented in Chapter 36, in which we saw that, whenever opportunity costs differ among countries, specialization and trade will raise world living standards. Free trade allows countries to specialize in producing commodities in which they have a comparative advantage.

Free trade allows the maximization of world production, thus making it possible for every household in the world to consume more goods than it could without free trade.

This does not necessarily mean that everyone will be better off with free trade than without it. Protectionism could allow the citizens of some countries to obtain a larger share of a smaller world output, so that they would benefit even though on average everyone would lose. If we ask whether free trade makes it possible to improve everyone's well-being, the answer is yes. But if we ask whether free trade is, in fact, *always* advantageous to *everyone*, the answer is no.

There is abundant evidence to show that significant differences in opportunity costs exist and that large gains are realized from international trade due to these differences. What needs explanation is the fact that trade is not wholly free. Why do tariffs and non-tariff barriers to trade continue to exist two centuries after Adam Smith and David Ricardo stated the case for free trade? Is there a valid case for protectionism? Before addressing these questions, let us examine the methods used in protectionist policy.

Methods of Protection

Two main types of protectionist policy are illustrated in Figure 37-1. Both cause the price of the imported good to rise and its quantity to fall. They differ, however, in how they achieve these results. The caption to Figure 37-1 analyzes the general effects of these policies; Box 37-1 analyzes the specific effects of these policies on economic efficiency.

FIGURE 37-1
Methods of Protecting Domestic Producers

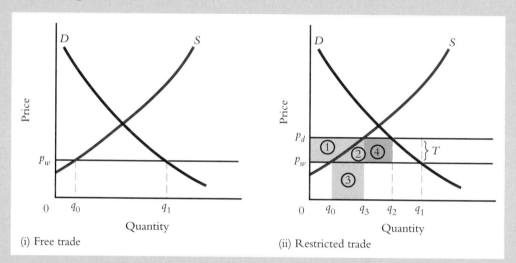

(i) Free trade   (ii) Restricted trade

The same reduction in imports and increase in domestic production can be achieved by using either a tariff or a quantity restriction. In both parts of the figure, D and S are the domestic demand and supply curves, respectively, and p_w is the world price of some commodity that is both produced at home and imported.

Part (i) of the figure shows the situation under free trade. Domestic consumption is q_1, domestic production is q_0, and imports are q_0q_1.

Part (ii) shows what happens when protectionist policies restrict imports to the amount q_3q_2. When this is done by levying a tariff of T per unit, the price in the domestic market rises by the full amount of the tariff to p_d. Consumers reduce consumption from q_1 to q_2 and pay an extra amount, shown by the shaded areas 1, 2, and 4, for the q_2 that they now purchase. Domestic production rises from q_0 to q_3. Since domestic producers receive the domestic price, their receipts rise by the three light shaded areas, labeled 1, 2, and 3. Area 3 is revenue that was earned by foreign producers under free trade, while areas 1 and 2 are paid by domestic consumers because of the higher prices that they must now pay. Foreign suppliers of the imported good continue to get the world price, so the government receives as tariff revenue the extra amount paid by consumers for the q_3q_2 units that are still imported (shown by the dark shaded area, 4).

When the same result is accomplished by a quantity restriction, the government—either through a quota or a *voluntary export agreement (VER)*—reduces imports to q_3q_2. This drives the domestic market price up to p_d and has the same effect on domestic producers and consumers as the tariff. Since the government has merely restricted the quantity of imports, both foreign and domestic suppliers get the higher price in the domestic market. Thus foreign suppliers now receive the extra amount paid by domestic consumers (represented by the shaded area labeled 4) for the units that are still imported.

Policies That Directly Raise Prices

The first type of protectionist policy directly raises the *price* of the imported commodity. A tariff, also often called an *import duty,* is the most common policy of this type. Other such policies are any rules or regulations that fulfill three conditions: They are costly to comply with; they do not apply to competing, domestically produced commodities; and they are more than is required to meet any purpose other than restricting trade.

As shown in part (i) of Figure 37-1, tariffs affect both foreign and domestic producers, as well as domestic consumers. The initial effect is to raise the domestic price of the imported commodity above its world price by the amount of the tariff. Imports fall, and, as a result, foreign producers sell less and so must transfer resources to other lines of production. The price received on domestically produced units rises, as does the quantity produced domestically. On both counts domestic producers earn more. However, the cost of producing the extra production at home exceeds the price at which it could be purchased on the world market. Thus, the benefit to domestic producers comes at the expense of domestic consumers. Indeed, domestic consumers lose on two counts: First, they consume less of the product because its price rises, and second, they pay a higher price for the amount that they do consume. This extra spending ends up in two places: The extra that is paid on all units produced at home goes to domestic producers, and the extra that is paid on units still imported goes to the government as tariff revenue. Box 37-1 deals with some of the effects of these tariffs on consumers and producers using the concept of consumers' and producers' surplus from microeconomics.

Policies That Directly Lower Quantities

The second type of protectionist policy directly restricts the *quantity* of an imported commodity. A common example is the **import quota,** by which the importing country sets a maximum of the quantity of some commodity that may be imported each year. Increasingly popular, however, is the **voluntary export restriction (VER),** an agreement by an exporting country to limit the amount of a good that it sells to the importing country.

The European Community (EC) and the United States have used VERs extensively, and the EC also makes frequent use of import quotas. Japan has been pressured into negotiating several VERs with the EC and the United States in order to limit sales of some of the Japanese goods that have had the most success in international competition. For example, in 1983 the United States and Canada negotiated VERs whereby the Japanese government agreed to restrict total sales of Japanese cars to these two countries for 3 years. When the agreements ran out in 1986, the Japanese continued to restrain their automobile sales by unilateral voluntary action. This episode is further considered in Box 37-2 on pages 794–795.

Fallacious Trade-Policy Arguments

We saw in Chapter 36 that there are gains to be had from a high volume of international trade and specialization. Later we shall see that there can be valid arguments for a moderate degree of protectionism. However, there are also many claims that do not advance the debate. Fallacious arguments are heard on both sides, and they color much of the popular discussion. These arguments have been around for a long time, but their survival does not make them true. We examine them now to see where their fallacies lie.

Fallacious Free-Trade Arguments

Free trade always benefits all countries. This is not necessarily so. We have just seen that some countries may gain by restricting trade in order to get a sufficiently favorable shift in their terms of trade. Such countries would lose if they gave up these tariffs and adopted free trade unilaterally.

Infant industries never abandon their tariff protection. As we saw in Chapter 36, there may be a case for protecting industries subject to scale economies since while they are young their costs are high, but when they mature their costs are low. It is sometimes argued, however, that granting protection to infant industries is a mistake, because these industries seldom admit to growing up and will cling to their protection even when they are fully grown. However, infant industry tariffs are a mistake *only* if these industries never grow up. In this case permanent tariff protection would be required to protect a weak industry that would never be able to compete on an equal footing in the international market. However, if the industries do grow up and achieve the expected scale economies, the fact that, like any special interest group, they cling to their tariff protection is not a sufficient reason for denying protection to other, genuine infant industries. When economies of scale are realized, the real costs of production are reduced and resources are freed for other uses. Whether or not the tariff or other trade barriers remain, a cost saving has been effected by the scale economies.

Box 37-1

The Efficiency Effects of Import Restrictions

Students who have studied consumers' and producers' surplus in microeconomics can use these tools to study the efficiency effects of restrictions placed on imports. Others should omit this box.

The figures below reproduce the two parts of Figure 37-1, except that some different areas are shaded (where common areas are shaded, they are given the same numbers). Part (i) shows the situation under free trade, with the consumers' surplus shaded in darkly and the producers' surplus accruing to *domestic* producers shaded in lightly. (The white area below the S curve between 0 and q_0 is revenue to cover the variable costs of domestic producers, and the white area between q_0 and q_1 is revenue of foreign producers.)

Part (ii) shows the situation after the restriction of imports has occurred. The shaded areas, labeled 1, 2, 4, and 5, are consumers' surplus, lost by domestic consumers. The light shaded area 1 is gained as producers' surplus by domestic producers. The dark shaded area 2 goes to pay direct costs of production on the extra amount, q_0q_3, produced at home. This represents inefficient production because these units could have been obtained abroad at a cost that was lower by the amount indicated by area 2. The light shaded area 4 goes to the government as tariff revenue on the imports in the case of a tariff, and to foreign producers as extra revenue in the case of a quantity restriction. The dark shaded area 5 is gained by no one. It is lost consumers' surplus on the units no longer consumed, and, because they are not produced, there is no one to gain that surplus.

The term *deadweight loss* (of the tariff or quantity restriction) refers to the sum of the two dark shaded areas: area 5, which measures the surplus that is lost by consumers and not gained by anyone else, and area 2, which measures the unnecessary cost incurred by producing at home rather than buying abroad.

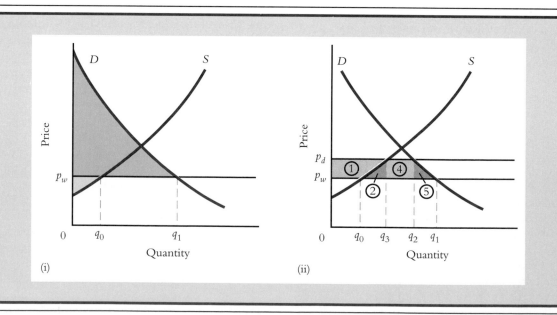

Fallacious Protectionist Arguments

Prevent exploitation.   According to the exploitation theory, trade can never be mutually advantageous; any gain going to one trading partner *must* be at the other's expense. Thus, the weaker trading partner must protect itself by restricting its trade with the stronger partner. However, the principle of comparative advantage shows that it is possible for both parties to gain from trade and thus refutes the exploitation doctrine of trade.

Protect against low-wage foreign labor.   Surely, the argument runs, the products of low-wage countries will drive U.S. products from the market, and the high U.S. standard of living will be dragged down to that of its poor trading partners. Arguments of this sort have swayed many voters through the years. Its latest manifestation is found in the argument that the United States should not enter a free-trade agreement with Mexico because high-wage U.S. producers will be unable to compete against low-wage Mexican producers. In this section we consider the average effects on the country as a whole. Later we will consider how tariffs may benefit particular subgroups within a country.

As a prelude to considering such arguments, consider what the argument would imply if it were taken out of the international context and put into a local one, where the same principles govern the gains from trade. Is it really impossible for a rich person to gain from trading with a poor person? Would the local millionaire be better off if she did all her own typing, gardening, and cooking? No one believes that a rich person cannot gain from trading with those who are less rich.

Why, then, must a rich group of people lose from trading with a poor group? "Well," you say, "the poor group will price its goods too cheaply." Does anyone believe that consumers lose from buying in a discount house or a supermarket just because the prices are lower there than at the old-fashioned corner store? Consumers gain when they can buy the same goods at a lower price. If the Indonesians and Mexicans pay low wages and sell their goods cheaply, Indonesian and Mexican labor *may* suffer, but U.S. consumers will gain because they obtain their goods at a low cost in terms of the goods that must be exported in return. The cheaper our imports are, the better off we are in terms of the goods and services that are available for domestic consumption. In this case, low wages usually means low productivity. Economic forces will

usually cause wages to follow productivity relatively closely.

Stated in more formal terms, the gains from trade depend on comparative, not absolute, advantages. World production is higher when any two areas, say, the United States and Mexico, specialize in the production of the goods for which they have a comparative advantage than when they both try to be self-sufficient.

Might it not be possible, however, that Mexico will undersell the United States in all lines of production, leaving the United States no better off, or even worse off, than if it had no trade with Mexico? The answer is no. The reason for this depends on the behavior of exchange rates, which we shall study in Chapter 38. As we shall see, equality of demand and supply in foreign-exchange markets ensures that trade flows in both directions so that one country cannot undersell another in all lines of production.

What we shall see in greater detail in Chapter 38 is the following. Imports can be obtained only by spending the currency of the country that makes the imports. Claims to this currency can be obtained only by exporting goods and services or by borrowing. Thus, lending and borrowing aside, imports must equal exports. All trade must be in two directions; countries can buy only if they can also sell.

In the long run, trade cannot hurt a country by causing it to import without exporting.

Trade, then, always provides scope for international specialization, with each country producing and exporting those goods for which it has a comparative advantage and importing those goods for which it does not.

Exports raise living standards; imports lower them. Exports add to aggregate demand; imports subtract from it. Thus, *other things being equal,* exports tend to increase national income, and imports tend to reduce it. Surely, then, it is desirable to encourage exports and to discourage imports. This is an appealing argument, but it is incorrect.

Exports raise national income by adding to the value of domestic output, but they do not add to the value of domestic consumption. In fact, exports are goods produced at home and consumed abroad, whereas imports are goods produced abroad and consumed at home. The standard of living in a country depends on the goods and services available for *consumption*, not on what is produced.

Box 37-2

Import Restrictions on Japanese Cars: Tariffs or Quotas?

In the early 1980s, imports of Japanese cars seriously threatened the automobile industries of the United States, Canada, and Western Europe. While continuing to espouse relatively free trade as a long-term policy, the U.S. and Canadian governments argued that the domestic industry needed short-term protection to tide it over the period of transition that it faced as smaller cars became the typical North American vehicle. Voluntary export restrictions (VERs) seemed the easiest route to achieve this protection. An agreement was reached whereby the Japanese government agreed to organize Japanese auto firms to limit severely the number of Japanese cars that could be exported to the United States and Canada.

What does economic theory predict to be the effects of VERs and tariffs? In both cases, imports are restricted, and the resulting scarcity supports a higher market price. With a tariff, the extra market value is appropriated by the government of the importing country—in this case the U.S. and Canadian governments. With a VER, the extra market value accrues to the goods' suppliers—in this case the Japanese car makers and their U.S. retailers.

Both cases are illustrated in the accompanying figure. We assume that the North American market provides a small enough part of total Japanese car sales to leave the Japanese willing to supply all the cars that are demanded in the United States and Canada at their fixed list price. This is the price p_0 in both parts of the figure. Given the U.S. demand curve for Japanese cars, D, there are q_0 cars sold before restrictions are imposed.

In part (i) the United States places a tariff of T per unit on Japanese cars, raising their price in the United States to p_1 and lowering sales to q_1. Suppliers' revenue is shown by the light shaded area. Government tariff revenue is shown by the dark shaded area.

In part (ii) a VER of q_1 is negotiated, making the supply curve of Japanese cars vertical at q_1. The market-clearing price is p_1. The suppliers' revenue is the whole shaded area (p_1 times q_1).

In both cases the shortage of Japanese cars drives up their price, creating a substantial margin over costs. Under a tariff, the U.S. and Canadian governments capture the margin. Under a VER policy, however, the margin accrues to the Japanese manufacturers.

Although this is a simplified picture, it captures the essence of what actually happened. First, while sellers of North American cars were keeping prices as low as possible, and sometimes offering rebates on slow-selling models, Japanese cars were listed at healthy profit margins. Second, while it was always possible for the buyer of a North American car to negotiate a good discount off the list price, Japanese

---

If exports were really good and imports really bad, a fully employed economy that managed to increase exports without a corresponding increase in imports should be better off. Such a change, however, would result in a reduction in its current standard of living because, when more goods are sent abroad and no more are brought in from abroad, the total goods available for domestic consumption must fall.

The living standards of a country depend on the goods and services consumed in that country. The importance of exports is that they permit imports to be made. This two-way international exchange is valuable because more goods can be imported than could be obtained if the same goods were produced at home.

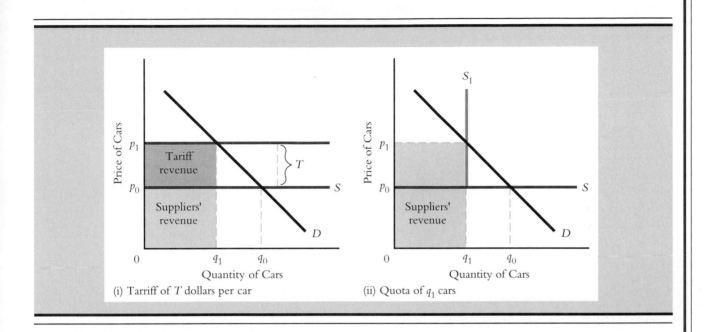

(i) Tarriff of T dollars per car

(ii) Quota of q_1 cars

cars usually sold for their full list price. Third, because Japanese manufacturers were not allowed to supply all of the cars that they could sell in the United States, they had to choose which types of cars to supply. Not surprisingly, they tended to satisfy fully the demand for their more expensive cars, which have higher profit margins. This change in the "product mix" of Japanese cars exported to the United States raised the average profit per car exported.

The VERs were thus very costly to North American consumers and an enormous profit boon to Japanese auto manufacturers. Indeed, it was estimated that North American consumers paid about $150,000 per year for each job that was saved in the U.S. automobile industry, and that most of this went to Japanese producers! (This cost to consumers per job saved is typical of what is found in many industries where VERs or their equivalents have been used.) Of course, this amount is spread over many consumers, so each does not notice the amount of his or her contribution. Nonetheless, $150,000 per year could do a lot of things, including fully retrain the workers and subsidize their movement to industries and areas where they could produce things that could be sold on free markets without government protection.

Create domestic jobs and reduce unemployment. It is sometimes said that an economy with substantial unemployment, such as that of the United States in the 1930s or the early 1990s, provides an exception to the case for freer trade. Suppose that tariffs or import quotas cut the imports of Japanese cars, Korean textiles, Italian shoes, and French wine. Surely, the argument maintains, this will create more employment for Detroit automobile workers, Tennessee textile workers, New York shoe factories, and midwestern farm workers. The answer is that it will—initially. But the Japanese, Koreans, Italians, and French can buy from the United States only if they get U.S. dollars from those who have goods in the United States. The decline in their sales of automobiles, textiles, shoes, and wine will decrease their purchases of U.S. machinery, aircraft, grain, and vacations in the United States. Jobs will be lost in export industries and gained in industries that formerly faced competition from imports. The likely long-term effect is that overall unemployment will not be reduced but will merely be redistributed among industries. Because the export industries that contract tend to be more efficient than the import-competing industries that expand, this policy tends to reallocate resources from more to less efficient lines of production and hence to reduce overall GDP.

The Case for Protectionism

We now come to arguments for protection that have some validity in that the protection may well achieve the goals that are being sought. Two kinds of arguments for protection are commonly offered. The first concerns national objectives other than national income; the second concerns the desire to increase domestic national income, possibly at the expense of total world income.

Objectives Other Than Maximizing National Income

It is quite possible to accept the proposition that national income is higher with free trade and yet rationally to oppose free trade because of a concern with policy objectives other than maximizing per capita national income.

Noneconomic advantages of diversification. Comparative advantage might dictate that a small country should specialize in producing a narrow range of commodities. Its government might decide, however, that there are distinct social advantages to encouraging a more diverse economy. Citizens would be given a wider range of occupations, and the social and psychological advantages of diversification would more than compensate for a reduction in living standards by, say, 5 percent below what they could be with specialization of production according to comparative advantage.

Risks of specialization. For a very small country, specializing in the production of only a few commodities—though dictated by comparative advantage—may involve risks that the country does not wish to take. One such risk is that technologi-. cal advances may render its basic product obsolete.

Everyone understands this risk, but there is debate about what governments can do about it. The pro-tariff argument is that the government can encourage a more diversified economy by protecting industries that otherwise could not compete. Opponents argue that governments, being naturally influenced by political motives, are, in the final analysis, poor judges of which industries can be protected in order to produce diversification at a reasonable cost.

Another risk is that cyclical fluctuations in the prices of basic commodities may cause a country to face depressed prices for years at a time and then enjoy periods of very high prices. The national income of a country that specializes in the production of such commodities will be subject to wide fluctuations. The average income level over a long period of time might be higher if specialization in the production of a few basic commodities were allowed. The serious social problems associated with a widely fluctuating national income might, however, induce the government to sacrifice some income in order to reduce fluctuations. The government might use protectionist policies to encourage the expansion of several less cyclically sensitive industries.

National defense. Another noneconomic reason for protectionism concerns national defense. It is sometimes argued, for example, that the United States needs an experienced merchant marine in case of war and that this industry should be fostered by protectionist policies, even though it is less efficient than that of the foreign competition. The Jones Act provides this protection by requiring that all cargoes moving between two U.S. ports be carried in U.S. ships. In the past (before the first OPEC shock), national defense was also used as a reason for protecting domestic oil producers. Imports of foreign oil were restricted on the grounds that national defense required a domestic oil industry of at least a certain minimum size.

Protection of specific groups. Although free trade will maximize per capita GDP over the whole economy, some specific groups may have higher incomes under protection than under free trade. An obvious example is a firm or industry that is given monopoly power when tariffs are used to restrict foreign competition. If a group of firms, and possibly their employees, find their incomes increased by, say, 25 percent when they get tariff protection, they may not be concerned that the country's per capita income falls by, say, 2 percent. They get a much larger share of a slightly smaller total income and end up better off.

Even large groups can gain in the same way. Consider a country rich in capital and land but with scarce labor. The scarcity will result in high wages. The opening of free trade brings competition from countries where labor is plentiful and may reduce the wage rate in the labor-scarce country. As a result, its labor will get a smaller share of the larger total income that trade makes possible. The larger are the gains from trade, the less likely is it that such changes in relative factor price earnings will actually lower real incomes of any large group within the country.[1]

Conclusion. Although most people would agree that, other things being equal, they would prefer more income to less, a nation may rationally choose to sacrifice some income in order to achieve other goals. Economists can do three things when they are faced with such reasons for imposing tariffs. First, they can see if the proposed tariff really does achieve the goals suggested. Second, they can calculate the cost of the tariff in terms of lowered living standards. Third, they can check policy alternatives to see if there are other means of achieving the stated goal at a lower cost in terms of lost output.

The Objective of Maximizing National Income

Next we consider five important arguments for the use of tariffs when the objective is to make national income as large as possible.

To alter the terms of trade. Trade restrictions can sometimes be used to turn the terms of trade in favor of countries that produce and export a large fraction of the world's supply of some commodity. They can also be used to turn the terms of trade in favor of countries that constitute a large fraction of the world demand for some commodity that they import.

When the OPEC countries restricted their output of oil in the 1970s, they were able to drive the price of oil up relative to the prices of other traded goods. This turned the terms of trade in their fa-

vor: For every barrel of oil exported, they were able to obtain a much larger quantity of imports. When the output of oil grew greatly in the mid-1980s, the relative price of oil fell dramatically, and the terms of trade turned unfavorably to the oil-exporting countries. These are illustrations of how changes in the quantities of exports can affect the terms of trade.

Now consider a country that provides a large fraction of the total demand for some product that it imports. By restricting its demand for that product through tariffs, it can force the price of that product down. This turns the terms of trade in its favor, because it can now get more units of imports per unit of exports.

Both of these techniques lower world output. They can, however, make it possible for a small group of countries to gain, because they get a sufficiently larger share of the smaller world output. However, if foreign countries retaliate by raising their tariffs, the ensuing trade war can easily leave every country with a lowered income.

To protect against "unfair" actions by foreign firms and governments. Tariffs may be used to prevent foreign industries from gaining an advantage over domestic industries through the use of predatory practices that will harm domestic industries and hence lower national income. Two common practices are the payment of subsidies by foreign governments to their exporters and dumping by foreign firms. Such practices are called *unfair trade practices,* and the laws that deal with them are called *fair-trade laws.* The circumstances under which foreign subsidization and dumping provide a valid argument for tariffs are considered in detail later in this chapter.

To protect infant industries. The oldest valid argument for protectionism as a means of raising living standards concerns economies of scale. It is usually called the **infant industry argument.** If an industry has large economies of scale, costs and prices will be high when the industry is small but will fall as the industry grows. In such industries the country first in the field has a tremendous advantage. A newly developing country may find that in the early stages of development its industries are unable to compete with established foreign rivals. A trade restriction may protect these industries from foreign competition while they grow. When they are large enough, they may be able to produce as cheaply as

---

[1] Models that show this possibility usually assume static technology and constant returns to scale. The presence of dynamic scale, learning effects, and induced improvements in technology increase the total gain and make it less likely that any large group will lose absolutely through free trade.

foreign rivals and thus be able to compete without protection.

To encourage learning by doing. Learning by doing, which we discussed in Chapter 36, suggests that the existing pattern of comparative advantage need not be taken as immutable. If a country can learn enough by producing commodities in which it currently is at a comparative disadvantage, it may gain in the long run by specializing in those commodities and developing a comparative advantage in them as the learning process helps to lower their costs. Learning by doing is an example of what in Chapter 36 we called *dynamic comparative advantages.* The successes of such *newly industrializing countries* (the so-called NICs) as Brazil, Hong Kong, South Korea, Singapore, and Taiwan seemed to many observers to be based on acquired skills and government policies that created favorable business conditions. This gave rise to the theory that comparative advantages can change and can be developed by suitable government policies.

Protecting a domestic industry from foreign competition may give its management time to learn to be efficient and its labor force time to acquire needed skills. If so, there may be a long-term payoff to protecting the industry against foreign competition while a dynamic comparative advantage is being developed.

Some countries clearly have succeeded in developing strong comparative advantages in targeted industries, but others have failed. One reason such policies have sometimes failed is that protecting local industries from foreign competition may make the industries unadaptive and complacent. Another reason is that it is difficult to identify now the industries that will be able to succeed in the future. All too often the protected infant industry grows up to be a weakling that requires permanent tariff protection for its continued existence, or else its rate of learning is slower than for similar industries in countries that do not provide protection from the chill winds of international competition. In these instances the anticipated comparative advantage never materializes.

To create or to exploit a strategic trade advantage. A major new argument for tariffs or other trade restrictions is to create a strategic advantage in producing or marketing some new product that is expected to generate pure profits. To the extent that all lines of production earn normal profits, there is no reason to produce goods other than ones for which a country has a comparative advantage. Some goods, however are produced in industries containing a few large firms where large scale economies provide a natural barrier to further entry. Firms in these industries can earn extra-high profits over long periods of time. Where such industries are already well established, there is little chance that a new firm will replace one of the existing giants.

The situation is, however, more fluid with new products. The first firm to develop and market a new product successfully may earn a substantial pure profit over all of its opportunity costs and become one of the few established firms in the industry. If protection of the domestic market can increase the chance that one of the protected domestic firms will become one of the established firms in the international market, the protection may pay off. This is the general idea behind the modern concept of strategic trade policy, and it is treated in more detail in the next section.

Strategic Trade Policy and U.S. Competitiveness

Implications of high development costs. Many of today's high-tech industries have falling average total cost curves due to their large fixed costs of product development. For a new generation of civilian aircraft, silicon chips, computers, artificial-intelligence machines, and genetically engineered food products, a high proportion of each producer's total costs go to product development. These are fixed costs of entering the market, and they must be incurred before a single unit of output can be sold.

In such industries the actual costs of producing each unit of an already developed product may be quite small. Even if average variable costs are constant, the large fixed development costs mean that the average total cost curve has a significant negative slope over a large range of output. It follows that the price at which a firm can expect to recover its total cost is negatively related to its expected volume of sales. The larger are the sales that it expects, the lower is the price that it can charge and still expect to recover its full costs.

In such industries, there may be room for only a few firms, and those firms may make large profits. A large number of firms, each of which has a relatively small output, could not recover their fixed costs. A small number of firms, each of which has a high output, can do so. Furthermore, it is possible for these firms to make large profits, whereas the entry of one more firm would cause everyone to suffer losses. In this case, the first firms that become established in the market will control it and will earn the profits.[2]

The production of full-sized commercial jets provides an example of an industry that possesses many of these characteristics. The development costs of a new generation of jet aircraft have risen with each new generation. If the aircraft manufacturers are to recover these costs, each of them must have large sales. Thus, the number of firms that the market can support has diminished steadily, until today there is room in the world aircraft industry for only two or three firms producing a full range of commercial jets.

Argument for subsidies.   The characteristics just listed are sometimes used to provide arguments for subsidizing the development of such industries. Suppose, for example, that there is room in the aircraft industry for only three major producers of the next round of passenger jets. If a government subsidizes a domestic firm, this firm may become one of the three that succeed. In this case the profits that are subsequently earned may more than repay the cost of the subsidy. Furthermore, another country's firm, which was not subsidized, may have been just as good as the three that succeeded. Without the subsidy, however, this firm may lose out in the battle to establish itself as one of the three surviving firms in the market. Having lost this one battle, it loses its entire fight for existence. The firm, and the country's possibility of bring represented in the industry, are gone for the foreseeable future.

This example is not unlike the story of the European Airbus. The European producers received many direct subsidies (and they charge that their main competitor, the Boeing 767, received many indirect ones). Whatever the merits of the argument, several things are clear: The civilian jet aircraft industry

remains profitable; there is room for only two or three major producers; and one of these would not have been the European consortium if it had not been for substantial government assistance.

Argument for tariffs.   The argument for tariffs is that a protected domestic market greatly reduces the risks of product development and allows successful firms to achieve sufficient scale on the domestic market to be able to sell at competitive prices abroad. The classic example here is the victory in the 1970s of the Japanese semiconductor producers over their U.S. rivals. From the beginning of the industry, U.S. firms held a large competitive edge over all others. Then the Japanese decided to develop their industry. To do so, they shielded their domestic market from penetration by U.S. firms. The Japanese, who at first were well behind the U.S. firms, caught up and were then able to penetrate the open U.S. market. In the end, the Japanese succeeded with the next generation of silicon chips, and the once-dominant U.S. industry suffered greatly. (This does not seem to have stopped the U.S. firms from being successful in the round of competition over the next generation of chips in the 1990s.)

A combination of domestic subsidization and tariff protection allowed the Japanese semiconductor industry to score a major victory in terms of market share over their U.S. competitors. The strategy, however, entailed large costs, both for product development and aggressive, below-cost pricing policies. Currently, there is debate as to whether the long-run profits resulting from this policy were sufficient to cover all these costs.

Debate over strategic trade policy.   Generalizing from this and similar cases, some economists advocate that the United States adopt a *strategic trade policy,* which means, for high-tech industries, government protection of the home market and government subsidization (either openly or by more subtle back-door methods) of the product development stage. These economists say that, if the United States does not follow their advice, it will lose out in industry after industry to the more aggressive Japanese and European competition—a competition that is adept at combining private innovative activity with government assistance.

Opponents argue that strategic trade policy is nothing more than a modern version of the age-old, and faulty, justifications for tariff protection. They

---

[2] The reason for this is found in the indivisibility of product development costs. If, say, $500 million is required to develop a marketable product, a firm that spends only $300 million gets nothing. To see why this creates the potential for profits, assume that the market is large enough for the product to be sold at a price that would cover variable costs of production and also pay the opportunity costs of $1.25 billion worth of capital. Further assume that the capital required for actual production is negligible. In this case two firms with a total of $1 billion of capital invested in development costs will enter the market and earn large profits. However, if a third firm entered, making the industry's total invested capital $1.5 billion, all three firms would incur losses.

argue that, once all countries try to be strategic, they will all waste vast sums trying to break into industries in which there is no room for most of them. U.S. consumers would benefit most, they say, if their government lets other countries engage in this game. Consumers could then buy the cheap, subsidized foreign products and export traditional, lower-tech products in return. The opponents of strategic trade policy also argue that democratic governments that enter the game of picking and backing winners are likely to make as many bad choices as good ones. One bad choice, with *all* of its massive development costs written off, would require that many good choices also be made, in order to make the equivalent in profits that would allow taxpayers to break even overall.[3]

Advocates of strategic trade policy reply that a country cannot afford to stand by while others play the strategic game. They argue that there are key industries that have major "spillovers" into the rest of the economy. If a country wants to have a high living standard, it must, they argue, compete with the best. If a country lets all of its key industries migrate to other countries, many of the others will follow. The country then risks being reduced to the status of a less-developed nation.

This is a debate about dynamic comparative advantage and the effects of key industries on growth and living standards. It is a difficult issue, and one that is hotly debated in the United States today. The debate is an important one because it concerns nothing less than the place of the United States in the world of the future. Over the next few decades, will the United States maintain its place as a leading industrial producer and innovator and as one of the world's highest-income countries? Will it, instead, go the way other leading countries have gone in the past—from a burst of dynamism, when its society was young and vibrant, to a period of relative stagnation? This happened to Spain in an earlier century and to the United Kingdom in this century. Will the United States be next? The debate over strategic trade policy is a debate over the best way to ensure a negative answer to this question. Should unaided market forces or government assistance through strategic trade policy be relied upon?

---

[3] Let each investment be $100 and, when successful, return $125, for a 25 percent return. Nine investments cost $900, and seven successes and two total losses yield $875. This is an overall loss of $25 on a $900 investment.

How Much Protectionism?

So far we have seen that there is a strong case for allowing free trade in order to realize the gains from trade, but that there are also reasons for departing from completely free trade.

It is not necessary to choose between free trade on the one hand and absolute protectionism on the other. A country can be trade-oriented and protectionist, too.

Free Trade Versus No Trade

Undoubtedly, it would be possible to grow coffee beans in Michigan greenhouses and to synthesize much of the oil that we consume (as Germany did during World War II). However, the cost in terms of other commodities forgone would be huge, because these artificial means of production require massive inputs of factors of production. It would likewise be possible for a tropical country currently producing foodstuffs to set up industries to produce all the manufactured products that it consumes. However, for a small country without natural advantages in industrial production, the cost in terms of resources used could be enormous. It is thus clear that there is a large gain to all countries in having specialization and trade. The real output and consumption of all countries would be very much lower if each country chose to produce domestically all of the goods that it consumed.

In an all-or-nothing choice, almost all countries would choose free trade over no trade.

A Little More Trade Versus a Little Less Trade

Today we have trade among nations, but this trade is not perfectly free. Table 37-1 shows the levels of tariffs on selected commodities in force today.

Would we be better off if today's barriers to trade were reduced or increased a little bit? This question shifts the focus of our discussion considerably, for it is quite a jump from the proposition that "Free trade is better than no trade" to the proposition that "A little less trade restriction than we have at present is better than a little more."

To see this latter issue more clearly, compare the effects of a 10 percent uniform effective rate of tariff with those of free trade. Tariffs of 10 percent will protect industries that are up to 10 percent less

TABLE 37-1 Tariffs on Selected Commodity Groups (*ad valorem rates*)

Commodity	United States	European Community	Japan
Weighted average of all manufactured items	4.4	5.5	3.6
Fruits, vegetables	1.7	3.4	14.5
Tea, coffee, and spices	5.3	1.8	34.1
Paper, paperboard	0.3	4.0	1.4
Textiles	15.9	9.0	8.0
Transport vehicles	2.5	6.2	2.1
Tobacco	13.0	0.0	54.3
Petroleum and coal products	0.0	6.3	1.4
Oil and natural gas	4.0	0.0	0.0
All commodities (trade weighted)	3.2	3.7	5.4

Source: Post-Tokyo Round tariff rates, courtesy Special Trade Representatives Office, U.S. government.

The United States is a low-tariff country overall, yet tariffs on selected items are plainly designed to be protective of important domestic industries. These tariffs, the lowest in history, result from the General Agreement on Tariffs and Trade (GATT) Tokyo Round negotiations. They were phased in during the 1980s and will apply until further tariff cuts are phased in after the end of the Uruguay Round of GATT negotiations. Notice the U.S. use of tariffs for protection on textiles and tobacco. In Japan the high tariffs on tobacco, tea, coffee, and spices are for revenue, because Japan does not produce these commodities. In contrast, the high Japanese tariffs on fruits and vegetables serve to protect a very high-cost domestic agricultural industry.

efficient than foreign competitors. If the costs of the various tariff-protected industries were spread out evenly, some would be 10 percent less efficient than their foreign competitors, and others would be only 1 percent less efficient. Their average inefficiency would be about one-half the tariff rate, so they would be on average about 5 percent less efficient than their foreign competitors.

Suppose that, as a result of tariffs, approximately 20 percent of a country's resources are allocated to industries that are different from the ones to which they would be allocated if there were no tariffs. This means that about 20 percent of a country's resources would be working in certain industries only because of tariff protection. If the average protected industry is 5 percent less efficient than its foreign rival,

approximately 20 percent of a country's resources are producing on average about 5 percent less than they would be if there were no tariffs. This causes a reduction in national income on the order of 1 percent as a result of tariff protection.[4]

Suppose then that the economic costs of existing tariffs are 1 percent of national income. Is this sacrifice of national income large or small? Expressed as a percentage of GDP, the loss seems small, yet in 1990 it was $57 billion per year in the United States. That amount every year forever could buy a lot of hospitals, schools, medical research, urban renewal, solar energy research—or even imported oil.

The previous calculations refer to gains from exploiting comparative advantage when costs are given and constant. More recent calculations allow for unexploited economies of scale in specific product lines and for some forms of dynamic comparative advantages. They show gains from reducing the world's remaining tariffs that are much larger than the smaller ones suggested before. These gains can approach 10 percent of the national incomes of small and middle-sized countries, although, for large countries such as the United States, the gains tend to be somewhat smaller, because many of the scale and dynamic economies can be exploited within the large domestic market.

Longer-run considerations. Some readers may be tempted to conclude that the seemingly small economic costs of the current amount of protectionism make it worthwhile to give in to the clamor to provide more protection for some of the United States' hard-pressed industries. Before rushing to this conclusion, however, some long-run political and economic possibilities need to be considered. The world prosperity of the entire period following World War II has been built largely on a rising volume of relatively free international trade. There are real doubts that such prosperity could be maintained if the volume of trade were to shrink steadily because of growing trade barriers. Yet the pressure to use trade restrictions in troubled times is strong. If countries begin to raise barriers moderately when the initial economic costs are not large, so strong are the political forces involved that there is no telling where the process, once begun, will end.

---

[4] This rough calculation is meant only to give some intuitive understanding of why the many careful measures of the cost of moderate tariffs commonly lead to figures that are closer to 1 percent than to 10 percent of the United States' national income.

addressed five key issues: (1) the growing worldwide use of nontariff barriers to trade; (2) the need to develop rules for liberalizing trade in services, which is the most rapidly growing component of foreign trade; (3) the distorting effect on trade in agricultural products caused by heavy domestic subsidization of agriculture, particularly in the European Community; (4) the need to develop more effective methods of settling disputes that arise from violations of GATT rules; and (5) the desire of developed nations to gain better copyright protection for intellectual property—a desire that pitted the rich, innovating nations against the poorer nations with a self-interest in gaining access to intellectual property on terms as favorable as possible. (Intellectual property is a property right resulting from mental effort, such as discovery, product development, or the creation of a work of art, and resulting in a right of ownership conferred by a document such as a patent or a copyright.)

Negotiations dragged on, missing several deadlines in 1990, 1991, and 1992.

Regional Agreements

Three standard forms of regional trade-liberalizing agreements are free trade areas, customs unions, and common markets.

A **free-trade area (FTA)** is the least comprehensive of the three. It allows for tariff-free trade between the member countries, but it leaves each member free to levy its own tariffs and other restrictions on imports from other countries. As a result, members must maintain customs points at their common borders (if they have any) to make sure that imports into the free-trade area do not all enter through the member that is levying the lowest tariff on each item. They must also agree on rules of origin to establish when a good is made in a member country, and hence is able to pass duty-free across their borders, and when it is imported from outside the FTA, and hence is liable to pay duties when it crosses borders within the FTA.

A **customs union** is a free-trade area plus an agreement to establish common barriers to trade with the rest of the world. Because they have a common tariff against the outside world, the members have no need for customs controls on goods moving among themselves.

A **common market** is a customs union that also has free movement of labor and capital among its members.

Free-trade areas. The first important free-trade area in the modern era was the European Free Trade Association (EFTA). It was formed in 1960 by a group of European countries that were unwilling to join the EC because of its all-embracing character. Not wanting to be left out of the gains from trade, they formed an association whose sole purpose was tariff removal. They removed all tariffs on trade among themselves. Each of the EFTA countries also signed a free-trade-area agreement with the EC. This makes the EC-EFTA market the largest tariff-free market in the world (over 300 milion people). Most of the EFTA countries are now moving to enter the EC some time in the 1990s.

In 1985 the United States signed a limited free-trade agreement with Israel. In 1988 a sweeping agreement was signed with Canada, instituting free trade on all goods and many services, and covering what is the largest flow of international trade between any two countries in the world. Australia and New Zealand have also entered into an association that removes restrictions on trade in goods and services between the two countries.

In 1991, at Mexico's behest, the United States, Canada, and Mexico began negotiations for a North American Free Trade Area, a so-called NAFTA. In September 1992 agreement was reached among the three countries' negotiators. This agreement was followed within a month by the publication of the full legal text of the agreement. The new NAFTA was, as expected, closely patterned on the existing U.S.-Canada agreement, although it was somewhat more protectionist in a few sectors. Notably, it significantly increased the difficulty for imported automobiles, textiles, and apparel to compete with similar products produced within the three NAFTA countries. The agreement also exempted Mexico's oil industry from the conditions already agreed upon between Canada and the United States. The reason was that the Mexican industry is shielded from foreign influence by the Mexican constitution. Although this was a bargaining victory for Mexico, it was not clear that Mexico would gain from the exclusion of foreign influences in such a key industry.

The full legal text also contained an accession clause allowing other countries to enter the agreement. The text itself was longer and more complex than the U.S.-Canada agreement because it was meant to be able to accommodate all Latin American countries so that it could grow into a full-scale Western Hemispheric Free Trade Agreement (WHFTA). In the United States the agreement comes to Congress under the "fast-track" procedure by which Congress can only vote to accept or reject the entire agreement but cannot amend it.[7]

Mexico's willingness to enter a free-trade agreement with the United States is the outcome of the remarkable liberalization of its economy that began in the 1980s. For decades Mexico experimented with policies of high tariffs and quota restrictions and attempts to build up infant industries, plus heavy domestic subsidization and deficit financing that resulted in inflations often exceeding 10 percent *per month*. Then, as is explained in detail in Chapter 40, in the 1980s these policies finally were recognized to be failures, and an outward-looking stance was adopted. Tariffs, often as high as 100–200 percent, were slashed unilaterally. Quotas were eliminated on most imports. Subsidies for domestic firms were cut, inflationary financing was brought nearly under control, and a general reliance on the market system over state control was accepted. The effects on the Mexican economy were dramatic, and exports and imports grew rapidly. To secure its liberalization, guarantee its access to wider markets, and make Mexico an attractive place for foreign investment, the government sought the free-trade agreement with the United States and Canada.

The Mexican example of liberalization is being followed by many other countries of Latin America. The decades of inward-looking, state-interventionist policies have been declared failures, and the countries are moving to adopt more market-oriented, outward-looking policies. Imports are no longer restricted, and exports are growing where the countries have comparative advantages rather than where the government subsidizes most. Like Mexico, these countries are seeking to consolidate their outward-looking policies by entering full trade-liberalizing agreements with their neighbors. The first move is with immediate neighbors. But if the NAFTA goes through, these countries may well join with it to form a wider Western Hemispheric Free Trade Agreement (WHFTA). This lies far in the future, but the remarkable movement toward market-oriented policies in Latin American countries makes it a distinct possibility. If the whole hemisphere were to join into one free-trade area, this would create a single market currently of 600 million people, in which goods and services moved tariff-free.

Common markets. The most important example of a common market came into being in 1957, when the Treaty of Rome brought together France, Germany, Italy, Holland, Belgium, and Luxembourg in what was first called the European Common Market (ECM), then renamed the European Economic Community (EEC), and finally just called the European Community (EC). The original six countries were joined in 1973 by the United Kingdom, the Republic of Ireland, and Denmark; Greece entered in 1983, and Spain and Portugal joined in 1986.

This organization is dedicated to bringing about free trade, complete mobility of factors of production, and the eventual harmonization of fiscal and monetary policies among the member countries. Many tariffs on manufactured goods have been eliminated, and much freedom of movement of labor and capital has been achieved. Substantial monetary integration has also been achieved, but there is still a long way to go to fully integrate the various national monies and monetary institutions into a single European monetary system with a single European currency.

A major push for greatly increased integration was made over several years and completed by a treaty in 1992. If, as is still uncertain at the time of writing, that treaty is ratified by all the member countries, "Europe 1992" will be a much more fully integrated market than the Europe of a decade earlier. The goal is tariff-free movement of goods and services, complete factor mobility, and, eventually, a single European currency. If that finally happens, Europe will be as much a single integrated market as is the United States today.

Trade Remedy Laws and Nontariff Barriers

Early rounds of negotiations under the GATT that started in 1949 concentrated on the reduction of tariffs. As these were lowered, countries that wished to

---

[7] Before the fast-track procedure was introduced, the U.S. and foreign negotiators working on some treaty would carefully balance their compromises to come to a mutually acceptable balance. The agreement then went to the Senate, which could strike down the clauses it did not like—generally those embodying U.S. compromises—and accept those clauses it did like—generally those embodying foreign compromises. Not surprisingly, foreign governments became unwilling to negotiate complex agreements with the United States under such a procedure, and the fast track provided the way of restoring the willingness of foreign countries to negotiate with the United States.

protect domestic industries began using, and abusing, a series of trade restrictions that came to be known as nontariff barriers (NTBs). Most NTBs are ostensibly levied for purposes other than protectionism. These other purposes are often called trade relief.

An effort to control the growing use of NTBs was made in the Tokyo Round of GATT negotiations. These measures were classified, and the circumstances under which their use was legitimate were laid down. The ironic result was that by making all countries aware of these measures, and by making their use respectable under some circumstances, these GATT agreements seem to have led to an increased use of NTBs for purposes of trade restriction.

Escape clause. One procedure that can be used as an NTB is the so-called escape clause action. A rapid surge of imports may temporarily threaten the existence of domestic producers. These producers may then be given temporary relief by raising tariff rates above those agreed to during the GATT negotiations. The trouble is that, once imposed, these "temporary" measures are hard to eliminate.

One "temporary" measure that is still in force provides a cautionary tale. In the late 1950s the textile and clothing industries in many advanced industrial nations saw their market shares reduced by a rising volume of imports from Hong Kong, Korea, the Philippines, and other newly industrializing nations. In response to a United States initiative, international meetings were held in 1961. Out of these meetings came the *multifiber agreements* (MFAs), which provided maximum annual quotas for each exporting textile-producing country for a 20-year period. Starting in 1981, many of these agreements were renegotiated, generally leading to more, rather than less, restrictive policies.

Dumping. When a commodity is sold in a foreign country at a price that is lower than the price in the domestic market, it is called **dumping.** Dumping is a form of price discrimination studied in the theory of monopoly. Most governments have antidumping duties, which protect their own industries against unfair foreign pricing practices.

Dumping, if it lasts indefinitely, can be a gift to the receiving country. Its consumers get goods from abroad at less than their real cost. Dumping is more often a temporary measure, designed to get rid of unwanted surpluses, or a predatory attempt to drive competitors out of business. In either case,

domestic producers complain about unfair foreign competition. In both cases, it is accepted international practice to levy *antidumping duties* on foreign imports. These duties are designed to eliminate the discriminatory elements in their prices.

Unfortunately, antidumping laws have been evolving over the last few decades in ways that allow antidumping duties to become barriers to trade and competition, rather than redresses for unfair trading practices. The United States has been a leader in making these changes, but many other countries, including those of the EC, have been quick to imitate the United States.

Two features of the antidumping system that is now in effect in many countries make it highly protectionist. First, *any* price discrimination is classified as dumping and thus is subject to penalties. Thus, prices in the producer's domestic market become, in effect, minimum prices below which no sales can be made in foreign markets, whatever the circumstances in the domestic and foreign markets. Second, following a change in the U.S. law in the early 1970s, many countries' laws now calculate the "margin of dumping" as the difference between the price that is charged in that country's market and the foreign producers' "full allocated cost" (average total cost). This means that, when there is global excess demand so that the profit-maximizing price for all producers is below average total cost (but above average variable cost), foreign producers can be convicted of dumping. This gives domestic producers enormous protection whenever the market price falls temporarily below average total cost. Furthermore, it is very difficult to allocate overheads among individual products in many multiproduct industries. This is particularly true in industries such as chemicals, where fixed costs are a high proportion of total costs and there are tens of thousands of individual products that have widely differing development costs.

Countervailing duties. Countervailing duties provide another case in which a trade relief measure can sometimes become a covert NTB. The countervailing duty is designed to act, not as a tariff barrier, but rather as a means of creating a "level playing field" on which fair international competition can take place. U.S. firms rightly complain that they cannot compete against the seemingly bottomless purses of foreign governments. Subsidized foreign exports can be sold indefinitely in the United States at prices that would produce losses in the absence of the subsidy.

The original object of countervailing duties was to contract the effect on price of the presence of such foreign subsidies.

If a U.S. firm suspects the existence of such a subsidy and registers a complaint, the U.S. government is required to make an investigation. For a countervailing duty to be levied, the investigation must find, first, that the foreign subsidy to the specific industry in question does exist and, second, that it is large enough to cause significant injury to competing U.S. firms.

There is no doubt that countervailing duties sometimes have been used to remove the effects of "unfair" competition that are caused by foreign subsidies. Other governments complain, however, that countervailing duties are often used as a thinly disguised barrier to trade. At the early stages of the development of countervailing duties, only subsidies whose prime effect was to distort trade were possible objects of countervailing duties. Even then, however, the existence of equivalent domestic subsidies was *not taken into account* when decisions were made to put countervailing duties on subsidized imports. Thus, the United States has some countervailing duties against foreign goods where the foreign subsidy is less than the U.S. subsidy. This does not create a level playing field.

Over time, the type of subsidy that is subject to countervailing duties has evolved until almost any government program that affects industry now risks becoming the object of countervailing duty. Because all governments, including most U.S. state governments, have many programs that provide some direct or indirect assistance to industry, the potential for the use of countervailing duties as thinly disguised trade barriers is enormous.

The Crisis in the Multilateral Trading System

At the end of World War II, the United States took the lead in forming the GATT and in pressing for reductions in world tariffs through successive rounds of negotiations. Largely as a result of this U.S. initiative, the world's tariff barriers have been greatly reduced, while the volume of world trade has risen steadily.

The 1980s saw a serious crisis evolve in this multilateral trading system. The most important single force that led to this was a shift in the attitudes of many U.S. citizens toward protectionism. There are at least two key reasons for this shift.

The Growth of Protectionist Sentiment

First, under the impact of the persistent trade deficit, which is further discussed in Chapters 38 and 39, many influential U.S. leaders have become protectionist, a sentiment that has not prevailed to such a degree since the early 1930s. Second, the stiff competition coming from Japanese and European industry has led many U.S. citizens to fear a loss of U.S. competitiveness. Many seem to feel that U.S. industry cannot compete effectively in the free market. This concern leads some to support *managed trade* as a protectionist device.

The growth of protectionist sentiments is not confined to the United States. Similar changes have been occurring in Europe for similar reasons. The great success of Japanese exporters in penetrating the EC market, while helping consumers, has caused trouble for many producers and has led to a search for ways to protect firms in the EC. The EC has made use of quotas, antidumping duties, and VERs. Because fighting an antidumping case can be time-consuming and expensive, the mere registering of an antidumping complaint can often lead a foreign firm to raise its prices to the levels that are charged by domestic producers. This has the effect, desired by the domestic producers, of preventing a more efficient foreign supplier from underselling them.

The Pressure to Manage Trade

In the free-market system, competitive prices determine what is imported and what is exported. Under managed trade, the state has a major influence in determining the direction and magnitude of the flow of trade. The voluntary export agreement that we have discussed is a typical example of the tools of managed trade. To fulfill a VER, the government of the exporting country must form its exporting firms into a cartel so that they can divide up the portion of the foreign market that they are allowed to serve, as well as collectively ensuring that they do not violate the export ceiling.

Another current example of the influence of managed trade is the judging of trade balances bilaterally rather than multilaterally. Pressure is being exerted to manage trade so as to reduce large bilateral imbalances; some would impose strict bilateral trade balances between pairs of countries. The essence of the multilateral trading system, however, is that one country does not have to buy the same amount from another country as it sells to it. Enforcing bilateral balances would impose this requirement on each pair of trading countries. Such a requirement makes no more economic sense, however, than requiring that the barber only cut the butcher's hair to the value of the meat that he buys from her, and so on for each supplier with whom the barber deals. To achieve bilateral balances, the state must intervene in the market to regulate exports and imports.

Regional Trading Blocks

The current trading world is dominated by the countries of *the triad*. These include the three great trading areas of (1) Japan; (2) the countries of the European Community (EC) and the European Free Trade Area (EFTA); and (3) the countries of North America (the United States, Canada, and Mexico, who are partners in the North American Free-Trade Area).

Some observers are concerned with the possible growth of more and more formally negotiated regional trading blocks. Such agreements need not conflict with the multilateral trading system. The United States–Canada agreement, for example, is consistent with increased trade between the rest of the world *and* these two countries. Such regional trading arrangements can, however, become inward looking, in the sense that they encourage trade between members while discouraging trade with the rest of the world. If the growth of protectionist sentiment in the United States and the EC were to greatly restrict the access of the countries of other areas, such as the Pacific Rim, to the markets of Europe and North America, some of them might form their own trading block, in which they could at least trade freely with each other.

Will the Multilateral Trading System Survive?

The next decade will be critical for the future of the multilateral trading system, which has served the world so well since the end of World War II. The dangers are, first, a growth of regional trading blocks that will trade more with their own member countries and less with others, and second, the growth of state-managed trade. The 1920s and 1930s provide a cautionary tale. Arguments for restricting trade always have a superficial appeal and sometimes have real short-term payoffs. In the long term, however, a major worldwide escalation of tariffs would lower efficiency and incomes and restrict trade worldwide, while doing nothing to raise employment. Both economic theory and the evidence of history support this proposition. This does not imply that pressure should not be put on countries that restrict trade. It does suggest, however, that such measures are best applied using the multilateral institution of the GATT. Unilateral imposition of restrictions in response to the perceived restrictions in other countries can all too easily degenerate into a round of mutually escalating trade barriers.

It is notable that in the United States, one of the staunchest defenders of the free-market system, many voices are being raised to advocate moves that reduce the influence of market forces on international trade and increase the degree of government control over that trade. It is ironic to see enthusiasm for state-managed trade growing just at the time when the former Socialist countries of Eastern Europe have at last agreed that free markets are better regulators of economic activity than is the state. How far this movement will go will become clearer during the 1990s.

SUMMARY

1. The advantage of free trade is that world output of all commodities can be higher under free trade than when protectionism restricts regional specialization.
2. Domestic industries may be protected from foreign competition by tariffs and other policies that affect the prices of imports, or by import quotas and voluntary export agreements, which affect the quantities of imports. Both sets of policies end up increasing prices in the domestic market and lowering the quantities of imports. Both harm domestic consumers and benefit domestic producers of the protected commodity. The major difference is that the extra money paid for imports goes to the domestic government under tariffs and to foreign producers under quantity restrictions.

3. Protection can be urged as a means to ends other than maximizing world living standards. Examples of such ends are to produce a diversified economy, to reduce fluctuations in national income, to retain distinctive national traditions, and to improve national defense.

4. Some fallacious free-trade arguments are that (a) because free trade maximizes world income, it will maximize the income of every individual country, and (b) because infant industries seldom admit to growing up and thus try to retain their protection indefinitely, the whole country necessarily loses by protecting its infant industries.

5. Some fallacious protectionist arguments are that (a) mutually advantageous trade is impossible, because one trader's gain must always be the other's loss; (b) buying abroad sends our money abroad, whereas buying at home keeps our money at home; (c) our high-paid workers must be protected against the competition from low-paid foreign workers; and (d) imports are to be discouraged because they lower national income and cause unemployment.

6. Protection also can be urged on the grounds that it may lead to higher living standards for the protectionist country than would a policy of free trade. Such a result might come about by using a monopoly position to influence the terms of trade or by developing a dynamic comparative advantage by allowing inexperienced or uneconomically small industries to become efficient enough to compete with foreign industries.

7. An important recent argument for tariffs concerns strategic trade policy. This is based on the belief, held by some economists, that protecting the domestic market will allow domestic firms that are producing new products to develop quickly, so that they can then compete strongly in the hope of becoming one of a few world-scale producers of the product.

8. Almost everyone would choose free trade if the only alternative were *no* trade. Cutting existing tariff barriers offers gains, expressed as a percentage of GDP, that may seem small but are large in terms of the total of goods and services involved.

9. Trade is vitally important in the national incomes of many countries. It is relatively less important to the United States. Nonetheless, trade is vital to particular U.S. industries, and few economists doubt that U.S. living standards would be lowered significantly if the United States tried to make itself fully self-sufficient.

10. Although the most industrialized countries now have low tariffs, their recent tendency to institute nontariff barriers, either by negotiation (as in textiles) or by unilateral policies (such as the misuse of antidumping and countervailing duties), causes concern that the 50-year trend to ever-freer trade is being reversed.

11. Multinational and regional trade-liberalizing agreements have succeeded in lowering trade barriers from the high levels of 50 years ago. After World War II, the GATT began a series of multinational rounds of tariff reductions that have greatly lowered tariffs and is now trying to address nontariff barriers as well. The

United States has free-trade agreements with Israel and Canada and has recently negotiated one with Mexico. The European Community is a common market with free trade among its members. Nonetheless, the recent clamor for protection in many trading nations threatens the trade-liberalizing trend that the GATT has fostered.

TOPICS FOR REVIEW

Free trade and protectionism

Tariff and nontariff barriers to trade

Voluntary export agreements

Fallacious arguments for free trade

Fallacious arguments for protectionism

Dumping and antidumping duties

General Agreement on Tariffs and Trade (GATT)

Free-trade areas, customs unions, and common markets

Countervailing duties

DISCUSSION QUESTIONS

1. "Pay $68,000, save a shoemaker," said an editorial in the *New York Times*, pointing out that a quota on shoe imports would save only 33,000 U.S. jobs at a cost in higher shoe prices of $68,000 per job. It has been calculated that the voluntary export agreement to reduce the import of Japanese cars into the U.S. market cost U.S. consumers $150,000 per job saved in U.S. automobile firms. Do consumers pay the cost? Who benefits? What alternatives are there to protecting jobs in the shoe or auto industry?

2. "What unfair trade had done to an American community" was the headline of a recent full-page ad in the *New York Times*. The ad claimed that subsidized and "dumped" steel imports from unstated foreign countries were unfairly driving U.S. steel plants out of business. What foreign practices might justify this claim? What apparent dumping might represent perfectly fair competition? What U.S. legislation or other practices could provide relief, whether justified or not, to the U.S. firms?

3. The policy of "aggressive reciprocity" has recently been urged on the U.S. government. Under it, every time a foreign government introduced a new barrier to trade, the U.S. government would reciprocate aggressively by introducing a new barrier of its own. Discuss the likely outcome of such a policy. What are some alternative policies for enhancing world trade?

4. What are some of the things that would happen if all countries tried to increase their domestic employment by imposing large tariffs on all imports?

5. "U.S. consumer is seen as big loser in new restraints on imported steel," said a recent *Wall Street Journal* headline. The big gainers from the quota limitations on imported steel were predicted to be U.S. producers, who would sell more, and foreign producers, who would sell less but at a higher price; the big losers would be U.S. consumers. Explain carefully why each of these groups might gain or lose.

6. Suppose the United States had imposed prohibitive tariffs on all imported cars over the last three decades. How do you think this would have affected the following?
    a. The U.S. automobile industry
    b. The U.S. public
    c. The kinds of cars produced by U.S. manufacturers

7. Lobbyists for many industries argue that their products are essential to national defense and therefore require protection. Suppose that supplies of a certain commodity are indeed essential in wartime. How does restricting imports solve the problem? Are there alternatives to import restrictions? If so, how might the alternatives be evaluated?

8. Import quotas are often used instead of tariffs. What real difference (if any) is there between quotas and tariffs? Explain why lobbyists for some U.S. industries (cheese, sugar, shoes) support import quotas while lobbyists for others (pizza manufacturers, soft drink manufacturers, retail stores) oppose them. Would you expect labor unions to support or oppose quotas?

9. There is much current concern that the United States is losing international competitiveness. Do countries that fall behind in the competitiveness race cease to reap the gains from trade?

10. The United States has greatly reduced tariffs since Congress passed trade legislation authorizing the president to negotiate tariff concessions with foreign countries. Why might Congress find it desirable to give the president this authority rather than reserve the authority to itself?

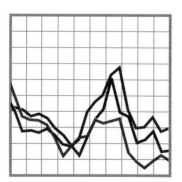

38

Exchange Rates and the Balance of Payments

As we saw in Chapter 23 (see Figure 23-8 on page 477), the value of the dollar in terms of foreign currencies has fluctuated considerably over the past 22 years, and especially in the last decade or so. It rose sharply in the early and mid-1980s, creating a competitive disadvantage for U.S. firms competing with foreign producers in international markets. The fall of the dollar in 1987 and 1988 eased some but not all of the concerns. The dollar fluctuated considerably from 1988 through 1992, and it experienced a sustained decline in 1991 and 1992. Its value remains a topic of concern among policymakers and commentators.

Fluctuations in the value of the dollar are a matter of concern to such varied groups as Japanese firms that want to build factories in the United States, U.S. citizens who want to buy French government bonds, German exporters who send automobiles to the United States, and U.S. citizens who hope to sell computers in Saudi Arabia. They also matter to U.S. tourists who cash their traveler's checks in London, Athens, or Bangkok. Some of the causes of these fluctuations are well understood, and some are still a source of debate and even controversy.

In this chapter we ask what it means to speak of the "external value of the dollar," what causes this value to change, and what implications such changes have for the economy. The discussion will bring together material on three topics studied elsewhere in this book: the theory of supply and demand (Chapter 4), the nature of money (Chapter 29), and international trade (Chapter 36).

The Nature of Foreign Exchange Transactions

We have seen that money is vital in any sophisticated economy that relies on specialization and exchange. Yet money as we know it is a *national* matter, one that is closely controlled by national governments. If you live in Sweden, you earn kronor and spend kronor; if you run a business in Austria, you borrow schillings and meet your payroll with schillings. The currency of a country is acceptable within the bounds of that country, but usually it will not be accepted by households and firms in another country. The Stockholm bus company will accept kronor for a fare but not Austrian schillings. The Austrian worker will not take Swedish kronor for wages but will accept schillings.

U.S. producers require payment in dollars for their products. They need dollars to meet their wage bills, to pay for their raw materials, and to reinvest or to distribute their profits. There is no problem when they sell to U.S. purchasers. However, if they sell their goods to Indian importers, either the Indians must exchange their rupees to acquire dollars to pay for the goods or the U.S. producers must accept rupees. They will accept rupees only if they know that they can exchange the rupees for dollars. The same holds true for producers in all countries; they must eventually receive payment in the currency of their own country.

In general, trade between nations can occur only if it is possible to exchange the currency of one nation for that of another.

The Exchange Rate

International payments involve the exchange of currencies between people who have one currency and require another. Suppose that a U.S. firm wishes to acquire ¥3,000 for some purpose (¥ is the symbol for the Japanese yen). The firm can go to its bank or to some other seller of foreign currency and buy a check that will be accepted in Japan as ¥3,000. How many *dollars* the firm must pay to purchase this check will depend on the value of the dollar in terms of yen.

The exchange of one currency for another is called a *foreign exchange transaction*. The term *foreign exchange* refers to the actual foreign currency or various claims on it, such as bank deposits or promises to pay, that are traded for each other. The *exchange rate* is the value of the dollar in terms of foreign currency; it is the amount of foreign currency that can be obtained with one unit of the domestic currency. For example, if one can obtain ¥125 for $1, the exchange rate is 125.[1]

A rise in the external value of the dollar (that is, a rise in the exchange rate) is an **appreciation** of the dollar; for example, if one can now obtain ¥150 for $1, the dollar has *appreciated*. A fall in the external value of the dollar (that is, a fall in the exchange rate) is a **depreciation** of the dollar; for example, if one can now obtain only ¥100 for $1, the dollar has *depreciated*.[2]

Because the exchange rate expresses the value of one currency in terms of another, when one currency appreciates, the other must depreciate.

When the dollar appreciates from ¥125 to ¥150, the yen depreciates in terms of the dollar, because ¥1 has fallen from being worth eight-tenths of one cent to being worth only two-thirds of a cent. Similarly, when the dollar depreciates from ¥125 to ¥100, the yen *appreciates* in terms of the dollar; ¥1, which was worth eight-tenths of a cent, is now worth one cent.

The Balance of Payments

Later in this chapter we discuss the determination of the exchange rate by analyzing the demand and supply that arise in the foreign exchange market as a result of international transactions. It is useful to start by reviewing the major categories of international transactions that occur; in so doing we encounter the balance of payments accounts.

Balance-of-Payments Accounts

In order to know what is happening to the course of international trade, governments keep track of the transactions among countries. The record of such transactions is made in the *balance-of-payments accounts*. Each transaction, such as a shipment of exports or the arrival of imported goods, is classified according to the payments or receipts that would typically arise from it. Table 38-1 shows the major items in the U.S. balance-of-payments accounts for 1991.

Transactions that lead to a receipt of foreign exchange, such as a commodity export or a sale of an asset abroad, are recorded in the balance-of-payments accounts as a credit item. In terms of our later objective of analyzing the market for foreign exchange, these transactions represent the supply of foreign exchange and the demand for dollars on the foreign exchange market. Transactions that lead to a payment of foreign exchange, such as a commodity import or the purchase of a foreign asset, are recorded as a debit item. These transactions represent the demand for foreign exchange and the supply of dollars on the foreign exchange market.

Current Account

The **current account** records transactions arising from trade in goods and services and from income accruing to capital owned in one country and in-

---

[1] Alternatively, one could express the relative values of the two currencies in terms of the dollar price of one yen, which in this example is $0.008; that is, one yen is worth eight-tenths of one cent.

[2] When the external value of the currency changes as a result of explicit policy of the central bank, it is often said to have been *devalued* when it falls and *revalued* when it rises.

TABLE 38-1 U.S. Balance of Payments, 1991
(billions of dollars)

Current account		
Merchandise exports	+416	
Merchandise imports	−489	
Trade balance		−73
Services exports	+164	
Services imports	−118	
Services balance		+46
Net investment income		+16
Unilateral transfers		+8
Balance on current account		−4
Capital account		
Net change in U.S. investments abroad [increase/capital outflow (−)]	−68	
Net change in foreign investments in U.S. [increase/capital inflow (+)]	+49	
Balance on capital account		−19
Balance on current plus capital accounts		+23
Official financing		
Change in liabilities to official foreign agencies [increase (+)]	+18	
Use of official reserves [increase (−)]	+6	
Statistical discrepancy[a]	−1	
Overall balance of payments[b]		0

Source: Survey of Current Business, June 1992.

[a]In balance-of-payments accounts there is a "statistical discrepency" item that results from the inability to measure some items accurately.

[b]Always zero. (Details may not add up because of rounding.)

The overall balance of payments always balances, but the individual components do not have to. In this example the United States shows a negative (deficit) trade balance (merchandise imports exceed merchandise exports) and a smaller negative (deficit) balance on current account. There is also a negative (deficit) balance on capital account because capital exports exceeded capital imports. The capital *plus* current account surplus is what is commonly referred to as the *balance of payments*, and in 1991 there was a negative (deficit) overall balance of $23 billion. This is exactly matched by the balance in the official accounts.

vested in another. The current account is divided into two main sections.

The first of these, variously called the **visible account**, the **trade account**, and the **merchan-dise account**, records payments and receipts arising from the import and export of tangible goods, such as computers, cars, wheat, and shoes. U.S. imports require the use of foreign exchange and hence are entered as debit items on the visible account; U.S. exports earn foreign exchange and hence are recorded as credit items.

The second section, called the **invisible account** or the **service account**, records payments arising out of trade in services and payments for the use of capital. Trade in such services as insurance, shipping, and tourism is entered in the invisible account, as are payments of interest, dividends, and profits that are made for capital used in one country but owned by residents of another country.[3]

As shown in Table 38-1, U.S. merchandise exports were $416 billion in 1991, and U.S. merchandise imports were $489 billion; thus the trade account balance had a deficit of $73 billion. As can also be seen in the table, the service account had a net surplus of $46 billion. The current account balance, the sum of the two plus net investment income and transfers, had a deficit of $4 billion. This current account deficit represented a net demand for foreign exchange of $4 billion; the way in which such funds are obtained is often referred to as *financing* the current account deficit.

Capital Account

The second main division in the balance of payments is the **capital account**, which records transactions related to international movements of financial capital. U.S. investment in foreign assets, called a *capital outflow* or a *capital export*, uses foreign exchange and so is entered as a debit item in the U.S. payments accounts.[4] Foreign investment in U.S. assets, called a

---

[3] The symbols *X* and *IM* as used in this book refer to exports and imports of both tangible goods and services but do not include payments of interest, dividends, and profits.

[4] It may seem odd that, whereas a merchandise export is a credit item on current account, a capital export is a debit item on capital account. To understand this terminology, consider the export of U.S. funds for investment in a German bond. The capital transaction involves the purchase, and hence the *import*, of a German bond, and this has the same effect on the balance of payments as the purchase, and hence the import, of a German good. Both items involve payments to foreigners, and both use foreign exchange. Both are thus debit items in U.S. balance-of-payments accounts.

capital inflow or a *capital import*, earns foreign exchange and so is entered as a credit item.

As shown in Table 38-1, in 1991 U.S. citizens increased their investments abroad by $68 billion, resulting in a capital outflow of that amount, while foreigners increased their investments in the United States by $49 billion, resulting in a capital inflow of that amount. The net capital inflow resulted in a deficit in the capital account of $19 billion.

Short-term and long-term capital flows. The capital account is often divided into two categories that distinguish between movements of short-term and long-term capital. Short-term capital is money that is held in the form of highly liquid assets, such as bank accounts and short-term treasury bills. If a nonresident merchant buys dollars and places them in a deposit account in New York, this represents an inflow of short-term capital into the United States, and it will be recorded as a credit item on short-term capital account. Long-term capital represents funds coming into the United States (a credit item) or leaving the United States (a debit item), to be invested in less liquid assets, such as long-term bonds, or in physical capital, such as a new automobile assembly plant.

Portfolio investment and direct investment. The two major subdivisions of the long-term part of the capital accounts are *direct investment* and *portfolio investment*. **Direct investment** relates to changes in nonresident ownership of domestic firms and resident ownership of foreign firms. Thus, one form of direct investment in the United States is capital investment in a branch plant or a subsidiary corporation in the United States in which the investor has voting control. Another form is a takeover, in which a controlling interest in a firm, previously controlled by residents, is acquired by foreigners. **Portfolio investment,** on the other hand, is investment in bonds or a minority holding of shares that does not involve legal control.

Official Financing Account

The final section in the balance-of-payments account represents transactions in the *official reserves* that are held by a country's central bank, and is called the *official financing account* or the *official settlements account*. These transactions reflect the financing of the balance on the remainder of the accounts. The central banks of most countries hold financial reserves that they use in the foreign exchange market. Some of these reserves are held in gold, some in foreign currencies or claims on them, and some in an international currency, called *special drawing rights* or *SDRs* (which are discussed further in the appendix to this chapter).

The Federal Reserve Board, operating on behalf of the government, can intervene in the market for foreign exchange to influence the dollar's exchange rate. For example, to prevent the value of the dollar from falling, the Fed must buy dollars and sell gold or foreign exchange. It can do so only if it holds reserves of gold or foreign exchange. When the Fed wishes to stop the value of the dollar from rising, it enters the market and sells dollars. In this case, the Fed buys foreign exchange, which it then adds to its reserves.

The Meaning of Payments Balances and Imbalances

We have seen that the payments accounts show the total of receipts of foreign exchange (credit items) and payments of foreign exchange (debit items) on account of each category of payment. It is also common to calculate the *balance* on separate items or groups of items. The concept of the balance of payments is used in a number of different ways, so we must approach this issue in a series of steps.

The Balance of Payments Must Balance Overall

Notice that the payments accounts record *actual* payments, not *desired* payments. For example, it is quite possible that, at the existing exchange rate between dollars and yen, holders of yen would want to purchase more dollars than holders of dollars would want to sell in exchange for yen. In this situation, the quantity of dollars demanded exceeds the quantity supplied. However, holders of yen cannot actually buy more dollars than holders of dollars actually sell; every yen that is bought must have been sold by someone, and every dollar that is sold must have been bought by someone.

It follows that, if we add up all the receipts arising from (1) payments received by U.S. residents on account of U.S. exports of goods and services, (2) capital imports, and (3) purchase of foreign exchange or gold by the Fed, these must be exactly equal to all payments made by holders of dollars arising from

Box 38-1

An Illustration of How the Balance of Payments Always Balances

Trade Between Two Countries

Suppose that the sole international transaction made this year by a small country called Myopia was an export to the United States of Myopian coconuts worth $1,000. Further suppose that the Myopian central bank issues a local currency, the stigma, but does not operate in the foreign exchange market, so there is no official financing. Finally, suppose that Myopia's self-sufficient inhabitants want no imports. Surely, then, you might think that Myopia has an overall favorable balance of $1,000, which is a current account receipt (C_R) with no balancing item on the payments side.

To see why such a conclusion is wrong, we must ask what the exporter of coconuts did with the dollars that he received for his coconuts. Let us suppose that he deposited them in a New York bank. This transaction represents a capital export from Myopia. Myopians have accumulated claims on foreign exchange, which they hold in the form of a deposit with a foreign bank. Thus, there are two entries in the Myopian accounts: One is a credit item for the export of coconuts ($C_R = \$1,000$),

and the other is a debit item for the export of capital ($K_P = \$1,000$). The fact that the same firm made both transactions is irrelevant. Although the current account shows a credit balance, the capital account exactly balances this with a debit item. Hence, looking at the *balance of payments as a whole*, the two sides of the account are equal. The balance of payments has balanced—as it must always do.

Consider now a slightly more realistic case. If the coconut exporter wants to turn his $1,000 into Myopian stigmas so that he can pay his coconut pickers in local currency, he must find someone who wishes to buy his dollars in return for Myopian currency. However, we have assumed that no one in Myopia wants to import, so no one wants to sell Myopian currency for current account reasons. Now suppose that a wealthy Myopian landowner would like to invest $1,000 in New York by buying shares in a U.S. firm. To do so, she needs $1,000. The coconut exporter can sell his $1,000 to the landowner in return for stigmas. Now he can pay his local bills. The landowner sells her stigmas to the exporter in return for dollars. Now she can buy the U.S. shares.

(1) U.S. imports of goods and services, (2) exports of capital, and (3) sale of foreign exchange or gold by the Fed.[5]

This relationship is so important that it is worthwhile to write it out in symbols. We let C, K, and F stand for current account, capital account,

and official financing account, respectively, and use R for receipts (credit items) and P for payments (debit items). Now we can use these symbols to write an expression showing that the sum of all receipts in the foreign exchange market must equal the sum of all payments:

$$C_R + K_R + F_R = C_P + K_P + F_P \qquad [1]$$

The three terms on the left of the equal sign represent all receipts of foreign exchange, and the three terms on the right represent all payments. Because any receipt by one person or firm is a payment by some other, the two must be equal.

---

[5] The services exported and imported in item (1) of each list include payments for capital services. As with the National Income Accounts presented in Chapter 24, measurement errors mean that measured payments do not exactly equal measured receipts, so the accounts include a balancing item, called a statistical discrepancy.

Once again, the Myopian balance of payments will show two entries, equal in size, but one is a credit and the other is a debit. There is a credit item for the export of coconuts (the sale of coconuts earned foreign exchange) and a debit item for the export of capital (the purchase of the U.S. shares used foreign exchange).

Trade Involving Many Countries

In the preceding example, Myopia had a balance in what is called its *bilateral payments account* with the United States. The *bilateral balance of payments* between any two countries is the balance between the payments and the receipts flowing between them. If there were only two countries in the world, their overall payments would have to be in bilateral balance; that is, one country's payments to the other would be equal to its receipts from the other. However, this is not true when there are more than two countries involved.

Suppose that in the year following the one just discussed, Myopia again sells $1,000 worth of coconuts to the United States, that the landowner does not wish to invest further in the United States, but that the Myopian people wish to buy 200,000 yen worth of parasols from Japan. (Assume also that in the foreign exchange market $1 trades for 200 yen.) Finally, assume that a Japanese importer wishes to buy $1,000 worth of skateboards from a U.S. company.

Now what happens, in effect, is that the Myopian coconut exporter sells his $1,000 to the Japanese skateboard importer for 200,000 yen, which the coconut exporter then sells to the Myopian parasol importer in return for Myopian stigmas. (In the real world the exchanges are all done through banks, but this is what happens, in effect.) Now the Myopian payments statistics will show a $1,000 bilateral payments surplus with the United States—receipts of $1,000 from the United States on account of coconut exports, and no payments to the United States—and a bilateral deficit with Japan of 200,000 yen (equal to $1,000)—$1,000 of payments to Japan on account of parasol imports and no receipts from Japan. However, when both countries are considered, Myopia's multilateral payments are in balance.

We can convert this into an expression relating the various balance of payments account simply by rearranging terms. Subtracting the three payments items (C_P, K_P, and F_P) from both sides of Equation 1 yields

$$(C_R - C_P) + (K_R - K_P) + (F_R - F_P) = 0 \qquad [2]$$

The three terms in parentheses are the current account surplus, the capital account surplus, and the balance on official financing; Equation 2 shows that the three balances must sum to zero. Box 38-1 illustrates this with an example.

Payments on Specific Parts of the Accounts Do Not Need to Balance

Although the overall total of payments must equal the overall total of receipts, the same zero balance does not have to hold on subsections of the overall accounts. We now look at the balances on *parts* of the accounts—balances that may be positive or negative. We do this first in relation to particular countries and then in relation to particular subsectors of the account.

Country balances.   When all foreign countries are taken together, a country's balance of payments must balance, but a country can have bilateral surpluses or deficits with individual foreign countries or with groups of countries. In general, the **multilateral balance of payments** refers to the balance between one country's payments to and receipts from the rest of the world. When all items are considered, every country must have a zero multilateral payments balance with the rest of the world, although it can have bilateral surpluses or deficits with individual countries.

Subsection balances. The *balance of payments on current account* is the sum of the balances on the visible and invisible accounts. As a carryover from a long-discredited eighteenth century economic doctrine called *mercantilism*, a credit balance on current account (where receipts exceed payments) is called a **favorable balance,** and a debit balance (where payments exceed receipts) is called an **unfavorable balance.** Mercantilists, both ancient and modern, hold that the gains from trade arise only from having a favorable balance of trade. This misses the point of the doctrine of comparative advantage, which states that countries can gain from a balanced increase in trade because it allows each country to specialize according to its comparative advantage. The modern resurgence of mercantilism is discussed in Box 38-2.

The balance on capital account gives the difference between receipts of foreign exchange and payments of foreign exchange arising out of capital movements. A surplus, or "favorable" balance, on capital account means that a country is a *net* importer of capital, whereas a deficit, or "unfavorable" balance, means that a country is a *net* exporter of capital. Notice that a deficit on capital account, which is referred to as an unfavorable balance, merely indicates that a country is investing abroad. For a rich country to invest abroad and accumulate assets that will earn income in the future may be a desirable situation. So once again we observe that there is nothing necessarily unfavorable about having an "unfavorable" balance on any of the payments accounts.

A credit balance on official financing account means the Fed has bought more gold and foreign exchange than it has sold. This adds to its reserves of foreign exchange. A deficit balance means the Fed has sold more gold and foreign exchange than it has bought. This reduces its foreign exchange reserves.

The Relationship Between Various Balances

Two important implications follow directly from our observation that the overall payments must balance:

1. The terms "a balance-of-payments *deficit*" and "a balance-of-payments *surplus*" must refer to the balance on some part of the payments accounts.
2. A deficit on any one part of the accounts implies an offsetting surplus on the rest of the accounts.

We now consider two important applications of these statements. The first application concerns the balances on official financing account and the combined balance on the capital plus current accounts; the second concerns the balances on current and capital accounts.

Official financing and the rest of the accounts. When people speak of a country as having a balance-of-payments deficit or surplus, they are usually referring to the balance of all accounts *excluding* official financing, that is, to the combined balance on current and capital accounts.

We can express the relationship between the balance of payments and balance on official financing by subtracting the official financing balance $(F_R - F_P)$ from both sides of Equation 2. This yields

$$(C_R - C_P) + (K_R - K_P) = (F_P - F_R) \qquad [3]$$

The two terms on the left-hand side are the current account balance and the capital account balance; their sum is what we have called the balance of payments. When the left-hand side is positive, the balance of payments is in surplus, which means that transactions on the current and capital accounts generate net receipts of foreign exchange. Equation 3 shows that in this case the Fed must be buying more foreign exchange than it sells.

A balance-of-payments surplus means that the central bank is adding to its holdings of foreign exchange reserves; a balance-of-payments deficit means that the central bank is reducing its reserves.

Only if the central bank intervenes in the foreign exchange market can the balance of payments be in deficit or surplus. If the central bank does not intervene in the foreign exchange market so that the official financing balance is zero, then there can be no deficit or surplus on the balance of payments; as we shall see in the next section, this imposes a strict relationship between the capital and current accounts.

Box 38-2

The Volume of Trade, the Balance of Trade, and the New Mercantilism

Media commentators, political figures, and much of the general public often judge the national balance of payments as they would the accounts of a single firm. Just as a firm is supposed to show a profit, the nation is supposed to secure a balance-of-payments surplus, with the benefits derived from international trade measured by the size of that surplus.

This view is related to the exploitation doctrine of international trade: One country's surplus is another country's deficit. Thus one country's gain, judged by its surplus, must be another country's loss, judged by its deficit.

People who hold such views today are echoing an ancient economic doctrine called *mercantilism*. The mercantilists were a group of economists who preceded Adam Smith. They judged the success of trade by the size of the trade balance. In many cases this doctrine made sense in terms of their objective, which was to use international trade as a means of building up the political and military power of the state, rather than as a means of raising the living standards of its citizens. A balance-of-payments surplus allowed the nation (then and now) to acquire foreign exchange reserves. (In those days the reserves took the form of gold. Today they are a mixture of gold and claims on the currencies of other countries.) These reserves could then be used to pay armies to purchase weapons from abroad, and generally to finance colonial expansions.

People who advocate this view in modern times are called *neomercantilists*. Insofar as their object is to increase the power of the state, they are choosing means that could achieve their ends. Insofar as they

are drawing an analogy between what is a sensible objective for a business, interested in its own material welfare, and what is a sensible objective for a society, interested in the material welfare of its citizens, their views are erroneous, because their analogy is false.

If the object of economic activity is to promote the welfare and living standards of ordinary citizens, rather than the power of governments, then the mercantilist focus on the balance of trade makes no sense. The law of comparative advantage shows that average living standards are maximized by having individuals, regions, and countries specialize in the things that they can produce comparatively best and then trading to obtain the things that they can produce comparatively worst. The more specialization there is, the more trade occurs.

On this view the gains from trade are to be judged by the volume of trade. A situation in which there is a *large volume* of trade but in which each country has a *zero balance* of trade can thus be regarded as quite satisfactory. Furthermore, a change in commercial policy that results in a balanced increase in trade between two countries will bring gain, because it allows for specialization according to comparative advantage, even though it causes no change in either country's trade balance.

To the business interested in private profit and to the government interested in the power of the state, it is the balance of trade that matters. To the person interested in the welfare of ordinary citizens, it is the volume of trade that matters.

The current and capital account balances. Suppose that the Fed does not engage in any foreign exchange transactions. This means that the official financing account is zero, because both F_R and F_P in Equation 3 are zero.

Now any deficit or surplus on current account must be matched by an equal and opposite surplus or deficit on capital account. For example, if a country has a current account surplus, the net foreign exchange receipts from that account must be matched by net foreign exchange payments in the capital account. The foreign exchange may be used to buy foreign assets or merely stashed away in foreign bank accounts. In either case there is an outflow of capital from the United States (which, as we saw earlier, is recorded as a debit item because it uses foreign exchange).

We can see this clearly if we return to Equation 3 and set F_R and F_P equal to zero to indicate no transactions by the Fed. This gives us

$$(C_R - C_P) + (K_R - K_P) = 0 \qquad [4]$$

Now subtract the capital account surplus $(K_R - K_P)$ from both sides of Equation 4 to get

$$(C_R - C_P) = (K_P - K_R) \qquad [5]$$

This expresses in equation form what we have just stated in words: A surplus on current account must be balanced by a deficit on capital account (an outflow of capital). The equation also shows that if a deficit on current account occurs (that is, the left-hand side is negative), it would have to be matched by a surplus on capital account (an inflow of capital).[6]

One important implication relates to situations where there are capital transfers into or out of a country. For example, since the early 1980s the United States has been importing capital and hence experiencing a surplus on capital account. Equation 5 tells us that it must therefore have had a deficit on current account. Because of the borrowing requirements of a massive government budget deficit, and because the boom made the United States an attractive place for private sector investment, there was a massive capital inflow into the United States, making a current account deficit inevitable. This issue is considered in more detail in Chapter 39.

National asset formation.   In Chapter 26 we defined national asset formation to include net exports. Equation 5 allows us to restate the logic of this definition quite directly. According to Equation 5, a current account surplus implies a capital account deficit

of the same magnitude. This capital account deficit arises because U.S. residents are acquiring assets abroad, and these assets are part of U.S. national asset formation. The current account balance itself consists of both net exports and payments for capital services, such as interest, dividends, and profits on investment abroad.[7] Generally, any change in the current account, whether due to a change in net exports or to a change in net payments for capital services, will cause a one-for-one change in the capital account and in national asset formation.

Actual and desired transactions.   The discussion in this section has focused on *actual* transactions as measured in the balance of payments accounts. How do these relate to *desired* transactions in international markets? As we shall see, the exchange rate plays a key role in reconciling actual and desired transactions. As a first step in understanding this, we now turn to a discussion of how the exchange rate is determined.

The Market for Foreign Exchange

For the sake of simplicity, we continue using an example involving trade between the United States and Japan and the determination of the exchange rate between their two currencies, dollars and yen. The two-country example simplifies things, but the principles apply to all foreign transactions. *Thus, yen stands for foreign exchange in general, and the value of the dollar in terms of yen stands for the foreign exchange rate in general.*

When   ¥125 = $1, a Japanese importer who offers to buy $4.00 with yen must be offering to sell ¥500. Similarly, a U.S. importer who offers to sell $4.00 for yen must be offering to buy ¥500.

Because one currency is traded for another in the foreign exchange market, it follows that a demand for foreign exchange implies a supply of dollars, while a supply of foreign exchange implies a demand for dollars.

---

[6] If the Fed engages in foreign exchange transactions, the relationship that is given in Equation 4 does not need to hold exactly. The sum of the current and capital account balances can diverge from zero by the balance on official financing account, as can be shown using Equation 2. In this case, a current account deficit must be matched by a combination of capital inflows and official financing.

---

[7] These payments for capital services are exactly the difference between GDP and GNP. GNP includes payments for capital services that accrue to, or are incurred by, domestic residents, whereas GDP does not.   .

For this reason a theory of the exchange rate between dollars and yen can deal either with the demand for and the supply of dollars or with the demand for and the supply of yen; both need not be considered. We will concentrate on the demand, supply, and price of dollars (quoted in yen).

We develop our example in terms of the demand-and-supply analysis first encountered in Chapter 4. To do so, we need only to recall that *in the market for foreign exchange*, transactions that generate a receipt of foreign exchange represent a demand for dollars, and transactions that require a payment of foreign exchange represent a supply of dollars. We focus only on the demand and supply of dollars arising from the current and capital accounts. Later we turn to the important role of official financing.

The Demand for Dollars

The demand for dollars arises from all international transactions that generate a receipt of foreign exchange.

U.S. exports. One important source of demand for dollars in foreign exchange markets includes foreigners who do not currently hold dollars but who wish to buy U.S.-made goods and services. A Japanese importer of lumber is such a purchaser; an Austrian couple planning to vacation in the United States is another; the Russian government seeking to buy U.S. steel is a third. All are sources of demand for dollars, arising out of international trade. Each potential buyer wants to sell its own currency and buy dollars for the purpose of purchasing U.S. exports.

Capital inflows. A second source of a demand for dollars comes from foreigners who wish to purchase U.S. assets. In order to buy U.S. assets, holders of foreign currencies must first buy dollars in foreign exchange markets.[8]

In recent years foreign households and firms have invested billions of dollars in U.S. securities and real estate. This has required the conversion of foreign currencies into U.S. dollars. The resulting transactions are called *long-term capital flows.*

When interest rates in the United States soared in the early 1980s, floods of "foreign money" came into the United States to buy short-term treasury bills and notes, certificates of deposit, and so on. The buyers of these securities were seeking a high return on their liquid assets, but first these buyers had to convert their lire, guilder, marks, and francs into dollars in the foreign exchange market. When people sell financial assets in one country for foreign exchange that they then use to buy short-term financial assets in another country, the transactions are called *short-term capital flows.*

A medium of exchange. Certain currencies, the most important of which is the U.S. dollar, have come to be accepted by nations, banks, and ordinary people as an international medium of exchange. These currencies are readily acceptable among buyers and sellers who might be less willing to trade with each other if they were using less well known kinds of currency. For example, a Norwegian exporter of smoked fish, selling to a Turkish wholesaler, may quote prices in dollars and expect payment in dollars. There is therefore a demand for currencies that can act as an international medium of exchange. Some of the trading in the U.S. dollar exists to provide a medium of exchange that is quite independent of the flow of U.S. imports or exports.

Reserve currency. Firms, banks, and governments often accumulate and hold foreign exchange reserves, just as individuals maintain savings accounts. The government of Nigeria, for example, may decide to increase its reserve holdings of dollars and reduce its reserve holdings of yen; if it does so, it will be a demander of dollars (and a supplier of yen) in foreign exchange markets.

The Total Demand for Dollars

The demand for dollars by holders of foreign currencies is the sum of the demands for all of the purposes just discussed—for purchases of U.S. exports, for long- or short-term capital movements, for purchases of the dollar to use in other transactions, or for adding to currency reserves.

Furthermore, because people, firms, and governments in all countries purchase goods from, and invest in, many other countries, the demand for any one currency will be the aggregate demand of individuals, firms, and governments in a number of different countries. Thus, the total demand for dollars, for

---

[8] Capital inflows also arise when U.S. citizens sell foreign assets, because they enter the foreign exchange market and sell the foreign currency received for the assets and buy dollars.

example, may include Germans who are offering marks, Japanese who are offering yen, Greeks who are offering drachmas, and so on. For simplicity, however, we continue with our two-country example and use only Japan and the United States.

The Shape of the Demand Curve for Dollars

The demand for dollars in terms of yen is represented by a negatively sloped curve, such as the one shown in Figure 38-1. This figure plots the value of the dollar (measured in yen) on the vertical axis and the quantity of dollars on the horizontal axis. Moving down the vertical scale, the dollar is worth fewer yen and hence is depreciating in the foreign exchange market. Moving up the scale, the dollar is appreciating.

Why is the demand curve for dollars negatively sloped? Consider the demand for dollars that is derived from foreign purchases of U.S. exports. If the dollar depreciates, the yen price of U.S. exports will fall. The Japanese will buy more of the cheaper U.S. goods and will require more dollars for this purpose. The quantity of dollars demanded will rise. In the opposite case, when the dollar appreciates, the price of U.S. exports rises in terms of yen. The Japanese will buy fewer U.S. goods and thus demand fewer U.S. dollars.

Similar considerations affect other sources of demand for dollars. When the dollar is cheaper, U.S. assets and securities become attractive purchases, and the quantity purchased will rise. As it does, the quantity of dollars demanded to pay for the purchases will increase.

The demand curve for dollars in the foreign exchange market is negatively sloped when it is plotted against the yen price of dollars.

The Supply of Dollars

The sources of supply of dollars in the foreign exchange market are merely the opposite side of the demand for yen. (Recall that the *supply* of dollars by people who are seeking yen is the same as the *demand* for yen by holders of dollars.)

Who wants to sell dollars? U.S. citizens, seeking to purchase foreign goods and services or assets, will be supplying dollars and purchasing foreign exchange for this purpose. Holders of U.S. securities may decide to sell their U.S. holdings and shift them into

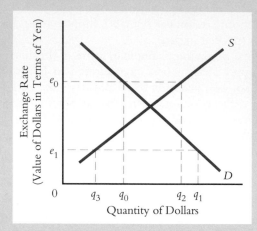

FIGURE 38-1
The Market for Foreign Exchange

The demand for dollars is negatively sloped, and the supply of dollars is positively sloped, when drawn against the exchange rate, measured as the value of the dollar in terms of foreign exchange. The demand for dollars in the market for foreign exchange is given by the negatively sloped blue line, D. It represents the sum of transactions giving rise to receipts of foreign exchange, C_R and K_R. When the exchange rate is e_0, the quantity of dollars demanded is q_0. A depreciation of the dollar is indicated by a fall in the exchange rate to e_1; foreign demand for U.S. goods and assets rises, and hence the quantity of dollars demanded also rises, from q_0 to q_1. An appreciation has the opposite effect; a rise in the exchange rate from e_1 to e_0 causes the quantity of dollars demanded to fall from q_1 to q_0.

The supply of dollars in the market for foreign exchange is given by the positively sloped red line, S. It represents the sum of transactions that require payments of foreign exchange, C_P and K_P. When the exchange rate is e_0, the quantity of dollars supplied is q_2. A depreciation of the dollar causes the exchange rate to fall to e_1; U.S. demand for foreign goods and assets falls, and hence the quantity of dollars that they supply to the foreign exchange market also falls, from q_2 to q_3. An appreciation has the opposite effect; a rise in the exchange rate from e_1 to e_0 causes the quantity of dollars supplied to rise from q_3 to q_2. (As discussed in footnote 9, we are assuming that the response of demand to the change in the exchange rate is *elastic*.)

foreign assets. If they do, they will sell dollars; that is, they will be supplying dollars to the foreign exchange market. Similarly, a country with dollar reserves of foreign exchange may decide that the dollar is "weak" and sell dollars in order to buy another currency.

The Shape of the Supply Curve of Dollars

When the dollar depreciates, the dollar price of Japanese exports to the United States rises. It takes more dollars to buy the same Japanese good, so U.S. citizens will buy fewer of the now more expensive Japanese goods. The amount of dollars being offered in exchange for yen in order to pay for Japanese exports (U.S. imports) will fall.[9]

In the opposite case, when the dollar appreciates, Japanese exports to the United States become cheaper, more are sold, and more dollars are spent on them. Thus more dollars will be offered in exchange for yen to obtain the foreign exchange needed to pay for the extra imports. The argument also applies to purchases and sales of assets.

The supply curve of dollars in the foreign exchange market is positively sloped when it is plotted against the yen price of dollars.

This is also illustrated in Figure 38-1.

The Determination of Exchange Rates

Recall that the demand and supply curves in Figure 38-1 do not include official financing transactions. The demand curve represents the transactions in the current and capital accounts generating receipts of foreign exchange (C_R and K_R); the supply curve represents the transactions in the current and capital accounts requiring payments of foreign exchange (C_P and K_P).

---

[9] As long as the price elasticity of demand for imports is greater than 1, the fall in the volume of imports will swamp the rise in price and hence fewer dollars will be spent on them. This condition is related to a famous, long-standing issue in international economics. In what follows, we adopt the standard case of the condition's being met. In a more general form, it is called the *Marshall-Lerner condition,* after two famous British economists who first studied the problem.

In order to complete our analysis, we need to incorporate the role of official financing transactions. Three important cases need to be considered:

1. When there are no official financing transactions by the central bank, the exchange rate is determined by the equality between the supply and demand for dollars arising from the capital and current accounts. This is called a *flexible exchange rate*.
2. When official financing transactions are used to maintain the exchange rate at a particular value, there is said to be a *fixed exchange rate*.
3. Between these two "pure" systems are a variety of possible intermediate cases, including the *adjustable peg* and the *managed float*. In the adjustable peg system, governments set and attempt to maintain par values for their exchange rates, but they explicitly recognize that circumstances may arise in which they will change the par value. In a managed float, the central bank seeks to have some stabilizing influence on the exchange rate but does not try to fix it at some publicly announced par value. (These are discussed further in the appendix to this chapter.)

Flexible Exchange Rates

Consider an exchange rate that is set in a freely competitive market, with no intervention by the central bank. Like any competitive price, this rate fluctuates according to the conditions of demand and supply.

Suppose that the current price of dollars is so low (say, e_1 in Figure 38-2) that the quantity of dollars demanded exceeds the quantity supplied. Dollars will be in scarce supply; some people who require dollars to make payments to the United States will be unable to obtain them; and the price of dollars will be bid up. The value of the dollar vis-à-vis the yen will appreciate. As the price of the dollar rises, the yen price of U.S. exports to Japan rises and the quantity of U.S. dollars demanded to buy Japanese goods decreases. However, as the dollar price of imports from Japan falls, a larger quantity will be purchased and the quantity of U.S. dollars supplied will rise. Thus a rise in the price of the dollar reduces the quantity demanded and increases the quantity supplied. Where the two curves intersect, quantity demanded equals quantity supplied, and the exchange rate is in equilibrium.

FIGURE 38-2
Fixed and Flexible Exchange Rates

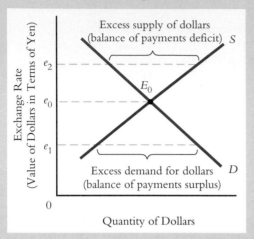

The exchange rate adjusts so that the balance of payments is equal to the level of official financing; in the absence of any official financing there is a flexible exchange rate and the balance of payments is zero. The demand for and supply of dollars reproduce those in Figure 38-1. If official financing is zero, there is a flexible exchange rate. The exchange rate will adjust to equate the demand and supply of dollars; this occurs at E_0 with an exchange rate of e_0. If the exchange rate is lower than that, say e_1, then the demand for dollars will exceed the supply. (This means that desired receipts of foreign exchange exceed desired payments.) The exchange rate will rise (the dollar will appreciate) until it reaches e_0, where balance is achieved at E_0.

If the exchange rate is above e_0, say at e_2, the demand for dollars will be less than supply. (This means that desired receipts of foreign exchange will be less than desired payments.) The exchange rate will fall (the dollar will depreciate) until it reaches e_0, where balance is achieved at E_0.

The government can fix the exchange rate by using its official financing transactions to meet the excess demands or supplies that arise at the fixed value of the exchange rate. For example, if it chooses to fix the exchange rate at e_1, there will be a balance of payments surplus because receipts of foreign exchange will exceed payments. The central bank will thus accumulate foreign exchange and supply dollars to meet the excess demand. Alternatively, if the central bank chooses to fix the exchange rate at e_2, there will be a balance of payments deficit, because receipts of foreign exchange will be less than payments. The central bank will thus pay out foreign exchange and absorb the excess supply of dollars.

What happens when the price of dollars is above its equilibrium value? The quantity of dollars demanded will be less than the quantity supplied. With the dollar in excess supply, some people who wish to convert dollars into yen will be unable to do so.[10] The price of dollars will fall, fewer dollars will be supplied, more will be demanded, and an equilibrium will be reestablished.

A foreign exchange market is like other competitive markets in that the forces of demand and supply lead to an equilibrium price in which quantity demanded equals quantity supplied.

Note that when official financing transactions are zero, the statement that the market for foreign exchange is in equilibrium is identical to the statement that the balance of payments accounts add up to zero; this follows directly from the equivalence between Equation 1 and Equation 4 (recalling that both F_R and F_P are zero). Equation 1 thus sets the demand for dollars equal to the supply, and Equation 4 thus states that the current and capital accounts add up to zero.

Fixed Exchange Rates

When official financing transactions are used to fix the exchange rate at a particular value, the balance of payments is generally not zero. Rather, it is just equal to the sum of the current and capital account balances that arise at the fixed value of the exchange rate. The balance on official financing has to be whatever is necessary to offset the balance of payments deficit or surplus that arises.[11] This is also shown in Figure 38-2.

The gold standard that operated for much of the last century and the early part of this one was a fixed exchange rate system. The Bretton Woods system, established by international agreement in 1944 and operated until the mid-1970s, was a fixed exchange

---

[10] Equivalently, we could say that there is an excess demand for foreign exchange.

[11] This can be seen directly from Equation 3. Note that the central bank is often said to give up control of its foreign exchange reserves when it chooses to fix the exchange rate.

rate system that provided for circumstances under which the par value of the currency had to be lowered (a devaluation) or raised (a revaluation). It was thus an adjustable peg system; the International Monetary Fund (IMF) has its origins in the Bretton Woods system, and one of its principal tasks was approving and monitoring exchange rate changes. (The operation and decline of both systems are discussed in the appendix to this chapter.) The European Exchange Rate Mechanism (ERM) is also a fixed exchange rate system between countries in the European Community; their exchange rates are fixed to each other but float as a block against the U.S. dollar and other currencies.

In the remainder of this chapter we focus on flexible exchange rates.

Changes in Exchange Rates

What causes exchange rates to vary? The simplest answer to this question is changes in demand or supply in the foreign exchange market. Anything that shifts the demand curve for dollars to the right or the supply curve for dollars to the left leads to an appreciation of the dollar. Anything that shifts the demand curve for dollars to the left or the supply curve for dollars to the right leads to a **depreciation** of the dollar. This is nothing more than a restatement of the laws of supply and demand, applied now to the market for foreign currencies; it is illustrated in Figure 38-3.

What causes the shifts in demand and supply that lead to changes in exchange rates? There are many

FIGURE 38-3
Changes in Exchange Rates

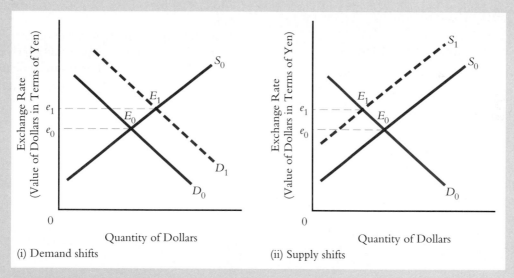

(i) Demand shifts

(ii) Supply shifts

An increase in the demand for dollars or a decrease in the supply will cause the dollar to appreciate; a decrease in the demand or an increase in supply will cause it to depreciate. The initial demand and supply curves, D_0 and S_0, are reproduced from Figures 38-1 and 38-2. Equilibrium is at E_0 with an exchange rate of e_0. An increase in the demand for dollars as shown by a rightward shift in the demand curve from D_0 to D_1 in part (i), or a decrease in the supply of dollars as shown by a leftward shift in the supply curve from S_0 to S_1 in part (ii), will cause the dollar to appreciate. In both parts the new equilibrium is at E_1, and the appreciation is shown by the rise in the exchange rate from e_0 to e_1.

A decrease in the demand for dollars as shown by a leftward shift in the demand curve from D_1 to D_0 in part (i), or an increase in the supply of dollars as shown by a rightward shift in the supply curve from S_1 to S_0 in part (ii), will cause the dollar to depreciate. The equilibrium shifts from E_1 to E_0, and the depreciation is shown by the fall in the exchange rate from e_1 to e_0 in both parts.

causes, some of which are transitory and some of which are persistent; we mention several of the most important ones.

A Rise in the Domestic Price of Exports

Suppose that the dollar price of U.S. electronic equipment rises. What this will do to the demand for dollars depends on the price elasticity of foreign demand for the U.S. product.

If the demand is elastic, perhaps because other countries supply the same product in world markets, the total amount spent will decrease and thus fewer dollars will be demanded; that is, the demand curve for dollars will shift to the left and the dollar will depreciate. This is illustrated in part (i) of Figure 38-3.

If the demand is inelastic (say, because the United States is uniquely able to supply the product for which there are no close substitutes), then more will be spent, the demand for dollars to pay the bigger bill will shift the demand curve to the right, and the dollar will appreciate. This is also illustrated in part (i) of Figure 38-3.

A Rise in the Foreign Price of Imports

Suppose that the yen price of Japanese-produced televisions increases sharply. Suppose also that U.S. consumers have an elastic demand for Japanese televisions because they can easily switch to Korean, Taiwanese, or U.S. substitutes. They thus spend fewer yen for Japanese televisions than they did before. Hence they supply fewer dollars to the foreign exchange market. The supply curve of dollars shifts to the left, and the dollar will appreciate. (If the demand for Japanese televisions were inelastic, spending on them would rise and the supply of dollars would shift to the right, leading to a depreciation of the dollar.) This is illustrated in part (ii) of Figure 38-3.

Changes in the Overall Price Levels

Suppose that, instead of a change in the price of a specific export, such as electronic calculators, there is a change in all prices because of inflation. What matters here is the change in the U.S. price level *relative* to the price levels of its trading partners. (Recall that in our two-country example, Japan stands for the rest of the world.)

An equal percentage change in the price level in both countries.   Suppose that there is a 10 percent in-flation in both the United States and Japan. In this case, the yen prices of Japanese goods and the dollar prices of U.S. goods both rise by 10 percent. At the existing exchange rate, the dollar prices of Japanese goods and the yen prices of U.S. goods will each rise by 10 percent. Thus the relative prices of imports and domestically produced goods will be unchanged in both countries. There is now no reason to expect a change in either country's demand for imports at the original exchange rate, so the inflation in the two countries leaves the equilibrium exchange rate unchanged. (This argument forms the basis of what is called the *purchasing power parity* theory of exchange rates, which will be discussed in more detail later.)

A change in the price level of only one country.   What will happen if there is inflation in the United States while the price level remains stable in Japan?[12] The dollar price of U.S. goods will rise, and they will become more expensive in Japan. This will cause the quantity of U.S. exports, and therefore the quantity of dollars demanded by Japanese importers, to diminish.

At the same time, Japanese exports to the United States will have an unchanged dollar price while the price of U.S. goods sold at home will increase because of the inflation. Thus Japanese goods will be more attractive compared with U.S. goods (because they have become *relatively* cheaper), and more Japanese goods will be bought in the United States. At any exchange rate, the quantity of dollars supplied in order to purchase yen will be increased.

A U.S. inflation, unmatched in Japan, will cause the demand curve for dollars to shift to the left and the supply curve of dollars to shift to the right. As a result the equilibrium price of dollars must fall; there is a depreciation in the value of the dollar relative to that of the yen.

Inflation at unequal rates.   The two foregoing examples are, of course, just limiting cases of a more general situation in which the price levels change

---

[12] When we consider price *level* changes, the elasticity of demand is relevant, as in the case just studied when a *particular* price changes. We maintain the assumption, outlined in footnote 9, that the foreign and domestic demands for imported goods are *elastic;* this assumption is quite plausible when applied to goods in general as opposed to particular goods.

in both countries. The arguments can readily be extended when we realize that it is the *relative* size of the changes in prices in two countries that determines whether home goods or foreign goods look more or less attractive. If country A's inflation rate is higher than country B's, country A's exports are becoming relatively expensive in B's markets while imports from B are becoming relatively cheap in A's markets. This will shift the demand curve for A's currency to the left and the supply curve to the right. Each change causes the price of A's currency to fall.

If the price level of one country is rising relative to that of another country, the equilibrium value of its currency will be falling relative to that of the other country.

Capital Movements

Major capital flows can exert strong influences on exchange rates. For example, an increased desire by U.S. citizens to invest in Japanese assets will shift the supply curve for dollars to the right, and the dollar will depreciate. This is illustrated in part (ii) of Figure 38-3.

A movement of investment funds has the effect of appreciating the currency of the capital-importing country and depreciating the currency of the capital-exporting country.

This statement is true for all capital movements—short term or long term. Because the motives that lead to large capital movements are likely to be different in the short and long terms, however, it is worth considering each separately.

Short-term capital movements.   A major motive for short-term capital flows is a change in interest rates. International traders hold transactions balances just as domestic traders do. These balances are often lent out on a short-term basis rather than being left idle. Naturally, the holders of these balances will tend to lend them, other things being equal, in those markets where interest rates are highest. Thus, if one major country's short-term rate of interest rises above the rates in most other countries, there will tend to be a large inflow of short-term capital into that country in an effort to take advantage of the high rate, and

this will tend to appreciate the currency. If these short-term interest rates should fall, there will most likely be a sudden shift away from that country as a source of transactions balances, and its currency will tend to depreciate.

A second motive for short-term capital movements is speculation about a country's exchange rate. If foreigners expect the dollar to appreciate, they will rush to buy assets that pay off in dollars; if they expect the dollar to depreciate, they will be reluctant to buy or to hold American securities.

Long-term capital movements.   Long-term capital movements are largely influenced by long-term expectations about another country's profit opportunities and the long-run value of its currency. A Japanese firm would be more willing to purchase a U.S. factory if it expected that the dollar profits would buy more yen in future years than the profits from investment in a Japanese factory. This could happen if the U.S. firm earned greater profits than the Japanese firm, with exchange rates remaining unchanged. It could also happen if the profits were the same but the Japanese firm expected the dollar to appreciate relative to the yen.

Structural Changes

An economy can undergo structural changes that alter the equilibrium exchange rate. *Structural change* is an all-purpose term for a change in cost structures, the invention of new products, or anything else that affects the pattern of comparative advantage. For example, when a country's products do not improve as rapidly as those of some other country, consumers' demand (at fixed prices) shifts slowly away from the first country's products and toward those of its foreign competitors. This causes a slow depreciation in the first country's currency, because the demand for its currency is shifting slowly leftward as illustrated in part (i) of Figure 38-3.

The Behavior of Exchange Rates

One surprise to those who supported the move to floating exchange rates following the demise of the Bretton Woods system in the early 1970s has been the degree of exchange rate volatility. Although we have just seen that there are many potential sources of exchange rate changes, the degree of exchange rate variability experienced over the past decade and a half is generally thought to exceed that which can be explained by variations in the above determinants of exchange rates.

Why have exchange rates been so volatile? This question remains at the center of debate and controversy among researchers and policy commentators. In this section we provide only a cursory view of this and related questions about the behavior of exchange rates.

First, we look at one measure of the value that the exchange rate would take on if it were subject to the influence of what might be called the underlying, or fundamental, market determinants. We can then compare this with the actual value of the exchange rate. Second, we provide one explanation for the divergence.

Purchasing Power Parity

Purchasing power parity (PPP) theory holds that over the long term the average value of the exchange rate between two currencies depends on their relative purchasing power. The theory holds that a currency will tend to have the same purchasing power when it is spent in its home country as it would have if it were converted to foreign exchange and spent in the foreign country.

If, at existing values of relative price levels and the exchange rate, a currency has a higher purchasing power in its own country, it is said to be *undervalued*; there is incentive to sell foreign exchange and buy the domestic currency in order to take advantage of its higher purchasing power in the domestic economy. This will put upward pressure on the domestic currency.

Similarly, if a currency has a lower purchasing power in its own country, it is said to be *overvalued*; there is incentive to sell the domestic currency and buy foreign exchange in order to take advantage of the higher purchasing power abroad. This will put downward pressure on the domestic currency.

The PPP exchange rate is determined by relative price levels in the two countries.

For example, assume that the U.S. price level rises by 20 percent, while the Japanese price level rises by only 5 percent over the same period. The PPP

value of the yen then appreciates by approximately 15 percent. This would mean that in Japan the prices of all goods (both Japanese-produced and imported U.S. goods) would rise by 5 percent, measured in yen, while in the United States the prices of all goods (both U.S.-produced and imported Japanese goods) would rise by 20 percent, measured in U.S. dollars.

The PPP exchange rate adjusts so that the relative price of the two nations' goods (measured in the same currency) is unchanged, because the change in the relative values of two currencies compensates exactly for differences in national inflation rates.

If the actual exchange rate changes along with the PPP rate, the competitive positions of producers in the two countries will be unchanged. Firms that are located in countries with high inflation rates will still be able to sell their outputs on international markets, because the exchange rate adjusts to offset the effect of the rising domestic prices.

Figure 38-4 shows that the exchange rate between U.S. dollars and three major currencies has followed the PPP rate over the long run. Notice also, however, the large fluctuations around the PPP rate.

Many economists, in particular those who advocate floating rates, have argued that speculators would stabilize the actual value of exchange rates within a narrow band around the PPP value. The argument was that, because everyone knew the normal value was the PPP rate, speculators who were seeking a profit when the rate deviated from its PPP level would quickly force the rate back to that level. To illustrate, suppose the PPP rate of the dollar in terms of yen is $1 = ¥100, and that the dollar appreciates so that the actual rate is $1 = ¥125 (¥1 = 0.8¢). Speculators would rush to buy yen and sell dollars at $1 = ¥125, expecting to sell yen for dollars later when the rate returned to its PPP level of $1 = ¥100. This very action would raise the demand for the yen and help push its value back toward its PPP level.

Such speculative behavior would stabilize the exchange rate near its PPP value if speculators could be sure that the deviations would be small and short-lived. However, as illustrated in Figure 38-4, the experience with flexible exchange rates has been that the swings around the PPP rate have been wide and have lasted for long periods. Whatever the causes of these wide and persistent swings, they serve to reduce the inherent stabilizing nature of speculation. For example, if the yen fell below its PPP value of $1 = ¥100, speculators would know that it could go lower and stay there for quite a while before returning to PPP. In that case it might be worth speculating on a price of, say, $1 = ¥90 next week rather than a price of $1 = ¥125 in some indefinite future.

The wide swings in exchange rates that have occurred mean that speculative buying and selling cannot be relied on to hold exchange rates close to their PPP values.

Why have these wide fluctuations occurred? One of the most important reasons is associated with international differences in interest rates.

Exchange Rate Overshooting

Differences in interest rates between countries, due to differences in monetary and fiscal policies as well as other factors, can trigger large capital flows as investors seek to place their funds where returns are highest. These capital flows in turn will result in swings in the exchange rate between the two countries. Some economists argue that this is the fundamental reason for the wide fluctuations in exchange rates that have been observed.

To illustrate, suppose that the Fed introduces a tight monetary policy, perhaps in order to restrain U.S. inflation. As we saw in Chapter 31, this will lead to an increase in U.S. interest rates. Suppose that this tight monetary policy causes U.S. interest rates to rise 4 percentage points above those in Tokyo.

The interest rate differential will lead to a capital inflow into the United States. U.S. and foreign investors alike will sell assets denominated in Japanese yen and buy U.S. dollar assets that earn higher interest. These capital inflows will lead to an increased demand for dollars on the foreign exchange market as investors exchange yen for dollars to buy U.S. assets. The increased demand will in turn lead to an appreciation of the U.S. dollar.

A tight monetary policy will lead to higher interest rates, a capital inflow, and an appreciation of the currency.

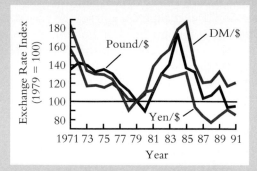

**FIGURE 38-4
The Dollar and Purchasing Power Parity, 1973–1991**

Deviations from PPP can be substantial in the short run, but over the long run exchange rates tend to converge to their PPP values. The figure shows the dollar's bilateral value in terms of three major currencies—the Japanese yen, the West German deutsche mark (DM), and the U.K. pound sterling. The series are calculated by multiplying the nominal exchange rate by the relative price levels of the two countries, and an index number is then calculated by setting the value for 1979 equal to 100. (In 1979 the U.S. current account was roughly in balance, and many economists argue that PPP roughly held then.)

If PPP always held, the series would be constant. However, as can be seen, the real value of the dollar fell steadily through the 1970s, and then in the early 1980s the dollar rose sharply in terms of all three currencies. This increase reflected a sharp rise in the foreign exchange value of the dollar that was not offset by relatively high foreign inflation. As a result, there was a real appreciation of the U.S. dollar, and U.S. goods became expensive relative to those produced in the other countries.

In 1985 the real value of the dollar started to fall. By 1986 it had returned to its 1979 value in terms of the yen *adjusted for changes in the relative price levels.* and by 1988 it had done so relative to the pound. In 1991 the U.S. dollar was actually lower in real terms relative to the yen and the pound than it had been in 1979, and it had almost fallen to its 1979 real value in terms of the deutsche mark.

When will the process stop? It will stop only when expected return on U.S. and foreign assets are again roughly equalized; as long as the return on

U.S. assets is above that on foreign assets, the capital inflows will continue, and the upward pressure on the dollar will continue. The key is that the expected return includes not only the interest earnings but also the gains or losses that might arise because of changes in the exchange rate during the period of the investment. A foreign investor holding a U.S. asset will receive U.S. dollars when the asset is sold, and will at that time want to exchange U.S. dollars for foreign exchange. If the value of the dollar has fallen, that will be a source of loss that has to be balanced against the interest income in assessing the net return on holding the asset.

Equilibrium occurs when the rise in value of the U.S. dollar in foreign exchange markets is large enough that investors will expect a future depreciation that just offsets the interest premium from investing funds in U.S. dollars.

Suppose investors believe that the PPP rate is US$1 = ¥100, but as they rush to buy dollars to take advantage of higher U.S. interest rates, they drive the rate to, say, US$1 = ¥125. (Because $1 now buys more yen, the dollar has appreciated, and because it takes more yen to buy $1, the yen has depreciated.) They do not believe this rate will be sustained and, instead, expect the U.S. dollar to lose value. If foreign investors expect the dollar to depreciate at 4 percent per year, they will be indifferent between lending money in New York and doing so in Tokyo. The extra 4 percent per year of interest that they earn in New York is exactly offset by the 4 percent that they expect to lose when they turn their money back into their own currency.

Any policy that raises domestic interest rates above world levels will cause the external value of the domestic currency to appreciate enough to create an expected future depreciation that will be sufficient to offset the interest differential.

If interest differentials are to persist, the exchange rate must change relative to its equilibrium or PPP value; this is often referred to as *overshooting* of the exchange rate.

One implication of this theory is that a central bank that is seeking to use its monetary policy to attain its domestic policy targets may have to put up with large fluctuations in the exchange rate. In the example the high U.S. interest rates were the result of a restrictive monetary policy, resulting in appreciation of the dollar. The overshooting of the dollar beyond its PPP rate would put export- and import-competing industries under temporary but severe pressure from foreign competition because U.S. goods would be expensive relative to imported goods. The resulting fall in demand for U.S. goods would open up a recessionary gap, thus providing a further mechanism by which the restrictive monetary policy was transmitted to the rest of the economy. This was discussed in Box 30-3 on page 638.

The other side of this coin is that the high value of the U.S. dollar creates inflationary pressure in other countries. U.S. goods become much more expensive abroad, thus putting upward pressure on foreign prices and wages. Authorities in other countries are faced with the uncomfortable choice of accepting this increased inflation or raising their own interest rates and thus dampening the fall in their exchange rates in terms of the U.S. dollar. In the early 1980s many foreign central banks chose this latter option, and tight monetary policies, initiated in the United States, were quickly imitated in other countries. This combined monetary contraction contributed to the severity of the world recession. Some related issues are discussed further in Box 38-3.

The overvaluation of the dollar meant that the recession was particularly severe in the United States and that U.S. export- and import-competing industries suffered enormously. Not surprisingly, this spurred many calls for protectionist measures to save jobs in those sectors. The relatively low values of many foreign currencies and, in particular, the Japanese yen, contributed to the view that foreign competition in such traded-goods sectors was indeed unfair and hence protection was justified.

As the U.S. economy recovered during the rest of the decade, it might have been expected that the pressures for protection would have subsided. However, while the U.S. current account deficit shrank, pressures for protection remained strong. As we saw in Chapter 37, major protectionist legislation was passed in 1988, and, as the 1990s proceed, it remains to be seen what further protectionist measures will be introduced.

Box 38-3

Beggar-My-Neighbor Policies, Past and Present

During the Great Depression of the 1930s, concern over massive unemployment came to dominate economic policies in almost every country. All measures, including exchange rate manipulations, seemed fair game for dealing with unemployment. Many of the policies adopted were acts of desperation. Governments, hoping to gain short-term advantages before their policies provoked the inevitable reaction from others, tended not to consider the long-term effects that the policies they adopted would have on trade or on their trading partners.

The use of devaluations to ease domestic unemployment rested on a simple and superficially plausible line of analysis: If a country has unemployed workers at home, why not substitute home production for imports and thus give jobs to one's citizens instead of to foreigners? One way to do this is to urge U.S. citizens to "buy American." Another, probably more effective, way is to lower the prices of domestic goods relative to those of imports. Putting a tariff on imports does this, as does devaluation of one's currency—both make foreign goods more expensive. Of course, if this policy works, other countries will find *their* exports falling and unemployment rising as a consequence. Because such policies attempt to solve one country's problems by inflicting them on others, they are called **beggar-my-neighbor policies**, often described as attempts to "export one's unemployment."

In a situation of inadequate world demand, a beggar-my-neighbor policy on the part of one country can work only in the unlikely event that other countries do not react by changing their policies to protect themselves.

During the 1930s industrialized countries engaged in a series of *competitive devaluations*. One country would devalue its currency in an attempt to reduce its imports and stimulate exports, but because other countries were suffering from the same kinds of problems of unemployment, retaliation was swift, and devaluation followed devaluation. The simultaneous attempt of all countries to cut imports without suffering a comparable cut in exports is bound to be self-defeating.

These policies, along with other restrictive trade policies such as import duties, export subsidies, quotas, and prohibitions, led to a declining volume of world trade and brought no relief from the worldwide depression because they did nothing to raise world aggregate demand.

To avoid a recurrence of the beggar-my-neighbor policies of the 1930s, trading nations designed some important institutions. The International Monetary Fund (IMF) was supposed to reduce the chances of competitive devaluations, and the General Agreement on Tariffs and Trade (GATT) was supposed to reduce the chances of competitive increases in tariffs and other trade restrictions. These institutions worked well for over 30 years.

Throughout the 1980s it was clear that great pressure was being put on the whole postwar fabric, designed to encourage trade and discourage beggar-my-neighbor policies. U.S. voters showed strong support for advocates of increased tariffs. Many countries, including the United States, negotiated unofficial quotas that restricted the importation of Japanese cars. European agricultural protectionism threatens to wreck the GATT negotiations and remains the focus of considerable debate in the United States and elsewhere. Less-developed countries sought covert ways of protecting their own infant industries and complained, with some justice, that the developed nations paid lip service to, rather than really acted on, the slogan of "trade, not aid."

SUMMARY

1. International trade normally requires the exchange of the currency of one country for that of another. The exchange rate between two currencies is the amount of one currency that must be paid in order to obtain one unit of another currency. Where more than two currencies are involved, there will be an exchange rate between each pair of currencies.

2. Actual transactions among the firms, households, and governments of various countries are kept track of and reported in the balance-of-payments accounts. In these accounts any transaction that uses foreign exchange is recorded as a debit item, and any transaction that produces foreign exchange is recorded as a credit item. If all transactions are recorded, the sum of all credit items necessarily equals the sum of all debit items, because the foreign exchange that is bought must also have been sold.

3. Major categories in the balance-of-payments accounts are the trade account, current account, capital account, and official financing. The so-called balance-of-payments account is the balance of the current plus capital accounts; that is, it excludes the transactions on official financing account. If official financing is zero, a balance on current account must be matched by a balance on capital account of equal magnitude but opposite sign.

4. There is nothing inherently good or bad about deficits or surpluses. Persistent deficits or surpluses cannot be sustained, because the former will eventually exhaust a country's foreign exchange reserves and the latter will do the same to a trading partner's reserves.

5. The demand for dollars arises from U.S. exports of goods and services, long-term and short-term capital flows into the United States, and the desire of foreign banks, firms, and governments to use U.S. dollars as an international medium of exchange or as part of their reserves.

6. The supply of dollars to purchase foreign currencies arises from U.S. imports of goods and services, capital flows from the United States, and the desire of holders of dollars to decrease the size of their holdings.

7. A depreciation of the dollar lowers the foreign price of U.S. exports and increases the quantity of dollars demanded; at the same time, it raises the dollar price of imports from abroad and thus lowers the quantity of dollars supplied to buy foreign exchange to be used to purchase foreign goods. Thus, the demand curve for dollars is negatively sloped and the supply curve of dollars is positively sloped when the quantities demanded and supplied are plotted against the price of dollars, measured in terms of a foreign currency.

8. When the central bank does not intervene in the foreign exchange market (zero official financing), there is a flexible exchange rate. Under fixed exchange rates, the central bank intervenes in the foreign exchange market to maintain the exchange rate at or near an announced par value. To do this the central bank must hold sufficient stocks of foreign exchange reserves.

9. Under a flexible, or floating, exchange rate, the exchange rate is market-determined by supply and demand for the currency. This

is simply an application of the laws of supply and demand, which we studied in Chapter 4; the item being bought and sold is a nation's money.

10. A currency will tend to appreciate in foreign exchange markets if there is a shift to the right of the demand curve or a shift to the left of the supply curve for its currency. Shifts in the opposite directions will tend to depreciate the currency. Shifts are caused by changes in such things as the prices of imports and exports, the rates of inflation in different countries, capital movements, structural conditions, expectations about future trends in earnings and exchange rates, and the level of confidence in the currency.

11. Since their adoption in the mid-1970s, flexible exchange rates have fluctuated substantially. As a result central banks have often intervened to stabilize the fluctuations. Thus the present system is called a *managed*, or *dirty, float*.

12. Fluctuations in exchange rates can be understood as fluctuations around a trend value that is determined by the purchasing power parity (PPP) rate. The PPP rate adjusts in response to differences in national inflation rates. Deviations from the PPP rate are related, among other things, to international differences in interest rates.

TOPICS FOR REVIEW

Foreign exchange and exchange rates

Appreciation and depreciation

Balance of trade and balance of payments

Current and capital account

Official-financing balance

Mercantilist views on the balance of trade and volume of trade

Sources of the demand for and supply of foreign exchange

Effects on exchange rates of capital flows, inflation, interest rates, and expectations about exchange rates

Fixed and flexible exchange rates

Adjustable pegs and managed floats

Purchasing power parity

Exchange rate overshooting

DISCUSSION QUESTIONS

1. What is the probable effect of each of the following on the exchange rate of a country, other things being equal?
   a. The quantity of oil imports is greatly increased, but the value of imported oil is higher due to price decreases.
   b. The country's inflation rate falls well below that of its trading partners.
   c. Rising labor costs of the country's manufacturers lead to a worsening ability to compete in world markets.

APPENDIX TO CHAPTER

38

The Gold Standard and the Bretton Woods System

Two episodes with fixed exchange rates occurred during the twentieth century. The gold standard, the origins of which are as old as currency itself, was used until the late 1920s and early 1930s. The Bretton Woods system, which was the only payments system ever to be designed and established by conscious action, was born out of World War II and collapsed a little less than 30 years later. These histories are instructive, not least because many people continue to propose returning to one or the other of these systems.

The Gold Standard

The gold standard was not *designed;* it just happened. It arose out of the general acceptance of gold as the commodity to be used as money. In most countries paper currency was freely convertible into gold at a fixed rate. In 1914 the U.S. dollar was worth 0.053 standard ounces of gold, while the British pound sterling was worth 0.257 standard ounces of gold. This meant that the pound was worth 4.86 times as much as the dollar in terms of gold, thus making £1 worth US$4.86. (In practice the exchange rate fluctuated within narrow limits set by the cost of shipping gold.) As long as all countries were on the gold standard, a person in one country could be sure of being able to make payments to a person in another.

The Gold-Flow, Price-Level Mechanism

Under the gold standard, the balance of international payments was maintained by adjustments in price levels within individual countries. Consider a country that had a balance-of-payments deficit because the value of its imports (i.e., purchases) from other countries exceeded the value of its exports (i.e., sales) to other countries. The demand for foreign exchange would exceed the supply in this country's foreign exchange market. Some people who wished to make foreign payments would need to convert their domestic currency into gold and ship the gold. Therefore, some people in a surplus country would receive gold in payment for exports. Thus, deficit countries would be losing gold, while surplus countries would be gaining it.

Under the gold standard, the whole money supply was linked to the supply of gold. The international movements of gold would therefore lead to a fall in the money supply in the deficit country and a rise in the money supply in the surplus country.

If full employment prevailed, changes in the domestic money supply would cause changes in domestic price levels. Deficit countries would thus have falling price levels, while surplus countries would have rising price levels. The exports of deficit countries would become relatively cheaper, while those of surplus countries would become relatively more expensive. The resulting changes in quantities bought and sold would move the balance of payments toward equilibrium.

Actual Experience of the Gold Standard

During the half century before World War I, the adjustment mechanism just described seemed to work well. Subsequent research has suggested, however, that the gold standard succeeded during that period mainly because it was not called on to do much work. No major trading country found itself with a serious and persistent balance-of-payments deficit, so no major country was called on to restore equilibrium through a large change in its domestic price level.

During the 1920s the gold standard was called on to do a major job. It failed utterly, and it was abandoned. How did this happen? During World War I most belligerent countries went off the gold standard. Most countries suffered major inflations, but the degree of inflation differed from country to country, which led to changes in the equilibrium (or purchasing power parity) exchange rates.

After the war, countries returned to the gold standard. Many returned to the prewar rates. This meant that some countries' goods were overpriced and other countries' goods were underpriced. Large deficits and surpluses in the balance of payments inevitably appeared, and the adjustment mechanism required that price levels should change in each of the countries in order to restore equilibrium. Exchange rates were not adjusted, and price levels changed very slowly. By the onset of the Great Depression, equilibrium price levels had not yet been attained. The financial chaos brought on by the Depression destroyed the existing payments system.

We may ask whether an altered gold standard, based on more realistic exchange rates, might not have succeeded. Some economists think that it would; most others believe that the gold standard suffered from the key weakness that the price adjustment process worked too slowly and too imperfectly to cope with large and persistent disequilibrium.

Furthermore, gold as the basis for an international money supply suffered several disadvantages: a supply that could not be expanded as rapidly as increases in the volume of world trade required, an uneven distribution of existing and potential new gold supplies among the nations of the world, and a large and volatile speculative demand for gold during periods of crisis. These factors could cause disruptive variations in the supply of gold that was available for international monetary purposes.

The Bretton Woods System

The one lesson that everyone thought had been learned from the 1930s was that a system of either freely fluctuating exchange rates or fixed rates with easily accomplished devaluations was a sure route to disaster. In order to achieve a system of orderly exchange rates that would facilitate the free flow of trade following World War II, representatives of many major countries met at Bretton Woods, New Hampshire, in 1944.

The Bretton Woods system had three objectives: (1) to create a set of rules that would maintain fixed exchange rates in the face of short-term fluctuations; (2) to guarantee that changes in exchange rates would occur only in the face of "fundamental" deficits or surpluses in the balance of payments; and (3) to ensure that, when such changes did occur, they would not

spark a series of competitive devaluations. The basic characteristic of the system was that U.S. dollars, held by foreign monetary authorities, were made directly convertible into gold at a price fixed by the U.S. government while foreign governments fixed the prices at which their currencies were convertible into U.S. dollars. It was this characteristic that made the system a **gold exchange standard**. Gold was the ultimate reserve, but other currencies were held as reserves, because directly or indirectly they could be exchanged for gold.

To maintain the convertibility of their currencies at fixed exchange rates and to be able to support the exchange market, the monetary authorities had to have reserves of acceptable foreign exchange.[1] In the Bretton Woods system, the authorities held reserves of gold and claims on key currencies, mainly the U.S. dollar and the British pound sterling. When a country's currency was in excess supply, its authorities would sell dollars, pounds sterling, or gold. When a country's currency was in excess demand, its authorities would buy dollars or pounds sterling. If they then wished to increase their gold reserves, they would use the dollars to purchase gold from the Fed, thus depleting the U.S. gold stock.

The United States therefore needed to have enough gold to maintain fixed price convertibility of the dollar into gold, as demanded by foreign monetary authorities. Other countries needed to maintain convertibility (on either a restricted or unrestricted basis) between their currency and the U.S. dollar at a fixed exchange rate.

Problems of the Adjustable Peg System

Three key problems of the Bretton Woods system hampered its functioning and contributed to its eventual collapse.

Reserves to accommodate short-term fluctuations. The Bretton Woods period witnessed a strong upward trend in the volume of overall international payments, and hence there was also a strong upward trend in the demand for foreign exchange reserves.

The ultimate reserve in the Bretton Woods system was gold, and this led to serious problems during the 1960s and early 1970s. The world's supply of

---

[1] The exchange rates were not quite fixed; they were permitted to vary by 1 percent on either side of their par values. Later the bands of permitted fluctuation were widened to 2.25 percent on either side of par value.

monetary gold did not grow as fast as the volume of trade; the world's stock of monetary gold during the 1960s grew at less than 2 percent per year while trade grew at nearly 10 percent. Gold, which had been 66 percent of the total monetary reserves in 1959, was only 30 percent by 1972. Over this period, reserve holdings of dollars and pounds sterling rose sharply. At the same time, during this period the United States lost substantial gold reserves to other countries. By the late 1960s, the reduction in U.S. reserves was sufficiently large to undermine confidence in the continued ability of the United States to maintain dollar convertibility.

Adjusting to long-term disequilibria. The second characteristic problem of a fixed-rate system is the adjustment to long-term disequilibria that develop because of secular shifts in the demand for and supply of foreign exchange.

These disequilibria developed slowly. At first they led to a series of speculative crises, as people expected a realignment of exchange rates to occur. Finally, they led to a series of realignments that started in 1967. Each occurred amid quite spectacular flows of speculative funds that thoroughly disorganized normal trade and payments.

Speculative crises. The adjustable peg system often leads to situations in which speculators are presented with one-way bets. In these disequilibria situations, there is an increasing chance of an exchange rate adjustment in one direction, with little or no chance of a movement in the other direction. Speculators then have an opportunity to secure a large potential gain, with no corresponding potential for loss. Speculative crises, associated with the need to adjust to fundamental disequilibria, were the downfall of the system.

Collapse of the Bretton Woods System

Although the Bretton Woods system worked reasonably well for nearly 20 years, the problems inherent in the adjustable peg system ultimately proved insurmountable. The system was beset by a series of crises of ever-increasing severity that reflected the system's underlying weaknesses.

The two key currencies in the system, the pound sterling and the dollar, each experienced speculative attacks that reflected a loss of confidence in the ability of the respective governments to maintain exchange

rates at the stated par values. A devaluation of the pound in 1967 set off a series of other devaluations, and the subsequent period witnessed increasing flows of speculative funds out of dollars and into other currencies, including the German mark and the Japanese yen. In 1968 central banks stopped pegging the free-market price of gold, although the price for official settlements between central banks continued to be set at $35 an ounce. (The free-market price quickly soared above this level.) In August 1971 the United States suspended convertibility of the dollar in terms of gold, and this led quickly to a sharp devaluation of the dollar.

An agreement among the major trading nations was signed at the Smithsonian Institution in Washington, D.C., in December 1971. The main element of the agreement was a 7.9 percent devaluation of the dollar against their currencies. Following the Smithsonian agreement, the world was on a de facto **dollar standard**. Foreign monetary authorities held their reserves in the form of dollars and settled their international debts with dollars. However, the dollar was not convertible into gold.

The Smithsonian agreements did not lead to a new period of international financial stability. U.S. inflation continued unchecked, and the deficit in the U.S. balance of payments persisted. In January 1973 speculative movements of capital once again occurred, and in February 1973 the United States proposed a further 11 percent devaluation of the dollar—to be accomplished by raising the official price of gold to $42.22 per ounce. Intense speculative activity followed the announcement.

Five member countries of the European Community then decided to stabilize their currencies against each other but to let them float together against the dollar. This joint float was called the *snake*. Some other European countries soon joined the snake, and other countries (including notably Italy, the United Kingdom, and Japan) announced their intention to allow their currencies to float in value.[2]

Fluctuations in exchange rates were severe. By early July 1973, the snake currencies had appreciated

---

[2] In June 1972 the Bank of England had abandoned the de facto dollar standard with the announcement that it had "temporarily" abandoned its commitment to support the pound sterling at a fixed par value against the U.S. dollar. The events of 1973 led "temporarily" to become "indefinitely."

about 30 percent against the dollar, but by the end of the year they had nearly returned to their February 1973 values.

The dollar devaluation formally took effect in October 1973. Most industrialized countries maintained the nominal values of their currencies in terms of gold, thereby appreciating them in terms of the U.S. dollar by 11 percent. The devaluation quickly became redundant, though: Despite attempts to restore fixed rates, the drift to flexible rates had become irresistible by the end of 1973.

The European Exchange Rate Mechanism

The countries of the European Community (EC), with varying degrees of commitment and varying degrees of success, have pursued a "block" approach to fixed exchange rates over the past two decades, maintaining fixed exchange rates among themselves but allowing their currencies to float as a block against other currencies such as the U.S. dollar and the Japanese yen. In the late 1960s the EC countries adopted the "snake," which worked well in "normal" circumstances but was subject to speculative crises and increasingly frequent realignments of relative values of national currencies.

These problems created the perception of a need for a more formal arrangement with a stronger commitment to the agreed-upon parities. The snake thus evolved into the European Exchange Rate Mecha-

nism (ERM), which also witnessed the creation of a European currency. National currencies were valued in terms of this European Currency Unit (ECU). In principle, all countries were committed to intervention in order to maintain the parities, but in practice the German central bank, the Bundesbank, assumed a hegemonic role. The Bundesbank was a committed and proven "inflation fighter," and for a period of time the ERM functioned quite well, with other central banks apparently willing to take advantage of the Bundesbank's credibility. Indeed, in the early 1990s, the so-called Maastricht Treaty created considerable momentum toward creation of a currency union with permanently fixed exchange rates and a common currency. In 1992, however, the momentum toward this goal suffered a sharp setback with a defeat of a referendum on the Maastricht Treaty in Denmark and a speculative crisis in the week leading up to the September 20 French referendum.

That crisis was led at least in part by the inconsistency of the monetary policies being pursued in the various countries with the commitment to fixed exchange rates. Britain, for example, faced the choice between raising interest rates to defend the pound or lowering them to stimulate the flagging economy. It tried the former, but in short order it gave in to speculative pressures and adopted the latter.

The crisis led to sharp changes in parities and interest rates, and even to Britain's withdrawal from the ERM. Many commentators felt that these events dealt a blow not only to the movement for the creation of a single European currency but perhaps even to the survival of the ERM itself.

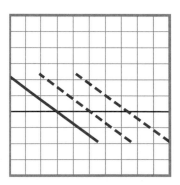

39

Macroeconomic Policy in an Open Economy

I n the early 1980s the U.S. economy slid into a deep recession as the external value of the U.S. dollar soared. How were these two events related? Later in the decade, and indeed, into the early 1990s, large government budget deficits were accompanied by large current account deficits. Why did economists refer to these as the *twin deficits*? Was the current account deficit the inevitable consequence of the government budget deficit?

In this chapter we explore these and other issues that arise in an *open* economy. When we focus on *open-economy* issues, new complications arise. These include the behavior of the exchange rate and its influence on the balance of trade and national income, the nature and extent of foreign borrowing, and the impact on the economy of changes in the terms of trade or in foreign national income, interest rates, and inflation. As we shall also see, the response of the economy to economic policies may be altered in an open economy, as opposed to the closed–economy response emphasized so far in this book.

In the first section of this chapter, we focus on the relationship between the balance of trade, aggregate demand, and national income, and on the role of the exchange rate. We then turn to a discussion of the implications of international movements of capital, or *capital mobility*.

The Balance of Trade and National Income

Suppose that there are no international capital flows in the world economy, so that the only international activities involve the exchange of goods and services across national boundaries. What are the implications of this international trade for the determination of national income and for the role of economic policies?

We start by comparing the basic macroeconomic equilibrium condition (in which national income equals desired aggregate expenditure) for a closed economy with that for an open economy. In each case we also use that equilibrium condition to analyze the multiplier relating changes in equilibrium national income to changes in autonomous expenditure. When we consider the multiplier in an open economy, we distinguish between an open economy that maintains a fixed exchange rate and one that has a flexible exchange rate.

In studying national income under these various circumstances, we find that changes in the price level arising as a result of movements along a positively sloped aggregate supply curve complicate but do not change the basic results.[1] Thus,

---

[1] Because the *SRAS* curve does not shift following a change in autonomous spending, the size of the resulting change in national income will be directly related to the size of the shift in the *AD* curve. (This issue is discussed further in Box 39-1 on page 845.)

for simplicity we focus our discussion on shifts in the *AD* curve *with a given price level*; in terms of the terminology in Chapters 25 and 26, we will focus on the size of the *simple* multiplier.

A Closed Economy

For a closed economy (that is, an economy that does not engage in international trade), the only sources of demand are domestic expenditure: consumption (*C*), investment (*I*), and government (*G*). Thus the equilibrium condition is that in which real national income equals the sum of these three expenditure categories:

$$Y = C + I + G \qquad [1]$$

We saw in Chapter 27 that this equation underlies the aggregate demand (*AD*) curve; see Figure 27-2 on page 553. Recall in particular that the *simple* multiplier gives the size of the horizontal shift in the *AD* curve following a change in autonomous spending. The simple multiplier is equal to $1/(1 - z)$, where *z is the marginal propensity to spend*. As we saw in Chapter 27, for our closed economy *z* is equal to $b(1 - t)$, where *b* is the marginal propensity to consume and *t* is the marginal tax rate.

We want to study what happens when the government changes its fiscal and monetary policies. A simple case of an expansionary fiscal policy is when the government increases its purchases (*G* rises). A simple case of an expansionary monetary policy is when the Fed increases the money supply. As we saw in Chapter 31, this sets in motion the transmission mechanism; the interest rate falls and hence interest-sensitive expenditures (as represented by *I*) *increase*. Thus expansionary fiscal and monetary policies both lead to a rightward shift in the *AD* curve, and hence to an increase in national income as illustrated in part (i) of Figure 39-1 by the shift from AD_0 to AD_{closed}.

An Open Economy with a Fixed Exchange Rate

Now consider an open economy (that is, one that engages in international trade). For the moment, we suppose that the government adjusts its official financing transactions so as to maintain a fixed exchange rate. As we saw in Chapter 38, this means that the balance of payments can take on a value different from zero; because we have also simplified our analysis at this stage by supposing that there are no international capital movements, the balance of payments is equal to the balance of trade.

FIGURE 39-1
The Simple Multiplier in an Open Economy with a Fixed Exchange Rate

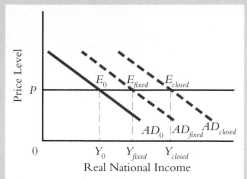

(i) Aggregate demand

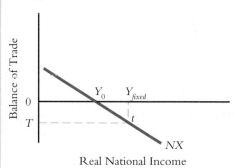

(ii) Net exports

Under fixed exchange rates and zero capital mobility, the simple multiplier is smaller than it would be in a closed economy; the responsiveness of net exports to national income provides an automatic stabilizer. In part (i), aggregate demand is initially given by the negatively sloped line AD_0, and the price level is *P*. Equilibrium is at E_0 and the equilibrium level of national income is Y_0. An increase in autonomous spending then shifts the *AD* curve to the right; the size of the horizontal shift is given by the simple multiplier. In a closed economy, the *AD* curve shifts to AD_{closed}, the new equilibrium is at E_{closed}, and the new equilibrium level of national income is Y_{closed}.

In an open economy with fixed exchange rates and no capital mobility, the simple multiplier is smaller. The *AD* curve shifts by less, to AD_{fixed}; the new equilibrium is at E_{fixed} and the new equilibrium level of national income is Y_{fixed}, less than Y_{closed}.

In part (ii), the balance of trade is shown by the negatively sloped line *NX*. At the initial equilibrium level of national income, there is a zero balance of trade; the rise in income to Y_{fixed} in the open-economy fixed-exchange-rate case causes a movement along *NX* to *t*, and there is a balance-of-trade deficit of *T*.

In Chapter 26 we saw that incorporating exports (X) and imports (IM) into the analysis results in the equilibrium condition:

$$Y = C + I + G + (X - IM) \qquad [2]$$

The inclusion of the balance of trade or net export term, $(X - IM)$, in the determination of desired aggregate expenditure has two important implications.

Automatic stabilizer. Because imports rise with national income, the simple multiplier is reduced; that is, there is a smaller horizontal shift in the AD curve following an increase in autonomous spending than would occur in a closed economy. Recall that the simple multiplier is given by $1/(1 - z)$ where z is the marginal propensity to spend; in an open economy the marginal propensity to spend is reduced because of *marginal propensity to import.* This reduction in z increases the denominator $(1 - z)$ and thus reduces the size of the multiplier. The simple open-economy multiplier is shown in part (i) of Figure 39-1 as the shift from AD to AD_{fixed}, which is smaller than the closed-economy multiplier shown by the shift from AD_0 to AD_{closed}.[2]

As we saw in Chapter 28, anything that reduces the size of the multiplier, and thus reduces the sensitivity of national income to autonomous changes in spending, is called an *automatic stabilizer.*

Under fixed exchange rates, net exports act as an automatic stabilizer.

The source of the difference between the closed and open economy multipliers is shown in part (ii) of Figure 39-1. In an open economy, the increase in national income following an increase in G causes a movement along the net export function. Thus, following the shock there is a deterioration in the balance of trade as a result of the increase in imports. From Equation 2 we can see that the fixed exchange rate multiplier is smaller because an increase in I or G is partially offset by a decrease in $(X - IM)$.[3]

Export multiplier. Equation 2 shows (as we discussed in Chapter 26) that in an open economy a change in the level of exports will cause national income to change. A change in the level of exports can occur for many reasons, including a change in the terms of trade (i.e., a change in the value of a county's exports relative to its import goods) or a change in the level of economic activity in a country's trading partners. These will lead to a shift in the AD curve and hence to a change in the equilibrium level of national income.

Under fixed exchange rates, changes in exports cause changes in aggregate demand and equilibrium national income.

This is often referred to as the *export multiplier.* The importance of the export multiplier is that it links the levels of economic activity of trading partners. For example, a boom in one country is transmitted to its trading partners via increased demand for the second country's exports.

The operation of the export multiplier is shown in Figure 39-2. As shown in part (i), a change in exports (X) leads to a shift in the AD curve. As shown in part (ii), it will also lead to a *larger* shift in the net export function; in contrast to the effects of an increase in domestic spending, a rise in exports will lead to a balance-of-trade *surplus* rather than a balance-of-trade deficit. **[46]**

In Figures 39-1 and 39-2, the shifts in the AD curves are superimposed on a given price level. A more complete analysis would take account of the effects of a positively sloped SRAS curve; as noted before, this complicates but does not change the basic results. For those who wish to work through this more complicated case, the analysis is presented in Box 39-1.

Flexible Exchange Rates

The automatic stabilizer role provided by the balance of trade and the potential for the export multiplier to transmit disturbances from one economy to another are key aspects of a fixed exchange rate system. As such, they may be relevant to the historical analysis of periods earlier in this century when the world was essentially on fixed exchange rates, and to a study of the economies of particular states within the United States or of countries that are part of the European Exchange Rate Mechanism.

However, in order to study the economies of countries such as the United States and most other

---

[2] The simple open-economy multiplier is $1/[1 - b(1 - t) + m]$, where m is the *marginal propensity to import.* Because m is positive, the denominator is increased and hence the simple open-economy multiplier is smaller than the simple closed-economy multiplier $1/[1 - b(1 - t)]$.

[3] The change in the balance of trade accompanying the change in national income may be undesirable. Thus, under fixed exchange rates there is a potential conflict for domestic policymakers between their objectives in terms of domestic (or *internal*) policy variables and international (or *external*) ones.

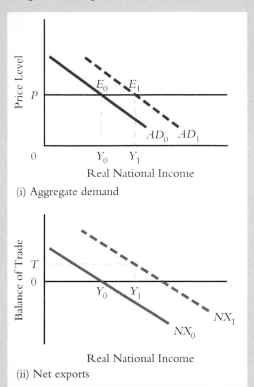

FIGURE 39-2
The Export Multiplier

(i) Aggregate demand

(ii) Net exports

An autonomous increase in exports leads, under fixed exchange rates, to an increase in equilibrium national income and to a balance-of-trade surplus.

Initially, aggregate demand is given by AD_0 in part (i) and the net export function is given by NX_0 in part (ii). The price level is P, equilibrium is at E_0, equilibrium national income is Y_0, and there is a zero balance of trade.

Following an autonomous increase in exports, the aggregate demand curve shifts to the right to AD_1 in part (i), and the net export function shifts to the right to NX_1 in part (ii). The new equilibrium is at E_1, with equilibrium national income rising to Y_1. Because the shift in NX is larger than the shift in the AD curve, at the new equilibrium level of income there is a balance-of-trade surplus of T.

the simplified model of this section, where there are no international capital flows, this means that the balance of trade must be zero. As we will see, this has dramatic implications for open-economy multiplier analysis.

Automatic stabilizer. Look again at Figure 39-1, which shows the situation following an increase in autonomous spending. (In this section we restrict our attention to the implications for changes in *domestic* spending, G or I; we return to the implications of changes in export spending, X, later.) Following an increase in autonomous domestic spending, aggregate demand and national income have increased, *and* the increase in income has caused a balance-of-trade deficit; this analysis is reproduced in parts (i) and (ii) of Figure 39-3.

Under flexible exchange rates, the balance-of-trade deficit following an increase in domestic spending cannot be sustained.[4] The increased demand for imports resulting from the stimulus to aggregate demand means that there is an excess supply of dollars in the foreign exchange market as U.S. citizens try to sell dollars in order to obtain foreign exchange with which to buy imports. (Equivalently we could have said that there is an excess demand for foreign exchange.) As a result, the dollar depreciates.

The depreciation of the dollar will lead to an increase in exports as U.S.-produced goods become more competitive on world markets, and to a decrease in imports as imported goods become more expensive.[5] This in turn leads to a shift up and to the right of the net export function; the depreciation of the dollar means that at any level of national income, net exports are higher. This is shown in part (ii) of Figure 39-3.

How much does the dollar depreciate, and how much does the net export function shift?

As we saw in Chapter 38, the dollar must depreciate by enough to ensure that the market for foreign exchange clears, which means that net exports are zero. Thus if national income were to remain constant at its new level (Y_1 in Figure 39-3), the answer would be that the net export function would shift by enough

industrialized countries outside of Europe, it is important to examine flexible exchange rates.

As we saw in Chapter 38, a flexible exchange rate means that official financing transactions are zero, so the balance of payments must be zero. In

---

4 In fact, it would never occur. There would be a tendency for a deficit to emerge, and this would set in motion the reactions discussed in the rest of this section.

5 We continue to suppose that the elasticity condition in footnote 9 in Chapter 38 is met.

FIGURE 39-3
The Simple Multiplier in an Open Economy with a Flexible Exchange Rate

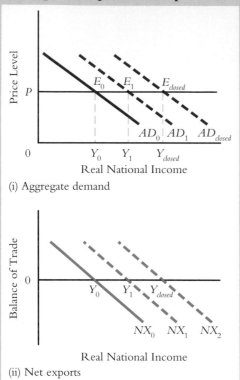

(i) Aggregate demand

(ii) Net exports

Under flexible exchange rates and zero capital mobility, the balance of trade is always zero, and hence the open-economy multiplier is identical to the closed-economy multiplier. There is no automatic stabilizer role provided by net exports. In part (i), aggregate demand is initially given by negatively sloped line AD_0, and the price level is P. Equilibrium is at E_0, and the equilibrium level of national income is Y_0. In part (ii), the balance of trade is shown by the negatively sloped line NX_0; there is a zero balance of trade.

An increase in autonomous spending then shifts the AD curve to the right; at the initial exchange rate the shift is the same as that shown in Figure 39-1 for a fixed exchange rate; this is shown in part (i) by the shift to AD_1. Thus at the initial exchange rate national income would rise to Y_1 and there would be a balance-of-trade deficit. The resulting depreciation of the dollar causes the NX curve to shift to the right, say to NX_1. This in turn causes the AD curve to shift to the right, thus increasing national income and opening up another trade account deficit. This in turn causes a further depreciation of the dollar.

At the new equilibrium, income and the exchange rate must be such that the balance of trade is zero. This occurs when the AD curve shifts by the amount it would shift in a closed economy, that is, to AD_{closed}, so that the new equilibrium is at E_{closed} and the new equilibrium level of national income is Y_{closed}. The dollar must depreciate by enough that there is a zero balance of trade at that level of income; that is, so that the NX curve shifts to NX_2.

to make the balance of trade zero at that new level of national income. The dollar would depreciate by the amount necessary to cause just that shift in the net export function. ·

However, there is a complication. The improvement in the balance of trade following the depreciation leads to a further increase in aggregate demand. (See Equation 2 above.) This of course leads to a further increase in national income, which in turn causes a movement along the new net export function. This deterioration in the balance of trade then gives rise to a further depreciation of the dollar.

This process comes to a halt when the new level of national income and the new exchange rate are compatible with equilibrium in the market for domestic output (as required by Equation 2) and the balance of trade is zero (as required by the flexible exchange rate in the absence of international capital flows). It might appear that finding the new equilibrium, and assessing the final multiplier impact of the increase in autonomous

spending, will be difficult. But further examination of Equation 2 reveals a surprising and simple answer.

Because the balance of trade is zero before and after the increase in autonomous spending, the economy behaves as if there were no foreign sector.

This means that the AD curve shifts until it is coincident with the closed economy curve AD_{closed} in Figure 39-1, and the equilibrium level of income is equal to Y_{closed}, the level that would have occurred in the closed economy. This is illustrated in part (i) of Figure 39-3. The NX curve shifts so that the balance of trade is zero when income is at its new equilibrium level. This is illustrated in part (ii) of Figure 39-3.

With zero capital mobility and flexible exchange rates, the simple multiplier in an open economy is the same as that for a closed economy.

Box 39-1

Aggregate Supply and the Open-Economy Multiplier

In this box we consider the implications of incorporating a positively sloped *SRAS* curve into the analysis of the open-economy multiplier of Figure 39-1.

The basic analysis is presented in the figure. Because the *SRAS* curve does not shift in response to the change in autonomous spending, the change in national income is directly related to the shift in the *AD* curve. Hence the results from the fixed-price-level analysis of Figure 39-1 appear to carry through to this case.

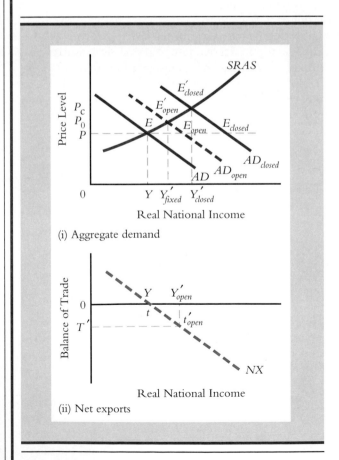

(i) Aggregate demand

(ii) Net exports

One complication is that the slopes of the *AD* and *SRAS* curves might change in the open-economy case. This is difficult to analyze, which is the reason we have focused on the fixed-price case in the text.

The effect of the openness of the economy on the slope of the *SRAS* curve is likely to be minor and, in any event, secondary to our discussion. For simplicity we do not consider it further.

The implications of changes in the domestic price level effects on *AD* are perhaps more central. When national income *and the price level* change in response to a change in autonomous spending, the components of aggregate demand—*C, I,* and $(X - IM)$—will be affected by the change in the price level. As a result:

The change in national income following a change in autonomous expenditure is smaller because of the positively sloped *SRAS* curve; the rise in the price level leads to a reduction in aggregate demand.

But this is true in both the closed economy and the open economy. Further, the presence of the positively sloped *SRAS* curve does not alter the relative change in national income in the two cases—the multiplier is still smaller in the open economy than in the closed economy.

In the open economy, the rise in national income following an increase in *G* or *I* also leads to a balance-of-trade deficit. From the discussion in Chapter 38, it might appear that the *NX* curve in part (ii) of the figure should shift as a result of the effect of the change in the price level on exports and imports. However, this effect can be incorporated in the slope of the *NX* curve (which changes the magnitude of the slope but not the sign), so that the *NX* curve does *not* shift in response to changes in autonomous spending. **[47]**

This means that the expansion of imports associated with the increased income resulting from an increase in domestic autonomous spending does not provide an additional automatic stabilizer for the economy (as it did under fixed exchange rates). This is true because the currency depreciation that accompanies the expansion of income serves to maintain a zero balance of trade. That is, the depreciation leads to increases in exports and decreases in imports that exactly offset the increase in imports resulting from the expansion of income.

Export multiplier.   Now consider the effects of an increase in exports resulting, say, from a boom in one of the country's trading partners. The effects under fixed exchange rates, shown in Figure 39-2, are an increase in national income and a balance of trade *surplus*.

Again, the nonzero balance of trade is not sustainable under flexible exchange rates. In this case the surplus leads to an appreciation of the dollar and a deterioration of the balance of trade; the fall in net exports in turn reduces aggregate demand, causing the *AD* curve to shift to the left. The fall in national income associated with the reduction in aggregate demand causes a trade account surplus and thus leads to a further appreciation of the dollar.

Once again, the solution to this apparently complicated interaction can be seen quite simply by reference to Equation 2, and again the answer is a surprising one.

Because the balance of trade is zero before and after the increase in exports, the economy behaves as if there were no foreign sector.

In terms of Figure 39-2, the appreciation causes the *NX* and the *AD* curves to shift to the left until they have been restored to their original position.

With zero capital mobility and flexible exchange rates, the export multiplier is zero.

The initial autonomous increase in *X* is offset by a combination of a decline in *X* and an increase in *IM* due to the appreciation of the dollar. As a result, the trade account remains in balance and there is no net change in desired aggregate expenditure or, hence, in national income.

The insulation properties of a flexible exchange rate.   These results led many economists to argue that a flexible exchange rate would *insulate* an economy from foreign disturbances that cause the demand for the home economy's exports to change. Thus a flexible rate was often said to cushion the domestic economy against cyclical variations in economic activity in other countries.

Suppose, for example, that Europe goes into a recession. The decline in European income will lead to a reduction in demand for goods exported from the United States. The fall in exports will reduce income in the United States through the multiplier effect. However, if the value of the dollar is allowed to respond to market forces, it will depreciate, because the trade account deficit reflects an excess supply of dollars on the market for foreign exchange. This fall in the external value of the dollar will stimulate demand for U.S. exports and encourage the substitution of U.S. goods for imports. Thus, the depreciation will provide a stimulus to demand in the United States that will, at least partially, offset the depressing effect of the European recession.

This insulation property, combined with the result that flexible exchange rates increase the multiplier for changes in domestic expenditure (which enhances the effectiveness of domestic stabilization), provided the basis for many economists to advocate flexible exchange rates. However, as we shall see in the next section of this chapter, these results depend crucially on the simplifying assumption that there is no capital mobility.

International Capital Mobility

As we saw in Chapter 38, capital flows are influenced by domestic interest rates. An increase in U.S. interest rates will attract an inflow of short-run capital. A fall in U.S. interest rates will have the opposite effect, as capital moves elsewhere to take advantage of the now relatively higher foreign rates. (Although long-term capital flows are typically less sensitive to interest rate differentials than short-term flows, they also show some response.)

When foreign investors buy securities that are issued by U.S. corporations or governments, or when they invest in U.S. industry, the capital inflow causes an increase in the demand for U.S. dollars in the foreign exchange market. Conversely, the acquisition of foreign assets by U.S. citizens represents a capital outflow and causes an increase in the supply of dollars in the foreign exchange market.

As we shall now see, this interest responsiveness of international capital flows affects the mechanism by which monetary and fiscal policies influence the economy and thus alters the effectiveness of those policies. The operation of these policies can not only differ sharply from the closed-economy results emphasized earlier in this book, but also differ from the simplified open-economy results with no international capital mobility that we have studied so far in this chapter.

We continue to focus on the flexible exchange rate case.

Flexible Exchange Rates

Capital mobility complicates the analysis in the first part of this chapter in two related ways. First, the balance of payments is no longer equal to the balance of trade; it is equal to the sum of the balances on the trade and capital accounts. Second, the effect of a domestic demand disturbance on the balance of payments, and hence on the exchange rate, depends on not only its impact on national income but also its impact on interest rates.

Here we focus on the different effects that monetary and fiscal policy have when there is a flexible exchange rate and international capital flows. The key to this difference is something we have already encountered earlier in this book—the different effects the two policies have on interest rates.

In a closed economy monetary and fiscal policies that have the same influence on income have opposite effects on interest rates.

We saw in Chapter 31 that expansionary monetary policy exerts its influence on income primarily by reducing interest rates and thus stimulating interest-sensitive expenditure. We saw in Chapter 34 that fiscal-policy-induced increases in national income are accompanied by increases in interest rates. (See page 730.)

Because monetary and fiscal policies have opposite effects on interest rates, it is important to distinguish between them when considering an open economy with interest-sensitive international capital flows.

Fiscal policy and the capital account. The effects of fiscal policy on the capital account of an open economy are related to the interest rate effects that it would have in a closed economy. Expansionary fiscal policy, for example, pushes interest rates up; in an open economy, this leads to a capital inflow as foreign and domestic investors seek to sell foreign assets and buy higher-yield U.S. assets. In summary:

An expansionary fiscal policy will put upward pressure on interest rates and lead to an inflow of foreign capital, thereby moving the capital account toward a surplus. A contractionary fiscal policy will have the opposite effects.

Monetary policy and the capital account. Because monetary policy influences interest rates in a closed economy, it will also influence the capital account in an open economy:[6]

An expansionary monetary policy will put downward pressure on interest rates and lead to an outflow of capital, thereby moving the capital account toward a deficit. A contractionary monetary policy will have the opposite effects.

The Effectiveness of Fiscal Policy

Suppose that the government seeks to remove a recessionary gap by expansionary fiscal policy. An increase in government expenditures or a reduction in taxes, or both, will increase income through the multiplier effect and reduce the size of the gap. As we saw earlier in this chapter, this also will cause a movement along the net export function, leading to a deterioration of the trade account.

In the absence of capital mobility, the deterioration of the trade account leads to a depreciation of the dollar; the resulting increase in net exports reinforces the fiscal stimulus and thus increases the size of the fiscal multiplier. With the introduction of capital mobility, we need to consider the impact of the fiscal stimulus on the capital account of the balance of payments.

Capital flows and the crowding-out effect. In a closed economy, a fiscal stimulus causes domestic interest rates to rise. This causes interest-sensitive private

---

[6] Typically, a fall in U.S. interest rates will lead to a fall in interest rates in many foreign countries. However, the interest rate differential still leads to a deficit on capital account. For the sake of simplicity, we can thus safely ignore changes in foreign interest rates in this and subsequent discussions.

expenditures to fall, thus partially offsetting the initial expansionary effect of the fiscal stimulus. As we saw in Chapter 34, this *crowding-out effect* plays an important role in the analysis of fiscal policy in a closed economy.

In an open economy, the crowding-out effect involves an additional channel because of induced effects of international capital flows on net exports. Higher domestic interest rates will induce a capital inflow; if—as is likely—this capital inflow is larger than the balance-of-trade deficit induced by the expansion of national income, it will cause the domestic currency to appreciate.[7] This will depress demand by discouraging exports and by encouraging the substitution of imports for domestically produced goods. The initial expansionary effect of the fiscal stimulus will be offset to a considerable extent by the effects of currency appreciation; crowding out of fiscal policy will be achieved in part by decreased net exports.

Under flexible exchange rates and capital mobility, there will be a crowding out of net exports that will reduce the effectiveness of fiscal policy.

It is possible for the crowding-out effect of fiscal policy to be mitigated by an accommodating monetary policy. Suppose that, in response to the increase in the demand for money induced by the fiscal expansion, the Fed increases the money supply so as to maintain domestic interest rates at their initial level. There will then be no capital inflow and no tendency for the currency to appreciate. Equilibrium national income will increase, just as in the zero capital mobility case.

The Effectiveness of Monetary Policy

Suppose that the Fed seeks to stimulate demand through an expansionary monetary policy. The Fed buys bonds in the open market, thereby increasing bank reserves and the money supply and reducing interest rates. This stimulates interest-sensitive expenditure and leads to an increase in national income. With zero capital mobility, as shown earlier in this chapter, the increase in national income leads to a

balance-of-trade deficit, a depreciation of the dollar, and a further increase of aggregate demand and national income.

When capital is mobile internationally, lower interest rates will cause an outflow of capital and thus a deficit on the capital account. This will reinforce the deficit on the trade account and will reinforce the pressures for the dollar to depreciate, stimulating exports and reinforcing the expansion in national income. Income and employment will be stimulated not only by the fall in interest rates, but also by the increased demand for domestically produced goods that has been brought about by a depreciation of the currency. The initial monetary stimulus will be *reinforced* by the effects of currency depreciation.

Under flexible exchange rates, monetary policy is a powerful tool for influencing national income and employment. Because capital flows are interest sensitive, a depreciation of the currency is an additional channel through which an increase in the money supply stimulates aggregate demand.

A Monetary-Fiscal Mix for Growth

Monetary and fiscal policy can be used in combination to influence the economy's growth.

Suppose that the current equilibrium involves low national saving, perhaps because of a large government deficit. Can anything be done to alter the level of savings and investment, while maintaining the current level of income, so as to generate a higher rate of growth in the economy?

Figure 39-4 shows how this can be achieved by changing the mix of monetary and fiscal policy. A fiscal contraction (in the form of a reduction in government purchases, G, or an increase in taxes, T) increases net savings at the current level of income. A monetary expansion increases national asset formation (reduced interest rates lead to higher investment, I, and depreciation of the currency leads to higher net exports, $X - IM$, and hence smaller capital outflows).

A move toward fiscal restraint and monetary ease can leave national income unchanged while increasing national saving and national asset formation.

Note that the fall in the government budget deficit (due to the reduction in G or the increase in T) is accompanied by a fall in the trade deficit; this link

---

[7] It is theoretically possible that the increase in the current account deficit will exceed the increase in the capital inflow, so that the overall balance of payments moves into deficit. However, the rapid integration of world capital markets in recent years has made capital flows very sensitive to interest rates, so the case treated in the text is the more likely one.

FIGURE 39-4
Growth and the Monetary-Fiscal Policy Mix

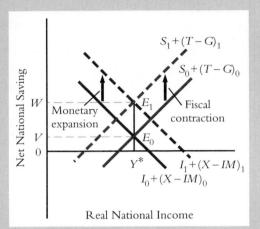

Changes in the mix of monetary and fiscal policy can maintain national income while changing savings, investment, and the balance of trade so as to increase growth. With the initial settings for monetary policy, the net national asset formation function is given by the solid blue line $I_0 + (X - IM)_0$; with the initial setting of fiscal policy, the net national saving function is given by the solid line $S_0 + (T - G)_0$. Equilibrium is at E_0, and national income is at its capacity level, Y^*. The equilibrium level of net national savings is V.

Monetary ease shifts the net national asset formation function to the dashed blue line $I_1 + (X - IM)_1$; fiscal contraction shifts the net national saving function to the dashed red line $S_1 + (T - G)_1$. Equilibrium is at E_1, and national income remains at its capacity level, Y^*. The equilibrium level of net national savings increases to W.

between the two deficits, as we saw in Chapter 34, leads to their being called the *twin deficits*.

The Insulation Properties of Flexible Exchange Rates Revisited

We have seen that international capital mobility enhances the effectiveness of monetary policy under flexible exchange rates but mitigates the effectiveness of fiscal policy. Consider the implications for the effects of an export boom; recall that, in the absence of capital mobility, flexible exchange rates insulate the economy from the effects of such a boom because the export multiplier is zero.

The initial effect of an increase in exports on national income and the balance of trade is as shown

in Figure 39-2; national income rises and there is a balance-of-trade surplus. The rise in national income causes an increase in the demand for money, an increase in the domestic interest rate, and hence a capital inflow. This reinforces the pressures caused by the trade account surplus for the currency to appreciate, and therefore to offset the expansionary impact of the export boom.

Capital mobility does not upset the ability of flexible exchange rates to insulate an open economy from the effects of shifts in the demand for its exports.

Suppose, however, that the boom in the foreign country also gave rise to an increase in foreign interest rates. This would lead to a capital outflow from the United States as funds moved in response to the higher foreign interest rates, and hence to a *depreciation* of the U.S. dollar. The depreciation in turn would lead to an improvement in the balance of trade and an increase in national income.

International capital mobility, by linking domestic and foreign interest rates, provides a channel by which business cycles tend to be correlated across countries.

This accords with the experience of the international economy over the past two decades when the widespread adoption of flexible exchange rates has witnessed a continued correlation of booms and recessions in the major industrial economies.

Policy and Performance During the 1980s

Events in the U.S. economy during the last 20 years or so provide a rich variety of experience that sheds some light on the theory outlined so far in this chapter; in turn, this theory can help us to understand and to interpret the controversies that surround those events. The key developments in the economy (many of which we have already encountered) were as follows:

1. The U.S. economy went into a severe recession during 1981–1982 and then experienced a sustained recovery in output and employment.

Inflation fell from its double-digit levels at the start of the decade to stabilize in the 4–5 percent range for the latter half of the 1980s. Inflation fell further during the recession that began in 1990, although fears of increases in inflation were widespread in 1992 as the Fed relaxed monetary policy in an attempt to speed up a sluggish recovery.

2. The current account deficit soared from a position of approximate balance at the start of the 1980s to reach a peak of about $160 billion in 1987; it then fell in each successive year through 1991.

3. During the first half of the 1980s the external value of the U.S. dollar soared dramatically; it then fell gradually for several years, and then stabilized in a relatively narrow range during the late 1980s and early 1990s.

The major policy developments were as follows:

1. As we saw in Chapter 31, the United States introduced sharply contractionary monetary policy at the start of the 1980s in an effort to halt inflation and was subsequently geared to providing sufficient monetary growth to meet the demand for money resulting from real income growth and steady but low inflation.

2. As we saw in Chapter 34, the federal budget deficit soared to record levels during the decade, despite a prolonged recovery in the last half of the 1980s and a great deal of political rhetoric directed toward deficit reduction. In 1992 it remained large and was projected to continue at near record levels well into the decade.

3. Protectionist sentiment emerged during the decade, leading to the passage of the Omnibus Trade Bill in 1988, to numerous measures enacted against specific trading partners in the late 1980s and 1990s, and to fears and threats of more protectionist measures in the coming years.

Monetary Contraction and Disinflation

We have seen earlier in this chapter that monetary policy exerts a very powerful influence on the economy under flexible exchange rates. Contractionary monetary policy operates in part through higher interest rates and in part through an appreciation of the domestic currency. This accords well with what happened during the first few years of the 1980s.

The dramatic rise in interest rates in 1981–1982 curtailed consumption and investment expenditure,

and the high value of the dollar placed U.S. firms that produce traded goods (i.e., goods for export and goods that face competition from imports) at a cost disadvantage relative to foreign producers. Falling production, rising unemployment, and many business failures resulted, but inflation also fell sharply.

Monetary contraction worked as expected: High interest rates and an appreciation of the dollar led to a recession and reduced inflation. The appreciation of the dollar during this period discouraged exports and encouraged imports, and it thus contributed to the emergence of a large current account deficit.

Fiscal Deficits

The dollar became overvalued during the period of tight monetary policy that began in 1980. If a temporary *overshooting* of the exchange rate (as discussed in Chapter 38) had been all that was involved in that overvaluation, the dollar would have come down shortly thereafter. Indeed, many economists expected it to do so. However, the dollar remained high throughout the 1981–1985 period, accompanying the record current account deficits that occurred over the same period.

Many observers argue that the dollar remained high because of large capital inflows into the United States. These were partly a result of the record government budget deficit, which at one point exceeded 5 percent of GDP. Some of the fiscal deficit was financed by private domestic savings, but much also had to be financed by foreign capital inflows.

The foreign borrowing in turn resulted in the current account deficit. As we saw in Chapter 38, equilibrium in the foreign exchange market means that a capital inflow is *necessarily* matched by a current account deficit (see page 819). Only when these two are equal will the demand for dollars by foreign investors who wish to buy U.S. capital assets be matched by the supply of dollars by those U.S. citizens who wish to import foreign goods and services. Thus:

The fall in national savings rates, precipitated by the federal budget deficit, meant that capital had to be imported from abroad; capital inflows were accompanied by high interest rates, a strong dollar, and a current account deficit.

Note that in this view the government deficit is the *cause* of the current account deficit, and the influence of the high dollar on exports and the demand for imports is the *mechanism* by which the current account deficit is brought about. In one study, it is estimated that about two-thirds of the U.S. current account deficit during the 1980s and about two-thirds of the appreciation of the dollar between 1980 and 1985 can be explained by the U.S. policy mix of fiscal ease and monetary tightness, combined with fiscal restraint in Germany, Japan, the United Kingdom, and France.[8]

The association of the government budget deficit with a current account deficit caused many commentators to speak of the *twin deficits* problem, as noted earlier. According to this view, the current account deficit was the necessary counterpart to the massive capital inflows that the U.S. economy experienced over this period, and the fall in national saving resulting from the fiscal deficits was one important cause of the capital inflows.

Other economists have emphasized that the large capital inflows that occurred were primarily responding not so much to high interest rates but to the combination of low inflation and relative prosperity in the United States, which made the country a safe and profitable place in which to invest, and that the current account deficit was a necessary by-product of these inflows.

With the help of Figure 39-4, we can see that the two explanations of the capital inflows are not mutually exclusive. The high government deficits decreased national saving, and the enhanced investment opportunities increased net national asset formation; both lead to capital inflows and a current account deficit.

Whatever the cause of the capital inflows, it is widely acknowledged that, given those inflows, a current account deficit also had to occur.

The evidence is that the fiscal deficits contributed to the sustained recovery that occurred during the second half of the 1980s. Although there was crowding out as discussed above, the record fiscal deficits provided a significant fiscal stimulus. Further, expansionary monetary policy reinforced the fiscal stimulus.

The monetary expansion occurred in two ways. First, there was some easing of monetary policy,

especially relative to the disinflationary stance of 1980–1981. (See the discussion in Chapter 31, pages 660–664.) Second, the appreciation of the dollar in the early stages of the recovery meant that import prices were sharply lower than they would have been otherwise; this meant that the price level was lower than it would otherwise have been and hence that the *real* money supply was larger. The increase in the real money supply amounted to monetary stimulus. As Harvard economist and former chairman of the Council of Economic Advisers Martin Feldstein said, "While expansionary fiscal policy therefore did contribute to the greater-than-expected rise of real GDP in 1983–84, it was through the unusual channel of dollar appreciation. The fiscal expansion raised output because it caused a favorable supply shock to prices—not because it was a traditional stimulus to demand."[9]

The latter part of the decade witnessed falling U.S. interest rates and a falling value of the U.S. dollar. The lower interest rates, and the increased U.S. saving resulting from the recovery in national income, led to a reduction in capital inflows. In turn, this, in conjunction with the depreciation of the dollar, led to a substantial reduction in the current account deficit.

Protectionism and the Current Account Deficit[10]

In spite of the vigorous expansion of the economy that occurred in the second half of the 1980s, many export- and import-competing sectors (often called the traded-goods sectors, in contrast with sectors that produce goods that do not enter into international trade, call nontraded goods) remained depressed. The plight of these traded-goods industries was, to many observers, obviously related to the current account deficit. Not surprisingly, this led to a call for protection.

Pressure was put on major trading partners (in particular, Japan, Germany, and Canada) to reduce their current account surpluses, and a number of steps were taken to curb imports. Some steps were specific, such as the tariff that was imposed in May

---

[8] Peter Hooper and Catherine Mann, "The Emergence and Persistence of the U.S. External Imbalance: 1980–87," Princeton University, International Finance Section, 1988.

[9] Martin Feldstein and Douglas Elmendorf, "Budget Deficits, Tax Incentives, and Inflation: A Surprising Lesson from the 1983–84 Recovery," National Bureau of Economic Research, Working Paper No. 2819, 1989.

[10] It would be useful to review the discussion in Chapter 37 of the rise of protectionism that occurred in this period.

1986 on Canadian cedar shakes and shingles. Some were very broad in scope; the highest profile was the Omnibus Trade Bill, passed in 1988. Although the current account deficit fell in the late 1980s and early 1990s, it remained historically high, and the pressures for protectionism persisted.

The motivation for these protectionist measures was easy enough to understand, but many economists felt that the measures were seriously misguided. First, they threatened to upset the fabric of international trading relations and cooperation that had been carefully built up through multilateral negotiation during the post–World War II period. Second, the measures were likely to be largely ineffective in terms of their goal of reducing the current account deficit. As we have seen, the current account deficit is a necessary counterpart to the capital inflows that the U.S. economy is experiencing, and unless the root causes of the capital inflows are dealt with, the current account deficit will persist, with or without protectionist measures.

To see this important point, assume that import tariffs, surcharges, and quotas reduced imports by enough to bring the current account into balance. This would appear to achieve the goals of the policy.[11] However, suppose that after the introduction of the protectionist measures and "correction" of the current account deficit, people still wished to bring capital into the United States. With a balanced current account, there would not be anyone willing to supply the dollars to the would-be capital importers. Consequently, the dollar would start to appreciate. This would lead to a reduction in exports and an increase in imports until the original current account deficit, equal to the desired capital inflow, was reestablished.

---

[11] But note that it does *not* mean that U.S. national income or, hence, the economic well-being of U.S. citizens, would be enhanced; as we saw in Chapter 37, protectionism is generally counterproductive for these purposes.

SUMMARY

1. Under fixed exchange rates and zero capital mobility, the responsiveness of imports to national income reduces the size of the autonomous spending multiplier and thus acts as an automatic stabilizer. In this case national income and the balance of trade surplus move in opposite directions; increases in national income are accompanied by a deterioration in the balance of trade.

2. Under fixed exchange rates and zero capital mobility, changes in the demand for exports lead to a change in equilibrium national income; this is called the export multiplier. In this case national income and the balance of trade surplus move in the same direction; increases in national income are accompanied by an improvement in the balance of trade.

3. Under flexible exchange rates and zero capital mobility, the balance of trade is zero, so net exports do not influence desired aggregate expenditure. As a result the economy behaves as if there were no international trade; there is no automatic stabilizer role played by imports and the export multiplier is zero. The latter is argued to mean that flexible exchange rates insulate the domestic economy from foreign disturbances.

4. International capital mobility means that capital flows, and hence the capital account balance, depends on interest rates. This means that the capital account is influenced by both fiscal and monetary policy, because both influence domestic interest rates. Capital mobility also means that the current account balance can be different from zero; the current account deficit will equal net capital inflows.

5. Under a flexible exchange rate, fiscal policy will be offset by a crowding out of net exports unless it is accompanied by an

accommodating monetary policy that prevents changes in interest rates and the exchange rate.

6. Under a flexible exchange rate, monetary policy is effective in influencing national income. When capital flows are highly interest-elastic, the main channel by which an increase in the money supply increases demand for domestically produced goods is through a depreciation of the exchange rate, which in turn leads to an increase in net exports.

7. Tight monetary policy during 1980–1981 had the predicted effects of high interest rates, a strong dollar, a severe recession, and a reduction in inflation. During the next several years, fiscal deficits contributed to a recovery of output and employment and also to sustained high interest rates and a strong dollar. These fiscal deficits were also accompanied by persistent current account deficits, and the two were referred to as the twin deficits.

TOPICS FOR REVIEW

Net exports as an automatic stabilizer

Export multiplier

Flexible exchange rates and insulation of the domestic economy

Fiscal and monetary policy and capital flows

Fiscal and monetary policy under flexible exchange rates

Twin deficits

The current account and protectionism

DISCUSSION QUESTIONS

1. Explain how a country can influence the external value of its currency by (a) direct intervention in the foreign exchange market, (b) fiscal policy, and (c) monetary policy.

2. It is often the case that, despite a formal commitment to flexible exchange rates, central banks try to stabilize the exchange rate and to "mimic" policies of other major countries. Why might a central bank oppose both a depreciation and an appreciation of its currency? Can you cite any episodes in which the Fed has faced this dilemma in the past two or three years?

3. In 1992 a widely read bank newsletter stated that "The continued existence of U.S. trade deficits reflects an imbalance of national saving and investment, not any fundamental decline in U.S. national competitiveness." Do you agree? Explain why or why not.

4. Suppose that the government deficit remains high, so that national savings remain low, but that the rising U.S. national debt and the fear of inflation cause a sharp fall in the desire on the part of foreigners to invest in the United States. Outline the key macroeconomic effects of this shift. What policies might you recommend to deal with these consequences?

5. In a column in the May 16, 1989, issue of the *Wall Street Journal*, economist Herbert Stein argued that much of the concern about the current account deficit is misplaced because the accompanying capital inflow has resulted in a stock of productive capital in the United States that is $700 billion higher than it would otherwise have been. What is the basis for such a statement? Should we worry about the current account deficit?

6. Consider the question posed by economist Fred Bergsten in a monograph that was published in 1988, *America in the World Economy: A Strategy for the 1990s*. What would be the implications for the current account positions and policies of other countries if the U.S. current account deficit had shrunk from $155 billion in 1987 to $5 billion by 1992?

7. Consider the following two potential sources of dollar appreciation: (a) contractionary monetary policy followed by the Fed and (b) foreign inflation. Explain how each could lead to dollar appreciation. What are the differences for the economy? How would you distinguish between the two?

8. In a speech in December 1980, the governor of the Bank of Canada stated that "the rapid run-up of U.S. short-term [interest] rates is bound to have a major impact on Canada through increases in interest rates [in Canada] or through a fall in the foreign exchange value of the Canadian dollar, or some combination of the two." Why must one of these responses occur? What policies could the Bank of Canada have followed in order to influence which of the possible responses occurs? Which would have been preferable?

40

Growth in the Less-Developed Countries

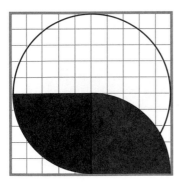

I n the civilized and comfortable urban life of today's developed countries, most people have lost sight of the fact that a short time ago—very short in terms of the life span of the earth—people were nomadic food gatherers, catching an existence as best they could from what nature threw their way. It has been only about 10,000 years since the first agricultural revolution, when people changed from food gatherers to food producers. Throughout most of subsequent human history, civilizations were based on a comfortable life for a privileged minority and unremitting toil for the vast majority. It has been only within the last century that ordinary people have been able to expect leisure and high consumption standards—and then only in the world's economically developed countries.

The Uneven Pattern of Development

Close to 6 billion people are alive today,[1] but the wealthy parts of the world—where people work no more than 40 or 50 hours per week, enjoy substantial leisure, and have a level of consumption at or above *half* that attained by the United States—contain no more than 20 percent of the world's population. Many of the rest struggle for subsistence. Many exist on a level at or below that endured by peasants in ancient Egypt or Babylon.

The richest countries with the highest per capita incomes are referred to by the United Nations as **developed countries.** These include the United States, Canada, most of the countries of Western Europe, Australia, New Zealand, Japan, and a few others. The poorer countries are referred to by the UN as the **developing countries**[2] and include a diverse set of countries. Some, such as Thailand and Indonesia, are growing very rapidly, while others, such as Ethiopia and Papua New Guinea, actually have negative growth rates of per capita real income. Between these two is another group of nations, variously called **newly industrialized economies (NIEs)** or newly industrialized countries (NICs). They include South Korea, Singapore, Taiwan, and Hong Kong. They have grown rapidly and typically have per capita incomes close to 50 percent of those found in the developed nations.

---

[1] The current rate of population growth is so high that the statement in the text will be correct when you read it, even though Table 40-1 correctly shows only 5.2 billion as the population in 1989.

[2] The terminology of development is often confusing. *Underdeveloped, less developed,* and *developing* do not mean the same thing in ordinary English, yet each has been used to describe the same phenomenon. For the most part, we shall use the term *developing,* which is the term currently used by the United Nations to describe the lower-income countries. Some of them are making progress, that is, developing in the ordinary sense of that word; others are not.

Seeing the problem of raising per capita incomes in a poorer country as one of economic *development* recognizes that the whole structure of its economy often needs to be altered to create economic growth. This is a complex task; many countries remain undeveloped today in spite of decades of effort by their governments to get them on a path of sustained growth.

Data on per capita incomes throughout the world (as shown in Table 40-1) cannot be accurate down to the last $100.[3] Nevertheless, the data reflect enormous real differences in living standards that no statistical inaccuracies can hide. The *development gap*—the discrepancy between the standards of living in countries at either end of the distribution—is real and large.

Figure 40-1 provides another way of looking at inequality. It shows the geographic distribution of per capita income. Modern political discussions of income distribution distinguish between richer and poorer nations as "North" versus "South." The map reveals why.

The consequences of low income levels can be severe. In a rich country such as the United States,

variations in rainfall are reflected in farm output and farm income. In poor countries variations in rainfall are often reflected in the death rate. In these countries, many people live so close to a subsistence level that slight fluctuations in the food supply bring death by starvation to large numbers. Other, less dramatic characteristics of poverty include inadequate diet, poor health, short life expectancy, and illiteracy.

For these reasons, reformers in developing countries feel a sense of urgency not felt by their counterparts in rich countries. Yet, as Table 40-2 shows, some of the poorest countries in the world are among those with very low or negative growth rates of per capita GDP. As a result:

The development gap has been widening for the very poorest countries.

As we shall see, this is a problem of both output and population. It is also an international political problem.

What are the causes of underdevelopment, and how may they be overcome?

Barriers to Economic Development

Income per capita grows when aggregate income grows faster than population. Many forces can impede such growth.

---

[3] There are many problems when we compare national incomes across countries. For example, home-grown food is vitally important to living standards in underdeveloped countries, but it is excluded, or at best imperfectly included, in the national income statistics of most countries. In the United States, significant amounts of GDP go to heating houses during cold winters. Such heating is not necessary in countries that have warm climates.

TABLE 40-1   Income and Population Differences Among Groups of Countries, 1989

GNP per capita (US$)	(1) Number of countries	(2) GNP (US$ millions) 1989	(3) Population (millions) 1989	(4) GNP per capita (US$) 1989	(5) Percent world population	(6) Percent world GNP
Less than $500	46	970,000	2,915	330	56.1	5.0
$500–$1,499	43	459,000	500	920	9.6	2.4
$1,500–$3,499	34	1,344,000	578	2,330	11.1	6.9
$3,500–$5,999	14	1,554,000	374	4,160	7.2	8.0
$6,000 or more	48	15,170,000	830	18,280	16.0	77.8
World[a]	185	19,497,000	5,197	3,750	100.0	100.0

Source: World Bank Atlas 1990, The World Bank, Washington, D.C.
[a]World Bank staff estimate

The unequal distribution of world income is shown in columns 5 and 6. The poorest half of the world's population earns only 5 percent of world income. The richest 16 percent earns nearly 80 percent of world income.

FIGURE 40-1
Countries of the World, Classified by Per Capita GNP, 1985

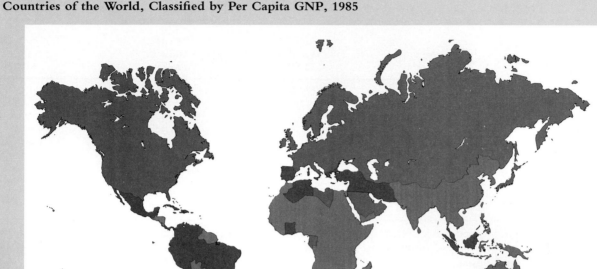

Key:
Per capita GNP

[■] $5,000 or more   [■] $1,001 – 4,999   [■] Less than $1,000

There is a sharp geographical division between "North" and "South" in the level of income per capita.
The nations of the world are classified here according to three levels of measured per capita GNP. The poorest group, shown in green, represents 31 percent of the world's population. The middle group, shown in red, represents about 41 percent of world population. The wealthiest group, shown in blue, includes all of North America, Europe, the (then) Soviet Union, and Japan and represents only 25 percent of the world's population. Areas in white indicate that no data are available. See Table 40-1 for more detail.

Rapid Population Growth

Population growth is one of the central problems of economic development. For example, in the decade 1980–1990 Ecuador, Ethiopia, and Papua New Guinea had growth rates of population of 2.7, 2.9, and 2.4 percent per year alongside GDP growth rates of 2.2, 1.8, and 1.8 percent, respectively. Hence, they experienced *negative* rates of growth of GDP *per capita* (of –0.5, –0.8, and –0.7 percent per year). Many less-developed countries have rates of population growth that are nearly as large as their rates of growth of GDP. As a result, their standards of living are barely higher than they were 100 years ago. They have made appreciable gains in aggregate income, but most of the gains have been literally eaten up by

the increasing population. This is illustrated in Table 40-2.

The critical importance of population growth to living standards was perceived early in the nineteenth century by the Reverend Thomas Malthus. He asserted two relations concerning rates of increase. First, food production tends to increase in an arithmetic progression (e.g., 100, 103, 106, 109, 112, where the increments in this example are *three units per period*). Second, population tends to increase in a geometric ratio (e.g., 100, 103, 106.09, 109.27, 112.55, where the increase in this example is 3 *percent per period*). As a result of these relations Malthus argued that, under conditions of natural growth, population will always tend to outrun the growth in food supply. The difference in the above example may

TABLE 40-2   The Relationship Between the Level and the Rate of Growth of Per Capita Income, 1980–1989

Growth of GNP per capita 1980–1989	Number of countries[a]	GNP (US$ millions) 1989	Population (millions) 1989	GNP per capita (US$) 1989
Less than 0%	64	899,000	820	1,100
0%–0.9%	16	654,000	393	1,660
1.0%–1.9%	21	2,209,000	244	9,050
2.0%–2.9%	16	9,575,000	673	14,230
3.0% or more	29	4,384,000	2,441	1,800
No data	39		626	—

Source: *World Bank Atlas 1990*, The World Bank, Washington, D.C.
[a]Countries with more than 1 million population

The very poorest countries spend much of their increase in income on a rising population. Thus, their increase in income per capita is less than half that of the countries that are already richer. The gap in income between rich and many of the very poor countries is not closing.

not seem like much after only 5 periods. But after 20 periods the arithmetic increase in food supply has increased it to 160 while the geometric increase in the population has increased it to 181.

Malthus' prediction gave economics the name of "the dismal science." In some poor areas of the world, the predictions seem all too accurate, even today. There, agricultural methods are fairly traditional so that food production increases only slowly while population tends to increase at more rapid rates. The result is subsistence living, with population held in check by low life expectancies and periodic famines.

Fortunately over most of the world, Malthus' predictions have been proved false. Two reasons are paramount. First, Malthus underestimated the importance of technological change, which has increased productivity in agriculture at a *geometric* rate far higher than the rate at which the demand for food has been growing in most advanced countries. Second, he underestimated the extent of voluntary restrictions of population growth due to the widespread use of birth control techniques, from delayed marriages to various mechanical devices. As a result, population has grown more slowly than has the production of food (and most other things) in developed countries. For them, living standards have been rising rather than falling.

For the more advanced industrialized countries, Malthusian pressures are not a problem today. For many poor countries, where people subsist on what they grow for themselves, the tendency for the growth in population to outstrip the growth in the food supply makes Malthusian pressures a current threat.

Figure 40-2 illustrates actual and projected world population. By now, the population problem is almost completely limited to developing countries. About 97 percent of the expected growth in the world's population between now and 2050 will be in the developing countries of Africa, Asia, and Latin America.

Inadequate or Inefficiently Used Natural Resources

A country's supply of natural resources is important. A country with infertile land and inadequate supplies of natural resources will find growth in income more difficult to achieve than one that is richly endowed with such resources.

How these resources are managed also matters. When farmland is divided into many small parcels, it may be much more difficult to achieve the advantages of modern agriculture than it is when the land is available in huge tracts for large-scale farming.

FIGURE 40-2
World Population Since A.D. 1

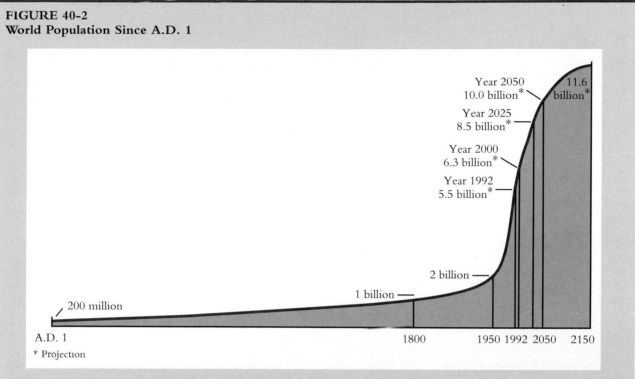

World population reached 5.5 billion in 1992 and is projected to rise to 10 billion by the middle of the next century. The population of industrialized countries has nearly stabilized. But in developing countries, population is skyrocketing. Up to 97 percent of population growth between now and 2050 will occur in developing countries. By that time, the 1992 population of 5.5 billion will have reached 10 billion. Birth and death rates among present populations allow estimates to be made up to about the middle of the next century with reasonable accuracy. The projection to 11.6 billion in 2150 is much more conjectural and highly uncertain. (*Source:* United Nations Population Fund.)

Fragmented land holdings may result from a dowry or inheritance system, or it may be politically imposed. One of the popular policies following the Mexican revolution early in this century was the redistribution of land from large landowners to ordinary peasants. Today, however, the fragmented land ownership prevents Mexican agriculture from producing in the 1990s at costs low enough to compete in international markets. The Mexican government now faces an agonizing choice between allowing its popular land reforms to be reversed or continuing to protect a large agricultural sector whose inefficiency is rapidly increasing relative to competing suppliers.

Although abundant supplies of natural resources can assist growth, they are neither sufficient to ensure growth nor always necessary for it. Some countries with large supplies of natural resources have poor growth performances because the economic structure encourages waste. Prime examples are the former USSR, Argentina, and Uganda over most of the last 50 years. In contrast, other countries have enjoyed rapid rates of economic growth based on human capital and entrepreneurial ability in spite of a dearth of natural resources. Prime examples are Switzerland in earlier centuries, Japan over the last 100 years, and Singapore, Hong Kong, Taiwan, and South Korea in the last 40 years.

When one discusses inefficiency in resource use, it helps to distinguish between two kinds of economic inefficiency, which are studied in microeconomics. *Allocative inefficiency* occurs when factors of production are used to make an inefficient combination of goods. There is too much of some goods and too little of others. This means that the society is at the "wrong" point on its production possibility boundary. If resources are reallocated to produce less of some and more of other types of goods, some people can be made better off while no one is made worse off.

Productive inefficiency occurs when factors of production are used in inefficient combinations. Given the prices of capital and labor, some production processes use too much capital relative to labor, while others use too little. This means that the society is inside its production possibility boundary (as shown in Chapter 1). If factor combinations are altered, more of all goods can be produced.

Monopolistic market structures, as well as taxes, tariffs, and subsidies, are some important sources of the distortions that lead to both allocative and productive inefficiencies.

Another kind of inefficiency, called **X-inefficiency**, occurs either when firms do not seek to maximize their profits, or when owners of factors of production do not seek to maximize their material welfare. X-inefficiency also puts the society inside its production possibility boundary.

Professor Harvey Leibenstein of the University of California, the economist who developed the concept, has studied X-inefficiency in developing countries. He cites psychological evidence to show that nonmaximizing behavior is typical of situations in which pressure that has been placed on decision makers is either very low or very high. If the customary living standard can be obtained with little effort, according to this evidence, people are likely to follow customary behavior and spend little time trying to make optimal decisions. When pressure builds up, so that making a reasonable income becomes more difficult, optimizing behavior becomes more common. Under extreme pressure, however, such as very low living standards or a rapidly deteriorating environment, people become disoriented and once again do not adopt optimizing behavior.

X-inefficiency may be typical of industries, and whole economies, where customary behavior leads to acceptable living standards or where the challenges become overwhelming.[4]

---

[4] Although such behavior is no doubt often found in some LDCs, it is also sometimes found in advanced countries. For example, studies of monopolies have often suggested a preference on the part of their managers and workers for the "quiet life" rather than an active search for profit and income-maximizing forms of behavior.

Inadequate Human Resources

A well-developed entrepreneurial class, motivated and trained to organize resources for efficient production, is often missing in poor countries. The cause may be that managerial positions are awarded on the basis of family status or political patronage (leading to X-inefficiency); it may be the presence of economic or cultural attitudes that do not favor acquisition of wealth by organizing productive activities; or it may simply be the absence of the quantity or quality of education or training that is required.

In today's world, much production is knowledge-intensive. This puts a premium on a well-educated work force. The ability to read, do basic calculations, operate electronic equipment, and follow relatively complex instructions are important requirements for much modern labor. Failure to create such essential labor skills can be an important cause of lack of growth.

Poor health is another source of inadequate human resources. When the labor force is healthy, less time is lost and more effective effort is expended.

Cultural Barriers

Traditions and habitual ways of doing business vary among societies, and not all are equally conducive to productivity. The late German sociologist Max Weber argued that the "Protestant ethic" encouraged the acquisition of wealth and hence encouraged more growth than systems of belief that directed activity away from the economic sphere.

Often in developing countries, cultural forces are a source of X-inefficiency. Sometimes personal considerations of family, past favors, or traditional friendship or enmity are more important than market incentives in motivating behavior. One may find a firm that is too small struggling to survive against a larger rival and learn that the owner prefers to remain small because expansion would require use of nonfamily capital or leadership. To avoid paying too harsh a competitive price for built-in inefficiency, the firm's owners may then attempt to influence the government to prevent larger firms from being formed, or try to secure restrictions on the sale of output—and they may well succeed. Such behavior will inhibit economic growth.

In an environment in which people believe that it is more important who your father is than what you do, it may take a generation to persuade employers to change their attitudes and another generation to persuade workers that times have changed. In a traditional society in which children are expected to stay in their parents' occupations, it is more difficult for the labor force to change its characteristics and to adapt to the requirements of growth than in a society in which upward mobility is itself a goal. (These are aspects of the traditional economy that we first discussed in Chapter 1.)

Structuring incentives is a widely used form of policy action in market-oriented economies. However, if people habitually bribe the tax collector rather than pay taxes, they will not be likely to respond to policies that are supposed to work by raising or lowering taxes. All that will change is the size of the bribe.

There is lively debate on how much to make of the significance of differing cultural attitudes. Some analysts believe that traditional considerations dominate peasant societies to the exclusion of economic responses; others suggest that any resulting inefficiency may be relatively small.

The fact that existing social, religious, or legal patterns may make growth more difficult does not in itself imply that they are undesirable.

Instead, it suggests that the benefits of these patterns must be weighed against the costs, of which the limitation on growth is one. When people derive satisfaction from a religion whose beliefs inhibit growth or when they value a society in which every household owns its own land and is more nearly self-sufficient than in another society, they may be quite willing to pay a price in terms of growth opportunities forgone.

Inadequate Infrastructure

Key services, called **infrastructure**, such as transportation and a communications network, are necessary to efficient commerce. Roads, bridges, railways, and harbors are needed to transport people, materials, and finished goods. Phone and postal services, water supply, and sanitation are essential to economic development.

The absence, for whatever reason, of a dependable infrastructure can impose severe barriers to economic development.

Many governments feel that money spent on a new steel mill shows more impressive results than money spent on such infrastructure investments as automating the telephone system. Yet private, growth-creating, entrepreneurial activity will be discouraged more by the absence of good telephone communications than by the lack of domestically produced steel.

Financial Institutions

The lack of an adequate, trustworthy, and trusted system of financial institutions is often a barrier to development. Investment plays a key role in growth, and an important source of funds for investment is the savings of households and firms. When banks and other financial institutions do not function effectively, the link between private saving and investment may be broken, making it difficult to raise funds for investment.

Many people in poor countries do not trust banks—sometimes with good reason, but often without. Either they do not maintain deposits, or they panic periodically, drawing them out and seeking security for their money in mattresses, in gold, or in real estate. When banks cannot count on their deposits being left in the banking system, they cannot engage in the kind of long-term loans that are needed to finance investments. When this happens, savings do not become available for investment in a productive capacity.

Developing countries not only must create banking institutions but also must develop enough stability and reliability so that people will trust their savings to them.

Development Policies[5]

The past decade has seen a remarkable change in the views of appropriate policies for industrial development. The views that dominated development policies during the decades from 1945 to the early 1980s have given way to a new set of views that reflect the experience of the earlier period.

The Evolution of Views

The Older View

The dominant views on appropriate development strategies from 1945 to the early 1980s were inward looking and interventionist.

---

[5] This section draws heavily from "Globalization and Developing Countries," Main Discussion Paper for the United Nations Symposium in The Hague, 30 March 1992, report by the Rapporteur.

The policies were inward looking in the sense that local industries were fostered primarily to replace imports. These local industries were usually protected with high tariffs (usually well into the three-digit range) and supported by large subsidies and favorable tax treatment. The exchange rate was almost always pegged, usually at an overvalued rate. As we saw in Chapter 38, fixing the exchange rate above its free-market level raises the prices of exports and lowers the prices of imports, which leads to an excess demand for foreign exchange. The argument for keeping export prices high was that foreign demand for traditional exports was inelastic so that (as we saw in Chapter 5) raising their prices would raise the amount received by their sellers. The excess demand for foreign exchange caused by the overvaluation of the currency led to a host of import restrictions and exchange controls such as import licenses and quotas issued by government officials.

Many governments were hostile to foreign investment and made it difficult for multinational firms to locate in their countries. For example, many had local ownership rules requiring that any foreign firm wanting to invest there must set up a subsidiary in which local residents would own at least half of the shares. Much new investment was undertaken by government-owned industries, while subsidization of privately owned, local industries was often heavy and indiscriminate. Industrial activity was often controlled, with a license being required to set up a firm or to purchase supplies of scarce commodities. Much investment was financed by local savings, which were sometimes made voluntarily and sometimes forced by the state. One way of doing the latter was for a state marketing board to be empowered to buy all the outputs of traditional export industries (such as cocoa in Ghana) at very low prices, sell them abroad at high prices, and use the profits so generated to finance government-owned industries.

This whole battery of measures is often referred to as being *inward looking* and based on *import substitution*. Strictly, import substitution refers to the attempt to build local industries behind protectionist walls to replace imports. Often, however, the term is used to refer to the entire battery of related measures just described.

These interventionist measures gave great power to government officials and, not surprisingly, corruption was rife. Bribes were needed to obtain many things, including state subsidies, licenses, and quotas. As a result, many resources were allocated to those who had the most political power and were willing to pay the highest bribes, rather than to those who could use the resources most efficiently.

Heavy subsidization of private firms and state investment in public firms required much money, and the tax structures of many poor countries could not provide sufficient funds. As a result, inflationary finance was often used.[6] Persistent inflation was a major problem in many of these countries. Inflation was almost always in the two-digit range and quite often soared to figures of several hundred percent per year.

Most of the economies where these policies were employed fell short of full central planning and full state ownership of resources. As a result, there was still some private initiative and some profit seeking through normal market means. But the overall policy thrust was interventionist and inward looking.

During the 1980s many governments became skeptical of this development model. Four important events contributed to the reappraisal. First, developing countries that had followed these policies most faithfully had some of the poorest growth records. Second, the GDP growth rates of the more industrialized countries of Eastern Europe and the USSR that had followed interventionist, nonmarket approaches to their own growth were visibly falling behind those of the market-based economies. Third, the countries of Taiwan, Singapore, South Korea, and Hong Kong, which had departed from the accepted model by adopting more market-based policies, were prospering and growing rapidly. Fourth, the globalization of the world's economy led to an understanding that countries could no longer play a full part in world economic growth without a substantial presence of multinational corporations within their boundaries. Given the size of developing countries, this mainly meant the presence of foreign-owned multinationals. We discuss each of these four events in more detail in the next four sections.

Experience of the Developing Countries

Highly interventionist economies fared poorly in the 1950s, 1960s, and 1970s. Economies as varied as Argentina, Burma, Tanzania, Ethiopia, and Ghana

---

[6] Under inflationary finance, the government sells newly created bonds to the central bank, which pays for them with newly created money. The large increase in money supply creates rapid inflation, as we saw in Chapter 31.

were all interventionist and all grew slowly, if at all. In Ethiopia, the emperor was overthrown, and the new government adopted rigid Soviet-style policies. Attempts to collectivize agriculture led, as they had 50 years previously in the USSR, to widespread famine. Some countries, such as Ghana and Nigeria, started from relatively strong economic positions when they first gained their independence but later saw their GDPs and living standards shrink. Other countries, such as India and Kenya, sought a middle way between capitalism and socialism. They fared better than their more highly interventionist neighbors, but their development was still disappointingly slow.

Experience of the Socialist Countries

Underdevelopment is as old as civilization. Concern with it as a remediable condition, however, became a compelling policy issue only within the present century. One incentive behind this new attention to development was the apparent success of planned programs of "crash" development, of which the Soviet experience was the most remarkable, and the Chinese the most recent. Not surprisingly, therefore, the early successes of the growth policies of many Socialist countries provided role models for many of the early development policies of the poorer countries. Their governments sought to copy the planning techniques that appeared to underlie these earlier Socialist successes.

In recent decades, however, the more developed Socialist countries began to discover the limitations of their planning techniques. Highly planned government intervention seems most successful in providing infrastructure and developing basic industries, such as electric power and steel—where these are needed, and where the technology can be copied from more market-oriented economies. It is now seen to be much less successful in providing the entrepreneurial activity, risk taking, and adaptivity to change that are key ingredients to *sustained* economic growth and technological change.

The discrediting of the Soviet approach to development was given added emphasis when the countries of Eastern Europe and the former USSR abandoned their system *en masse* and took the difficult path of rapidly introducing market economies. Although China, the last major holdout, has been posting impressive growth figures, two very "non-Socialist" reasons are important in explaining its performance. First, over 90 percent of the population is engaged in basically free-market agriculture—

because that sector has long been free of the central planning apparatus that so hampered agriculture in the former USSR. Second, while the state-controlled industries suffer increasing inefficiencies and absorb ever-larger proportions of the state budget in subsidies, a major investment boom is going on in China's South-East coastal provinces. Here foreign investment, largely from Japan and the Asian NIEs, is introducing a rapidly growing, and highly efficient, industrialized market sector.[7]

The Experience of the NIEs

South Korea, Taiwan, Hong Kong, and Singapore are often called the Asian Tigers. All four have turned themselves from poor countries to relatively high-income industrialized countries in the course of 40 years or less.

During the early stages of their development, they used import restrictions to build up local industries and to develop labor forces having the requisite skills and experiences. In the late 1950s and early 1960s, however, each of the four abandoned many of the interventionist aspects of the older development model. They created market-oriented economies with little direct government intervention compared with other developing economies, who stuck with the accepted development model.

Korea and Singapore did not adopt a *laissez faire* stance. Instead both followed quite strong policies that targeted specific areas for development and encouraged those areas with various economic incentives. In contrast, Hong Kong and Taiwan have had somewhat more *laissez faire* attitudes toward the direction of industrial development.

After local industries had been established, all four adopted outward-looking, market-based, export-oriented policies. This tested the success of various policies to encourage specific industries by

---

[7] Karl Marx predicted that the state would wither away under communism, whereas it actually became ever more powerful. Ironically, communism may be withering away in China (rather than being swept away in one grand gesture as it was in Eastern Europe). If the Communist government continues to turn a blind eye to the growth of foreign investment and market-oriented production in its coastal regions, the government will soon be unable to eliminate this dynamic sector because it will generate too large a proportion of China's GDP and employment. In contrast, the state-owned industries continue to languish, requiring ever larger subsidies merely to keep their inefficient operations in existence.

their ability to compete in the international marketplace. With industries designed to serve a sheltered home market, it is all too easy to shelter inefficiency more or less indefinitely. With export-oriented policies *not based on subsidies,* the success of targeted firms and industries is tested in international markets, and unprofitable firms fail.

Each country has experienced great successes and some failures of policy. Taiwan was typical in demonstrating the value of the new market-oriented approach when, in the period 1956–1960, following the advice of the Western-trained Chinese economist S. C. Tsiang, they abandoned most of the apparatus of the older development model and moved to market-oriented policies. Before long their growth rate increased, and they started on a path that has taken them from a per capita GDP of about 10 percent of that of the United States in 1955 to one of about 50 percent in 1990. Today Taiwan has become a major foreign investor as its less skill-intensive industries migrate to mainland China and other locations in Southeast Asia. In Taiwan, wages are rising, making low-skill-intensive manufacturing uneconomic and pushing local industries to higher-value-added lines of production that can support higher wages and hence higher living standards for the workers.

Not far behind the NIEs is a second generation of Asian and Latin American countries that have also adopted more market-oriented policies and have seen substantial growth follow. Indonesia, Thailand, the Philippines, Mexico, Chile, and Argentina are examples. Even Vietnam and Laos are liberalizing their economies as Communist governments come to accept that a market economy is a necessary condition for sustained economic growth.

Globalization of Trade and Investment

We discussed globalization briefly in Chapter 1; you may find it useful to reread that discussion at this time. At the heart of globalization lies the rapid reduction in transportation costs and the revolution in information technology that has characterized the last two decades. One consequence has been that the internal organization of firms, whether multinational or not, is changing to become less hierarchial and rigid, and more decentralized and fluid. *Another consequence is that the strategies of transnational corporations (TNCs), which span national borders in their organizational structures, are driving globalization and much of economic development.* Because most trade, and much investment, is undertaken by TNCs, no country can develop into an integrated part of the world economy without a substantial presence of TNCs within its borders. This is now recognized, and most aspiring developing countries generally put out a welcome mat for TNCs. Some countries, such as India, still put obstacles in the way of foreign investment. But even in these cases, the attitudes are softening so that foreign investment is increasingly tolerated, and even encouraged.

History has seen at least three great periods of foreign direct investment (FDI) (which was first described in Chapter 15). In the first period, dated about 1880–1914, the FDI occurred mainly in natural-resource-based sectors and was largely directed to colonies of the investing countries. Most of the high-value-added secondary processing was done at home.

The second burst, dated about 1945–1970, accompanied a period of falling trade barriers and falling transportation costs, which led to the gradual globalization of markets. A rising flow of FDI created an increasing number of multinational corporations. Their investment was primarily designed to produce and sell in *foreign markets* the same goods that were already being sold in their home markets. Later a second motive arose. This was to move low-value-added production to lower-wage countries (a movement that is still going on). For the most part, innovation was undertaken in each firm's home country.

In the third burst, from around 1970 to the present, many multinational firms are becoming true *transnationals.* In some cases even their nationality sometimes becomes blurred as they span borders with loosely knit groups of activities and their shares become increasingly owned by people in many countries. The most pronounced motives for FDI are now (1) to restructure existing investments to gain from the increased regional economic integrations discussed in Chapter 37, (2) to avoid growing nontariff barriers to trade (also discussed in Chapter 37), and (3) to acquire new technological or marketing assets that relate to the TNC's global competitive position. This last motive encourages TNCs to establish a substantial R&D presence in each of the major economic areas: Europe, North America, and Japan.

In industries that sell undifferentiated products such as steel and paper, and in industries with substantial scale economies such as aircraft, production tends to be concentrated in the home country while the output is exported. In contrast, FDI tends to be high in industries selling differentiated products not subject to major scale economies, which includes many consumers goods. The FDI allows the local market to be served with suitable product variations and often creates multidirectional trade in different varieties of the same basic product, much of which is intrafirm trade.

TNCs increasingly operate in high-tech sectors, in complex manufacturing, and in services. TNCs that produce in these sectors tend to concentrate in countries where the productivity of capital is high, the business environment is favorable, and other investors are present. This FDI is often undertaken by domestic firms that have built up some advantage in the local market, such as patents and know-how, that gives them advantages when they move into foreign markets.

Although some countries, such as Japan and Taiwan, did industrialize without major infusions of FDI, they did so before the globalization of the world's economy. It is doubtful that many (or any) of today's poor countries could achieve sustained, rapid growth paths without a substantial amount of FDI brought in by foreign-owned transnationals. Without such FDI, both the transfer of technology and foreign networking would be difficult to achieve.

Developing countries have gradually come to accept the advantages to dropping their traditional hostility to foreign direct investment (FDI). First, the FDI often provides somewhat higher-paying jobs than might otherwise be available to local inhabitants. Second, it provides investment that does not have to be financed by local savings. Third, it links the local economy into the world economy in ways that would be hard to accomplish with new firms of a purely local origin. Fourth, it provides training in worker and management skills that come from working with large firms linked into the global market. Fifth, it can provide advanced technology that is not easily transferred outside of the firms that are already familiar with its use.

Today virtually all developing economies encourage foreign TNCs to locate within their borders. Where governments used to worry that their countries had too much FDI, they now worry that there may be too little.

The Newer View

As a result of the above experiences, a new consensus on development policy is emerging. The revised model calls for a more *outward-looking, international-trade-oriented, market-incentive-based route to development*. It calls for accepting market prices as an instrument for the allocation of resources. This means abandoning both the heavy subsidization and the pervasive regulations that characterized the older approach.

One of the most important parts of this new consensus is an acceptance of the beneficial role played by competition (in its broadest sense) as a defender of the public interest and as a stimulus to growth-creating innovation. The other side of the coin is recognition of the harmful role played by monopolies (in the broadest sense), whether of private firms, closed-shop union agreements, communications media, government institutions, or government-owned industries.

Another important part of the consensus is that it is more efficient to locate economic activities in the private rather than the public sector (unless there are compelling reasons for doing otherwise, as there may be with a range of "social services" such as medical and hospital care). Some of the reasons that lie behind this presumption are (1) the incentives for efficiency when managers are responsible to owners who are risking their own wealth; (2) the constraint provided by the need to be profitable, which acts as a rapid cutoff device when failure is evident; and (3) the corrective for inefficiency provided by the possibility of a hostile takeover.

Part of the consensus concerns those activities that are required of the government. Two basic classes of activity are important.

First, the government needs to provide the framework for the market economy that is given by such things as well-defined property rights secure from arbitrary confiscation; security and enforcement of contracts; law and order; a sound money; ensuring the basic rights of the individual to locate, sell, and invest where, and how, he or she decides; and the provision of infrastructure.

Second, state activity is needed to resolve conflicts of interest, to handle market failures, and to redistribute income in line with currently accepted ideas of social justice. Redistributive policies cannot be judged in isolation (nor can growth policies). Instead they must be constantly scrutinized for their impacts on growth and, where these are significant, trade-offs need to be consciously made.

The New View in Detail

The new view has many aspects, and we touch on only a few of the most important. The first concerns the changed attitude to foreign direct investment undertaken by TNCs. FDI is now understood to be capable of changing a country's comparative advantages and of improving its competitiveness in many ways.

The Importance of FDI

FDI provides a major source of capital. This capital tends to be allocated to areas where experienced international operators feel the chances of success are best. The capital brings with it up-to-date technology that would be hard to develop domestically or even transfer to home-owned firms. It would be difficult to generate this capital through domestic savings and, if it were so generated, it would be difficult to import the necessary technology from abroad. The modern growth research discussed in Chapter 35 has shown that the transfer of technology to firms with no previous experience of using it is a far more difficult, risky, and expensive task than was formerly thought. Also, when capital is obtained through loans or grants from foreign governments, there is a risk that its allocation will be in the hands of administrators inexperienced in commercial activities and motivated by political concerns.

Over a longer period of time, the FDI creates many externalities—benefits available to the whole economy that the TNCs cannot appropriate as part of their own income.

These include transfers of general knowledge and of specific technologies in production and distribution, industrial upgrading, work experience on the part of the labor force, the introduction of modern management and accounting methods, the establishment of finance-related and trading networks, and the upgrading of telecommunications services. FDI in services affects the host country's absolute advantage and competitiveness by raising the productivity of capital and enabling host countries to attract new capital on favorable terms and by creating services that can be used as strategic inputs in the traditional

export sector to expand the volume of trade and to upgrade production through product and process innovation.

In today's world, the competitiveness of a country appears to be affected less and less by its relative factor endowments and the inherent abilities of its labor, and increasingly by the nature of its investment. It is difficult to compete in globalized trade without being a part of the vast, informal but powerful network of information and communications among TNCs.

By altering a country's comparative advantages and improving its competitiveness through technology transfer and the effects of myriad externalities, foreign as well as domestic investment can alter a country's volume and pattern of trade in many income-enhancing directions.

The Washington Consensus

What John Williamson of the Institute for International Economics in Washington, D.C., has called the Washington Consensus describes the conditions that, according to the newer views, are necessary for a poorer country to get itself on a path of sustained development. These views are accepted by a number of international agencies, such as the World Bank, the IMF, and several UN organizations. The main elements of this consensus are as follows.

1. Sound fiscal policies are required. Large budget deficits financed by bonds sold to the central bank can lead to rapid inflation and financial instability. For example, Brazil ended an excellent growth performance largely as a result of unsound macro policies.
2. The tax base should be broad, and marginal rates should be moderate.
3. Markets should be allowed to determine prices and the allocation of resources. Policies designed to affect resource allocation should work through price incentives rather than either the principles of a command economy (as described in Chapter 1) or price-distorting interventions. Exchange rates should be determined by market forces. Trade liberalization is desirable and, in particular, import licensing, with its potential for corruption, should be avoided.

4. The desirability of free trade, however, is subject to the qualification of the infant industry justification discussed in Chapter 37. This allows targeted protection for specific industries and a moderate general tariff, say, 10 to 20 percent, to provide a bias toward widening the industrial base of a less-developed country. Such protection should be for a specified period that is not easily extended.

5. In today's world, however, measures to insulate the home market from domestic protection should be held to the minimum possible consistent with developing strategic clusters of new industries. Industrial development should rely to an important extent on local firms and on attracting FDI and subjecting it to a minimum of local restrictions *that discriminate between local and foreign firms*. (Of course, restrictions will be required for such things as environmental policies, but these should apply to all firms whether foreign-owned or locally owned.)

6. An export orientation provides a powerful impetus to the development of national capabilities (as long as exports do not rely on permanent subsidies). It provides competitive incentives for the building of skills and technologies geared to world markets; it permits realization of scale economies; it furnishes the foreign exchange required for needed imports of capital; and it provides access to valuable information flows from buyers and competitors in advanced countries.

7. Education, health (especially for the disadvantaged), and infrastructure investment are desirable forms of public expenditure. Creating the appropriate factors of production is critical to creating comparative advantages in products that can be exported. This means general education, trade schools, and other appropriate institutions for formal education as well as assistance to increase on-the-job training within firms. Because future demands are hard to predict and subject to rapid change, a balance must be struck between training for specific skills and training for generalized, and adaptive, abilities.

8. Growth must be sustainable in the meaning given that term by the Brundtland Commission. (See Box 35-3 on page 764.) *Using existing technology* to raise the world's present population to the standards of living now found in the developed nations would put intolerable strains on the world's resources and its ecological systems. Therefore, the main hope for raising living standards of the developing countries to those of the developed countries (as well as not stopping growth completely in the developing countries) is through continued development of new technologies. Research into technological change provides the good news that most new technologies use less of all resource inputs per unit of output than do the older technologies that they replace.

9. Finally, emphasis needs to be placed on poverty reduction for at least two reasons. First, poverty can exert powerful antigrowth effects. People in poverty will not develop the skills to provide an attractive labor force, and they may not even respond to incentives when these are provided. Malnutrition in early childhood can affect a person's capacities for life.

Second, although economic growth tends to reduce the incidence of poverty, it does not eliminate it. Commonly accepted views of equity call for some of the benefits of growth to be made available to those who do not gain from it through the normal operations of the market. Self-interest calls for avoiding growing inequality in the distribution of income as those who benefit from growth (including employed workers) enjoy rising incomes while major groups are untouched by the growth process and suffer static or declining incomes.

Beyond the Washington Consensus

The basic Washington Consensus on outward-looking, market-oriented, fiscally sound economic policies provides what, in today's world, are probably necessary conditions for a country to achieve a sustained growth path—which in most cases will require that it is able to attract quite a large volume of FDI.

The policies suggested by the Washington Consensus relate primarily to the behavior of governments themselves.

Sufficient or Just Necessary?

There is substantial debate around one crucial issue: Are the conditions of the Washington Consensus *sufficient* to encourage the kinds and volumes of both domestic and foreign investments needed to develop dynamic comparative advantages in higher-value-added industries, or are they merely necessary?

Some observers believe that these are sufficient. In their view, all a country needs to do is to meet these conditions. Domestic savings will finance domestic investments, FDI will flow in, and a sustained growth path will be established. Other economists worry that many countries may have only limited ability (1) to attract FDI, (2) to benefit from it, and (3) to create sufficient domestic investment, even after fulfilling the necessary conditions of the Washington Consensus. The latter set of economists point to the experience of some African countries where TNCs operated extractive industries that despoiled the countryside and left little permanent benefit behind them; they merely extracted the available resources and then left. Others point out that there is a major difference between pure extractive enterprises and manufacturing enterprises, the latter having more potential spillovers to the local economy than the former.

What does happen after the conditions of the consensus are fulfilled will partly depend on the existing endowments of the country in question. If large supplies of natural resources or cheap, reasonably well-educated labor are available, fulfilling these conditions may be sufficient. Those who call for policies beyond those of the Washington Consensus argue that for some countries, a past history of nongrowth, plus the absence of externalities that go with a reasonably developed industrial sector, may call for the government to adopt a more active set of *integrated* trade, technology-transfer, and innovation policies. This set of policies would be aimed at encouraging the development of human and technological capabilities and building international competitiveness.

Policies that go beyond the Washington Consensus are directed at *the interactions between governments and the private sector,* **particularly as represented by TNCs.**

They relate, in British economist John Dunning's words, to the "interface between the global strategies of TNCs designed to advance corporate profitability and growth, and the strategies of national governments intended to promote the economic and social welfare of their citizens."

Implications of Modern Growth Theory

What is at issue in the debate just described is related to the newer views on economic growth that were discussed in Chapter 35 and that are now gaining acceptance among many economists. The key new view is that *endogenous* technological innovation is the mainspring of economic growth. Things emphasized by economists for centuries, such as aggregate savings and investment, are still essential, but technological change is now seen to lie at the core of the growth process.

As we saw in Chapter 35, technological change is a costly process that is undertaken mainly by firms in pursuit of profit and that responds to economic incentives. Research and development are in their nature highly risky and highly uncertain activities. The technological path followed by firms and industries is evolutionary in the sense that it develops as experiments and errors are made.

For developing countries, one of the most important of the many new insights stemming from research into the growth process is that adopting someone else's technology is not a simple, costless task. Substantial R&D capacity is needed to adapt other people's technology to one's own purposes, and to learn how to use it. For one reason, much of the knowledge required to use a technology is tacit; it can be obtained only from learning by doing and learning by using. This creates difficulties in imitating the knowledge, as well as uncertainty regarding which modifications will work in any new situation. This is true even when technology moves from one firm to another in the same industry and the same country. The problems are greater when technology moves across industrial or national borders. The difficulties of adopting new technologies also become more difficult the more complex and information-intensive the technology becomes.

It follows that all knowledge is not freely tradeable. Neither a firm nor a government can go out and buy it ready to use. Acquiring *working* technological knowledge requires both investment (sometimes in large, indivisible lumps) and the experience that allows workers and management slowly to acquire the needed tacit knowledge.

Usable new knowledge comes to a less-developed country through a slow, costly diffusion process.[8]

What May Be Needed

The above view of technological change suggests to some economists a major reason why active government policies that go beyond the Washington Consensus may be needed. These would do more than just attract FDI and create favorable market conditions. It is argued that some countries have achieved this much but then got little technological spin-off from the TNCs to the local economy. When the TNCs subsequently moved away, little of lasting benefit was left behind. To avoid this result, the policies would be designed to encourage the diffusion of technological capacities into the local economy so that all parts of the economy could benefit and grow. For this, public assistance may well be necessary. It was provided in varying degrees by the governments of all four of the Asian Tigers.

Such policies work by developing the externalities that come from initial investment in the local economy, and that give benefits not captured by the firms who help to confer them. The policies also take account of the fact that technology is not bought in competitive markets and imported ready to go.

Experience suggests, however, that the appropriate set of policies is usually highly country-specific. What works well in one environment may fail in another. Many local details need to be assessed before appropriate policies can be designed for one country. These depend, among many other things, on location, size of economy, existing natural and human resources, infrastructure, social and cultural attitudes, and development stage.

Protection of the domestic market.   Such policies can work at the early stages by establishing a protected domestic market through tariffs and other import restrictions. Virtually every country that has moved to a sustained growth path in the past, including the United States, Canada, Japan, and all of the NIEs,

has done so using import substitution in its early stages of industrialization. A protected home market provides a possible solution to the problem of coping with the enormous externalities involved in building up an infrastructure of physical and human capital as well as the required tacit knowledge and abilities. Even if all the specific infants that are protected by the import-substitution policy do not grow into self-sufficient adults, the externalities may still be created and become available for a second generation of more profitable firms.

Protection of the home market from international competition can, however, pose serious problems unless it is selective and temporary. Investment may occur mainly in areas where comparative advantage never grows. High costs of protected industries may create a lack of competitiveness of other domestic industries whose inputs are the outputs of the protected industries. Some potential comparative advantages may not be exploited because of the distorting effects of existing tariffs, and—as always—consumers bear much of the cost in terms of high prices of protected outputs.

Trade restrictions do not provide the only route to building an industrial and R&D capacity by encouraging technological diffusion and creating structural competitiveness. Other methods include the much-needed public investment in infrastructure and human capital, and many other things such as the provision of adequate financial schemes to favor investment in physical and intangible assets, procurement and tax incentives, provision of technical and marketing information, consulting services for assisting firms in industrial restructuring and in the adoption of new technologies and organizational techniques, support services in design, quality assurance and standards, schemes for training and retraining personnel, and facilities for start-up companies.

Those who advocate such a policy package stress the importance of having the above incentives as a part of a more general innovation and competition policy in order to encourage technological transfer to the local economy (such transfers are riddled with market failures arising from their externalities). Linkages among firms, and between firms and universities and research institutions, both within the country and with the rest of the world, are also important.

Policies that encourage the development of small and medium-sized enterprises are important to any development strategy. These tend to be locally

---

[8] An important characteristic of formal (nonlinear) models that capture some of this process of innovation is that they show extreme sensitivity to small alterations in their initial conditions, which have enormous effects a little later on. In such circumstances, public policy that alters the present in only small ways can have large effects in the future.

Box 40-1

Rediscovering the Middle of Africa

A recent article in the *London Economist,* under the title used in this box, reports on a discussion paper called "Africa's Entrepreneurs," written for the International Finance Corporation by Keith Marsden.

This article argues that many countries are learning that private-sector entrepreneurs are often a better engine of economic growth than is public-sector investment. These countries are also learning that it is important to reduce growth-inhibiting tax policies.

Development economists sometimes...complain about a "missing middle": Africa, they say, has vast state companies and thousands of subsistence hustlers, but virtually nobody in between.

During the 1980s two-thirds of the countries south of the Sahara embarked on the market-freeing policies advocated by the IMF and the World Bank. They received more than $1 billion a year in aid. Yet private capital has fled. After nearly a decade of reforming, some wonder if banks and businesses will ever return.

For the foreseeable future, few foreign companies are likely to invest in Africa to produce for the local market. It is simply too poor: the continent's combined GDP is a tenth of that of the seven countries of Eastern Europe.

Yet some countries have managed to attract investment aimed at export markets. Mauritania has drawn in so much that it no longer depends on huge injections of aid.

There are plenty of Africans running medium-sized firms. Botswana (population 1.1m) has 13 competing manufacturers of metal furniture; Tanzania has 5,000 registered road-transport companies.

These medium-sized African firms are efficient. A World Bank study in Kenya in 1986 found that private, Kenyan-owned enterprises earned an average return of 20%, compared with 18% for foreign private firms and 15% for public enterprises.

Entrepreneurs bring more expertise and motivation to such work than government consultants. Public funds, Mr. Marsden suggests, are better spent on tax incentives that promote the private sector. In Botswana, for example, new investment projects attract tax relief and selective wage subsidies. This is probably the biggest reason why private employment has grown much faster there than in the highly taxed Ivory Coast.

Mr. Marsden's main recommendation is for more lending to go to entrepreneurs rather than to governments. Many standard sorts of finance are denied to African businessmen: stock exchanges are scarce; banks lend according to a client's assets, rather than judging his business's potential. On top of all that, government borrowing often crowds out private requests—from institutions both domestic and foreign.

(*The Economist,* 8 December 1991)

owned and tend to be the vehicle by which know-how and best practices are transferred from TNCs to the local economy. They are also the sector most vulnerable to excessive red tape, rules and regulations, profit taxes, and other interferences that raise the cost of doing business. This issue is discussed further in Box 40-1.

A cautionary note. There is no doubt that the governments of many poor countries have been highly interventionist—and some still are. Thus, a good first strategy is often to diminish the government's place in the economy. There is no point adopt-ing a new, relatively rational, technology-promotion strategy if existing government interventions are irrational and heavy. What is then needed is to clear away the unproductive interventions first. This does not demonstrate, however, that if a government were starting from scratch, the best objective would be to minimize its place in the economy.

Whatever methods are chosen, selective intervention is a delicate instrument, highly dangerous when used by inept hands, and, even when in practiced hands, much damage can be done.

The intervention needs to be carefully tailored to get specific results and to reduce the opportunities for small groups to gain at the expense of others, and most assistance should, as a rule, be terminated after specified periods of time. It is also important to leave room for the market to generate, and support, unforeseen opportunities.

Box 40-2 provides a case study of South Korea's experience with some of the policies that go beyond the Washington Consensus.

Policy Issues Common to New and Old Views

Any government interested in encouraging development must take a stand on certain issues not covered in the debates reviewed in the previous section. Here we mention a few of these issues by way of illustration: population, agriculture, domestic saving, and the social structure.

Population

The race between population and GDP has been a dominant feature of many less-developed countries. Where population is growing rapidly, there are only two possible ways for a country to win this race. One is to achieve an income growth rate that is well in excess of the population growth rate. The other is to control population growth.

The case for population control.   The problem *can* be solved by restricting population growth. However, the issues of whether and how to do so are controversial, because considerations of religion, custom, and education are involved.

Customs can be changed to raise the average marriage age and hence lower the birthrate. Prohibition of child labor and the establishment of compulsory education alters the costs and benefits of having children and may reduce the desired family size. Providing the education that women are often denied in poor countries, changing their role, and providing career alternatives outside the home can also lower the birthrate, in some cases dramatically.

University of Maine Professor Johannes Overbeck has reported that a comprehensive family planning program—involving the provision of a broad selection of birth control techniques, a broad range of social services, and accelerated research to develop more effective and cheaper contraceptives—would have an annual cost of $1 per capita in a typical less-developed country. Excluding mainland China, this amounts to less than $3 billion per year for all developing countries combined, a relatively modest sum equal to around 5 percent of the vast sums currently spent on armaments. If this estimate is roughly accurate, population policy offers a high return on spending to promote per capita growth in developing countries.

Different countries have adopted very different positions with respect to population. Kenya, with a birthrate of 50 per 1,000, until recently rejected any serious national policy of population control. Mexico, with nearly as high a birthrate during the early 1970s, began to dispense free contraceptives and family planning information and saw its annual rate of population growth drop from 3.2 percent to 2.5 percent in less than five years.

The Chinese—today one-quarter of the world's population—have reduced their rate of population growth from more than 3 percent to less than 1 percent in the past 25 years by promoting later marriages and exhorting parents to value daughters as well as sons and thus to be content with fewer children. In 1980 China began more aggressive steps in an announced attempt to achieve zero population growth by the year 2000. Families that have only one child receive bonuses and preferential treatment in housing and in education for their offspring. (Housing space is allocated to all families as though they had one child.) Families that do not comply with the policy have their salaries decreased and are promoted less frequently.

The case against population control.   The above case is not without its critics. The critics argue that the view allows little place for the enjoyment value of children by their parents. In their view, the psychic value of children should be included as a part of the living standards of their parents. They also point out that in rural societies, even young children are a productive resource. Furthermore, in many developing countries, where state help for the aged is negligible, fully grown children provide old-age security for their parents.

The argument for positive population control is also criticized for assuming that people breed blindly,

Box 40-2

South Korea's Development Policy: A Case Study*

In the late 1950s South Korea seemed unable to generate adequate levels of exports and savings. Policymakers solicited foreign aid and sought to manage the flow of imports. The currency was overvalued at a fixed rate on the foreign exchange market, tariff rates were high, and quantitative import restrictions abounded. These policies, which discouraged exports and encouraged import substitution, were close to the old model of appropriate development policy discussed in the text.

The economy was dominated by agriculture and mining, and the manufacturing sector supplied only simple consumer products. Exports amounted to about 3 percent of GNP and consisted almost entirely of primary products and various minerals.

Then came policy reforms that stretched over several years, starting in 1960. They centered on fostering exports from both existing and new industries.

Today South Korea is dominated by the manufacturing sector. Major industries established since 1960 range from chemicals and electronics to automobiles and heavy electrical equipment. Exports exceed 40 percent of GNP, with manufactured products constituting over 90 percent of the total.

Existing Industries

For well-established industries, the reforms ensured that production for export would be no less profitable than production for the domestic market. This was accomplished by insulating export activity from the adverse consequences of policies motivated by domestic concerns.

Capital and intermediate inputs used in export production could be imported without tariffs and were not bound by the quotas that applied to imports for other purposes. Tradeable inputs were exempt from indirect taxes. Exchange was managed at rates that were no longer overvalued.

The government enabled exporters to borrow

---

* This box is based on Larry E. Westphal, "Industrial Policy in an Export-Propelled Economy: Lessons from South Korea's Experience," *Journal of Economic Perspectives* (Summer 1990).

working capital from state-owned banks in proportion to their export activity. Additional incentives were granted in the form of direct tax reductions, preferential interest rates, and privileged access to import licenses. The export incentives were administered fairly uniformly across all industries. They were granted equally to "indirect exports"—inputs produced and sold domestically that are destined to be used in export production. (This policy was a major innovation rarely found in developing nations.)

The government has also used publicly announced, quarterly export targets for individual commodities, markets, and firms. At a minimum, the targets have been useful in keeping the government well informed about export performance so that timely changes could be made in incentives.

These measures seem on balance to have been neutral among specific established export industries. They encouraged exports in general without the government having to pick specific winners in advance. No doubt, however, the policies encouraged producers to move to the export sector from the competing import sector, where the distortional policies still applied.

New Industries

The South Korean government has selectively intervened to promote targeted infant industries, typically by supporting the creation of large-scale establishments that were accorded temporary monopolies and received access to credit on preferential terms, as well as exemptions from most taxes (including tariffs).

Protection for nonexport sales has been the dominant incentive to infant industries. Targeted industries have been protected by import controls, which enable them to practice discriminatory pricing. Export targeting requires that infant industries sell a swiftly growing proportion of their output at world prices, either as direct or indirect exports. This forces them to increase productivity rapidly.

The first producers of fertilizer, petrochemicals, and refined petroleum products were public-owned enterprises. So was the first integrated steel mill, which is generally considered to be one of the most efficient mills in the world. *New public enterprises have been expected to achieve international competitiveness quickly.* They have been managed as autonomous profit-seeking entities and have contributed to government revenues.

The Contribution of Industrial Policy

The South Korean experience shows that industrial policy can work. Selective intervention seems to have contributed to the nation's remarkable success by accelerating the rate of growth with little if any compensating loss in efficiency.

The enormous uncertainty in selecting infant industries for promotion was resolved by using information gained during implementation to evaluate intentions and by judging new industries on their ability to export (in a regime in which export promotion policies were neutral with respect to specific exports).

Viewing this apparently successful experience, an economist will naturally ask: What South Korean market failures has selective intervention successfully overcome?

Some economists argue that market imperfections associated with technological transfer are unimportant because less-developed countries face an abundant supply of available technology. But (as we have seen in the text of Chapters 35 and 40) elements of technology are far from being perfectly tradeable. Moreover, the tacitness of much technology creates problems in communication over long distances and across social boundaries, problems that can be overcome only at substantial cost.

1. The tacitness of much knowledge makes some elements inherently nontradeable. Peculiarities in local resources, institutions, and local technological practices cannot be understood without being experienced.
2. Because of the imperfect tradeability of technology, externalities related to technological de-

velopment can be quite extensive. There are economies of scope in the application of many of the capabilities acquired in the course of industrialization.
3. An initial entrant's investments to master new technology may greatly reduce costs for subsequent, nearby entrants. The returns to particular technological efforts may be largely inappropriable because a significant share of them derives from the application of the newly acquired element in a cascade of subsequent technological changes.

In short, if it is used appropriately, selective intervention seems able to increase a country's ability to capture dynamic economies associated with the introduction and exploitation of modern technology.

Lessons

South Korea's industrial performance owes much to the government's reliance on free-market institutions to provide for flexibility in resource allocation. It has resulted in many highly profitable ventures that were either not foreseen or not actively promoted by the government.

But South Korea's industrial performance also owes a great deal to the government's promotional policies toward exports and to its initiatives in targeting industries for development. Selective intervention has driven the fast-paced evolution of South Korea's industrial structure by fostering vertical integration at the national level and by promoting greater diversification of end-product mix.

The belief that selective intervention has outlived its usefulness led the South Korean government to alter its policies. Selective intevention has lost the support of the South Korean public, who prefer democratic government to economically enlightened dictatorship. The trend appears to be away from selective interventions, and it remains to be seen whether South Korea's economic performance will continue to be exceptional.

as animals do. The critics point out that traditional methods of limiting family size have been known and practiced since the dawn of history. Thus, they argue that large families in rural societies are the result of choice, not ignorance.

The population explosion did not come through any change in "breeding habits" but as a result of medical advances that greatly extended life expectancy (which surely must be counted as a direct welfare gain for those affected). Critics of an active population policy argue that, once an urban society has developed, family size will be reduced voluntarily. This was certainly the experience of Western industrial countries; why, critics ask, should it not be the experience of the developing countries as well?

Agriculture

A developing country whose labor force is mainly devoted to agriculture has little choice but to accept this basic allocation of resources. It can build up its industrial sector, and if its efforts are successful, the proportion of the population devoted to urban pursuits will rise. But the change will come slowly, leaving a large portion of the country's resources in rural pursuits for a long time to come.

It follows that policies to help the agriculture sector raise productivity are an important part of the development strategy in any agricultural-based, poor country. These can fill the dual purposes of raising incomes of rural workers and reducing the cost of food for urban workers.

A developing country's government may choose to devote a major portion of its resources to stimulating agricultural production, say, by mechanizing farms, irrigating land, and using new seeds and fertilizers. If successful, the country will stave off starvation for its current population, and it may even develop an excess over current needs and so have a crop available for export. A food surplus can earn foreign exchange to buy needed imports.

In the last two decades, India, Pakistan, Taiwan, and other Asian countries have achieved dramatic increases in food production by the application of new technology and the use of new seed in agricultural production. This has been labeled the *green revolution*.

The gains from this strategy, while large at first, are subject to diminishing returns. Further gains in agricultural production have an ever-higher opportunity cost, measured in terms of the resources needed to irrigate land and to mechanize production. Critics of reliance on agricultural output argue that newly developing economies must start at once to develop other bases for economic growth.

Many developing countries (as well as many developed ones) suffer from misguided government intervention in the agriculture sector. In India, for example, the government has encouraged crops such as oilseeds and sugar cane, in which India has a comparative disadvantage, and discouraged crops such as rice, wheat, and cotton, in which India has a strong comparative advantage. It has subsidized food prices, thus giving large benefits to the urban population. About 8 percent of all Indian government spending is on subsidies that go to fertilizers, to farmers' debt payments, and to urban food consumption.

Domestic Savings

Although modern development strategies call in many instances for a large infusion of foreign capital imported by TNCs, the rise of domestically owned firms, which will reap some of the externalities created by foreign technology, is one key to sustained development. This requires a supply of domestic savings to finance their growth.

If more domestic capital is to be created at home by a country's own efforts, resources must be diverted from the production of goods for current consumption. This means a cut in present living standards. If living standards are already at or near the subsistence level, such a diversion will be difficult. At best, it will be possible to reallocate only a small proportion of resources to the production of capital goods.

Such a situation is often described as the *vicious circle of poverty:* Because a country has little capital per head, it is poor; because it is poor, it can devote few resources to creating new capital rather than to producing goods for consumption; because little new capital can be produced, capital per head remains low, and the country remains poor.

The vicious circle can be made to seem an absolute constraint on growth rates. Of course, it is not; if it were, we would all still be at the level of the early agricultural civilizations. The grain of truth in the vicious-circle argument is that some surplus must be available somewhere in the society to allow saving and investment. In a poor society with an even distribution of income, in which nearly everyone is at the subsistence level, saving may be very difficult, but this is not the common experience. Usually, there is at least a small middle class that can save and invest if opportunities for the profitable use of funds arise. Also, in most poor societies today, the average household is above the physical subsistence level. Even the poorest households will find that they can sacrifice some present living standards for a future gain. For example, presented with a profitable opportunity, villagers in Ghana planted cocoa plants at the turn of the century, even though there was a seven-year growing period before any return could be expected.

An important consideration is that in less-developed countries one resource that is often *not* scarce is labor. Profitable home or village investment that requires mainly labor inputs may be made with relatively little sacrifice in current living standards. Unfortunately, this kind of investment often does not appeal to local governments, which are too often mesmerized by large and symbolic investments, such as dams, nuclear power stations, and steel mills.

International Debt

The 1970s and early 1980s witnessed an explosive growth in the external debt of many developing nations. Since the mid-1980s most of these countries have experienced difficulties in making the payments required to service their debt. "Debt rescheduling"—putting off until tomorrow payments that cannot be made today—has been common, and many observers feel that major defaults are inevitable unless ways of forgiving the debt can be found.

The trend to increased debt started when OPEC quadrupled the world price of oil in 1973. Because many developing nations relied on imported oil, their balance of trade moved sharply into deficit. At the same time, the OPEC countries developed massive trade surpluses. Commercial banks helped to *recycle* the deposits of their OPEC customers into loans to the developing nations. These loans financed some necessary adjustments and some worthwhile new investment projects. However, a large part of the funds were used unwisely; wasteful government spending and lavish consumption splurges occurred in many of the borrowing countries.

A doubling of energy prices in 1979 led to a further increase in the debt of developing nations. The severe world recession that began in 1981 reduced demand for the exports of many of these countries. As a result, they were unable to achieve many benefits from the adjustments and investment expenditures that they had made. Furthermore, sharp increases in real interest rates led to increased debt service payments; as a result, many countries could not make their payments.

The lending banks had little choice but to reschedule the debt—essentially lending the developing nations the money to make interest payments while adding to the principal of the existing loans. The International Monetary Fund played a central role in arranging these reschedulings, by making further loans and concessions conditional on appropriate policies of adjustment and restraint. These conditions were intended to limit wasteful government expenditure and consumption and thus to increase the likelihood that the loans eventually would be repaid. Critics of the IMF's role argued that much of the restraint resulted in reduced investment and, thus, that the IMF's conditions were counterproductive.

During the mid-1980s, the world economy recovered and interest rates fell. As a result, the LDCs' export earnings grew, their debt-service obligations stabilized, and the crisis subsided. The sharp *fall* in the price of oil, which started in late 1985, further eased the problems of the oil-importing nations, but it also created a new debt problem.

Throughout the period of rising energy prices in the 1970s, a number of *oil-exporting* developing nations—including Mexico, Venezuela, and Indonesia—saw in those high prices new opportunities for investment and growth. Based on their high oil revenues, their ability to borrow improved. Their external debt grew, and they were able to avoid many of the adjustments that the oil-importing developing nations had been forced to undertake. When oil prices fell, these oil exporters found themselves in very difficult positions. Today, although the debt is no longer rising, it remains an enormous burden on developing nations. Often the borrowed money produced little or no benefit, going either to develop industries that did not turn out to be viable or to provide graft to the ruling classes. Today those who benefited little or not at all from the funds are saddled with the need to pay taxes to service the debt. This produces an enormous drag on further development.

Social Attitudes

Authoritarian and interventionist governments can sometimes overcome specific sources of X-inefficiency. They may suppress social and even religious institutions that are barriers to growth, and they may hold on to power until a new generation grows up that did not know and does not value the old institutions. It is much more difficult for a democratic government, which must command popular support during each election, to do currently unpopular things in the interest of long-term growth. Whether the gains in growth that an authoritarian government can achieve are worth the political and social costs is, of course, an important value judgment.

Another example concerns saving. Where social attitudes do not sanction the sacrifice of current living standards needed to generate a large volume of domestic saving, a government can impose compulsory saving. Such forced saving policies were one of the main aims of most development plans of Socialist governments, such as those of the former USSR and China. The goal of such plans was to raise savings and thus lower current consumption below what it would be in a market economy.

A less authoritarian method is to increase the national savings rate through fiscal and monetary policies. The object, however, is the same: to increase investment in order to increase growth and thus to make future generations better off.

Unfortunately, even where the governments of developing countries have succeeded in raising their national savings rate, much of the savings were wasted in inefficient state-owned enterprises that could never become profitable. If the funds had been invested in needed infrastructure that only the government can create, the government intervention might have been effective in encouraging development.

Many critics argue that development plans, particularly when imposed by economists coming from advanced countries, pay too little attention to local cultural and religious values. Even when they are successful by the test of rising GDP, this may be at too great a cost in terms of social upheaval for the current generation.

A country that wants development must accept some alteration in traditional ways of doing things. However, a trade-off between speed of development and amount of social upheaval can be made. The critics argue that such a trade-off should be made by local governments and not be imposed by outsiders who understand little of local customs and beliefs. An even more unfavorable possibility is that the social upheaval will occur without achieving even the expected benefits of a rising GDP. If the development policy does not take local values into account, the local population may not respond as predicted by Western economic theories. In this case, the results of the development effort may be disappointingly small.

Conclusion

According to the World Bank's *World Development Report* of 1991, about 1.1 billion residents of the developing countries were in poverty in the year 1985. In reviewing this report, the *London Economist* argued: "With luck and a lot of policy changes in rich and poor countries alike, that figure might be cut to about 800 million by the year 2000."[9] That may not seem like a large change at first sight, but it is when put into the perspective of the rapidly growing world population. The 1.1 billion that the World Bank reckoned to be in poverty in 1985 made up about one-third of the developing countries' total population. The 800 million would be only 18 percent of the estimated population of these same countries in the year 2000. The predicted change would substantially reduce the probability that a person born into the developing world in 2000 would be born into poverty and condemned to a life of acute deprivation.

According to the *Economist,* the World Bank's prescriptions fall into two categories:

> Create new economic opportunities for the poor. Since the poor's main source of income is what they are paid for their labor, this means promoting labor-intensive economic growth.
>
> Equip the poor to grasp these opportunities. This calls for adequate provision of basic social services such as primary education, health and family planning.

The Bank also points out that one of the most damaging economic distortions in many developing countries is excessive taxation of farming. This hits

---

[9] All equations from the *Economist* in this section are from 21 July 1991.

the very part of the economy upon which most of the poor depend for their livelihood.

In sub-Saharan (i.e., black) Africa, 53 percent of the population was above the poverty line while only 56 percent of the current young attended primary school. This suggests that few of the poorer children were attending. Higher education is utilized almost exclusively by the middle- and upper-income groups. Commenting on these facts, the *Economist* argued:

> It might, at first sight, seem crazy to argue that fees for education and hospital care are a good way to help the poor. In developing countries, however, they can indeed serve this purpose. If governments recovered the cost of higher education and hospital health-care from consumers, they would not be hurting the poor because they never set foot in universities and hospitals. The revenue could then be used for spending that really would help the poor—like better provision of cheap primary education and village health-posts.

It used to be claimed that economic growth hurt the poor—a claim since disproved by the success of the Asian Tigers. Labor-intensive growth helps the poor, rest assured. However, governments do have a trade-off to wrestle with—not between overall growth and the well-being of the poor, but between the poor and the not-poor.

The World Bank's report and the *Economist's* commentary suggest that a major reduction in poverty is possible worldwide. What is needed is the acceptance of the new consensus on the importance of market determination and of reducing state control and state ownership of business activity. This, plus a large dose of enlightened policies to bring education, health, and jobs to ordinary people and improved technology to the nations' firms, could pay enormous dividends in reducing poverty and suffering. The next decade will show how much of that hopeful potential will be realized.

SUMMARY

1. About one-fourth of the world's population still exists at a level of bare subsistence, and nearly three-fourths are poor by American standards. Although some poorer societies have grown rapidly, the gap between the very richest and very poorest remains large and is not decreasing.

2. Impediments to economic development include excessive population growth; resource limitations; inefficient use of resources, particularly those that are related to X-inefficiency; inadequate infrastructure; excessive government intervention; and institutional and cultural patterns that make economic growth difficult.

3. The older model for development policies included (1) heavy tariff barriers and a hostility to foreign direct investment to protect the home market for local firms, (2) many government controls over, and subsidization of, local activities, and (3) exchange rates pegged at overly high values with imports regulated by licenses.

4. During the 1980s many governments became skeptical of this model as a result of observing the poor growth performances both of the planned economies and of those developing countries that adhered closely to this model, the good performances of those who did not follow the model, and the globalization of the world economy, which made transnational corporations and foreign direct investment increasingly important. Today, no developing country can play a part in the global trading system without some significant presence of TNCs within its borders.

5. The newer view holds that (1) heavy indiscriminate protection of home markets should be avoided, (2) protection that does

exist should be targeted to sectors that have a real chance of creating comparative advantage and that the protection be only for a moderate period of time so that market tests of success and failure can be allowed to operate, (3) competition is an important spur to efficiency and innovation, (4) quantitative controls should be avoided and exchange rates set at a market-clearing volume, and (5) production of most goods and services should be in the private sector, except where there are strong reasons for preferring the public sector, as might be the case in, say, medical and health services.

6. Part of this new view is given in the Washington Consensus, which calls for (1) sound fiscal and monetary policies, (2) broad-based taxes levied at moderate rates, (3) market determination of prices and quantities, (4) discriminating use of infant industry protection for moderate time periods, (5) an acceptance of FDI and the presence of TNCs, (6) active government provision of education, health care, and infrastructure, and (7) antipoverty programs to help in human resource development and to aid those who are left behind by the growth process.

7. An active debate turns on whether the conditions of the Washington Consensus are sufficient, or just necessary, to establish a country on a sustained growth path. Those who regard it as sufficient feel that, once unleashed, natural market forces will create sustained growth.

8. Those who regard the conditions of the Washington Consensus as just necessary point to substantial externalities and pervasive market failures in the diffusion of technological knowledge from advanced to less-advanced nations. They argue that foreign firms will not invest enough because they cannot capture in their profits many of the benefits they confer on the local economy (externalities) and that much of the technological know-how will not diffuse to local firms because such knowledge is not easy to transfer (market failure). These economists call for active government innovation policies to augment investment and to assist the transfer of technological know-how and practice to the local economy.

9. All developing economies must decide on policies with respect to population, agriculture, the encouraging of domestic savings, and whether to attempt to alter social attitudes to be more conducive to growth-creating activities.

TOPICS FOR REVIEW

Barriers to development

The vicious circle of poverty

The NIEs

TNCs and FDI

The Washington Consensus

Externalities and market failures in the diffusion of technology

DISCUSSION QUESTIONS

1. Discuss the following statements, which were made by economists from developing countries attending a recent UN conference on development strategies for the 1990s. Which ones illustrate points made in the chapter?

   a. "While the quantity of flows to developing countries as a whole, and Asia and the Pacific and Latin America and the Caribbean in particular, continued to increase, the share of FDI going to developing countries declined over time, reflecting strategies of TNCs that increasingly favor the locational advantages of developed market economies."

   b. "Investment flows to Africa fell to $2.2 billion in 1990—slightly more than what Portugal received in that year—a decrease of 50 percent from 1989."

   c. "In recent years, a number of countries in Africa have sought to attract greater amounts of FDI, primarily by reducing or removing legal and regulatory restrictions on the activities of foreign companies. Despite these extensive efforts at liberalization, the quantity of FDI flowing to the region has remained small."

   d. "The 1990s may well see the maturing of the global economy, the emergence of which began in the 1960s, faltered in the 1970s, and was resuscitated in the 1980s. A major reason for this optimism is the renaissance of the international market economy, and the positive role which both TNCs and national governments can play in facilitating and using this tried and tested mechanism to create sustainable and balanced economic development; and in a way which is both humanly acceptable and environmentally friendly."

   e. "As TNC activities have shifted into high-technology sectors, in complex manufactures and into technology-based services, their global operations have tended to create significant externalities for the host countries. These are associated with the use and diffusion of technology, with the extent and direction of knowledge-transfers regarding production, management or distribution, and with the ability of host countries to enter established, regional or global, finance-related or trading networks."

   f. "What a developing country can do to increase its ability to attract and benefit from FDI is: liberalize its trade and investment policies; improve domestic political and economic stability; aggressively promote itself to potential investors, especially in the NIEs; by making strategic investments in infrastructure and human capital; and explore regional linkages with neighboring countries. Most of these policies will also encourage domestic private investment and stimulate economic growth, and are thus worth undertaking even if the prospects for attracting FDI are not particularly good."

   g. "According to what is becoming conventional neoliberal wisdom, if market forces can fully operate in a stable macroeconomic environment, sooner or later the entrepreneurial spirit will flourish and productive investments are going to be made. However, the received literature and the experiences of the OECD and some Asian developing countries, clearly suggest that the process of achieving international competitiveness by increasing productive investment and creating dynamic comparative advantages is a far more complicated process than that depicted by prevailing neoliberal approach in Latin America."

2. In 1990 India had masses of people living at or near the poverty level. Yet surveying recent major reforms in that country, the *London Economist* had this to say:

The experience of the 1980s showed that poverty begins falling swiftly in India when the rate of growth reaches 5%. A sustained GDP growth rate of 9% a year would free most Indians from truly grinding poverty by 2000, and make 1 billion of them middle-class by 2020. That is not impossible. India has plenty of entrepreneurs—and plenty of savings. Yet the government may lack the will to seize the chance. The government has so far shrunk from four huge challenges: reform of the labor market, of the financial system, of agriculture and of its own finances."

   a. Why can developing nations such as India hope (if they get the conditions right) for sustained growth rates as high as 8 to 9 percent while developed countries such as the United States or Germany cannot?
   b. Which of the possible obstacles to growth discussed in this chapter does the *Economist* not seem to think important?
   c. What does the *Economist* see as the major obstacle to rapid growth in India?
   d. Given the last sentence in the quotation, can you guess what some of India's policies with respect to the labor market, the financial system, agriculture, and public debt might have been at the time of writing in May 1992?

3. "This natural inequality of the two powers of population and of production in the earth...form[s] the great difficulty that to me appears insurmountable in the way to perfectibility of society. All other arguments are of slight and subordinate consideration in comparison of this. I see no way by which man can escape from the weight of this law which pervades all animated nature. No fancied equality, no agrarian revolutions in their utmost extent, could remove the pressure of it even for a single century" (T. R. Malthus, *Population: The First Essay*).

   Discuss Malthus' "insurmountable difficulty" in view of the events of the past 100 years.

4. To what extent does the vicious circle of poverty apply to poor families that are living in developed countries? Consider carefully, for example, the similarities and differences facing a poor family living in Appalachia and one living in Ghana, where per capita income is less than $400 per year. Did it apply to immigrants who arrived on Ellis Island with $10 in their pockets?

5. Would removing all restrictions on immigration into the advanced countries help to improve living standards in the developing nations? How might this change in policy affect living standards in the advanced countries?

6. "Just about the most important thing the advanced countries could do to help the developing nations is to remove all restrictions on imports from those countries." Is this good advice from the point of view of the LDCs? Which groups in advanced countries do you think might support such advice, and which might oppose it?

7. "High coffee prices bring hope to impoverished Latin American peasants," reads the headline. Mexico, Kenya, and Burundi, among other LDCs, have the right combination of soil and climate to increase their coffee production greatly. Discuss the benefits and risks to them if they pursue coffee production as a major avenue of their development.

Mathematical Notes

1. The rule of 72 is an approximation, derived from the mathematics of compound interest. Any variable X with an initial value of X_0 will have the value $X_t = X_0 e^{rt}$ after t years at a continuous growth rate of r percent per year. Because $X_t/X_0 = 2$ requires $r \times t = 0.69$, a "rule of 69" would be correct for continuous growth. The rule of 72 was developed in the context of compound interest, and if interest is compounded only once a year, the product of r times t for X to double is approximately 0.72.

2. Because one cannot divide by zero, the ratio $\Delta Y/\Delta X$ cannot be evaluated when $\Delta X = 0$. However, as ΔX *approaches* zero the ratio $\Delta Y/\Delta X$ increases without limit:

$$\lim_{\Delta X \to 0} \frac{\Delta Y}{\Delta X} = \infty$$

3. Many variables affect the quantity demanded. Using functional notation, the argument of the next several pages of the text can be anticipated. Let Q^D represent the quantity of a commodity demanded and

$$T, \overline{Y}, N, Y^*, p, p_j$$

represent, respectively, tastes, average household income, population, income distribution, the commodity's own price, and the price of the jth other commodity.

The demand function is

$$Q^D = D(T, \overline{Y}, N, Y^*, p, p_j), \quad j = 1, \ldots, n$$

The demand schedule or curve is given by

$$Q^D = q(p)\Big|_{T, \overline{Y}, N, Y^*, p_j}$$

where the notation means that the variables to the right of the vertical line are held constant.

This function is correctly described as the demand function with respect to price, all other variables being held constant. This function, often written concisely as $q = q(p)$, shifts in response to changes in other variables. Consider average income: if, as is usually hypothesized, $\partial Q^D/\partial \overline{Y} > 0$, then increases in average income shift $q = q(p)$ rightward and decreases in average income shift $q = q(p)$ leftward. Changes in other variables likewise shift this function in the direction implied by the relationship of that variable to the quantity demanded.

4. Quantity demanded is a simple, straightforward but frequently misunderstood concept in everyday use, but it has a clear mathematical meaning. It refers to the dependent variable in the demand function from note 3:

$$Q^D = D(T, \overline{Y}, N, Y^*, p, p_j)$$

It takes on a specific value whenever a specific value is assigned to each of the independent variables. The value of Q^D changes whenever the value of any independent variable is changed. Q^D could change, for example, from 10,000 tons per month to 20,000 tons per month as a result of a *ceteris paribus* change in any one price, in average income, in the distribution of income, in tastes, or in population. It could also change as a result of the net effect of changes in all of the independent variables occurring at once. Thus a change in the price of a commodity is a sufficient reason for a change in Q^D but not a necessary reason.

Some textbooks reserve the term *change in quantity demanded* for a movement along a demand curve, that is, a change in Q^D as a result of a change in p. They then use other words for a change in Q^D caused by a change in the other variables in the demand function. This usage is potentially confusing, because it gives the single variable Q^D more than one name.

Our usage, which corresponds to that in more advanced treatments, avoids this confusion. We call Q^D *quantity demanded* and refer to *any* change in Q^D as a *change in quantity demanded*. In this usage it is correct to say that a movement along a demand curve is a change in quantity demanded, but it is incorrect to say that a change in quantity demanded can occur only because of a movement along a demand curve (because Q^D can change for other reasons, for example, a *ceteris paribus* change in average household income).

5. Continuing the development of note 3, let Q^S represent the quantity of a commodity supplied and

$$C, X, p, w_i$$

represent, respectively, producers' goals, technology, the products' own price, and the price of the *i*th input.

The supply function is

$$Q^S = S(G, X, p, w_i), \quad i = 1, 2, \ldots, m$$

The supply schedule or curve is given by

$$Q^S = s(p) \Big|_{G, X, w_i}$$

This is the supply function with respect to price, all other variables being held constant. This function, often written concisely as $q = s(p)$, shifts in response to changes in other variables.

6. Continuing the development of notes 3 through 5, equilibrium occurs where $Q^D = Q^S$. *For specified values of all other variables,* this requires that

$$q(p) = s(p) \tag{1}$$

Equation 1 defines an equilibrium value of p; hence, although p is an *independent* variable in each of the supply and demand functions, it is an *endogenous* variable in the economic model that imposes the equilibrium condition expressed in Equation 1. Price is endogenous because it is assumed to adjust to bring about equality between quantity demanded and quantity supplied. Equilibrium quantity, also an endogenous variable, is determined by substituting the equilibrium price into either $q(p)$ or $s(p)$.

Graphically, Equation 1 is satisfied only at the point where demand and supply curves intersect. Thus supply and demand curves are said to determine the equilibrium values of the endogenous variables, price and quantity. A shift in any of the independent variables held constant in the q and s functions will shift the demand or supply curves and lead to different equilibrium values for price and quantity.

7. The definition in the text uses finite changes and is called *arc elasticity*. The parallel definition using derivatives is

$$\eta = \frac{dq}{dp} \times \frac{p}{q}$$

and is called *point elasticity*. Further discussion appears in the Appendix to Chapter 5.

8. The propositions in the text are proved as follows. Letting TR stand for total revenue, we can write

$$TR = pq$$

It follows that the change in total revenue is

$$dTR = qdp + pdq \tag{1}$$

(Recall that total revenue of the firm and total expenditure by consumers are identical, so the following applies equally to total expenditure.) Multiplying and dividing both terms on the right-hand side of Equation 1 by $p \cdot q$ yields

$$dTR = \left(\frac{dp}{p} + \frac{dq}{q} \right) pq$$

Because dp and dq are opposite in sign, one positive and one negative, dTR will have the same sign as the term in parentheses on the right-hand side that dominates, that is, on which percentage change is largest.

A second way of arranging Equation 1 is to divide both sides by dp to give

$$\frac{dTR}{dp} = q + p\frac{dq}{dp} \tag{2}$$

From the equation in note 7, however,

$$q\eta = p\frac{dq}{dp} \tag{3}$$

which we can substitute in Equation 1 to obtain

$$\frac{dTR}{dp} = q + q\eta = q(1 + \eta) \tag{4}$$

Because η is a negative number, the sign of Equation 4 is negative if the absolute value of η exceeds unity (elastic demand) and positive if it is less than unity (inelastic demand).

Total revenue is maximized when dTR/dp is equal to zero, and as can be seen from Equation 4, this occurs when elasticity is equal to -1.

9. The axis reversal arose in the following way. Marshall theorized in terms of "demand price" and "supply price," these being the prices that would lead to a given quantity being demanded or supplied. Thus

$$p^d = D(q) \qquad [1]$$
$$p^s = S(q) \qquad [2]$$

and the condition of equilibrium is

$$D(q) = S(q)$$

When graphing the behavioral relationships expressed in Equations 1 and 2, Marshall naturally put the independent variable, q, on the horizontal axis.

Leon Walras, whose formulation of the working of a competitive market has become the accepted one, focused on quantity demanded and quantity supplied *at a given price.* Thus

$$q^d = q(p)$$
$$q^s = s(p)$$

and the condition of equilibrium is

$$q(p) = s(p)$$

Walras did not use graphical representation. Had he done so, he would surely have placed p (his independent variable) on the horizontal axis.

Marshall, among his other influences on later generations of economists, was the great popularizer of graphical analysis in economics. Today we use his graphs, even for Walras' analysis. The axis reversal is thus one of those historical accidents that seem odd to people who did not live through the "perfectly natural" sequence of steps that produced it.

10. The relationship of the slope of the budget line to relative prices can be seen as follows. In the two-commodity example, a change in expediture (ΔE) is given by the equation

$$\Delta E = p_C \Delta C + p_F \Delta F \qquad [1]$$

Along a budget line, expenditure is constant; that is, $\Delta E = 0$. Thus, along such a line,

$$p_C \Delta C + p_F \Delta F = 0 \qquad [2]$$

whence

$$-\frac{\Delta C}{\Delta F} = \frac{p_F}{p_C} \qquad [3]$$

The ratio $-\Delta C/\Delta F$ is the slope of the budget line. It is negative because, with a fixed budget, to consume more F one must consume less C. In other words, Equation 3 says that the negative of the slope of the budget line is the ratio of the absolute prices (i.e., the relative price). Although prices do not show directly in Figure 7-1, they are implicit in the budget line: Its slope depends solely on the relative price, while its position, given a fixed money income, depends on the absolute prices of the two goods.

11. Because the slope of the indifference curve is negative, it is the absolute value of the slope that declines as one moves downward to the right along the curve. The algebraic value, of course, increases. The phrase *diminishing marginal rate of substitution* thus refers to the absolute, not the algebraic, value of the slope.

12. The distinction made between an incremental change and a marginal change is the distinction for the function $Y = Y(X)$ between $\Delta Y/\Delta X$ and the derivative dY/dX. The latter is the limit of the former as ΔX approaches zero. Precisely this sort of difference underlies the distinction between arc and point elasticity, and we shall meet it repeatedly—in this chapter in reference to marginal and incremental *utility* and in later chapters with respect to such concepts as marginal and incremental *product, cost,* and *revenue.* Where Y is a function of more than one variable—for example, $Y = f(X, Z)$—the

marginal relationship between Y and X is the partial derivative $\partial Y/\partial X$ rather than the total derivative.

13. The hypothesis of diminishing marginal utility requires that we can measure utility of consumption by a function $U = U(X_1, X_2, \ldots, X_n)$ where $X_1, \ldots, X_n$ are quantities of the n goods consumed by a household. It really embodies two utility hypotheses: first, $\partial U/\partial X_i > 0$, which says that for some levels of consumption the consumer can get more utility by increasing consumption of the commodity; second, $\partial^2 U/\partial X_i^2 < 0$, which says that the marginal utility of additional consumption is declining.

14. *Marginal product,* as defined in the text, is really *incremental product.* More advanced treatments distinguish between this notion and *marginal product* as the limit of the ratio as ΔL approaches zero. Marginal product thus measures the rate at which total product is changing as one factor is varied and is the partial derivative of the total product with respect to the variable factor. In symbols,

$$MP = \frac{\partial TP}{\partial L}$$

15. We have referred specifically both to diminishing *marginal* product and to diminishing *average* product. In most cases, eventually diminishing marginal product implies eventually diminishing average product. This is, however, not necessary, as the accompanying figure shows.

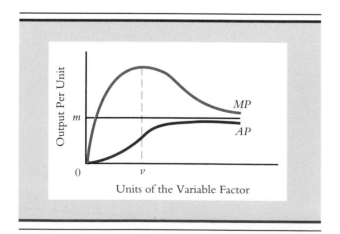

16. Let q be the quantity of output and L the quantity of the variable factor. In the short run,

$$TP = q = f(L) \tag{1}$$

We now define

$$AP = \frac{q}{L} = \frac{f(L)}{L} \tag{2}$$

$$MP = \frac{dq}{dL} \tag{3}$$

We are concerned about the relationship between these two. Where average product is rising, at a maximum, or falling is determined by its derivative with respect to L:

$$\frac{d\frac{q}{L}}{dL} = \frac{L\frac{dq}{dL} - q}{L^2} \tag{4}$$

This may be rewritten

$$\frac{1}{L}\left(\frac{dq}{dL} - \frac{q}{L}\right) = \frac{1}{L}(MP - AP) \tag{5}$$

Clearly, when MP is greater than AP, the expression in Equation 5 is positive and thus AP is rising. When MP is less than AP, AP is falling. When they are equal, AP is at a stationary value.

17. The text defines *incremental cost.* Strictly, marginal cost is the rate of change of total cost, with respect to output, q. Thus $MC = dTC/dq$. From the definitions, $TC = TFC + TVC$. Fixed costs are not a function of output. Thus we may write $TC = K + f(q)$, where $f(q)$ is total variable costs and K is a constant. From this we see that $MC = df(q)/dq$. MC is thus independent of the size of the fixed costs.

18. This point is easily seen if a little algebra is used:

$$AVC = \frac{TVC}{q}$$

In this case marginal product diminishes after v units of the variable factor are employed. Because marginal product falls toward, but never quite reaches, a value of m, average product rises continually toward, but never quite reaches, the same value.

but

$$TVC = L \times w$$

and

$$q = AP \times L$$

where L is the quantity of the variable factor used and w is its cost per unit. Therefore,

$$AVC = \frac{L \times w}{AP \times L} = \frac{w}{AP}$$

Because w is a constant, it follows that AVC and AP vary inversely with each other, and when AP is at its maximum value, AVC must be at its minimum value.

19. A little elementary calculus will prove the point:

$$MC = \frac{dTC}{dq} = \frac{dTVC}{dq}$$

$$= \frac{d(L \times w)}{dq}$$

If w does not vary with output,

$$MC = \frac{dL}{dq} \times w$$

However, referring to note 16, Equation 3, we see that

$$\frac{dL}{dq} = \frac{1}{MP}$$

Thus

$$MC = \frac{w}{MP}$$

Because w is fixed, MC varies negatively with MP. When MP is a maximum, MC is a minimum.

20. As we saw in note 17, $MC = dTVC/dq$. If we take the integral of MC from zero to q_0, we get

$$\int_0^{q_0} MC \, dq = TVC \, q_0 + K$$

The first term is the area under the marginal cost curve; the constant of integration, K, is fixed cost.

21. Strictly speaking, the marginal rate of substitution refers to the slope of the tangent to the isoquant at a particular point, whereas the calculations in Table 11A-1 refer to the average rate of substitution between two distinct points on the isoquant. Assume a production function

$$Q = Q(K, L) \qquad [1]$$

Isoquants are given by the function

$$K = I(L, \overline{Q}) \qquad [2]$$

derived from Equation 1 by expressing K as an explicit function of L and Q. A single isoquant relates to a particular value $(\overline{Q})$ at which Q is held constant. Define Q_K and Q_L as an alternative, more compact notation for $\partial Q / \partial K$ and $\partial Q / \partial L$, the marginal products of capital and labor. Also, let Q_{KK} and Q_{LL} stand for $\partial^2 Q / \partial K^2$ and $\partial^2 Q / \partial L^2$, respectively. To obtain the slope of the isoquant, totally differentiate Equation 1 to obtain

$$dQ = Q_K dK + Q_L dL$$

Then, because we are moving along a single isoquant, set $dQ = 0$ to obtain

$$\frac{dK}{dL} = -\frac{Q_L}{Q_K} = MRS$$

Diminishing marginal productivity implies Q_{LL}, $Q_{KK} < 0$, and, hence, as we move down the isoquant of Figure 11A-1, Q_K is rising and Q_L is falling, so the absolute value of MRS is diminishing. This is called the *hypothesis of a diminishing marginal rate of substitution*.

22. Formally, the problem is to maximize $Q = Q(K, L)$ subject to the budget constraint

$$p_K K + p_L L = C$$

To do this, form the Lagrangean

$$Q(K, L) - \lambda(p_K K + p_L L - C)$$

The first-order conditions for finding the saddle point on this function are

$$Q_K - \lambda p_K = 0; \quad Q_K = \lambda p_K \qquad [1]$$

$$Q_L - \lambda p_L = 0; \quad Q_L = \lambda p_L \qquad [2]$$

$$-p_K K - p_L L + C = 0 \qquad [3]$$

Dividing Equation 1 by Equation 2 yields

$$\frac{Q_K}{Q_L} = \frac{p_K}{p_L}$$

That is, the ratio of the marginal products, which is (-1) times the *MRS*, is equal to the ratio of the prices, which is (-1) times the slope of the isocost line.

23. Marginal revenue is mathematically the derivative of total revenue with respect to output, dTR/dq. Incremental revenue is $\Delta TR/\Delta q$. However, the term *marginal revenue* is used loosely to refer to both concepts.

24. For notes 24 through 26, it is helpful first to define some terms. Let

$$\pi_n = TR_n - TC_n$$

where π_n is the profit when n units are sold.

 If the firm is maximizing its profits by producing n units, it is necessary that the profits at output q_n be at least as large as the profits at output zero. If the firm is maximizing its profits at output n, then

$$\pi_n \geq \pi_0 \qquad [1]$$

 The condition says that profits from producing must be greater than profits from not producing. Condition 1 can be rewritten as

$$TR_n - TVC_n - TFC_n \\ \geq TR_0 - TVC_0 - TFC_0 \qquad [2]$$

However, note that by definition

$$TR_0 = 0 \qquad [3]$$
$$TVC_0 = 0 \qquad [4]$$
$$TFC_n = TFC_0 = K \qquad [5]$$

where K is a constant. By substituting Equations 3, 4, and 5 into Condition 2, we get

$$TR_n - TVC_n \geq 0$$

from which we obtain

$$TR_n \geq TVC_n$$

This proves Rule 1.

 On a per unit basis, it becomes

$$\frac{TR_n}{q_n} \geq \frac{TVC_n}{q_n} \qquad [6]$$

where q_n is the number of units produced.

 Because $TR_n = q_n p_n$, where p_n is the price when n units are sold, Equation 6 may be rewritten as

$$p_n \geq AVC_n$$

25. Using elementary calculus, we may prove Rule 2.

$$\pi_n = TR_n - TC_n$$

each of which is a function of output q. To maximize π, it is necessary that

$$\frac{d\pi}{dq} = 0 \qquad [1]$$

and that

$$\frac{d^2\pi}{dq^2} < 0 \qquad [2]$$

From the definitions,

$$\frac{d\pi}{dq} = \frac{dTR}{dq} - \frac{dTC}{dq} = MR - MC \qquad [3]$$

From Equations 1 and 3, a necessary condition for attaining maximum π is $MR - MC = 0$, or $MR = MC$, as is required by Rule 2.

26. To prove that for a negatively sloped demand curve, marginal revenue is less than price, let $p = p(q)$. Then

$$TR = pq = p(q) \times q$$

$$MR = \frac{dTR}{dq} = q\frac{dp}{dq} + p$$

For a negatively sloped demand curve, dp/dq is negative by definition, and thus MR is less than price for positive values of q.

27. The equation for a downward-sloping straight-line demand curve with price on the vertical axis is

$$p = a + bq$$

Total revenue is price times quantity:

$$TR = pq = aq + bq^2$$

Marginal revenue is

$$MR = \frac{dTR}{dq} = a + 2bq$$

Thus the MR curve and the demand curve are both straight lines, and the slope of the MR curve ($2b$) is twice that of the demand curve (b).

28. A monopolist, selling in two or more markets, will set its marginal cost equal to marginal revenue in each market. Thus the condition $MC = MR_1 = MR_2$ is a profit-maximizing condition for a monopolist that is selling in two markets. In general, equal marginal revenues will mean unequal prices, because the ratio of price to marginal revenue is a function of elasticity of demand: The higher the elasticity, the lower is the ratio. Thus equal marginal revenues imply a higher price in the market with the less elastic demand curve.

29. The marginal revenue produced by the factor involves two elements: first, the additional output that an extra unit of the factor makes possible and, second, the change in price of the product that the extra output causes. Let Q be output, R revenue, and L the number of units of labor hired. The contribution to revenue of additional labor is $\partial R/\partial L$. This, in turn, depends on the contribution of the extra labor to output $\partial Q/\partial L$ (the marginal product of the factor) and $\partial R/\partial Q$ (the firm's marginal revenue from the extra output). Thus,

$$\frac{\partial R}{\partial L} = \frac{\partial Q}{\partial L} \cdot \frac{\partial R}{\partial Q}$$

We define the left-hand side as marginal revenue product, MRP. Thus,

$$MRP = MP \cdot MR$$

30. The proposition that the marginal labor cost is above the average labor cost when the average is rising is essentially the same proposition proved in math note 16. Nevertheless, let us do it again, using elementary calculus.

   The quantity of labor depends on the wage rate: $L = f(w)$. Total labor cost is wL. Marginal

cost of labor is $d(wL)/dL = w + L(dw/dL)$. Rewrite this as $MC = AC + L(dw/dL)$. As long as the supply curve slopes upward, $dw/dL > 0$; therefore $MC > AC$.

31. Let t be the tax rate applied to the profits, π, of the firm. Thus, after-tax profits are $(1 - t)\pi$, where π is a function of output, q. To maximize profits after tax requires

$$\frac{d(1 - t)\pi}{dq} = 0$$

or

$$(1 - t)\frac{d\pi}{dq} = 0$$

Dividing through by $(1 - t)$, we see that $d\pi/dq = 0$ depends on the level of q and is independent of the tax rate.

32. If prices grow at a rate of 0.87 percent per calendar quarter, prices in any given quarter will be 1.0087 times their level in the previous quarter. Start with a price level of P_0. One quarter later the price level will be $P_0 \times 1.0087$; the following quarter it will be $P_0 \times 1.0087 \times 1.0087$. In general, for any growth rate per unit of time, g, and starting value, P_0, the price level at time t, P_t, will be $P_0 \times (1 + g)^t$. This is the formula for *compound* growth at rate g per unit of time. Thus, $P_t = (1.0087)^4 = 1.0353$, and prices will have risen by 3.53 percent. For small values of g, $(1+g)^t$ will be very close to $(1+tg)$. In this example, $1 + tg = 1 + 4(0.0087) = 1.0348$. But as g gets larger, so does the difference. For example, if prices are growing at 2 percent per month, the annual growth will be $(1.02)^{12} = 1.268$, yielding a growth rate of 27 percent per year. This is considerably more than 24 percent, which is just the monthly rate times 12. Generally, annual rates of growth are calculated by compounding rates of growth that are measured over shorter or longer periods than one year.

33. In the text we define MPC as an incremental ratio. For mathematical treatment it is sometimes convenient to define all marginal concepts as derivatives: $MPC = dC/dY_d$, $MPS = dS/dY_d$, and so on.

34. The basic relationship is

$$Y_d = C + S$$

Dividing through by Y_d yields

$$Y_d/Y_d = C/Y_d + S/Y_d$$
$$1 = APC + APS$$

Next, take the first difference of the basic relationship to get

$$\Delta Y_d = \Delta C + \Delta S$$

Dividing through by ΔY_d gives

$$\Delta Y_d/\Delta Y_d = \Delta C/\Delta Y_d + \Delta S/\Delta Y_d$$
$$1 = MPC + MPS$$

35. The total expenditure over all rounds is the sum of an infinite series. If we let A stand for the initiating expenditure and z for the marginal propensity to spend, the change in expenditure is ΔA in the first round, $z\Delta A$ in the second, $z(z\Delta A) = z^2\Delta A$ in the third, and so on. This can be written as

$$\Delta A(1 + z + z^2 + \cdots + z^n)$$

If z is less than 1, the series in parentheses converges to $1/(1-z)$ as n approaches infinity. The change in total expenditure is thus $\Delta A/(1-z)$. In the example in the box, $z = 0.80$; therefore, the change in total expenditure is five times ΔA.

36. This involves using functions of functions. We have $C = C(Y_d)$ and $Y_d = f(Y)$. So, by substitution, $C = C[f(Y)]$. In the linear expressions that are used in the text, $C = a + bY_d$, where b is the marginal propensity to consume. $Y_d = hY$, so $C = a + bhY$, where bh is thus the marginal response of C to a change in Y.

37. This is easily proved. In equilibrium the banking system wants sufficient deposits (D) to establish the target ratio (v) of deposits to reserves (R). This gives $R/D = v$. Any change in D of size ΔD has to be accompained by a change in R of ΔR of sufficient size to restore v. Thus $\Delta R/\Delta D = v$, so $\Delta D = \Delta R/v$, and $\Delta D/\Delta R = 1/v$.

This can be shown also in terms of the deposits created by the sequence in Table 29-8. Let v be the reserve ratio and $e = 1 - v$ be the excess reserves per dollar of new deposits. If X dollars are initially deposited in the system, the successive rounds of new deposits will be X, eX, e^2X, e^3X, ... The series

$$X + eX + e^2X + e^3X + \cdots$$
$$= X[1 + e + e^2 + e^3 + \cdots]$$

has a limit

$$X\frac{1}{1-e} = X\frac{1}{1-(1-v)} = \frac{X}{v}$$

This is the total new deposits created by an injection of $\$X$ of new reserves into the banking system. For example, when $v = 0.20$, an injection of $\$100$ into the system will lead to an increase of $\$500$.

38. Suppose that the public wishes to hold a fraction, c, of deposits in cash, C. Now suppose that X dollars are injected into the system. Ultimately, this money will be held either as reserves by the banking system or as cash by the public. Thus we have

$$\Delta C + \Delta R = X$$

From the banking system's reserve behavior, we have $\Delta R + v\Delta D$, and from the public's cash behavior, we have $\Delta C = c\Delta D$. Substituting into the above equation, we get the result that

$$\Delta D = \frac{X}{v + c}$$

From this we can also relate the change in reserves and the change in cash holdings to the initial injection:

$$\Delta R = \frac{v}{v + c}X$$
$$\Delta C = \frac{c}{v + c}X$$

For example, when $v = 0.20$ and $c = 0.05$, an injection of $\$100$ will lead to an increase in reserves of $\$80$, an increase in cash in the hands of the public of $\$20$, and an increase in deposits of $\$400$.

39. The argument is simply as follows, where prime marks stand for first derivatives:

$$M^D = F_1(T), \qquad F_1' > 0$$

$$T = F_2(Y), \qquad F_2' > 0$$

Therefore,

$$M^D = F_1(F_2(Y))$$

$$= H(Y), \qquad H' > 0$$

where H is the function of the function combining F_1 and F_2.

40. Let $L(Y, r)$ give the real demand for money measured in purchasing power units. Let M be the supply of money measured in nominal units and P an index of the price level, so that M/P is the real supply of money. Now the equilibrium condition requiring equality between the demand for money and the supply of money can be expressed in real terms as

$$L(Y, r) = \frac{M}{P} \qquad [1]$$

or by multiplying through by P in nominal terms as

$$PL(Y, r) = M \qquad [2]$$

In Equation 1 a rise in P disturbs equilibrium by lowering M/P, and in Equation 2 it disturbs equilibrium by raising $PL(Y, r)$.

41. The relations involved here are discussed in note 1 above.

42. The time taken to break even is a function of the *difference* in growth rates, not their level. Thus had 4 percent and 5 percent or 5 percent and 6 percent been used in the example, it still would have taken the same number of years. To see this quickly, recognize that we are interested in the ratio of two growth paths: $e^{r1t}/e^{r2t} = e^{(r1-r2)t}$.

43. A simple example of a production function is GDP $= z(LK)^{1/2}$. This equation says that to find the amount of GDP produced, multiply the amount of labor by the amount of capital, take the square root, and multiply the result by the constant z. This production function has positive but diminishing returns to ei-

ther factor. This can be seen by evaluating the first and second partial derivatives and showing the first derivatives to be positive and the second derivatives to be negative. For example, $\partial \text{GDP}/\partial K = (\frac{1}{2}zL^{1/2})/(K^{1/2}) > 0$ and $\partial^2 \text{GDP}/\partial K^2 = (-\frac{1}{2}zL^{1/2})/K^{3/2} < 0$. The production function also displays constant returns to scale, as can be seen by multiplying both L and K by the same constant, λ, and seeing that this multiplies the whole value of the function, that is, the value of GDP, by λ: $z(\lambda L \lambda K)^{1/2} = z(\lambda^2 LK)^{1/2} = \lambda z(LK)^{1/2} = \lambda(\text{GDP})$.

44. The figures are derived from the production function, output $= 4(KL)^{1/2}$, in which both factors have the same average and marginal products.

45. In the neoclassical production function, which allows for growth, we have

$$\text{GDP} = z(L^\alpha K^{1-\alpha})$$

The parameter z is a constant that relates given inputs of L and K to a specific GDP. Increases in factor productivity cause z to rise so that given amounts of L and K are associated with higher GDP. Exogenous technical progress at a constant rate can be shown as

$$\text{GDP}_t = z^t(L_t^\alpha K_t^{1-\alpha})$$

where z grows at a constant rate as time passes.

46. The shift in the AD curve, and hence the change in national income, is given by the simple multiplier, which in this case is $1/[1 - b(1 - t) + m]$, times the change in exports, dX.

The shift in the NX curve is given by the solution for dY in the condition $dX - mdY = 0$, which is $1/m$ times dX. Because $1/m$ is larger than $1/[1 - b(1 - t) + m]$, the shift in NX is larger than the shift in AD.

The change in net exports, dNX, is given by the change in exports, dX, minus the change in imports, dIM. The latter is equal to the marginal propensity to import, m, times the change in national income, dY. Thus

$$dNX = dX - [m/[1 - b(1 - t) + m]]dX$$

Because $m/[1 - b(1 - t) + m]$ is less than one, dNX is positive.

47. Net exports equals exports minus imports.

$$NX = X - IM \quad [1]$$

Exports depend on foreign income, Y^f, and on the terms of trade.

$$X = X_0 + m^f Y^f - b^f \left(\frac{P}{eP^f}\right) \quad [2]$$

where X_0 is autonomous exports, m^f is the foreign marginal propensity to import, b^f is the response of exports to a change in relative prices, P is the domestic price level, e is the exchange rate, and P^f is foreign prices. Imports depend on domestic income and the terms of trade.

$$IM = M_0 + mY + b\left(\frac{P}{eP^f}\right) \quad [3]$$

Combining Equations 1, 2, and 3, we can write

$$NX = (X_0 - M_0) + m^f Y^f - mY - c\left(\frac{P}{eP^f}\right) [4]$$

where $c = b + b^f$. In Chapter 26 we considered this relationship in isolation, and hence the slope of the NX curve when it was drawn against national income was taken to be $dNX/dY = -m$, where the other variables in Equation 4 were held constant. Now we have to take into account the fact that P changes as Y changes.

Writing the $SRAS$ curve as

$$P = g(Y), \quad g' > 0 \quad [5]$$

and substituting Equation 5 into Equation 4, we eliminate P to yield

$$NX = (X_0 - M_0) + mY^f - mY - c\left(\frac{g(Y)}{eP^f}\right) [6]$$

The slope of the NX curve is now given by

$$\frac{dNX}{dY} = -(m + u') < 0 \quad [7]$$

where $u = cg'/ep^f > 0$. Hence as Y rises, NX falls, both because of the marginal propensity to import and because of substitution away from domestic goods as P rises.

Glossary

absolute advantage When a given amount of resources can produce more of some commodity in one country than in another.

absolute price The amount of money that must be spent to acquire one unit of a commodity. Also called *money price*.

acceleration hypothesis The hypothesis that when national income is held above potential, the persistent inflationary gap will cause inflation to accelerate, and when national income is held below potential, the persistent recessionary gap will cause inflation to decelerate.

actual GDP The gross domestic product that the economy, in fact, produces.

adjustable peg system A system in which exchange rates are fixed in the short term but are occasionally changed in response to persistent payments imbalances.

administered price A price set by the conscious decision of the seller rather than by impersonal market forces.

ad valorem tariff An import duty that is a percentage of the price of the imported product.

ad valorem tax See *excise tax*.

adverse selection Self-selection, within a single risk category, of persons of above-average risk.

AE See *aggregate expenditure*.

agents Decision makers, including households, firms, and government bodies.

aggregate demand Total desired purchases by all the buyers of an economy's output.

aggregate demand (AD) curve A curve showing the combinations of real national income and the price level that makes aggregate desired expenditure equal to national income; the curve thus relates the total amount of output that will be demanded to the price level of that output.

aggregate demand shock A shift in the aggregate demand curve.

aggregate expenditure (AE) Total desired expenditure on final output of the economy; $AE = C + I + G + (X - M)$, representing the four major components of aggregate desired expenditure.

aggregate expenditure (AE) function The function that relates aggregate desired expenditure to national income.

aggregate production function The relation between the total amount of each factor of production em-ployed in the nation and the nation's total output, its GDP.

aggregate supply Total desired sales of all the producers of an economy's output.

aggregate supply (AS) curve See *short-run aggregate supply curve* and *long-run aggregate supply curve*.

aggregate supply shock A shift in the aggregate supply curve.

allocation of resources See *resource allocation*.

allocative efficiency A situation in which no reorganization of production or consumption could make everyone better off (or, as it is sometimes stated, make at least one person better off while making no one worse off).

antitrust policy Policies designed to prohibit the acquisition and exercise of monopoly power by business firms.

appreciation A rise in the external value of the domestic currency in terms of foreign currencies; i.e., a rise in the exchange rate.

a priori Literally, "at a prior time" or "in advance"; that which is prior to actual experience.

arc elasticity A measure of the average responsiveness of quantity to price over an interval of the demand curve. For analytical purposes it is usually defined by the formula

$$\eta = \frac{\Delta q / q}{\Delta p / p}$$

An alternative formula often used where computations are involved is

$$\eta = \frac{(q_2 - q_1)/(q_2 + q_1)}{(p_2 - p_1)/(p_2 + p_1)}$$

where p_1 and q_1 are the original price and quantity and p_2 and q_2 are the new price and quantity. With negatively sloped demand curves, elasticity is a negative number. The above expressions are therefore usually multiplied by -1 to make measured elasticity positive.

automatic fiscal stabilizers See *automatic stabilizers*.

automatic stabilizers Anything that automatically lessens the magnitude of the fluctuations in national income caused by changes in autonomous expenditures, such as investment.

automatic transfer service (ATS) A savings deposit from which funds are transferred automatically to the depositor's demand deposit to cover checks as they are drawn.

autonomous expenditure In macroeconomics, elements of expenditure that do not vary systematically with other variables, such as national income and the interest rate, but are determined by forces outside of the theory.

autonomous variable See *exogenous variable*.

average cost (*AC*) See *average total cost*.

average fixed cost (*AFC*) Total fixed costs divided by the number of units of output.

average product (*AP*) Total product divided by the number of units of the variable factor used in its production.

average propensity to consume (*APC*) The proportion of income devoted to consumption; total consumption expenditure divided by total disposable income ($APC = C/Y_d$).

average propensity to save (*APS*) The proportion of disposable income devoted to saving; total saving divided by total disposable income ($APS = S/Y_d$).

average revenue (*AR*) Total revenue divided by quantity sold; this is the market price when all units are sold at one price.

average tax rate The ratio of total taxes paid to total income earned.

average total cost (*ATC*) Total cost of producing a given output divided by the number of units of output; it can also be calculated as the sum of average fixed costs and average variable costs. Also called *cost per unit, unit cost, average cost*.

average variable cost (*AVC*) Total variable costs divided by the number of units of output. Also called *direct unit cost, avoidable unit cost*.

balanced budget A situation in which current revenue is exactly equal to current expenditures.

balanced budget multiplier The change in income divided by the tax-financed change in government expenditure that brought it about.

balance-of-payments acounts A summary record of a country's transactions that involve payments or receipts of foreign exchange.

balance of trade The difference between the value of exports and the value of imports of visible items (goods).

bank notes Paper money issued by commercial banks.

barter A system in which goods and services are traded directly for other goods and services.

beggar-my-neighbor policies Policies designed to increase a country's prosperity (especially by reducing its unemployment) at the expense of reducing prosperity in other countries (especially by increasing their unemployment).

benefit–cost analysis A technique for evaluating government policies. The sum of the opportunity cost to all parties is compared with the value of the benefits to all parties.

black market A situation in which goods are sold illegally at prices that violate a government price ceiling.

bond An evidence of debt carrying a specified amount and schedule of interest payments and (usually) a date for redemption of its face value.

boom A period in the business cycle characterized by high demand and increasing production at a level that exceeds potential GDP.

bread-and-butter unionism A union movement whose major objectives are higher wages and better conditions of employment rather than political or social reform.

break-even price The price at which a firm is just able to cover all of its costs, including the opportunity cost of capital.

budget balance The difference between total government revenue and total government expenditure.

budget deficit Any shortfall of current revenue below current expenditure.

budget line Graphical representation of all combinations of commodities or factors that a household or firm may obtain if it spends a specified amount of money at fixed prices of the commodities or factors. Also called *isocost line*.

budget surplus Any excess of current revenue over current expenditure.

business cycle Fluctuations of national income around its trend value, after seasonal fluctuations have been removed, and that follow a wavelike pattern.

C See *consumption expenditure*.

capacity The level of output that corresponds to the firm's minimum short-run average total cost.

capital A factor of production consisting of all manufactured aids to further production, including plant, equipment, and inventories.

capital account A part of the balance-of-payments accounts that records payments and receipts arising from the import and export of long-term and short-term financial capital.

capital consumption allowance An estimate of the amount by which the capital stock is depleted through its contribution to current production. Also called *depreciation*.

capital-labor ratio A measure of the amount of capital per worker in an economy.

capital stock The aggregate quantity of capital goods.

cartel An organization of producers who agree to act as a single seller in order to maximize joint profits.

CD   See *certificate of deposit.*

ceiling price   See *price ceiling.*

central bank   A bank that acts as banker to the commercial banking system and often to the government as well. In the modern world, usually a government-owned and -operated institution that controls the banking system and is the sole money-issuing authority.

centrally planned economy   See *command economy.*

certificate of deposit (CD)   A negotiable time deposit carrying a higher interest rate than that paid on ordinary time deposits.

ceteris paribus   Literally, "other things being equal"; usually used in economics to indicate that all variables except the ones specified are assumed not to change.

change in demand   An increase or decrease in the quantity demanded at each possible price of the commodity, represented by a shift in the whole demand curve.

change in quantity demanded   An increase or decrease in the specific quantity bought, represented by a change from one point on a demand curve to another point, either on the original demand curve or on a new one.

change in quantity supplied   An increase or decrease in the specific quantity supplied, represented by a change from one point on a supply curve to another point, either on the original supply curve or on a new one.

change in supply   An increase or decrease in the quantity supplied at each possible price of the commodity, represented by a shift in the whole supply curve.

classical unemployment   See *real wage unemployment.*

clearing house   An institution where interbank indebtedness, arising from transfer of checks between banks, is computed, offset against each other, and net amounts owing are calculated.

closed economy   An economy that has no foreign trade.

collective bargaining   The process by which unions and employers arrive at and enforce agreements.

collective-consumption goods   Goods or services that, if they provide benefits to anyone, can, at little or no additional cost, provide benefits to a large group of people, possibly everyone in the country. Also called *public goods.*

collusion   An agreement among sellers to act jointly in their common interest, for example, by agreeing to raise prices. Collusion may be overt or covert, explicit or tacit.

command economy   An economy in which the decisions of the government (as distinct from households and firms) exert the major influence over the allocation of resources.

commercial bank   Privately owned, profit-seeking institution that provides a variety of financial services, such as accepting deposits from customers, which it agrees to transfer when ordered by a check, and making loans and other investments.

commercial policy   A government's policy involving restrictions placed on international trade.

commodities   Marketable items produced to satisfy wants. Commodities may be either *goods*, which are tangible, or *services*, which are intangible.

common market   A customs union with the added provision that factors of production can move freely among the members.

comparative advantage   The ability of one nation (region or individual) to produce a commodity at a lesser opportunity cost of other products forgone than another nation.

comparative statics   Short for comparative static equilibrium analysis; the derivation of predictions by analyzing the effect of a change in some exogenous variable on the equilibrium position.

complement   Two commodities are complements when they tend to be used jointly with each other. The degree of complementarity is measured by the size of the negative cross elasticity between the two goods.

concentration ratio   The fraction of total market sales (or some other measure of market occupancy) controlled by a specified number of the industry's largest firms, four-firm and eight-firm concentration ratios being most frequently used.

conglomerate merger   See *merger.*

constant-cost industry   An industry in which costs of the most efficient size firm remain constant as the entire industry expands or contracts in the long run.

constant-dollar GDP   Gross national product valued in prices prevailing in some base year; year-to-year changes in constant-dollar GDP reflect changes only in quantities produced. Also called *real GDP.*

constant returns to scale   A situation in which output increases in proportion to inputs as the scale of production is increased. A firm in this situation, and facing fixed factor prices, is a *constant-cost firm.*

Consumer Price Index (CPI)   A measure of the average prices of commodities commonly bought by households; compiled monthly by the Bureau of Labor Statistics.

consumers' durables   See *durable good.*

consumers' surplus   The difference between the total value that consumers place on all units consumed of a commodity and the payment that they must make to purchase that amount of the commodity.

consumption   The act of using commodities, either goods or services, to satisfy wants.

consumption expenditure In macroeconomics, household expenditure on all goods and services. Represented by the symbol C as one of the four components of aggregate expenditure.

consumption function The relationship between total desired consumption expenditure and all the variables that determine it; in the simplest cases, the relationship between consumption expenditure and disposable income and consumption expenditure and national income.

contestable market A market is perfectly contestable if there are no sunk costs of entry or exit, so that *potential* entry may hold profits of existing firms to low levels—zero in the case of perfect contestability.

cooperative solution A situation in which existing firms cooperate to maximize their joint profits.

corporation A form of business organization in which the firm has a legal existence separate from that of the owners, and ownership and financial responsibility are divided, limited, and shared among any number of individual and institutional shareholders.

cost (of output) To a producing firm, the value of inputs used to produce output.

cost-effectiveness analysis Analysis of program costs with the purpose of finding the least-cost way to achieve a given result. See also *benefit-cost analysis*.

cost minimization An implication of profit maximization that the firm will choose the method that produces specific output at the lowest attainable cost.

CPI See *Consumer Price Index*.

cross elasticity of demand (η_{xy}) A measure of the responsiveness of the quantity of a commodity demanded to changes in price of a related commodity, defined by the formula

$$\eta_{xy} = \frac{\text{percentage change in quantity demanded of one good } X}{\text{percentage change in price of another good } Y}$$

crowding out effect The offsetting reduction in private expenditure caused by the rise in interest rates that follows an expansionary fiscal policy.

current account A part of the balance-of-payments accounts that records payments and receipts arising from trade in goods and services and from interest and dividends that are earned by capital owned in one country and invested in another.

current-dollar GDP Gross national product valued in prices prevailing at the time of measurement; year-to-year changes in current-dollar GDP reflect changes both in quantities produced and in market prices. Also called *nominal GDP*.

customs union A group of countries who agree to have free trade among themselves and a common set of barriers against imports from the rest of the world.

cyclical unemployment Unemployment in excess of frictional and structural unemployment; it is due to a shortfall of actual national income below potential national income. Sometimes called *deficient demand unemployment*.

cyclically adjusted deficit (*CAD*) (or surplus (*CAS*)) An estimate of the government budget deficit (expenditure minus tax revenue), not as it actually is but as it would be if national income were at its potential level. The cyclically adjusted surplus (*CAS*) is the negative of the *CAD*.

debt Generally, amounts owed to one's creditors. From a firm's point of view, that portion of its money capital that is borrowed rather than subscribed by shareholders.

decision lag The period of time between perceiving some problem and reaching a decision on what to do about it.

decreasing returns A situation in which output increases less than in proportion to inputs as the scale of a firm's production increases. A firm in this situation, with fixed factor prices, is an *increasing cost* firm.

deflation A reduction in the general price level.

deflationary gap See *recessionary gap*.

demand The entire relationship between the quantity of a commodity that buyers wish to purchase per period of time and the price of that commodity.

demand curve The graphical representation of the relationship between the quantity of a commodity that buyers wish to purchase per period of time and the price of that commodity, other things being equal.

demand deposit A bank deposit that is withdrawable on demand (without notice of intention to withdraw) and transferable by means of a check.

demand for money The total amount of money balances that the public wishes to hold for all purposes.

demand inflation Inflation arising from excess aggregate demand, that is, when national income exceeds potential income.

demand schedule A table showing for selected values the relationship between the quantity of a commodity that buyers wish to purchase per period of time and the price of that commodity, other things being equal.

deposit money Money held by the public in the form of demand deposits with commercial banks.

depreciation (of capital) See *capital consumption allowance*.

depreciation (of a currency) A fall in the external value of domestic currency in terms of foreign currency; that is, a fall in the exchange rate.

depression A persistent period of very low economic activity with very high unemployment and high excess capacity.

derived demand The demand for a factor of production that results from the demand for the products that it is used to make.

developed countries The higher-income countries of the world, including the United States, Canada, most of the countries of Western Europe, Japan, Australia, and South Africa.

developing countries The lower-income countries of the world, most of which are in Africa, Asia, and Latin America. Also called *underdeveloped, less developed*, and the *South*.

differentiated product A group of commodities that are similar enough to be called the *same* product but are dissimilar enough so that all of them do not have to be sold at the same price.

diminishing marginal rate of substitution The hypothesis that the marginal rate of substitution changes systematically as the amounts of two commodities being consumed vary.

direct burden Amount of money for a tax that is collected from taxpayers.

direct investment In balance-of-payments accounting, nonresident investment in the form of a takeover or capital investment in a domestic branch plant or subsidiary corporation in which the investor has voting control.

discount rate (1) In banking, the rate at which the central bank is prepared to lend reserves to commercial banks. (2) More generally, the rate of interest used to discount a stream of future payments to arrive at their present value.

discouraged workers People who would like to work but have ceased looking for a job and hence have withdrawn from the labor force, because they believe that no jobs are available for them.

discretionary fiscal policy Fiscal policy that is a conscious response (not according to any predetermined rule) to each particular state of the economy as it arises.

disembodied technical change Technical change that raises output without the necessity of building new capital to embody the new knowledge.

disequilibrium The absence of equilibrium. A market is in disequilibrium when there is either excess demand or excess supply.

disequilibrium price A price at which quantity demanded does not equal quantity supplied.

disposable personal income (Y_d) GNP minus any part of it not actually paid to households minus personal income taxes paid by households plus transfer payments to households; personal income *minus* personal income taxes.

distributed profits Profits paid out to owners of a firm. For incorporated firms, the distributed profits are called *dividends*.

dividends Profits paid out to shareholders of a corporation.

division of labor The breaking up of a production process into a series of specialized tasks, each done by a different worker.

dollar standard A system under which countries hold reserves in, and settle debts with, U.S. dollars, but the dollar is not backed by gold or any other physical source of monetary value.

double counting In national income accounting, adding up the total outputs of all the sectors in the economy so that the value of intermediate goods is counted in the sector that produces them and every time they are purchased as an input by another sector.

dumping In international trade, the practice of selling a commodity at a lower price in the export market than in the domestic market for reasons that are not related to differences in costs of servicing the two markets.

duopoly An industry that contains only two firms.

durable good A good that yields its services over an extended period of time. Often divided into the subcategories *producers' durables* (e.g., machines, equipment) and *consumers' durables* (e.g., cars, appliances).

economic efficiency The least costly method of producing any output.

economic growth Increases in real, or constant-dollar, potential GDP.

economic profits or **losses** The difference between the revenues received from the sale of output and the opportunity cost of the inputs used to make the output. Negative economic profits are economic losses. Also called *pure profits* or *pure losses*, or simply *profits* or *losses*.

economic rent The surplus of total earnings over what must be paid to prevent a factor from moving to another use.

economies of scale Reduction of costs per unit output resulting from an expansion in the scale of a firm's operations so that more of all inputs are being used.

economies of scope Economies achieved by a firm that is large enough to engage efficiently in multiproduct production and associated large-scale distribution, advertising, and purchasing.

economy A set of interrelated production and consumption activities.

effective rate of tariff The tax charged on any imported commodity expressed as a percentage of the value added by the exporting industry.

elastic demand The situation in which, for a given percentage change in price, there is a greater percentage change in quantity demanded; elasticity greater than unity.

elasticity of demand (η) A measure of the responsiveness of quantity of a commodity demanded to a change in market price, defined by the formula

$$\eta = \frac{\text{percentage change in quantity demanded}}{\text{percentage change in price}}$$

With negatively sloped demand curves, elasticity is a negative number. The above expression is therefore usually multiplied by −1 to make measured elasticity positive. Also called *demand elasticity, price elasticity*.

elasticity of supply (η_S) A measure of the responsiveness of the quantity of a commodity supplied to a change in the market price, defined by the formula

$$\eta_S = \frac{\text{percentage change in quantity supplied}}{\text{percentage change in price}}$$

embodied technical change Technical change that is intrinsic to the particular capital goods in use, and hence that can be utilized only when new capital, embodying the new techniques, is built.

employment The number of adult workers (16 years of age and older) who hold full-time jobs.

endogenous expenditure See *induced expenditure*.

endogenous variable A variable that is explained within a theory.

ends The goals that we seek to attain.

entry barrier Any natural barrier to the entry of new firms into an industry, such as a large minimum efficient scale for firms, or any firm-created barrier, such as a patent.

envelope Any curve that encloses, by being tangent to, a series of other curves. In particular, the *envelope cost curve* is the *LRAC* curve, which encloses the *SRATC* curves by being tangent to each without cutting any of them.

equilibrium condition A condition that must be fulfilled if some market or sector of the economy, or the whole economy, is to be in equilibrium.

equilibrium differential A difference in factor prices that would persist in equilibrium, without any tendency for it to be removed.

equilibrium price The price at which quantity demanded equals quantity supplied.

equity capital Funds provided by the owners of a firm the return on which depends on the firm's profits.

excess burden The value to taxpayers of the changes in behavior that are induced by taxes; the amount that taxpayers would be willing to pay, over and above the direct burden of taxes, to abolish the taxes.

excess capacity The amount by which actual output falls short of capacity output (which is the output that corresponds to the minimum short-run average total cost).

excess capacity theorem The property of long-run equilibrium in monopolistic competition that firms produce on the falling portion of their average total cost curves, so that they have excess capacity measured by the gap between present output and the output that coincides with minimum average total cost.

excess demand A situation in which, at the given price, quantity demanded exceeds quantity supplied. Also called a *shortage*.

excess reserves Reserves held by a commercial bank in excess of the legally required minimum.

excess supply A situation in which, at the given price, quantity supplied exceeds quantity demanded. Also called a *surplus*.

exchange rate The price in terms of one currency at which another currency, or claims on it, can be bought and sold.

excise tax A tax on the sale of a particular commodity; may be a *specific tax* (fixed tax per unit of commodity) or an *ad valorem tax* (fixed percentage of the value of the commodity).

execution lag The time that it takes to put policies in place after the decision has been made.

exhaustible resource See *nonrenewable resource*.

exogenous expenditure See *autonomous expenditure*.

exogenous variable A variable that influences endogenous variables but is itself determined by factors outside the theory.

expectational inflation Inflation that occurs because decision makers raise prices (so as to keep their relative prices constant) in the expectation that the price level is going to rise.

expectations-augmented Phillips curve The relationship between unemployment and the rate of increase of money wages or between national income and the rate of increase of money prices that arises when the demand and expectations components of inflation are combined.

external economies of scale Scale economies that cause the firm's costs to fall as *industry output* rises but that are external to the firm and so cannot be obtained by the firm's increasing its own output.

external value of the dollar The value of the dollar expressed in terms of foreign currencies; changes in the dollar's external value are measured by changes in the exchange rate.

externalities Effects, either good or bad, on parties not directly involved in the production or use of a commodity. Also called *third-party effects*.

factor markets Markets in which the services of factors of production are sold.

factor mobility The ease with which factors can be transferred between uses.

factor services The services of factors of production that are used to produce outputs.

factors of production Resources used to produce goods and services to satisfy wants; frequently divided into the basic categories of land, labor, and capital.

fair trade laws Laws providing import duties intended to eliminate unfair competition from foreign goods caused by foreign-government subsidies or predatory pricing by foreign producers. Also called *trade remedy laws*.

falling-cost industry An industry in which the lowest costs attainable by a firm fall as the scale of the industry expands.

favorable balance of payments A credit balance on some part of the international payments accounts (receipts exceed payments); often refers to a favorable balance on current plus capital account (that is, everything except the official settlements account).

fiat money Paper money or coinage that is neither backed by nor convertible into anything else but is decreed by the government to be accepted as legal tender and is generally accepted in exchange for goods and services and for the discharge of debts.

final demand Demand for the economy's final output.

final goods Goods that are not used as inputs by other firms, but are produced to be sold for consumption, investment, government, or exports during the period under consideration.

financial capital See *money capital*.

fine tuning The attempt to maintain national income at or near its full-employment level by means of frequent changes in fiscal or monetary policy.

firm The unit that employs factors of production to produce goods and services.

fiscal policy The use of the government's tax and spending policies in an effort to influence the behavior of such macro variables as the GDP and total employment.

fixed cost A cost that does not change with output. Also called *overhead cost, unavoidable cost*.

fixed exchange rate An exchange rate that is maintained within a small range around its publicly stated par value by the intervention of a country's central bank in foreign market operations. Also called a *pegged rate*.

fixed factor An input that cannot be increased beyond a given amount in the short run.

fixed investment Investment in plant and equipment.

flexible exchange rate An exchange rate that is left free to be determined by the forces of demand and supply on the free market, with no intervention by the monetary authorities. Also called *floating exchange rate*.

floating exchange rate See *flexible exchange rate*.

foreign exchange Actual foreign currencies or various claims on them, such as bank balances or promises to pay, that are traded for each other on the foreign exchange market.

foreign exchange market The market where different national monies, or claims to these monies, are traded against each other.

45° line In macroeconomics, the line that graphs the equilibrium condition that aggregate desired expenditure should equal national income ($AE = Y$).

fractional reserve system A banking system in which commercial banks are required to keep only a fraction of their deposits in cash or on deposit with the central bank.

free good A commodity for which the quantity supplied exceeds the quantity demanded at a price of zero; therefore, a good that does not command a positive price in a market economy.

free-market economy An economy in which the decisions of individual households and firms (as distinct from the government) exert the major influence over the allocation of resources.

free reserves See *net unborrowed reserves*.

free trade The absence of any form of government intervention in international trade, which implies that imports and exports must not be subject to special taxes or restrictions levied merely because of their status as "imports" or "exports."

free-trade area An agreement among two or more countries to abolish tariffs on all, or most, of the trade among themselves, while each remains free to set its own tariffs against other countries.

frictional unemployment Unemployment caused by the time that is taken for labor to move from one job to another.

full employment See *high employment*.

function Loosely, an expression of a relationship between two or more variables. Precisely, Y is a function of the variables $X_1, \ldots, X_n$ if, for every set of values of the variables $X_1, \ldots, X_n$, there is associated a unique value of the variable Y.

functional distribution of income The distribution of total national income among the major factors of production.

G See *government expenditure*.

gains from trade The increased output due to the specialization according to comparative advantage that is made possible by trade.

Giffen good An inferior good for which the negative income effect outweighs the substitution effect, so that the demand curve is positively sloped.

GDP deflator See *implicit GDP deflator*.

GDP gap See *output gap*.

gold exchange standard A monetary system in which U.S. currency is directly convertible into gold and other countries' currencies are indirectly convertible by being convertible into the gold-backed U.S. dollar at a fixed rate.

goods   Tangible commodities, such as cars or shoes.

goods markets   Markets in which outputs of goods and services are sold. Also called *product markets*.

government   All public officials, agencies, and other organizations belonging to or under the control of state, local, or federal governments.

government purchases   Includes all government expenditure on currently produced goods and services and does not include government transfer payments. Represented by the symbol G as one of the four components of aggregate expenditure.

Gresham's law   The theory that "bad," or debased, money drives "good," or undebased, money out of circulation, because people keep the good money for other purposes and use the bad money for transactions.

gross domestic product (GDP)   National income as measured by the output approach; equal to the sum of all values added in the economy or, what is the same thing, the values of all final goods produced in the economy. It can be valued at *current prices* to get *nominal GDP*, which is also called *GDP at current*, or *market, prices*; or it can be valued at base-year prices to get *real GDP*, which is also called *GDP at constant prices*.

gross investment   The total value of all investment goods produced in the economy during a stated period of time.

gross national product (GNP)   The value of total output produced, and incomes earned, by domestically based producers and factors of production. Measured from the expenditure side of the national accounts, it is the sum of consumption, investment, government expenditure on final output, and net exports; measured from the income side of the national accounts, it is the sum of factor incomes, plus depreciation, plus indirect taxes net of subsidies.

gross national product at market prices   See *gross national product*.

gross tuning   The use of macroeconomic policy to stabilize the economy such that large deviations from high employment do not occur for extended periods of time.

high employment   Employment that is sufficient to produce the economy's potential output; at high employment, all remaining unemployment is frictional and structural.

high-employment GDP (Y^*)   See *potential GDP*.

high-employment national income (Y^*)   See *potential GDP*.

homogeneous product   In the eyes of purchasers, every unit of the product is identical to every other unit.

horizontal merger   See *merger*.

household   All of the people who live under one roof and who make, or are subject to others making for them, joint financial decisions.

human capital   The capitalized value of productive investments in persons; usually refers to value derived from expenditures on education, training, and health improvements.

hypothesis of diminishing returns   See *law of diminishing returns*.

I   See *investment expenditure*.

IM   A country's total expenditure on imports.

implicit GDP deflator   An index number derived by dividing GDP, measured in current dollars, by GDP, measured in constant dollars, and multiplying by 100. In effect, a price index, with current-year quantity weights, measuring the average change in price of all the items in the GDP. Also called *gross product domestic deflator*.

import quota   A limit set by the government on the quantity of a foreign commodity that may be shipped into that country in a given time period.

imputed costs   The costs of using factors of production already owned by the firm, measured by the earnings they could have received in their best alternative use.

income-consumption line   (1) A curve showing the relationship for a commodity between quantity demanded and income, *ceteris paribus*; (2) a curve drawn on an indifference curve diagram and connecting the points of tangency between a set of indifference curves and a set of parallel budget lines, showing how the consumption bundle changes as income changes, with relative prices being held constant.

income effect   The effect on quantity demanded of a change in real income.

income elasticity of demand   A measure of the responsiveness of quantity demanded to a change in income, defined by the formula

$$\eta_Y = \frac{\text{percentage change in quantity demanded}}{\text{percentage change in income}}$$

incomes policy   Any direct intervention by the government to influence wage and price formation.

increasing returns   A situation in which output increases more than in proportion to inputs as the scale of a firm's production increases. A firm in this situation, with fixed factor prices, is a *decreasing cost* firm.

indexation   The automatic change in any money payment in proportion to the change in the price level.

index number   An average that measures change over time of such variables as the price level and industrial production; conventionally expressed as a percentage relative to a base period, which is assigned the value 100.

indifference curve A curve showing all combinations of two commodities that give the household an equal amount of satisfaction and between which the household is thus indifferent.

indifference map A set of indifference curves based on a given set of household preferences.

induced expenditure In macroeconomics, elements of expenditure that are explained by variables within the theory. In the aggregate desired expenditure function, it is any component of expenditure that is related to national income. Also called *endogenous expenditure*.

industry A group of firms that produce a single product or group of related products.

inelastic demand The situation in which, for a given percentage change in price, there is a smaller percentage change in quantity demanded; elasticity less than unity.

infant industry argument for tariffs The argument that new domestic industries with potential for economies of scale, or learning by doing, need to be protected from competition from established, low-cost foreign producers, so that they can grow large enough to achieve costs as low as those of foreign producers.

inferior good A good for which income elasticity is negative.

inflation A rise in the average level of all prices. Sometimes restricted to prolonged or sustained rises.

inflationary gap A situation in which actual national income exceeds potential income.

information asymmetries Sources of market failure that arise when one party to a transaction has more information relevant to the transaction than does the other party.

infrastructure The basic installations and facilities (especially transportation and communications systems) on which the commerce of a community depends.

injections Income earned by domestic firms that does not arise out of the spending of domestic households and income earned by domestic households that does not arise out of the spending of domestic firms.

innovation The introduction of an invention into methods of production.

inputs Intermediate products and factor services that are used in the process of production.

interest The payment for the use of borrowed money.

interest rate The price paid per dollar borrowed per period of time, expressed either as a proportion (e.g., 0.06) or as a percentage (e.g., 6 percent). Also called the *nominal interest rate* to distinguish it from the *real rate of interest*.

intermediate products All outputs that are used as inputs by other producers in a further stage of production.

intermediate targets Variables that the government cannot control directly and does not seek to control ultimately, yet that have an important influence on policy variables.

internal economies of scale Scale economies that result from the firm's own actions and hence are available to it by raising its own output.

internal value of the dollar The purchasing power of the dollar measured in terms of domestic goods and services; changes in the internal value of the dollar are measured by changes in an index of U.S. prices.

internalization A process that results in a producer or consumer taking account of a previously external effect.

invention The discovery of something new, such as a new production technique or a new product.

inventories Stocks of raw materials, goods in process, and finished goods, held by firms to mitigate the effect of short-term fluctuations in production or sales.

investment expenditure Expenditure on the production of goods not for present consumption.

investment goods Goods that are produced not for present consumption, i.e., capital goods, inventories, and residential housing.

invisible account A form of balance-of-payments account that records payments and receipts arising out of trade in services and payments for the use of capital. Also called *service account*.

invisibles All those items of foreign trade that are intangible; services as opposed to goods.

involuntary unemployment Unemployment due to the inability of qualified persons who are seeking work to find jobs at the going wage rate.

isoquant A curve showing all technologically efficient factor combinations for producing a specified amount of output.

isoquant map A series of isoquants from the same production function, each isoquant relating to a specific level of output.

Keynesians A label attached to economists who hold the view, derived from the work of John Maynard Keynes, that active use of monetary and fiscal policy can be effective in stabilizing the economy. Often the term encompasses economists who advocate active policy intervention in general.

Keynesian short-run aggregate supply curve A horizontal aggregate supply curve, indicating that, when national income is below potential, changes in national income can occur with little or no accompanying changes in prices.

kinked demand curve A demand curve facing an oligopolistic firm that assumes its competitors will match its price reductions but will not respond to its price increases. At the firm's current price-output combination, its demand curve is kinked and its marginal revenue curve is discontinuous.

k percent rule The proposition that the money supply should be increased at a constant percentage rate year in and year out, irrespective of cylical changes in national income.

labor A factor of production consisting of all physical and mental efforts provided by people.

labor force The total number of persons employed in both civilian and military jobs, plus the number of persons who are unemployed.

labor force participation rate The percentage of the population of working age that is actually in the labor force (i.e., either working or seeking work).

labor union See *union*.

Laffer curve A graph relating the revenue yield of a tax system to the marginal or average tax rate imposed.

laissez faire Literally, "let do"; a policy advocating the minimization of government intervention in a market economy.

land A factor of production consisting of all gifts of nature, including raw materials and "land," as understood in ordinary speech.

law of demand The assertion that market price and quantity demanded in the market vary inversely with one another, that is, that demand curves are negatively sloped.

law of diminishing returns The hypothesis that, if increasing quantities of a variable factor are applied to a given quantity of fixed factors, the marginal product and average product of the variable factor will eventually decrease. Also called *hypothesis of diminishing returns, law of variable proportions*.

law of variable proportions See *law of diminishing returns*.

learning curve A curve showing how a firm's costs of producing at a given rate of output fall as the total amount produced increases over time as a result of accumulated learning of how to make the product efficiently using given equipment.

legal tender Anything that by law must be accepted for the purchase of goods and services or in discharge of a debt.

less-developed countries (LDCs) The lower-income countries of the world, most of which are in Asia, Africa, and South and Central America. Also called *underdeveloped countries, developing countries*, the *South*.

leveraged buyout (LBO) A buyout of a firm largely financed by borrowed money.

life-cycle theory A hypothesis that relates the household's actual consumption to its expected lifetime income rather than (as in early Keynesian theory) to its current income.

lifetime income See *permanent income*.

limited liability The limitation of the financial responsibility of an owner (shareholder) of a corporation to the amount of money that the shareholder has actually invested in the firm by purchasing its shares.

limited partnership A form of business organization in which the firm has two classes of owners: general partners, who take part in managing the firm and who are personally liable for all of the firm's actions and debts, and limited partners, who take no part in the management of the firm and who risk only the money that they have invested.

liquidity preference (LP) function The function that relates the demand for money to the rate of interest.

logarithmic scale A scale in which equal proportional changes are shown as equal distances (for example, 1 inch may always represent doubling of a variable, whether from 3 to 6 or 50 to 100). Also called *log scale, ratio scale*.

logrolling The political practice in which two or more voters agree to support the other's programs in exchange for support for his or her own.

long run A period of time in which all inputs may be varied, but the basic technology of production cannot be changed.

long-run aggregate supply (LRAS) curve A curve showing the relationship between the price level of final output and the total quantity of output supplied when all markets have fully adjusted to the existing price level; a vertical line at $Y = Y^*$.

long-run average cost (LRAC) curve The curve relating the least-cost method of producing any output to the level of output when all inputs can be varied.

long-run industry supply (LRS) curve A curve showing the relationship between the market price and the quantity supplied by a competitive industry when all the firms in that industry are in full, long-run equilibrium.

Lorenz curve A graph showing the extent of departure from equality of income distribution.

M1 Currency plus demand deposits plus other checkable deposits.

M2 M1 plus money market mutual fund balances, money market deposit accounts, savings accounts, and small-denomination time deposits.

M3 M2 plus large-denomination time deposits (CDs), term repurchase agreements, and money market mutual funds held by institutions.

macroeconomics The study of the determination of economic aggregates, such as total output, total employment, the price level, and the rate of economic growth.

marginal cost (*MC*) The increase in total cost resulting from raising the rate of production by one unit. Mathematically, the rate of change of cost with respect to output. Also called *incremental cost*.

marginal cost pricing Setting price equal to marginal cost so that buyers are just willing to pay for the last unit bought the amount that it cost to make that unit.

marginal efficiency of capital (*MEC*) The marginal rate of return on a nation's capital stock. The rate of return on one additional dollar of net investment, that is, an addition of one dollar's worth of new capital to capital stock.

marginal efficiency of investment (*MEI*) function The function that relates the quantity of investment to the rate of interest.

marginal physical product (*MPP*) See *marginal product*.

marginal product (*MP*) The change in quantity of total output that results from using one unit more of a variable factor. Mathematically, the rate of change of output with respect to the quantity of the variable factor. Also called *incremental product* or *marginal physical product (MPP)*.

marginal-productivity theory of distribution The theory that factors are paid the value of their marginal products so that the total earnings of each type of factor of production equals the value of the marginal product of that factor multiplied by the number of units of that factor that are employed.

marginal propensity to consume (*MPC*) The change in consumption divided by the change in disposable income that brought it about; mathematically, the rate of change of consumption with respect to disposable income ($MPC = \Delta C / \Delta Y_d$).

marginal propensity not to spend The fraction of any increment to national income that is not spent on domestic production (1 − the marginal propensity to spend; that is, $1 - \Delta AE / \Delta Y$).

marginal propensity to save (*MPS*) The change in total desired saving related to the change in disposable income that brought it about ($\Delta S / \Delta Y_d$).

marginal propensity to spend The fraction of any increment to national income that is spent on domestic production; it is measured by the change in aggregate expenditure divided by the change in income ($\Delta AE / \Delta Y$).

marginal rate of substitution (*MRS*) (1) In consumption, the slope of an indifference curve, showing how much more of one commodity must be provided to compensate for the giving up of one unit of another commodity if the level of satisfaction is to be held constant. (2) In production, the slope of an isoquant, showing how much more of one factor of production must be used to compensate for the use of one less unit of another factor of production if production is to be held constant.

marginal revenue (*MR*) The change in a firm's total revenue resulting from a change in its rate of sales by one unit. Mathematically, the rate of change of revenue with respect to output. Also called *incremental revenue*.

marginal revenue product (*MRP*) The addition of revenue attributable to the last unit of a variable factor ($MRP = MP \times MR$). Mathematically, the rate of change of revenue with respect to quantity of the variable factor.

marginal tax rate The amount of tax that a taxpayer would pay on an additional dollar of income; that is, the fraction of an additional dollar of income that is paid in taxes.

marginal utility The additional satisfaction obtained by a consumer from consuming one unit more of a good or service; mathematically, the rate of change of utility with respect to consumption.

margin requirement The fraction of the price of a stock that must be paid in cash, while putting up the stock as security against a loan for the balance.

market Any situation in which buyers and sellers can negotiate the exchange of a commodity or group of commodities.

market-clearing price Price at which quantity demanded equals quantity supplied, so that there are neither unsatisfied buyers nor unsatisfied sellers, that is, the equilibrium price.

market economy A society in which people specialize in productive activities and meet most of their material wants through exchanges voluntarily agreed upon by the contracting parties.

market failure Failure of the unregulated market system to achieve optimal allocative efficiency or social goals because of externalities, market impediments, or market imperfections.

market for corporate control An interpretation of conglomerate mergers, leveraged buy outs, and hostile takeovers as mechanisms that place the firm in the hands of those who are able to generate the most value product.

market rate of interest The actual interest rate in effect at a given moment.

market sector That portion of an economy in which commodities are bought and sold and in which producers must cover their costs from sales revenue.

market structure All those features of a market that affect the behavior and performance of firms in that market, such as the number and size of sellers, the extent of knowledge about each other's actions, the degree of freedom of entry, and the degree of product differentiation.

means The methods of achieving our goals.

means-tested programs Means-tested programs pay benefits only to persons who are sufficiently poor to be eligible. Medicaid is the largest federal means-tested program. Aid to Families with Dependent Children (welfare) is the most well known.

median The value within any set of data at which half of the observations are greater and half are less. Thus, half of a population earns income above the median income, and half earns income below the median.

medium of exchange Anything that is generally acceptable in return for goods and services sold.

merchandise account See *trade account*.

merger The purchase of either the physical assets or the controlling share of ownership of one firm by another. In a *horizontal* merger both firms are in the same line of business; in a *vertical* merger one firm is a supplier of the other; if the two are in unrelated industries, it is a *conglomerate* merger.

merit goods Goods such as housing and medical care that are deemed to be especially important.

microeconomic policy Activities of governments designed to alter resource allocation and/or income distribution.

microeconomics The study of the allocation of resources and the distribution of income as they are affected by the workings of the price system and by government policies.

minimum efficient scale (*MES*) The smallest output at which long-run average cost reaches its minimum because all available economies of scale in production and/or distribution have been realized. Also called *minimum optimal scale*.

minimum wages Legally specified minimum rate of pay for labor in covered occupations.

mixed economy An economy in which some decisions about the allocation of resources are made by firms and households and some by the government.

monetarists A label attached to economists who stress monetary causes of cyclical fluctuations and inflations and who believe that an active stabilization policy is not normally required.

monetary equilibrium A situation in which the demand for money equals the supply of money.

monetary policy An attempt to influence the economy by operating on such monetary variables as the quantity of money and the rate of interest.

money Money acts as a medium of exchange and can also serve as a store of value and a unit of account.

money capital Money that a firm raises to carry on its business, including both equity capital and debt. Also called *financial capital*.

money income Income measured in monetary units per period of time.

money market deposit Checkable deposit accounts at nonbank financial institutions that earn relatively high interest rates.

money market mutual fund (MMMF) Liquid financial instruments that earn high yields, are checkable, but are subject to transaction restrictions.

money rate of interest See *interest rate*.

money substitute Something that serves as a temporary medium of exchange but is not a store of value.

money supply The total quantity of money in an economy at a point in time. Also called *the supply of money*.

monopolist A firm that is the only seller in some market.

monopolistic competition (1) A market structure of an industry in which there are many firms and freedom of entry and exit but in which each firm has a product somewhat differentiated from the others, giving it some control over its price; (2) More recently, any industry in which more than one firm sells differentiated products.

monopoly A market containing a single firm.

monopsony A market situation in which there is a single buyer.

moral hazard A situation in which an individual or a firm takes advantage of special knowledge while engaging in socially uneconomic behavior.

multilateral balance of payments The balance of payments between one country and the rest of the world taken as a whole.

multiplier The ratio of the change in national income to the change in autonomous expenditure that brought it about.

NAIRU (Short for *nonaccelerating inflationary rate of unemployment*.) The rate of unemployment associated with potential national income and at which a steady, nonaccelerating or nondecelerating inflation can be sustained indefinitely. Also called *the natural rate of unemployment*.

Nash equilibrium In the case of firms, an equilibrium that results when each firm in an industry is currently doing the best that it can, given the current behavior of the other firms in the industry.

national asset formation The sum of investment and net exports.

national debt The current volume of outstanding federal government debt.

national income In general, the value of total output and the value of the income that is generated by the production of that output.

national saving The sum of public saving and private saving. All of national income that is not spent on government purchases or private consumption.

natural monopoly An industry characterized by economies of scale sufficiently large that one firm can most efficiently supply the entire market demand.

natural rate of unemployment See *NAIRU*.

natural scale A scale in which equal absolute amounts are represented by equal distances.

near money Liquid assets that are easily convertible into money without risk of significant loss of value and can be used as short-term stores of purchasing power, but are not themselves media of exchange.

negotiable order of withdrawal (NOW)   A checklike device for transferring funds from one person's time deposit to another person.

net domestic product   Gross domestic product less capital consumed in the production of GDP.

net exports (NX)   The value of total exports minus the value of total imports. Represented by the expression $(X - IM)$ as a component of aggregate expenditure, where X is total exports and IM is total imports.

net investment   Gross investment minus replacement investment.

net taxes   Taxes minus transfer payments.

net unborrowed reserves   The total reserves of the commercial banking system minus required reserves minus the reserves that have been borrowed from the central bank; that is, excess reserves minus borrowed reserves. Also called *free reserves*.

neutrality of money   The doctrine that the money supply affects only the absolute level of prices and has no effect on relative prices and hence no effect on the allocation of resources or the distribution of income.

newly industrialized economies (NIEs)   Countries that have industrialized and grown rapidly over the past 30 years to achieve per capita incomes roughly half of those achieved in the United States. Also called *newly industrializing countries* (NICs).

nominal national income   Total national income measured in dollars; the money value of national income. Also called *money national income* or *current-dollar national income*.

nominal rate of interest   See *interest rate*.

nominal rate of tariff   The tax charged on any imported commodity.

noncooperative equilibrium   An equilibrium reached when firms calculate their own best policy without considering competitor's reactions.

nonmarket sector   The portion of the economy in which goods are provided freely so that producers must cover their costs from sources other than sales revenue.

nonrenewable resource   Any productive resource that is available as a fixed stock that cannot be replaced once it is used.

nonstrategic behavior   Behavior that does *not* take account of the reactions of rivals to one's own behavior.

nontariff barriers   Restrictions, other than tariffs, designed to reduce the flow of imported goods.

normal good   A good for which income elasticity is positive.

normal profits   The opportunity cost of capital and risk taking just necessary to keep the owners in the industry. Normal profits are usually included

in what economists, but not businesspersons, call *total costs*.

normative statement   A statement about what ought to be—in an ethical sense—as opposed to what actually is, in a positive sense.

NOW   See *negotiable order of withdrawal*.

oligopoly   An industry that contains two or more firms, at least one of which produces a significant portion of the industry's total output.

open market operations   The purchase and sale on the open market by the central bank of securities (usually short-term government securities).

opportunity cost   The cost of using resources for a certain purpose, measured by the benefit given up by not using them in their best alternative use.

organization theory   A set of hypotheses that predicts that the substance of the decisions of a firm is affected by its size and form of organization.

output gap   Potential national income minus actual national income. Also called the *GDP gap*.

outputs   The goods and services that result from the process of production.

Pareto-efficiency   See *Pareto-optimality*.

Pareto-optimality   A situation in which it is impossible by reallocation of production or consumption activities to make all consumers better off without simultaneously making others worse off (or, as it is sometimes put, to make at least one person better off while making no one worse off). Also called *Pareto-efficiency*.

partnership   A form of business organization in which the firm has two or more joint owners, each of whom takes part in the management of the firm and is personally responsible for all of the firm's actions and debts.

paternalism   Intervention in the free choices of individuals by others (including governments) to protect them against their own ignorance or folly.

pegged rate   See *fixed exchange rate*.

per capita output   GDP divided by total population.

perfect competition   A market structure in which all firms in an industry are price takers and in which there is freedom of entry into and exit from the industry.

perfectly contestable market   See *contestable market*.

permanent income   The maximum amount that a household can consume per year into the indefinite future without reducing its wealth. (A number of similar, but not identical, definitions are in common use.) Also called *lifetime income*.

permanent-income theory   A hypothesis that relates actual consumption to permanent income rather than (as in the original Keynesian theory) to current income.

personal income Income earned by, or paid to, individuals before allowance for personal income taxes on that income.

Phillips curve Originally, a relationship between the percentage of the labor force unemployed and the rate of change of money wages. Now often drawn as a relationship between the percentage of the labor force employed and the rate of price inflation or between actual national income and the rate of price inflation.

point elasticity A measure of the responsiveness of quantity to price at a particular point on the demand curve. The formula for point elasticity of demand is

$$\eta = \frac{\Delta q}{\Delta p} \times \frac{p}{q}$$

With negatively sloped demand curves elasticity is a negative number. Sometimes the above expression is multiplied by -1 to make elasticity positive.

point of diminishing average productivity The level of output at which average product reaches a maximum.

point of diminishing marginal productivity The level of output at which marginal product reaches a maximum.

policy instruments The variables that the government can control directly to achieve its policy objectives.

policy variables The variables that the government seeks to control, such as real national income and the price level.

portfolio investment In balance-of-payments accounting, foreign investment in bonds or a minority holding of shares that does not involve legal control. See also *direct investment*.

positive statement A statement about what actually is (was or will be), as opposed to what ought to be in an ethical sense.

potential GDP (Y^*) The real gross domestic product that the economy could produce if its productive resources were fully employed at their normal levels of utilization. Also called *potential national income, national income, high-employment GDP, high-employment national income*.

potential income See *potential GDP*.

poverty gap The number of dollars per year required to raise everyone's income that is below the poverty level to that level.

poverty level The official government estimate of the annual family income that is required to maintain a minimum adequate standard of living.

precautionary balances Money balances held for protection against the uncertainty of the timing of cash flows.

present value (*PV*) The value now of one or more payments to be received in the future; often referred to as the *discounted present value* of future payments.

price ceiling A government-imposed maximum permissible price at which a commodity may be sold.

price-consumption line A line connecting the points of tangency between a set of indifference curves and a set of budget lines where one absolute price is fixed and the other varies, money income being held constant.

price controls Government policies that attempt to hold the price in a particular market at a disequilibrium value.

price discrimination The sale by one firm of different units of a commodity at two or more different prices for reasons not associated with differences in cost.

price elasticity of demand See *elasticity of demand*.

price floor A government-imposed minimum permissible price at which a commodity may be sold.

price index A number that shows the average of some group of prices; expressed as a percentage of the average ruling in some base period. Price indexes can be used to measure the price level at a given time relative to a base period.

price level The average level of all prices in the economy, usually expressed as an index number.

price makers Firms that administer their prices. See *administered price*.

price taker A firm that can alter its rate of production and sales without significantly affecting the market price of its product.

price theory The theory of how prices are determined; competitive price theory concerns the determination of prices in competitive markets by the interaction of demand and supply.

principal-agent problem The problem of resource allocation that arises because contracts that will induce agents to act in their principals' best interests are generally impossible to write or too costly to monitor.

principle of substitution Methods of production will change if relative prices of inputs change, with relatively more of the cheaper input and relatively less of the more expensive input being used.

private cost The value of the best alternative use of resources used in production as valued by the producer.

private saving Saving on the part of households—that part of disposable income that is not spent on consumption.

private sector The portion of an economy in which goods and services are produced by nongovernmental units, such as firms and households.

procyclical Movements of economic variables in the same direction as the business cycle—up in booms and down in slumps.

producers' durables See *durable good*.

producers' surplus The difference between the total amount that producers receive for all units sold of a commodity and the total variable cost of producing the commodity.

product differentiation The existence of similar but not identical products sold by a single industry, such as the breakfast food and the automobile industries.

production The act of making commodities—either goods or services.

production function A functional relation showing the maximum output that can be produced by each and every combination of inputs.

production possibility curve A curve that shows which alternative combinations of commodities can just be attained if all available resources are used; it is thus the boundary between attainable and unattainable output combinations. Also called the *production possibility boundary*.

productive efficiency Production of any output at the lowest attainable cost for that level of output.

productivity Output produced per unit of some input; frequently used to refer to *labor productivity*, measured by total output divided by the amount of labor used.

product markets Markets in which outputs of goods and services are sold. Also called *goods markets*.

profit (1) In ordinary usage, the difference between the value of outputs and the value of inputs. (2) In microeconomics, the difference between revenues received from the sale of goods and the value of inputs, which includes the opportunity cost of capital, so that profits are *economic profits*. (3) In macroeconomics, profits exclude interest on borrowed capital but do not exclude the return on owner's capital.

progressive tax A tax that takes a larger percentage of income the higher the level of income.

proportional tax A tax that takes a constant percentage of income at all levels of income and is thus neither progressive nor regressive.

protectionism Any government policy that interferes with free trade in order to give some protection to domestic industries against foreign competition.

proxy An order from a stockholder that passes the right to vote to a nominee, usually an existing member of the board of a firm.

public goods See *collective consumption goods*.

public saving Saving on the part of governments. Public saving is exactly equal to government budget surpluses, or government revenues less government expenditures.

public sector The portion of an economy in which goods and services are produced by the government or by government-owned agencies and firms.

purchasing power of money The amount of goods and services that can be purchased with a unit of money. The purchasing power of money varies inversely with the price level. Also called *value of money*.

purchasing power parity (PPP) exchange rate The exchange rate between two currencies that adjusts for relative price levels.

quantity demanded The amount of a commodity that households wish to purchase in some time period.

quantity supplied The amount of a commodity that producers wish to sell in some time period.

rate base The total allowable investment to which the rate of return allowed by a regulatory commission is applied.

rate of inflation The percentage rate of increase in some price index from one period to another.

rate of return The ratio of net profits earned by a firm to total invested capital.

rational expectations The theory that people understand how the economy works and learn quickly from their mistakes, so that, while random errors may be made, systematic and persistent errors are not made.

ratio scale See *logarithmic scale*.

real capital The physical assets that a firm uses to conduct its business, composed of plant, equipment, and inventories. Also called *physical capital*.

real GDP See *constant-dollar GDP*.

real income Income expressed in terms of the purchasing power of money income, that is, the quantity of goods and services that can be purchased with the money income; it can be calculated as money income deflated by a price index.

real national income National income measured in constant dollars, so that it changes only when quantities change.

real product wage The proportion of each sales dollar accounted for by labor costs (including the pretax nominal wage rate, benefits, and payroll taxes).

real rate of interest The money rate of interest corrected for the change in the purchasing power of money by subtracting the inflation rate.

real-wage unemployment Unemployment caused by too high a real product wage. Also called *classical unemployment*.

recession In general, a downturn in the level of economic activity.

recessionary gap A positive output gap; that is, a situation in which actual national income is less than potential income. Also called a *deflationary gap*.

regressive tax A tax that takes a lower percentage of income the higher the level of income.

relative price The ratio of the money price of one commodity to the money price of another commodity; that is, a ratio of two absolute prices.

renewable resources Productive resources that can be replaced as they are used up, as with physical capital; distinguished from nonrenewable resources, which are available in a fixed stock that can be depleted but not replaced.

rent seeking Behavior in which private firms and individuals try to use the powers of the government to enhance their own economic well-being.

replacement investment The amount of investment that is needed to maintain the existing capital stock intact.

required reserves The reserves that a bank must, by law, keep either in currency or in deposits with the central bank.

reserve ratio The fraction of its deposits that a commercial bank holds as reserves in the form of cash or deposits with a central bank.

resource allocation The allocation of an economy's scarce resources of land, labor, and capital among alternative uses.

retained earnings See *undistributed profits*.

revenue sharing The return of some of the revenue collected by the federal government to a state or local government for unrestricted expenditure; a noncategorical or general grant-in-aid.

rising-cost industry An industry in which the minimum cost attainable by a firm rises as the scale of the industry expands.

satisficing A hypothesized objective of firms to achieve levels of performance deemed satisfactory rather than to *maximize* some objective.

saving See *private saving, public saving, national saving*.

scarce good A commodity for which the quantity demanded exceeds the quantity supplied at a price of zero; therefore, a good that commands a positive price in a market economy.

scatter diagram A graph of statistical observations of paired values of two variables, one measured on the horizontal and the other on the vertical axis. Each point on the coordinate grid represents the values of the variables for a particular unit of observation.

search unemployment Unemployment caused by people continuing to search for a good job rather than accepting the first job that they come across after they become unemployed.

sectors Parts of an economy.

securities market See *stock market*.

selective credit controls Controls on credit imposed through such means as margin requirements, restrictions on installment buying, and minimum down payments on mortgages.

sellers' preferences Allocation of commodities in excess demand by decisions of those who sell them.

service account See *invisible account*.

services Intangible commodities, such as haircuts or medical care.

shareholders See *stockholders*.

short run A period of time in which the quantity of some inputs cannot be increased beyond the fixed amount that is available.

short-run aggregate supply (*SRAS*) curve A curve showing the relation between the price level of final output and the quantity of output supplied on the assumption that all factor prices are held constant.

short-run equilibrium Generally, equilibrium subject to fixed factors or other things that cannot change over the time period being considered. For a competitive firm, the output at which market price equals marginal cost; for a competitive industry, the price and output at which industry demand equals short-run industry supply and all firms are in short-run equilibrium. Either profits or losses are possible.

short-run supply curve A curve showing the relationship between quantity supplied and market price, with one or more fixed factors; it is the horizontal sum of marginal cost curves (above the level of average variable costs) of all firms in a perfectly competitive industry.

shut-down price The price that is equal to a firm's average variable costs, below which it will produce no output.

simple multiplier The ratio of the change in equilibrium national income to the change in autonomous expenditure that brought it about, *calculated for* a constant price level.

single proprietorship A form of business organization in which the firm has one owner, who makes all the decisions and is personally responsible for all of the firm's actions and debts.

size distribution of income The distribution of income among households, without regard to source of income or social class of households.

slope The ratio of the vertical change to the horizontal change between two points on a curve.

social benefit The contribution that an activity makes to the society's welfare.

social cost The value of the best alternative use of resources available to society as valued by society. Also called *social opportunity cost*.

social insurance program Government programs that tax eligible workers and that pay those workers when the workers qualify for benefits. Social Security and Medicare are the two most important examples.

social regulation The regulation of economic behavior to advance social goals when competition and economic regulation will fail to achieve those goals.

special drawing rights (SDRs) Financial liabilities of the IMF held in a special fund generated by contributions of member countries. Members can use SDRs to maintain supplies of convertible currencies when these are needed to support foreign exchanges.

specialization of labor The specialization of individual workers in the production of particular goods and services, rather than producing everything that they consume.

specific tariff   An import duty of a specific amount per unit of the product.

specific tax   See *excise tax*.

speculative balances   Money balances held as a hedge against the uncertainty of the prices of other financial assets.

stabilization policy   Any policy designed to reduce the economy's cyclical fluctuations and thereby to stabilize national income at, or near, a desired level.

stagflation   The coexistence of high rates of unemployment with high, and sometimes rising, rates of inflation.

stockholders   The owners of a corporation who have supplied money to the firm by purchasing its shares. Also called *shareholders*.

stock market   An organized market where stocks and bonds are bought and sold. Also called *securities market*.

strategic behavior   Behavior designed to take account of the reactions of one's rivals to one's own behavior.

structural unemployment   Unemployment due to a mismatch between characteristics required by available jobs and characteristics possessed by the unemployed labor.

substitute   Two commodities are substitutes for each other when both satisfy similar needs or desires. The degree of substitutability is measured by the magnitude of the positive cross elasticity between the two.

substitution effect   A change in the quantity of a good demanded, which results from a change in its relative price, eliminating the effect on real income of the change in price.

supply   The entire relationship between the quantity of some commodity that producers wish to make and sell per period of time and the price of that commodity, other things being equal.

supply curve   The graphical representation of the relationship between the quantity of some commodity that producers wish to make and sell per period of time and the price of that commodity, other things being equal.

supply of effort   See *supply of labor*.

supply of labor   The total number of hours of work that the population is willing to supply. Also called the *supply of effort*.

supply of money   See *money supply*.

supply schedule   A table showing for selected values the relationship between the quantity of some commodity that producers wish to make and sell per period of time and the price of that commodity, other things being equal.

tacit collusion   Collusion that takes place with no explicit agreements. See also *collusion*.

takeover   When one firm buys another firm.

takeover bid   See *tender offer*.

tariff   A tax applied on imports.

tax expenditures   Tax provisions, such as exemptions and deductions from taxable income and tax credits, that are designed to induce market responses considered to be desirable. They are called *expenditures* because they have the same effect as directly spending money to induce the desired behavior.

tax incidence   The location of the burden of a tax; that is, the identity of the ultimate bearer of the tax.

tax-related incomes policy (TIP)   Tax incentives for labor and management to encourage them to conform to wage and price guidelines.

technical change   See *technological change*.

technological change   Any change in the available techniques of production. Also called *technical change*.

tender offer   An offer to buy directly, for a limited period of time, some or all of the outstanding common stock of a corporation from its stockholders at a specified price per share, in an attempt to gain control of the corporation. Also called *takeover bid*.

term   See *term to maturity*.

terms of trade   The ratio of the average price of a country's exports to the average price of its imports, both averages usually being measured by index numbers; it is the quantity of imported goods that can be obtained per unit of goods exported.

term to maturity   The period of time from the present to the redemption date of a bond. Also called simply the *term*.

theory of games   The theory that studies rational decision making in situations in which one must anticipate the reactions of one's competitors to the moves one makes.

time deposit   An interest-earning bank deposit, legally subject to notice before withdrawal (in practice the notice requirement is not normally enforced) and until recently not transferable by check. Also called *savings deposits*.

time series   A series of observations on the values of a variable at different points in time.

time-series data   A set of measurements or observations made repeatedly at successive periods (or moments) of time. Contrasted with *cross-sectional data*.

total cost (TC)   The total cost to the firm of producing any given level of output; it can be divided into total fixed costs and total variable costs.

total fixed cost (TFC)   All costs of production that do not vary with level of output. Also called *overhead cost* or *unavoidable cost*.

total product (TP)   Total amount produced by a firm during some time period.

total revenue (TR)   Total receipts from the sale of a product; price times quantity.

total utility   The total satisfaction resulting from the consumption of a given commodity or group of commodities by a consumer in a period of time.

total variable cost (TVC) Total costs of production that vary directly with level of output. Also called *direct cost* or *avoidable cost*.

tradeable emission permits Government-granted rights to emit specific amounts of specified pollutants that private firms may buy and sell among themselves.

trade account A section of the balance-of-payments accounts that records payments and receipts arising from the import and export of tangible goods. Also called the *visible account* and the *merchandise account*.

trade remedy laws See *fair trade laws*.

transactions balances Money balances held to finance payments because payments and receipts are not perfectly synchronized.

transactions costs Costs incurred in effecting market transactions (such as negotiation costs, billing costs, and bad debts).

transfer payment A payment to a private person or institution that does not arise out of current productive activity; typically made by governments, as in welfare payments, but also made by businesses and private individuals in the form of charitable contributions.

transmission mechanism The channels by which a change in the demand or supply of money leads to a shift of the aggregate demand curve.

transnational corporations (TNCs) Firms that have operations in more than one country. Also called *multinational enterprises (MNEs)*.

treasury bill The conventional form of short-term government debt. A promise to pay a certain sum of money at a specified time in the future (usually 90 days to 1 year from date of issue). Although treasury bills carry no fixed interest payments, holders earn an interest return because they purchase them at a lower price than their redemption value. Also called *treasury note*.

two-part tariff A method of charging for a good or a service, usually a utility such as electricity, in which the consumer pays a flat access fee and a specified amount per unit purchased.

undistributed profits Earnings of a firm that are not distributed to shareholders as dividends but are retained by the firm. Also called *retained earnings*.

unemployment (U) The number of persons 16 years of age and older who are not employed and are actively searching for a job.

unemployment rate Unemployment expressed as a percentage of the labor force.

unfavorable balance of payments A debit balance on some part of the international payments accounts (payments exceed receipts); often refers to the balance on current plus capital account (that is, everything except the official settlements account).

union An association of workers authorized to represent them in bargaining with employers. Also called *trade union, labor union*.

unit costs Costs per unit of output, equal to total variable cost divided by total output. Also called *average variable cost*.

utility The satisfaction that a consumer receives from consuming a commodity.

value added The value of a firm's output minus the value of the inputs that it purchases from other firms.

value of money See *purchasing power of money*.

variable Any well-defined item, such as the price of a commodity or its quantity, that can take on various specific values.

variable cost A cost that varies directly with changes in output. Also called *direct cost, avoidable cost*.

variable factor An input that can be varied by any desired amount in the short run.

velocity of circulation National income divided by quantity of money.

vertical merger See *merger*.

very long run A period of time that is long enough for the technological possibilities available to a firm to change.

visible account See *trade account*.

visibles All those items of foreign trade that are tangible; goods as opposed to services.

voluntary export restriction (VER) An agreement by an exporting country to limit the amount of a good exported to another country.

wage and price controls Direct government intervention into wage and price formation with legal power to enforce the government's decisions on wages and prices.

wage-cost push inflation An increase in the price level caused by increases in labor costs that are not themselves associated with excess aggregate demand for labor.

wealth The sum of all the valuable assets owned minus liabilities.

withdrawals Income earned by households and not passed on to firms in return for goods and services purchased, and income earned by firms and not passed on to households in return for factor services purchased.

X Exports; the value of all domestic production sold abroad.

X-inefficiency The use of resources at a lower level of productivity than is possible, even if they are allocated efficiently, so that the economy is at a point inside its production possibility boundary.

X − IM See *net exports*.

Index